MEDICAL MISADVENTURES

The Author

Medical Student, St Thomas' Hospital 1960-65,
MRCS, LRCP (1965), MBBS (London 1967),
FRCS Eng, FRCS Edin, FRCS A&E, DCH, D Obst, RCOG, ATLS.
Serving Brother Officer, St Johns Ambulance Brigade,
Appointed Casualty Consultant, Derbyshire Royal Infirmary (1978), later
renamed Emergency Consultant.
Retired 2007.
Clinical Teacher 2007-2015.

MEDICAL MISADVENTURES

Fifty-four years at the cutting edge of the NHS

Alistair Fraser-Moodie

Matador
9 Priory Business Park,
Wistow Road, Kibworth Beauchamp,
Leicestershire LE8 0RX
Tel: 0116 279 2299
Email: books@troubador.co.uk
Web: www.troubador.co.uk/matador
Twitter: @matadorbooks

ISBN 978 1788037 907

British Library Cataloguing in Publication Data.
A catalogue record for this book is available from the British Library.

Printed and bound by CPI Group (UK) Ltd, Croydon, CR0 4YY
Typeset in 11pt Minion Pro by Troubador Publishing Ltd, Leicester, UK

Matador is an imprint of Troubador Publishing Ltd

This book is dedicated to my five grandchildren – Angus, Rory, Louisa, Mirren and Thomas. (They all can be seen on page 597.) Included in the dedication are any future grandchildren.

Contents

List of Figures

PREFACE

Health is not everything, but without health everything is nothing.

A wise man ought to realise that health is his most valued possession.

Hippocrates

At practically the end of my medical career I came to realise that I did not want to stop. My ageing brain still buzzed. A few neurones still synapsed. I was impatient, but for what, I thought? I recalled that in my medical life I had met a lot of patients, and witnessed a lot of changes. This book is of a 54-year medical journey that I have found fascinating.

Things did not always work out. I have failed more than my share of examinations. I have been forced into a change of career specialty. I ended up idyllically happy working as an emergency consultant for over 30 years. I had the best job in the world. In view of my patchy academic record some people might say I was lucky to become a consultant. Several of my medical colleagues failed to progress up the ladder.

Finally I came to realise that, nearly retired, I did not have to stop. This was because I was spurred on. This book was inside me. It wanted to escape and spread itself over page after page after page.

So I got out a blank piece of lined paper and a biro. Hey presto – this book exploded into life. I did not write it. This book wrote itself. All of it is true, though admittedly there are a few stories and facts included that I have been told by others. Names have occasionally been changed, and sometimes a patient or doctor may recognise himself or herself, so pseudonyms disguise identity. Nobody else will know who you are – unless you have given me permission to use your name or, in a few instances, I didn't think a friend would mind. Apologies to one and all. Most patients are entirely anonymous and I defy anybody to be able to trace them through this narrative.

The reader may be amazed that occasionally patient confidentiality has been breached. This is because a few patients wanted to be identified. Some edited my script and others wrote it for me. Thank you, patients, one and all. I have worked in 30 district general hospitals and so my patients written up here come from all over the country.

I have quoted extensively, and definitely not consciously plagiarised, as I have referenced each quote. Imitation may be the sincerest form of flattery, but I have tried hard to avoid this pitfall. Apologies if, in error, I have strayed in this direction. I am guilty of self plagiary!

There is repetition, but this I feel is inevitable – for example, my agreement on mandatory training of doctors, which is referred to in a reference on private finance initiatives and again on medical education. The reason for this is that my feelings on all these topics are so strong, they need emphasising and repeating, especially at the end of the book.

Gradually, more stories were added. I reflected upon some bizarre anecdotes that jolted my memory. Retrospectively, this book behaved like a malignant tumour that spreads. I had no control. New ideas materialised, just like a cancer. I recognised secondary ideas and these spread everywhere. The jigsaw of words, ideas and recollections grew and grew. It was not difficult to start. The hardest part has been knowing when to stop. The literacy gestation period from start to finish has been over ten years. This book, in my opinion, is educational throughout!

Apologies to the reader in advance for my primitive punctuation. I had originally intended to announce that this book did not contain a single colon, as I have only one colon – and it connects my small bowel to my anus. That claim is not true, as the wretched things were too difficult to avoid! Apologies, too, for the puerile poems and the amateur alliteration, but I could not stop myself!

> *Above all, it is a true story because that is the only kind worth telling.*
> Nicholas Monserrat, *The Cruel Sea*, Pg. 11

ACKNOWLEDGEMENTS

I t is hard to recall all the people who have helped me. My secretary, the lovely Mrs Samantha Whittingham, has been patient, helpful and hardworking throughout. Initially, Mrs Sue Pollicott, another gifted secretary, helped me. Thank you both.

My thanks go to Phil Stubbs of Stubbs PR Limited. He has edited my book extensively and brought it from the 20th to the 21st century.

Countless friends have read the manuscript. Many have read their 'part'. Thank you, one and all. Their comments have been mixed and so honest. My particular thanks go to Sir Stephen Moss, Richard Lindop, Alan Passmore and my daughter Lindsay. Each of them has 'specialist knowledge' on a particular subject that I have touched on in this book. They have, all four, taken time to read this book, and then provided me with helpful advice and comments.

Kate Smith, a professional illustrator, has drawn some excellent pictures. All the illustrations are hers, apart from the X-ray of the 'drug mule'. This was drawn by an amateur, and it shows!

Will Stone, a professional photographer helped with these pictures over and over again. He and his colleagues from the medical illustration department of the Derby Royal Hospital were so kind to me.

Ms Gemma Adlington from the Plastic Surgery Office at the Royal College of Physicians sent me the picture of Sir Harold Gillies. I was encouraged by Victoria Wilcox, picture editor of the *Derby Evening Telegraph* and also by the editor of the *Annals of the Royal College of Surgeons (England)*. Melanie Sambells of Mirror Pictures sold me the pictures of Mike Hawthorn. I discussed this chapter with a former police officer, and an expert in accidents, Anthony Pickering.

I had help from the librarians at the Derby Royal Hospital, the Surrey History Centre, Woking, the Local Studies Centre, Matlock and Daniel Gee of the *Farnham Herald*. Thanks also go to Graeme McAlister and HM du Preez of the Royal College of Physicians of Edinburgh for the information of Dr 'James Barry'. Thanks to Dr Jacqueline Banerjee, the editor of the Victorian Web. Dr Henry Oakley FRCP, the Garden Fellow of the Royal College of Physicians, Regent's Park, wrote a book about all the graduates of our year (and non-graduates too). I have plagiarised this tome ad nauseam for this publication. Many apologies, Henry. Please don't sue for this indiscretion.

My thanks to Sage Publications for allowing me to publish extracts of *Study Skills for Dyslexic Students* by Sandra Hargreaves.

I am a digital dinosaur and Martyn Taylor, a computer whizz, helped me over and over again. Well done, Martyn – what patience!

I thank Professor Neil Mortensen for permission to publish information from Dr James Barry: 'The woman who fooled the RCS and deceived the world' by Michael du Preez and Jeremy Dronfield and printed in *The Bulletin* of the Royal College of Surgeons in October 2016.

I wish to thank my friend Giorgio Rimi from Sydney for his support on the fishing trip from Lord Howe Island. He took the fishy pictures. What a great guy.

My thanks also go to my teenage neighbour Ashley Heath for his help with my many pictures. Also thanks to Troubador Publishing Ltd.

My thanks to my family – Christine, Lindsay, Isabel and Duncan – for their help and support.

My friends Chris and Viv Ring have kindly proofread this to me – thank you.

Finally, my thanks go to an excellent firm of solicitors from Derby, Flint Bishop. They gave me wise advice on how to steer clear of defamation, plagiarism, perjury, copyright and slander, to say nothing of falling foul of medical etiquette. They kept me from sinking into the quicksands of intellectual property – a court case could do wonders for the circulation of my book, but it could cost me dear!

Thank you, one and all, Alistair.

Writing is easy. All you do is stare at a blank piece of paper until drops of blood form on your forehead.

Gene Fowler

CHAPTER ONE

Interviews for
Medical School (1960)

Listen to what your father teaches you, my sons. Pay attention and you will have understanding.

Proverbs 4

Aged 17 years I was about to be interviewed for a medical school place. I was very apprehensive. I was driven to St Thomas' Hospital, London by my father through the then light London traffic. It was a late spring afternoon in 1960. The sun shone brightly.

For the very first time in my life I was wearing a suit. It felt strange. This new garment looked good, but I felt uncomfortable. My mop of red hair had been savagely hacked, and I now had a parting. Thanks to my hair colouring I got away without shaving regularly. My chin this day, however, felt like an advertisement for Gillette. I did not feel or look like me at all. I was the victim of this charade.

I was being tutored by my father as he drove the car. I did not understand how my medical father knew the questions I would be asked. He asked me the following questions:

"Well, they will say, why do you want to be a doctor? What will you answer?"

Fig 1 – Me, pre-interview.

I stumbled out a pathetic answer saying I was interested in helping people and that I was fascinated by zoology (an A-level subject).

"No, that's not good enough," he said. "You should say you are interested in human anatomy, physiology and biochemistry. Then you go on to say you are interested in the pathology of disease."

"Oh, Dad," I said, "I don't know all those long words. That's not my answer but yours!" We did not agree. I sulked. So, he tried another tack.

"Well," he said, "what will you say if he asks you why you want to come to this hospital?"

I had no answer. They all smelt the same to me (of antiseptic). Also they were full of busy people rushing about in all directions. I had not been a patient but had watched my father operate in another hospital.

"Well," he said, "you should reply that this hospital has a wonderful reputation and its medical school is one of the very best."

"Well, how do I know?" I said.

"Because I have told you," said my father.

I was not happy with this answer as this was hearsay and I had no independent opinion. Anyway, I thought, how does he know what questions I will be asked? Secretly I thought I might get a tricky medical question, such as a tough anatomy question. I would not know the answer and be chucked out! (I mean, not considered for a place.)

Forty-five minutes later, after an annoying wait outside the hospital secretary's office, I was summoned in. "They," to my great surprise, turned out to be just one sandy-haired man. I could hardly see him, as the setting sun shone through a window onto the polished table in front of him and effectively blinded me as it reflected onto my face. He had a paper before him, presumably my application form. I affirmed my name, age and school. He paused and then said: "Well, why do you want to be a doctor?" I blurted out that I was interested in helping people and wanted to know more of the working of the human body. No question was asked of this reply. He paused and made notes. Then he said, "Why do you want to come to this hospital?" I said, "Because it has a very good reputation both as a hospital and as a medical school." This went down well. He smiled and wrote something.

"I see both your parents are doctors." (At this time, having a medical relative was an advantage. It has subsequently become less of an advantage. At least I knew what I was letting myself in for.) "Yes," I said. "My mother is a single-handed practitioner and holds surgeries in our home. My father is an oral surgeon."

"Has your father taken you to his hospital?" he asked.

"Oh yes," I said. "I have watched my father operate several times. Last time he plated a jaw, and then on another patient he dissected a tumour from the neck."

"And what can you do to help your mother?" he asked.

"Oh," I said, "I take messages from patients, their names, addresses and their complaints. I write this all down and pass the information on when my mother comes in."

I recalled that on two occasions a patient's relative telephoned in some distress, but my mother had gone out on her visits. In this emergency situation I telephoned another general practitioner and he did the visit. (This was the 1950s. The GP was in charge of the patient away from the hospital. The patient must only be referred to hospital with a letter and following a telephone call to the hospital. The new emergency ambulance service run by county councils had just begun with the birth of the National Health Service.[1] So now a new ambulance service existed but for years was underused and not abused!)

He wrote something again.

"And you play sport," he asked. I felt myself relax. I was on safer ground now.

"Yes. I play golf."

"Oh, your handicap is 16?" he said.

"No, it's now down to 14," I said.

"Well, we have a good golf team," he said. (That was the understatement of the century I later learned. There was a captain, a scratch county player, also another, the current holder of the President's putter, another one who was later thrown out of the medical school and turned pro instead, plus several others who were nearly as good.)

"You also play rugby," he said. "What position are you?"

"Oh," I said, "I am a hooker."

"Oh, that's a great shame as we have lots of hookers," he said, and paused for thought. "Can't you play in any other position?"

"No," I said. "That's it. I have never played in another position."

"Oh dear," he said, "oh dear, oh dear," and made a note.

Well, that was the end of the interview. I trooped out to be met by my 'expectant' father.

"How did it go?" he asked anxiously.

"Oh," I said, "they have plenty of hookers here."

He gave me a funny look!

There was a story about rugby and medical school interviews: as you entered, you were thrown a rugby ball – catch it and you are in; drop it and you are not selected. However, if you catch it and then drop kick it back to the thrower, you get a scholarship!

My father drove me back to our family home in Richmond upon Thames. He asked me about the interview. I told him about the neck operation I had witnessed. "You should have called it a cancer and not a tumour, as the latter means a swelling." Oh, I thought, I had made another mistake.

As I had entered the interview, I recall having glanced at a copy of my CV. I had passed ten O-levels, each of which had a pass rate of less than 50% (a close friend who attended another school, St Paul's Boys' School, had not passed any). I even passed Latin which was a 'must-have' for medicine. Gosh, I struggled at this. There was a rhyme we used to chant: "Latin is a language as dead as dead can be. It killed the ancient Romans, and now it's killing me." This was so true for me. I struggled through the first paper in Latin, getting about 40% – a fail. Then in the second paper, our master Mr Harwood told us which bit of Caesar's Gallic Wars we would get. Well I knew that bit by heart – one long paragraph – and, amazingly, he was right. So I just wrote it out in about ten minutes. The really difficult bit was the Virgil, but I knew the English translation by heart (23 foolscap pages that I read every day). So I got nearly 100% for the second paper, giving me an overall pass. But would Latin O-level really help me in medicine, I wondered? How?

I was graded into the third stream for O-levels. We felt inferior to the first and second streams. But my two friends in the third stream and I did quite well in retrospect. Barry got an open scholarship to Cambridge in English and Bill got a double first at Oxford! Well, what were the first stream like? Read on.

I had already witnessed time and time again other boys I knew fall by the wayside. For example, I knew that only one in three boys passed the entrance examination to my school. One boy I met on the bus quite often was at another school. He then failed to get into my school. He was bitter about it. Another friend at school, Stephen, failed some O-levels that I passed. He wanted to become a doctor had but had to then change his mind and become a solicitor instead.

Caro sat on my left for A-level Zoology. He was likely to fail this examination and join his father's business instead. But if I got into medical school I could be chucked out if I failed further examinations! My academic record was patchy – both highs and lows. But why? I worried about being thrown out of medical school in this way, before I had even got there – it was a definite possibility!

References

1. Alexander Pollock. Ambulance Services in London and Great Britain from 1860 to today. A glimpse of history gleaned mainly from the pages of contemporary journals. *Emergency Medicine Journal*. 2013;30:218-222.

Another Friend's Interview

Education, education, education.

Tony Blair

The interview process for medical school was a lot less predictable in the 1960s than it is today. My contemporaries have shared numerous experiences over the years, both of the interviews themselves and the routes they took to achieve a place in medical school. Many of them would not get into medical school like that today.

Bill was bright. A schoolboy at Lancaster Grammar School and an outstanding hooker in the First XV. He was very heavily built but not very tall – perfect for that position.

After he sat his A-levels he went abroad touring the continent – backpacking. He had a provisional place at Manchester to read Medicine. When the results came out he had straight As. Bill could not be contacted at the time. His father and his housemaster together discussed these excellent results. These two decided by themselves to cancel the place at medical school and send Bill back to school. They hoped he would then get into Cambridge the following year.

Bill returned home. He was very, very unhappy to be going back to school. He was doubly unhappy at the prospect of more exams. He had no choice – it was a fait accompli. At school all of his contemporaries had left. He played and helped coach the rugby team he thought he had left behind him. He was unhappy academically. He had passed his exams with flying colours, but here he was back in the same classrooms doing the same lessons with younger boys. His heart was not in it.

One day a letter arrived for him. He had an interview for Cambridge University. He told nobody but took the day off. At Cambridge he sat in a room divided into two parts by a thin partition. Candidates were interviewed in the other part of the room. He was the last to be interviewed that day. He was preceded by a foreign student and English was not his first language. He could hear the interviewer speaking loudly and clearly to the candidate.

"What is, in your opinion, the greatest advance in medicine today?"

Gosh, he thought, I would not like that question: it's difficult. Scattered around him were some scientific journals to read. He picked one up and saw an interesting article. An eminent professor wrote that interferon, in his opinion, was the greatest advance in medicine today. He read on. Two minutes later he was called in to be introduced to several grey-haired professors.

"Well," said the question master, "what in your opinion is the greatest advance in medicine today?"

Bill answered confidently.

"Well, Professor Whatsit writing in the *New Scientist* recently explained that it is, in his opinion, interferon. I am inclined to agree because it can cure infections that otherwise would be fatal, for example.

As Bill spoke on and on he could see the grey-haired old men nodding gently to each other.

Next question: "If you came to our college, would you continue playing rugby?" He explained that his interest in the game was as strong as ever.

Two days later he had a letter offering him an unconditional place at Cambridge. So he did not have to sit any more examinations. He told nobody at school. That day in Chemistry, Bill had difficulty paying attention. He kept looking outside to the rugby pitch. His inattention did not go unnoticed. At the end of the lesson the teacher said, "Class dismissed, except you," and pointed at Bill. He then had a lecture on concentrating for the examinations ahead that wouldn't be easy. After this Bill said, "Excuse me, sir."

"What is it, boy?"

"I would like you to know that I received a letter today. In it, Cambridge College offered me an unconditional place. So you see, sir, I don't have any more exams this year!" Bill got up and walked out of class!

He got a blue at rugby as, of course, a hooker. He later captained the United Hospitals side and became an eminent medical consultant.

Sometimes a candidate for an interview is asked a question for which they cannot have prepared an answer. The examiner wants to know if they are bright and quick enough for medicine.

For example: "Tell me which is the odd one out of these: a coconut, a plum, an apple, a gooseberry or a banana."

Well, a coconut is the only one with a hard shell; a plum is the only one with a big stone; an apple is the only one with pips; a gooseberry is the only one to grow on a bush; a banana is the only one that is not round.

(The point is, any of these answers will do – you just have to have a reason – something to say – rather than stony silence.)

A candidate may not have time to work this out, however. An answer is expected, and quickly. One answer would be to say an apple: "I only eat them." Or a banana "I hate them!" This is better than nothing. The ability to think quickly is the key – as well as being able to display some initiative. One candidate, for example, was deemed to show initiative by spelling medicine phonetically – MEDECINE. He got into medical school.[1]

The questioner may digress and ask a question on reasoning.

For example, "The tomato. Now, is it a fruit or a vegetable?"[2] Or the questioner could say, "Your CV is full of your good points. Do you have any weaknesses?"

Finally, the questioner could ask a question on the history of medicine:
Question: "Who invented penicillin?"
Answer: "Sir Alexander Fleming."

Reference:

1. Alan Bailey FRCP. Letter to *The Times*: 20. 10. 09:31.
2. The Tomato Question. *The Times*. 9. 20. 5:14.

A-Levels

Discipline was strict at my large public school, King's College School, in Wimbledon. Although there were nearly 1,000 boys in the school, the headmaster taught just Latin and ancient Greek to a couple of sixth-formers. He drove to school daily. This was barely 100 yards! Every evening he drove home the same way. I should know, as he pulled out on me twice. Luckily, my Lambretta swerved just in time.

The head was grey-haired and balding, with a small moustache, so he looked very old, and had a severe speech impairment. He stammered and could not pronounce an O. So when he opened the new science block to a large crowd of parents, pupils and staff, he stuttered, "I declare... th-these labratries, err, open!" I chuckled (to myself).

We had to wear starched, detachable collars on our shirts – held on with two awkward studs. Initially, we wore cufflinks too. Out of school we had to wear caps with our uniforms. We then had to touch our caps to all parents and teachers, as a sign of respect. Failure to comply with the dress code, or this accepted behaviour, led to a caning from the prefects – very sore indeed!

* * *

Our masters were nearly all brilliant teachers. My English master, Mr R K G MacEwen, was the current Scottish international hooker. I sang in the school choir for eight years. Our music master was John Carol Case, who died recently. He was a singer of international repute, and much admired by Benjamin Britton. However, Mr Case's voice has not been forgotten. In 1968, for example, he recorded Faure's Requiem with the choir of King's College, Cambridge and the new Philharmonia Orchestra conducted by Sir David Willcocks. I have a CD of this recording. It is still on sale today!

* * *

Back at school I tried to work as hard as I could on my three A-level subjects. There was just one set of examinations in June after two years of study, so they were not modular. For Zoology, Physics and Chemistry there were written examinations and then a practical examination. Our Chemistry master wore a wig. One day the wig fell off. He was bald and did not notice. How we laughed! I was taught brilliantly in Zoology and Chemistry. I had regular tests. Beside me in Zoology sat Roger and Clive (both from the first stream). Physics was a problem, however. We had a different syllabus after the first year of study and had to do all calculations in calculus. We rarely had Physics tests – and we were behind on the syllabus. I struggled and struggled with calculus.

However, the Physics masters excelled in eccentricity. Daily, on my way to school, I passed my Physics master painfully cycling up Wimbledon Hill. I can picture him now – pink, panting, perspiring profusely. So surely, so slowly, sir suffered so. 'Twas terrible to watch; tantamount to torture.

The senior Physics master was a notoriously fast driver. One day he was driving the school minibus full of boys, thundering along the motorway. One boy asked, "What is the purpose of the small lane beside the motorway?"

"That is an escape road," was the reply and the teacher thought a practical demonstration was needed. It took several hours for the AA to pull the minibus out backwards. The boys were very amused.[1]

Then a letter arrived for me; St Thomas' wanted me! All I had to do was to get three A-level passes. This might sound easy today, but then less than half the A-level students passed each subject.

9

As relaxation between hours of study, I played and enjoyed sport. The day after my St Thomas' interview we had an important house rugby game. We had to win. I was hooker and pack leader. Our best player, and captain, was our scrum half. We started so well. The trouble was that we won the ball at every scrum. I had no opposition. The referee was a confident master who I knew did not know the rules well. The previous month I had a loose ball bounce in front of me. I grabbed it and touched down five yards away. "No try!" he called out. "You must touch down with more weight. I give the other side a 25 drop out." I thought this was nonsense. A few years before, the same master had told me that the main function of a hooker was to push in the scrum. Then, to improve our scrummaging, he (wearing a beautiful blue sweater and shorts) pushed against our scrum. Well, he was pushed over backwards in the mud. I had the dubious honour of planting my muddy boots on his sweater. "So sorry, sir," I said. (Lying hound.)

So, back to this important house match. This so-called 'impartial' referee let the opposition break from the scrum before the ball was out. The direct result was that our captain was soon carried off and, without him, 14 players had no chance. Single-handedly he managed to hand us a defeat in the face of almost certain victory. Very unfair, but also something I viewed as a personal failure at the time.

I ran cross-country races every week and trained in between-running in Richmond Park. My goal was to do the senior cross-country (five-and-a-half miles of mud) in under 30 minutes. It rained and rained before the race so I failed by 30 seconds (came 20th out of 300). Another failure!

I did not play cricket much as I could not see the cricket ball bowled fast at me. The reason for this would be explained to me 12 years later. I captained our house sprint team at sports day. Unfortunately, one member of the team threw the baton to the next member, who dropped it. We were in last place – and were disqualified. Another failure.

On the last day of school I was expecting the headmaster to announce in assembly that I had won the school golf competition and to give me a few golf balls. This had happened to a predecessor of mine a year before. The golf captain, however, forgot to tell the head and I was handed them as we trooped out! Yet another failure.

But what about the A-levels? Remember, I needed to pass all three. Well, Zoology and Chemistry went fine but, guess what, Physics was a disaster – especially the second paper.

In August the results came:

Zoology – pass   Chemistry – pass   Physics – fail.

I telephoned the secretary's office at St Thomas'. Yes, they would have me. But I would be the only student sitting Physics at Christmas. I had to pass it then. I agreed. Another failure looming? Would I fail again?

What would the future hold? – five years of study. Would I pass Physics at Christmas? – no idea.

But I was interested in the working of the human body. I wanted to know more. The medical school had some confidence in me or they would not have offered me a place. Yet I needed more motivation and confidence to succeed and become a really good doctor. Lots more examinations loomed, even after Christmas. Could I acquire all this knowledge? I did not know. What about all those skills? Did I expect to acquire them all too? I did not know. If I qualified, would my patients trust me and like me, or would I frighten and upset them? I did not know!

I was different from average. At just five feet seven inches, I was below average height. I had bright red curly hair and very fair skin. In summer, everybody else got brown sunbathing and I just burnt and went red like a beetroot. I was shy on meeting people, particularly compared to some of my confident, extrovert friends. So would I actually enjoy being a doctor? I did not know! Could I keep professional secrets? I did not know! Patients had complications. Things did not always go to plan. My parents had responsibilities for the lives of their patients. Could I cope with the responsibility? If I qualified, could I work as hard as my parents – both on call 24/7? I did not know!

I listened to my parents talking. A colleague had been struck off by the General Medical Council. What publicity! What a disgrace! What a waste! How upset their friends and family were! Total income lost!

So, before I got to medical school, apprehension gripped me hard – very hard. Even if I qualified and got on the register in five years' time, would there be a job for me? Could I stay on the register of doctors? I simply did not know!

11

My poor parents had paid for my private education. Gosh, how they had paid (I once saw a bill from the school. It was outrageous. My poor dad had to pay £50 a term). Now they had to pay for me at medical school. I lived in Richmond upon Thames. None of my friends ever got grants to university from there. (Though I met somebody in my medical year from Norfolk. None of his friends went to university. He got a full grant even though his dad was a surgeon too!)

Two of my friends from school also went onto further training and in doing so got paid. One worked in a bank (George) and the other was a trainee solicitor (Stephen). I later learnt that medical students had to do something a bit awkward to get paid (volunteer to be a guinea pig in a medical experiment or donate sperm). Not surprisingly to those who know me, I have done neither.

Another way to get paid as a medical student, I later learnt, was to join one of the armed services. You were expected to spend one evening a week and one weekend a month in that service training. At least once a year you then had to stay full time in that service for usually two weeks. My friend Alex did that. He got a generous grant, a free uniform, free kit bag and kit. He was delighted to be in the Navy. He got off the train at Portsmouth in full uniform. He was going to his ship. He saluted everyone else on the platform in uniform. He was busy, and loved every second. Then a petty officer came up to him from behind and commented, "That's very good saluting, sir, but we in the Navy use our other hand." Oh dear.

When qualified fully, you are expected to spend five years or so full time in that service. So Alex was paid by the Navy all the time he was a medical student.

Reference:

1. *Old King's Club Newsletter* No 117 and Facebook.

CHAPTER TWO

Who Influenced This Choice of Career?

I was waiting to go to medical school at St Thomas' and knew exactly what I was letting myself in for: a lot of hours and a lot of hard work. My father was a surgeon, employed part-time by the NHS but on call all the time. My mother was a full-time, single-handed general practitioner with over 1,000 patients. She, too, was on call all the time. My older sister Janet was a medical student at the Middlesex Hospital.

Yet these three did not deter me from my aim to become a doctor. There are always people and circumstances in one's life that will directly or indirectly influence a choice of career or a course of action. I was no different. I had some obvious influences on my decision to become a doctor, including my great uncle Henry Fraser, a physician who was spoken of in awe. But there were also the less obvious, or at least less predictable, influences that helped to spur me on, such as a chance meeting with Sir Harold Gillies, the 'father of plastic surgery', who made me realise that medicine had no boundaries. I was also intrigued by the real reason behind the sudden death of world champion racing driver Mike Hawthorn back in 1958 – a controversial subject on which I dedicate a chapter towards the end of this book.

So let's look at some of my influences…

My Late Father, Dr William (Bill) Fraser-Moodie

A Glaswegian, Bill was born in 1903. By the age of 17 he had decided to study medicine and he was very intelligent. His parents were told that Bill should have no trouble with his "Highers" – similar to A-levels. However, throughout his school years at Allan Glen's School, Glasgow, he had health problems with severe intermittent abdominal pains. He had had an appendicectomy and was subsequently told that his pain was 'psychological'.

Bill was frequently absent from school due to this pain. He was criticised for this by the teachers. The school was short-staffed because of the First World War. Discipline had to be very strict. A friend of his, Jack, was expelled one day simply for dancing on the library table. But this harsh act was the catalyst for Jack's future success. He emigrated to the United States after the war and danced into Hollywood films. He starred in many and became world famous. Jack indeed was the most successful old boy from his school, to the ignominy of the teachers who had expelled him. Nobody knows if he would have succeeded had he not been expelled. This man was Jack Buchanan. The other, less well known, old boys of this school include Dirk Bogarde the actor, and Alastair Kellock, a former Scottish rugby captain.

Meanwhile, my own father's non-medical parents discussed Bill's future career with their general practitioner, who had seen Bill on several occasions for his abdominal pain. "Oh," said the doctor, "Bill is not fit enough for medicine. He must try another degree."

Bill was very unhappy, but in 1920 he heeded the advice of his parents. So he went to Glasgow University as planned and studied the next best thing to medicine – dentistry. He had been there only a short time before he made a lot of friends. One morning, one of them said to him, "Hey, Bill, you have a free period; come and listen to my lecture."

So Bill went along to a big lecture theatre. The subject was anatomy and Bill was fascinated. Whilst concentrating hard on the teaching, a large book was pushed into Bill's hands.

"Just sign in," said his friend, and so he did. The lecture finished. Bill was still enthralled by the subject of anatomy.

"Well," said his friend, "now you are a medical student as well as a dental student!"

Bill said nothing of this to his parents. By now he was just 18 years of age. He found time to continue with both the medical and dental studies. Dental practicals were time-consuming, but he often did them in the evenings. He passed examinations separately in both these subjects – medicine and dentistry. He still suffered bouts of abdominal pain but just learnt to live with them.

Bill worked hard every evening and his parents were very proud of him. In 1926 at the age of 23, his father, a chemist, had a conversation with Bill.

"Well, Bill," said his father, "you have your dental finals soon. Good luck."

"Dad," he said, "I've got something to tell you."

"Yes?" said his father anxiously.

"Well, Dad, I've got some more exams later this year. I'm sitting my medical finals too."

His parents were dumbfounded. True to form, he passed both sets of examinations, although the courses were separate. He practised both medicine and dentistry throughout his life. He must have been one of the first people to be doubly qualified (if not *the* first – 1926).

He married my mother Christina, another doctor, in 1935 and became a consultant oral surgeon at the Central Middlesex Hospital, with responsibilities to several other local hospitals. He still had bouts of abdominal pain during the Second World War. He was barred from enlisting in the services but told to work in the hospital instead. There were no junior doctors during the war in the hospital, just a skeleton staff of senior doctors working together. He recalled and published one interesting case:

In October 1940 he was seeing casualties from an air raid. A 77-year-old lady had a fractured neck of her left femur. So she had a broken hip and could not walk… but on the other hip was an old surgical scar. Had she had a fracture on the other side?

"Oh no," she said, "that scar was made by Joseph Lister at King's College Hospital in 1884." She had had a gluteal abscess that followed a road traffic accident (hit by a horse-drawn carriage). Mr Lister had drained the abscess. It took two months to heal. He used penicillium

Fig 2 – Lord Lister.

in the wound. She remained an inpatient for two months. It finally healed but she continued as a probationer at the hospital. She qualified as a nurse and became a ward sister on Mr Lister's own ward – Fergusson. She had a scrapbook containing the word penicillium.

My late father confirmed this story by finding the hospital records showing that this lady had been admitted to King's College Hospital on 2nd November 1884 after having been knocked down by a cab. Further research showed that in 1880 there was correspondence between Lister and Pasteur on the subject. Pasteur made reference to Penicillium Glaucum – known for hundreds of years and reputed by the peasants of Brittany to heal sores contracted in the field.

Many years later, Professor Sir Alexander Fleming wrote a letter to the President of the Royal College of Surgeons about Lord Lister: 'What a pity that his experiments of 28th November 1871 did not come off. He had the idea of Penicillin but he had the wrong mould, or the wrong bacteria, or both. If fate had been kind to him medical history might have been changed and Lister might have lived to see what he was always looking for – a non-poisonous antiseptic.'

So, this elderly lady showed that Lord Lister might not only have been known for the discovery of antiseptics but also penicillin. My father reported this case in detail.[1]

My late father finally had his abdominal pain diagnosed after over 30 years of intermittent pain. He had gallstones, and a cholecystectomy cured him. (This dangerous diagnosis of psychological abdominal pain was disproved at last!)

My father travelled from London to Scotland to visit his own mother regularly just before she died. He even signed his own mother's death certificate!

Due to the surprising fact that my father's NHS pay, and later his pension, was very poor, he was forced to take a second job in industrial medicine. Prior to his death, he had been employed in a food production factory. I could not tell the directors of this food factory, who came to his funeral, how old he was because my father, aged 80, was doing a job where he should have retired at 65!

Today, there are many teaching hospitals that combine a medical and dental course. These combined courses are for those who wish to become maxillo-facial surgeons (previously called oral surgeons). My dear father was very good to me. For example, he was my dentist and orthodontist for 30 years, and never charged me. We played a lot of golf together and enjoyed each other's company.

Reference:

1. W Fraser-Moodie. 'It is good occasionally to unroll the pages of the past...' *British Journal of Oral Surgery* November 1967:5;2;77-85.

Dr Christina Fraser-Moodie

My mother was born in 1906. She was absolutely determined to become a doctor. Her father, an engineer, had never met or even heard of a lady doctor. Neither had any of his friends or acquaintances. My mother was told by her father, "But look, medicine – it's just not the right thing for a young lady to do. I forbid it."

She ignored him, passed some examinations and got into the only medical school in London that took ladies – the London School of Medicine for Women – later to be called the Royal Free Hospital. This hospital took only ladies, whilst all the other London hospitals took only men to train as doctors.

My mother took a year out of medical school to nurse her father who then died. All his finances were tied up in the family engineering

Fig 3 – My parents dining at the Central Middlesex Hospital one evening.

business. Unfortunately, my grandfather's partner then took over all the firm's assets, leaving my mother's family penniless! (It took a High Court action years later to restore the family's rightful financial state!)

Meanwhile, my mother resumed her medical studies – unpaid of course – qualifying in 1929. Once she had qualified she had to do house jobs. These, at this time, were honorary too, i.e., unpaid. The doctors did get free board and lodging. The only time a house surgeon or house physician got paid was if they went to court. On returning to the doctors' mess they were expected to help their friends out financially! One of her hospital jobs was in Liverpool. Three people did a ward round every day, seeing all the patients under the watchful eye of the boss – the ward sister. These people were my mother the doctor, then the priest and then finally the bookmaker!

After two years of hospital jobs, all unpaid, my mother (heavily in debt) aged 26 years went into general practice – to get some money. The senior partner in each general practice usually had a higher qualification – an FRCS or an MRCP. They all had their own beds in hospital and often their own operating lists. They frequently did emergency operations and delivered babies in the district. There was no ambulance service as we know of today. At one practice the only way of getting a patient to hospital in a hurry was by train! My mother rang the local stationmaster and he arranged for the signalman to stop the next train to take the patient about 20 miles from Grantham to Nottingham. After she married, she moved to Northolt and the Second World War started.

Hitler invaded Poland and the Polish Air Force flew to England. Here they joined fighter command and were stationed at Northolt. But after a few drinks some night, the Poles got a bit excited and clashed with some Irish pilots. If there were any injuries then, Casualty, as we know it, had not been invented – anyway, there was a blackout. So the local GP was called. Barely five feet tall, with bright red hair, my mother sorted out the fracases. She patched and stitched them up. Now, today, is the modern GP equipped and trained for such cases? A doctor nowadays would plead, 'Oh, that's not in my job description!" The GP's receptionist would say, "Call 999 and not us!"

The ambulance service, as we know it, only started with the National Health Service in 1948. This was too late for some patients. My mother was bitter about no ambulance service before then. During the blitz she had been delivering a baby in the blackout one night in Greenford. There was a rare complication. The baby's umbilical cord presented first before the head. The only chance for the baby was to push the cord back inside and perform a caesarean section urgently. With a skeleton ambulance service this was impossible. The baby, as expected, died. The relatives blamed my mother and were vicious. Home confinements are less frequent nowadays. Why is this? Well, this particular complication is only one of the many reasons why!

In 1948, the very day when the new National Health Service was starting, my parents decided to visit a local attraction in Northolt – the dog racing track. They were amazed. Well, lots of patients owed my mother money, as she had treated them. All of these people who owed her money were there at the track betting heavily on the dogs. Many of them never paid her. Cash flow in medicine was a problem then. It remains a problem in our National Health Service to this very day.

My Great Uncle, Dr Henry Fraser MRCP

Henry Fraser went to Aberdeen to train as a medical student in 1895. Soon after starting he was awarded the Pharmacological Society's medal for coming 1st in Pharmacology. In 1900 he was awarded the John Murray medal and scholarship, as the most distinguished graduate in medicine of his year.

Henry Fraser qualified and then passed his MRCP – a higher qualification. Dr Henry Fraser was a physician sent by the Colonial Office in London to Malaya in 1906. This was to become the Director of the Institute for Medical Research Federation of Malaya. The Colonial Office told him to find the cause of beriberi which they knew to be a bacteria. Beriberi could affect the heart, leading to collapse. Often it affected the brain, leading to hallucinations and fits. It was often fatal.

Dr Fraser was aided by five scientific staff, including a bacteriologist. He failed to find the bacterium, but was interested in a theory about rice already published by Dr W L Braddon, a State Surgeon of Negri Sembilan. Fraser decided he had to put this theory to the test. We now call such things 'clinical trials', but this phrase had not been invented then.

Fraser, working with two other doctors, Stanton and Fletcher, divided 300 Javanese labourers into two groups.[1] These men were employed in road construction in remote villages. 150 men were fed white rice, a polished variety. The other 150 were given Indian rice, with the husks intact. After 87 days beriberi broke out in the white rice group and this continued until the rougher Indian rice was substituted. The Malayan authorities were jubilant. A plaque to Fraser and Stanton was erected at the institute commemorating their 'pioneer work on beriberi carried out at the institute'. It is there still. The nutritional cure for beriberi (lack of B vitamins) was attributed to Dr Braddon, who started it all.

Dr Fraser was urgently recalled for medical services during the First World War. Strangely, and possibly due to poor communication methods in those days, he was held in disgrace by the Colonial Office. Despite what we might view now as a very successful clinical trial, Dr Fraser was told that he had failed to find the bacteria that caused beriberi, and he had also experimented with human lives by sending workers into the jungle to get beriberi.

Having spent nearly ten years in the tropics he was sent to Salisbury Plain with the army in the winter of 1915. He contracted pneumonia under canvas and died – still in disgrace!

Despite this, he was a figure of some awe and respect in my family, and certainly had some influence on my career choice.

Reference:

1. The Institute for Medical Research 1900-1950, Kuala Lumpur. Printed at the Government Press 1951. Chap 3: pg. 88.

Sir Harold Gillies

When I was 14, my father was more than a little worried about my schoolwork (could do a lot better, as reported in my school reports). I enjoyed sports but never was good enough to make them a career. I showed some aptitude in art and could draw a lot better than most of my contemporaries.

"Perhaps you could make a medical artist," my dad said. And he took me to an art exhibition at the Royal College of Surgeons, Lincoln's Inn Fields. I spent a fascinating afternoon. There were a huge variety of sketches, watercolours and oils. Most, but not all, were by doctors.

I can recall looking at some very simple pencil sketches of army life in North Africa during the Second World War. The draughtsmanship was superb. On close inspection, just a squiggle here and there, yet it then became something on taking a step back. There

Fig 4 – Sir Harold Gillies.

were plenty of tents, tanks and soldiers, all beautifully drawn in pencil on ordinary white paper.

"Oh, do you like them?" an old grey-haired man asked.

"Gosh, they are fantastic," I said, wishing I had half the talent of the artist.

"Well," said the old man, "we had plenty of time when there wasn't anything else to do."

"Are they yours?" I asked in astonishment.

"Oh yes," he replied.

I was in the presence of greatness. I was totally overawed.

"Do you draw?" he asked.

"Oh yes," I replied, "but not like you."

My father interrupted: "He is playing with me in the Father and Son Golf Tournament at West Hill next week."

The old man beamed a broad smile.

"Always play short of the third green with your second shot," he said.

"Oh, thank you," I said. (My golf ball had already visited the stream in front of the green.)

"What is your handicap?" the old man asked.

"Oh, 18," I said.

"What was yours?" my father asked the old man.

"Well, I was scratch for a long time. I played for England but failed to get into the Walker Cup Team (British team against America). I was busy in Harley Street and took the night train to Liverpool on the Friday. I had to play 36 holes on the Saturday. I had no sleep and got tired. I lost on the last green and so missed the team."

I was flabbergasted. This fantastic artist played golf better than I could ever dream.

"Oh that's nothing," he said. "I invented a club that hit the golf ball further. My tees were very high and I could even hit the ball off the top of a bottle. But the Royal and Ancient Rules Committee changed the rules and outlawed all my equipment. You can read these changes in the front of the rules book."

I was just bowled over. I stood aghast. My father had spent many hours in his youth fly fishing. He made his own flies and there was a glint in his eye when talking about it.

"They tell me you never worked anywhere unless there was a good fly fishing river nearby?" he asked the old man.

"Oh yes," was the reply, and he reeled off a list of rivers where he had spent hours and hours thrashing the water with enticing flies. He wished me "good luck in the Father and Sons." We parted. Dad and I chatted in the car on the way home.

"Gosh, that old boy is a fantastic artist and golfer," I blurted out.

"Oh, he's a surgeon too," said Dad.

"Oh that," I replied (not impressed).

I had just met Sir Harold Gillies, the father of plastic surgery. He repaired so many faces and other areas damaged in the First and Second World Wars. As a surgeon he was a colossus. He is still spoken of in awe. Such a modest man too. He found time to talk to an ignorant schoolboy like me. Perhaps it's a good job that he did.

Mike Hawthorn

As a teenager in the 1950s, like several of my friends, I had an interest in motor racing. The sports page of papers and the newsreels in cinemas reported motor racing regularly. One of my role model heroes was a young man called Mike Hawthorn. He was doing well in the World Motor Racing Formula One Championship.

Then a newspaper article ran a strange story all about motor racing. The reporter, male of course, was apparently at a complete loss to understand why a huge number of young ladies had started to flock to watch motor racing. Prior to this, it had been a sport followed and watched almost exclusively by men. What had happened? Even stranger to this reporter was that none of these ladies knew anything at all about car engines! I puzzled over this article too. The previous week, my older sister had asked me when the next race was. I thought it a bit strange at the time as she had no interest in cars whatsoever.

The answer was actually very simple. A good-looking, blond hunk called Mike Hawthorn had captivated their hearts. This high-heeled brigade just wanted to catch a glimpse of their hero. They did not worry who won the race. All that mattered was that 'Mike was safe' at the end.

In 1958, Mike Hawthorn became World Motor Racing Formula One Champion – and retired almost immediately. This was to the intense

Fig 5 – Mike Hawthorn.

relief of many ladies, as motor racing was more dangerous in those days.

Then, a few months later – on 22nd January 1959 – the newspaper headline read 'Mike Hawthorn killed'. He had had a road traffic accident on the A3 close to Guildford. He was carried from his car unconscious. He was laid down on his back and then later died. A massive head injury was suspected. The article concluded, 'A post mortem will be carried out'. The female population of the planet went into mourning.

I was upset too. Each day subsequently I scanned the paper, eager for the result of the post mortem. Several days later, right at the bottom of the front page, was one little paragraph. The post mortem on Mike Hawthorn showed 'a significant head injury'. But, even then, I was dissatisfied with the lack of detail. It didn't really explain fully why he had died.

My interest had been aroused. What was it that happened in a head injury that could cause death? Could it have been prevented?

More than 50 years later I have given an answer to those two questions about Mike Hawthorn in a later chapter. Am I right? – we will probably never know!

So, all these people in some way or another attracted me to a career in medicine. From my father and his abdominal pain I learnt that establishing the right diagnosis was always the key to correct treatment. My mother taught me how to juggle three jobs – her single-handed practice, running a house and bringing up three children. She also walked the Scottie dog, was a keen gardener and taught Scottish country dancing. What a dynamo. My older sister Janet, a medical student at the Middlesex Hospital, taught me to pass all my examinations first time. But I failed to follow that example!

Fig 3 shows my parents dining at a 'consultants' evening dinner' at the Central Middlesex Hospital. Most consultants dined at such events, which were frequent. Well, most consultants were on call – my father was always on call. The doctors all paid for their meals and the hospitals catered for them. It was good for hospital morale, as the consultants got to know each other well. The patients benefitted too. My father's juniors often called in to discuss an X-ray or ask him to see an emergency.

My mother was on call 24/7 too – but as a GP. When my parents got home after the meal, my mother would frequently go out to visit a patient at 11pm, if a telephone message had been left in her absence.

Today, consultant numbers have exploded. The workload is great, but they complain if they are on call once a week. The doctors' dining room and the doctors' coffee room are all gone – labelled elitist. Social events are rare and morale is poor. The consultants don't know each other, and all rush home at the end of the day.

My uncle Henry did fantastic research and never was acknowledged for it. I had met Sir Harold Gillies, in that brief encounter. What a multi-talented genius he was. I doubt if medicine has ever seen such a brain before or since. He fired my enthusiasm. I still did not understand how or why Mike Hawthorn had died. Would I ever learn about head injuries?

CHAPTER THREE

Medical School

In teaching the medical student, the primary requisite is to keep him awake.

Chevalier Jackson

So, I had gone for it – medicine was going to be my career. I swapped one school for another – King's College School, Wimbledon for St Thomas' Hospital Medical School, beside the Thames, opposite the Houses of Parliament (fig. 7 and 8). St Thomas' was steeped in history – the second oldest teaching hospital in London. It was an imposing large stone building with huge windows facing Big Ben. The hospital was named after Thomas à Becket, who was canonised in 1173. But the institution that received his name was in being from 1106 – originally called St Mary Overie. In 1212 it burnt down and was rebuilt. In 1658 Samuel Pepys attended St Thomas'.

I was to be incarcerated with other students in the medical school beside the hospital for the first 18 months. We were all subjected to a stream of lectures, practicals, tutorials, vivas, tests and examinations. A viva is an oral examination with the examiners.

It was fixed by law that 15% of medical students had to be female. It was a standing joke that our sandy-haired doctor, who originally interviewed me, liked female redheads. There were two in our year alone.

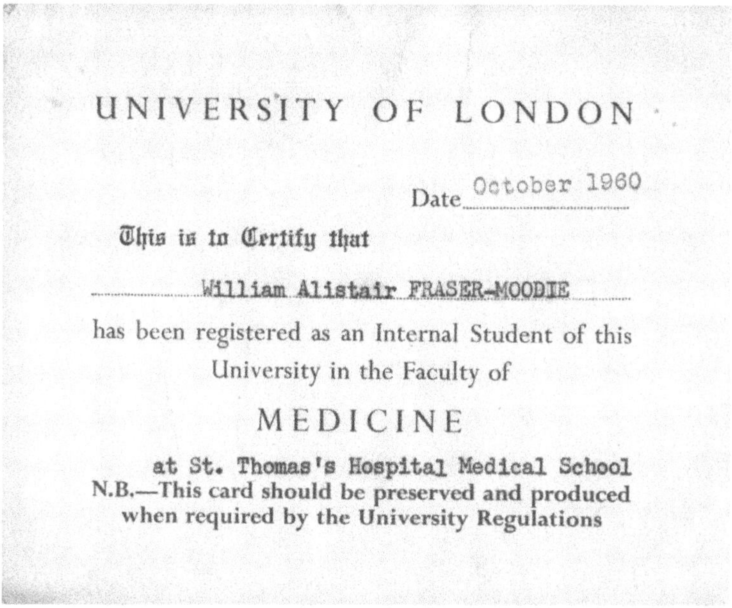

UNIVERSITY OF LONDON

Date October 1960

𝔗𝔥𝔦𝔰 𝔦𝔰 𝔱𝔬 ℭ𝔢𝔯𝔱𝔦𝔣𝔶 𝔱𝔥𝔞𝔱

William Alistair FRASER-MOODIE

has been registered as an Internal Student of this
University in the Faculty of

MEDICINE

at St. Thomas's Hospital Medical School
N.B.—This card should be preserved and produced
when required by the University Regulations

Fig 6 – My London University registration card.

So, there were 43 male and eight female students starting to read medicine
in October 1960 (fig 9). In retrospect, the ratio of applicants to places was
19:1 for men, 40:1 for women and 100:1 for overseas students. This was
before equal opportunities legislation!

Of the 51 students starting medicine at St Thomas' in October 1960,
only two (males) were the product of state education. Our main subjects
for the first 18 months were anatomy, physiology and biochemistry. We
were split up into small groups for our main subject, anatomy. On the first
afternoon we were directed to the Army and Navy stores – to buy long
white coats. Each group dissected a body injected with the preservative
formalin. We wore white coats but no gloves. Most of these bodies were
very old and thin. However, our group of four students, Di, David, Graham
and I dissected a muscular Chinaman. Any time between lectures would
find us dissecting the body and checking with anatomical pictures and
learned texts. We had lectures all morning from 9am till 1pm, including
Saturday. Indeed, the professor of Anatomy gave us a lecture at 9am every
Saturday. In the afternoon we had physiology or biochemistry practicals.
We also did anatomical dissection in the afternoon. Then we went to the
library. We all had a thorough physical examination on entry. Well, it was

27

Fig 7 – The Medical School at St Thomas' Hospital, 1960.

Fig 8 – St Thomas' Hospital, 1960. Since then it has been partially rebuilt.

a requirement for all students to be of sound health on entry.[1] The medical school wanted to be sure we were not carriers of disease, like tuberculosis, or suffering from other conditions, for example congenital heart disease.

At the end of the first term I came fourth in one subject – physiology. Gosh, was I pleased. But then this was the first time I had competed directly against girls. I looked again – oh no, the three ahead of me were all female!

Also at the end of the first term, I had to sit the Physics examination, 1st MB. The professor of Physics was superb. He gave me several one-to-one tutorials. He could teach, and for once I could understand. Above all, no calculus – this made it easy. This was DIFFERENT!

Fifty or so of us from all over the country sat the 1st MB examination. I did not think I had done well. What a noodle I was; I only came top by a long way (if my old physics teacher only knew)!

But not everything that term went according to plan. In an experiment in physiology we had to show that smoking inhibits urination. I smoked one cigarette and drank two litres of water. I did not pee at all, so it worked. I went to the library for one hour afterwards – still nothing. I was gridlocked in my Morris 1000 on Wandsworth High Road at 7pm. Then I realised I had a problem. My bladder was bursting. I finally relieved myself by diving into a bush on Wimbledon Common, to the consternation of a blonde in a 4x4 behind me. I'm so surprised that my kidneys work at all now, as I later went on a low salt diet for one week (boiled rice, etc.) After one week of this diet, my body wanted to conserve salt, so I only produced a few drops of urine in 24 hours. This was the other extreme.

One of my more notable fellow students at St Thomas' was Dave MacSweeney. Dave had played rugby for Ireland. He struggled at Chemistry. I tried to help him, but he really floundered. All the professors wanted to pass Dave. He was, after all, in the rugby team for the medical school! This was all just part of the colourful and often chaotic life of a medical school in those days.

One Friday night, another student, Jim, and I took two of the young ladies in our year to a ball. What a relaxation. What fun. We all had a great time. After dropping the girls off at 2am I realised that public transport had stopped. I could not get Jim back to his lodging that night as he lived miles away. So I took him home to my parents' house in Richmond. I lent him a toothbrush, though my clothes did not fit him as he was tall and slim.

Fig 9 – My fellow students at St Thomas' Hospital, 1960. Note that there are five women but twenty-eight men. A few students are missing.

At 9am on the next day, Saturday morning, we were waiting for the Prof's anatomy lecture. As he came in he glanced at Jim, still in his dinner jacket. He remarked, in his dry Welsh manner, "Well, I'm pleased to see that at least one of you is coming to my lecture properly dressed." Jim beamed.

When we all started at medical school in London not one student had a car. Living in Richmond, I was the only student who lived outside London, so after about a year my father bought a car for me to use. This Morris 1000 cost the princely sum of £300 – brand new. It's a very different story now, in the 21st century, when so many university students run cars. How times have changed!

Reference:

1. St Thomas' Hospital Medical School Prospectus 1958-9 (revised).

Medical School Sport

Guinness Brewery sponsored an annual walk from London (Tower of London) to Brighton (seafront) – about 56 miles. All of the London medical schools competed, and I was registered as number 980. This number was pinned to the front and back of my chest. After walking a few minutes I realised I was starving. I had rushed from the medical school to the start. As I passed a fish and chip shop my feet turned left and led me in. My large cod and extra chips was generous. I weaved my way out of the crowded shop, clutching the precious bag in front of me, held up between my cupped hands. Several pairs of hungry eyes followed me out. A wag called out, "Number 980, after that you will never make it to Brighton!" They all laughed. But I was determined to succeed.

The most memorable feature was dawn breaking over the South Downs – idyllic. I had done no training and walked through the night, getting there in 13 hours, having started at 7pm on a Friday night.

I learnt three things from this experience: my feet were really sore for the last ten miles and two soluble aspirins were fantastic. So I learnt the value of adequate analgesia (first thing). Secondly, in Brighton at 7.30am I was crossing a minor road. A motorcycle roared round a corner. I did not have any acceleration to jump out of the way and I was nearly flattened. So, fatigue predisposes to injuries (second thing). Thirdly, I did not learn

Fig 10 – My two numbers from the walks that I did from London to Brighton. Gosh, my feet hurt after each walk, but no blisters, thanks to that treatment.

by my mistake of walking the first time, and repeated the exercise the following year. I finished quite early in the field, and no girls beat me on either occasion.

By Monday morning I had fully recovered. Unlike most of my contemporaries I had no blisters, while they still struggled in pain. This was because prior to this event I had hardened my feet. Surgical spirit did not work, so I had contacted a dermatologist – a friend.

"Soak your feet in water with a few crystals of potassium permanganate," he said. Yes, it worked. My feet were stained a dark purplish brown but they were so hard. As I removed my socks in the male changing room of the operating theatre, a short-tempered, extrovert surgeon spied my feet.

"Get out of theatre at once with those dirty feet!" he cried. "You are absolutely disgusting. Get out now. How the hell do you have the gall to appear in my clean theatre with such filthy feet?"

I protested my innocence. He knew nothing of the skin-hardening treatment. My friends, instead of supporting me, just laughed – well, most of them had blisters! Finally, after much debate, this consultant let me stay. He was still not convinced of my explanation for the colour of my feet. But he had to write an official assessment of me at the end of his surgical firm and send it to the Dean. Did he write: 'Fraser-Moodie has made at least one appearance to my operating theatre, but sadly I, myself, have grave concerns about his personal hygiene?' I will never know what he wrote, but I was very worried.

The main sporting event annually was the Rugby Cup – a knockout event between the medical schools. So much has been lost by the amalgamation of London medical schools. There was a competition on and off the pitch.

One year we were to play the London Hospital in the final. Its students were enterprising enough to hire a boat and moor it in the Thames at high tide, right opposite St Thomas'. On the vertical part of the bank, below the Houses of Parliament, they painted, in huge white letters, 'LONDON → CUP'. As these huge letters were painted on the bank below the Houses of Parliament they were visible only from the other side of the river, i.e., from St Thomas'. Well, that was too much for our students, who then hired another boat and at high tide added the word 'DEFEAT'. So the message now read, 'LONDON → CUP DEFEAT'.

Mindless vandalism can take a bit of thought.

Banksy

The London students were incensed and went along with copious amounts of turps to rub out the word 'Defeat'. The River Police caught them and they were in trouble (Ha ha).

It's always easier to get forgiveness than permission.

Banksy

After one Rugby Cup Final, students from Guy's Hospital battled with our students. They had already won playing rugby – and now off the pitch in a battle too. Our mascot was an old oxyacetylene cylinder mounted on wheels, and we called it our cannon. The victorious Guy's students stole it and put it on the back of their lorry as they travelled along the Upper Richmond Road from Richmond to Putney. This was a bus route and all those waiting for a bus were pelted with flour by jubilant Guy's students. A police road block in Putney caught them all. They went to court and were each fined £50. They were then up before their Dean. What a disgrace!

It was not all bad though. I know of one student who had his fine paid for by his mother, then again by his grandfather, and finally again by his maiden aunt!

We got our mascot back – erroneously reported in *The Times* as a Boer War cannon!

At half time in that rugby match one of our forwards, Di, had a very sore face. So he went to the president of the rugby club, a doctor called Professor Wrigley. He was the professor of obstetrics and gynaecology. After a brief examination he assured Di that, 'nothing was wrong.'

"Get back to the pitch and win," Di was told by the professor.

Unfortunately, we lost the match. A few pints later and Di's face was fine. But the next morning he was in agony. He went to Casualty. Diagnosis: fractured jaw.

So the moral of the story is, if you have a facial injury, don't go to a gynaecologist!

Despite the occasional injury, sport was a big part of many students' lives at medical school, not least my own. It was great for camaraderie, for mutual trust and respect, and provided a welcome release from the long hours and hard work. In hindsight, it has also provided some fabulous memories.

Douglas MacMillan was my 'partner' at the medical school. We were paired together on medical and surgical firms, which, to non-medical readers, are teams of students who work together to look after a list of patients. Each student was given patients to learn about. If either Douglas or I was absent from a teaching round then the other presented the case.

Douglas was also cox of the St Thomas' Hospital rowing eight. He asked me to help at the hospital bumps (rowing races). I agreed. Of all the hospitals in London, our first eight was currently 'head of the river' – carried over from the previous year. The race itself took place on three consecutive evenings.

I drove three other St Thomas' medical students to the start – on the Thames, a mile above Kew Bridge. Now the Thames is familiar to us all from viewing the Oxford and Cambridge boat race on television. That course is a boat race upstream from Putney to just below Chiswick Bridge. Kew Bridge is the next bridge upstream from Chiswick Bridge. This boat race was downstream and finished under Kew Bridge. Officially, cars are banned from the towpath, but I managed to drive my Morris 1000 up the steep bank and onto it. We found our rowing crew – the first of a long line of eights, and each cox manoeuvred his boat to his team's respective stake. All the stakes were separated equidistantly. Each cox grasped a length of rope attached to their stake.

I held our boat steady in the water, ensuring it was pointing downstream. It was tense. A flag went up – two minutes to go. The wind and the current easily pushed the boat off line. One second the boat was heading for the nearside bank and the next diagonally across the river! The cox, the crew and even passers-by were full of advice for me. Then the gun went off. Shouting abounded. As I pushed the eight off, muddy water poured into my wellies. Douglas shouted orders and let the rope go. The eight shot off – rowing hard. One mistake would spell disaster.

I splashed through the mud, up the bank and into my car – tooting the horn. My three friends shouted encouragement out of the windows as we flew along. Driving was not easy! The towpath sloped steeply away on each side. Pedestrians and cyclists were obstacles to the progress of my car.

Eight after eight shot by us. One crew bumped the one in front of them. They would change places the next evening. One crew had overtaken another, but contact had not taken place – not a bump yet. One fast crew had gone past the crew in front and was trying to bump the next crew ahead. What chaos!

A mile or so downstream at Kew Bridge the race stopped. St Thomas' was still head of the river. All the crews were shattered. Amazingly, I avoided a mishap in my car. I emptied the water from my wellies and drove in normal shoes to the boathouse to congratulate my friends.

The following evening another student, Carol Minty, pushed our eight off very enthusiastically. As she did so, she fell forwards. The eight had a very good view of her going right under the water as they pulled away. She survived but, surprisingly, never volunteered to help again!

After three races our eight were still head of the river. And what fun we had then.

Car Accident and Medical Student Life

Carriages without horses go and accidents fill the world with woe.

Anon

During my time as a medical student, I was driving to St Thomas'. My fellow passenger Andy and I had an anatomical viva that morning. She was studying *Gray's Anatomy* as I drove and she asked me question after question. The anatomy book was open on her knees, and looking down she read from it. Whilst stationary at a junction, a Wandsworth refuse lorry cut across in front of us obliquely. The front of the lorry was close to us. I could not back the car as there was a car behind us. The lorry passed slowly by, getting a bit close for comfort. Eventually the back of the lorry removed most of the front of my Morris 1000 and drove on – without stopping! I could not follow as there was traffic following the lorry, though I recorded the number of the lorry.

That evening, the car owner and main driver on the insurance, my father, and I reported the accident to a dozy police constable at Richmond Police Station. The station sergeant, also standing nearby behind the desk, was half listening.

35

Question from PC to me: "Were there any other witnesses apart from you?"

Answer from me: "No, I had a passenger who saw nothing."

My father, to clarify matters, said, "No, at that time she was looking at her anatomy."

The sergeant exploded with laughter for about five minutes. The constable and my father saw nothing funny. I was just very embarrassed.

My father too was embarrassed when I told him what he had said, once we'd arrived back outside the station. "I didn't say that, did I?" he asked.

"I'm afraid you did, Dad," I replied.

The council paid for my repairs. The dustmen refused to admit who was driving. The viva was a nightmare, conducted over a dead, dissected body. Andy and I must have passed, as we both qualified, but it was a big struggle.

After 18 months at medical school we were tested in a formal examination on anatomy, physiology and biochemistry. My brain was in overdrive but I performed so badly. My first attempt at my hospital examinations had failed. So I tried to take an alternative examination called the conjoint examinary board – but I failed again.

I crammed and crammed facts and, three months later, I finally passed the hospital examination.

One story I recall at the time, relayed to me later by my friend Dave MacSweeney, illustrated just how hard we had to study for these examinations. The night before we sat the examination that I finally passed, Dave was swotting hard. He was studying his biochemistry notes. If he failed he would be thrown out of medicine. His wife called out, as it was getting late:

"Are you coming to bed, Dave?" A pause.

"Could I have a coffee please?" he replied.

She stripped off and brought him a cup. She stood close beside him – stark naked!

He sipped his coffee and carried on reading. "Do you notice anything, Dave?" she asked.

Pause.

"Oh yes," he said, "there's no sugar in my coffee!"

We got the results read out to us on Friday 13th. Although I had passed, several friends had failed. So it was a day of mixed emotions.

I'd succeeded on this occasion, but why was I so bad at examinations? I either seemed to do brilliantly or fail completely. There was nothing in between. This was not normal behaviour. It would take years before I found out why.

So, I had at last passed 2nd MB, as it is called, Physiology, Biochemistry and Anatomy. I was told that the reason why Latin was essential for medicine was that it was supposed to help with the understanding of anatomy. What rubbish, I say. For example, flexors flex the fingers towards the palm, and extensors are a group of muscles that pull the fingers straight again (extended). Nobody needs to suffer Latin to learn this. I hear some learned anatomy professor cry out, "There are lots of lessons from Latin that help in anatomy." Well, none of them helped me at all. One example of Latin applied to anatomy is in the brain. We all have a hippocampus. Everybody has a hippocampus. It is a Latin word, I suppose. It means seahorse, or sea monster with a horse-like head. So everyone has a sea monster in their brain. This translation I find just very odd and rather confusing. Latin never helped me learn or understand anatomy.

Soon after coming to St Thomas', the hospital embarked on a major rebuilding programme. The sound of pneumatic drills filled the air and cranes towered above us. Despite the chaos, the hospital continued to function and rapidly expanded. Nota bene – private finance initiatives had yet to be invented! Thank goodness, this development was financed the old way with cash up front. And it worked of course! The old wards with no partition and high ceilings were replaced, as were the graceful corridors and staircases. A new hospital, fit for purpose, emerged to meet the needs of the 21st century.

Clinical Medicine

To celebrate our passing of the 2nd MB examination, the Dean, Mr Bob Nevin, invited all the successful students to a cocktail party. We all formally accepted his invitation and turned up well-dressed. (Well, the Dean had the power to sack any student! So we all had to behave.)

Fig 11 – My first clinical year. This was before equal opportunities legislation so there are very few ladies present. The Dean is in the middle of the front row with the professor of anatomy and the hospital secretary to the medical school. Note the chief executive did not exist.

I was chatting to Dave MacSweeney (fig 13). He was an extreme extrovert who, in addition to being a former Irish rubgy star and launching a career in medicine, also became a novelist and was a great friend of the actor Richard Harris. One of Dave's three wives once described him as a 'novelist, poet and wit!' Dave had previously studied at Trinity College, Dublin, and Cambridge. His staple diet most evenings was beer – and plenty of it. He told me that the Dean's sherry glasses were far too small. Well, that evening I saw him down at least six glasses of sherry.

The Dean approached smiling and said, "You know I come from Ireland too, MacSweeney?"

"Oh no you don't," retorted Dave. "You come from bloody occupied Ireland, you do." The Dean retreated very quickly. I was very embarrassed.

So I started on the wards (fig 12). I bought a stethoscope and had to learn how to use it. Gradually, we were introduced to other strange objects – the sphygmomanometer, otoscope and ophthalmoscope – and learnt to use them.

The wards at St Thomas' were modelled on the old Nightingale model. At the entrance door you could see the whole length of the ward – all the beds. The ceilings were high and the windows large. At the far end of the ward we had views over the river to the Houses of Parliament. Big Ben kept us on time. Sister's office was a large table in the centre of the ward.

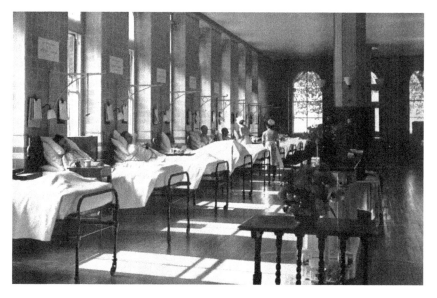

Fig 12 – A ward at St Thomas' Hospital. Please note the high ceiling, the flowers in abundance and those old-fashioned beds with so many pillows.

She was in charge of her ward. All persons, patients, doctors, visitors and especially students were admitted only with her permission. So she could and would refuse to allow a medical ward round to come in, e.g. if a bed pan round was going on or the medicine trolley was out.

As students, we did student clerking, mirroring the medical clerking. We were supposed to examine our patients. On teaching rounds we had to present our patients. We went from one firm to another. We were paired together and, as before, my partner was Douglas. My first medical firm was three months on the surgical unit. We were taught extensively on one topic: lymphoedema. This is an uncommon condition where patients are born with very few or no blood vessels to carry a body fluid called lymph round the body. These patients have swollen legs due to problems they have been born with concerning blood vessels called lymphatics. Every ward round included something about lymphoedema. We went to theatre and watched a lot of operations to do with lymphoedema. In retrospect, the vast majority of the surgery we saw concerning lymphoedema is not carried out today. So a lot of these operations are now obsolete.

I had two patients of my own. One had Hunter Hurler Syndrome. This is a rare complicated hereditary condition, that the patient was born with.

Fig 13 – Dave MacSweeney: novelist, poet and wit. Yes, he was a larger-than-life character, and he played rugby!

He had multiple abnormalities. I knew all about it and every ward round I was asked to speak on it. My patient was in for several weeks, mainly for the benefit of students. Then the surgeons opened him up. There was nothing that they could do. He was closed up, recovered from the operation and sent home. I have not seen another case since and never been asked about this condition in any examination or even heard of another case.

All of this teaching predated the modern scan. My other patient would have benefitted from one. He came in as he had a lump in his abdomen. This disappeared so he was sent out again. He returned later with a much bigger lump there. He had a retroperitoneal sarcoma that is uncommon. It is a nasty form of cancer arising from deep within the abdomen. Nothing could be done then but surgery could be done today? We would get the diagnosis earlier and try various treatments.

I recall going out on the wards one day to take blood samples, as requested by the house surgeon. He had written the forms. I needed to take the blood (venesection). I was well used to taking blood for tests. We had a routine that we all followed as directed. In the middle of the ward a large metal steriliser was full of boiling water bubbling away. We then grasped a long pair of forceps – the two pincer ends were in antiseptic.

We looked into the steriliser and fished out a needle from the bottom with the pair of forceps. These needles were a bit blunt – well, the same needles had been used for generations! We were able to sharpen any very blunt needles on a nearby carborundum stone. If we did this, then the needle had to go back into the steriliser for a bit longer.

Finally we attached our cooled needle to the glass syringe (used repeatedly too) and set off in search of blood. Once we had finished, the glass syringe went off to be sterilised and the needle popped back again into the steriliser.

This particular day was different. I had never seen such chaos on that ward. There was pandemonium. People were rushing everywhere.

Fortunately, a kindly staff nurse came to me and said, "Oh, it's chaos today. Please go away and come back tomorrow."

"What is going on?" I asked.

"Oh," she said, "it's something new – they've got to try all these strange new things – I don't agree at all."

"Well, what's it all about?" I asked.

"Don't you know?" she said.

"No," I replied.

"Oh," she said. "All the old glass syringes have been declared obsolete. We now have disposable plastic ones. We even have disposable needles. Use them and throw away. How costly. It will never catch on."

I agreed and left the pandemonium as requested. *Plastic syringes*, I thought. *I agree; whatever next?*

In the early 1960s, intravenous-giving sets were delicate. These were used to transport fluids including blood from a bottle into the bloodstream. They were made up of a metal needle connected to glass and rubber tubing – all sterilised of course. A rubber tube connected a glass bottle with the intravenous fluid to the intravenous-giving set. Gosh, plastic has revolutionised all of this.

My next firm was medical. The first patient I clerked had had a coronary thrombosis. Well, I thought, this was a medical condition. This history, the medical tests (electro-cardiogram and blood tests), all confirmed that he had had a definite coronary thrombosis (this is another term for a heart attack). It was only in retrospect that I realised how very rare he was. He was a teetotal, non-smoking, theology student aged 21 years! Poor chap. His prognosis was terrible.

Most of our bedside teaching was excellent, particularly in general medicine. I recall one physician, Dr Hector Goadby, teaching us cardiology. A dozen medical students watched him tape the diaphragm of his stethoscope to a patient's chest. He then attached the earpiece of this stethoscope onto a small portable box. He himself had put together the contents of this box. It was his invention. The box contained an amplifier and a loudspeaker. He switched the box on and the whole ward heard this patient's heart sounds plus a cardiac murmur over and over again. Without this box we could have only listened individually with our own stethoscopes. Dr Goadby then pointed out the heart sounds and the murmur. We all heard the same sounds. Such teaching would be of value today, but I suspect Health and Safety have banned it on the grounds of invasion of patient's privacy.

The stethoscope was invented by a Breton, Professor Laennac, in the early 19th century. He listened to the air going in and out of the lungs through a simple tube held to the chest. The modern stethoscope is more versatile, and indispensable to today's doctors, apart from a few, like orthopaedic surgeons and psychiatrists. For these pariahs, it is completely obsolete!

The modern version of the stethoscope is only of use to the professional classes – the physician and the safe-breaker.

My medical father was a typical Scot and hated wasting money. A water board official informed him that the dribble of water from our taps was due to a leak. This leak was from the water supply pipe to our house. A trench needed to be dug along a path from the front gate, under the back gate and to the rear of the property. The householder was, of course, to meet the full cost. It would not be cheap!

My father, on his knees, put his stethoscope to the ground along this path. In one area he heard a trickling noise and recalled the official. Sure enough, one little hole over this area found the leak.

Thank you, Professor Laennec!

Our numbers were swelled at medical school by Oxbridge medical students. One, Pete, was a good friend from Oxford. I took him canoeing once or twice from Teddington to the Black Swan at Thames Ditton. We had a couple of pints and canoed back. It was very restful. We chatted and he once remarked he had an identical twin brother who was reading

Medicine at the Middlesex. His brother was the extrovert ladies' man. We both laughed. Pete was quiet, behaved sensibly and dressed accordingly.

We were in the middle of a general surgical teaching round one morning. We had been deserted by the doctors teaching us, for five minutes, so they could write the surgical operating list for the next day. We were abandoned at the entrance to a ward. Pete as always had known all the answers to the questions posed to him. Yours truly had struggled with his answers. We were still good friends.

A tall, elegant staff nurse passed us. "Well, hello," said Pete. "I don't believe we have met before." There then followed a very smooth set of chat-up lines. She stopped and listened, faintly smiling at this impudent student. After he had flattered her and smiled appealingly at her, she then flatly refused a date. "I only go out with doctors," she said, turning him down flat. She stuck her beautiful nose in the air and hurried on.

I was absolutely amazed. "Pete, what are you doing?" I looked closely at him. Yes, that is my Pete, but his attitude is foreign to me. Then I looked closer, and closer. He had a red, flashy tie on – oh no, that's not Pete. I sidled up to him really close, and whispered in his ear, "You are not Pete, you are his brother." He went pale and whispered back, pleading with me, "Don't tell please, please; we will be in such trouble."

So the twins had swapped for the day. Pete was a student at the Middlesex Hospital and his brother had come to St Thomas'. If the deans had found out, the brothers would have been for it. They were bright enough to get away with it. I was a brick and told no-one (until now).

Pete became a professor of psychiatry and so did his brother!

CHAPTER FOUR

More Medical Student Days and Nights

Education never ends, Watson. It is a series of lessons with the greatest for the last.

Sir Arthur Conan Doyle MD

As a medical student, you have knowledge but no licence to practice. Some people trust you completely and others not at all.

I was driving through Battersea one day. Quite close to the dogs' home, on the Battersea Park Road, a cyclist had suffered a head injury. So I stopped to help. He was confused and bleeding. His airway was not good, lying on his back. I supported his head and neck and turned him gently onto his side. His airway improved. A female passer-by asked who I was.

"Are you a doctor?" she asked.

"No," I honestly replied. "I am a medical student."

"Not qualified. Oh help," she said. "Don't touch him if you are only a student," she said.

She then put her not-inconsiderable frame between me and the patient. I was told to go away.

"I will protect you from him," she said to the man (still not conscious!).

He still had an airway but only just. Fortunately an ambulance turned up before things got nasty. She felt very strongly that she had 'done her duty', and she told me so as I left. The patient could have died if I had not improved his airway.

I had had a lot of teaching about airway maintenance, principally in theatre from anaesthetists. Gradually I came to realise that this is how my boyhood hero Mike Hawthorn may have died. Had he been laid on his back following a minor head injury, which obstructed his airway? His tongue may have fallen back and blocked his airway. How tragic, and yet how very simple. This also sparked an interest in First Aid. More people should know about maintaining an airway – not just doctors. That is why I became involved in teaching First Aid.

In our training, we rotated through all the different medical specialties. Each teacher emphasised that their particular specialty was so very important. This included dermatology, ear nose and throat (ENT), and even genito-urinary medicine. The latter is better known as the 'Special Clinic'.

We did not know of the achievements of many of our teachers. For example, Mr Harold Ridley taught us all ophthalmology. But previously, in the Second World War, Mr Ridley had treated several spitfire pilots. They each had plastic embedded in their eyes from escaping through the shattered canopies of their planes. He noted surprisingly that this plastic – poly methyl meth acrylate (PMMA) – had not caused any inflammation at all. So he decided to use this plastic to make an intraocular lens. In November 1949, as a consultant at St Thomas' Hospital, he removed a cataract and implanted the very first plastic lens. This pioneering surgery was so controversial – attracting huge criticism at the time.[1]

The plastic lens and the surgical technique have subsequently been refined. This operation is successfully performed worldwide to this day. His critics have long since been silenced. Bizarrely, Mr Ridley himself benefitted from his own invention. In later life, he developed cataracts and underwent his own operation – very successfully!

This totally unexpected medical discovery was not the only one from the Second World War. For example, it is well known that, in Holland, some children thrived during the German occupation, only to regress on a better diet after the war. They were all subsequently found to have a gluten sensitivity (Coeliac disease). Once wheat, barley, rye and oats were excluded from their diet, they thrived again!

Reference:

1. Spitfires and Cataracts. *MDU Journal* April 2012; 28: Pg. 16.

Medical School – Psychiatry

Anyone who spends money on a psychiatrist should have his head examined.

Samuel Goldwyn

As medical students we were attached to a psychiatric firm and I soon banished any thoughts about a career in psychiatry.

I had to clerk a psychiatric patient. Poor man, he had been certified insane and was an inpatient. I found him excellent company and empathised with him. If I had had my way he would have been discharged immediately. He was a complete victim of circumstances and his detention was monstrous.

He was a lorry driver in his forties. He went to deliver a load at the docks. He was stopped at the dock gates. Somebody was very, very rude to him. So this 16-stone, six feet two inches driver dismounted his cab and gave the other man verbal and then physical abuse. In the circumstances I agreed that he had been provoked. So he landed up in hospital. How unjust, I thought.

A few days later there was a meeting of consultant psychiatrists from our hospital and elsewhere. There were lots of junior doctors and many more students. We waited and listened to learn.

This first case was my poor friend, the lorry driver.

"Let's hear from the medical student first," the senior consultant said. I stood up and spoke up for my friend. How unjust to keep him in hospital. He had suffered verbal abuse and should be let out now. There are many disturbed patients in the world and he is definitely not one of them.

My thoughts were accepted – and then entirely ignored. The psychiatric registrar smirked in response to my words. Several eminent consultant psychiatrists spoke, as did, eventually, a visiting professor of psychiatry. Their verdict – a dangerous psychopath. He had paranoid delusions and was very violent. Somebody suggested Broadmoor.

I never discovered the driver's actual fate, but that episode determined that I would definitely not become a psychiatrist. I was upset!

The very next day I was offered an escape from the psychiatric firm. *Oh terrific*, I thought. *Let's go.*

The psychiatric registrar said, "we need a male student to escort a patient to Epsom. You will enjoy the trip."

I waited for my patient outside an ambulance, having been given a little warning by the psychiatric registrar:

"Watch out, he's dangerous. Very dangerous."

Suddenly my trip to the country did not sound so jolly (this patient had been certified insane and needed to be detained as an inpatient until he was better).

Three male nurses and a sister escorted a tall, slim young man to the ambulance. I was standing by. The patient wore a brown corduroy jacket and had an open-neck shirt. I said a friendly, "Hello." He did not introduce himself, but climbed in. I followed, expecting an ambulance man to follow. None did.

The doors were slammed shut and locked. I was locked in with this 'very dangerous' man – help! The two ambulance men climbed into the front. One peeped through a small window and then pulled something over it. The ambulance started off gently. They turned their radio onto light music and we were on our way.

"God, I hate those doctors," said my cellmate. "I want to kill them all." "You'll never get out," he said, "never; you will be in for life – for life."

I realised he had taken me for another patient. Hurriedly, I turned away from him so I could deftly unclip my name badge and put it discreetly into my pocket.

"Oh, you might get out," I said.

"Oh no I won't," he said, raising his temper. "I hate them all. You wait. You don't understand, I want to kill all these doctors. All of them."

He ignored any remarks about the weather, the journey, etc. It was tense. It was slow. The tirade against the medical profession continued unabated.

I tried to calm him but nothing worked. I pretended to be a patient. He asked no questions of me. He was totally absorbed in his predicament. If he shouted and shouted, the ambulance men just turned their radio up. *Oh help*, I thought. *If he goes berserk I will be dead before they can save me!*

As he shouted again, the ambulance man just looked once through his window. *I could be killed*, I thought. *They won't come to my rescue.* Then I am sure the dance music was turned up once more. It was a long journey to Epsom. When we got there, four burly male nurses and a buxom sister came to meet us and take him away. It was relief at last. My tachycardia was still going strong. Well, I felt as if my heart was racing. I was so anxious for my own safety. I could not calm down.

I am definitely not, not, not going to be a psychiatrist.

Medical Student – Obstetrics

Fair fa' your honest sonsie face, Great Chieftain o' the puddin' race.

Robert Burns – *Ode to the Haggis*

I was one of four medical students sent to West Middlesex Hospital for obstetrics for a few weeks: two from St Thomas' and two from the Middlesex Hospital. We went on ward rounds, into theatre and had formal teaching. Also, there was a bleep (a pager). When a baby was due, the medical student on call was bleeped by the midwife and we had to run to the delivery suite (half a mile away)!

We would deliver the baby once we were gowned and gloved up. The midwife would supervise and give the appropriate injections, e.g. pethidine (a painkiller). We then checked the mother and examined the baby. Finally we looked at the placenta in the sluice, to see it was complete. We sometimes had to stitch up the mother if there had been a tear or cut around the vagina (an episiotomy).

We then washed the floor, the delivery couch and, the best bit of all, its bathed the baby. We then dressed the baby and took the baby to its mother. It was all great fun but time-consuming. The midwives gave us a rough time. They were in charge of us! They were qualified and we were only students.

One day we realised that all four of us were of Scottish descent and wore the kilt. My partner, as usual, was Douglas MacMillan. Burns Night was imminent and four female student nurses said they would join us. We could use the dining room in their nurses' home!

Everything was organised. It sounded perfect, apart from being on an on-call rota.

I was late turning up as a mother was so slow to deliver. Then I had to clean up and bathe the baby. By the time I got there, all kilted up, the other seven were well into the wine brought by the nurses.

We had to eat soon after. Soup was followed by, of course, haggis, neeps and tatties. Somebody supplied copious amounts of gravy (whisky).

I gave the 'Ode to the Haggis' – a Burns poem (all the verses and actions too). This was followed by cake and coffee. Then I organised the dancing. At that time I happened to be chairman of a local Scottish country dancing club (Sheen and District). None of the other students could dance – it was dire. To the correct music we had Dashing White Sergeant, Strip the Willow, The Duke of Perth (my favourite) and finally an eightsome reel. This was thirsty work – more whisky. I was exhausted pushing and pulling the dancers.

At about 10pm the student nurses (sticking together for safety) all said they were on an 'early' (whatever that is). They disappeared and informed us the front door would be locked by matron. (Ha, ha.) A curfew – what nonsense is this?

After a bit more intelligent discussion and whisky, it was about 11pm when the bleep bleeped. Up staggered a Middlesex medical student, only to be confronted by a locked front door. There was nobody about. The windows were locked too!

About ten minutes later – in complete panic – we found the top window over the toilet hinged open a bit. If one climbed onto the toilet seat and then the windowsill one could put one leg outside and heave oneself through the window. It was a tight fit. He managed it with the three of us pushing the last bare leg through and stopping him from falling back! Then all was quiet till the bleep went off again and again. Off went the kilted students into the night with advice like, "Don't drop the baby!" Suddenly, I was alone. After clearing up I had difficulty getting out on my own, balancing on one leg on the windowsill, and found the drop down was more than I thought. It was dark outside.

I had just got into bed when my bleep exploded and I ran off bleary-eyed to catch the baby at 9am. I was greeted by the midwife with, "What, no kilt?"

The immortal bard would have been proud of us. We had celebrated his birth in style.

* * *

About five years later, whilst working at the Central Middlesex Hospital, there was a fire one night in the nurses' home. All 40 female student nurses had to climb onto the roof (they were locked in and had no fire escape!). To everybody's surprise they found 20 men with the female nurses. Now, what were they doing there at 3am?

* * *

Some medical students were attached to the obstetrics unit at St Thomas'. They were bored one dark night. One student, Julian, unceremoniously smuggled Lord Lister's marble bust into a laundry basket. The 'patient' was put to bed. When the student nurse felt the patient's cold brow she nearly fainted. The ward sister summoned all the students for a dressing down at 6am. Later, the professor of obstetrics, with a twinkle in his eye, thanked Julian for removing the heavy ward laundry basket.

CHAPTER FIVE

The Long Hot Summer and Cold Winter of 1963

Medical student Paediatrics, ward rounds, golf and running. In a hospital with students… The patients are more carefully looked after, their diseases are more fully studied and fewer mistakes made.

Sir William Osler MD (St Thomas')

Something was different about the summer of 1963. I felt liberated. I did not see the obvious reason. Well firstly, I was at last doing what I enjoyed – clinical medicine – meeting patients and finding out what was wrong. Their responses to treatment and their follow-up were interesting. You never know if you are going to like something till you are doing it. I was happy learning, not from boring lectures that I never got on with, but face to face. I knew that medicine was my right career of choice.

Secondly, I had a summer free of examinations – well, the occasional test, but that was all. In 1958, it had been all O-levels. In 1959, they had found me two more O-levels to do and we had exams for first year A-level. In 1960, we sat A-levels. It was the anatomy, physiology and biochemistry exams in 1961. And 1962 had been 2nd MB – which I passed at my second attempt in July. I enjoyed the summer of 1963 a lot. No examinations at last.

As students we studied paediatrics. I loved it. My partner Douglas was so very keen – and never off the ward. Gosh, was I impressed. Until I discovered the true reason for his regular attendance – an attractive student nurse Sarah, whom he later married.

One paediatrician had a habit of calling all the children George, including the girls. One four-year-old girl reacted angrily to this, not surprisingly: "I'm called Melissa," she bellowed at him, "and not, not, not George!"

We were sitting down being taught in a group (firm), when the consultant paediatrician brought in a seven-year-old boy. He limped badly with a stiff left knee and right elbow.

"Tell us what happened to you, George," was the doctor's introduction. George knew what to say and his delivery was superb. He had spoken of this before.

"Well, I was playing at my house in the garden. Mum was in the kitchen washing and cooking. Dad was at work. I was so bored; I had no-one to play with. Then I opened our garden shed. Inside, my dad had about a hundred red plant pots (terracotta). I picked one out and put it on our patio. I jumped on it. It was great – it exploded – bits went everywhere. So I got another out and then another. At last all the pots were smashed. I had made a big mess. It was great fun. My mum heard nothing as the washing machine was on. Then I heard a car; my dad had come home. I was in for it. I hid in the now empty garden shed. I crouched down in a ball and kept quiet. My dad was upset at the mess. He shouted for me. I kept quiet. He opened the door and was upset with me. Then I found my back hurt, my left knee was stiff and my right arm. So I was sent by my own doctor to this hospital."

We laughed and laughed at this boy's antics, but we had no idea what was wrong with him.

It turned out that he was a haemophiliac. This is a hereditary condition that even blighted the Russian royal family. He had bled into his joints, leaving some residual stiffness. St Thomas' was a haemophilia centre.

I was upset to discover that he would not regain full function in his limbs again. So this hereditary bleeding disorder can cause permanent disability. Spontaneous internal bleeding can be fatal.

All intellectual improvement arises from leisure.
Samuel Johnson – *Life of Boswell.* Vol 2, pg. 219 (13. 4. 1773)

On 15th May 1963 I was asked to play in a golf match for the university second team at Stanmore Golf Club, playing against the club members. Their hospitality was generous and the hilly course in excellent condition. My putter was magic. I won easily. Our captain Martyn was pleased, and I now found myself in a team.

But my newly-found team members were all in poor spirits. They were glued to the radio. Spurs were playing badly in the European Cup football final. At half time they were one goal down. Hence their dismay. After dinner the radio was turned on again. Danny Blanchflower, their captain, got things going. Spurs won 5-1. The celebrations began.

I was on the beer all evening – well, ginger beer. At 11.30pm I discovered, to my horror, that I was driving six team members home. Martyn, our captain, had a car, but nobody would travel with him.

"Why?" I asked.

"He dislikes roundabouts!"

"What do you mean?"

"He goes straight across!"

So my Morris 1000 was packed tighter than a tin of sardines. One sober driver (me), six inebriated passengers, seven golf bags, other bags, golf trolleys, umbrellas, shoes, coats etc. I finally got back to Richmond, shattered, after 2am.

University golf, here I come.

My golf and my social life improved (to the detriment of my medical studies).

Never let schooling interfere with your education.
Mark Twain

Professor H Webb

Mediocrity knows nothing higher than itself, but talent immediately recognises genius.
Sir Arthur Conan Doyle

Fig 14 – Me playing a shot against Oxford University. We beat them, and also we beat Cambridge University when I beat a two handicap player playing on level terms.

I marched onto the 10th tee at Rye Golf Club in 1964 to play a friendly game of golf against Professor H Webb, a professor of neurology at St Thomas'. Then, for two days, we had a friendly golf match – medical students vs consultant staff of St Thomas'. I had an eight handicap that I could easily play to. I had played and beaten many players of lower handicaps, playing on level terms (fig 14). I played twice a week and regularly in the London University team (fig 15), as well as captaining the medical student team for St Thomas' and the university second team.

Professor Webb was about 20 years older and joked, correctly, that he had not touched his golf clubs for a year.

"I dug them out of the back of a cupboard under the stairs," he said. They were very old-fashioned and dusty clubs. His first golf shot was at least 30 degrees off line – a long way out of bounds down a nearby empty road. He laughed and laughed at this.

"Caught at mid-off," he muttered. "A cricket stroke."

He then proceeded to stroke the golf ball round the course like a professional golfer. Every stroke was a perfect strike. He thrashed me.

Fig 15 – London University Golf Team, 1964. On my left is Di Adams, a Welsh international, and in front of me is Clive Clarke, the current English amateur champion before he turned professional!

I walked off the last green having played well, but was soundly beaten. I did not understand how this man could play so well with rubbish clubs and no practice at all. All was explained to me by a chance remark to Professor Webb at lunch the next day.

"How many blues did you get, Hugh?" he was asked by another consultant.

"Oh, a dozen or so," he said modestly.

We all wanted to know how he did it. It sounded absolutely impossible to us. We asked him how he did it. He began slowly, "Well, I was in the cricket team anyway (1). I played golf and squash and got into the teams at the trials (2). I missed the tennis trial. The team had been picked but not announced. I challenged the captain to a game. I beat him and the other two members of the team (3). The hockey trial was fun and I had a few good runs (4). Football needed my services (5). Rackets and fives were a problem, as I did not know the rules, but I got into these two teams too (6).

I eventually got over 12 blues – the record," he said.

So I had witnessed raw talent at its very best.He had wonderful hand and eye co-ordination. His job as a professor was demanding on his time, likewise his family life. He had little time for sport. I once witnessed him playing cricket. The dangerous fast bowler he faced was soon dispirited as a succession of shots flew to the boundary. I later left St Thomas'.

Twenty years later I opened a newspaper and read of the Oxford vs Cambridge annual cricket match. The cricket correspondent was about to retire after about 40 years. A student had scored a century in this match. He praised the young batsman. He wrote: 'Yes, that was the best century I have seen since H Webb in 1948.'

I knew exactly what those bowlers must have been through. (In the Varsity match in 1948, he scored 145 not out, playing for Oxford.[1])

Professor Webb was a legend. He was so friendly and not at all aloof like some professors. Years later, I heard of two students who attended his outpatients clinic on a hot summer's day. The professor protested, "You two should not be here on a hot day like today. You need to be in the fresh air." At this, he handed them two tickets for Wimbledon that day. They left at once for the Centre Court.

Reference:

1.   J Webb. Hughie Webb. *BMJ* 2011; 342: 1152.

Skiing as a Medical Student

Snow, snow, thick, thick, snow.

Apologies to dancers.

Back to 1963.

My friend Bob told me in choir practice that year that he was organising a skiing holiday. Bob was two years behind me at medical school but a qualified accountant before he started medical school.

"Great," I said, "count me in." This was my fourth year as a medical student. A few weeks later found us in Victoria Station very early but all kitted up for skiing. Our numbers were made up by four wild Scottish nurses from Edinburgh. We took the night sleeper to Austria. The train was packed, especially the carriage with music and a bar.

Skiing was fun and wild. One of the big pop hits at the time was the tune 'Bobby's Girl'. Every time Bob joined a ski lift queue, the four nurses started singing it loudly and pointed him out. He cringed.

Fig 16 – Well, we did go skiing in ski school...

I was on holiday in Austria (fig 16) with second-year medical students. As a fourth-year student they considered me 'practically qualified'!

My first ever patient was a blonde in our skiing party in her early twenties. I was called to see her about 10pm by her room mate. I left the bar in an excited state – well, I'd just won a drinking contest. I rushed upstairs to her room and to her side. I saw she was unwell. I felt for her pulse – I could not feel it. (*How drunk am I?*) *Can I feel my pulse?* Yes. Still can't feel hers! She smiled at me. She was breathing normally. I realised she had a fast pulse, that I could not feel.

So I tried rubbing her neck to stimulate a nerve (vagus) to slow the heart – nothing. Still no pulse.

I decided she needed a different stimulus – cold air. So we opened the window. She leaned out. "I feel a little better," she said. To improve matters we held her out of the window. Her friend held her bottom and I anchored her thighs with a very firm grip.

About ten minutes later I was suffering the dual effects of ethanol inebriation and acute onset hypothermia. We hauled her in. She felt better.

She had a normal pulse. I was paid with kisses all round, and staggered back to the bar to great acclaim! She made a full recovery, and this cardiac problem did not recur.

We had lunchtime rugby in the snow as students. It was great fun packing down in a mixed scrum, especially when it collapsed. What a surprise! We used as a ball several woolly hats pushed one inside another (and not one of the nurses). The game stopped when our winger dislocated his shoulder. My GP mother had told me once how to put a shoulder back. I gave him a shot of morphine (carried illegally by me through customs – my mother had supplied me with it). The shoulder went back easily, using the Hippocratic method first described by Hippocrates himself and still the safest method to this very day. (My second ever patient!)

I continued to carry morphine on the slopes for years and years afterwards, always supplied by my mother and only used in an emergency. As a student, I could not be struck off the medical register as I had yet to get on it. My mother, who was, of course, a fully registered practitioner would have been in trouble with the General Medical Council (GMC) if they had found out – but they never did.

I continued to carry morphine in my pocket when skiing long after I had qualified in medicine. I can recall coming down an icy gully with three friends, me at the back. A large German had fallen at the side in thick snow. He had dislocated his shoulder too. My so-called friend pointed me out and said I was a doctor and had morphine. I could therefore not ski by. I was forced to give the morphine, reduce the shoulder and tell the patient to pass on the information that he had had morphine to anybody seeing him, so he did not get it twice and suffer an overdose.

I was obsessive at checking my bindings and never suffered a fractured leg. Time and time again I saw people with a fractured leg with their bindings done up too tightly. I altered my release mechanism every now and then to ensure my bindings always released. Today's bindings are more scientific (figs 17 and 18).

My best patient on the slopes was a nurse called Rickie, married to one of my medical friends, John. Rickie was 30 weeks pregnant and wanted to go skiing with her husband.

Fig 17 – A view of the Matterhorn. The snow conditions are not always this perfect.

Fig 18 – My skiing party. Six glasses and all are empty!

"Oh yes," said her obstetrician, "the sunshine and gentle exercise will do you both (mother and baby) a lot of good."

It was very cold in January. Unfortunately, the only good snow was at the top of the mountain. So Rickie in the beginners' class of ski school was taken to the top via the cable car. It was cold and windy. It was 20 degrees centigrade below freezing, plus wind factor. I just happened to be passing soon after she had fallen badly. It was bitterly cold skiing. She was very cold indeed, lying still and in pain, and what about the baby? We could not tell. Her leg was broken. I loosened her boot to help the circulation to her foot and removed the ski. We discussed the situation. We agreed what to do.

She was given morphine by me. She had it intravenously. My fingers were lumps of ice. Morphine here had two functions. One to relieve her pain and two to stop her going into labour. A very premature baby was the very last thing we wanted at 3,000 metres in a gale force ten at minus 20 degrees centigrade.

Rickie received excellent treatment. The leg healed. She had a lovely baby girl. The only thing that went wrong was her marriage (her husband strayed) but she has since then happily remarried.

Casualty as a Medical Student

I can well recall working very hard as a medical student in Casualty. As students, and indeed later as doctors, we all followed the routine of history first and then examination. The history has to be in the patient's words.

A lady whose words I recorded in 1963 was very upset. This was natural as she had been in a car involved in a road traffic accident. The history I wrote in the Casualty records was as follows:

"I was a front-seat passenger wearing a seat belt. Another car appeared from nowhere. It hit us and then disappeared. My Norman was driving. It wasn't his fault!"

One medical student had just finished examining a 15-year-old girl in a Casualty cubicle, suitably chaperoned by her mother. On leaving, the students overheard some muttering inside the cubicle. Then came the mother's loud voice, "Well, what did you expect? Dr Kildare?"

One thing struck me at the time, and it seems more relevant today. This was the strong bond of the family. Often a family of Lambethians would convey their matriarch to Casualty. So all the family came – sometimes 12 or 15 of them.

One night there was a list of minor operations to be performed. This included stitching of wounds, drainage of abscesses and removal of toenails. The Casualty officer was overworked so we two students were told to "get on with it".

"Yes, sir," we said.

My partner, Douglas, gave the local anaesthetic and I operated. We entered these cases in a large tome signing ourselves as surgeon and anaesthetist respectively. We discharged the lot of them and as far as we know they all did well! Such actions by students of today would be impossible without intense supervision.

Fast-forward 50 years to today. Junior doctors working in the emergency department, as it is now known, do not have the surgical experience of old hands like me. Recently I was told by such a doctor that they don't stitch! What lunacy is this?

Well, Casualty then was busy, but with what? There were large numbers of patients who had had minor wounds. We were worried that they could develop tetanus. None knew their immune status. So they were each given a test dose of anti-tetanus serum (ATS). This was developed in horses and injected into us to boost our immune status. Many casualties collapsed after the test dose due to allergy to the foreign protein. These then had to be resuscitated. Then they never got the injection of the full dose 20 minutes later.

So preventing tetanus was dangerous, haphazard and time-consuming.

Tetanus is an infection. Spores of tetanus are in the soil. So in any dirty wound these spores can multiply. As this bacterial infection develops, a powerful chemical is released. This chemical then attacks our nervous system. We go to great lengths to avoid the spasms of tetanus as these have a high mortality.

My last medical firm as a student

We were all more than a little worried. Medical finals were not too far away. As a group we were attached to a general medical firm. Now, general medicine is the backbone of medicine. It is vital that to become a good doctor you should have a good grasp of clinical medicine on a general medical firm. The centre point of this teaching was a round every Wednesday morning at 10am.

We all turned up to the first teaching round, our stethoscopes and notebooks ready. The consultant in charge of the firm never showed up, nor did a deputy. We sat about and then went and drank coffee before going back to the library. He failed to appear at all in the three months we were attached to his firm. We complained to the Dean's office – no response. There were no feedback forms either.

I discussed this with my father. He arranged for me to have some teaching from a slim young medical registrar at the Central Middlesex Hospital – Dr Peter Golding. He was excellent.

CHAPTER SIX

Queen Square and Finals

We had at the examination board one afternoon a charming but extremely slow-witted student who had appeared before us several times already and of whom we were rather very fond. He had a quality of devoted plodding seriousness which would have made him a good doctor if only he could learn to carry enough of the necessary information in his head at a time. One of us held a bone to him and asked what it was. The student replied correctly, "A femur, sir." Delighted with the correct answer my colleague pursued the matter: "And how many of these have you got?" After a little cogitation, "Four, sir."

"Oh come on, old chap, think again, and be careful when you answer."

"Four, sir, two in my body, this one I'm holding and another I've got to work on at home."

Lord Thomas Horder

On one side of Queen Square, in the centre of London, is a large stone examination hall. For generations, undergraduate medical students and doctors have been tested here. My late mother was a medical student at the Royal Free (then called the London School of Medicine for Women).

She can recall standing outside the same examination hall, that has not changed since then, waiting to do her final examinations.

Important people go in the front door after they have ascended an impressive flight of steps. These include all those working in the building, especially examiners, administrative staff and patients. Candidates for examination are sent to the tradesmen's entrance round the back!

Many years ago my late mother, Christina, had stood waiting for her clinical final examinations. She chatted to one of her extrovert female friends, also a candidate, Ursula. They saw a very elderly, frail, grey-haired man with a stick stagger towards the front steps. He mounted the steps slowly with great difficulty. Ursula rushed forward and accosted him very politely.

"Please help me," she said. "I am a candidate for this examination and we might meet in the clinical. If you told me what is wrong with your leg it would help me."

"Oh yes, oh yes, it would help you," he said.

"What is wrong?" she asked.

"Well, it's a long story," he said. "I had tuberculosis of the lung as a boy and was hospitalised for over six months. This infection spread to my right hip. The bone was affected so my right leg is three inches shorter. My right hip is fixed. My right shoe is built up, so I still limp badly as a consequence."

"Oh thank you, thank you," she said. "I do so hope we meet in the exam."

"So do I," said the old man with a smile. "Goodbye, young lady."

The good news was that Ursula met the old man in the examination hall. The bad news was that he was not a patient to be examined, but the examiner himself.

Ursula and Christina both passed.

Denis

My friend Denis had a bad time in finals at Queen Square. He was asked about a syndrome called by an eponymous name. He blurted it out.

"Well," said the examiner, "who is it named after?"

"Oh," said Denis, "the surgeon is dead."

The examiner called across to the next table.

"George, how are you feeling?"

"Fine thank you, Tom."

"Well, that's strange," said Tom; "there is a candidate here who has just told me you are dead." Denis cringed. Things then got a whole lot worse.

"Look out of the window," Denis was asked at the next try at finals.

"Now, what do you see?"

"Trees, sir."

"Very good, my boy. Now, what colour are they?"

"Green, sir," said Denis.

"Very good."

"Now, we will see you again when they are brown."

Failed again!

Denis was a likeable fellow who would grace every social gathering at the medical school and well supported the bar. On his return from one of the many occasions he graced Queen Square for his finals he told us he had been asked the anatomical length of a delicate piece of female anatomy – the female urethra down which ladies pass urine. (Denis did not know the answer was one and a half inches). He paused.

"Come on, boy, how long is it?" The bell sounded but the examiners would not let him go till he had answered. "How long is it?" was repeated.

"Oh, six inches," said Denis in desperation.

The two male examiners fell about laughing.

"Congratulations, my boy," said the examiner who always faced Denis across the table. "You must have some fantastic women at St Thomas'." Denis cringed and fled. Failed again.

They eventually took pity on Denis and passed him!

(That last question according to 'examination gossip' has been banned.)

Christopher was a medical student with no interest in surgery whatsoever. He rarely graced the operating theatre with his presence and missed the anaesthetic course completely. But he had to pass surgery finals. In the viva he was passed a curved rubber tube. This tube was of a type used by anaesthetists to supply patients under anaesthesia with vital gases.

"Well, what is this?" he was asked.

He declared with certainty that this was a flatus tube, lifting it up to demonstrate. So according to this student the tube had a function to relieve wind from the bowel.

His examiner, Mr Guy Blackburn, was flabbergasted. Christopher still passed and quickly went into private general practice.

Years later, by chance, he met Guy Blackburn at the Garrick Club. Chris was not forgotten. The surgeon even bought him dinner.

One medical student was a perpetual student. John knew everybody and anybody at St Thomas'. He was well-connected and well-liked by everybody. He played rugby and umpired the cricket matches. He was always in the bar every evening. He knew everybody. If I returned to the bar years later, he was still there. What a fine fellow.

The Dean had been very, very patient with John, as this longest-ever serving medical student failed finals over and over again. However, you could not get annoyed with John, by now about forty years of age. He was always in the hospital but rarely on the wards (or in the library).

The Dean summoned him.

"John, you are sitting your finals next week and I forbid you to play rugby tomorrow. Do you understand?"

"Yes, sir. I will not play rugby."

"Good," said the Dean.

Like the fine fellow he was, John did what the Dean had asked. So he refereed a rugby game instead of playing in it. He never qualified in medicine! One of his excuses was that this examination always clashed with a more important event – Royal Ascot!

He never passed his finals but propped up the bar at St Thomas' for the rest of his life. Such a likeable fellow! He knew everybody and greeted us all. He was the life and soul of any party.

We had arrived at medical school all having sat and passed quite a few exams already. Years later, Professor O'Higgins, past President of the Irish College of Surgeons, recalled to me once the story of a mathematics test his sister had sat at school. She got all the answers right, so scored 96%. However, the Irish Matriculation Board gave 10% more if you answered in Irish Gaelic! She had done this and so scored 106%. (It could only happen in Ireland!) This bizarre fact is true and illustrates the fact that if examinations are not organised properly, they can become a farce.

I became a regular attender at examinations as I failed to satisfy examiners on several occasions. We were told that 40% would fail 2nd MB after 18 months of study. I had scraped through at the second attempt. Finals had a high failure rate and I duly took three goes to get it. None of us passed surgery finals if we saw a certain patient. He refused to let us examine him – result, failure! I failed pathology finals for a technical reason. I had just finished an infectious disease course two weeks previously. I had acute abdominal pain the day before the examination. If there are any medical students reading this you may like to make a differential diagnosis:

I was a 23-year-old man with previously no ill health now with abdominal pain. I had no hernias, normal genitalia and normal bowel sounds. My chest was clear. But I had vague abdominal tenderness and the pain was getting worse. I did not lay still.

Differential diagnosis: Constipation? Gastroenteritis? Appendicitis? Peptic ulceration?

Now, carry on. The diagnosis is none of those.

How about gall bladder disease? Pancreatitis? Rectus haematoma?

No, none of these either. What is the diagnosis???

Ureteric colic?

Wrong again.

Clues: Many rare and unusual presentations occur in doctors. I had been on an infectious disease course. Have you any ideas? Spots, raised, red and itchy, appeared all over me 12 hours later. They were very irritating and itchy, especially at muco-cutaneous junctions. The only area I could count them was on my palms – 36 of them on my right palm. I could not recognise myself in the mirror. My neck was as broad as my head.

I had chicken pox. The incubation period is up to 21 days. My abdominal pain had been in the prodromal time, i.e., before the spots came out. I lost my fee for the examination as I was infectious and so I was forbidden to take it! So I 'failed again'. I must have been in contact with chicken pox on the infectious disease course. Chicken pox is a very rare cause of abdominal pain.

* * *

Later, as I waited for my pharmacology viva, I saw a friend from the Middlesex Hospital.

"How did you get on?" I asked.

"Oh, dreadful," he confided in me. "One of the examiners spoke in a thick German accent and the other had a bad Bell's palsy."

I did not believe a word – what rubbish. I laughed at him. Exactly ten minutes later I was ushered in.

"Vellvhotvillve be talking about, sen?" asked my examiner. I panicked and looked around. The other examiner just grinned, except his mouth was near his left ear. Oh help – failed again.

Nowadays the pass rate for finals is at least 90% – a lot easier. I wonder why.

* * *

My friend Alex McDonald had a bad time in his viva for Obstetrics and Gynaecology in finals. Poor chap, his mind went blank and the lady examiner was distraught. Finally she wrote something down and asked Alex to "please sign this piece of paper". Then, as agreed, she passed him! What had he signed? The lady had written on the paper: 'If I pass finals, I promise that I will never ever practise Obstetrics and Gynaecology'.

In those days, for medical students there were three ways to qualify in England:

Their own university.

The College of Surgeons of England exams (conjoint).

The apothecaries' examination held at their hall in London.

I qualified initially by the conjoint examination, and on my third attempt a year later passed my own university final examination.

I had finished my final examinations. I had worked for months with no break. I was waiting for the results. I needed fresh air and exercise. For the first time in about four months I went down to the local golf club, Royal Mid Surrey. It is in Richmond. I hit quite a few golf shots on the practice ground. One other was there – a schoolboy.

I was bored and wanted to play some golf. I got chatting to this lad. He was 14 years old and had a ten handicap. We arranged to play 18 holes the next day. He would receive two shots from me (so I handicapped myself by two shots).

We had chosen a cold wet windy afternoon. The greenkeepers had

68

put all the tees right back. So the course was playing long. It was October and nobody else was on either course. This was because of the weather.

Our game was close. We both played well. Considering the conditions, we both were striking the ball well. Gosh, this lad could play. What promise he showed! So young and yet really talented.

He beat me on the very last hole. I lost one down. We shook hands. We went in to the clubhouse to the warm. I bought him a tall lemonade. Two other senior members were drinking whisky. I was greeted with: "You haven't been playing golf in that?" one old guy asked rudely.

"Oh yes," I said. "I went round in 79 and was beaten by this young man, aged 14."

In disbelief this man went to tell his drinking friend. I heard one say, "Impossible." They both laughed and left. We ignored them. I told the lad he would go far in golf. He had talent and plenty of it.

I went home. Soon I was thrown into medicine proper. I hardly touched a golf club for years and years. But I was able to follow my opponent's progress on the golfing grapevine and later in the press. He soon made the county golf team. Then he became English amateur champion and won countless competitions.

His greatest moment was playing for the British Isles in the Walker Cup. He had the deciding rubber and beat the American champion Melnick, before my friend turned professional.

I had played with Warren Humphreys.

"The choice of a putter," as P G Wodehouse noted wisely, "is so much more important than the choice of a wife."

CHAPTER SEVEN

Junior Posts

My First Ward Round Ever

*The education of the doctor which goes on after he has his
degree is, after all, the most important part of his education.*
John Shaw Billings

I was aged 23 and had just qualified as a doctor in October 1965. I was unemployed. My own hospital had no jobs for me. I telephoned the local hospital. They needed a locum house surgeon. I had work for two weeks. I was told I had to run the bar at the doctors' mess too. I disliked the beer – Watneys Red Barrel – and ordered Worthington E immediately. I clerked patients and ran the ward for the first day. None of my patients was very ill. I took all the blood tests myself. So I had no phlebotomists to help me. Then came the first ward round on the second day.

My three medical colleagues all had the Fellowship of the Royal College of Surgeons qualification. So they were experienced surgeons, one consultant, one senior registrar, and one registrar Ian. I was put firmly in my place (very low down). As the very inexperienced newcomer only provisionally registered, I was there to learn. I had to do the telephoning, arranging the day to day tasks, little but important tasks. I took a lot of blood tests and arranged X-rays, etc. In return for me running about and arranging things I was taught on this ward round.

I was shown a 50-year-old man with a hard lump that seemed to be within his left biceps muscle. I can recall I had not the slightest idea what it was. I had seen nothing like this before. As this patient was examined his gown fell open on his side, and I could see, and felt quickly, a fatty lump (lipoma) on his right hip.

"Well, what is the lump on his arm?" I was asked.

"Er, a lipoma," I said (as they are sometimes multiple).

There was an awkward silence. I was led away whilst the other two made small talk.

"It's definitely a hard lump in his biceps," said Ian. "This is a sarcoma of the muscle. It cannot possibly be a lipoma." A sarcoma is a rare cancer while a lipoma is common and usually benign.

I had made yet another error! Oh dear!

Just then my bleep sounded. I apologised. The call told me a drayman had come to the doctors' mess and I had to go to help him join up the new barrel. He could not do it! I fled to the doctors' mess where a large red-faced man from the brewery knew exactly what he was doing.

"We need to test the first pint, doctor," he explained. "Well, come on, then," he said.

He quickly drew two pints. I had barely started my pint before he drew two more pints (at 11am).

"We need to test the second pint, doctor," he said. "It might not be good."

Two pints later I staggered back to my round, now in the mortuary. The others commented on the funny smell (my breath). We then had coffee and I rushed off to sort out some errands on patients and sober up.

I had failed again – or had I?

At 3pm on the ward I had a bleep. Ian called me from the theatre. Our patient did not have a sarcoma, as the other three had thought, but an innocent intermuscular lipoma. Good news for the patient and for me too. As he told me, Ian said he was, "in a state of shock". I just laughed (figs 19 and 20).

Maybe I was not so stupid after all, I thought. (This man had a soft lump that felt hard because it was surrounded by muscle.)

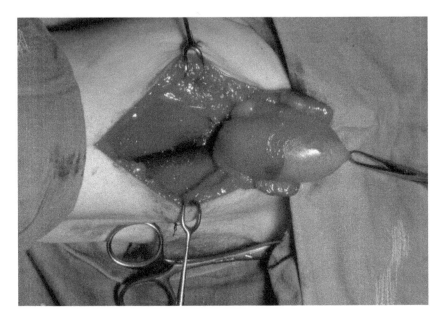

Fig 19 – Lipoma in situ. It felt so hard in between two muscles.
Usually a lipoma feels so soft.

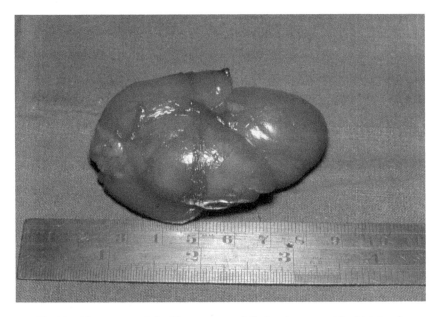

Fig 20 – Lipoma once it had been removed (before it was sent for histology).

* * *

The administrator to the hospital told me to contact the department of work and pensions. I was not registered. "Come down between 9am and 5pm any weekday this week to register," I was told over the telephone. I told them I was working and couldn't come.

"Oh, that is awkward of you," I was told. I was telephoned back half an hour later. "Our boss will call into the hospital this evening at 6pm," I was told.

He was curt and annoyed at being called out. He told me so. I explained I could not have the time off.

He took my details – name, age, etc. Then he paused and sighed. "Well, I must say I am absolutely disgusted at you. You are aged 23 years and have never done a day's work in your life. I started work from school at 15. I hope you are ashamed of yourself."

He shook his head. He gathered up his papers and left. He went home, I presume. I was soon bleeped for an emergency and rushed off to Casualty. I worked really hard for two weeks – the locum. I found this a big shock to the system – more was to come!

First Job: Orthopaedic House Surgeon

I at last had a full-time job. I had applied to this same hospital for a full-time post for six months. I was a house surgeon in orthopaedics. I was on call Monday to Friday, 8am to 6pm daily. I was also on call alternate nights and alternate weekends. These on-call alternate nights came round too often. I lived in the hospital and slept and slept on nights off. (A weekend off in those days did not start until Saturday lunchtime!)

The hospital was Queen Mary's, Roehampton (fig 21). This is part of the Westminster group of hospitals. It had been a war pension hospital before 1948 – the war pensions officer came on all the medical ward rounds. A remedial gymnast came too – to keep the amputees fit! Our proximity to the then largest limb-fitting unit in the United Kingdom meant that we frequently had patients for lower limb amputation, usually above or below the knee. These operations were uneventful and the

Fig 21 – Christmas 1965 at Queen Mary's Hospital, Roehampton. Please note the doctor's white coat, the excessive alcohol and even one nurse smoking! Oh, how times have changed. But who has the red nose and the beard? That is me!

patients so grateful. Well, artificial limbs were first recorded by the Greek historian Herodotus in the 5th century BC!

Historically, amputation has for decades been the province of the doyen surgeon. In Victorian times it was frequently performed through the hip joint (hind quarter). These operations had complications galore. Surgery had to be so swift to give the patient any chance at all of recovery. Following one such infamous operation by Robert Liston, a Professor of Surgery, the patient succumbed. The surgeon's assistant had been mortally lacerated in the fray (his fingers had been cut off) and he passed away too. Finally, an onlooker was so shocked that he too collapsed. Well, the surgeon's flaying scalpel had slashed through his coat tails. The poor terrified spectator thought it had pierced his vital organs and he died of shock. So this one operation gave a mortality rate of 300% – truly a record![1]

I had four wards to look after, a quarter of a mile apart. A lady physiotherapist asked me if I had seen the children on Gillies ward. I had not, so we made a detour to that ward. As we approached, the noise was deafening. The air was full of happy noises. Inside was a hive of activity. The children of all ages were playing together helped by the nurses. Then the penny dropped – each child had at least one limb deformity – this was the thalidomide ward.

A two-year-old scuttled across the floor chased by an older boy with one normal arm. The other arm stopped at the elbow. The two-year-old scuttled on his bottom as he had no legs. He was laughing at being chased.

Sister was a smiling happy lady. She had just had a visit from a dentist who complained to her that, "A lot of these children will not be able to look after their own teeth."

She disagreed and, to prove a point, called over a tall girl. "Emily, show this man how you clean your teeth," she said. Emily had no arms, just tiny fingers sprouting from her shoulders. Emily grasped the toothbrush between her big and second toe, balancing on her other leg. She proceeded to clean her teeth. As an encore she picked up a pen with her toes and wrote her name on the paper on the floor.[2] I was just amazed. It was a very happy, lively ward.

I had witnessed the victims of one of the worst, or perhaps the very worst, iatrogenic mistake ever – the thalidomide disaster. This, amazingly, was first reported in an obscure Australian medical journal. These children had come to Queen Mary's for intensive, specialised physiotherapy assessment and treatment, combined with possible limb fitting. They were so happy and they shared a common bond of deformity. I shall never forget the joy of those young souls and the noise – laughter, singing, clapping and shouting.

Life is not easy or straightforward if you have no deformity. It is far more difficult with one. Soon they were to leave this sanctuary, this oasis of care, and go out individually to face an uncertain future in our wide world.

We now know that the drug thalidomide, given to pregnant ladies in the late 1950s and early 1960s, caused birth defects. Official statistics in the UK are that 2000 babies were born to ladies who had been prescribed thalidomide during pregnancy, and only 466 babies survived.

Martin Johnson, a former director of the Thalidomide Trust, has calculated that due to this drug in the UK alone, there were 6,000 miscarriages, 2,000 stillbirths and 2,000 babies that died in infancy. Their poor parents would have been largely ignorant of the connection with thalidomide. There was also no birth defects register.

The whole thalidomide saga is bizarre from the beginning to the end. This drug was developed by Grunenthal in Germany in the early 1950s. It was aggressively marketed as a safe drug, as it was thought that no drug could cross the placental barrier. At its height, this drug was distributed under license to 37 different countries, largely as a treatment for morning sickness in pregnant ladies.

Nobody would believe the scientific evidence, even when an Australian obstetrician, William McBride, and a German paediatrician, Widukind Lenz, independently showed the association between thalidomide and birth defects. The association between the development of birth defects and thalidomide was independently suggested in a letter to the *British Medical Journal*. On 31st December 1960, Dr Leslie Florence wrote 'Is Thalidomide to Blame?'; she quoted four cases of birth defects. Each mother had been treated with thalidomide. There was a delay before this drug was withdrawn in the UK in November 1961. Other countries were slow to follow suit.

Mr Enoch Powell, the Health Minister from 1960 to 1963, flatly refused a public enquiry. The thalidomide victims had to wait 50 years before the British government and the German manufacturers issued apologies.

We will never know the full toll of misery caused by this drug worldwide. The victims of this disaster have yet to be compensated!

Today the survivors of this iatrogenic disaster are still suffering physically, mentally and financially. Many need round-the-clock assistance. Once again, action had been too little and too late.[2] But these people have special skills demonstrated today – the Mouth and Foot Painting Artists, with their own gallery.[3] One victim of thalidomide is Tony Melendez. An award winning singer, he plays the guitar with his feet!

* * *

I was overpaid (£31 a month after tax). This means I was paid about ten pence for each hour that I was doing some work.

Every other night, from 6pm to 8am, another doctor, called the senior house officer, was on call. However, he went off on study leave and did not come back for over a month. I was not expecting this and neither was anybody else. I was therefore on call till he came back. So I was on 24/7. I was given no apologies, no locums, no nothing. I had a friend, George, doing rheumatology. He went off sick suddenly with tuberculosis. At the same time, my consultant, behind my back, arranged for me to do George's work. I was told by my senior registrar that this was arranged. I needed a reference from my boss, so I could not argue. I just did that job with ward rounds too. It was interesting as many patients had been prisoners of war under the Japanese.

Very soon after I started, a strange incident occurred. It was the first of many to confront me during my medical career. I was in a cubicle in Casualty clerking an old lady with a fractured neck of femur. So she had broken the upper end of her thigh bone and could not walk. She needed an operation to pin her fracture. My job was to see she was fit for the general anaesthetic.

On the other side of the curtain in the next cubicle there was a 'dispute'. An anxious father had brought in his own toddler. He suspected she had eaten deadly nightshade berries (belladonna). These are highly poisonous and contain atropine. He was worried and brought in a sprig of deadly nightshade to confirm his story.

The locum doctor spoke English as a second language. His female nurse and this male doctor were slow-witted. He failed to find deadly nightshade in the authorative textbook on botany kept for reference, to the exasperation of the father. "It's on page 38," said the father curtly. "Oh look," said the nurse, "the patient has the same surname as the book's author."

I could contain myself no longer. I interrupted the other doctor and introduced myself to the father.

"Is this your book?" I asked (noting that the author was a Ph. D).

"Oh yes," said the father modestly.

I had to explain to the doctor that the patient's father had written the textbook held in his hands. So the toddler had had close contact with this poison. The toddler was admitted overnight and discharged the next day. She can't have swallowed any berries.

I learnt not to underestimate the patient or their relatives!

* * *

As a very junior doctor in my first registration year I had been 'volunteered' by my orthopaedic surgeon (consultant boss) to help the rheumatology and rehabilitation consultant (his junior had developed tuberculosis!).

Quite simply, I did what I was told. I expected to see a lot of patients with various forms of arthritis. Not so. I was working in Queen Mary's Hospital, Roehampton in 1965-66. This rehabilitation consultant was following up men who had been prisoners of war under the Japanese.

These poor men had outwardly recovered from their starvation and beatings. They initially had returned to the UK, I was told, full of diseases and parasites. They were treated for these. They had all subsequently put on weight and seemed healthy 20 years later. These men each had physical examinations by me. Then they had a chest X-ray. They were still vulnerable to tuberculosis and other infections. Apart from routine blood tests they had stool examinations and cultures. I was told that they all had been 'riddled with amoebae and intestinal worms'. There was a real danger that intestinal amoebiasis could recur even after repeated courses of treatment. We treated such recurrences, but they were uncommon.

What really upset me was the mental state of these men over 20 years after the war. They never talked about their time in captivity. They all seemed withdrawn 'to some degree'. They never really relaxed. Conversely, the amputees from the war in my orthopaedic ward laughed and joked a lot. They each had an obvious memento from the war – an artificial limb. However, none of the amputees were withdrawn or upset mentally. There was a difference.

* * *

I had just finished work one Sunday evening at 10pm and I wandered into the doctors' mess hoping I got to bed that night. I was shouted at by the Casualty officer and he told me he was going to the Coroner's Court at 9am the following morning. He was senior to me. I was supposed to do his job in his absence. It was too late to alert my senior doctors. I was too tired to.

At 9.15am the next day I was in Casualty on my own. I had had two patients and each had had a cardiac arrest. I was the only doctor. Both had died and I was trying to resuscitate a third poor chap. He died too. To the intense annoyance of the nursing staff my, bleep was going over and over again. I could not answer. I was busy. Messages were related to me, to the dismay of the nurses.

"Come to my ward round at once, or I shall report you to your boss," said the rheumatology consultant via the nurse.

"Get your butt end down here, you lazy bastard," said my registrar from theatre. "I want you now to hold the leg." (These were his exact words.) So I was reported to my boss for not doing my job – twice over. I heard nothing at all. No apologies, nothing. Suddenly I was let off all these extra duties, and a few days later that senior house officer I was covering for just appeared – all smiles. (He had failed his examination in Surgery.)

A lot of our patients suffered from chronic bone infections (osteomyelitis). They had been in the Second World War and suffered leg fractures. These fractures had often been slow to heal as this was the pre-antibiotic era and their legs were full of shrapnel. As an aid to recovery, apart from surgery and antibiotics, I had to give them hyperbaric oxygen treatment. I put them in an oxygen tank and increased the pressure from one to two, or even three, atmospheres. I did this most days. Unfortunately, this treatment did not help them. It was thought that more oxygen getting to the injured area would promote healing. It did not.

This treatment took a lot of organising. It was very useful in two other conditions – crushed hands with poor circulation, and carbon monoxide poisoning. Both these conditions improved at once. As I was the only doctor to use this machine, I was asked to help out. Today hyperbaric chambers have a different use. They can be used to cut detox times for drug addicts.[4]

I was due to finish my first job at Queen Mary's Roehampton after a weekend on call at 9am Monday. But I had a second job at Barnet General starting at 9am that same Monday. Clearly, I could not be in both places at once. So I telephoned Barnet General and talked to a senior administrator in staffing.

He was unhelpful: "If you are not here at 9am on that Monday morning we will sue you for breach of contract."

I protested in vain.

"Sort it out at that other hospital," I was told. "I will personally check you are not late." End of telephone call!

The hospital secretary at Queen Mary's, Roehampton was even less helpful.

"Oh yes, doctor," he said. "I know your predicament. Your consultant is on sick leave. He is the only one who can sign your form to say you have done the six months satisfactorily to meet the GMC regulations. We won't sue you if you leave early that day, but I personally will ensure that nobody at all signs that form." He laughed and put the phone down on me.

In a flat panic I telephoned my future boss at Barnet to explain my predicament. I was very upset indeed. The boss was busy but I spoke to his registrar, Dr Geof Robb. At last I spoke to a sensible person.

"Well, you can't be in two places at one time," he said. "Administrators are lazy. They each have a long lunch break and often go home early. None do nights or weekends. Just forget them. No, I will hold your bleep till you turn up at, say, 10am. See you then. Bye."

I worked closely with Geof for six months.

My boss, an orthopaedic surgeon, never gave me a reference.

He was on extended sick leave. He never returned to work and later died. On his desk sat my form from the General Medical Council. As my consultant, all he had to do was sign it and I was credited with having completed a six-month pre-registration job. My boss's secretary had cleared his desk of everything but this form! A consultant physician, who I had never worked for and only briefly met, happened to pass by. "What's this?" he said, picking up the form – and he promptly signed it. I will always be eternally grateful to this doctor, who committed perjury, on my behalf, to my intense relief. A lady from the General Medical Council had informed me the previous week that I would probably have to do the six-month job again.

I discovered that I still had plenty of motivation and confidence to succeed as a doctor. Knowledge is acquired gradually I found. This learning curve is lifelong and never ceases. Examinations do accelerate this process. I had a few skills and hoped to acquire a lot more. I could keep professional secrets. I did not let my guard slip.

I was nearly on the medical register – just provisionally at that time. Fingers crossed. The really difficult thing was responsibility. I had a lot. In time, I would have more, i.e., when fully registered. I could not leave medical problems at work. My mind still stored this worrying information. The general public will never know how much their doctor cares. Above all, I enjoyed being a doctor. Most patients and most fellow staff are pleasant and courteous to their doctor. It all helped me, as life is not all 'plain sailing'. My brush with the General Medical Council and those hospital administrators illustrates how junior doctors are treated by those running our National Health Service.

Well, looking back, this job that I had was strange. The boss was off sick, initially neither of his registrars were qualified surgeons and I got landed doing three medical jobs as well as resuscitating in Casualty.

References:

1. Robert Liston by Bill Thomas. Saints and Sinners. *Royal College of Surgeons (Bulletin)* 2012. 94. 64-65.
2. The Mouth and Foot Painting Artists. 9 Inverness Place, London, W2 3JG.
3. M Barrow. Thalidomide babies plead for help to last a lifetime as they enter their 50s. *The Times* 7.5.2012: 3.
4. Lindsay McIntosh. Divers' Recovery Chamber used to help City Addicts. *The Times.* 14.4.12:13.

CHAPTER EIGHT

Second Job: General Medicine House Physician, Barnet General Hospital

It was spring 1966. I was a house physician on call alternate nights for six months and every weekday from 9am until 6pm, Monday to Friday. Every other weekend I was continuously on call for the wards and emergencies from 5pm Friday to 9am Monday. There was no time off, then I started the next week. Everyone worked hard. I telephoned my boss at 10pm every evening on call to tell him about the patients I had admitted. If I ever saw a medical patient in Casualty late at night and this patient had old records, I was given the keys. I had to open up medical records. I went in alone, I found the old notes, I put a tracer card in the place of the notes and came out clutching the old records. They could not afford staff to do this.

I recall one prize patient, a retired professor of pathology, who had had a coronary thrombosis and was attached to a cardiac monitor. He was doing well.

Unfortunately, in the next room was an eccentric man who said he had taken an overdose of tablets. He was very well and all the tests showed no evidence of any drugs in his body. I suspected he was a liar and an attention-seeker. His marriage was having problems, but his wife was now dancing attention to him 'so ill' in hospital. At 10pm this madman jumped out of the ground-floor window and ran across the village green. He was caught on the lounge bar of the local pub – well, half the hospital staff were there! He was brought back to Casualty by a friendly male radiographer.

"Well, doctor," the patient said, "are you going to get me a consultant psychiatrist? I need one right now."

"Not at 11pm," I answered. "Get back to bed, sir," I added.

The real worry here was the professor of pathology. He had heard the madman escape and had chased after him across the green. Now, this violent exercise is not recommended for post-coronary thrombosis patients. My boss went pale when I told him the next day. I was not popular at all. Well, I did let his prize patient go for a sprint in the middle of the night. Another black mark to me.

I looked after children as well as adults. One 12-year-old boy came in with headaches and a nosebleed. I admitted him and did routine blood tests. The haematology junior doctor bumped into me that evening and told me the boy had acute leukaemia. Leukaemia is cancer of the white cells of the blood. I told the boss at 10pm.

"Oh, I'll see him in the morning," was his reply. The boy, who had been playing tennis the day before, collapsed and died at 2am. In leukaemia the clotting of the blood can fail, and so he bled into his brain and died.

We had several children with acute leukaemia. They all died. None of them lived very long. I found this distressing.

My boss had an unusual treatment for haematemesis (vomiting blood). Endoscopy had not got as far as Barnet General Hospital then. Endoscopy is looking into the body through an aperture with a lighted tube. If the bleeding did not stop I followed a strict protocol. Stypven and adrenaline went down the nasogastric tube. The blood pressure went crazy. This was charted every 15 minutes.

Surprisingly, no-one died from this treatment. If the bleeding failed to stop we contacted the surgeons.

Stypven was a topical astringent. It was used to stop bleeding and could be bought over the counter at some chemists. Adrenaline, however, is a very powerful drug. In life and death situations, small amounts of adrenaline are injected into patients, for example, in cardiac arrest or acute anaphylaxis. Minute doses of adrenaline injected subcutaneously causes vasoconstriction of arterioles and capillaries (one part of adrenaline diluted many, many times). However, it has effects on the cardiovascular system. These are both powerful and dangerous. Any patient given adrenaline down a nasogastric tube could absorb the lot into his body through a bleeding raw area. This could result in hypertension, and this could cause a stroke or myocardial infarct. Also, the function of the heart could be altered, leading to heart failure of some type. So this therapeutic Blitzkrieg could kill. I hoped that if this happened my consultant would support me. I would wave his protocol at the coroner.

Fortunately, this treatment given to less than a dozen patients by me usually worked. A couple of patients went to the surgeons as the bleeding did not stop. The rest recovered.

This treatment by this maverick consultant is definitely given no more.

* * *

"Come at once to Casualty," the sister from Casualty told me.

I flew there to find a poor lady deeply unconscious. As I got there the casualty officer left. He should have stayed to help. He did not. The patient then stopped breathing. I was very junior and asked the nurses to call for help. I had just got a tube into her trachea when somebody said, "Oh, I'll take over." To my relief an anaesthetic registrar took over. I had just got a drip up to give her fluids and drugs intravenously when my registrar appeared. The poor lady had only taken huge amounts of alcohol, sleeping tablets (barbiturates) and aspirin. This was a serious suicide attempt. With all the drugs she had taken, nobody gave her a hope. She spent ages on the intensive care unit. She needed artificial ventilation. Then I heard she had gone to the renal unit for dialysis – her kidneys had packed up. Things were bad. How badly was her brain damaged?

I kicked myself – so slow getting to Casualty – so slow intubating my patient, i.e., getting a tube into the lungs to help her breathe – so slow getting the drip up. What a failure I was!

Several weeks later I had a strange encounter with my patient. She turned up with countless relatives looking so glamorous. I was amazed. What did she say?

"Where is my designer gown?" she asked. "What have you done with it?"

The hospital administrators insisted that everybody concerned give a written signed statement with emphasis on the gown. I know she was wearing something when I first saw her, but what, I can't recall.

The hospital had to pay out a huge sum for losing her clothes. Well, in our frantic attempts to resuscitate her, clothes were torn and probably later thrown out.

Her treatment might well have cost as much as the gown! Life has surprises – its ups and its downs!

I was tied to the hospital working and on call most of the time. However, to be honest, so too was my consultant close to retirement. I telephoned him to tell him about patients when I was on call at 10pm every evening. So portly and moustached, he worked hard too. He was pleasantly eccentric. He was known nationally for his orchid growing. Several times after the 10pm phone call he would come in to see a very ill patient.

These occasions I found amusing. I would stand outside Casualty, close to the hospital entrance, taking the cool evening air after the stuffy hospital. My boss drove a Mini Cooper S at a furious speed. I listened and the quiet evening stillness would be shattered by the tones of his rapidly approaching engine. He timed his run and always looked at his watch as the little machine screeched to a halt beside me. I only had this onerous job for six months, but he had had it for his medical life. So the junior doctors were not the only workaholics.

I personally found my professional life filled most of my days as well as a lot of my evenings, weekends and nights. I tried to study for my MBBS examination retakes. I only passed this – third attempt – at the end of this six-month medical appointment. My social life was fragmented.

Occasionally I had a drink at the bar in the doctors' residence. I sometimes went out for a meal with friends. I had no time at all for my pastimes of golf and Scottish dancing. I hoped someday I would take them up again.

As a medical student I had taken out a lot of girls. Usually they shared my interests and were of a similar age. I took nurses out occasionally, but

I had no firm attachments; I lacked the time for it and the inclination. I had not met the right girl and I knew it. Then a very annoying incident happened. Cathy my ward sister told me to 'watch out' for one of the night sisters: "She is after you."

She was told at a meal in the sisters' common room that this older woman was going to seduce me! This night sister was about 30 years of age – slim and blonde. I could not recall having more than a cursory conversation with her. This attraction was not shared by me. I laughed at Cathy.

A couple of days later, a much older and senior ward sister from another ward called me into her office for a chat. I thought I had done something wrong or upset a nurse.

"It's very embarrassing," she said, "but one of the night sisters is after you. To be honest, she has told all the other sisters that she will get you into her bedroom, pull off your trousers and seduce you over and over again. She always gets her man she says and won't take no for an answer." I was shocked. *Help. Help. How much will it hurt me?*

Now, I was just a pre-registration house physician. I was very junior. This lady called Sister Spall was a senior nurse. I was also at her beck and call. I was determined to escape her clutches.

Late one evening I had a telephone call from Sister Spall.

"Oh, doctor," she cooed, "could you please come to Ward 3 and write a night sedation for Mr Stephen Jones. He can't sleep." I panicked. She had me cornered. This was a large ward with a secluded sister's office. She would send the student nurse off on some fool errand and I would be trapped. On the other hand, I had to go.

"I'm not coming," I said.

"But you must come," she replied, very upset.

"No, I am not," I said, and I put the phone down on her.

Then I knew what I must do and quickly. My only hope was to be quick and escape her clutches.

Sister Spall would know where the night superintendent was. She would rush to her and then rush back to the ward with her. Then the night superintendent would phone me herself. I would then be in trouble and have to go there at once.

I flew out of the medical residency and up a path into the ward. A student nurse said, "Oh, I thought you were not coming. The patient has fallen asleep waiting for the night sedation." I quickly wrote up the night sedation. This very attractive student nurse smiled knowingly as I wished her good night, and I shot back to the safety of the residency. I was safe at last.

Sister Spall left me alone after that.

* * *

At the end of this post I applied to my old teaching hospital St Thomas' to be a Casualty officer. I attended for an interview. On the main corridor I bumped into a medical friend, Peter Cotton. We had played a lot of golf together, both for the hospital team but also for the university. We talked. He had just returned from Japan where he had learnt a new technique. This was how to do endoscopy with new fibre optic scopes. He joked at how conspicuous he was in Japan. Well, the Japanese are short and dark-haired. Peter is over six feet two inches tall and very blond! I was confused. As a medical student I had been taught by Mr Barratt, a chest surgeon, how dangerous this investigation was. Mr Barratt was a large man – not fat, just well built. Like all his contemporaries he was always immaculately dressed on the wards in a three-piece suit, a tie and cufflinks, etc. He was called Pasty by all his colleagues because of his pallid complexion. We called him Pasty, but only behind his back. He was an excellent teacher, who spoke clearly and concisely from great experience.

Mr Barratt used a rigid oesophagoscope to investigate his patients. Flexible instruments had not yet reached England. The symptomatic oesophagus is often tortuous and the opening small. The diseased oesophageal walls were thin – all predisposing to perforation. He explained the procedure in great detail. The poor patient was sedated for this investigation in theatre. This rigid scope was inserted by Mr Barratt with great care and skill. The main aim was to take biopsies so oesophageal cancer could be diagnosed or disproved. The dreaded complication was perforation.

If this happened – absolute panic! The poor patient was immediately given a general anaesthetic. The chest was then opened (thoracotomy) and the hole in the oesophagus repaired. Failure to do this, at once, leads to a serious infection in the chest from escaping fluid (mediastinitis), often with fatal consequences.

But my friend Peter, who had graduated a year or so before me, wanted to carry out endoscopy more frequently with modern scopes! He would investigate lower down – the stomach and small bowel. Would this work? The danger of perforation was still there. Well, anything was better than the blunderbuss treatment of stypven and adrenaline for vomiting blood.

CHAPTER NINE

The ECFMG Examination

Go west, young man, go west.

The year was 1966. I was just finishing my second job as a doctor. After the registration year I would hopefully be fully registered as a doctor. I had completed an orthopaedic job and then a general medical job. There was a serious omission on my CV – no general surgical appointment. I applied for several of these posts. I had no luck. Why? Well, it was a chicken and egg situation. I had not had the experience to be appointed. Reality dawned on me. There were a lot fewer doctors around at that time but, even worse, medical appointments of all sorts were highly contested and scarce.

This scarceness of jobs was brought home to me very hard after I had been appointed as a house physician in General Medicine at Barnet General Hospital. My medical boss congratulated me on being appointed. Then as an aside he said, "You know of course that well over 100 doctors applied for this appointment. That is why we had to shortlist 12 of you." I was shocked.

The ECFMG examination stands for the Educational Certificate for Foreign Medical Graduates. This is the entry qualification for all doctors wishing to work in the United States. I decided as an insurance to take the test. Well, I was conditioned to take examinations. I had studied for over two years quite hard on my nights off to eventually, recently, get my final qualification from London University MBBS (third attempt). Another examination – well, I was so used to them. The pressure was not on me too much. I did not have to pass but obviously wanted to very much indeed.

There was bitterness amongst many of my contemporaries. You may ask why. Well, they too struggled and struggled to get a job. They were all applying for stand-alone appointments, and no rotations for several years as nowadays. The pay was derisory. After one year of working hard my total income was well under £400. I tried to run a car on that. I went out occasionally too.

I recall that during my first job my next door neighbour in the doctors' residency kept his wife and child in the room. They must have been very cramped. In such a room there was a single bed, a small table and chair, and a wash basin. There was no en suite, no luxuries, just basic single accommodation. On our salary, he could not afford to do anything else. He could not wait to get into general practice and earn some 'real money'.

I was reading the *British Medical Journal* one day. A large advertisement was in the journal for the ECFMG. I was looking out for it and applied at once.

Three weeks later found me in the East End of London on a day off for 'examination purposes'. I did not know the area well. I soon discovered that several men of roughly my age in that street were also looking for the same examination hall. We were directed and soon I was in a football-type crowd, all going to the same place.

Suddenly, a large friendly arm was put around my shoulders from behind.

"Alistair!" he boomed out in a familiar Southern Irish accent. "We will have a pint at lunchtime."

I wished Dave MacSweeney, my old classmate, good luck, and we split up to go to our respective seats in the hall. What a huge crowd, I thought. This hall had several levels, all full of doctors seated behind desks. *This examination must be very hard,* I thought. I concentrated to get a good start. This is vital, especially in multiple choice. I recall the first question very clearly:

THE HEART IS PART OF THE...
CARDIOVASCULAR SYSTEM
RESPIRATORY SYSTEM
NERVOUS SYSTEM

I stared in total disbelief. What is the catch? Why a question any five-year-old can answer? I ploughed on. To my utter amazement it took a few pages for the questions to get any harder. I was insulted. *Everybody here must pass,* I thought.

There were a few complicated questions on biochemistry I did not know. I left them blank, rather than guess the answer. After three hours I staggered out into the daylight.

"Alistair, come along," Dave called out. "We just have an English test this afternoon," he reassured me. True to form I had not looked at the examination schedule except to know when it all started – 9am. Dave was bigger than me – a lot bigger! He was also an extrovert, drawing customers in the public house into our conversation. I relaxed totally. *Well,* I thought foolishly, *an English test; what rubbish. I am English – it will be a doddle – a complete walkover.*

Dave bought me a pint. To be polite I bought him one for the second round. He was well ahead of me. To my surprise, I turned my back and found he had bought me a third one. Well, I was confident now – very confident. But 2pm was upon us. Just a simple little English test. I supped up and quickly strode back to the hall.

A young American examiner stood before us. This was, according to him, an English comprehension test. All the room was in a relaxed and happy mood. Everybody I had met spoke English well, but to an Indian on my right English was obviously not his first language. We had chatted though, and I understood this friendly courteous man perfectly.

The American explained that he would read out only 20 questions. We had to get 16 right to pass the comprehension test. He would not, definitely not, repeat any questions. We all had papers in front of us on which to write the answers to his questions.

Question one. He said, "WHAT IS A BAWL?"

Panic! I thought to myself. *Is he talking about a bowl?* Or a ball?

The American refused to repeat anything. There was a lot of stamping of feet. I tried to sober up fast.

More questions passed. His diction was appalling. I concentrated hard. Several obscenities were hurled at him. An Australian at the back was very rude indeed.

Then the American gave us a short story. At the end we had to answer some questions about his dictation. I listened and at last this was a lot easier. My Indian friend did not understand. He tried to write the dictation down as he talked, all on the back of an envelope. Surprisingly, he failed to keep up and swore out loud!

Soon it was all over. Well, 20 questions does not take long. For the first time that day I was very worried, not about the medicine test but the English comprehension test. Just to call it that was a complete travesty.

There was a pause. I went to leave. Oh no. We had another three hours of examinations. I tried vainly to sober up and concentrate. This was not going to be easy. It was not.

The following day in *The Times* there was a picture of us all trooping into the examination hall. The reporter wrote that 700 doctors had sat the test. He was shocked and disgusted at us. This country had spent a lot of money (he suggested £10,000) training each one of us, and what did we do? Shoot off to the States to supplement their system. He called us traitors in so many words. I was mortified.

I awaited the results eagerly and was annoyed with myself over those three pints of beer. Then a letter came. I had passed with a mere 83%. That was a fantastic result for me. I celebrated and read on. English comprehension test – Pass. Now, that is what I was really worried about.

I never went to the States but kept it in reserve if I found myself on the dole – a real possibility in those days! Perhaps I should adopt this as an examination technique. Before every further exam – three pints of beer please.

So the 700 of us were all tested solely on our basic theoretical medical knowledge. There were no clinical scenarios and indeed no patient contact whatsoever. I found this very strange indeed.

CHAPTER TEN

Third Job: Casualty, St Thomas'

Life is a joke that's just begun.

Gilbert

As a Casualty officer in the 1960s all the doctors and the porters were male. All the nurses were female. Male trolley patients were wheeled into the male trolley area where the doctors examined them. However, the student nurses, being all female, guarded the female trolley area fiercely. Porters could bring the female patients in and then had to leave immediately. The doctors were only allowed in to see the female patients when suitably chaperoned and after this they too had to leave. Rules were rules. The nurses were in charge – especially over the students! Above all, the female patients must be protected from the male doctors, male porters and male medical students.

About midnight there was a commotion. Five victims of a road traffic accident were brought in. One man and four screaming ladies. The man was in a grey chauffeur's uniform with yellow writing on it and wore a peaked cap – very smart.

"What happened?" I asked him.

"Oh," he said, "it was a low speed impact; a bus pulled out on us."

He had no injuries. His job was to drive the 'four cabaret stars' from one nightclub to another.

I wandered round to the female trolley area. It was in absolute chaos. The four 'cabaret stars' were being undressed by the nurses. The patients spoke no English and screamed and screamed. The stars waved their arms and legs, making the process difficult.

"Don't cut these clothes," said sister. "They are beautiful. Be careful."

The stars were smartly dressed in bright costumes and stunk of cheap perfume. I decided to help. One of the stars grabbed my right arm. The arm was very slim but the grip was vice-like. The last time I had been gripped that hard was at school when we were going for a push over try in rugby years ago. They were slim patients but on careful scrutiny lacked the gentle curves of a female. So there were four men in the ladies' trolley area dressed in ladies clothing!

"Excuse me," I said, "there has been a mistake here. Stop, nurses, and listen to me." They did not stop. They were busy with buttons. Before I could say anything more, a student nurse complained to sister about my interfering.

"Doctor, leave at once," sister told me.

"But, sister, there is some mistake," I said.

"Go now doctor. This is the ladies' trolley area. Ladies only. Now, leave at once."

I left, walked slowly round the corner and sat down at a table. Although late at night a student nurse was finishing an essay.

"I have sister's permission to finish my essay," she said anxiously.

"Listen," I said, "your nurses are undressing four men in the female trolley area."

"Oh," she said, not registering at all, and carried on writing furiously. Then she stopped and asked me to repeat what I had just said.

"You are kidding?" she said.

"No," I said. "Let's wait and listen." We waited and waited.

A nurse screamed out and then another.

"Sister, sister, come quickly," they called out. She came running. She passed me. Sister came back to me slowly.

"Doctor, I am ashamed at you. You knew they were men, yet you allowed my nurses to undress them in the ladies' trolley area. I will inform your consultant of your disgusting behaviour."

Another black mark for me!

More Casualty, 1966

The nakedness of woman is the work of God.

William Blake

A shout called my attention to the waiting room at midday. Through the throng of waiting seated patients ran a very large, naked, dark skinned lady at full speed. As she flew past me her legs pounded the floor and her arms flayed the air. Her flesh bounced about in all directions. Her abdominal pendulous apron of fat flew up and down over her genitalia. Her nipples made circles in the air. Two student female nurses gave chase enthusiastically. Two porters followed half-heartedly. As they disappeared round the corner I started to go back to work. Before I could, I was alerted by another call of: "Here she comes again."

The large lady was still running but puffing loudly as she flew past on her second circuit. The first nurse was gaining ground. The second porter was walking. Two elderly ladies complained.

"Stop her," they called out; "it's disgusting." Of course, if I had tackled her I could have been accused of assault. One little man in the corner did not even look up from his newspaper throughout. A few seconds later she reappeared very puffed out. She staggered in. The student nurse caught her arm. She was led to a cubicle. I was called to see her. The lady refused to speak. She had no signs of injury or drugs.

I diagnosed schizophrenia and certified her. (I later learnt I had the correct diagnosis.) She was referred to a consultant psychiatrist. This lady destroyed one cubicle by smashing the mirror and pulling off fitments, so the nurses put her in another. She destroyed that too. She refused clothes and the first ambulance refused to take her.

"She is not our sort of patient," they said. "You need a psychiatric ambulance." (Whatever that is!) Later, a second ambulance came and took this poor lady away for psychiatric help. I never saw her again. So this mental condition, schizophrenia, caused her to act in a very strange way.

One small practical point for all non-doctors reading this. That is, if you meet a doctor socially, stay off the medical complaints. We need time to switch off. Let me give an example.

My friend Dai was at a posh cocktail party. He met a gorgeous blonde in a skimpy and tight-fitting, yellow dress. Well, he was a warm-blooded Welshman who was still single. He was immediately attracted to her. Unfortunately, she discovered he was a doctor. She then started off on all her medical complaints. She ended up complaining of abdominal pain and pointed to her umbilicus. Was her dress too tight? Dai had had enough. He was no longer interested in this neurotic woman.

So he said, "Well, madam, just take your dress off and we will all see what the problem is!" She screamed and ran off.

Two Casualty Mistakes

It is better to learn from other people's mistakes, than your own!

A saying

I was busy in Casualty at 1am (I was working a night shift: 10pm to 9am). A lot of patients were waiting. An elderly man presented complaining of a sore penis. Nil else. He had a male companion: "Oh, his wife has just died, poor chap," he told me. Well, what was it all about? The patient would not stop crying. I learnt no more history. The patient cried and cried and cried.

The offending organ was red and swollen. I diagnosed cellulitis and rushed off to the next patient after prescribing penicillin.

I had just got to bed and fallen asleep at 9.15am when I was then telephoned by the GU medicine consultant. Gosh, he was so aggressive:

"You idiot," he said. "This man went and visited a prostitute after his wife died. Didn't he? The result of course was venereal disease. And you gave him penicillin. No tests. Nothing. What a shambles. We can't test him for syphilis now. What a fool you are." Phone put down!

So, my mistake. I never got the right history. The patient had returned and given a better history. So the moral of the story is 'contact with prostitutes can lead to venereal disease'!'

Here is another of my mistakes:

A middle-aged man presented with backache. He worked in the City. It was far more convenient for him to come to the hospital than to see his GP. He was well otherwise. The man had a slightly stiff back on examination. Nothing else was wrong.

I sent this man for physiotherapy. Sometime later, I was telephoned by a consultant, Dr Cyriax. He was confused as the patient was no better – "Could you please X-ray his back." An x-ray showed secondary deposits of cancer in his bones. Dr Cyriax told me off for an inappropriate referral. I tended to X-ray all patients with back pain after this. I referred this man for further investigation. Backache is a very rare presentation for a patient with cancer.

Dr Cyriax had an unusual consultant position – he was a 'Consultant in Orthopaedic Medicine'. I cannot recall seeing anybody else ever with this title. Dr Cyriax was balding with a double chin. He always wore a long white coat.

Patients with joint, neck or back problems were referred to him. He made brilliant diagnoses and proceeded to manipulate or inject the patient. As scans had yet to be invented, these diagnoses could not be proved or disproved.

He wrote extensively on his subject. He taught doctors, medical students and physiotherapists. Indeed, as a student, his out patient sessions were extremely popular. You would have thought that these prospective doctors wanted to learn about manipulation. Well, no. As 85% of students were male there was another reason. Dr Cyriax was always assisted by at least two physiotherapists. He always chose the best-looking assistants, (female of course!). They were absolutely gorgeous. We concentrated hard.

Dr Cyriax was not liked universally. He treated patients who would otherwise have gone to orthopaedic surgeons, osteopaths or chiropractors. He had no friends in these 'camps'.

Dr Cyriax was very successful in private practice. Patients flocked to him. Of all the consultants at St Thomas', however, one surgeon was far the busiest in private practice. I assisted him – one of a small army that did so. Mr Frank Cockett specialised in vascular surgery. Rumour had it he had become bored with so much varicose vein surgery. So he doubled his private patient fees. He then got more patients than ever. His private operating list was very long. He did one varicose vein case after another, on and on. His car registration was VV1. His yacht was called Saphena and the dinghy Varix! (The prominent leg vein in varicose veins is called the saphenous vein, and a bulging of the vein is called a varix.)

Another Hard Day in Casualty

The chapter of accidents is the longest chapter in the book.
John Wilkes

I was doing the late morning shift. My confidence in human nature was to be badly shaken that day. When I came on duty as instructed at 11am I handed over to the orthopaedic doctors a city gent for admission. He had been hit crossing the road by a car that had shot across traffic lights on red. It had failed to stop. His leg was broken as a result and put in a plaster backslab. He was naturally very upset.

At teatime some gypsies came in with three children. The adults then walked out, leaving the children behind. We had no contact details, etc. There was nothing medically wrong with the children. They had to be admitted to hospital initially and Social Services were informed but were not interested. The parents returned three days later.

Later, an ambulance with an admission for another hospital had to stop on passing as an emergency, because their casualty had severe chest pains. I noted he had a very swollen leg. I thought he had had a pulmonary embolus, and I was about to relieve his pain and suffering with a large syringe of morphine, when sister stopped me. She pushed my syringe away. (A pulmonary embolus is a clot of blood usually in a leg vein that breaks off and can travel to the lung, causing chest pain and sometimes death.)

"He's a regular," she said. "He is a morphine addict. His leg is always swollen from an old injury. He never had a deep vein thrombosis. I know him well."

I felt an idiot and quickly flushed the morphine down the sink.

I was showered with abuse by the patient. He then got up and walked out. There was no chest pain. Another mistake by me!

At nearly 10pm an attractive blonde lady patient was in tears. She had been beaten up by her husband who had come home drunk. I noted carefully in the records the size and distribution of her injuries. Her aggressive husband then turned up and she refused to press charges. She quickly went home with him willingly and against my medical advice. I was having a bad day.

An alcoholic is a man who drinks more than his doctor.
Alvan Barack

Then something happened that restored my faith in human nature completely. A very smart middle-aged lady had been attacked by a vile drunk. He came in singing loudly, clutching a milk bottle half full of methylated spirits. He had attacked her and she had fought this drunk off, cutting his face badly with the rings on her fingers. A young man passing by had come to her help. He escorted the 'bleeding' drunk to Casualty. I could not find a porter to help me. In desperation I shouted for help, but they had all disappeared in a flash! With great difficulty the drunk was held down on the couch by this passer-by and myself. The body odour was nauseating. I could not find the cut on his face initially because of his dirty thick matted beard. As I cleared this area of dirt, blood and old vomit, two fleas jumped out of the overgrowth and gambolled about on the clean white pillow. They were joined by lice trundling over the pillow. How kind of this vagrant to act as a host for such creatures. I had to remove stitches from a previous, now healed, cut before inserting some new ones. The beard was trimmed around the cut. This was not a cosmetic operation. The haemorrhage had to be stemmed. Local anaesthetic was not necessary as he had taken sufficient meths to kill the pain. So, being drunk, he could feel no pain.

The passer-by commented that his surname of Scottish descent – Fraser – was the same as mine. I glowed with pride. I was pleased to have help from one of my clan. Most of this young man's contemporaries were in the pub, but he had chosen to help this poor lady. She, in turn, sobbed and sobbed, comforted by a nurse. Her smart clothes, a matching suit, reminded me of a typical child's mother at a school open day. But I was not paying attention to my potentially violent patient. Only Fraser held him down now as I was busy with the wound. The drunk sat up, swore and tried to escape. In a flash, Fraser and I leant on the drunk and back down onto the couch he went. To hold him there I had to press on his chest with my left arm and shoulder, whilst stitching with my right hand. It was not easy. My nose was close to the drunk's face; wave upon wave of repugnant body odour filled my nostrils. I suppressed my thoughts of vomiting only with great difficulty.

The insect party was all around us. Oh, please don't hop into my hair! I felt itching – was this psychological or pathological? After a few seconds I had finished the sewing, the wound was cobbled together – the haemorrhage staunched. Once released, the drunk sprang to life again like an uncaged wild animal, cursing us all and spitting. He grabbed his milk bottle containing the meths, made a beeline for the door and swayed out of the department singing loudly. He paused only briefly to utter more oaths to startled patients in the waiting room.

My namesake comforted the lady old enough to be his mother. He volunteered to escort her away from the hospital and "a long way from the drunk." I thanked him for his help. I watched the two of them leave together from a window. The drunk could be seen and heard going off in the opposite direction. Gosh, he really could sing as he zigzagged his way along. A rich baritone voice was giving a rendering of the toreador's song from Bizet's *Carmen*. He had voice control and held his notes well – perhaps a throwback to a previous existence. He was rolling along the deserted, wet pavement, and I was the sole member of his audience.

Then suddenly, as if by magic, a porter appeared at my side. "Do you know them two, doc?" he asked, pointing in the direction the young man and the older lady had gone.

"No," I said, "but he was a big help."

"Well," he said, "she is the local prostitute and he is her pimp!"

So all three players were explained. She was in uniform plying her trade in the oldest profession. The drunk had a moth-to-the-flame attraction for the 'lady'. Finally, Fraser had a financial interest in her wellbeing. We can put men on the moon, but, as ever, we could not keep this Scot from his money!

* * *

I was the night Casualty officer. It was after midnight and chaos. Patients were everywhere. I was fighting a losing battle. But I had help. Four medical students were helping me. Students of today, note that the students of yesteryear were there in the thick of it after midnight – and early on Sunday morning!

The students were doing quarter-hourly head injury observations (the Glasgow Coma Score had yet to be invented) on a young man aged 26. He had been hit by a bus and was deeply unconscious, but responded to a painful stimulus. I had done an X-ray that showed a fractured skull on the right parietal bone. His airway was secure. At 1.30am they came running to me. He had 'gone off'.

His right pupil was bigger and unreactive, his left arm and left leg were rigid, and he was unresponsive to any stimulus of pain. (These were all new findings.)

Diagnosis: An extra dural haematoma (blood clot pressing on the brain).

I called my registrar who telephoned the on-call consultant neurosurgeon. There was only one on call all the time – a consultant at home. No reply. My general surgery registrar was pale and sweating. He was not neurosurgically trained, i.e., he had done no brain surgery. He was in a state of emotional shock. Just then one of the nicest and best consultant general surgeons walked through casualty at 1.30am. He had called in to see a private patient. This surgeon had an international reputation as a colo-rectal surgeon. He was always courteous and polite. I never ever saw him any other way.

Roger, the general surgery registrar, saw this surgeon and said, "Good evening, sir."

"Good morning, Roger," said Mr Lockhart-Mummary correctly.

"Excuse me, sir," said Roger, "but I wonder if I could show you an interesting case."

"Of course, Roger," said the consultant. Yes, always the gentleman.

My patient with the extra dural haematoma was shown. A few minutes later he was in the main theatre. I took French leave and went up to see the operation from the students' gallery. The rectal surgeon did burr holes and removed the clot. The first burr hole was through the fracture and that was how the clot was detected.

The patient made a complete recovery with no residual problem.

What had happened here? This man had suffered a fractured skull in the initial impact, and bruising (contusion) of the brain. This accounted

101

for his initial condition, i.e. unwell. The brain is in a closed box called the skull. The injured brain then bled from an artery. Now sometimes other wounds bleed, but elsewhere it does not matter much. But the brain is in a closed box – no way out. The bleeding caused a clot (haematoma). This caused pressure on the right side of the brain, that affected the left side of our body as the nerves cross over. (That's just the way it is.)

The burr holes let this clot out and so there was no pressure on the brain. The patient got better as a result.

Mr Lockhart-Mummery was a general surgeon of the old school and indeed a proper general surgeon. These have been replaced by lots and lots of different surgeons: vascular surgeons, hepato-biliary surgeons, back trauma surgeons, hand surgeons, neurosurgeons, urologists – the list is long and still growing!

It is amazing, but all these branches of surgery originated in general surgery. In many parts of the world, even today, general surgeons also practise orthopaedics, ENT, gynaecology, obstetrics, as well as the list above.

* * *

As a Casualty officer I found that for the very first and subsequently last time in my medical career I did not get on well with two of my fellow doctors. In retrospect this was not surprising, but at the time I was annoyed with both of them. I tried hard, but failed. My blood pressure rose whenever I encountered them. But we had to work together!

One, Charles, was a ladies' man. He was, as he told me several times, "Tall, dark and handsome. They flock to me," he said. "They can't get enough of me."

Well, he was not just words. I watched him one lunchtime and two female medical students were hanging on his every word. When he was on call in Casualty at least one female a night would ask the sister, "Can you direct me to the Casualty officer's room?" – and that was at 1.30am! Sister was not amused. His medicine was not too hot. He sent one young man with a painful testicle home as he had 'nothing wrong'. The poor man returned with a gangrenous testicle from torsion. This is a classic serious error. I made mistakes too, but not of this magnitude as far as I recall.

The other was Richard. He upset me over and over again. He was, however, very, very clever. To some patients he saw he gave them his medicine.

"Now, you must take it," he said. "Finish the bottle." Secretly between ourselves this was his 'go away medicine'. It was unpleasant, but harmless. When they took the medicine he hoped the patient would go away permanently. In retrospect I have never ever seen or heard of this being done by anybody else.

One night on call alone it was bedlam. Then yet another call from the police but not about a road accident victim or an assault, for once. The river police had been busy. A passer-by had seen a body floating in the Thames. This person was coming in by ambulance now. I expected the worst.

The young man seemed unconscious, but with no sign of a head injury! He was breathing and had a good pulse. He was not hypothermic, and a drug screen was negative. What was going on? He had been found floating face upwards and not face downwards. Were his lungs full of water? An Xray would not help me at all. I did not know how to proceed!

Then a medical friend passed by. He was John Schilling who informed me he could use a bronchoscope. (Bronchoscopy involves visualising the air passages in the lungs with the passage of an instrument down the windpipe, always under a general anaesthetic. It is useful to do biopsies of conditions like tuberculosis or cancer.) We suspected that this man was suffering from hysteria.

John passed the instrument into the patient's lungs. He did not wake up at all! There was no water in his lungs. The fact that he allowed this procedure with no anaesthetic made the diagnosis of hysteria more likely. The patient was admitted and observed in hospital. At 3am he 'woke up' and felt fine, so he discharged himself.

Hysteria is difficult to diagnose and to treat.

John became an eminent ophthalmic surgeon.

There is no-one on earth who does what is right all the time,
and never makes a mistake.
 Good News Bible. Ecclesiastes Chapter 7, verse 20.

Towards the end of my Casualty officer's six-month stint I became tired. Now, I was very fit and healthy normally. I was sleeping 12 hours a night and was still tired. My throat was sore. I could not speak properly sometimes. Now under normal circumstances, I would have gone to my GP, who just happened to be my mother. I could not have wished for a better service. My father often was called for a second opinion. Well, two doctors were better than one. As I was qualified we now were three doctors!

My father had had a diaphragmatic hernia secondary to a road traffic accident. He had had surgery. My mother took him off to the sun for three weeks. Her locum at the surgery in my parents' house was a retired haematologist. He just did blood tests and never examined anybody. I had no trust in him. Tired, I sought a second opinion.

I was so ill that I felt terrible. It was the summer of 1966. I was offered a ticket for the World Cup football final and turned it down! I was shattered and just wanted to sleep. I referred myself to an ENT registrar at St Thomas'. I walked slowly to his clinic, feeling rough.

Richard (my medical colleague who gave out the go-away medicine) saw me in the corridor. "How the hell have you got the bloody impudence to turn up here?" he asked. Now, he could have said, "How are you?" (No, he was not that sort of person.) The other Casualty officers were covering my work and that is why Richard was fed up with me. I walked by.

The registrar examined me. Yes, I had a very sore throat. "You do not have tonsillitis as there is no pus on the tonsils. We will do a blood test," he said.

I waited for the blood test result. Maybe I was wrong. I knew the differential diagnosis and tried not to think about it. So I went to the medical school library to reassure myself that I was completely and utterly wrong. Unfortunately I was right.

Most likely diagnosis: Infectious mononucleosis. Known to all as glandular fever. This is a virus. An infection of young person's, 'characterised by pharyngeal inflammation and fever. Convalescence is sometimes slow and may be associated with marked prostration'. It is thought to be spread by kissing. Well, I had a few female friends – quite a few! But could it be anything else? Yes, I thought. I read on:

Agranulocytosis (no or few white cells in the blood): 'characterised by severe sore throat and marked prostration'. It got worse still:

Acute myeloblastic leukaemia: 'characterised by rapidly developing fatigue and fever… with or without bacterial infections'.

I returned to the registrar. My relief was profound when he announced the blood test showed glandular fever. My doctor, alias my mother, was upset on her return to find I had glandular fever and she had not been there to help.

CHAPTER ELEVEN

First-aiders

Life is a joke that's just begun.

Gilbert

The consultant physician with an interest in cardiology looked just like a City gent in his suit, carrying a rolled-up umbrella and briefcase. He was on the Guildford to Waterloo train due to arrive at 7.56am.

He looked through the current *British Medical Journal*. There was a leader on cardiac arrhythmias written anonymously. He did not read it because he had written it himself!

As the train pulled into Waterloo he put the BMJ away. He looked at his watch. The train was on time and he would be able to dictate an urgent reference for his senior registrar, Dr Jones, for a consultant interview the following week. As he walked down a passageway from Waterloo Station he noticed a young man in front of him stagger. He then fell as they got into the daylight. The consultant knelt at the young man's side. The patient was pale and breathing. He was semi-conscious and moving his arms a little. He had a faint fast pulse, about 200 beats a minute. Supraventricular tachycardia (SVT) seemed the most likely diagnosis. The consultant gave carotid massage that stimulates the vagus nerve that in turn may slow the pulse to normal.

At that moment the consultant was pushed over on the pavement by a burly navvy in blue dungarees. "First-aider!" he shouted, and pushed his equally large friend at the casualty.

"What is it, Bert?" he asked his friend.

"Oh, it's a heart attack," said Bert, the second navvy.

The consultant picked himself up. "Excuse me," he said, "but I am.. ." He was then interrupted by the first garrulous navvy.

"Can't you hear? This is a first aider. Get out." He was pushed away again.

The consultant saw the patient moving a bit more and his colour was improving. An ambulance was heard coming in their direction. He picked up his briefcase and umbrella, brushed the dust off his clothes and walked quickly to work at St Thomas'. The first-aider handed the casualty to the professional – the ambulance lady. She took charge, taking the patient to the casualty department. The ambulance lady then handed the patient to the nurse who then took responsibility. I was asked to see the patient by the nurse. I was the doctor working in Casualty that day in 1966. By then the patient was fully alert but did not know what had happened. He did recall waking up with a man in a dark suit pressing on his neck. He now seemed fine. I could find no abnormality. An electrocardiogram (heart tracing) was absolutely normal. I asked the nurse to do a long run on the electrocardiogram, i.e., a longer rhythm strip. There it was – 30 seconds of paroxysmal supraventricular tachycardia (SVT) that reverted to a normal cardiac rhythm spontaneously. So there was an intermittent problem with this man's heart. The heart suddenly beat quickly.

I referred the patient to the house physician on call for the day. He came with the senior registrar, Dr Jones.

"Yes, very interesting," Dr Jones said. "Get him upstairs to the ward at once. The boss starts his ward round in half an hour."

The consultant had had a busy clinic that morning. He started his ward round at 2pm. Dr Jones introduced the third patient who had just been transferred up from Casualty.

"Please don't bother, Dr Jones," said the boss. "I know this man. Carotid massage worked well on his SVT (supra ventricular tachycardia)." He told his part of the story and the house physician told me later. Dr Jones was dumbfounded.

The following week Dr Jones was appointed a consultant at St Elsewhere's.

Bert (& co) were none the wiser!

More First-aiders in the 1970s

These are wonderful people. They give up their spare time at nights or weekends to help anybody at public events. Their enthusiasm and dedication is an example to us all. In return, the first-aider might get, at best, his travelling expenses, cups of tea or just a pat on the back.

As a first-aider with St John, and a doctor, I volunteered for one duty at an international three-day event at Locko Park in Derby over ten years later, soon after I had been appointed a consultant. We had three casualties all afternoon. Just before I had arrived, the front runner in the event, Lady Whatsit, had come with a painful toe. The first-aider had seen the toe and was about to give advice.

"Are you a doctor?" asked her Ladyship.

"No," said the first-aider. "I am a qualified first-aider."

"Well," said her Ladyship, "I won't let any man touch me ever who is not a doctor." With that, she stormed off. (Did she know what she had just said?)

The next casualty was in a dreadful state.

"I need your help urgently," he said. "This is an emergency."

"What is the matter?" I asked.

"Oh, well, I am the only male judge; all the rest are female. You see, the zip has gone on my trousers. Please can I have a safety pin or two?"

We obliged with this 'emergency'.

The third case was more complicated. A middle-aged lady rushed up.

"Can you help with a bone down the throat?"

"Yes," I said. "We will do our best."

"Oh good," she cried. "I have a very highly bred dog with a long pedigree. He loves to snap at people, but he is large and highly strung. He's friendly really but other people, well, just don't understand him. Can you get his bone out of his throat?"

With that she was gone. I waited for my patient, trembling at the thought of a dog bite. Fortunately he must have coughed it out as she never came back. Thank goodness.

The Annual Review

Conduct to the prejudice of good order and military discipline.

Army Act 40

Soon after this last event I was appointed the doctor to the transport division of St John in Derby. Like all first-aiders this was honorary, i.e. I was not paid.

A Sunday afternoon was picked for the St John Ambulance Brigade Annual Review. Quite a few of the adult members of the brigade pleaded gardening duty. However, their numbers were more than made up for by hordes of adolescents who filled the ranks. A large field was the venue. It was dry and sunny with a gentle breeze. I was the transport division medical officer. The transport division were excluded from the parade. This was because we had the stretcher. In the unlikely event of anybody fainting, our job was to pick them up and bring them to the ambulance on the stretcher. So we were onlookers. Another officer, John Davis, was in charge of the transport division.

The ambulance had been recently presented to the transport division by the NHS county ambulance service. The milometer had been twice round the clock and the engine was badly worn, but to us it was 'the new ambulance'. It certainly looked the part of a new ambulance. The volunteers had painted and polished the vehicle till it shone brightly like a new pin.

At the end of the parade the surgeon-in-chief would review the 'new ambulance'. This was to be the high spot of the parade. Everyone wanted to show him the new vehicle. At 2pm Mr David Thomas, the county surgeon, emerged from a building to review the lines of first-aiders that stood at ease. He was an imposing figure who filled the uniform very well. (This uniform has not been filled that well before or since!)

I hoped he would walk briskly round and we would all be home for tea. We had no such luck. Mr Thomas was deep in conversation with one and then another adolescent. *This could take a long time*, I thought. Then things got worse, the breeze died. It got hotter – very hot.

The first-aiders started to faint. Just one or two at first. Then more and more and more (like flies). Oblivious to the carnage around him, DT kept to his game plan. He did not waiver. Certainly he did not speed up. Soon the ambulance was full, the shade was full and all around the ambulance were first aiders all recovering from fainting.

I calculated that if DT went any slower all the parade would be horizontal and not vertical. Nearly all the casualties got better quickly. I refused to allow any to get back on parade. It was very hot and one faint each was quite enough for one day. However, one spotty twelve-year-old still looked pale. He had a fast pulse and complained of chest pain. (As doctors, we are trained to examine patients in private in a little room, and definitely not trained to examine people in public in a large field.) I mistakenly thought that as he was a first-aider he must know where his chest was. Surely? Anyway, myocardial infarcts in 12-year-olds are about as rare as 'rocking horse shit.'

Finally, I said, "Could you point to where you feel the chest pain?" and he touched his lower right abdominal wall.

"I was in the Children's Hospital with suspected appendicitis till this morning," he said. "I am under Mr Thomas' care. The junior doctors let me out just to take part in the parade, but I feel so sick and the pain is a lot worse than it has ever been!"

He was flushed and tachycardic (fast pulse). I decided I had no alternative but to send him back to the hospital. I watched the 'new ambulance' disappear with the spotty casualty in it. Two minutes later DT had finished. He rushed up to me. "Where is the ambulance?" he asked, rather upset.

"Taking one of your patients back to your ward," I said.

First-aid Examinations and Lectures

There are some who speak one moment before they think.
Jean de la Bruyere

As a junior doctor and later as a consultant I often did first-aid lectures or examinations.

I picked up a small pile of first-aid examination papers. The first candidate headed the paper 'First Ade'. All his answers matched his first statement. He failed.

I was invited to the Red Cross headquarters in Central London. I was greeted by two tall elegant ladies. They wore long flowery dresses, necklaces, long gloves and high-heeled shoes. They had just taken their hats off! They looked as if they were off to the Ladies' Day at Ascot. Instead they made it quite plain that they wanted me to pass a candidate for the highest level of first-aid training. In confidence they told me quietly that a previous doctor had, "failed him against their wishes. After all, doctor, he has been to all our meetings." I judged that I had failed them in the elegance stakes in my sports jacket, shirt and tie.

They brought in the candidate and then insisted on sitting one on each side of him throughout the test. The candidate was a charming African man dressed in a smart suit, white shirt and a tie. I found their presence intrusive, but had no option. They smiled broadly throughout and said nothing. I started with a basic question in first-aid that he would certainly know easily.

Question:	"Tell me about the circulation of blood round the body."
Reply:	...long pause... "Well, err... erm... it goes round the body." Long pause, silence.
Question:	"How does the blood get round?"
Reply:	...long pause... "Well... err, erm..." Long pause. Silence.
Question:	"We have types of blood vessels, don't we?"
Reply:	"Oh yes." Silence.
Question:	"Well, what are these blood vessels called?"
Reply:	"Well, well, err... err..." Silence.
Question:	"Some are called arteries, are they not?"
Reply:	"Yes." Silence.
Question:	"What are the other vessels called?"
Reply:	"Oh, I have just forgotten."
Question:	"Well, are they called veins?"
Reply:	"Oh yes, that's it. Veins."
Question:	"Well, what do arteries do?"

110

Reply:	"Well, err… erm, err… erm, they take dark blood back to the heart."
Question:	"No, that's what veins do. Well, one does carry red blood."
Reply:	"Oh yes, that's it."
Question:	"So what do arteries do?"
Reply:	"I've forgotten." Silence.
Question:	"What does the heart do?"
Reply:	Silence.
Question:	"Can I help you at all?"
Reply:	"I was not expecting such a very difficult question. It is very complicated."
Question:	"What other blood vessels are there?"
Reply:	"There are veins and arteries and more veins and arteries."

I tried a different approach to the same question.

Question:	"Have you ever heard of the double circulation – a figure of eight?"
Reply:	"No. I want another question please."
Question:	"Well, tell me a fracture or type of fracture that is likely to occur in a child."
Reply:	"Oh yes," he said, "I've heard of bean stick fractures."

Throughout these proceedings the ladies leant forward intently, hanging on every word.

"Have you finished, doctor?" one said.

"He has passed, hasn't he?" the other asked. My silence followed this question. I could not understand how he had got through previous levels of first-aid examinations. To have passed him would have been an insult to the whole examination – a complete travesty.

"No," I said, "he has failed, I am sorry to say."

"Doctor, we are very disappointed in you. We have been let down."

I was quickly shown the door and no refreshments were given to me. I was never asked to return. I wonder if he ever passed this test.

* * *

I gave a course of first-aid lectures to a St John Ambulance first-aid course in Ashford, Middlesex in 1972. Some first aiders had to attend for a refresher course. They were all keen to learn, with one exception. A small elderly man called Fred with a Yorkshire accent, wearing a faded St John uniform, always sat at the back. His eyes wandered round the room and I knew he was not listening.

One evening I gave an illustrated talk on burns. I stressed resuscitation but not before it was safe to do so. So, check the electrical current is not still going through the patient. The acid, especially hydrofluoric, should be washed off first. Thick smoke should not be breathed by the first-aider, or the patient approached in a dangerous position, e.g., under a train or in the middle of a motorway, till it was safe to do so, etc., etc.

The talk over-ran, but I was thanked profusely. Then this old chap, Fred, started to speak as always. He had a knack, like some politicians, of commanding everyone's attention immediately. He was holding a cup of tea at the time.

"A man at our works," he began. A hush fell and he started again. "A man at our works, the electric grid fell on him." Gasps from the audience. "Oh it was bad, very bad." More gasps.

"What did you do, Fred?" someone asked.

"What could we do?" said Fred. "He had 10,000 volts right through him." Silence.

"What did you do, Fred?" was asked again. Everybody was listening and you could hear a pin drop.

"Oh," said Fred, "we couldn't do anything. We just picked him up and took him straight to the mortuary." Fred finished his tea and left.

Somehow, just somehow, I felt Fred had undermined my talk!

CHAPTER TWELVE

Fourth Job: Gynaecology & Obstetrics

Maternity is a matter of fact – Paternity is a matter of speculation.

H Gideon Wells

In 1967 I left Casualty and started work as a senior house officer in gynaecology at the Central Middlesex Hospital. Historians will know this date as it was just before the Abortion Law was passed. I was on call every third night. Illegal abortions were performed regularly in the backstreets of Wembley and Southall by gamps – the name given to back street abortionists. I admitted these patients who had had these illegal acts performed upon them. It was obvious on examination as there were marks of surgical forceps on the necks of their wombs (cervix). They always denied this as these abortions were illegal but it was quite clear clinically. I had to do the haemoglobin blood test myself when they presented. (The haematology technician would not do these tests. He simply refused. I never knew why but I suspected it was because these patients flooded in. He would never get to bed if he did them.) The patients had a stormy course with bleeding and sepsis. They were often still bleeding and very shocked when they came in. What a price to pay. The local papers recorded several cases of such ladies who had died as a direct result of this butchery. So I was very glad indeed when the Abortion Law came in.

Survival following an illegal abortion by a gamp could lead to permanent problems. These included sterility due to pelvic infection, or subsequent late abortions due to damage to the cervix (called incompetence).

A clear example of how desperate these ladies were to have an abortion was demonstrated to me one day. A young physiotherapist was seen by me with vaginal bleeding. On speculum examination I saw a huge hole into her rectum from her vagina. She had done this with knitting needles. She had failed to give herself an abortion. The pregnancy was secure. She needed major surgery under a general anaesthetic. This resulted in the patient having a temporary colostomy, and the wound between her rectum and vagina was closed. She recovered from this injury. She had a normal full-term delivery of a healthy baby.

I had decided that gynaecology was not for me. Well, I had a ward full of ladies with gynaecological problems. Every day I did a ward round with sister and another nurse. This consisted of a consultation and examination for each patient. This always culminated in me performing an internal vaginal examination. Well, I wore gloves, but somehow, just somehow, a lifetime of repeated vaginal examinations I felt was not for me. So this appointment was good experience, but I decided that three months would be my limit. My junior colleagues were career gynaecologists. They looked after other wards or were on call when I was off. So I was the amateur gynaecologist, and they reminded me by their actions that they were the professionals. So be it.

One young lady, 15 years old, who had been admitted with vaginal bleeding, seemed different from all the others. I was confused. She was sure of her dates – absolutely certain, in fact. However, her uterus was much bigger than I expected. Her blood pressure was raised. On testing her urine, there was protein, and the pregnancy test was very positive indeed.

The round was expected the next morning with all the doctors. I wrote in the notes '? Hydatidiform mole'. This is a strange occurrence where the male sperm at conception fertilizes an empty ovum. So without an ovum (or egg) a pregnancy cannot happen. For a pregnancy to occur, a live sperm and a live egg must fuse together. In a hyatidiform mole, only a grape-like structure grows in utero – there is no foetus. It only occurs once every 500 pregnancies or so.

My notes were ridiculed by my junior professional colleagues. They changed their minds when the boss agreed with me. We were right. The patient had an evacuation of this 'thing' and recovered well.

On my evening off we had rehearsals for the Christmas revue (figs 22 & 23).

The young liberal MP David Steel introduced a private members' bill in Parliament. This subsequently became the Abortion Act (1967). Mr Peter Diggory, the gynaecologist, acted as medical advisor to Mr Steel throughout the bill's progress. This gynaecologist subsequently published a series of 1,000 abortions he had carried out, many performed prior to this act. He risked prosecution for this. Mr Diggory cited the typical case of the 'poor woman admitted to an NHS hospital, whose neighbours had injected soap, whisky, or even toothpaste into the uterus.'[1] He was right. I was learning fast.

Fig 22 – The whole cast of the Christmas Revue at the Central Middlesex Hospital, 1967.

115

Fig 23 – Me with a student nurse on my right and a sister on my left. They are lead dancer and producer respectively.

One evening on the ward at visiting time a very large West Indian man sought me out. He told me that Mrs Smith in Bed 8 was his and, "You tell her, doc, to come home with me." He was intimidating. He stood over me.

He continued: "My brother got married with my name so that lady is mine, all mine. You tell her, doc." I was a bit frightened but told him that Mrs Smith would go home with whoever she liked.

"Oh no, doc," he said, "you've got it all wrong. You tell her that she goes home with me."

I cringed and repeated, "She goes home with whoever she likes." He left a very unhappy man.

If I had told him that the original marriage of his brother was not legal he would have killed me. He was fired up.

Around ten minutes later a pleasant, elderly lady came.

"You have been expecting me," she said. "I am Josephine Brown's mother and she wanted me to know all about her condition." Sure enough, Josephine Brown had written in the notes and given permission for this talk. Josephine had extensive cancer from her uterus. It had spread to her liver and the outlook was grim, I explained.

"Thank you," she said and went to comfort Josephine.

Half an hour later another lady came in, also saying she was Josephine's mother. I was confused. It turned out the first lady was a busybody from down the street. We apologised. We are not used to looking at ID for this but probably do need to.

After three months in gynaecology, I did an obstetrics job. I loved the babies. One antenatal clinic, I was accosted by a rather rude lady.

"I don't know why I am here," she said. "I can't be pregnant. I have a coil in situ."

I organised an X-ray that did indeed show the coil in situ but also a rather large foetus. She was informed and was not happy. My boss had this X-ray on his wall. He told me the baby always comes out clutching the coil and laughing.

Contraceptives are fairly recent, are they not? Well, it is well known that Henry VIII used a pig's bladder as a condom. However, a vaginal plug of lint and honey was used as a contraceptive as long ago as 1500 BC, as referred to in an Egyptian papyrus!

Some weeks after I had left this job, I was nearly called back. Well, I did an occasional clinic on my own and I saw a lot of very grateful elderly ladies. They all had vaginal prolapse with symptoms, but had refused or were unfit for surgery. Quite a large ring pessary was inserted into the vagina. This cured their symptoms. In the clinic I changed the pessary regularly.

I had put one pessary in and subsequently left the job. Then nobody could get it out! How they struggled. They nearly called me back. This lady needed a general anaesthetic to undo what I had done in a few seconds!

Reference

1. Paul Diggory. Peter Diggory; Obituary. BMJ 2010; 340: 479: c1081.

The Diploma in Obstetrics

I was finishing my post in obstetrics and gynaecology after six months. My boss was a kindly Scot. We seemed to get on well together. My boss advised me to sit the Diploma in Obstetrics (D Obst RCOG). He explained that all his juniors pass this test. He told me that it is an added qualification and quite straightforward.

I took his advice and sat the written examination. It was straightforward. The viva went well too. I just seemed to know most of the answers. I only had the clinical to do.

My long clinical case was an unfortunate lady. She had been in hospital throughout her pregnancy and was close to term. She had vomited throughout the time she was pregnant. Doctors love to coin long names for all medical conditions. This one is called hyperemesis gravidarum – she had been very ill indeed.

I took a long detailed history and a relevant examination.

This lady had been chosen as a long case as, quite simply, there are a lot of causes of vomiting in pregnancy but they usually settle well. She was a very good talking point. Firstly, she may have some form of infection – classically a urinary tract infection. There may be other infections to upset her. She may have high blood pressure, diabetes, hepatitis, renal failure, a brain tumour or a diaphragmatic hernia. The list is very long indeed. There may be a cause concerning the foetus – twins is a classical cause, or an abnormality to the baby causing excessive (amniotic) fluid.

However, this lady according to my calculations started vomiting for the first time around the time of conception. Now, that is very early in the pregnancy for this to occur. She had not stopped vomiting!

Unfortunately, I had seen one such case on my own ward at the Central Middlesex Hospital. It was so similar, it was uncanny, identical in every way. My boss kept her in for the whole pregnancy and tried test after test – all negative. The vomiting carried on and on. In desperation as a very last resort my kind boss asked a psychiatrist to see his patient. She seemed normal mentally to us. The psychiatrist was quite definite, however. He announced that this lady was not normal mentally. The psychiatrist went a lot further. In his mind he was sure that mental illness was the cause of the vomiting. After delivery he took the lady to his ward and cured her vomiting with drugs. My boss was very grateful.

In the Diploma of Obstetrics examination I had to present my history and my examination to my examiner. This man was serious and not at all friendly.

"Well, tell me about her," the examiner said.

I gave the briefest of histories and I outlined a cursory examination of her. He grew restless. I wondered why he seemed upset.

"She has vomited from conception," I said. "All your tests have proved negative. So she has been an inpatient for nearly nine months. So, you have excluded all the common causes. Now, in her case, I don't think you have asked a psychiatrist to see her!"

My examiner went red in the face. He told me abruptly to start again.

"I want a full history and full examination," he said. And he finally got it. I listed all the causes but said nothing about a psychiatrist.

I passed the examination despite my big mouth. I had been far too clever. I was probably right. He knew it and I knew it. So, clearly, he knew that I knew that he knew. How dare I tell him how to investigate his case? He was the examiner, not me.

Although the pass rate was 70%, he might have failed me. It was my big mouth. I had been impudent and had showed him up.

CHAPTER THIRTEEN

Paediatrics

Children are a third of our population and all our future.
US Select Panel for the Promotion of Child Health

I spent 18 months doing paediatrics from the autumn of 1968 until summer 1970. I loved it. There were many lovely children I treated. I had six months working on a neonatal unit, six months doing plastic surgery in the country at Banstead, Surrey, and six months Casualty work.

My hospital was Queen Elizabeth's Hospital in Hackney Road. I realised it was tough when I got there as all the policemen went round in fours – yes, four walking together! On my first morning I was getting to know the children in a ward on the fourth floor. We looked down on the surrounding buildings.

One child said, "There is a man," whilst looking out the window.

Another said, "There is another man." After a while I went to this window to see the child, and happened to look out.

To my surprise there were two lorries parked in the road beneath us. Two separate gangs of men were stripping lead off the roofs of two houses nearby. We saw it all from high up above them on the opposite side of the road.

There was a lookout at the corner.

I asked the hospital switchboard to phone the police. Ten minutes later, no action – no police.

I telephoned again. The hospital telephone operator told me, "We don't call the police here. The last time we did that was when the local jewellers were robbed. The gang came back the next night and did us all in. So we keep ourselves to ourselves."

The police eventually came, sirens sounding, but the two gangs made a quick getaway.

The Kray brothers were operating in the area at the time. The East End was tough.

So was our hospital accommodation. I had a glass of water by my bed at night. I found I could not drink it a few times. Well, it was frozen!

In the East End of London in the 1960s I discovered that none of the patients arriving at hospital after 6pm had a GP letter. These general practitioners had surgeries that were locked up at about 6pm – they opened again in the morning. The doctor was uncontactable for that time. Previously, the vast majority of my evening and night patients had letters from their doctor and often a prior phone call. This self referral to hospital out of hours by patients has become more and more common since then.

On call for paediatrics was very busy indeed. The children flooded in. I was so busy that twice I never got to bed. I just worked solidly through the night. Wearing yesterday's clothes I worked through the next day, till I had to collapse in bed by 4pm.

I recall at breakfast one day I came across a colleague, Mike, who looked dreadful.

"Oh, was it that bad?" I enquired.

"It was far worse than that," he explained. "I was telephoned twice by night sister to see emergency children. Then I got back to bed the third time, but fell into a deep sleep. I had this nightmare: in it, Rosie the night sister was bouncing up and down on my bed. I was screaming. I awoke and it was true. She was bouncing on my bed to wake me up to see another emergency. I had slept through her phone calls and bleeps. I remained shaken and never got back to sleep again!"

I commiserated. Well, Rosie had a nickname: Scatty. She was a caring nurse – the children loved her. But her appearance let her down badly. Short and plump, she unwisely wore very short skirts. Her hair was pinned up but bits fell down. Every day was a bad hair day. Her glasses kept falling off her nose – she had a knack of catching them! I understood why Mike was in such a state.

My four months of the rotation working in the county branch at Banstead, Surrey, were idyllic. I was rarely telephoned at night. The hospital was purpose built by the Victorians. The second floor had the baby ward. I looked after the first floor – the surgical ward. A medical ward and reception area were on the ground floor. We had plenty of children suffering from fibrocystosis. I was one of two resident doctors.

This hospital was approached via a sweeping drive past rhododendron bushes. On the back was a huge lawn and a tennis court. The grounds were extensive; I could walk in the grounds for half an hour admiring the flowers and trees. Such hospitals were commonplace in the 1960s. Most have long since been sold off.

For once I had a spacious bedroom that looked out over a courtyard and the nurses' home. I noted one consultant paediatrician was very keen – how impressive. He regularly called to this hospital – out of hours too. Surprisingly, this married man only visited the nurses' home!

After four months in the county I returned to Hackney and really hard work.

George was a well-covered two-year-old who nearly died of bronchiolitis. On follow-up he failed to attend. He was called again and again – no reply, but I had just seen him in the waiting room and sought him out with his mother. She protested, "He was George last week but this week he is called Adam," she said. No wonder the child was a bit confused!

Once I was called to an eye injury. A female had been at a local night-club and got mascara in her right eye. It was 1am. She was scantily dressed, exposing a lot of thigh and most of her breasts. She smelt of alcohol and cheap perfume.

I protested, "This is a children's casualty department. You have no right to be here at all."

The gamine snarled back, "I'm 12, ain't I?"

Oh gosh, wrong again!

A very large West Indian lady brought her four-year-old boy to the paediatric Casualty unit. Jimmy was the last of many children I saw that day.

"He has a cold, doc," was her history.

122

Apart from a runny nose this rather miserable child seemed fine. Apyrexial, chest clear, throat and ears clear, abdomen soft. No tachycardia or heart murmurs.

"Well," I said, "he has a cold. Keep him warm and give him clear fluids."

She knew better as she left: "It's just like the other one," she said, opening the door to go out.

"What other one?" I asked, rather bored.

"The one what died, doc," she said.

I closed the door and brought mum and Jimmy back to the desk.

"What one?" I asked.

"Oh, you know," she said, "the one that died."

"No, I don't know what one," I said.

"Well," she said, rather surprised, "you know the Social – they moved us."

I was amazed. Here I was working in Hackney, a very deprived area. There was damp poor housing all around. There were many poor people; lots of the children had asthma. Despite writing letter after letter none of them seemed to get better housing. Therefore, to move a family it had to be something different and something dangerous. But what? I made a verbal stab in the dark.

"Did he have lead poisoning?" I asked.

"Oh yes, that's what I'm telling you," she said.

Now I enquired, "You haven't moved back to the same house, have you?"

"Oh yes," she said.

"Don't tell me Jimmy is eating the paint from the wall?" (lead paint).

"Oh yes, that's what I said."

"Did your other child do that?"

"Oh yes, doctor; don't you know?"

Jimmy was admitted. He had a blood test that showed a very high lead level. Mum told every doctor that she explained her boy had lead poisoning. He survived and recovered well. I so nearly missed the diagnosis. There were no clinical signs. It was all on the history.

I was upset by the children with cancer. In particular, those with leukaemia all did badly, and most died.

I decided to sit the Diploma in Child Health examination and go to Glasgow (to avoid my bogey place – Queen Square). Everybody was so polite to this Englishman from London. I was warned to expect a case of rickets by my registrar Mike. Now, what a laugh – I had never heard of a case. But I looked rickets up in my paediatric textbook. Rickets is caused by lack of vitamin D, i.e., lack of sunlight. How impossible can you get? In the clinical I was shown a good-looking smiling Pakistani lad of four.

"Look at his arms," I was told. His wrists were swollen bilaterally.

"Have you fallen?" I said. Laughter all around.

"No," came the answer.

"Does any joint problem run in the family?"

"No," was the answer again – and more laughter.

"May I see an X-ray?" I asked. There was the classic X-ray appearance of rickets. (If I had said it first time they would have suspected I had been tipped off.)

I still failed that time.

And I'm still looking for my second case of rickets!

I retook and passed the DCH in London. My long case had had rheumatic fever and the heart valves were affected. Two examiners pressed me on this. They were like tigers. The bell sounded and I went to leave. Two children had screamed and I could not listen to the heart.

"No, come away and listen again," said one examiner.

A minute later I said, "Well, in the mitral area there is mitral stenosis and mitral incompetence." (So this valve had been damaged by rheumatic fever.)

"Good, good, very good," they said, "and what else did you hear?"

"In the aortic area?"

"Yes, yes," they said.

"There is stenosis." This valve had been damaged too.

"Very good," they said. And then one of them said, "What else?"

"Oh, incompetence," I said.

"Yes," said one. "No," said the other. I felt they could be arguing to this day.

I fled the examination hall. I had passed.

Today, rheumatic fever is rare thanks to modern antibiotics.

Medicine is an art. There are a lot of clever investigations that help the

124

clinician nowadays. We can see the inside of the patient clearly displayed with scans nowadays. There are many blood tests designed to elicit diseases. Nothing, however, has replaced the clinical history. A lot of patience is needed, the intensity and quality of the complaint evaluated carefully. The other systems of the body are looked into as well.

A careful history is complemented by a thorough clinical examination. It is hardly surprising that clinical history-taking is an integral part of final medical examinations and also higher examinations as well.

* * *

HE'S GOING TO CUT IT OFF, DAD.

By the end of my time as a paediatric Casualty officer, I had collected a series totalling 12 patients with a condition and treatment unreported as yet in the whole world's medical literature! I never got to publish – until now!

All were boys aged between three and 12 years. All were engrossed in something; a game or TV. Each felt an urge to relieve themselves and rushed to the toilet. After quickly passing urine they each zipped up their own penis! In each case the foreskin of the child's penis was caught up in the trouser zip!

The presenting features to hospital were practically identical in every case. In staggered an adult male, usually dad, bearing his son. Screams filled the air. Priority was always given to this patient, although the subsequent Manchester triage system today does not mention it. My consultation with a previous patient was often interrupted by a 'come at once'. My medical colleagues, all female, disappeared. The injured organ was protected by hands, clothing and even knees. I tried to calm the situation verbally. I refused repeated requests for a general anaesthetic. Well, the child's stomach was full and so a GA was out of the question.

A nurse would quietly place in my hands a very large pair of scissors. This act was always noticed.

"He's going to cut it off, Dad!" screamed at least one patient on seeing the scissors. Once the trousers were cut, the foreskin was easy to free from the metal zip. It always took a few seconds. The organ was a little red but undamaged. The trousers, however, were a write-off.

Each patient was carried home quickly after profuse thanks. Treatment time – less than ten minutes. Prognosis excellent. Possible complications nil. I never saw a recurrence. But what was really hurt? It was his pride!

* * *

In 1969, doing paediatric plastic surgery, I had an interesting registrar, Bob Acland. He had a particular interest in Microsurgery.

"What's that?" I asked.

"Oh," he explained, "it will become very big in surgery. The Chinese are the world leaders in this. They have done a lot of digital reattachments after trauma. Eventually I believe that free flaps will be quite common."

I was not convinced! How wrong could I be?

I had been fascinated by the plastic surgery I had seen. But to do this meant I had to get the FRCS. This meant primary and final examinations and lots of surgery training.

First stop primary FRCS, but the pass rate is well under 50% and sometimes as low as 10%-20 %. Oh dear, back to the grindstone (and more visits to Queen Square)!

CHAPTER FOURTEEN

The Primary FRCS (1971)

In examinations, those who do not wish to know ask questions of those who cannot tell.

Walter Raleigh

I stopped work in the summer of 1970. I had no income. I put a stamp on my employment card every week. I lived off my savings. This examination has a low pass rate. I was determined to pass.

I worked reading in bed from 6am to 8am. Then I got up and travelled to the Royal College of Surgeons, Lincoln's Inn Fields, London. There was a course for this examination. We had lectures, tutorials and vivas. I paid to go on this course. It was competitive.

I read a textbook on the tube going in. I read at lunchtime. I read in the library before going home. I read on the train going home. I read at home and got to bed about 9pm.

I took the examination in April 1971. Just before the examination I had headaches and sore eyes. I went to an optician who prescribed glasses.

"By the way," he said, "you never could see a fast ball coming at you at cricket, could you?" (I was bowled over by this comment!)

"No," I said astonished. "I could not see the ball."

"Well," he said, " you have astigmatism – a curved lens. We can correct this with glasses. A curved lens makes it impossible to follow fast objects."

Well, that would explain why I could never play cricket. I swung the bat and hoped.

The thing I still didn't know, because nobody had ever explained it to me, was why I had problems with examinations.

Spelling was always a problem. I could not spell inoculation in my final medical examination paper to qualify as a doctor, and changed this word to vaccination. The question was about immunisation and inoculation occurred many times. What a disaster!

Learning for examinations was a big problem. I could not take notes and follow the lecture. I either did one or the other – not both. I had difficulty learning principles, especially in mathematics or physics. I received a little private tutoring for common entrance. I then scored 93% for the three mathematics papers! My maths teacher wrote 'What an astounding result!' on my report.

I failed physics A-level, then had some good teaching and came top of London University in physics in the next examination. What a roller coaster.

Finally, for the second medical examination and my finals (twice), then the DCH once, I had failed again and again to learn facts. (I tried hard to fail the D Obst RCOG, but just failed to fail.) I knew I could sit through a lecture, take copious notes and no facts went into my brain. I struggled with my spelling too.

I knew I was up against it. So in these tests above I did not know the facts. That is why I failed. What was wrong with my brain? (I was to learn later!)

Incidentally, I had had an IQ test at school. The masters did this and refused to tell us the result. One boy found the tests in a cupboard and went round the school giving the results back to everyone. My IQ was 140 – not bad. So I was clever enough for most examinations, but needed to work on my memory and my spelling. The primary FRCS examination would be tough. Far more failed than passed!

In the meantime I tried a different approach. I would read a page or two and shut the book. I closed my eyes and tried to recall as many facts as possible. Often one fact led to another to another, etc. I counted on my fingers. At first I recalled fewer than ten facts. Then I remembered more and more. So I adopted this different strategy, all of my own. I thought about a subject and asked myself, "What facts have I remembered after reading this page?" I closed my eyes and started counting them. I remembered a few facts and counted them on my fingers. The next time I picked up this textbook, I would try to remember what I had learnt last time.

Just before the examination itself I sometimes closed my eyes and counted and counted and counted. I could recall two or three hundred related facts. All my friends thought I was asleep in the library, but my brain was working overtime recalling and storing facts, to be reproduced in the examination.

This technique worked well – I was prepared for this primary FRCS examination – low pass rate and all!

The examination was run by porters in uniform. For vivas they checked the candidates, and when the bell sounded we had a fixed time with our examiners, then the bell sounded again. Then we had to leave. We were face to face with our examiners – frightening! The longer we talked and talked with no questions the better. For the primary FRCS I had to sit three papers: anatomy, pathology and physiology. The first two were fine and the last was borderline. I walked into the physiology viva and met a professor who had lectured to me on a course. The bad news was that he had not passed anybody the day before, according to exam gossip – that usually is correct. There was worse to come. He should have had a second examiner. He was absent. Things could not have been worse for me.

"I apologise," he said, "but my surgical colleague has been called to the phone."

"Oh dear," I said boldly. "Does that mean I have you for 20 minutes on your own?"

He laughed and laughed (19 minutes left). Amazingly, he passed me.

In the anatomy viva I had to look at three slides under a microscope and try and say what organ they represented. I knew the first two slides at once (liver and kidney). I was unsure of the last slide, possibly heart. I needed to look carefully for the tissue that conducts the nerve impulse through the heart from the pacemaker. I looked and looked but could not find it. In desperation I took the slide out and turned it over. On the slide was written 'heart'. I found the nerve conducting tissue eventually as the bell sounded for the next part.

"Well," said the lady examiner, "you spent ages on the last slide; what is it?"

"Oh, heart," I replied.

"Why?" she inquired.

I was tempted to say because it is written on the back of the slide, but instead said, "Because I can recognise the conducting tissue (called Purkinje)."

The pathology viva should have been a doddle. I had done a good paper and answered the first few questions well. Then three extra professors walked in and I froze. I was handed a pot of a kidney with big empty holes in it. I did not have a clue. Then I tipped the pot up and a lot of white stuff filled the pot. It was like one of those little pots with a snow scene at Christmas. My mind went blank and I panicked.

In retrospect, I should have said, "Tuberculous kidney." However, I was thrown by the white-out in the pathology pot. I was completely confused by this white-out.

The room was full of candidates at the end of the vivas that day. A porter read out the numbers of those who had passed. My number was read out. We few trooped downstairs and we congratulated each other. We left the majority in depressed confusion upstairs. They had failed.

I was physically and mentally exhausted but very happy – as I had passed. Over 70% had failed. The next day I went to the local labour exchange to join the dole queue. They took my details and gave me no money. I was broke, I explained.

That afternoon the telephone rang. They had a job at the local hospital. I could start at 5pm – and I did. There is no peace for the wicked.

CHAPTER FIFTEEN

Working for the Final FRCS

I was working as a senior house officer in a district general hospital. I had passed the first part of the FRCS examination and was working on my alternate nights off for the second part. My registrar, Aspi, was working for the same examination. Aspi was an Indian – a Parsee (part Persian in origin). This was a minority tribe in India and none too popular with the rest. I could see why Aspi was a typical Parsee. He was the cleverest doctor I had ever met. His surname was Doctor, so he was Doctor Doctor. He told me all Parsees had funny names. (Farouk Engineer, the former Indian cricket captain, was a Parsee.)

Aspi came from a very poor village. His mother lived in a mud hut. He had a scholarship to school and then another to the higher school and yet another to university. We had tutorials together. I could talk on a subject I had prepared for five or at the most ten minutes. Then there was a pause. Aspi would say, "Is that it?" And I would say, "Yes." He then said, "Well," and started. Facts poured out of his mouth. I gasped and he continued. Finally he listed references over and over again, all from his head. His brain was a sponge, a walking medical encyclopaedia.

Aspi was training to be a cardiothoracic surgeon but needed to work for one year in general surgery to fulfil the requirements for the FRCS examination. He told me of his experience in medicine. When he worked

131

in a busy cardiothoracic unit in Leicester the boss wanted to watch Aspi operate as he had good references from India. So Aspi started to do a heart operation (mitral valvotomy). The boss was called to the phone and thought Aspi had stopped. He continued to operate though! When the boss returned Aspi was just putting in the last skin stitches. He had finished the operation. The boss was upset initially. Then when he subsequently discovered the operation was a complete success, he was very happy with Aspi.

Aspi and I had both passed the first part of the FRCS examination. He had sat this test whilst still working full-time, on call alternate nights. I conversely took six months off work and worked on average twelve hours a day. Exhausted, I just scraped through! However, after the written examination Aspi had an interesting time in his anatomy viva. As he entered, the two anatomy examiners muttered amongst themselves and then withdrew. In came two really ancient anatomy professors and one carried a foetal skull. They asked Aspi at what age the bones of the skull started to become true bone, i.e., ossify. Aspi knew all of that. At the end of the viva the two old men nodded once to each other. Not only did he pass, but Aspi was given the Hallett Prize for coming first in anatomy (I would have failed such a viva!).

Whilst doing general surgery together our consultant went on holiday. He told Aspi to do any cases on the waiting list. There were several patients each with a huge hiatus hernia, part of the abdominal contents protrudes into the chest through the diaphragm. Aspi sent for them all and operated on them. I assisted. He approached the surgery through the chest, whereas our consultant boss did these through the abdomen. The intensive care unit was full for two weeks just with our patients. They all did brilliantly. On his return from holiday the consultant boss was very surprised indeed to discover he no longer had these difficult patients on his waiting list. He just sat down and was given a cup of coffee.

He just repeated over and over again, "Gosh, you have done them all?"

In the summer of 1972, I was working hard for the final FRCS examination. My job as a senior house officer at Norwick Park Hospital was demanding. I worked 9-5 every weekday and on call alternate nights and weekends. I was contacted by my old school, King's College, and asked to play golf in a match for the old boys against the school. That day, I was on call, but Aspi, my registrar, told me to go for a few hours to play. I worked from 8am till 3pm. Just before I left, Fiona, the ward sister, offered me a cup of coffee. I accepted then rushed out of the door.

The London traffic was light in 1972 as I drove round the north circular road and then through Richmond Park to Wimbledon. As I neared my destination I was unwell. My bladder was bursting. I drove onto the club car park and rushed past team members to relieve myself in the toilet. Later, before playing, I needed a soft drink. What was happening? Have I suddenly developed diabetes?

On the way round I drank from two drinking fountains on the course. I felt washed out. Was I ill? I halved the golf game and later ate a meal with all the players. Then I drove back to Northwich Park Hospital. I told switchboard I was on call at 10.30pm. The following day on the wards Fiona casually asked me how I got on. I answered that I had halved my game. "You didn't play golf, did you?" she queried. "Oh yes," I replied (I was too embarrassed to tell her about my fleeting diabetes). "Well," she noted, "I hope you never get heart failure."

She went on to say, "Diuretics don't work on you, obviously."

"What do you mean?" I queried.

"Well," she replied "I put 40mgn of Frusemide (lasix) in your coffee. You should have peed all night!" (Frusemide is a diuretic and that dose would get rid of fluid on the lungs in congestive heart failure.)

Well, thanks a lot, sister – I thought.

That was the first, and last, cup of coffee she ever made for me!

The female of any species is always more dangerous than the male.

Fact

Aspi and I went to Edinburgh to sit the final FRCS Edinburgh examination. The written test was straight forward but then we had to face our examiners in clinical evaluation (cases) and vivas. This can be a bit tricky. I recall being shown a man with an arm injury. His biceps tendon was ruptured but this muscle has two tendons and one was intact. His arm worked well and he was a clerk with no strenuous hobbies. I knew that most orthopaedic surgeons would not operate – just treat the patient initially with rest and analgesics, followed by physiotherapy if required. The patient told me, however, he was to be operated upon the next day by the president of the college.

"Well, laddie," said the president to me, "how will you treat this man?"

"Well," I said, "some people would not operate here." His forehead furrowed. "But," I added, "just in his case, I would operate."

"Capital, laddie," said the president. "What operation do you favour?"

I had no idea. He passed me. I was later informed by a learned orthopaedic consultant colleague that no orthopaedic consultant would operate on such a case.

"Well," I said, "the president is urologist."

"Oh, that explains it," he retorted.

I went for the examination results later that day certain that I had failed. My name was read out. I had passed. In a state of shock and euphoria I rejoined the examiners. An Australian had also thought he had failed and turned up in an old sweatshirt, dirty jeans and trainers. To his surprise he had passed too. I recall asking a smiling Indian lady if she was now a Mrs or Miss. She gasped and pointed down. She was about 30 weeks' pregnant – definitely a Mrs.

The same president then greeted me like a close friend as he downed his fair share of sherry. He asked me to forgive him for the viva on the function of the peritoneum (lining of the abdomen). I thought at the time of the viva he was trying to pass a borderline case (me). In fact I had passed easily and he was finding out what I knew. Before I left I had to sign the college subscription to be paid annually ad infinitum.

Aspi had an interesting time! He was met by a pleasant surgeon who was supposed to quiz him on several short cases (usually four or five). He was left for five minutes with the first case and then the examiner returned apologetically: "Sorry to leave you – tell me about this lady."

"Well, she has a fracture of the shaft of her left humerus because I can feel and move the fracture," said Aspi, "but she should not be here."

"Why not?" asked the examiner, taken aback.

"She has no pulses at the wrist and she is likely to have damaged the brachial artery." Rarely, the artery to the arm is damaged by the fractured bone pressing on this main artery.

"Oh gosh," said the examiner, and he too examined her and just rushed off rather upset, to get help.

"Come back," said Aspi.

"Why?" asked the examiner

"Well," said Aspi, "she needs an arteriogram and surgery is likely, but she is also possibly a bad diabetic. I have just tested her urine for sugar and it's strongly positive."

"Oh, thank you, thank you," said the examiner, who rushed off again. Aspi had no more short cases, and passed!

I decided to sit the FRCS (Eng) in London. For this I had to attend Queen Square. This was in fact the eighth time I had attended this building for examination purposes! The chief porter greeted me before the clinicals like a long lost friend. "Oh blimey, sir," he said. "Not you again, sir. Well, good luck this time, sir."

In the short cases I was introduced to a man with very dark skin – black. But he had no associated Negroid features, i.e., protuberant lips. So in fact he was a white man with dark skin.

"Have you any African relatives?" I asked. Profuse laughter greeted my question.

"No," was his answer. Then I inspected his palms. He had dark streaks of melanin in the palmar creases.

"Addison's disease," I confidently replied. (An endocrine disorder that affects melanin).

"Oh, well done," said the examiner.

My long case was a child who was small. I had done plenty of paediatrics and reeled off a long list of causes of this. I mentioned renal causes and my examiner stopped me. He then asked me to tell him a list of these. I obliged.

"What if the kidneys themselves are normal?" he asked. "Could the function be impaired?"

"Oh yes," I said. "Urethral valves in boys and idiopathic bladder neck obstruction in girls (Marion's disease)."

He passed me. Well, I had done tons of paediatrics. So working for one examination helped me pass another – how fortunate!

Aspi telephoned me – he was engaged to the ward sister, Fiona. He did not drive and asked if I would drive him to the registry office on his wedding day – that was all! Of course, I agreed. Two days before the wedding to which I was invited, I rang him.

"Am I your best man?" I asked.

"Oh yes," he said, too shy to ask me. I spoke at the reception along with Aspi and Professor Kakkar from the Brompton, a surgeon of international repute.

CHAPTER SIXTEEN

My First Registrar Job

Surgery like lovemaking must be done gently and with adequate exposure.

Moshe Schein

I had applied for and got a locum registrar job in general surgery (Ashford, Middlesex). I wanted to impress my boss as there was a substantive job coming up. I met him on a Saturday morning on my way to a weekend orthopaedic course. After we chatted he said he would meet me on Monday at 8.30am on the ward round at the start of the two-week locum.

Monday morning found me at the hospital by 7.30am – the traffic was light. I ate breakfast and chatted with the other doctors.

One remarked, "I'm so sorry about your boss. Very unlucky."

"Oh," I said, not knowing what he was talking about. "Err. I'm sorry too. Err, what has happened?"

"Don't you know?" said my colleague.

"No, I don't. Please tell me," I said.

"He's in theatre now, having his Colles' fracture dealt with. He fell out of the loft last night."

"Oh," I said, not knowing what else to say.

I did not know what to do. I discovered he had fully recovered from the general anaesthetic by telephoning the ward. Well, I was on call, and he said he would see me at 8.30am. So, at 8.30 am I went to his side room and knocked on the door.

"Come in," he said.

I went in. He was in bed, of course, and we exchanged pleasantries. He said how silly he was to fall out of the loft. No operating for a bit, etc. It won't take long to heal, etc. Then my boss leant forwards.

"Can you help me?" he asked .

"Yes, sir," I said, "what is it?"

"Well," he said, "I have a new doctor starting today. He is not very experienced. Can you help him?"

"Oh yes," I said, "I will keep an eye out for him."

"Oh, thank you," he said.

I felt he had not fully recovered from the anaesthetic and took my leave. I went and did a ward round. Several consultants and a senior registrar offered to help me. At 12.30pm I returned to my boss in bed. He now knew exactly who I was. He had recovered. For the next few days my boss with his arm in plaster looked over my shoulder as I operated. He sometimes got a bit agitated because he could not do it himself. It was not easy for either of us.

Then something happened. I was on the ICU trying to help a patient who was paralysed and had bled per rectum. I had just stopped the bleeding. Then my fast bleep sounded. A baby had stopped breathing in the children's ward. I went there at once, ten yards away. A small fat baby had arrested breathing. The baby had croup. The paediatric registrar had started the operation making a low transverse cut. The child needed a tracheostomy. I was handed a scalpel with a plastic handle and the patient was in semi-darkness. So I had one plastic instrument and no decent light. I felt in the midline, and the trachea (the windpipe) was not there. In small babies the trachea can be mobile, as in this case, as the cartilage of the rings is soft. The first thing I felt was the backbone! I found the trachea – much narrower than my little finger – pushed to one side. I made a slit in it and called for surgical assistance – instruments, drapes and light. The baby started to breathe – how fantastic. At this point the night superintendent turned off all the lights, as it was the children's bedtime. There was darkness everywhere. We then had a frank exchange of views between the superintendent and myself. The lights stayed on, reluctantly, till the end of the procedure. The theatre sister came to help me and brought instruments. It took ages before we found a tube small enough to go into the trachea! (A tracheostomy tube.) The child recovered fully and completely with no neurological deficit.

I told my boss the next day. He just kept on saying, "Oh dear, oh dear. This has not happened before."

Pathologists often tell coroners, as reported in the media, what an easy operation this is, tracheotomy. No, not in small, fat babies away from theatre with no instruments and in the dark! Pathologists don't even have to treat patients.

> *Not having the right instrument at the right time is like not having a condom: no point in looking for it... because by the time you find it you won't need it.*
>
> Moshe Schein

I had written up a rare case of gas gangrene that I had seen as a doctor at St Helier in the *British Journal of Surgery*.[1] Very rarely, infection in a wound creates gas and it is called gas gangrene. I have not seen such a patient before, or since. I then received out of the blue a request for a reprint from my old classmate, Roger. He had sat on my right in sixth form. He was from the first stream. Aged 16 he had a scholarship to Cambridge to read medicine. He was too young to take it up. Oh, what a brain. He must have waited two years to go to Cambridge! But now this brainbox was an associate professor in New York – what a clever guy. He had overtaken me – the cream always came to the top!

I sent him a reprint of my article. He commented that the pictures were good (I had taken them!).

Then, complete disaster. Three months later, I read Roger's obituary in the old boys' magazine. He had walked into a bank in New York. There was a holdup. The police got there. Roger was killed instantly in the crossfire.

I was so upset. What a complete waste of a great guy with a brain the size of the planet. Unfortunately, several more of my own contemporaries were to die in strange circumstances. Four died in road traffic accidents (three of them abroad); five died of cancer; three committed suicide; one died scuba diving; one drowned; and one died of pulmonary oedema up Everest. I was upset each time – over and over again.

History repeats itself. On 24th August 2012, nine passers-by were wounded outside the Empire State Building. The Mayor of New York explained that they may have been hit by police bullets, when a gunman was shot dead![2]

* * *

I got the substantive registrar job in general surgery.

This surgery registrar job was straightforward. I worked only from 8.30am till about 5.30pm, Monday to Friday. Oh, a small point: I was resident on-call for emergencies on alternate nights and alternate weekends. I often worked till 1am and then fell into bed.

One night at 1.30am I was telephoned. *Oh no,* I thought, *not another emergency.* No, it was one of the night sisters. I knew them all professionally, but I must confess I had been seeing quite a bit of the senior night sister. She was, of course, single. The night sister on the phone was married and 'just wondered if I wanted a cup of coffee'. She could deliver this to my room pronto!

Social gossip had informed me that this night sister's marriage was unstable. Being named as a correspondent in a divorce would not help my career. Incidentally, I felt no attraction for her at all.

I quickly replied, "No thank you," and put the phone down. I felt very sorry for her. She was an excellent nurse. All she wanted was love and attention. As a doctor I try and help people. Somehow I felt that I was not the right person to give her this treatment.

References:

1. A Fraser-Moodie. An Unusual Presentation of Gas Gangrene. *Brit J Surg.* 1973:60:8; 621.

2. Tim Teeman. Nine passers-by injured in Empire State gun fight may have been shot by police. *The Times*: 25. 8. 12; 11.

Oops... Oops... Oops

If you can keep your head when all about you are losing
theirs and blaming it on you...

Rudyard Kipling, *If*

I was working as a surgical registrar at Ashford Hospital, Middlesex. We were a surgical team – on call every other night – my boss, me and a pre-registration house surgeon (Colin). Life was busy and fun.

At 11pm I had done a whole series of emergency procedures. All the usual sort of operations any general surgery registrar will do. I had in my right hand a piece of small bowel – another in my left. I had to join these two together. The patient had, three months before, refused repair of his inguinal hernia as it caused him "no problems – just a lump doctor!" A piece of small bowel had been caught in the hernia that day and was resected by me as it was black, i.e. it was dead. I was simply putting things together again. The hernia had been repaired. These bowel anastomoses just needed a bit of time. I had to be careful. I was not going to be hurried despite a lot of distractions. All hell broke loose around me. Shouting and distraction abounded. Let me explain:

A phone call relayed to me from a student nurse in Ward 2:

"Doctor, your post-operative appendicectomy is in trouble. I can't record his blood pressure! Otherwise he is fine – good pulse and respiration. He has a headache!"

This patient had had horrible appendicitis. I had removed it half an hour before. I had put a drain in. Only aged 28 and very fit, he should have been fine.

My anaesthetist commented to me, "Oh, your tie on his appendix has slipped and he must have bled. His blood pressure could have dropped as a result?"

I was dumbfounded. What was going on? This guy was very fit – very, very fit. I thought he could ooze and ooze from the operation site, and his blood pressure would not drop. Anyway, if he bled internally it should come up his drain.

I relayed a message to the student nurse: "Do the arrest team need to be called?"

Answer: "No."

"Call night sister, please."

Reply from student nurse: "Night sister is at lunch."

Next message from me: "Get her out of lunch."

Reply from student nurse: "She won't like it. You have upset her before – don't you remember?"

Reply from me: "Get night sister now, please."

Reply from student: "Don't blame me, doctor."

The theatre staff complained to me about using their runner as a telephonist.

My anaesthetist could not go to see the patient. He was giving the anaesthetic. I needed help from my junior. He could not go. I had something to do. I was slow doing the anastomosis – small wonder! Two minutes later I asked the nurse to telephone the ward and asked her to say: "How is the patient?"

The student nurse replied, "Blood pressure still unrecordable, patient's pulse bounding. He still has a headache. Night sister is finishing her coffee and will be two minutes."

Theatre sister complained to me about interruptions!

Next call, night sister is on the line: "Get here at once. His blood pressure is right off the top of the sphygmomanometer." I guessed the diagnosis. Now, what was it? Was I right?

Sherlock Holmes said, *"When you have eliminated the impossible, whatever remains, however improbable, must be the truth."*

(*Sign of Four*, Conan Doyle) Well, Conan Doyle was a doctor!

My diagnosis was a phaeochromocytoma. This is a rare, rare tumour that excretes adrenaline into the bloodstream. One of the 'tests' for such a tumour is to give the poor patient a general anaesthetic. This test is definitely not recommended ever.

The blood pressure takes off like no tomorrow. This poor man needed a general anaesthetic for one condition. It stimulated this tumour previously asymptomatic. Result: blood pressure 'high as a kite' (diastolic 190mm of mercury, systolic off the scale). That's why he had the headache!

I stitched the abdomen of my hernia patient with no assistance at all. My houseman went to see the patient and called the medical registrar.

This doctor was at home and refused to come in. Half an hour later he came, at my bidding, complaining that this was a surgical or anaesthetic problem. "Definitely not medical."

He took my man over and spent most of the night getting his blood pressure down. The medical registrar I knew well. He was a first class doctor. My patient could have had a stroke from such a high blood pressure, and died!

The 28-year-old was later investigated. And I was correct! His phaeochromocytoma was removed by a specialist surgeon at the Hammersmith Hospital. He had no more problems. He made a full recovery.

The hernia man recovered too.

My blood pressure went up that night too! Well, it felt like it!

So my job was straightforward as a general surgery registrar. In practice I got to bed by 1am when on call. There was a steady stream of emergency patients to be operated upon. There were ward rounds to follow patients up.

* * *

I don't know why, but I got tired!

I had alternate weekends off. I went home to my parents' house in Richmond and slept a lot till I went back to the hospital on Sunday evening. But my mother was still on call as a general practitioner aged about 70 years. So over a couple of years she was sometimes called out at night when I was there.

I accompanied my mother on these visits. She had always treated the family involved for years and knew all about her patients. She drove straight to the address and was greeted like a member of the family. I was introduced – well, two doctors are better than one! Repeatedly these calls were to general surgery emergencies. My mother would arrange emergency admission to the appropriate hospital and then turn to me.

"What should I write?" she would say. Well, I was a registrar in that specialty and it was easy for me to dictate a letter. My mother arranged an ambulance and then drove us home again afterwards.

At breakfast the next day, my father always expressed surprise that we had been called out. Well, he slept soundly through it all. Later, so often, the patient's family telephoned and told us what had happened at the hospital. They often said they were surprised and told us: "The surgeon at the hospital was amazed that the GP knew so much surgery." What a laugh. It was good to repay my mother in this small way for how she had helped me in the past. I cherish the memory of those happy jaunts into the cold night, not knowing what we would find at the patient's house.

In retrospect it was really surprising that all those calls were to surgical emergencies – well, surgery was the specialty that I had chosen. It was the 1970s. In my previous paediatric job I had experience of the children coming into the hospital with no GP letter. This was different. So in West London and the surrounding counties the general practitioner was on call 24/7 for his or her own patients. This doctor would rush out to do visits, and refer the patient as an emergency to a hospital when indicated. There was no GP on-call deputising service to my knowledge. The new GP contract had not even been dreamed of!

It is vitally important that doctors and nurses work closer and closer together to achieve the best results. I witnessed this togetherness early one morning. At 3am, I was rushing to bed through the doctors' mess. I expected to meet nobody, but a noise happened to draw my attention to a small group of seated doctors and nurses. This group togetherness seemed to have gone really, really well!

There were some playing cards on a low table. Around the table, concentrating hard, were three male doctors – all naked. Also together, sat two student nurses. They each had only their knickers on! Well, strip poker is a sort of team building exercise, is it not?

I exited quickly.

A Chinese Puzzle

The liver was at one time considered the seat of life: hence its name – liver, the thing we live with.

Ambrose Pierce

I had a call to Casualty. There was a Chinaman there, Mr Wong, who had puzzled the experienced Casualty officer. He spoke no English but had an interpreter, Mr Cheung. Mr Wong was a cook in Mr Cheung's Chinese restaurant. Mr Wong was in abdominal pain and was shocked. He was bleeding internally. His X-ray showed a big liver.

At surgery a big problem awaited me. I opened his abdomen under a general anaesthetic. Mr Wong had cirrhosis, that is common in the Chinese. He was bleeding from a huge tumour (hepatoma) in the centre of his liver (porta hepatis). A hepatoma is a rare cancer of the liver. This cancer was so big and in such a position that it could not be removed surgically. So this was a huge cancer in a place where it could not be removed as other vital structures were all around it. After one hour all my efforts to stop the bleeding had failed so I called the boss. After a few 'oh dears' he told me to pack the bleeding area and bring the pack out through the abdominal wall. I did this. I wanted to tie off the hepatic artery – this is the blood supply to the tumour and the liver – he told me not to. Mr Wong did well post-operatively. We later found we could not remove the pack post-operatively. It was stuck.

Mr Cheung, Mr Wong and I had several discussions. Then Mr Wong flew home to Hong Kong to die. Such a tumour cannot be removed, I thought. His family wanted to see him and he wanted to see them. His religion dictated that he must return home to die. Mr Cheung told me so.

I took my parents to Mr Cheung's restaurant. Mr Cheung drew up later in his white Mercedes. He told me Mr Wong had got to Hong Kong and then was referred to the University Hospital, Hong Kong. Why?

Mr Wong has had another operation, Mr Cheung said. But what? Resection of the tumour?

I opened the *British Medical Journal*, and read an article from the University Hospital, Hong Kong. 'A patient was transferred from a district general hospital in England to Hong Kong for treatment for a hepatoma. We tied off the hepatic artery. Six more such cases were described, etc.'

Another meal. Mr Wong was no better. He had been referred to Communist China 'to see what Mautse Cheung can do.'

Another meal. Mautse Cheung could do nothing.

"Mr Wong is dying," Mr Cheung said. Mr Wong died soon after.

By chance I met a relative of Mr Cheung's very recently. Mr Cheung of white Mercedes fame had lived another 30-plus years and died recently, aged 89.

A Ward Round (Chinese) 1973

No man is a good doctor who has never been sick himself.
Chinese Proverb

I was now a surgical registrar at the Hammersmith Hospital. I was on a ward round with the consultant surgeon and Tom Treasure (senior house officer). These rounds were formal. One patient only spoke Chinese (Mandarin). The patient or the hospital were unable to provide an interpreter. Tom had bought a medical phrase book in Chinese with help on pronunciation. After an operation the Chinese man was going home.

We came to him on the ward round but then the consultant took Tom aside.

"Look, Tom," he said, "I have never spoken Chinese. Can you help me?"

"Oh yes," said Tom. "What do you want to say?"

"Oh, just how do you do?" said the consultant.

Tom looked it up and took the consultant to a corner. They practised a phrase from the book. Then, when the surgeon had it, Tom told him to say it to the patient. Beaming broadly, the surgeon approached the patient and shaking hands he uttered this phrase... The patient too was excited and uttered a response as well as gesticulating with his right hand in front of his chest.

"What does he say, Tom?" asked the surgeon, while repeating his Chinese phrase over and over again. The Chinaman smiled too but still gesticulated with his right hand in front of his chest.

"He says, 'How are you?'" said Tom to his boss. "Oh good," said the surgeon. Finally, after five minutes of this pantomime, it slowed down. Tom informed the patient he was going home with that phrase 'home today'. The Chinaman nodded and repeated, "Home today, home today, home today," and smiled.

We later finished the round. In sister's office, a glasshouse in the middle of the ward, we all had a quick coffee. The boss and sister left us then. I then cornered Tom and asked him what the boss had said. He refused to answer at first. The senior registrar joined in – I had an ally. I told Tom that the book was full of medical phrases and how do you do was not one of them – I had seen the book. Tom tried to prevaricate but we had him cornered.

"Oh, all right," he said. "Well, the boss said 'Have you any wind today?'" We laughed – well, he did speak Chinese, though the boss was never told what he had said.

CHAPTER SEVENTEEN

More Snow and More Drinks

Working as a general surgical registrar, 8am to 6pm, Monday to Friday, and on call alternate nights and weekends, is rather tiring. At times there was little time for anything else but work and sleep. Frequently I got to bed at 3am on call. I needed another holiday. I went skiing for two weeks in a group from the Ski Club of Great Britain (figs 24 and 25). I had passed their representatives course and could lead groups off piste.

On the first day of skiing I was still tired. Sober and stationary, putting on my skis, I slipped on the ice, falling on my chest. I felt a soreness in my chest, but skied on. This soreness continued and in the bath that night I palpated the offending area. I had local bony tenderness. Oh dear, this meant fractured ribs.

The next day I was introduced to severe pain. I did not need a chest X-ray as I had not punctured a lung as I was not short of breath.

I had had plenty of analgesic tablets, but had given two lots to suffering members of our group. I had no more tablets left.

That morning every bump on the slopes sent a painful shock into my chest. I had paid to come here and paid for a lift pass. I was going to ski, and that was that.

I decided that a three-inch Elastoplast strapping round the fractured

Fig 24 – Here I am again, in a cable car this time. We are off to the top of the mountain, hoping to find lots of good snow.

Fig 25 – Yet another skiing party, and a different girl beside me again!

ribs would heal them. I got another doctor to strap me up. "As tightly as possible please."

The result had no effect on the pain, but I was short of breath. I took the bandage off.

That evening I was in even more pain. The skiing had been curtailed, painful and slow. There was no local pharmacy. In my bedroom, my eye alighted on a bottle of cherry brandy that I had intended to take back to England intact as a present. I changed my plans and opened the bottle for a little nip to help the pain.

Half an hour later after two generous tots I was fine and pain-free. A couple of beers and a small tot at bedtime gave me a good night's sleep.

The skiing on the next day was great. I was not going to drive as my car was over 1,000 miles away. Instead I was mildly inebriated in charge of two skis and two sticks. I kept my blood alcohol up for the rest of the holiday. The ribs were a little sore at times. I finished the cherry brandy just before I got back to the UK.

At work I felt a little down – something was missing. Then after a week I had two drinks at a mess party. I felt terrific. To my utter horror, I realised I had a problem. An alcohol problem. I knew that drug or alcohol addiction were much commoner in doctors than in the general population.

I had to do something drastic. I did not touch a drop of alcohol for six months. I made a full recovery. Incidentally, my two fractured ribs healed perfectly. As broken bones heal, they produce new bone formation (callus). I felt two lumps of callus on my injured ribs, confirming my diagnosis.

More Skiing

Doctors are not known for abstinence. I was once sharing a room in an annex with Sandy on holiday in Austria. At 5pm I was resting after skiing hard all day. We were all booked into a very smart restaurant that evening by Bob (our organiser).

"You must all be on your best behaviour," he told us. "It's upmarket."

My slumbers were broken at 5pm by Sandy crashing into the room.

149

Fig 26 – Me on skis waiting for a ski school race.

"I'm going to get bloody drunk tonight!" he shouted. He staggered around the room as I tried to hide our booze.

"What happened?" I asked.

"Well," said Sandy, "as you know, I'm in a ski class of Krauts. We all went to the bar at the bottom of the nursery slopes. After a few schnapps we had a competition of pulling middle fingers." (Sandy was our stroke in the first eight so I knew he must have strong hands and fingers.)

"Guess what?" he said. "I beat the skiing instructor, and he is the local champion at this. My prize was that everybody in the class bought me a drink. It was great."

He then crashed out of the door to tell our friends downstairs about it. I shouted out forlornly down the stairs.

"You forgot to put your trousers back on." He never heard. He walked through a downstairs room, where two maids were ironing, to get to the other bedroom. I heard the laughter from my room as he was sporting a fine pair of long johns. Sandy reappeared a few minutes later heralded by more laughter from downstairs. He admonished me for not reminding him that he was trouserless.

Sandy continued to be the life and soul of the party. We went for preprandial drinks, where Bob told me off for getting Sandy drunk. We finally entered the discreet, dimly lit and expensive restaurant. Sandy by now was fortunately rather quiet. He ate a delicious meal and then said he felt ill! Soon after, he was very, very sick all over the table, fellow guests and the waiter. He apologised profusely but said the food felt better going down than coming up.

Fig 27 – My skiing party, and just look at all those bottles on that table!

I took him back to our room with some difficulty. His airway was fine and I left him to sleep it off. I returned to my friends and continued to eat an excellent meal. Two hours later I took another person back to the annex. He was the hospital secretary of a London teaching hospital. Well, he did not look the part as I helped him home rather drunk, up steps and stairs. He thought he was a steam engine and all he said was, "Poop, poop, poop," in a loud voice like a whistle.

I helped him into bed. "Poop, poop, poop," he went and for some time after, till he ran out of steam. (I heard this 'train' from my room upstairs.)

Sandy, meanwhile, had woken up. Indeed, for the first and only time that evening he was wide awake. He knew he had been ill and he knew who I was.

"Tell me," he said, "when I was ill who was there?" At that time, when not on holiday in Austria, he was the Dean's house surgeon at St Thomas' in the UK.

"Oh," I lied, "tonight the Dean was there."

"Oh God," he said.

"Oh, and his wife," I added.

"Oh no," the reply.

151

Fig 28 – A student doctor, me, and a student nurse, Helen, are discussing the condition of the snow!

"And Sir John Richardson and his wife." (Currently he was the president of the College of Physicians.)

"Oh gosh," he said. "I will apologise to them all in the morning."

Sandy slept well and recovered well.

Sandy is now a consultant general surgeon and a pillar of society. The steam engine recovered well too. He joked his skiing got worse and worse and worse, but he was not upset. Instead he found something very special indeed that holiday – a wife!

* * *

A few years later:-

Someone special was missing from my life. I had had a girlfriend who was Scottish and wild. She was a nurse and a skier. I found that it did not work out. It was over.

So as a surgical registrar I threw myself into my work. I was also training hard for my next skiing holiday soon. I ran every night and went to dry ski slopes often.

"Can I come to the dry ski slope with you tomorrow," asked Liz, a fellow doctor. "Oh yes," I replied. She was a lively brunette, but definitely not my sort of girl. She went on to tell me that she could ski, and had a pair of ski boots. I looked forward to her company.

At the dry ski slope I had my own skis and so I was on the slopes first. After a few runs of mine she appeared clutching her hired skis. I then overtook her. *Oh horror, she can't ski! She can't move at all.* I gave her some help, but was told to go away. I carried on skiing but overtook her over and over again. (My last girlfriend would have overtaken me.)

Her posture was wrong. She was leaning back and her weight was on the wrong foot. Then it happened, she fell heavily. I went to help her. She had injured her right hand. That was the end of my skiing that evening!

I drove her back to the hospital.An Xray confirmed a complicated little injury that would need an operation soon. She had a fracture and tendon damage. She wore a sling and had analgesia. I carried her things to her room. I looked around for another female to help her. There was nobody.

"Well, good night," I said, "I hope that you manage."

"Please came back soon and check I am OK," she pleaded.

I returned ten minutes later, and cautiously knocked on her door.

"Come in," she said, "and come here."

She then opened her eyes and wriggled about in the bed. What was happening? Then she asked me to, "Hop in."

I was horrified and mumbled, "No thank you." I fled. I did not see that coming. Oh Help! Help! Help!

The next day, on the ward, a staff nurse asked me if I had enjoyed myself last night? I was confused! She then giggled. What was going on?

Later at tea time a nurse whispered to me, "You are so lucky to have escaped her clutches last night." She went on to say, "At tea, yesterday, Liz boasted to all the nurses that she had had a long long line of successful male seductions. You would be a pushover. She never failed to conquer! Just another victory for her."

I was amazed. I had never given Liz any encouragement at all.Our relationship was professional and nothing, nothing else. So that is why she endured the torment of the slopes. What she really wanted was not to ski, but me! She was selfish. Her hand healed well post-operatively. I hope she found happiness.

I was to find love a little later.

The Doctors' World Skiing Cup

My younger sister Sheila was a teacher at a well-known public school near Inverness. She was head of Geography and was often driving pupils all over Scotland on field trips. One day she got the Land Rover stuck in a ditch. A fifteen-year-old boy asked her politely to: "Wait over there, Miss." Several of the boys drove Land Rovers on farms and estates although all under age (they never drove on the road). A rug and a plank of wood got the Land Rover out of the ditch in no time. Teacher could then 'take over again'.

Sheila rang me in 1973 and explained she was due to take a mixed group of pupils on a skiing holiday to Austria. Unfortunately, the male teacher was ill and nobody from the school could help. Could I help her out? "Oh yes," I said.

I thought that 15-year-olds were all the same. No, not quite. On the plane over, two of the boys were spending money like water. They flashed their cheque cards over and over again. This was the first cheque card that I had ever seen. Before then, we had cash or cheques. They had bought two expensive cameras and had not stopped. I quickly told my sister.

"Oh, don't worry about them," she said. "Their respective parents own a very large part of New South Wales. When they fly to Sydney they are picked up by the family helicopter!"

On the first evening out, one of the other boys Peter (aged 16) seemed to be in charge of ordering in the restaurant. He always caught the waiter's eye and continued to take charge whenever we went out. I later discovered his dad owned a group of hotels. His son Peter went as an undercover guest and reported everything back to his dad. That explained his actions.

We went to Solden where there were large posters advertising 'Coupe de Monde de Ski des Medecins'. I went along to investigate. I hoped to watch the Doctors' World Cup Skiing Race.

I entered the lobby of a plush hotel and made discreet enquiries at the desk. I was not prepared for what followed.

A short, dark-haired Frenchman came rushing towards me with a beautiful brunette. Whilst I was ogling her, he told me he was Jean, the President of the Doctors' World Skiing. He was a gastroenterologist from Lille. I was still ogling the girl when Jean rushed at me. He held me in a tight embrace – my chest was crushed. I could not breathe. I felt faint. Worse was to follow.

He kissed me passionately on the left cheek – then the right cheek and then the left and right again. His cheeks felt like sandpaper (he had not shaved). His breath smelt of garlic and his oily hair rubbed my nose. I felt I was going blue when he finally unembraced me.

I turned towards the brunette in eager anticipation. She was called

Heidi. She was tall and slim, wearing a dark green dress, and had filmstar looks. As I moved expectantly towards her she smiled. The whole room lit up as a result. Then all she gave me was…

All she gave me was a very limp handshake. What a let-down. Worse was to come. She only spoke German. I don't speak German. That was the end of a beautiful friendship that never was.

The secretariat told me I was the only British doctor. I found myself in the race. I would also be the group leader and have to attend the group leaders' meetings. There were social events before.

I met a lot of doctors on the slopes and at parties, and we had a cocktail party, and a zither evening, a midnight buffet and Tyrolean evenings. A large group of tall Dutchmen adopted me as the only Englishman. They were mad and insisted on rising and giving the toast, "God Save the King," to which I replied, "God Save the Queen!" I saw all these men skiing, and on the whole I was not impressed. One even fell off the ski tow. I had done a bit of racing before and thought it would be like a ski school race. Not so! I was wrong – very wrong!

On Thursday evening at the group leaders' meeting, a Swedish orthopaedic surgeon, Lars Dakistedt, interpreted for me. It was strange – some German speakers could not understand other German speakers. The other leaders argued furiously in different languages and various dialects. They still could not understand each other. I was quietly amused. Then I began to learn about the race. You could get disqualified easily even before the start! There were 200 competitors from all over Europe (the name World Cup was pretentious). The race started at 8am. The lifts were open from 7am – very early, just for the race. At the top of the lifts we would get a tow to the start if we held onto the back of 'Piste Bashing Machines' with large caterpillar tracts (snowploughs) – they pulled us up a sharp incline to the start.

So, fresh piste on a steep, steep slope was prepared for the race. There were 44 gates (sticks between which we had to ski), each with a ski instructor checking we went through properly. The overall drop was over 1,380 metres. The overall length was 1,600 metres. They kept on repeating, "World Cup Rules, World Cup Rules" over and over again.

I was eating breakfast alone the next morning at 6.30am. It was dark outside. All the other guests in our hotel were still in bed. I eventually

Fig 29 – Dr John Harvey and me, the entire British Medical Ski Team, start to celebrate after our runs.

got to the start, but the snowplough's wheels were close to me going up. Where were my friends? I recognised nobody. It was really serious, but sunny by now. Two men discussed what wax they had used on their skis.

Another had got up early and skied the course at 7am (at dawn). I was surrounded by unfamiliar fit athletes. My worst dreams became a reality as the first few flashed down the course with a nimbleness that outclassed even the local instructors.

Finally my number was called. I edged to the start. I went through the electronic gates and people rang bells. People shouted.

Gravity took me down and through the first gates in a flash. I accelerated. I was going out of control. It was steep. I was very short of breath and had to slow down (or crash). My legs were like rubber and my eyes would not focus.

I got to the bottom in what seemed like an eternity (over two minutes). I was exhausted. It took me half an hour to recover my breath. At the last minute another British doctor turned up, Dr John Harvey. He got down too. He hoped to dazzle the opposition with a series of snowplough turns.

I only had to go to the last group leaders' meeting. This ordeal was over, thank goodness. Then, that evening, it was revealed that the second half of the race started at 8am next day. *Oh no*, I thought, *not again*. Once again, I ordered an early breakfast and trudged through the snow at dawn.

The same serious race-hungry group of doctors met me at the top. The gates flashed by. The mist descended and the course was very icy. The skis were noisy scraping on the ice. I finished really exhausted again. John had got down but missed a few gates. His fiancée Patsy patiently waited at the bottom with a schnapps that was never more welcome (fig 29).

I went along to the prize-giving that evening. A hundred

Fig 30 – A poster for the doctors' World Cup race with my skies, my number, and of course that cup!

people were expected and four hundred turned up. There were a lot of speeches in all sorts of languages! Cups were given out. I had not come in the top 50, but had beaten a lot of skiers. I had finished 53rd out of 93 starters, with a combined time of four minutes and 34 seconds. The winner was an Italian, Umberto Parrini (two minutes 34 seconds).

The Italians had been celebrating all day – as only Italians can celebrate. Come that evening, they were hysterical in their hour of triumph. The speeches droned on and cups were presented to a fanfare of trumpets, flashing cameras and tumultuous applause. Suddenly, my name was called out. I was given a cup as the first (and last) skier from Great Britain to finish. So I was rewarded with a cup although I had done no better than 53rd (the Italians on the next table to ours were highly amused by this). I smuggled this priceless cup through customs (fig 30).

We were not asked to prove we were doctors. I did not even have my GMC certificate with me.

Perhaps, as I had taken part in two international medical courses, I should have applied for study leave.[1]

On my return I tried to find more British doctors to compete. So I wrote articles about this race in the medical and skiing press.

Then on the piste at St Anton two years later, I bumped into Major Cranston of the British Army Ski Team. He had read this publicity and competed. He did better than me, and also got a cup as the first British skier. He had just returned from skiing with the British forces in Norway.

I said, "You ski a lot with the army, John, but when did you last see a patient?"

He paused and answered, "Oh, I last worked as a doctor about a year ago!"

* * *

Some years later, whilst visiting some German hospitals, I met two surgeons who were keen skiers. They were so impressed that I had skied in the Doctors' World Championships. I discovered that they had each failed to get in. They had to ski in local, regional and then national trials to be included. So, despite intensive training, they had missed out. It was frowned upon to enter as an individual. They had to earn a place in their team. That explained the standard of skiing. I, the idiot Englander, had gate-crashed their races completely by accident .

* * *

I skied every winter in the Alps for many years but always trained hard beforehand. At Frenchay two years later, I ran every evening for two months to get fit – even in old heavy ski boots to strengthen my legs. One evening I was joined by a tall slim theatre technician called Christopher (Chris). This teenager wore dirty kit, but seemed to glide along easily. I had run with county athletes before and so knew I could keep up.

We came to the bottom of a long hill. Chris took off and sprinted flat out to the top. I ran up gamely, but was totally and completely outclassed.

I was so short of breath that I could not speak till we got back to the hospital.

Question: "Who did you last run for, Chris?"

Answer: "English schoolboys."

Yes, it showed.

Transplants

At the end of the general surgery rotation at the Hammersmith Hospital I was a registrar attached to the urology department. This had an active dialysis unit and a renal transplant unit. I witnessed time and again the poor patients in renal failure trying to follow a normal life. But they were hooked up to a dialysis machine for several hours two or three times a week. They felt dreadful. They could not work or go on holiday. Their life expectancy was poor.[2]

Conversely, those who had had a successful renal transplant felt so much better. They were free to work and go on holiday. (Recently I played golf with a man who had had a heart transplant!) So transplant surgery can change a life dramatically and sometimes permanently. Transplants save the NHS money too. Many years later, whilst teaching medical students on patients in April 2014, I met a man who had had a heart transplant when he was six years old and that was 25 years ago! But the world record for survival of heart transplant patients was broken in 2014 by John McCafferty of Newport Pagnell, now aged 71 years. He received a new heart 31 years ago!

* * *

Has the reader heard of Kris Compton – an American professional golfer? As I write, in March 2013, this man has done well in the Honda Classic Golf Tournament. That's not bad for somebody who has had two heart transplants!

In the 1970s, I witnessed the complicated but efficient system for renal transplantation. Once a donor is found, the kidney is tissue-typed. This information from the UK and Europe is fed into a computer in Southmead, Bristol. The kidney is flown urgently to the appropriate recipient, who is called in. Transplant surgeons all over the country are always on call 24 hours a day.

Despite there being many patients awaiting a transplant, there are so few donors then and now. Indeed, in 2012, as I write this, even if the patient has given consent for a kidney donation after death, so many relatives override these wishes and refuse consent – perhaps from ignorance?[2] Transplantation of an organ to a donor from a recipient involves legal, medical, ethical and emotional issues for all those directly and indirectly involved.

Currently, 7,000 people are waiting for an organ. It is likely that 1,000 of them will die before they get one. According to the NHS Blood Transfusion Unit, most patients in life would agree to donate an organ after death. But after death only 57% of families consent to the donation of their loved one's organs. Why the selfishness?[3][5]

Conversely, recently I discussed donation with the parents of a teenage girl who had suffered a massive fatal head injury. Five adults benefitted from her death – two corneal transplants, two kidney transplants and a small bowel transplant. Her parents were comforted that their daughter did not die for nothing. More relatives need to come to terms with reality.

In life we all work for a living.
In death we also could be giving.

As I write in September 2016, it is ten years since living organ donation from strangers became legal. In those ten years, over 500 kidneys have been donated in this way. Most donors are family members.

But in 2016 there are over 5,000 patients in the UK on the waiting list for a new kidney.[6]

Is there any hope for the children and young adults in renal failure? They are condemned to be married to a dialysis machine for several hours a week until a donor is found. There is, however, one new possible answer to this problem, but it is still in its infancy. Harald Ott, a surgeon at Massachusetts General Hospital, has grown a new kidney, in rats, by injecting kidney and blood vessel cells! It's early days, but very exciting for those in kidney failure. Could we also develop a new lung, a new heart, a new pancreas or even a new brain?[4]

References:

1. A Fraser-Moodie. Le Coupe de Monde de Ski des Medicins. *Hammersmith News Sheet.* 1973: 16.
2. Nicholas Evans et al. Irreversible renal damage from mushroom poisoning. *BMJ* 2012; 345: 47-49.
3. Jason Allardyce and Gillian Bourditch. Families thwart organ donors. *Sunday Times.* 7.10. 12:1.
4. Hannah Devlin. Harald Ott; Nature Medicine, 15. 4. 13. Transplant breakthrough as scientists grow kidney in lab. *The Times.* 15. 4. 13:18.
5. Tom Peck. Opt out of organ donation? Don't be so selfish. Freeview from the editors at *i* 12. 7. 13;14.
6. 500 healthy donors give a kidney to save a stranger. *The Times.* 21. 9. 16:16.

CHAPTER EIGHTEEN

Plastic Surgery

The plastic surgeon sat in front of the fire. Unfortunately, he just melted away.

Joke

I left general surgery to pursue my career aim – plastic surgery – in 1974. I was initially very excited about the specialty. The work is probably ill understood by the general public. I worked at Queen Mary's, Roehampton and then as a registrar at Frenchay Hospital, Bristol.

Roughly a third of plastic surgery cases come from various accidents. This usually involves wound closure – flaps of various types or skin grafting. Many patients have been burnt. A lot are children.

A third of patients have congenital abnormalities, for example, cleft lip and palate.

A third of patients have malignancy. Malignant melanomas are dealt with by plastic surgeons.

Many people confuse plastic surgery with cosmetic surgery. The latter is usually carried out privately, but sometimes cosmetic surgery and plastic surgery are the same. For example, I did an eyelid reduction under the NHS for a lady. Cosmetic procedure, you cry. No, the folds of skin fell over the front of her eyes. She held them up with her fingers.

"I just bought a cow and I can't see the bugger," she said in her West

Country accent. Post-operatively she could see without using her hands, as the folds had gone. My colleague did a facelift on the NHS. The poor patient had had smallpox. His face was a mess but much better post-operation. You may disagree with breast reconstruction post-cancer surgery under the NHS. I saw such a patient receive this treatment, but she was only 19 years old post mastectomy. Gosh, she had suffered.

Many patients who had been burnt caused their injuries by being stupid. For example, the man who refused to pay his electricity bill, so his house was disconnected from the supply. He had no electrical knowledge but tried to reconnect the supply, with the obvious result.

The lady who threw a burning chip pan out of the window. The window was unfortunately shut.

The man who threw petrol on his bonfire and then lit it. Petrol vapour in the air is explosive. His trousers went up in flames. The next door neighbour (a lady) pulled his trousers off. She had never seen him before – what an introduction!

Finally, we had several suicide attempts. They all did it wrong. They turned on the gas and closed the doors. They then lay down in front of the cooker. But North Sea Gas is not poisonous. Oh dear, they woke up ten minutes later: *Is it heaven?* they thought. *Oh no, it is still my kitchen.* Failed again.

So, to compensate, they lit up a fag – BOOM! Into the burns unit they came.

Major burns are less frequent, as our houses are a lot safer. Cooking is becoming safer, especially in developed countries. In North America the latest electric cooking top called induction has four hobs incorporated in a flat plastic resin. Touching one part of the top activates one hob. If a magnetic pot full of water is put on that hob it soon boils. Amazingly, the pot itself stays cool to the touch, as does the cooking top! I have seen it myself – seeing is believing. So, burns from cooking are less likely with this new device.

Many of the plastic surgery patients were my own age. One a few years younger than me was James Partridge. He had been badly burnt on his face and hands when a Land Rover he was driving went into a ditch and caught fire. James had been to Cambridge and had had several operations. I told him I was going to Bristol to take up this new post as a registrar. We arranged to play golf together at Hankley Common – a wonderful golf course in Surrey.

I will never forget that occasion, for this reason. I had paid my green fee, but returned to the professionals' shop just as James was coming out. The young assistant then said to me, "Did you see that awful creature that was just in this shop?"

"Yes," I said, "he is a friend of mine."

The assistant refused to speak to me. There was nobody to complain to. The club secretary was not in. I had to ignore this rude remark.

James would go through life facing this active discrimination. But I would see him again later.

I saw James Partridge again when he read the news on Channel 5 in November 2009. Those years cannot have been easy for him.He now leads a charity, 'Changing Faces.' His 'Face Equality At Work' is now supported by 25 employers. I hope it will be accepted by everybody soon.

* * *

I saw one lady aged 32 and she was a private patient transferred from the Middle East. Quite honestly, I did not believe her story. She said that her father locked her in her bedroom all the time to stop her meeting men! One day he caught her talking to a male admirer out of her bedroom window. Her father was furious and boarded up the window. She said that if she remained single she would have to look after her father in his old age. So he kept her away from men. In desperation she set herself on fire and came to us for skin grafting. Looking back with the benefit of hindsight, she probably was telling the truth. When healed, she went back to her father in the Middle East. What a life she had!

* * *

I loved the staff, the patients and the operating. I took away from this three and a half years a lot of experience and something – or rather someone – very, very special indeed.

I had been working for two days and the hospital had given me a room. But on the third day at lunchtime I was told to leave immediately by a hospital administrator. Another doctor had come, and I had to go and find accommodation outside the hospital. It was very inconvenient. I did just that. I moved out that lunchtime, putting my things in my car.

At 10pm the same day I was on call and passing my old room of 48 hours. There was a light on. I called by to see if the new doctor had settled in. He was a she, and she was washing her hair when I called. After a brief conversation I realised my mistake and left. Sometime later, I met her again at the swimming pool. Well, ladies surprisingly look a lot more attractive in bikinis than when washing their hair. We fell in love. Yes, I got something, or rather someone, very special from plastic surgery – Christine.

Before we married I rediscovered Scottish country dancing with Christine's help. One New Year's Eve I left work, got kilted up and picked Christine up. She looked gorgeous. The dance started at 8pm in a large hall. All the men wore kilts – about 200 ex-pats. The band was terrific. Every dance is different and follows a set sequence. A clear head is essential. Dance followed dance. We really got into it – not missing one dance. I quenched my thirst with pints and pints – of orange juice!

At 10pm we ate, and Auld Lang Syne was at midnight. There followed a free for all – kisses all round. I was grabbed by so many ladies, and I had not even been introduced! There then followed lots of easy dances – eightsomes and the like. Chris and I loved every second. We were both on a high when the dance ended at 3am. What could we do? Well, I drove Chris back to the hospital and we woke up a couple of friends to celebrate New Year!

Then I took Chris to her flat and later went to my lodging. My tired head hit the pillow at 6am. I woke with tinnitus – bells ringing. Then I had a thumping noise in my head. Oh no, it's the telephone that rang, and my landlady was banging on my door! I staggered to the phone.

"Where are you?" It was my boss.

"Oh," I replied, "where am I?"

"Well, I want you on my ward round now."

I glanced at my watch – 7am. I dressed (no kilt) and drove to work. What was happening?

There was no scheduled ward round due, and I was not yet on duty!

As I arrived my boss was just finishing. He had impressed the nurses and patients. He was a brilliant surgeon but a very strict teetotaller. He stared at me suffering from acute sleep deprivation. His face clouded. He misdiagnosed me as a bad hangover. I decided not to wish him a Happy New Year.

He stated: "Well, I have finished the round without you. I will be out today, but at home this evening." He left.

So this talented genius, for once, was going out! His lightning ward round was simply to appease his conscience. I recalled this impromptu, pre-dawn round in the doctors' mess later. It generated incredulity and laughter.

I was very busy that day, but annoyed at being deprived of sleep and wrongly labelled an alcoholic.

* * *

"Will you join our rugby team this Saturday afternoon, Alistair?" asked a friend. "The student nurses have challenged us, the doctors. It will be great fun."

"OK," I said, not realising what I had let myself in for.

Saturday afternoon found me standing amidst 14 other male doctors. I thought I was the oldest player, till a consultant I hardly knew, in his sixties, turned up! Surely he was too old to play. Why was he there?

This three-acre field had no pitch marked out, no goal posts and no referee either! The opposition was over 30 female student nurses, and two large male student nurses who boasted of their ability to play rugby football.

Shrieks and shouts filled the air. They kicked off. The rugby ball bounced into my arms. I punted it away well over the heads of the advancing hordes. Relieved, I stood still, watching the ball come down beyond the opposition. Then I was tackled by the only two male members of the opposition. One took my knees and the other flew at my head, embedding his teeth for a second in my forehead. No apologies were given. My assailants ran off to rejoin the fray. I went off to get my wounds cleaned and for antibiotics as befits a human bite.

I returned to the match half an hour later after treatment. I felt guilty as I had hardly taken part at all. The nonstop action had resulted in all the players being exhausted. The rugby ball was then kicked deep into our half. I was fresh and rushed to pick it up. I ran well wide of the melee to touch down at the other end. This was the only try of the match. We had won!

Those front teeth that had embedded themselves illegally momentarily in my forehead became loose. They had to be extracted. I was not surprised.

The consultant left the field early. He was ordered off by the opposition for repeatedly handling in the scrum. No, not handling the ball, but handling the female nurses!

As a schoolboy I had met Sir Harold Gillies. As a plastic surgeon I was introduced to, and used, some of his instruments that he invented – the Gillies Hook and the Gillies Needle Holders – scissors and needle holders in one! (Figs 31,32 and 33.)

He is also quoted as being the first person to suggest that: "Anaesthetic gases could be given via a tube into the trachea." His remarks were initially treated with incredulity. Now this is a routine manoeuvre for all general anaesthetic cases. How times change.[1]

Sir Harold invented an operation to treat a common injury that had previously baffled other surgeons – the displaced fractured zygoma (malar) bone. We all have two of these small bones, one cradled below each of our eyes to provide support to the eye. These bones are fragile and attached to the larger bones on both sides, but unsupported below. Trauma to the

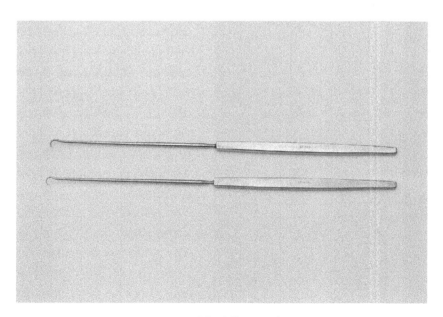

Fig 31 – The Gillies Hooks.

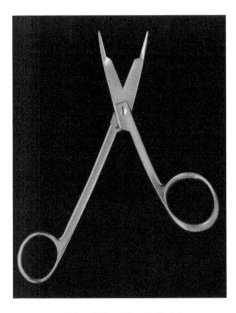

Fig 32 – The Gillies Needle holders and Scissors are combined as one instrument.

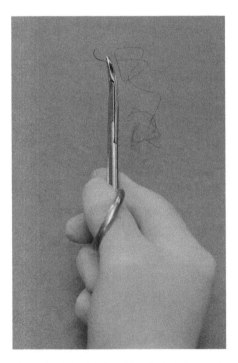

Fig 32 – The Gillies Needle holder with a suture.

cheek often leads to the force being transmitted. This can cause a downward, displaced, fractured zygoma. Now unsupported, the eye too slips down a little. So, untreated, the patient subsequently develops double vision! The face often looks different, and the displaced fracture is soon healed.

Previously, other surgeons had operated soon after the injury. They incised over the fracture and lifted it up. The fracture healed undisplaced – no double vision – but the facial scar was unsightly! No, a different operation was needed – but what?

Sir Harold adopted a novel approach. Under a general anaesthetic he made a small incision within the hair of the temple on the injured side. He then dissected bluntly round the cheekbone to make a passage to the zygoma. Through it, he inserted an instrument. One hand levered the end of the instrument protruding from the temple. The other hand guided the other end of the instrument to below the eye, through the skin. The zygoma could easily be lifted up these few millimetres, and it stayed there.

Sir Harold performed this operation over and over again – a success each time. But he needed a special instrument. It had to be metal for strength and sterilisation, flat for easy passage, blunt at the tip to avoid injuring tissues and curved to fit around the cheekbone. He did not possess such an instrument in his surgeon's bag, but he had the very thing in his garage! He used a small tyre lever (personal communication!).

In my lifetime I have had plenty of exposure to this injury, diagnosing and treating it – especially as a plastic surgery registrar. Today this approach to this fracture is adopted worldwide and is still called the 'Gillies' Lift'. A proper instrument is now used for this delicate operation. (Amazingly, it still looks to me like a small tyre lever.) Punches, falls or road traffic accidents tend to produce this fracture. In the absence of other injuries a punch is the most likely cause. Even celebrities are not immune. I know of at least one former world champion racing driver who has benefitted from the 'Gillies' Lift'. (He had other injuries too.) As always, the scar remains invisible, hidden in his hair.

Thank goodness Health and Safety never found out about this tyre lever or they would have cancelled all these facial operations, and probably got Sir Harold struck off for unprofessional conduct! Well, they never did because nobody filled in an IRI form (incident report). I recently read a eulogy of Sir Harold in an eminent surgical journal. He dared to criticise Sir Harold for not introducing arterial flaps as developed by a contemporary Dutch surgeon Johannes Esser. I can't understand it. All Sir Harold had to do was to google 'arterial flaps', or get hold of Johannes on Skype![2]

* * *

I worked for three and a half years in plastic surgery as a registrar. There were very few opportunities for promotion to senior registrar. I applied for about six posts over these years. Almost invariably at appointment a local candidate got the job. The two senior registrars I worked with could not gain promotion to consultant posts either.

Eventually, my senior consultant asked me, "Were you unsuccessful again?"

"Yes, sir," I said.

"Oh," he said, "you will have to make way for another trainee." I was eventually told I had to leave. I felt a failure. What could I do? Where could I work?

I expressed interest in a job in Holland in plastic surgery attached to a university. The salary was staggering, but I turned it down when offered to me! I was loyal to the NHS and the UK. After numerous visits and informal discussions, I decided on pursuing a career in Casualty. This was a new specialty. So I left my post in Plastic Surgery. I applied for a locum consultant job in Casualty in Derby.

Derby, here I come.

References:

1. *A Short History of Anaesthesia*. Butterworth, page 95.
2. Brian Morgan. Saints and Sinners Sir Harold Gillies. *Royal College of Surgeons Eng Bulletin* June 2013; 6:95:204-205.

CHAPTER NINETEEN

Derby, 1978

Carriages without horses go and accidents fill the world with woe.

Anon

So, I finally decided to change tack and become a Casualty doctor – a new emerging speciality. There was a locum consultant post going in Derby. Before I applied for this job I needed to look at it. It was a very foggy day so I travelled from Bristol to Derby by train because of this, leaving my very heavily pregnant wife Christine in Bristol.

I was greeted in Derby by the incumbent, Mr John Collins. He had designed the department and ran it single-handedly. This locum position was the second consultant post. I was shown round and introduced to everybody. Yes, it seemed fine.

Then a bell sounded loudly and all hell broke loose. Mr Collins shouted, "a squad, a squad!" He propelled me down the corridor at great speed, holding me by my collar. He was taller and heavier than me. I was pushed into the back of a large white Volvo.

"What is it?" I asked.

"A squad, a flying squad," everyone repeated. We shot off at great speed through Derby and onto a dual carriageway. Luckily I had had no lunch yet. I glanced over the shoulder of the driver in front of me to see

Fig 34 – The Derbyshire Royal Infirmary

our speed – 110mph. Oh gosh, I thought, and I came by train for safety. The fog had not lifted. The siren sounded and Mr Collins was on the loudhailer.

"Give way. Please give way. Give way. RPG 2649, give way please. Thank you." The car in front moved out of the way.

We soon came to an accident. A coach had come off the road and was in a ditch. A very nice lady – a nursing officer from elsewhere – had a fractured femur. Two nurses from our Volvo got out all the drugs and kit. What a lot. Mr Collins asked me to take over. "It's my eyes," he said. "I can't see well."

I put up a drip and she was given a fluid expander (so fluid went into her veins to treat shock) after taking routine blood tests. I gave her morphine intravenously, then put a splint on the leg. Then she had more morphine. The splint was adjusted. Mr Collins went back into the warm and cosy squad car. I went in the cold and draughty ambulance with our patient back to the hospital. Once back, I had to sign for the morphine, but I was not employed by the hospital. I had no contract and was not covered legally. I signed, and fortunately both the nurses with me countersigned in the drugs book – as decreed by the Dangerous Drugs

Act. The General Medical Council could have rightly told me off. But I had no alternative.

I got the job as a locum. At long last I had found the job that I was happiest doing.

So I became a Casualty consultant for over 30 years, up to my retirement.

My First Day

I was a locum emergency consultant in Derby. This was my first day as a consultant. I wandered round at 9am (I could not get a photo name badge till 10am, so I could not work normally until then)!

I came across a mother sitting by a baby, about nine months old. The mother talked a lot to her baby. The child was on her back, her right leg was strapped up and elevated, attached by a small cord to a pulley counterbalanced by a weight. This is the normal treatment for a fractured femur in a baby and relieves the pain. The child seemed happy and not in pain. No notes were available so I caught a passing nurse.

"What's happening here?" I asked.

"Oh," said the nurse, "this is a classic case. The child has a fractured femur and mum says the child fell over and that's impossible. She is really not bothered so it's a 'battered baby.'"

I was puzzled and went back to the mother.

"Are you worried about your child?" I asked.

"No, fractures don't bother me," she said.

I was even more puzzled. She seemed a very caring mother. Something was wrong.

"Have you fractured any bones?" I asked.

"Oh yes," she said, "fourteen times."

Then the penny dropped. I looked at mum's eyes and she had pale blue sclerae. (The normal white of the eye around the coloured iris.) She had fragilitas ossium, also known as brittle bone disease. It is inherited. Such patients suffer broken bones a lot. The baby had blue sclerae too – a sign of this condition. I told the nurse and the Casualty officer that this patient was not a 'battered baby' and wrote it in her notes. The fracture healed well in hospital.

This loving mother rarely left her baby's cot.

So I had left plastic surgery for good.

* * *

Soon after starting my new job, my registrar showed me a mole on the back of one of my junior doctors. I thought it was a malignant melanoma. We showed this mole to the local consultant plastic surgeon. He was convinced it was "definitely benign – not a serious mole at all". Well, he was the expert in a specialty I had failed to progress in. The consultant surgeon told us to ignore this mole. "Don't bother to remove it; just ignore it," he told us with great authority.

But we still decided to remove this mole under a local anaesthetic. It was shown to be a very nasty malignant melanoma after all. I was a trifle confused – well, if such an expert can be so very wrong, it shows how difficult this whole subject is.

My junior doctor had further surgery (skin grafting) and more treatment. He died a year later of malignant melanoma metastases. Such a waste. He was an excellent doctor, happily married with a young son. Such is life.

* * *

When I was first appointed a Casualty consultant (now Emergency Medicine), three conditions regularly flooded in, especially at night or on weekends. These were toothache, ingrowing toenails and psychiatric disorders. These patients all had three things in common. Firstly, they were usually an acute flare-up of a long-term problem, secondly, some specialist knowledge was required, and thirdly, they and their relatives complained a lot: "Urgent treatment now please".

We gave them all plenty of advice. The dental patients often had not seen a dentist in years! We arranged for a local dentist to see them urgently (for a price!)

The ingrowing toenail patients were referred to the hospital chiropodist who we arranged to come and do a clinic in our department. This has continued.

Finally, psychiatric disorders presented a more complex problem. Some have a suicidal risk. I sat on a Hospital Working Party and we finally developed a small part-time Mental Health Liaison Team. This has now expanded and is only now full-time 24/7.[1]

These actions freed our junior doctors to get on with seeing other patients.

Reference:

1. New 24/7 Mental Health Team to help patients in hospitals' A&E departments. *Derby Telegraph.* 25.10.13:6.

Out of the frying pan – and into the fire.

A saying

So I found myself a Casualty consultant. I had a colleague, Mr John Collins. He was close to retirement and he told me, "I leave the running of this department to you." I had 12 junior doctors. 12 junior doctors to assess and train. I started teaching formally and informally. After one year Mr Collins retired. So I was now on call 24 hours a day – every day!

Firstly I had two registrars, Sammy and Alec. Unfortunately, they were not on speaking terms with each other! I assessed their grasp of medicine. I tried to retrain them both, but they failed to improve. I just knew that there were potential trainees for this new Casualty specialty. I discussed these present registrars with medical staff in Human Resources. I was told that both these doctors were in post for as long as they liked. "Don't try and sack them!" The longer I worked with them the more I was convinced that neither of these doctors was in the right post. Rows between them were commonplace, as were complaints from patients.

I had eight very junior doctors called Casualty officers, all on short-term contracts. They were excellent. Indeed, one of them seemed to be running the department clinically when I arrived! Dave Rowley subsequently became a professor of orthopaedics and became head of orthopaedic training nationwide! He left to continue his training.

I finally had two clinical assistants – one, David, was brilliant. Unfortunately, David Wells left after a couple of years to pursue a career in industrial medicine. I envied him – guaranteed no night calls. The other clinical assistant had been in post for years and attracted numerous complaints from staff and patients alike! He had a job elsewhere as a general practitioner and only worked part-time for me. He had to go, I told Human Resources – they strongly disagreed!

Well, medical training is full of advice concerning patients, but nothing about how to deal with these three major problems – the wrong doctors in post. I desperately needed an ally to talk to. I got two that shared my problems and helped me out. They guided me. Well, I was in a mess. I was new and inexperienced in administration.

Firstly, I got approval and funding for a senior registrar. We appointed Sunil, an Indian surgeon with an FRCS (one ally). He came to me highly recommended by a surgical friend. He subsequently became a Casualty consultant in Birmingham.

The second ally came from an unexpected source – the chief nursing officer for the hospital. He had a similar problem – a nurse running a department who was very unpopular. This nurse refused to retrain nurses or employ any part-time. We were adamant on reflection that the three doctors and that one nurse had to go. How did we do it? Such things are in no medical or nursing textbook. Well, we did it legally, and I believe that all four of these professionals benefitted from this!

Firstly, I looked at the registrars' contracts that they had signed. As a training post, the registrars were supposed to be studying for a higher qualification. One registrar, Alec, confided that he had no intention of working for this. I informed him that he had violated his contract. He was blocking a training post. He wisely decided to go into general practice. He is happy there still.

The second registrar, Sammy, insisted that he was studying hard for his Primary FRCS. He was married with small children. I knew that things were not as they seemed.

One night Sammy was contracted to be the hospital resident on call, overnight. At 2am he crashed his car into a motorcyclist three miles away. Our accident flying squad, including me, was called, so I had numerous witnesses! I knew that he was visiting his mistress who lived nearby.

My senior registrar knew of the affair and told me. How did he find out? Well, the senior registrar, Sunil, was on call one night. At 4am he was asleep in the registrars' on-call room on the sixth floor. He was called to see a casualty and so he rushed across the residents' corridor into the lift. Here he was surprised to bump into this married registrar with a lady. This registrar was not on call that night and the only rooms on that floor are bedrooms! The lady was introduced to Sunil as a doctor (he knew she was not!). The purpose of the presence of these two in that lift, at that time, on that floor, left little to the imagination!

The next day after the road traffic accident Sammy had no explanation for this episode. I told him that he had broken his contract as he left the hospital whilst on call. I offered him a committee of inquiry. He refused and resigned. He went to work elsewhere. This was a long way from his mistress. He never passed his examinations. I hoped that I had saved his marriage. I felt very sorry for his wife.

Well, what about the clinical assistant who worked locally as a general practitioner? He insisted on staying. Well, we had a full-blown committee of inquiry at my insistence. Very reluctantly, Human Resources attended. They were worried that I could cost them money by insisting on an unfair dismissal. This doctor was well-represented by a professional well-versed in such affairs. The hospital gave me no help at all. All the administrators were scared stiff.

I proved that the clinical assistant's records were inconsistent with life! Many letters of complaint were read out. One said, 'He stitched my son with no analgesia of any sort.' Another said, 'He stitched my daughter, then stopped to pick his nose. Then he carried on stitching.'

As a consequence, this clinical assistant was advised to resign. His main job was in general practice. So all my three doctors had to leave. They were all replaced by excellent candidates. I was able to train dozens of registrars over the years. All have made fine consultants. I, myself, was joined by a second consultant, Paul, after two years. Paul and I worked together on call for alternate nights for over 20 years.

But what about the nurse? How did the chief nursing officer get that nurse removed? This nurse had not violated any contract and had little clinical contact. Well in their fifties, this nurse was offered promotion! This would really help their pension. They went off jubilant to a small peripheral hospital. Here they could 'do no harm' – a very big fish in a tiny pond!

CHAPTER TWENTY

Charity

It is better to give than to receive.
The Bible, Corinthians Chapter 13

I first experienced charity work as a plastic surgery registrar on call at Frenchay Hospital, Bristol. Four of our lady secretaries decided to raise money for a local children's charity. We treated a lot of children with a wide range of congenital abnormalities. Before the unit at Plymouth opened we saw patients in Bristol from all over the south west. One of the commonest abnormalities was cleft lip and palate. Many of these children came over 100 miles to our unit for treatment. Frequently, they had multiple attendancies, making treatment a financial and time-consuming burden. This charity helped patients affected in this way. Some money came to the unit itself for research to help such patients directly. It was a worthwhile cause that had proved its worth over and over again. Patients benefitted directly and indirectly. As it was a local charity, there was huge support.

I was needed briefly at about 8am 'for my muscles'. I humped large containers of second-hand ladies' and children's clothing. There were no male clothes on sale. After several journeys into the hall at the hospital, I was convinced there was no way this lot would be sold. There was far too much. Then somebody else brought some more clothes and then yet more. The ladies sifted the clothes into piles and put them on tables or on hangers. I left, convinced that it would not work. This was a hot Saturday morning in the summer of '76 – one of the very hottest that dry summer.

I missed my lunch as being on call I had to take a child with a dog bite to theatre for suturing and unfortunately skin grafting. I knew there were light refreshments, so at about 4pm I passed by for a cup of tea. I was starving. What bedlam awaited me. Half the female population of Bristol seemed to be there. They hunted and rooted over and over the clothes that were liberally spread about. I paid for a total of three cups of tea and two large pieces of cake. I felt a lot better and left to get some fresh air. Gosh, it was hot.

At 6pm I called by to take away all the unsold clothes. To my utter amazement there were just a few oddments left. Everything else was gone! The refreshments all went too.

I later learnt that they had raised well over £1,000. I was gobsmacked. What was their secret?

Well, they knew the market and got in plenty of clothes, different sizes and styles. There was no rubbish. The publicity had been superb. Everybody knew about it locally. The ladies had been organised and worked like beavers. Everybody had a specific job to do.

All were very happy. They had had a good day – with one small exception. One lady helper was a bit frantic.

"Where are they?" she said.

"What are you looking for, Beryl?" another said.

"My knickers," she explained. "I took them off round the corner when it got very hot. Now I can't find them!"

We soon realised what had happened. She took them off to cool down. Somebody else then picked them up and they were sold! (Beryl went home knickerless.) I think she felt no shame. She instead enjoyed the notoriety!

Charity work, I discovered, was very hard and at times amusing!

Eight years later I was a consultant in the accident and emergency department at the Derbyshire Royal Infirmary in Derby. The regional neurosurgical unit at our hospital was moving to a major teaching hospital, The Queen's Medical Centre in Nottingham, ten miles away. The neurosurgeons had been lured by promises of fantastic facilities and further finance. Many of these promises have remained unfulfilled. As a parting shot, the neurosurgeons promoted the possibility that the two accident and emergency consultants (of which I was one) should take over the management of head injury patients in their absence. We could then liaise with the neurosurgical unit when appropriate. Well, these patients came through our department anyway. We had a short-stay ward to observe these patients. We also had the support of the department of anaesthetics with an intensive care unit. The department of radiology, however, did not have a scanner. The hospital had no money for one. The neurosurgeons took an ageing head scanner with them to Nottingham, along with some anaesthetists and an experienced radiologist.

So my colleague and I had responsibility for head injuries, but no head scanner. We knew that without one we could not investigate patients properly. There was one extrovert general surgeon with experience of fundraising, David Thomas. This same man had been the county surgeon. I was a member of a group that went along to persuade him to raise the funds privately. He considered this carefully, sounded us all out and took the bait!

We launched a team effort, David at the helm as our chairman. He led from the front and like all natural leaders he did not consider failure as a possibility. He had a style somewhat reminiscent of Winston Churchill (without the cigar). I was one of a dozen founder governors of the Scanner Appeal. We could not start fundraising at once as at a meeting of the hospital doctors it was agreed that the MacMillan Unit fundraising should go first. Two big appeals at one time would not work.

I upset the organiser of the MacMillan appeal just before they finished raising money. An eccentric extrovert with long hair contacted the media unbeknown to me. He was going to run down the High Street in Derby with his hair on fire to attract attention. His mates would follow with buckets to collect money, all for the Scanner Appeal, but it had not been launched yet! I had to go along as he might have been burnt to death. Not to go would show disinterest and disloyalty. My presence was noted and my picture appeared in the press. Yes, the media had landed me in trouble. Not for the first or last time, I was unpopular with my peers!

This break before we started the Scanner Appeal properly gave us time to plan ahead. David told us to be ready to get hold of all our contacts and talk to as many people as possible about this appeal.

The day of the launch of the appeal came at last. David went to

Markeaton Park in Derby and let off many hot air balloons, all bearing our logo, in front of the press to get publicity. At the same time a presenter on Radio Derby invited me to speak about the launch of this appeal. (his wife had been a patient of mine). I clearly recall he told me beforehand exactly what questions he would ask live on air. When the time came he promptly asked me several different questions.

I hesitated 'live on air'. He turned off his mike and fell about laughing. Thanks a million, pal. What a complete set-up and I fell for it. The main thing was that we got publicity. I was reminded again not to trust completely presenters in the public spotlight, radio, TV and the press.

Slowly at first and then quickly, the money rolled in. We had regular governors' meetings. Well, they were fun. We were kept up to date, as to how much was raised, by our accountant Harold Bates. He was in his seventies but still working hard. He came in every day. We employed two ladies full-time who were in our scanner office. They liaised with everybody and did an excellent public relations job.

They talked to donors. They wrote letters of thanks. They arranged for us as governors to give talks on the scanner and to pick up cheques, usually in the evening. I vividly remember one occasion when I had written to an ex-private patient asking for money for the Scanner Appeal. He was the chief executive of an airline. He sent me a cheque for £1,000, but made out to me personally! I entered the scanner office proudly showing off my 'cheque'. They soon had it as they forced me to sign it on the back. I was not tempted to bank it myself!

These ladies finally gave all the cheques to Harold Bates, our accountant, who banked them the same day. He had previously founded the accountancy firm Bates Weston in Derby.

Harold put the money to work, earning interest. It started to mount up more and more. The interest was tax-free being a charity. Harold put large sums on the money market. Interest rates were better than today. At meetings he gave us accounts accurate to that day. Now, conversely, at ordinary hospital department meetings the hospital accountants were three or six months behind. That shows you the measure of Harold's worth and also the value of experience and hard work. (He was too old to work in a hospital normally!) All he got was a free car parking space – how generous was that?

Our deputy chairman was Margaret Cohen, a radiologist. She

provided technical knowhow. She scoured the country for information about scanners, and the very best value for money, which ones broke down and which ones were the most reliable and gave the best picture. She learnt at first hand – well, it's better to learn from other people's mistakes than your own. She finally got a really good deal and we knew our target – £800,000 – would we make it? Margaret was also the senior magistrate and gained a law degree after retiring from medicine!

I got involved with visiting various large firms to see if their employees would be interested in small regular pay roll deductions for our appeal. I was one of a group that visited the British Rail works. I visited two other large firms. We signed up a lot of people. The money came in regular monthly returns. Incidentally, some of these people were even contributing still 25 years later – now, that is loyalty.

I am sure that the reader is conversant with the usual ways of raising money for charity. There are whip-rounds in the pub, coffee mornings, cake sales, bring-and-buy sales or own-clothes days at school. I never ceased to be amazed by some folks' ingenuity and invention. There were whist drives, beetle drives, games of bridge or poker, tombolas, raffles and lotteries. Some paid or sponsored somebody to travel – walks, runs, swims, horse riding, motorcycle riding, bicycling, off-road vehicles, and even trips in a balloon. I clearly recall picking up one cheque, just after tea one day. I took my son, Duncan, along and we were then showed how the money was raised. We were bounced around a muddy field in an open-top four-wheel drive kit car. My tea fortunately stayed down – but only just.

The money also came from singing, dancing, dinners, concerts, music of all sorts, the theatre, employers and employees. We never knew where it would come from next or how much. Finally, it even came from undertakers and people's wills. I thought I had seen it all, until one particular evening I recall well. I was sent to pick up a cheque at a working men's club in West Hallam. I got there promptly at 7.30pm and was greeted enthusiastically. They had had a fundraising evening and enjoyed it very much indeed. They gave me a generous cheque for several hundred pounds.

"Come and have a drink, doc," one said. I sat down with the three organisers to chat. They all three were retired. They each ordered pints of beer. It was quite clear that this was their local and that they were regulars. I then asked them exactly how this money had been raised. "Oh, doc, you should have been there. We all had a great time," was the reply. One of them explained.

"Well, we filled this place. We had over a hundred chaps here. They had each paid £10 to get in." He was drooling into his beer as he spoke. "Two ladies came here from Nottingham. They then took their clothes off. They stripped naked. Oh, it was great."

I was shocked. Oh, I was so glad that I was not there. I told them so. They were upset.

"Aren't you interested in ladies then, doc?" One of them muttered something about, "Do you bat for the other side?"

I tried to explain about the work that I do.

"I am paid to see men, women and children who come to me with problems. After chatting to them, they take some or all of their clothes off. I am sorry, but ladies stripping off is a busman's holiday for me."

They simply could not understand me and my reluctance to share their passion. One of them then blurted out: "Then these ladies were paid a lot more money. We went into the next room and guess what they did?"

"No," I said. I did not want to know. I felt trapped and rather embarrassed at how they had raised this money for such a worthwhile cause. I dared not say anything more.

We paused and one of them said, "They should be here by now. I wonder where they have got to."

"Who are you waiting for?" I said.

"Oh, the *Ilkeston Echo* and the *Derby Evening Telegraph*," one said.

Panic gripped me. I was still wary about any media involvement. I could see myself on the front page of the *Derby Evening Telegraph* with the cheque. What would the caption read?

'Doc says carry on stripping'?

'Strippers worked hard, doc says'?

'Thank you, strippers'?

Oh no, I thought. I finished my drink and turned to my friends. "I am sorry but I have to go now. I have another appointment." "But you've only just come," said one. "Please stay for another drink," said another.

I thanked everybody and fled. The cheque was safely in my pocket. Well, it was legal, but definitely risque.

We reached our target in nine months. The scanner was bought.

There were yet more expenses concerning installation. The hospital had to commit to the running costs of the scanner and staffing. The great day came and the new whole-body scanner was up and running.

All the clinicians wanted to use it. There was great demand. The radiologists had to go back to school to learn to read the scans. Over the next few years the scanner needed speeding up and modules were added for example, radiotherapy. This was all paid for by the Scanner Appeal. We even took it back after a year and insured the scanner for a lot longer. Well, it would have been a disaster but – a possibility – that it would break down and could not be repaired.

Personally, I was very proud of the scanner. Our head injury patients benefitted directly. We paid for the facility to transmit scans down the telephone wires to the neurosurgeons at Nottingham – all out of the Scanner Appeal. They could then see the same head scans that we could and so easily discuss them. It worked well for over ten years. Thank you, people of Derby and Derbyshire.

Our Scanner Appeal branched out and became the Scanner and Medical Equipment Appeal. Vascular surgery, breast screening and ophthalmology were major benefitters from this diversity. David Thomas retired. Margaret took over as chairman, and when she retired I was chairman for six years, ably assisted by Di Holland. We were the last two of the original governors on the appeal. After over 25 years on the same committee I bowed out. I had had enough. I had met and worked with so many lovely people.

Harold Bates, our accountant, had carried on and on. He went from strength to strength. He was a very shrewd and gentle Christian man. I felt a certain affinity with him. Probably by his careful accounting and playing the money market, he had made more money himself for the Scanner Appeal than anybody else. He certainly was a trump card.

I did not realise what we both had in common until I wrote Harold's obituary in the hospital gazette. He had died aged 90!

"What had we in common?" you may ask. Well, we both had three Scottish grandparents. Our bond was of Highland blood! That explains it. He worked so hard and was paid absolutely nothing. Scots know the value of money and hate to see it wasted. An Englishman, Neil, trained by Harold, took over the accountancy reins.

Some years after the scanner was installed, a white paper was produced by the Royal College of Surgeons on the 'Management of Head Injuries'. It is known better as the Galasko Report after its chairman Professor Galasko. In it there was outlined a model for all district general hospitals to manage head injury patients. The Accident and Emergency consultants should be in charge of head injury patients in that hospital. They should work with the anaesthetists on the Intensive Care Unit to manage such patients. There must be a short-stay observation ward. There should be facilities for head scanning at that hospital. The A&E doctors should liaise with the neurosurgeons at the regional neurosurgical unit. But we had it all in place already in Derby. It had been there for years. I met other emergency consultants from other hospitals. When I told them we had had such a service in place for years, my words were greeted with incredulity. They struggled to implement such a service. Thank you, scanner.

The reader may have been struck by a very serious omission in the above. Lots of people are mentioned, but not one word about hospital administrators.

It's a very sad fact but, without them, things go really, really well!

CHAPTER TWENTY-ONE

The Derby Accident Flying Squad

Come fly with me, let's fly, let's fly away.

1st line of a popular song

Mr John Collins, before he retired, gave me the history of this unique service held in high esteem, quite rightly, by the people of Derby. The word flying is a misnomer. It was a fast vehicle, not an aeroplane. The original flying squads were obstetric flying squads. These started over a hundred years ago around Edinburgh. There was a high incidence of rickets, and antenatal care was not established. This led to a lot of problems in labour, hence the obstetric flying squad. Antenatal care has improved now and rickets is rare today. So the Obstetric Flying Squad is all but obsolete.

At the time Mr Collins became in charge of Casualty in the 1960s, the mines round Derby were still open. There were accidents down these mines. 80% of such accidents happened close to the coal face. Mr Collins took a mobile team to these casualties. They were conveyed underground in little trucks along railway lines. 'Keep your head down doctor,' he was told repeatedly. The police or the ambulance service took him there with other doctors and nurses. Gradually more

186

equipment was built up. It had to be checked repeatedly. It seemed to work well.

All the coalmines around Derby have closed. (However, we still had miners' helmets in the 1970s when I arrived.) The road traffic accident became commoner. The roads got busier and the traffic went faster and faster.

So the Derby Accident Flying Squad went out to road traffic accidents. They were initially conveyed by the police in squad cars. Mr Collins clearly recalled one incident coming back from a call in a police car (another doctor travelled in the ambulance with the patient). The police car stopped behind a line of traffic stationary at traffic lights. A female learner driver was first in the queue. The lights went to green and she stalled. Cars hooted. The lights went red again.

"Give her a chance," the police driver boomed over the loudhailer. Green again – oh, she stalled again. The loudhailer had not been switched off and the policeman told everyone, "Oh, the silly bitch has done it again!"

The police trained several men to be fast and safe drivers. They became our flying squad drivers. From 1975 the accident flying squad was given a vehicle of its very own. The Lions Club of Derby had raised the money and presented a new Volvo to Mr Collins at a ceremony in a plush hotel in Derby. The chief fundraiser and organiser was a very large gentleman called Ewan McWilliam. He arranged for the Volvo to be in the very centre of the dining room. Everybody was there sitting down enjoying a slap-up dinner.

Then a call came from the ambulance service. Flying Squad wanted now! Mr Collins shouted out, "Hurry up, let's go!" Tables were pushed aside. The specially trained flying squad driver started the engine. Ewan was pushed in the back of the vehicle. Others jumped in. Off they roared up the Burton Road. It was absolute chaos. The dining room was left in disarray.

A mile up the road they ran out of petrol! (Well, new cars often don't have much petrol in them.) Mr Collins called on his radio for an ambulance to get them to the incident. Ewan, who had no first-aid experience whatsoever, ran away. What a complete shambles.

The Derby Accident Flying Squad, for nearly 40 years overall, went out two or three times a week mainly to road traffic accidents. We had a lot of equipment and drugs. Many patients benefitted from this service. We brought them back to the Derbyshire Royal Infirmary in an ambulance. The good people of Derby and Derbyshire paid money to help run the squad. These people were very generous indeed. We got a second vehicle – a Range Rover.

We went out in all weathers and never refused a call. We covered the whole of Southern Derbyshire, sometimes going to North Derbyshire, Nottinghamshire, Leicestershire or Staffordshire. We resuscitated a lot of trapped drivers.

* * *

I recall giving one lorry driver trapped in his cab five pints of blood before we got him out on the A38 on Abbey Hill. Well, as doctors we are trained to take full histories and do a full examination before treatment. Trapped upright in his cab, that was compressed, he was in agony. I could only examine his right forearm and record a weak thready pulse. I guessed (quite rightly) that he was bleeding internally with multiple fractures.

When we finally got him back to the hospital he had multiple fractures – pelvis, both femurs, both tibias and a rare and awkward injury – a dislocated talus – notorious for problems. He even bled externally from a deep wound in his bottom. I treated him in a mast suit that compressed his pelvis and legs. He needed 15 more pints of blood in hospital! He needed multiple operations to fix his fractures. Even that horrible dislocated talus bone recovered. He was an inpatient for weeks.

He eventually returned to driving his lorry.

* * *

Another patient was a car driver who swerved off a road one evening. He rolled his car through a wooden fence and into a woodyard in Duffield. Bizarrely, he impaled his chest on a wooden post – 4"x 4" in cross section. As I got there a burly fireman was freeing him by sawing the post above and below him. The lower end of the post was still in the ground!!!

This man should have died, but did not. He was 20 years old and fit. He screamed in pain and was very much alive. His only injury was to his chest. The post went in at his right nipple and out below his right shoulder blade! So we had to lay him on his left side on the stretcher after giving him morphine and intravenous fluids.

This large foreign body in his chest meant we could not X-ray him. I called the surgeon on call. At operation, miraculously he found the wooden post had not penetrated into his chest cavity but pushed all his ribs to the left. So his right lung was in the midline.

Once the post was removed the ribs sprang back into place. The would was cleaned up and laid open. Days later the chest wound was closed. The patient made a full recovery and was just left with a large right-sided chest scar.

He was so very lucky! All the emergency services worked together so well.

* * *

On another occasion, a driver had had his face pushed right in. My junior was quicker than me (he was a dentist as well as a doctor). He pulled this man's fractured upper jaw out, improving the airway. He survived too. I once used a medical student to hold the infusion for a man trapped in his Mercedes in thick snow. When the fireman eventually got the man out, over an hour later, I found the student was suffering from early hypothermia. Both the student and the driver survived. Cardiac patients were defibrillated and children treated too.

For about 20 years after I first came to Derby we filled a niche that existed. Gradually the ambulance personnel became better trained. Indeed, when I first came to Derby, Mr Collins rudely called the ambulances 'Bread vans on wheels'. This was not surprising as the main training for the ambulance personnel initially was how to drive the vehicle!

Our flying squad drivers were terrific. They knew all the roads and had been trained by the police to a very high standard. They were all trained first-aiders. One once remarked to Mr Collins, "Do you know that the squad vehicle can do 100mph?"

"Yes, of course I do," said Mr Collins.

"But this was on a grass verge," said the driver.

* * *

We once had a call to Radio Derby – a politician had collapsed live on air! (It takes a lot to stop them talking.) I thought the squad driver had gone the wrong way, but he shot across the dual carriageway at a tiny gap I did not know of. The politician needed an injection as he was in heart failure. He quickly recovered. His wife was an ex-nurse and also was in local politics. This story was told in an edition of the *Reader's Digest*.[1]

Even I had to drive the flying squad vehicle myself once. I was familiar with Range Rovers as I drove one myself. I did not drive quickly despite using the blue flashing lights and the siren. If we ever got lost our senior receptionist Ann redirected us over the radio. You learn a lot about people when they direct you, "Turn right at the Coach and Horses, then left at the White Lion." I can hear her still!

* * *

We did have problems with onlookers. Once, in Alvaston on a Saturday night, we were treating a badly injured lady. I looked up and a few feet away were onlookers staring at us rudely as they each ate their bags of chips. Another time one policeman had a big bunch of keys that he proudly announced would open any car. He put them down to help us. He turned round and the keys were gone!

Twice in my fifties I found myself on call for the department and the flying squad throughout the night. On each occasion a registrar went sick and nobody else could cover the night Casualty officer. We felt each time that this doctor needed supervising. I was the consultant on call that night unfortunately. I had to do something, I was responsible.

So I drove home that afternoon to grab a toothbrush, pyjamas and a change of clothing. My day shift finished at 6pm. My night shift began at 6pm. After 9pm it was just the Casualty officer and me.

The first time I was forced to do this I worked till 4am. Then I felt tired. My knees were weak and my brain numbed. I was told of one last patient with a cut wrist who needed a couple of stitches. His hand had gone through a glass door. He was such a pleasant drunk. So courteous and embarrassed to be there. For fun he had swapped clothes with his girlfriend. His dress was a tight fit! What a laugh! But my junior had not examined the patient properly. Yes, the skin was cut and needed suturing. Unfortunately, all the nerves, arteries, veins and guiders had also been divided in the front of the wrist – the hand would not function.

"Re-examine the patient and call the hand surgeons," I barked as I staggered off to bed exhausted. So my presence on the shop floor that night was worthwhile – just for that one patient alone.

The second time I found myself doing an unscheduled night shift I only lasted till 3.30am. The junior doctor I was working with did really well – no mistakes at all.

About ten minutes after my head hit the pillow I was in a deep, deep sleep. Then the flying squad bleep exploded into life. Disorientated, and in the dark, I awoke and tried to get dressed. I rushed into the lift. Down I was taken into the department. I staggered out into the night still tired and still clutching the noisy bleep. The flying squad vehicle was waiting for me. I climbed in. One nurse, Sue, one driver, John, and sped off into the dark night. We had been called to a road traffic accident.

We flew along a deserted narrow lane that I knew well. We turned a corner to be met by dazzling lights.

Three fire tenders were parked together – one lighting up the scene like a filmset. Firemen were everywhere. A police car was parked nearby and the road was closed to all other traffic – well, we blocked it completely. A small car was buried in a wall. The driver had kept going straight on, at a bend. Little remained the car. The top had been removed. The driver was screaming from inside of the car and was very, very bossy. Two ambulance men were in attendance beside the casualty.

We parked at the bottom of the hill and walked up to the scene. It then started to rain and rain. The rescue operation had had to stop as the driver insisted on more analgesia. I refused him a general anaesthetic as his stomach was full it as could have killed him. I gave him plenty of morphine intravenously, and then gave instructions to carry on getting him out of the car.

The burly fireman had him out in a jiffy – still swearing and shouting at his rescuers. The ambulance men conveyed him to their ambulance on a stretcher. He just had a fractured tibia – undisplaced. This injury was painful but definitely not life-threatening. The patient was kept in hospital overnight with his leg in a back slab. He took his own discharge against medical advice the next day, when his friends wheeled him out of hospital. (Well, he had borrowed the car without consent and the police were very interested in him!)

Meanwhile, I had been driven back to the hospital. As I got there the day registrar had come in early – to help the old man (me). I put my hand in my pocket to give him the precious bleep. Oh dear, it was not there.

I looked everywhere – no bleep. After several hours' sleep I looked again – no bleep. One black mark to me!

I worked a normal day, then I drove home early that afternoon. As the light was just fading I made a detour to the ill-fated rendezvous of the previous night. The scene had been cleaned up – well done. I looked at where our flying squad vehicle had been parked. There at the side of the road where I had alighted was the precious bleep. I picked it up.

The next day at work this precious bleep was not functioning, so I took it to the telephone superintendent. "What have you done to this precious bleep, doctor?" she asked anxiously.

"Oh, nothing," I replied truthfully!

"But it won't work," she said after trying it again.

She removed the back of the bleep and poured out water. She gave me one of those looks. So the bleep was broken and could not be repaired. I nearly got the bill for a new bleep, but somebody took pity on me.

* * *

On another occasion, we were called out by the ambulance service to a small farm in Belper. There were new houses all around, but this farm remained. A 16-year-old boy had just left school and was working alone in this farm building with some machinery. Several hours earlier his left trouser leg had caught in the revolving mechanism. He was dragged in. He could not escape or turn the machinery off. Neither the ambulance nor the fire service could free him.

When we got there it was obvious that his left leg below the knee was non viable, i.e., dead. I gave him a huge dose of morphine intravenously and then put up a drip to counteract the shock with fluids. Once the pain had lessened we could free him. He had a crude surgical amputation of his left leg. I established haemostasis to the wound (stopped it bleeding) and dressed it. We transported him to the hospital where he had a formal left below-knee amputation under a general anaesthetic in theatre.

Despite the terrifying ordeal, this lad returned to farming, walking on an artificial limb. I kept in touch. He raised money for our accident flying squad and does farm contracting work to this day.

* * *

On another occasion on the Derby outer ring road a tree fell onto a car in a high wind. The driver was trapped. We could hear his screams. How badly was he injured? We had no idea. It was dark. Cutting and lifting gear was not available. All of us from the fire, police, ambulance and flying squad failed to lift the tree off the car! Then something happened. Men and ladies appeared from everywhere – onlookers on foot and onlookers from cars. An army of volunteers formed. Altogether we lifted that tree off the car. The driver was unhurt, but the car was a write-off!

* * *

Many of our Flying Squad calls had an unhappy outcome. The four young men, whose car one night crashed into a tree in Duffield, all died. All I could do was to certify them dead at the scene. The tree survives to this day. The five Ecclesbourne pupils who were in a Mini all died, when their car collided one evening with a taxi on the A6 near Allestree Park. The taxi driver just had a broken jaw!

Whenever that sort of disaster occurred, doom and gloom would descend on our department. But we could not reflect as, on return, the department had always filled up. This was 'catch-up time' and we threw ourselves into the chaos!

* * *

Just before I retired in 2007, we realised that the accident flying squad would soon cease to exist. The ambulance service was by now well trained and able to take over. Well, we were busy enough in the hospital. Our last call was to a man trapped in his bedroom. He had fallen, but they could not get him out through the door. The fire service made a hole in the wall. We gave him morphine and he was stretchered out.

He had not been outside 'for years' and weighed over 40 stone!

* * *

Mr John Collins wrote about accident flying squads in the *British Medical Journal*. He was awarded the MBE for this work.[2]

References:

1. Deborah Cowley. Derby's Life Saving Flying Squad. Reader's Digest. Vol 124: No 724. February 1984;56.
2. J Collins. Organisation and function of an Accident Flying Squad. *BMJ*: 1966; 2: 5515: 578-580.

CHAPTER TWENTY-TWO

Road Traffic Accidents

"Have wheels – will travel"

A saying

I worked for 30 years as a consultant in an emergency department. On many occasions I was in charge of the Derbyshire Royal Infirmary Flying Squad. The vast majority of patients that we treated at the scene were victims of road traffic accidents. The plight of these individuals was close to my heart.

Annually, about 1.3 million people die on the world's roads. About 40 times this number are seriously injured. Road accidents worldwide kill more five to 14-year-olds than malaria or AIDS. Road accidents on our planet every day cause a loss of life equivalent to ten jumbo jet crashes.[1]

There are three major factors involved in the cause of any road traffic accident – the driver, the environment and the vehicle they were travelling in. Except in extreme weather conditions, the environment is not usually the main cause of road accidents. (It is interesting to not, however, that in extreme weather conditions some countries, like Holland, can forbid travelling on roads except for local journeys!)

Thanks to regular servicing and other checks, the vehicle itself today is not usually the main factor in causing an accident. No, in about 80% of road traffic accidents, it is the driver who is to blame. He, or she, needs to be targeted all over the world because road crashes are commoner in developing countries. In some rich, Western countries road deaths are falling. The United Kingdom has the lowest casualty rate in the world when considering the size of our population. But nearly 2,000 people die on our roads each year!

Most accidents are caused by driver error – often going too fast.[3] The latest killer is drivers using their mobile phones whilst driving. Car drivers over the age of 85 years cause a lot of accidents too.[2] It is crazy really. We ask doctors to revalidate annually now. This is a lot of hassle – but important for the doctors and patients. But I passed my car and motorbike tests over 50 years ago. I had no further tests, even when I passed 70 years. This is absolute nonsense!

Finally, when will UK licence holders over the age of 70 years be retested for driving? There are over four million of us in 2015. Our response times to an emergency stop are getting slower! However, we have fewer accidents than drivers under 30 years of age. Research has shown that people over 70 are 9% of drivers, but only 6% of driver casualties. Conversely, drivers under 30 are 20% of drivers but 35% of casualties.[3] But surely the Ministry of Transport should be alerted to the high accident rate of the drivers under 30. To ban drivers under 30 from driving would cause chaos and be totally impractical, but they could all be banned from driving public service vehicles. This would immediately create a shortage of drivers for ambulances, fire engines and police cars. There is, however, a simple solution. These younger drivers could be replaced by safer, more experienced ones, i.e., old age pensioners!

There are many ways a reduction in accidents can be achieved. Politicians need to forget that the driver has the vote and do some drastic measures now.

The first is speed. We forget that, in the 1970s, there was a petrol crisis. I remember it well. Petrol was rationed. I produced my stethoscope and luckily got my car filled up. I could not get to work any other way. Many motorists had no petrol for their cars! The government reduced the speed limit on motorways to 50mph. Guess what – the accident rate fell and fell – how strange! And this is true today. In 2009 the results of 20mph limits in London were analysed. Over 20 years they estimated that over 4,000 casualties were prevented.[4] How crazy that we have cars that usually can travel at over 100mph, and many do. But our limit on motorways is 70mph. How mad is that? I suggest that if somebody is caught speeding, the magistrate can order the driver's car be adjusted to go a maximum of 80mph. It can be done! This could be done in Africa too. Speed needs to be controlled. Some police forces like those in Derbyshire have sought to re-educate and not prosecute car drivers caught speeding just over the maximum. Drivers are not prosecuted if they pay a small amount to attend a National Speed Awareness course. The course is a four-hour, interactive, road-safety presentation and discussion.[5] No driving is involved. I applaud this initiative that has been widely adopted.

The second cause is terrible drivers. No indicators used. No position sense on the road. No stopping at junctions, etc. However, the Transport and Road Research Laboratory did some work on this with advanced motorists. (I have to admit a personal interest here. I am such a driver.) These advanced motorists were shown to have a 25% lower accident rate than normal drivers. Every time a driver gets points on his licence the magistrate could say, "You must retake your driving test or do an advanced test." The roads would be safer as a result.

Finally, I personally have held a clean licence for a motorcycle and a car for over 50 years. In my first ten years after qualifying I lost three close medical friends to the road accident in separate crashes. I miss them. What a tragic loss. Annually, 1.3 million people will die on the world's roads. 90% of the deaths and injuries occur in developing countries.[1] All these governments need to take measures to make their drivers slow down and drive better. It is the biggest killer of 15 to 29-year-olds worldwide.

Recently, our British Government was considering putting up the speed limit on motorways from 70mph to 80mph. This is madness. Every driver will go faster. The ones doing 100mph will go up to 110mph! Accidents will increase and be worse. More and more precious petrol will get used up a lot quicker.

But the speed limit on motorways may still be put up to 80mph. How fast will everybody drive on these roads? This is a clear example of politicians pandering to the electorate. This policy was initially greeted with enthusiasm. It has recently been dropped – once reason had prevailed.

References:

1. G Robertson. What kills more children than AIDS? Roads. *The Times* 2.3.10: 20.
2. J Rowlatt& A Rani. How safe are Britain's Roads? BBC 2; 9pm: 31.10.12.
3. S Ameratunga. Traffic Speed Zones and road injuries. *BMJ* 2009; 339;b4743. doi: 10,1136/bmj. b4743 and C Grundy and Co. Effect of 20 mph traffic speed zones on road injuries in London 1986-2006: controlled interrupted time series analysis. *BMJ* 2009:339;b4469.
4. Willie Ryan. The Age-Old Debate. *Motoring*. Spring 2013 30-33.
5. AA Drive Tech, Driver Aware Division, PO Box 6838, Fanum House, Basing View, Basingstoke, RG24 4PX.

True Tales of Motoring Madness

A senior surgeon was on call for vascular surgery. This usually means the urgent repair of an abdominal aneurysm. These are infrequent but serious, requiring great skill and surgical speed.

From home he was called in. The patient's life was saved by the operation. A few days later the surgeon received a penalty notice for speeding at 36mph close to a hospital that evening. Result: penalty points and a fine!

* * *

A newly appointed surgeon was asked to do a domiciliary consultation (a home visit) for a general practitioner. In the dark, after the operating list had finished, he had great difficulty reading the house numbers in Rose Hill Street, Normanton. A policeman stopped him as he was kerb crawling. Well, he did not know he was in the middle of the red light district! Result: no action taken against him (this time).

* * *

Ann was the senior receptionist in Casualty. At that time she did the triage and generated all the Casualty hospital records by hand. She worked long hours and was highly efficient. She knew all the emergency personnel, but had a short fuse. Late, after a 12-hour shift, she was driving down a wide, well-lit, quiet road to catch up with her fragmented social life. She was upset to be caught in a speed trap. She then suffered the indignity of being told off for speeding by an 'underage' police officer. Who was this juvenile? She thought she knew all the traffic cops.

He finished his tirade with, "Your penalty, madam, is that Uncle Walter is going to smack your bottom." Result: Walter, the senior traffic cop, appeared from the shadows.

"On your way, Ann, and don't do it again," he said and smiled. She fled.

* * *

An integral part of the driving test is to prove to the examiner that the applicant has good eyesight by reading a car number plate about 20 yards away. My friend David failed his first driving test, as he could not read such a number plate. His eyesight was poor.

He re-applied to take the test and turned up at the test station very early. He wandered around memorising all the car number plates nearby. So when the examiner asked him what the car's number plate was, he knew immediately (without looking!).

So he passed his test the second time and for many years was an excellent driver. He drove me many times. David is not driving anymore unfortunately. Well, there is a slight problem; the poor chap is completely blind now!

Car Seat Belts and Car Safety

Please 'Belt Up'.

Publicity slogan

I was exposed to a few cases of windscreen glass injuries as a Casualty officer briefly for six months in 1967. The true horror of these injuries was revealed to me in 1974 when working as a plastic surgery junior.

For four years, I toiled regularly trying to put faces back together again when windscreen glass had caused havoc. Sometimes, sight had been lost or the facial nerve damaged so movement to the face was lost. This devastating injury changed people's lives permanently. They each had to come to terms with living with facial scarring for the rest of their lives. This burden changed the lives of each and every person forever. I empathised with them, but it was too late. The damage had been done.

I naturally became a strong supporter of the 'compulsory wearing of seat belt' campaign. Over ten years previously my medical student friends had presented me with car seat belts as a 21st birthday present. My car did not have seat belts fitted. I always subsequently used seat belts. The compulsory wearing of seat belts in cars was first introduced in Victoria, Australia. Other Australian states followed. The accident statistics plummeted. Not only was the restrained occupant less likely to suffer facial or head injuries, also the restrained casualty was not thrown around the inside of the vehicle. Most important of all, they stayed inside the vehicle. Once a casualty is thrown outside a car then the chances of being killed are increased dramatically.

The British politicians debated at length the introduction of 'compulsory seat belts'. They did nothing! Were they really concerned with the wellbeing of the electorate? Or were they more concerned at upsetting public opinion and not getting re-elected next time? I wrote a letter in the *British Medical Journal* that was published on 17th July 1976.[1]

'Sir, I read with interest Dr John Knight's letter from Victoria (5th June, *B. Med. J*). Their improved road accident statistics following the compulsory wearing of seat belts is encouraging in view of our government's pending legislation. Here, too, there is a strong lobby against the bill on several grounds, including the infringement of liberties. The views of statisticians and politicians are being voiced, but not those of road accident victims, particularly those who have been cut by windscreen glass. I have found it rewarding to study 20 such patients. None of them had been wearing a seat belt at the time of their accident. They were 12 men and eight women, of average aged 22 years. Eighteen of them had been on short journeys, within 20 minutes of home; only two were on longer journeys. Twelve were drivers and eight front-seat passengers.

Eighteen of the 20 volunteered the information that the wearing of seat belts would probably have prevented the injury caused by contact with the windscreen and facia. Only two patients disagreed. Sixteen of the patients attributed their non-wearing of seat belts to laziness, their hurry to get somewhere or the late hour. None found the seat belt uncomfortable. The remaining two of the patients did not have seat belts fitted in their cars.

Now, many months and years later, only ten of these patients regularly wear seat belts. Thus many of this select group of accident victims don't wear seat belts although they believe in their effectiveness to prevent injuries and have been injured through not wearing them. So what hope do we have in convincing the rest of the public to wear seat belts, short of government legislation?'

The above letter was, I suppose, 'preaching to the converted'. It was read by fellow doctors, the vast majority of whom were strong supporters of compulsory seat belts. In March 1978 I left plastic surgery and became an emergency medicine consultant (Casualty). Once again, I was presented with a steady stream of windscreen glass injuries. I had the necessary training. I spent hours and hours suturing them up – often at weekends, sometimes one after another. The patients remained devastated when they viewed their faces after the general anaesthetic.

The politicians, as always, talked and talked. Well, they are good at that! Actions speak louder than words. Finally, at long last, in 1983, the seat belt law came in. The accident statistics improved at once. The politicians congratulated each other for doing such a good job – well, they are the first to jump on the 'bandwagon' of any success. In my humble opinion, they should have done it years earlier! More refinements followed. Compulsory rear seat belts, compulsory child restraints and compulsory baby seats. All excellent innovations.

How many injuries could have been prevented in the UK if the seat belt law had been introduced from the start? The answer is A LOT. Well, 1899 saw the first fatal motor car accident in Britain. On Grove Hill, Harrow, the rear wheel of a Daimler collapsed. Two men, Edwin Sewell and Major Richer, were thrown right out of the car and both died. If seat belts had been fitted, the chances are that both of them would have survived. This is because seat belts would have kept them in the vehicle. Once anybody is thrown right out of a car in an accident then the chances of dying in that accident are increased several times.

The motor car in the UK has come on a long way since 1896. Then 14th January 1896 saw the formation of the Daimler Motor Company Limited. This was the UK's first serial production motor car company. They produced 89 vehicles in the first eight months of production from their site in Coventry. The British motor industry had officially begun.

In the late 19th century many automobiles (cars) were badly designed. Many had faults, making them dangerous to travel in. For example, some cars had no brakes. In other cars the driver's view was obstructed by passengers seated in front of him. The gears were notoriously difficult to engage and the driver often got the wrong one. Well, double declutching to change gear was difficult, my late mother had told me. So sometimes, in the wrong gear, the car shot forwards or backwards totally unexpectedly!

What is surprising is that people queued up to travel in these deathtraps. Comfort for passengers was a rarity. A few cars were fitted with a cocktail cabinet, a bed or even a flushing toilet! Well, how convenient is that?!

My late mother Christina was taught to drive by her father on private roads – round his factory. On 21st May 1924 – her 18th birthday – this redhead was allowed to drive on public roads for the first time. The roads were less busy then and lady car drivers somewhat of a rarity. She caused quite a stir as she drove her father and two of his friends down a main road in an open-top car. The police were telephoned and they set up a road block to catch the 'underage driver'. Once she had produced her birth certificate to the police officer she could carry on driving. She predated the driving test. She drove into her eighties and never ever had a test!

* * *

The motor car has seen serial improvements in safety and comfort. The importance of such innovations is only apparent when something 'goes wrong'. Improvements in car safety continue to this day. Foremost in this is the annual Stapp Car Crash Conference in the USA. This name honours the late Dr John Stapp, who used himself as a dummy in simulated car crashes![2]

* * *

My late mother was retired from general practice in her late seventies, 30 years ago. She had a saloon car two years old that had been regularly serviced and had had no accidents. She was driving alone down the A3 to visit her sister-in-law. The weather was warm and sunny and the car was going well. But she stopped in a layby, as she smelt burning. She walked round the car. All seemed fine so she was getting in to drive off. Another car stopped behind her.

"Get away from that car!" yelled the other driver. "There is a fire underneath." She looked and there was a fire right under the vehicle.

Within a short time the car was ablaze. As the flames shot 10 or 15 feet into the air a traffic policeman stopped to help.

"Move that car at once," he ordered my mother. At a loss to know what to do she contacted the AA. They towed away the burnt-out wreck.

So why had the blaze happened? She was shaking. She was nearly incinerated. It was later explained to my mother that the petrol feed pipe from the petrol tank to the engine must have leaked. Petrol had spilled onto the exhaust. The only car that detected this fault then was the Volvo. Once detected, this car engine stopped. My mother bought a Volvo. Cars need to continue to improve. This episode proved it.

∗ ∗ ∗

Recently I was driven down some quiet roads in the Scottish borders. I did not wear a seat belt! Well, none were fitted, as I was travelling in a 1937 Triumph Vitesse. It had been superbly restored to former glory and we travelled open top, as it was warm and sunny. I felt very safe as this car went along at a modest speed, compared to the cars of today. (Note: no anti-roll bars, no airbags and no side impact bars!) We are all in too much of a hurry today. That day I travelled in comfort and style. I really enjoyed it.

Today our roads, and our vehicles, continue to evolve. We regularly sacrifice prime agricultural land for new, better and faster roads. We all want to drive that new, better and faster car. So drivers are changing too. Record numbers of us have been caught speeding on our roads, and our fines have swelled government coffers. But that is not all.

New laws have been introduced in England and Wales banning driving with any of 17 controlled drugs in significant levels in our blood.

In 2016, 26 police forces responded to a freedom of information request by the *Daily Mail*. This showed that the police had performed 5,857 drug tests at the roadside, 3,718 drivers had tested positive – that is 63%.

So drug driving arrests have soared 800% in the past year. It is thought that the taking of drugs causes 200 deaths a year on our roads.

So our roads and our cars improve, but our drivers do not.

References:

1. Alistair Fraser-Moodie (letter), *BMJ* 17. 7. 1976; 2: 178.
2. Giles Chapman. In the Name of Road Safety. *IAM Journal* (iam. org. uk) Winter 2012: 15-16.

CHAPTER TWENTY-THREE

A Minor Disaster, 1970s

The truth is stranger than fiction.

A saying

In a North London hospital in the 1970s the question of the very much in fashion 'mobile medical teams' was raised and solved at a consultant meeting. They were about to advertise for a general surgery registrar. The hospital secretary added a paragraph on the job description. This would be replicated in all such appointments in the future. So, problem solved.

The paragraph: 'In the event of an emergency telephone call from County Ambulance Headquarters asking for surgical assistance at the scene of an accident, then the General Surgery Registrar on call will proceed at once to Casualty. There he will be given a case containing all the necessary equipment to deal with any such emergency. He will travel to the accident in a county ambulance.'

One of my contemporaries, the late Mr Simon Cox, went to such an emergency. He performed an amputation for which he was awarded an OBE. At our 'North London hospital' things did not go to plan. The successful applicant for the job was ecstatic at the interview. He was reminded of the said paragraph by the chairman of the appointments' committee. He then started the busy job.

A month or so later, 5pm on a Friday night found him finishing off a long general surgery list. The boss had left earlier. He muttered something about a meeting. That was partly true. He was meeting a private patient at the Nuffield Hospital for the direct benefit of his bank balance. The telephone rang. It was switchboard. The county ambulance was on the line and had been waiting ten minutes already until the general surgery registrar could be found. He must proceed at once to Casualty as an emergency had arisen. This was relayed to the registrar who was vainly trying to close an abdomen. After a few more stitches he handed over to the very inexperienced senior house officer to the startled dismay of the consultant anaesthetist.

The registrar, partly dressed, flew down the corridor to Casualty. He could not see a case. He said, "Excuse me. I am the general surgery registrar," to a Staff Nurse. "I'm looking for a case."

She said, "Oh good, at last. We've a child with diarrhoea and an old boy with a blocked catheter. He's in a lot of pain."

"No, no, no," he said. "I'm looking for a case. A case of instruments." The staff nurse shrugged her shoulders and walked off, very disillusioned and disappointed at this dishevelled registrar.

Just then an ambulance man called out from the front door, "Hey, doc. Hurry up. He's bleeding something chronic. We've had four cups of tea just waiting for you".

Then another ambulance man appeared: "What's up, Joe? Is that him? Oh, hurry up; it's got to come off, doc."

"Yes," said the first ambulance man "it's a mess. You will have to cut it off. Shame, but it's the only way."

"But I can't find my case," blurted out the surgical registrar.

"Is this it?" said the beaming ambulance man. "It was sitting by the door." He picked up a smart black case that was unattended.

Without hesitating, the ambulance man carried the shiny new case to the ambulance.

"What is the problem?" asked the registrar.

"Look," said the ambulance man, "we can't stand around here gossiping with you. We are on an emergency. You'll soon see, doc. Hop in."

The back doors of the ambulance were flung open.

In climbed the registrar plus case. The doors were then closed. The ambulance shot off, sirens blaring. The registrar landed up in a heap on the floor clutching his precious case. He thought about what he would need.

He thought out loud, "Will I have to give a general or a local anaesthetic? What intravenous fluids do I have? Are there any sterile drapes? Are the instruments sterile, and do I have a full set of instruments?" He opened the case. Yes, he did have a full set.

He had a full set of brand new plumber's tools.

Major Disasters – Three Crashes?

'So weary with disasters'

Shakespeare, *Macbeth*

Papa India – London Airport (Heathrow)

In 1972 I was a surgical registrar at Ashford Hospital at Middlesex. I had a weekend off and was definitely not on call. I was making a canoe with the aid of a mould that I had hired just for the weekend. During a critical stage of getting the canoe out of the mould my father had been watching television. He told me of a plane crash close to the hospital. It was a Sunday afternoon. Ashford Hospital is the nearest hospital to Heathrow and part of the major disaster plan.

I went to the hospital at once although it was my weekend off. The traffic was terrible. People go to the scene of major accidents just to gawp. They get in the way and are a nuisance. When I got there nothing could be done. A large group of us doctors stood together. Everybody from the plane was dead. It was depressing just standing there with nothing to do – how helpless. What a waste of life.

I later met a nurse who lived close to the scene of the crash. She had climbed on board the aeroplane before the emergency services had arrived. It was illegal but she had just done it on the spur of the moment. It was dire. Many people were still alive, but all died of multiple injuries.

She too was traumatised emotionally – poor lady.

Aer Lingus – East Midlands Airport

In about 1985 an Aer Lingus plane was landing at East Midlands Airport at night. As the plane came down, the pilot missed the runway but landed just inside the perimeter fence. You can imagine the panic in the control tower. One minute the plane was on the radar, then the pilot reported a landing. No plane on the runway.

Where was that plane?

In the plane, I was told by the passengers, there was panic too. One minute a planeload of Irish people had been having a party courtesy of duty free. Then the plane had missed the runway, landed bumped and stopped and the emergency exits had opened. They shot down the chutes to safety. More cause for celebration.

One Irishman I met was first out. "Everywhere was in darkness," he told me. Then he saw car headlights in the distance. He scaled the perimeter fence and rushed out into the road. A passing car had to stop. Well, a man had just jumped out in front of his car headlights. The Irishman asked the startled driver a simple question, "Please, where are we?"

The rescuers fared worse. The airport had just taken delivery of a fire tender costing £70,000. They had practised driving this all around the perimeter of the aerodrome but mainly in the daytime at reasonable speeds.

This was a great emergency. Adrenaline flowed. Where was that plane? They shot off at great speed laden with firemen. Unfortunately the fire tender rolled over and over. It was written off. Three of the firemen were seen at our hospital with back injuries. Nobody else was injured!

I personally was overjoyed. Nobody had died on this plane. It was a carnival time in Casualty. All the passengers, crew and Aer Lingus officials were there. What a party atmosphere.

* * *

In November 2009 in Zimbabwe, a plane hit a bush pig on the runway before it took off. The plane stopped and was evacuated in the dark. Two people were injured running into ditches.[1] Nobody else was injured.

History repeats itself over and over again!

Reference:

1. J Raath. Airline makes a complete pig's ear of take-off emergency. *The Times* 9. 11. 09:39.

The Kegworth Plane Crash, East Midlands Airport

British Midland Flight BD 92 – January 8th 1989

A Boeing 737-400 was attempting an emergency landing at East Midlands Airport. It had a fire in one engine. Another engine was turned off! It crashed beside the M1 at Kegworth. Nobody was injured on the motorway itself. I was once again not on call that Sunday evening. I was the first person called in to the hospital before the consultant on call went to the scene of the accident in our flying squad vehicle. It was a big help to communicate from the hospital to our flying squad driver at the scene on our own radios.

Communication in such situations is everything. It was many hours before all the extra hospital staff could be contacted to come in. The

Fig 35 – The Kegworth plane crash. What absolute chaos. No practices can prepare you for the real thing. So many people came out of this alive. Well done to one and all.

police came to our hospital and administrators came in – all to help communication. We had no idea how many casualties we were getting or their injuries. Twenty-eight casualties came to our hospital. The ambulance drivers who brought them were not front line and so had no idea where our hospital was, so they had difficulty finding it. Hospital staff not on call poured in too. Wards were cleared to accommodate the injured.

I was in charge of the emergency department. The sister in charge had been to the waiting room as soon as she knew of the crash. When she announced there had been an aircraft crash, all the waiting patients walked out. So how urgent were they?

After the Papa India incident years before, I was delighted to see anybody alive from the plane. Many were uninjured – the first patient I saw was a steward from the plane. He had been thrown out of the plane

Fig 36 – An invitation to meet the Queen, and a brochure about the hospital.

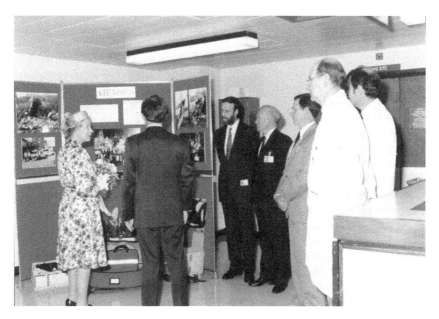

Fig 37 – My colleague Paul Pritty (back to the camera) talks to the Queen and shows her photographs of the plane crash.

Fig 38 – Two white-coated orthopaedic surgeons are on my left. On my right are an anaesthetist and the major incident officer.

and ended up in a tree. He was unharmed. Statistically, I knew at the time that this steward had survived because of an absolute miracle. If you are thrown out of a car in an accident then the chances of being killed in that accident are increased five times. So if you are thrown out of an aeroplane and survive unharmed – how lucky is that? Several patients had broken limbs and many more were uninjured. The latter went to local hotels for the night.

No hospital staff had identification, except the vicars who wore dog collars. I later learnt that one passer-by had pretended to be a doctor. This charlatan was prosecuted. We did not know how many casualties we were getting or their injuries. Confusion reigned! The police were excellent, checking names on the list of passengers against casualties in our hospital. The media were superb with one exception. One photographer who climbed up a drainpipe to take a photograph!

We later learnt that 47 people had died, but I was delighted to see anybody alive from the stricken plane. A total of 79 passengers survived.

Mrs Thatcher visited the accident department two days later. She thanked all the staff for their efforts. But Barry, a porter, asked her, "Can you get me two Cup Final tickets?" – not entirely appropriate in the circumstances. She laughed, and his remark 'broke the ice'.

Sometime later I was introduced to the Queen when she visited our hospital (figs 36, 37 and 38).

Out of this disaster a new brace position was recommended for aeroplane passengers in the event of air crashes. This arose from studies of injuries in this crash by two orthopaedic surgeons, Professor Angus Wallace and Mr John Rowles from Nottingham. So, hopefully, as a result there will be fewer deaths and injuries in future from such crashes.

A Tale of Two Cities

Confused alarms of struggle and flight.

Arnold (1867)

The Derbyshire Ambulance Service received a 999 call from East Midlands Airport: please come at once; a male passenger is very ill having just landed from Calcutta. The ambulance crew were directed onto the tarmac to an aeroplane beside the terminal buildings. All the other passengers had got off. This man was lying down, occupying three seats at the rear of the aircraft. He was in agony from his right leg. His right thigh was swathed in clothes and some bandages. Blood was seeping through this makeshift dressing.

This man spoke no English. He had a large hysterical family who were shouting and could not be understood. The ambulance crew were confused. Nobody seemed to know what had happened. The steward, who was in charge of the passengers throughout the flight, told the ambulance crew, "He was fine at the airport in Calcutta, when checking onto the flight. There was an argument between him and some family members who were not flying. He ran and later was hurt on the tarmac. His close family carried him on board. He has been in great pain ever since!" The ambulance crew, still mystified, put up a saline drip. They gave the man an injection of a morphine derivative and Entonox (nitrous oxide) by mouth. His legs were splinted together. He was transported to the Derbyshire Royal Infirmary. (Customs had been circumvented, I gather!)

I saw him at the Infirmary. His relatives were very upset and confused.

The clue as to what on earth was going on was only discovered when I examined his right thigh. There was a large gaping wound on the front of his right mid-thigh. It was bleeding, but not profusely. Scorch marks around this wound suggested he had been shot. The femoral artery was intact, as was the sciatic nerve.

An X-ray told us what we wanted to know. There were multiple small metal fragments in his thigh. The femur was shattered. So he had been shot probably by a shotgun! The X-ray suggested a low-velocity injury. Blood was cross-matched. He received six pints over the next 12 hours. He was given morphine intravenously.

He was admitted. That night the orthopaedic surgeons explored the wound and removed as much dead tissue and metal as possible. The wound was open and infected. So the fracture of the femur was treated with traction through the tibia, and various pulleys put over his bed. This is old fashioned, but internal fixation was contraindicated. This man was kept in under traction for nearly two months until the fracture healed. He made a slow steady recovery. He later walked with a limp.

But what had happened? Why the injury? Had he been shot?

He was head of his family as his brother was dead. He had brokered an arranged marriage between his niece and a man. Some relatives were very unhappy with this match. They said that the honour of the family had been compromised. He was escaping from them on the tarmac near the aeroplane in Calcutta when they shot him at point blank range with a sawn-off shotgun.

The British police were contacted, but the crime had been committed in Calcutta City, India and not Derby City, UK. He received all his treatment free under the NHS (that's why our taxes are so great!).

I had never ever realised before that our hospital had such a big catchment area!

CHAPTER TWENTY-FOUR

Coloured Patients

*His colours laid so thick on every place. As only showed the
paint and not his face.*

Dryden to Sir R Howard

The Happening

Locko Park is an estate on the outskirts of Derby. There was a happening
(an event) there each year. People from all over Europe went there and
camped in tents. Each person registered as a character and had to remain
'in costume' for the long weekend.

These costumes were bizarre. The people taking part covered
themselves with dye (apart from the whites of their eyes). They drank
copious amounts of alcohol and competed amongst themselves. Well,
they usually ended up fighting!

The first person I met from there was a very deep green – face, neck,
arms and legs. He had a dark green dress and a fetching green wig.
Although he himself was enamoured by his own sartorial elegance,
he went unnoticed amongst the melee of ordinary casualties. On
questioning, he was registered as a character and was called an 'Old
Crone'. He was drunk when he fell over the guy rope of a tent. He had

sprained his ankle – no fracture. I told him he was "in great danger of getting better". He told me to come along with him. He said, "The fun is really intense." (Or was it "in tents"?) He wanted to get back to fight the Norwegians!

On leaving the hospital for home that evening I met two more casualties covered in vivid dye. Well, they looked like Little Boy Blue and Will Scarlet!

One Coat Covers All

I have seen this scenario twice. It was almost identical each time, except the first case was with yellow paint and the second deep blue. Both times of presentation were about 10.30am on a Sunday morning. On each occasion the parents had slept in after a good night out. Each time they had two children – an older girl of about six and a boy toddler. I suspect that on each occasion the girl was jealous of the boy – he was the youngest

Fig 39 – One coat covers all – what fun they are having!

and a boy. She wanted to get her own back. She could just recall when she had been the centre of attention, before the boy had been born.

This is what happened in each case. Both parents slept, so she played with her lovely baby brother and then had a plan. She took off all his clothes. There was this bottle of gloss paint and a brush. She got to work painting him all over. She did not paint the eyes but put plenty on his willy! Girls love painting, don't they? After a half hour or so he grew tired of this game and wandered in to see his mother. She panicked and plonked him in the bath. DIY enthusiasts will know this has no effect on gloss paint. The child got cold and cried more. So the cold, coloured child was brought to Casualty. The nurses, advised by the pharmacist, put spirit-based cream on his skin but not near his eyes. The child was, in each case, still coloured on discharge at about midday – but less coloured than on arrival.

This is family trauma at its most colourful.

Never Say Dye

I was sitting relaxing in the staff room enjoying a nice cup of tea. Two nurses were chatting amongst themselves. One conversation caught my ear.

"I've never seen anything like it, no never," one said.

"Me neither. It just looks so odd. That blue colour," the other one said.

I could bear it no longer. I interrupted.

"Excuse me," I said, " What are you talking about?"

"Oh, this girl in the dressing's clinic," one nurse said. "She has this blue discharge from her wound!"

"Can I see her?" I asked.

"Oh yes," was the reply. "She comes every day."

The next dressings clinic, I attended. The patient called Melissa was a West Indian girl aged eleven years. From a small wound on her left shin there was a discharge coloured blue. I stared and stared. She was brought to hospital by her mother, a quiet lady. On questioning, both parties denied any interference or injury. Mother was very concerned about this blue discharge.

There was no evidence of any infection but I sent some of this blue fluid for microscopy and culture. The result from the microbiology department came back as no evidence of infection.

I sent another sample to haematology. A technician rang me to say this referral was inappropriate. So I sent a third sample to biochemistry. Another telephone call. This time from another technician: "Err, it's not blood so we won't be doing anything to it," he said.

Question from me: "Can you help me at all?"

Answer: "No."

"Can I speak to the senior technician or a consultant biochemist?"

Answer: "I am the senior technician, and the biochemist in charge has better things to do. If you don't mind we are busy."

Well, that was a blank. The patient's GP, Dr Tom Fraser, was a big encouragement. He said, "You yourself can find out the reason for this blue discharge. No, don't send the patient to the paediatricians. I am sure with your paediatric and plastic surgery experience you can find out the cause of this blue discharge. Good luck."

There is a large chemical factory on the outskirts of Derby called Courtaulds. I was treating one of the workers from there and I asked him if any chemists worked there. "Oh, there are lots," he said.

A month earlier I had organised a symposium on industrial injuries at our hospital. I was amazed as about 200 doctors attended from miles around and they all worked in industry. I had met there Dr Anne Llewellyn from Courtaulds. So I telephoned her about Melissa.

She was delighted to help. "I have two chemists between projects at present. They need something like this to do," she said. I cautioned her that the patient's information and results had to be kept secret by everybody concerned. She agreed and understood professional secrecy had to prevail. I sent a sample and waited nearly a month.

Then I got a letter from Anne. The sample was of a variety of ink. This ink had been tested several ways and shown to be rare. Chromatography showed it to be one particular type. Only one firm in Derby used this type of ink. It was not for sale anywhere. Melissa's mum worked at the firm that used this ink. I telephoned Tom, the GP. He was adamant I see the family and confront mum.

Mum came with Melissa and the third member of the family I had not met before, Junior. He was a typical loveable overactive two-years-old. He played and played on the floor as we talked. Melissa was listening but played a little with Junior. He had a cheeky woollen bobble hat on. On hearing Melissa's skin had blue dye from a bottle of ink, her mum became agitated. Melissa was very quiet – she knew that she had been rumbled.

Mum said, "Oh, it's just like Junior."

I said, "What do you mean?"

"Oh," she said, "he has hair at night and not in the morning."

"Does he swallow his hair?" I asked.

"Oh yes. That's what I said," she said. "He has one or two hairs at night and none by the morning, as he swallows them!"

"Come here, Junior," she said.

He obliged and she pulled off his hat – he was as bald as a coot! Junior cried. He was tired and upset. Melissa was still quiet. They left.

I told Tom I was referring Melissa to a paediatrician, who wrote back after the consultation to say, "Thank you for the referral. How fascinating. I have never seen or heard of anything like this before. The blue discharge stopped once the cause was found. I have therefore discharged her."

Melissa must have put the dye on her wound on purpose! This blue discharge episode, as well as the swallowing of hair, was probably a form of attention-seeking by both children who were looked after by mum. Melissa could recall when she had been the only child and had had mum's full attention. She no longer had it – hence the dye episode. There was no dad.

Down the Plughole

A 20-month-old girl presented to the senior registrar of our accident and emergency department, Dr D Esberger, in the arms of her mother. The child was upset and blue, wearing nothing but a nappy on her bottom and a plughole on her right hand. Whilst exploring the delights of the plughole her right index finger had to become stuck. She could not release it!

She screamed for her mother. She too was unable to release the now swollen digit. The fire brigade was called.

I had an opportunity to discuss what had happened with one of the

Fig 40 – Her finger was stuck in the plughole. She was very unhappy!

fire officers. They too were unable to release the offending digit initially. So the water was turned off to the house. The water was drained to the system. Then the two taps were disconnected. Once the bath was freed it had to be 'dismantled' to release the metal plughole.

In all it took six fire officers 48 minutes to free her.

The plughole was subsequently cut off the red and swollen right index finger under a general anaesthetic in the Hand Surgery theatre. The digit, the child, the mother and the bathroom each made a good recovery.[1]

_____

Reference:

1. D A Esberger. Down the plughole. *BMJ* Vol 307 Dec 93:1634.

CHAPTER TWENTY-FIVE

Accidents and the Wheeled Bin Refuse Collection

'More rubbish from Derby.'

In 1988, in Derby, the wheeled bin refuse system was introduced. This refuse bin is usually two and a half times the size of a normal bin that it replaced (several sizes of bin exist). The householder wheels the bin to the edge of their property. The refuse collector wheels the bin to the dust cart. The bin is clipped onto a hydraulic hoist and emptied mechanically.

Twenty-nine patients in 1991 attended the accident and emergency department of the Derbyshire Royal Infirmary with injuries suffered whilst using wheeled bins over an eight-month period. I studied them all.[1]

Nine refuse collectors attributed their injuries to one refuse bin being too heavy. Another eight injuries to refuse collectors happened when the heavy refuse bin fell off the dust cart.

Nine of the 12 householders injured were female. Eight householders were injured moving a bin, and six of them were female. Seven of these eight injuries happened whilst the patient was walking backwards pulling a bin behind them. Usually, either the bin ran over a foot, or the arm was crushed against a wall, or the bin fell back onto them.

Fig 41 – Wheelie bin injuries were very common initially.

The two most severe injuries were four fractured transverse lumbar vertebrae from falling after being lifted by the hoist, and a Colles' fracture from a householder falling over.

Investigations

The height and weight was recorded of all the eight householders injured whilst moving a bin. They were all, but one, of small stature.

A total of 100 wheeled bins were weighed just prior to the refuse collector arriving. The lightest bin weighed just under 25 kilograms and the heaviest was over 115 kilograms (one bin contained a fridge and another was full of soil!).

Conclusion

Over one period, 11 householders and only five refuse collectors were seen, suggesting that the injuries to householders were more frequent. Refuse collectors are more likely to come to hospital to record this injury. This system has resulted in fewer injuries for refuse collectors.[2]

In our opinion, refuse collectors should refuse to move a heavy bin, and leave a red sticker on it explaining why.

Householders should be advised to wheel their bin walking forwards and not backwards. None of the four old age pensioners injured in our series were aware that their bins could be pulled out for them. This is vital if they are of short stature. So better communication is needed here.

It was a lot easier to collect the names of injured refuse collectors. They knew each other, and one injured refuse collector told us of another, etc. I am not surprised that the refuse collectors suffered fewer injuries than previously. Now the bins are wheeled along and lifted mechanically by the lorry. Two refuse collectors were caught in this lifting mechanism and suffered more severe injuries.

Derby was one of the first cities in the UK to introduce this refuse collection system. Each time this system is introduced there is a spate of accidents to householders. Time and time again the main cause is from little old ladies wheeling full bins whilst walking backwards.

As I review this book and check and recheck references, in May 2013 I discovered from the local television news that wheelie bins were still being introduced, this time to parts of Birmingham!

References:

1. A Fraser-Moodie. More Rubbish from Derby. *Archives of Emergency Medicine*. March 1992.
2. J Key. Contracts Manager, Derby City Council. Personal communication, 1991.

World Cup Fever – Football Mania

In 1990, during the screening of England's World Cup football games, the doctors working in the accident and emergency department of the Derbyshire Royal Infirmary were not busy. A study was carried out to find out if this was true.

England played seven games of football – a total of 12 hours. The casualty cards were studied of all patients who had attended our department during these games. These patients were then grouped retrospectively into four triage groups:

1. Seriously ill.
2. Less serious, e.g., fracture.
3. Minor, e.g., sprained ankle.
4. Very minor, e.g., graze or bruise.

Their age and their sex was also recorded and, where possible, the duration of symptoms. The casualty cards were then got out for the same day of the week, one year previously (control period). The retrospective triage was done by one consultant and he did not know if he was looking at study or control cards. He did two runs of all the cards, with only two differences overall.

The chi-squared test was used to compare attenders in the two time periods. The total numbers of attenders during the 12 hours of football was 88, but 121 for the control period. This is significant statistically.

The total difference in numbers between these two groups is 33. Twenty-six fewer males aged 16-45 years attended during the football times compared to the control times. This is statistically significant. Also, statistically fewer young men with minor injuries (triage group four) attended during the football times compared to the control times.

So the fact that staff observed that fewer patients attended the accident and emergency department during the World Cup can be confirmed statistically. Those most likely to suffer from 'football mania' are young males, and during this 'footballing 12 hours', they were conspicuous by their absence.

As watching football on television is a low-risk activity, these young men would have a low incidence of injury anyway during this time.

However, we know from the duration of symptoms that most sufferers of minor injuries do not usually attend for several hours at least following their injury. So perhaps these young men endured their minor injury for the duration of the football match or came before the match.

A more frequent screening of the World Cup would lead to less busy accident and emergency departments everywhere. But could we stand it?

Reference:

1.   Presented to 25th International BAEM Meeting (1992) and published in *Archives of Emergency Medicine,* March 1992.

Sally

A young lady was playing hockey on a pitch that was muddy. There was a goalmouth scramble. She fell over and was brought to hospital by ambulance. She said she had been knocked out. She had a bad headache but was fully conscious and alert. At that time our one and only head scanner had broken and was being repaired. No neighbouring hospital had a scanner!

She insisted she had been hit on the head at hockey. She refused to let us talk to the other players. She hinted that lots of members of her family had died in middle age.

"Of what?" I asked.

"I don't know," she said, "and don't go bothering my folks either; leave them alone."

She got better after a couple of days on our ward and went home. I tried to pop in at visiting time just on the off-chance of meeting her folks or another member of her team. I had no luck.

She came back unconscious a month later. The GP wrote that according to her family and the hockey team she had collapsed at the game and had not hit her head. The scanner, now working, confirmed a massive bleed from a small aneurysm (swelling of an artery) in the base of the brain (Circle of Willis).

She died. If she had only let me take a proper history from her family and team before. Her family members had all died of this same condition too. That is rare but can happen.

If we had had an accurate history then there is a possibility that we could have tested her for this leaking aneurysm (a lumbar puncture) and even arranged for the neurosurgeons to tie it off. The history that she had had a head injury meant that a lumbar puncture was contraindicated.

I messed up here!

Casualty – Election Fever, 1979

Election fever gripped the country. The media was full of results of election polls. Television and radio interviewers had spent the day resting and were just getting ready to broadcast. Peter Snow was no doubt polishing his swingometer. I saw none of this as I was busy in Casualty as a doctor. The pubs were about to close.

A smart, elderly lady was refusing to go home by car. She had fallen down some steps coming out of the polling station. Her head was badly cut. This had been stitched. She was fully mobile with her stick. She was well-orientated and keen to get home.

"Just call me an ambulance," she said.

"But," protested the nurse, "a young man with a car is in the waiting room to take you home. He's got a suit on and you can't miss him. He's wearing a big blue rosette. He has been there an hour or two already."

"No," she said, "I'm not going home with him. No. No. No."

"Oh," said a student nurse, "he can take me home anytime!"

"Me too," said another nurse.

"Well, I'm not going," said the old lady.

Sister was called.

"What's all this?" she asked.

"Call me an ambulance or even a taxi," the old lady said.

"I don't understand," said sister. "What is the matter? Please tell me."

"Well," said the old lady, calming down, "it's like this. My son always takes me to the polls. I've voted the same ever since the Second World War. I must vote. It's my right, you know. My son rang this morning and said his shift had been changed and he could not take me. So I rang round and round, even the town hall. Finally this evening that man came and drove me to the polls. I've voted and want to go home now."

"Well, what is the problem?" asked sister.

"I can't go home with him," she said. "I just can't go."

"Why not?" asked sister.

"Well, none of you understand, do you?" she said.

"No," said sister, "we don't."

"But can't you see?" she said. "Oh dear, oh dear, oh dear."

"Look, what is the matter really?" asked sister, sympathetically.

"The matter? I will tell you what the matter is. I can't go home driven by him. You see, I've just voted Labour!"

* * *

That evening, just before the polls closed, a drunk who had been admitted at lunchtime decided to take his own discharge.

"I know," said sister. "You want to get to the pub before it closes."

"No," he said, "I want to vote; it's my democratic right to er, er, e-exercise m-my f-franchise," he stuttered.

"Who are you voting for?" asked sister.

"The Conservatives," he mumbled.

"What was that?" she asked.

"Oh, the Conservatives," he spoke up.

"Oh," she said. "Then in that case I'll keep you in another ten minutes." And she did!

He just missed the polls.

Mystifying Mutism

I literally bumped into a man walking about our Emergency department in an area reserved exclusively for minor injury patients. "Oh sorry," I said. There was no reply from him. He wandered on, looking around.

"What's wrong with him?" I asked a nurse.

"Oh," she said, "he's mad – refusing to speak. "He's been here some time."

I found his department records. I sat him down and started writing notes to him, confirming his name, address, GP, what happened, etc. Of course, he was Mr Smith and not registered with a general practitioner. He lived alone, and he had no relatives locally. He had got drunk two nights before, and woke up the day before unable to speak! He had a headache, possibly from drink and possibly from a head injury. He knew nothing of an injury. Full examination revealed tenderness to the back of his head. He was fully conscious and alert with no abnormal neurological signs. His blood was screened for drugs – none present.

I contacted the radiologists for a head scan. "But has he had a head injury?" was their question.

"I have no idea," was my reply. "Oh well, as it's you," the senior radiologist said, "we will do a head scan – but it's not the normal indication for this test. Don't go giving any of your junior's ideas."

The scan showed a fractured skull at the back of the head (occiput). It also showed a discrete area of contusion (bruising) over the speech area on the posterior aspect of his left cerebral hemisphere. This area of the brain controls speech in a right-handed person. We suspected that he had fallen over whilst drunk and suffered this injury.

Our man rested in hospital and had speech therapy. Gradually his speech returned to normal. There are other causes of mutism – strokes, schizophrenia or drugs.

Another case, another cause, reported in this article below.

1.   Melissa Maguire et al. Acute mutism: A Useful Lesson. *Emergency Medical Journal* – 1. 2011:28;82.

Shop Hopping

Shopping has never been easier. Oh, and forget the bill.

The following letter was published:[1]

'Napoleon called us a nation of shopkeepers. We are now, I believe, a

Fig 42 – A shop hopper collapses and, so soon she will get free food and even a lift in the direction of her home!

nation of shoppers. Some people shop unfunded. We call them shoplifters. They rely on a combination of stealth, speed and occasional force. Here are two cases of a variant of shoplifting that I call 'shop hopping'. A shop hopper is an individual with a habit of regularly faking collapse in shops to avoid payment.

Case Reports

Case One:

Elizabeth presented to our Accident and Emergency department at the Derbyshire Royal Infirmary in 1979. She had no general practitioner. She had a respiratory tract infection. She received antibiotics and soon recovered. She was then brought to our hospital roughly every few days by the ambulance service for the next four years. The story was always the same: she 'collapsed' with her shopping at the checkout of a food store. An ambulance was called. Well-meaning shoppers put her shopping in the ambulance too – all unpaid for. Once in our department, she usually recovered quite quickly and walked home. She lived nearby and rarely stayed long enough to be examined. No medical cause was ever found for these timely attacks. She became well known to all the emergency crews on the ambulances and was also well known to our staff. One of our sisters saw her collapsed at the checkout at Sainsbury's. When she shouted to her to "get up and get out", she was nearly lynched by the other shoppers!

The last time I saw Elizabeth in our accident and emergency department, she had collapsed with a stroke. She died soon after.

Case Two:

Patricia presented to our department in 1998 with chronic back pain, demanding analgesia. She had just come from Scotland and already had had a row with a general practitioner locally. She then expressed suicidal intent and was referred to a psychiatrist. Telephone calls to other hospitals confirmed her to be a 'hospital hopper', i.e., she faked a hospital attendance usually to get drugs! However, the ambulance service of several counties knew her better as 'the lady who collapsed in food stores at the checkout.' She then obtained free food as they conveyed her in comfort to the local hospital; this happened many times. She had come down south on a shopping and hospital hopping spree.

These two cases illustrate the habits of a 'shop hopper'. Neither patient had a good relationship with a general practitioner. These patients are a type of 'hospital hopper' who purposely abuse the ambulance and hospital services for their gain. We, the taxpayers, foot the bill. Circulating pictures of such patients to shops would breach medical etiquette. Challenging such patients in a store does not cure them. The store cannot send a bill to the patient, as the goods have not been through the till. The ambulance service cannot 'boycott' these people as they have a duty to convey collapsed patients to a hospital. We doctors have a duty to examine all such patients. Such a collapse may be genuine. Once in a hospital, recovery is rapid, and they take their own discharge prior to the police arriving. Shops, hospitals and the police need to recognise these people and become more vigilant.

I cannot think of a better way to shop!

Reference:

1. A Fraser-Moodie. Shop Hopping. *Journal of Accident and Emergency Medicine* 1998;15:288.

Postman's Finger

The fickle finger of fate.

A saying

I came across a patient who had been bitten delivering leaflets. As he'd pushed a leaflet through a letterbox his finger had been bitten by a dog waiting inside the house. I thought that this was a 'one off'. Then I saw another case. I read in the literature of a patient who had had the end of his finger bitten right off. A hand surgeon described another similar case to me. So I kept a look-out for such patients.[1]

A colleague and I collected these cases over two years. Between us we saw 16 patients. They had each been putting letters or leaflets through a letterbox when bitten from inside the property. They had all had their fingers cleaned and dressed, and they had all received antibiotics.

The average age of these patients was 41 years – 14 male and only two female. Twelve of the 16 patients were bitten on their dominant hand. Most of the injuries were minor. Two patients had surgery, and one year later three patients had ongoing symptoms.

The most striking feature was their occupations. Fourteen of the patients were amateur postmen. Only two were professional postmen. As they are training, postmen are taught not to insert any part of the hand through the letterbox. However, publicity from the police tells us to push

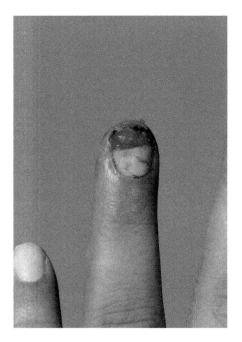

Fig 43 – Postman's finger injury. One of many that we saw.

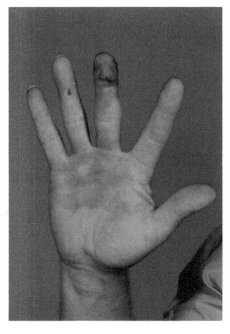

Fig 44 – Postman's finger strikes yet again – ow, ow ow!

any mail inside the letterbox as protruding mail advertises an empty property!

Of the 14 amateurs, 12 of them were delivering small items – leaflets or small cards. The letterbox was never high. Eight of them had letterboxes with a draft excluder, making posting more difficult.

There are many, many ways this painful little injury could be prevented or simply made less likely. People who deliver mail should know of this injury. Leaflets could be made stiffer and business cards bigger so that posting is easier, quicker and safer. 'Beware of the dog' stickers could make postmen wary.

Better still, a basket could be fitted inside the front door to catch the mail of all households with dogs. Alternatively, the letterbox opening could be made at the top of the door.

One lady had her finger bitten by a dog when posting a leaflet. Her husband finished the round. He posted the leaflets in with a wooden peg till this was bitten right off.

None of these postmen can sue the householder for

Fig 45 – Here is the crime scene. I pity the poor postman. He is in for a very big shock.

the injury. This is because once they stick their fingers through the letterbox, this constitutes trespass!

I read in the *Derby Evening Telegraph* in July 2012 that these injuries to post office employees have been recorded. The safety director for the Derby Post Office has issued these employees with plastic tongs. In total, 80,000 of them have been made nationwide!

Reference:

1. A Fraser-Moodie and M Ryatt. Postman's Finger. Presented to the British Association of Emergency Medicine Annual Meeting 2006 and published in the proceedings.

CHAPTER TWENTY-SIX

No Fixed Abode

There's no place like home.

From a song

A few people choose a 'homeless' nomadic life. But for the majority, homelessness is a misfortune that usually results from poverty/hunger, natural disasters, war/genocide or disease/overcrowding. The Bible records many such events – even Jesus was born in a stable (overcrowding) and was soon taken to Egypt to avoid Herod's slaughter of infants (genocide). I, myself, was evacuated to a caravan site in Pewsey, Wiltshire to avoid the Blitz (war). Sometime later (1952), my medical parents sent me for a stay in Scotland. This was to avoid contracting tuberculosis that was rife in Northolt (disease).

In January 2011, as I write this, there are officially over 10,000 people homeless in the United Kingdom. The real number is likely to be a lot more. Now in 2017 perhaps 20,000 are homeless. There are two million people waiting for council housing. This is a huge problem. Many of the homeless have given up altogether. They have a low esteem. Some are alcoholics. They are part of society, yet shunned by it. As we pass a cardboard box late at night we know it is somebody's home, just like a shell for a snail. These people have slipped from grace – clinging to life with the aid of benefits. There are handouts from the government. Like peers of the realm and the certifiably insane, they are disenfranchised. They cannot have a general practitioner and they cannot apply for a job as they have no address. So even if they are well suited for a job they cannot apply for one. They are trapped in society by society. Many charities try and help such people. There are soup runs. Advice is given about benefits. These charities try and get the homeless into sheltered accommodation. In the *British Medical Journal* in 2009 the life expectancy of a man living rough is England was calculated – only 42 years.

I first had contact with the homeless as a medical student in the 1960s. I was on call in Casualty. Nearby at Waterloo Station a huge number of homeless congregate. The large roof is a cover for them. There is plenty of food, drink and facilities. It is their home.

Many of these were alcoholics and mostly men. They frequently suffered minor head injuries and needed to be observed. This explained their presence in Casualty. Well, quite honestly, the hospital is warmer than the draughty station. Also, the nurses give you cups of tea.

I found myself saddled with up to a dozen of these vagrants. My remit from the Casualty officer was to do head injury observations overnight every 15 minutes. These men were in various stages of inebriation. I had to wake them and shine a light in their eyes regularly through the night (medical students of today are not seen after 9pm at the latest, please note). I was not popular. They swore at me regularly. Well, at least it meant they were not lapsing into a coma from a bleed into their brain secondary to their head injury!

Sometimes one of these men would 'open up'. I would get a clear conversation with one. "I was a tailor once," said one. "I was a jeweller," said another. Job lost and family relations became strained. They left home and drank. There was a familiar downward spiral in each life I explored.

Then suddenly they all woke up together at exactly 5.30am. This was because one of them proudly announced to all the others, "They're open." What he meant was that in Covent Garden Market, the public house opened every day at 5.30am for the porters. These alcoholics cashed in on the early opening times. They trooped out of Casualty en masse enticed by the lure of liquor. This was their lifestyle. What a waste.

They displayed total disregard for everybody else. Their actions were buoyed by a huge sense of entitlement. In fact they were just alcohol addicts.

I went to bed shattered.

London, that great cesspool into which all the loungers and
idlers of the Empire are irresistibly drained.
Sir Arthur Conan Doyle,
A Study in Scarlet (1888) Chapter 1

Soon after I became an Emergency consultant I was called to see an 'emergency' in our casualty department. I was met with screams and a pile of bodies, on top of which was a radiographer and a student nurse. I pulled them off the security man. He could not cope, and the ones on top had tried to help him by falling on him. Under the security man was a bearded man in shabby clothing – he had been sleeping rough. He was very aggressive, hence the other three had tried to overcome him.

"Who are you?" asked the beard.

"I'm the boss," I replied, and told him my name. He seemed to respect authority. I gave him a cup of tea and examined his minor injury. I treated this and asked why he was here and what all the aggression was about. He had a strong Glaswegian accent and did not want to talk. I told him my father was a Glaswegian and he mellowed a little. We talked about his life sleeping rough and he eventually opened up.

"It's like this," he said. "I'm a professional soldier in the Glasgow and Sutherland Highlanders, or rather was. We were in the forgotten war. Do you know that one?" he asked.

"Yes," I replied, "the Korean War."

"That's right," he said. "Well, we fought the Chinks over and over again all round one hill. First they took it and then we did. This went on and on for weeks. The Chinks just wanted things, not to kill us. There were dead bodies everywhere. We piled them up and hid behind them. There were fleas and lice all over them and the smell… Then one day, just out of the blue, it happened. An artillery barrage came from nowhere. All my mates were killed – blown up into pieces. I woke up and it was dark. The Chinks were stealing anything they could – watches, money or food. They were all around me, but it was dark. I crawled away and hid. Then crawled some more. I got away eventually'.

"I was not captured – well, they would have just shot me if found. I still have ringing in my ears, headaches and nightmares. No, I've not been right since. I was discharged from the Army on medical grounds and live rough. Nobody cares. I am always fighting and I have no friends."

I called him Jock. He attended intermittently for many years to our hospital. He was violent if challenged. I found him very likeable. He was not violent if I saw him. He respected authority and I felt like one of his officers. He had no friends and nowhere to go.

* * *

Another down and out I befriended was a lot younger, about 40. He was well spoken and polite.

"What happened?" I asked. "Why no abode?"

"Oh," he said, "I had a good job with good money. I longed for a wife. I went on holiday to Thailand and met this young lady. Gosh, she was beautiful. I went back again and fell for her. We were married six months later. We had no children but after two years she heard her dad was very ill and went back home. I left as soon as my work would let me. I never found her. I looked and looked. She was the love of my life. I told my work I was on extended leave without pay. I lost her! I came back to the UK six months later. My house was by then repossessed. I had lost my job and I could not get another. I was heavily in debt, so I ended up of no fixed abode – sleeping rough! No wife, no job, no friends, nothing."

* * *

Mr Holt had no fixed abode. He was tall and distinguished in manner, always wearing a coat. Our emergency department was warm and comfortable with an endless supply of cups of tea. So although he was never a casualty, Mr Holt would frequently be found in our waiting room any time of the day or night. He always sat in a prominent position in the middle of the room. He also had two strange habits.

In the first he would suddenly puff his cheeks out and give a loud, impromptu impersonation of a brass band. It was rhythmic, but tuneless and endless. This noise, combined with his excessive body odour, made him someone to avoid. One lunchtime I was queueing in the local post office. Suddenly this familiar cacophony assaulted my left ear. The lady in front of me jumped up and dropped her parcels. I shouted, "Come out, Mr Holt". He then appeared from behind a screen. He apologised, touched his forelock and scarpered.

His second habit was even more bizarre. Any time between early November and late January, he would approach a member of our department and ask them if they wanted a present. Well, this is the season of gifts and goodwill. Nobody could refuse. Then out of his pocket he would give each of us a Christmas card. It was always identically the same cheap card every year, never in an envelope and he wrote nothing inside it! This simple act of giving me a card gave him obvious pleasure. I suspect that he had found a job lot of cards somewhere and was working through them.

So Mr Holt was part of our society, but as a vagrant he was rejected. All his actions drew attention to himself. Was he trying to be accepted as normal by society? To my mind these vain attempts failed miserably, and only served to show that he was so very different from the rest of society.

* * *

Homelessness is a problem for all of us in society, not just the sufferers. It is in our natural instinct to run away from such a cardboard box. Benefits exist for these people. Money given to a beggar is likely to go on alcohol. What more can we do for these people?

There is sheltered housing in every city in the United Kingdom. There are charities who need helpers. Food, clothing, furniture and money are all wanted. If everybody did a little it would mean a lot.

There but for the grace of God go I.

So there are many homeless people, and a lot of them are young fit men. In England, and many other countries, this group has been 'explored'. Out of this has emerged the England Homeless Football Team. This has lifted the esteem of each and every one of its players. They played in Rio de Janeiro for the Homeless World Cup (Jan 2011)!

Over 600 admissions of the homeless were reviewed.[1] The average age of such admissions was 43 years – a lot younger than the non-homeless. 87% of these homeless were male. Nearly 40% of admissions were alcohol related and nearly 30% substance abuse related. As an Emergency consultant in England for 30 years, my experience was similar. We admitted a lot of homeless men, each with a minor head injury. They all had to be admitted for social reasons. Nobody else could keep an eye on them!

Many of the homeless people are stuck in a rut. They have lost all motivation to get out. There are homeless charities. A charity may help the homeless on to a career path. They fund networking events, seminars and conferences. So the homeless are eligible to obtain qualifications and even degrees. They aid the homeless primarily to gain employment. Abroad, some politicians have championed the homeless – reducing crime and homicides. For example, thanks to the late Pat Layton in Canada, downtown outreach workers monitor these individuals.[2]

George Orwell wrote *Down and Out in Paris and London* in 1933. This included his personal experiences of living with tramps during the Great Depression. Recently, in 2013, a healthy 26-year-old called Lee Halpin planned to spend a week on the streets of Newcastle. This was to film a documentary about the homeless. The overnight temperature fell to -4°C. Lee was found dead after three nights – hypothermia?[3]

Homelessness is the tip of the iceberg – the obvious bit. But the iceberg is a lot bigger. The web of poverty in the United Kingdom is huge. Poverty is defined as households that have an income below 60% of the national median wage. Approximately 13.5 million people fall into this group. Many of these adults are still working – but on a low wage.[4]

Matt Padley of Loughborough University's Centre for Research in Social Policy reports in 2017 that there is a steady growth of people with too little income. There is also an association between poverty and disease. For example, over 100,000 admissions annually to UK hospitals are for breathlessness (Chronic Obstructive Pulmonary Disease). There is an obvious association between this condition and smoking, poor air quality and asthma. But an even stronger association between breathlessness and poverty.

Many councils in the UK provide help for the homeless – particularly in winter. In the winter of 2012, rough sleepers in Barnstaple could access a centre but only if the temperature was below freezing for three nights in a row.[5]

In 2017, homelessness in the United Kingdom is increasing.

Thanks to the conflicts all around the world, global homelessness is a huge problem. But a team of refugees, displaced from their own country, competed in the 2016 Olympic Games under the Olympic flag. They consisted of six men and four women from Syria, South Sudan, the Democratic Republic of the Congo, and Ethiopia.

Our society may well be judged, in retrospect, by how well we look after our most vulnerable members.

A fact

References:

1. Profiling the medical admissions of the homeless. R Romero-Ortuno et al. *Acute Medicine.* 2012:11(4) 197-204.
2. Homeless help should be part of crime strategy, advocates say. M Ibrahim. *Edmunton Journal* 10.8.11:1.
3. Dead after three days, the man who tried to live like homeless. David Brown. *The Times.* 6.4.13:5.
4. Church Action on Poverty. Church Urban Fund, Church House, Great Smith Street, London, SW1P 3AZ.
5. Winter Help for the Homeless. North Devon. Connect 8.

CHAPTER TWENTY-SEVEN

History Repeats Itself

Thank heavens for little girls.
Words of song sung by Maurice Chevalier

P am was a specialist registrar in emergency medicine working a night
shift. She was very close to the end of a particularly long training,
as she was aiming for dual accreditation for emergency medicine, adults
and children. She was childless, but hoped to spend a lot of her working
life looking after other people's children.

Pam was tall, slim and attractive. She went about supervising the
work of the more junior doctors. The calm and quietness was about to
be broken.

The doors were flung open and in marched two burly ambulance
men wheeling an obese aggressive lady on a stretcher. "Ow, ow, ow," she
screamed at the top of her voice. And then she shouted, "Do something,
ow, ow, ow!!!"

The lady was pushed into the resuscitation area that was empty.
More screams and abuse followed, some more abuse and then she
finally calmed down. The lady's husband meekly followed, carrying
a handbag.

The specialist registrar Pam examined the lady, and politely told
her she was pregnant. "No I am not," she said indignantly. A fuller

241

examination followed, including with the foetal stethoscope and an internal examination.

"Not only are you pregnant, madam," the doctor said, "but you are about to deliver a full-term foetus."

"Rubbish," said the lady. "I'm not pregnant, do you hear me, doctor, NOT PREGNANT. I've already got two children!"

The doctor had a quick conversation with the sister in charge. A pack was opened, etc.

Five minutes later a fine baby girl was born. She cried immediately. The doctor delivered the placenta intact. Mother was fine.

All the time the patient's husband had sat in the corner. He missed nothing. He said nothing. The doctor turned her attention to the new arrival. The cord was attended to. Full examination revealed a healthy infant. Blood glucose normal. Now for the first feed of clear fluids.

"That's not my baby," said the mother. "Take that thing away."

"I'm very confused," said the husband.

The nurses were getting busier as a few more patients turned up. An ambulance was arranged to take the mother, baby and presumably the father to the maternity hospital. It would be some time.

The registrar had other patients to see and more junior doctors to supervise. She went off to attend to her duties. As the mother did not want her child, and the nurses were busy, she was given no alternative but to carry the baby everywhere. "How do you like my baby?" she said to everyone she met.

Some time later the ambulance turned up. Pam somewhat reluctantly had to give up the baby and return to her work. This registrar, Pam, passed all her examinations and is now an Emergency consultant with dual accreditation.

The pregnant lady had no previous psychiatric problems. A few days, after admission, she accepted her baby girl and took her home. She was a good mother!

* * *

Many years before, I was a Casualty officer at St Thomas' when a 16-year-old girl who had just left school was brought in. She was working at County Hall in the offices of the Medical Officer of Health for Surrey.

The lady had abdominal pain, and had a short letter from the deputy medical officer for Surrey, Dr Macgregor. This letter was brief, ending in the statement: '? pregnant, ? abortion'. I knew this doctor (we played golf together). I knew he was an administrator and, as he said, he "had given up examining patients years ago".

The girl's 17-year-old boyfriend was in attendance and he said she was just possibly aborting.

The pains were every three minutes and the only diagnosis on my history was labour. Examination confirmed that a full-term foetus was due in about five minutes. Sister and I shot the mother upstairs to the delivery suite.

The boyfriend was left to explain to her parents who were 'on their way'.

* * *

A New Arrival – A Tail of the Unexpected (1998)

Spasm supervening upon a wound is dangerous.
                                          Hippocrates

My daughters brought her home. I was not expecting this at all. "Well what about the mother?" I said. "Doesn't the mother want her own offspring?"

"No," they said. "She had twins and she can't cope. Not enough milk."

"Well, can't anybody else look after her?" I said.

"Oh no," said one of my daughters, Isabel. "The man in charge, Iain, told us just to take her home to you."

"Oh," I said. I wondered if the birth had been registered. We had not adopted her. Was this legal? Would the police call?

The little one thrived. My daughters and my wife took over most of the time, but late at night and first thing in the morning Dad was delegated to feed her. She thrived. She opened her eyes and gulped down the milk. It was a joy to hold her close to me.

It was on the fifth morning I was to feed her. Instead of her sparkling eyes I saw, to my horror, just a semi-conscious little body, frothing at the mouth. She twitched as she lay, full of involuntary movements.

243

I called the specialist who said, "Oh, how interesting. We don't see this very often."

"What is wrong?" I asked.

"Oh, it's tetanus, tetanus neonatorum – tetanus of the newborn."

No intensive care unit for her. No, just a shot of penicillin – not adequate to cure the condition.

She died a few hours later. No death certificate. No funeral. But I said a short prayer.

In the corner of a field I buried the lamb.

Tetanus

Prevention is better than cure.

Proverb

We forget how immunisation has revolutionised our whole lives. We are not born with any immunity to tetanus. The spores lie dormant in our soil and frequently contaminate our wounds. Before the First World War, up to one-third of all British casualties in wartime died of tetanus due to contamination of war wounds. So in any dirty wound, in time, the spores of tetanus, a bacterium, can multiply and multiply if the wound is not cleaned. A powerful chemical (an exotoxin) is released by these bacteria. This causes fits initially and if untreated death follows quickly.

A crude type of immunisation with horse serum started in the First World War and the mortality rate from tetanus fell to about 1%. We were still using the crude immunisation when I was in Casualty as a medical student and then a doctor in the 1960s. It was called anti-tetanus serum (ATS).

We now have a safe form of immunisation but immunity may not last.[1] Immunity is conferred by regular injections, throughout life, of tetanus toxoid. But tests show that only about 10% of our population currently have any immunity to tetanus.[2]

* * *

I have seen four people develop tetanus. One lady in Bristol pricked her finger on a rose thorn. She survived after a long period in ICU on a ventilator.

A second patient presented with a stiff painful jaw (lockjaw). She survived too.

A third was a gravedigger who refused immunisation. He died of tetanus.

A fourth patient was elderly and her birth predated the routine immunisation of the 1940s. This lady had a fractured forearm and a small graze to her upper arm. The fracture was treated well in hospital, when she went into severe spasms. She later died in ICU.

If one applies the Advanced Trauma Life Support guidelines and national guidelines, she was not a candidate for immediate preventative treatment against tetanus (an injection of immunoglobin). This is expensive and lasts only a few days. She just had a superficial graze – no infection or dead tissue.[3] Why she developed tetanus I did not know. If she had been given an injection of tetanus toxoid it would have boosted her immune system but taken up to a month to work! Her tetanus came on three days after injury!

She died though. The coroner's deputy, himself a doctor, at the inquest asked the relatives to talk to me in court. They were upset and naturally very aggressive towards me. I won't forget that torrid time.

So tetanus remains a constant threat even today. About 50 people die from tetanus in the United Kingdom annually, despite immunisation and modern wound management.

> *The superior doctor prevents sickness, the inferior doctor treats actual sickness.*
>
> Chinese proverb

References:

1. M Cooke. Are current UK tetanus prophylaxis procedures for wound management optimal? *Emergency Medicine Journal* 2009:26;845-8.
2. Jane McVicar. Should we test for tetanus immunity in all emergency

department patients with wounds? *Emergency Medicine Journal.*
2012:30;177-179.

3. Department of Health. Scottish Executive Health Department. Welsh
    Assembly Government. DHSSPS (Northern Ireland) Tetanus In: Salisbury
    DM, Ramsey ME, Moakes K eds. Immunisation against infectious diseases
    – 'The Green Book'. LONDON TSO 2006:367-84.

Allez Baa-Baa? (1990)

I met a young man, Paul, whilst I was buying some free range eggs
locally in Farnah Green, a mile up the road from where I live. He was a
shepherd keen to build up his flock of sheep. But he was short of grazing.
I suggested he put his flock in a field of mine. His friendly sheep could
eat down the grass and weeds, as well as fertilising the ground, to our
mutual benefit. The boundary was secure, the gate padlocked, there
was shelter from trees and a trough. So nothing at all could possibly go
wrong. But it did!

My wife telephoned me at work. She was upset: "A child has come
into our field and stabbed one of Paul's ewes. The sheep is in a bad way.
Paul has taken her home."

I felt guilty. Well, this field seemed to be so safe. There was a local
authority residential children's home nearby. I later learnt that a 'disturbed'
teenager from there had attacked this sheep. Paul's sheep were so friendly,
and did not run away when approached.

When I got home I telephoned Paul. "How is the ewe?"

"I've just been talking to my vet," Paul said. "He wants to come and
put her down. He gave her no chance to survive. Her guts are hanging out
with holes. It's hopeless! What a pity – she had twins this year, and one at
least is still suckling. She was a good ewe. I will miss her. Before she gets
put down could you just look at her? She is in my front garden. I'll be
home all evening."

I got everything ready: sterile instruments, retractors, forceps,
scalpel, antiseptics, sterile drapes, local anaesthetic and a variety of suture
materials. All these things were normally reserved for private patients.
Well, the ewe was not an NHS patient. No, she was a courtesy patient.

My patient was standing on Paul's lawn. Two pieces of torn small bowel protruded from her abdomen. There was a hole in the mesentery. There was no haemorrhage. The bowel was viable (alive).

I had not completely forgotten my time as a general surgery registrar. Antiseptics first, then injections of local anaesthetic. Saline soaks, chronic cat gut repair to bowel wall and mesentery. Paul held the patient down and whispered something soothing into her ears. The hardest thing was closure of the abdominal wall with a large hand-held silk needle. I covered the whole procedure with an intramuscular antibiotic. We feared the worst.

The patient made an amazing recovery. Back in the field she was soon grazing and suckling her lambs again. Her stitches were removed some time later. She had twins again the following year.

Well, this animal had better powers of recovery than any human.

Should I have been a vet?

* * *

I later learnt that I had committed a serious offence and could be prosecuted. Not by the farmer, the vet or the patient, but by the police. It is an offence, in this country, for anybody to operate on an animal, who is not a qualified veterinary surgeon. But the patient got better – no excuse. The veterinary surgeon wanted to put the animal down – irrelevant. I am qualified to do general surgery operations – yes, but only on humans.

I did not know this was an offence – ignorance of the law is no excuse. I would have pleaded guilty and awaited sentence! A caution? A fine? Imprisonment? We have abolished capital punishment, haven't we?

Strangely, however, if I was stabbed and a veterinary surgeon offered to operate, that is allowed by British law – as long as he did not pretend to be a doctor, and I agreed to this procedure.

Well, this law is an ass. This episode is a clear example of another medical misadventure – well, a female was involved – ewe all know who!

* * *

It was a wet windy evening in the accident and emergency department in Derby. The receptionist was clock watching. Well, she was off at 11pm and it had been a busy evening. The doctors were busy resuscitating two road traffic accident victims. The waiting room was nearly empty. A man in a raincoat came in.

"Can I help you?" she said.

"Oh, are you all busy?" was his reply.

"What is the problem?" she asked.

"Oh well, it's complicated," he said.

"Well, how can we help you?" She was getting a little impatient.

"Well," he said, unbuttoning his coat. "My rabbit is not well, I don't know what to do, and I'm worried."

A rabbit was produced. The receptionist was well-trained and resourceful. She called a flying squad driver, Vince, he loved animals. After a consultation and examination he gave some sound advice on diet. The rabbit had been fed the wrong diet. The man and patient left. No charge.

This NHS is a wonderful thing!

* * *

It was 9pm on a Sunday evening. Aged nearly 60, I had been on call since 9am Friday. I had just done a ward round with the experienced registrar and had handed over to him. I was ready for food and then my bed, hoping for no more interruptions.

Then the receptionist relayed a telephone call to me. The police asked for the most senior doctor in Casualty to stay. They wanted my opinion.

A few minutes later two senior policemen turned up with a small package. A dog had dug it up, beside, but not in, a local cemetery. "Is it human? Doctor, please tell us," was my remit.

I puzzled over the odourless, but partly decayed, piece of flesh for a full ten minutes or so. It was the size of a large paw or a small hand. The carpal bones (hand bones of the palm) did not feel human. There were five rays; the digits were missing.

Some skin was removed. The specimen was covered on one side in thick hair (or blanched fur). This clinched it for me. No human has thick hair on their hands.

"This is definitely not human," I said.

"Oh, thank goodness, doctor," they said. "We did not want to start

248

a murder inquiry tonight. We would have called in extra police and cordoned a wide area off. Thank you so much," they added, and left.

The moral of the story is, if your pet dies, dispose of the body properly or you may inadvertently spark off a murder investigation!

CHAPTER TWENTY-EIGHT

Three Lucky Escapes

Would seem a miracle, and exercise our admiration.

John Dunne

Willie (2010)

I have a friend, Willie (this is his real name), who plays golf professionally. I have known him, his wife and their family well, for years. At 56 years of age he was very fit. One morning we heard that Willie had collapsed.

Four days before, he was playing golf in Surrey with friends. He felt a sharp pain in his head, saw a flash of light and heard a bang. He looked about himself but saw nothing wrong. He is determined, and was able to finish the round of golf, and to drive in some pain up the M1 to Derby (about three hours). A niggling headache continued for two days. Then he took his wife out for a meal and he collapsed before he had had a drink. He was rushed to hospital. He fitted and stopped breathing. His breathing was assisted, and he had a head scan. He had bled into his brain from an aneurysm (he had been born with it). The flow of fluid (cerebro-spinal) around his brain was blocked by the blood. The neurosurgeons were contacted, and they gave a grave prognosis.

He spent a night on the Intensive Care Unit on a ventilator to assist

Fig 46 – Willie in the centre is our captain in 2012 on captain's day at Chevin Golf Club. I am on his left and a professor of public health is on his right.

his breathing, and the next day he was still alive. The neurosurgeons then took him and stopped the aneurysm bleeding by cannulating his carotid artery and putting fine platinum wires into the aneurysm i.e., from the inside. So they put a cannula into his neck in an artery that went up into his brain. This caused the aneurysm to clot and the bleeding to stop. Willie made a slow steady recovery with no paralysis or other serious problems.

I visited him whilst he was recovering in hospital. I was teaching at the time and so brought along a medical student. Willie was sleepy initially, but then he woke up completely. Was he just so pleased to see me? Or was it because my female medical student was 'blessed with great beauty?' He recovered completely with no further problems. He is back playing golf again – as well as ever. (fig 46).

If I had seen him before he took his wife out, I would have told him to have a scan – but this is not the classic history of a bleeding cerebral aneurysm. Usually the headache is the worst that they have ever had. But he had just had a mild headache.

It is strange that he was born with this aneurysm that gave him no problems for 56 years. An aneurysm is simply a localised bulge of an artery.

Probably as he got older his blood pressure rose slightly and the stress of playing golf pushed it up more, causing the aneurysm to burst and bleed. The loud noise that he heard must have been the aneurysm bursting inside his skull at the base of his brain!

However, he could have collapsed and died any time after the onset. He could have killed a lot of people on the motorway. He is a very lucky man.

Incidentally, whilst Willie was very ill in hospital, several well-meaning people sent letters of condolence to his wife!

> 'The report of my death was an exaggeration.'
>
> Mark Twain
>
> New York Journal. 2nd June 1897 (and often misquoted).

Tally Ho (1980)

A huntsman in his sixties was brought into the resuscitation room. He could not speak. His horse had rolled on his trunk. He looked grey. He was very short of breath. He could not speak as he was so ill.

Horse riding injuries tend to be severe because horse riders are often fearless. Perched high up, when the rider falls off, gravity takes over! The horse is heavy and can fall too, rolling on the rider. Jumping and hunting are dangerous. (Drag hunting is still legal.)

He was resuscitated. A mobile chest X-ray showed a bilateral pneumothorax. So on each side of his chest his lung had punctured. Air then escaped from inside the lung to around the lung and collapsed this organ. Once again, I shoved in the chest drains. This was before the modern protocols. The old way was quicker, with a metal spike (trocar) and cannula. Putting chest drains in today, the protocol has to be followed – it makes it slower but safer. But I never had any problems with the old way!

Once the bilateral chest drains were in, the air started bubbling out of his chest from around his lungs and into the underwater seal. (So the air can't go back – can only come out.) He was on his way to recovery. His lungs were expanding , and filling with air from his windpipe. The life-threatening injury became less serious. He would live.

He then said his first words, "I want to go private!"

This private patient was admitted under the private surgeons. We did not see him again, but before he left the hospital he had his prostate out!

Our treatment was life-saving under the good old NHS and cost him nothing… Well, that's life.

* * *

The reader may think that jumping horses is the most dangerous of all sports. Well, in my experience of seeing casualties over 50 years, there is one sport with a higher incidence rate of serious casualties. It is snooker.

I have seen six patients who played snooker and they all suffered fractured skulls as a consequence. Let me explain: they were crouching over the snooker balls and going for a big break and each time another player got jealous. He turned his cue round and hit the crouching player on the head. Result: fractured skull!

A Lover's Tiff (1985)

A 999 ambulance brought in a young man. He was covered in blood and not very well. His hand was held by his wife. She sobbed.

"Oh," she cried, "I have killed him; I did it."

The ambulance man told us that a large carving knife was at home covered in blood. The patient had strayed and been seduced by another woman. His wife found out and stabbed him. She had done a good job – puncture wounds to both sides of his chest anteriorly. Blood was everywhere. During quick resuscitation he had an X-ray. It showed a bilateral pneumothorax – both lungs punctured. A life-threatening injury.

I put in bilateral chest drains. In those days we had a long metal spike inside a plastic casing. This worked very well. The metal spike was then taken out and the plastic tube connected to an underwater seal. The air bubbled out. The lungs expanded. He healed and recovered. Many people have died of such an injury.

He made a full recovery in hospital.

I don't know what happened to the marriage in the long term.

What a Bloody Mess

A strange lady presented to our casualty department many years ago. She had a smear of blood on her right cheek and also on her jumper. There was blood on both hands and on her jeans. Her husband had blood on his trousers. This bloody man had just driven his bloody wife to the hospital.

As she walked into my consulting room I rose in anguish.

"Where are you bleeding from, madam?" I asked.

"Chaddesden," she replied.

Overstrenuous housework had led to bleeding from small cuts on her hands. Once they were cleaned, she recovered quickly.

CHAPTER TWENTY-NINE

Medico-legal

When I am King... the first thing we do, let's kill all the lawyers.

Shakespeare *Henry VI Part 2*

Preface

I have five children. I was looking forward to them all being educated in our excellent state-education system. Things did not work out that way at all.

Our eldest son was eight years of age. He had read all the books in his classroom. He was instructed by his teacher to go to the next class to get another book. He knocked on the door and on request the teacher in the year above gave him another book to read. This did not go unnoticed by the pupils. They realised this little boy from the year below was ahead of them at reading. They took it out on him at break time. He continued to be bullied. The teachers did nothing. The only alternative was private education. He went into private education and even a scholarship did not do much to soften the financial blow!

Soon after this, our next child was excelling at school to the envy of others. She was far less diplomatic than her brother. Well, she has always said her mind! One day, whilst the teacher was out of the room, she was assaulted by a much bigger boy. She came home extremely upset.

"I want to leave now."

Oh dear, more private education. Once again a small scholarship did little to help financially! (The boy who assaulted her was also outstanding – at setting alight telephone boxes – and so was granted special education!) So, the grand aim of sending all five children to state schools resulted in all of them being educated partly by the state and partly privately. Even then things got worse five to university (not helped by two girls extending five years to six-year courses each, with an extra BSc!) As I write, one other has started a second degree course – medicine of course. I had only one way of meeting this extra finance – medico-legal reports.

I was going to rely on the accuracy of the medical records to generate a medical report. The medical records are legal documents and belong to the British government. It is an offence to destroy or deface them. They are frequently produced in court. I have been asked to read out my records by judges and coroners. Indeed, the only valid reason for taking medical records from any hospital is for court purposes. Mistakes have been made when the history is not accurate. Patients have died as a result, and doctors struck off the medical register for this offence. But, occasionally, some leniency and perception is required. Twenty years ago I discovered this. Yes indeed, 'not under oath' I erred for the direct benefit of my patient.

I had worked a normal week and now was on call all the weekend before the next week's work! I loved the work but hated the long hours. Short of sleep found me at work on Sunday morning. At 9am after a ward round of inpatients and a review of the junior doctors' work, I could only find one patient waiting! But loads and loads of patients would pile in that day, usually around lunchtime. We joked that the bus had come! I ushered into a cubicle a dishevelled man aged 40, of short stature with a black eye.

"What happened?" I asked.

"Oh, I fell over," he replied. Silence followed.

"No," I said, "what really happened?" Silence again.

"Oh, I fell over," he repeated.

To explain, I had previously looked at an X-ray ordered by the triage nurse a few minutes before. He had a displaced fracture of the malar (cheek) bone. A fall was unlikely. This isolated injury would be from a punch in 99% of cases. The patient looked so tired and depressed. Then he 'opened up' and confessed:

"Last night I was on an evening shift that finished at 10pm. I usually get home about 10.15pm. There was no work for us. So just for once the foreman sent us all home at 8pm. I rushed home and went upstairs to see my wife. She was in bed with my best friend. They were both naked. There was a row. I got punched on the face and thrown out of my own house. They bolted the door. I have been walking all night."

I wrote for his benefit in the medical records: 'Fell over and hurt face.'

Medico-legal Cases

"The truth, the whole truth and nothing but the truth" or at times "Lies, lies and damn lies!"

Nothing could be simpler. On request from a solicitor I get out the records of a patient's injury. I discuss the history of the injury with the patient. Then I examine the patient and write a report addressed to the court, detailing the injury with a relevant prognosis. How could anything go wrong? Well honestly, quite easily! Our legal system is slow and cumbersome – especially when it comes to paying doctors! Income tax is paid on bills sent out, rather than money received! Patient compliance can be even worse. The history of the injury and the injury itself may not comply.

The Interview

I saw patients at my house. They often turned up on the wrong day, the wrong week or the wrong hour! I even transported some patients to my house for a report. On one such occasion a local man remarked on the nice area I lived in.

"I have not been here before," he said. I soon discovered that, aged 30 years, he had never left Derby before.

"No," he said, "I've never been anywhere at all. I don't see the point."
Well, how insular can you get?

Another patient left his car parked in my drive and not on the road.
Well, it was obvious his car was untaxed (and uninsured).

A girl insisted that she would only see me if her fiancé was present.

"Oh good," she said when I reluctantly agreed. The fiancé then learnt
a few things about her and broke off the engagement.

"Now look here doctor," her solicitor subsequently lectured me, "as
you well know, a fiancé is not a relative, and so you had no right to agree
to his coming too. My client's life has been ruined by your unprofessional
manner. I have instructed a barrister."

I just informed my medical defence union and heard no more.

* * *

In 1995, I soon discovered one patient had done time for burglary. It said
so in his GP records. As we walked towards his car after the consultation,
he looked about my house. He was noting the drainpipes, the windows,
the window ledges, etc. I was petrified he would return one night for a
'routine call'. Just then my dog barked.

"Oh, you have a dog?" he asked.

"Oh yes," I said. "Unfortunately he is rather large and at times very
aggressive." The patient turned a bit pale.

"The dog barked and barked late one night and so we let him out," I
said. "I think it was a prowler."

"Did you catch anybody?" he asked.

"No, unfortunately not," I said, "but the trail of blood went right down
to our wood."

"Was he all right?" he asked, going very pale indeed.

"Oh yes," I reassured him, as I helped him into his car, "the dog was
fine. Goodbye."

* * *

Some patients cancelled repeatedly. Then would ring up and tell me
they were not coming after all! One particular man said the time was
inconvenient.

"Well, when is it convenient?" I asked. He thought for a while and then told me, after some deliberation, that the only time he was free was 3am on a Tuesday morning.

"No other time is convenient at all," he argued. I declined to see him at that time and informed his solicitor who laughed and laughed.

* * *

One man had great difficulty coming to see me. Fergus O'Flattery telephoned me at 7pm one Friday evening. He wished to cancel his appointment at 3pm that day (he had not come) and make another. He was so polite and had a lovely southern Irish accent. I agreed to see him at 10am on the next morning (Saturday). He failed to come but at 10pm that night I received another courteous call. I could hear laughter in the background and a clink of glasses. He wished to cancel the appointment for that morning and wanted another.

I agreed to see him at 2pm on Sunday (after church and before a parents' evening at school). He failed to attend, and I had forgotten about him when the doorbell rang at 10.30pm on that Sunday evening. There was Fergus, smiling broadly in a striped jumper and dark purple trousers.

"I'm Fergus O'Flattery," he said. "Oh, doctor," he said, taking control of the situation, "why weren't you there? Where were you, doctor? Everybody else was there, oh everybody."

"Oh?" I said somewhat taken aback.

"It was such a wake, doctor, a wonderful wake." Pause. "She was a wonderful divorced lady," he said.

"Well," I said, thinking that the Catholic Church does not exactly approve of divorce. "Well, err, what did the Church think of her?"

"Oh, doctor, I've just left the priest. Poor chap, he was in such a bad way. Do you think I should go back to him now?"

"Well," I asked, "when did the funeral take place?" He paused and thought and thought.

"Oh, doctor," he said, "what a difficult question." He thought again. "Wednesday or Tuesday, I think," he said.

"Can I see you for your claim?" I said.

"Of course, of course," he said. "I'll just tell the taxi driver to wait. Don't worry, doctor, the solicitor is paying."

Fergus could recall very little of the accident. He came out of the public house and got into his car. The car collided with another car. Then the occupants of both cars were so upset they went back into the public house and had a few more beers. He felt better and drove home. The next day his right knee was painful.

"Oh, it was so painful, doctor," he said, suddenly starting to limp. I could not help noticing that by now his nose, that was red to start with, was very red indeed.

"Well," I said, trying to calm down this very excited Irishman, "why don't you sit down and I can examine this injured knee." Fergus tried to bend his back and legs to sit down. He could not sit. He apologised.

"You will have to examine my knee standing up, doctor," he said.

"Now, Mr O'Flattery," I said, "what about your other knee?"

"Oh, it's perfect," he said.

I had great difficulty examining his leg with him standing up, but somehow I sort of managed. He had some tenderness all over his right knee. His left knee was fine. I then showed him his hospital attendance the day after the accident for an injured left knee.

"Oh… it's wrong," he said.

"No," I said, "the receptionist, the triage nurse and the doctor all record the left knee as the injured one."

He left a bit upset. No limp now. Finally, on leaving, he turned round.

"Oh," he said, "I've another accident to see you about. I'm coming back next week. I fell down some steps that should not have been there!"

He left. He never returned. My factual report would not have helped his claim very much at all.

N.B. The reader may be surprised to learn that this factual report of the interview is accurate in every degree with one exception – I have changed his name.

Make sure you engage your brain before you open your mouth.

Bill McFarlan

Some patients insist that the doctor, i.e., me, goes to see them for a report. Each time, I made an appointment over the telephone and turned up. Occasionally such a meeting was unavoidable but on one occasion the patient was out – shopping! On another occasion I did not realise I had been tricked into a home visit when I asked about mobility.

"Oh my husband drives me everywhere."

"Well, did he drive you to the solicitors?"

"Oh yes," she said. "It would have been too expensive otherwise."

"But why didn't you drive to my house?"

"Oh," she said, "we don't think of you as being expensive at all. Doctors don't charge, do they?"

* * *

I saw one man in his twenties at the hospital for a medical report one evening when I was not on call. He staggered into the room in some pain from his left thigh.

"I was hit by a bus," he recalled. He seemed to be in agony. His only attendance for this injury to hospital was the next day when he could not wait to be seen and quickly went away. He only saw the receptionist. On examination for the report I found that he was so tender over his left thigh that I arranged an X-ray. He staggered there and back. Result: a normal X-ray.

"Well," I said, "I will write a report to your solicitors." We shook hands. He lunged for the door handle and pulled himself up. He limped down the corridor and out of sight, in agony and very slowly. In a flash I took off my white coat and donned my sports jacket. I left hurriedly by another exit. I saw my client hurrying too, across the car park with little trace of a limp. I sprinted to catch him up but he was moving fast! There is a pelican crossing outside the hospital. As he approached, it had just turned green. He had to really hurry now. No problem. He broke into a run. He shot past a lady wheeling a pram over the crossing. He overtook others. He was in buoyant mood. Once across the other side he continued to run down the road and round the corner out of sight. What a great athlete!

I telephoned the solicitors. They laughed at their client. No report was written.

* * *

Sometimes during an interview it is obvious the patient is lying. One such man claimed a waiter had dropped a knife and it had cut off his fingertip, also causing a fracture. I am a surgeon and have shortened fingers but only with the aid of bone cutters and nibblers. The truth became apparent on perusal of the hospital records:

'Patient drunk. Caught finger when closing toilet door, cutting off the tip.' Yes, that sounded far more likely. Claim failed.

* * *

The Daily Telegraph reported on its front page another failed claim. A man was annoyed with the Social Security office in Nottingham. His payments were insufficient. He was so upset he threw a brick at their window. Unfortunately the window was plastic. The brick rebounded and caused a head injury to the man. His claim was that there was no notice saying the window was plastic! His claim deserved to fail.

Some injuries were very strange. For example, the man at the swimming pool who swam to the edge of the pool and grasped the bar. It rotated, injuring his wrist. He claimed compensation, but I thought all the bars rotated?

Another lady fell down some steps. Were the steps steep? (No.) Were the steps slippery? (No.) Was there a rail? (Yes.) Was her fall due to her previous stroke (maybe), or her symptomatic varicose veins (maybe), or her established osteoarthritis of her knees on X-ray (maybe)? She recalled her glasses fell off as she fell. As she talked, her glasses fell down from the top to the bottom of her nose, and had to be replaced repeatedly. Her glasses were just like Eddie the Eagle's on a ski jump. Her claim failed too.

* * *

Some claims were strange. For example, when a wife was driving and the car crashed injuring her husband as he was a passenger. He then claimed from his wife for personal injuries! In one such case the wife kept her maiden name but called herself 'Mrs'. So 'Mrs Elizabeth Young' was married to 'Mr John Smith'. The solicitor, who may not have met the couple, continued to call her 'Mrs Elizabeth Smith', but that was not her name!

CHAPTER THIRTY

Writing a Report

This can be very tricky. For example, I once had to write a report on somebody who had suffered a whiplash injury to the neck two years before. The confusing thing here was that she had had four previous whiplash injuries! Then, before I could see her, she had two more!

"Now," said the solicitor in his letter, "tell us what symptoms the patient would have had if this accident had occurred in isolation!" Well nobody knows, is the answer. Before the case was settled she had two more whiplash injuries (were the brakes on her car too sharp?)!

In another case an epileptic fell downstairs and then fitted. He then recovered well. Did his epilepsy cause him to fall or the steepness and slipperiness of the steps? Was his epilepsy affected by the fall in the long term? Did his head injury cause the fit or his epilepsy cause it? Could his epilepsy have recovered if he had not fallen? The questions were endless.

It gets very complicated and I was very happy to refer such complicated cases to a specialist neurologist. I am well aware that many patients who have epileptic fits have no evidence of their medication in their blood afterwards. So they have not taken their tablets.

At other times their fits occur to order. I recall one such patient who always came to our church and sat in a prominent position. (She also came regularly to our Casualty department because of 'fits'.) She had a fit that always occurred in the middle of the sermon. There was no sleepiness afterwards and no proper convulsions during the fit. In other words the fit was staged to cause maximum effect. The preacher was unmoved by her histrionics and carried on. Another fake.

One poor lady was a backseat passenger involved in a road traffic accident. She was injured in the crash with another car. Then the occupants of the other car beat her up. The solicitor wrote: 'We want to know what injuries are due to the road traffic accident and what are due to the assault?' Another almost impossible question for the poor doctor, i.e., me.

Investigations

The records are often very revealing. One patient, a lady, denied any previous back problem. I consulted her GP records and showed them to her. She had been to her GP over 20 times with an identical back complaint. She greeted this with total and complete denial. These refer to "somebody else and not me" she said. The GP herself was consulted and confirmed her patient to be a regular attender with her back. The GP described the patient's appearance very accurately, so there was no mistake here.

Another such patient was a man with a terrible whiplash injury. The X-rays showed cervical spondylosis and the impact had been terrific, he informed me. I followed him up and despite physiotherapy he got worse and worse. The solicitor saved me though. Neither car was damaged, he confirmed. The impact was so very slight. So the patient's complaint was of cervical disc disease and not whiplash. His complaint failed.

Investigations include secret camera information on the complainant. I vividly recall seeing one video of a man who had complained of his back after an accident, for some time. Yet the other side showed me a video of him renovating a house recently. He wheeled a barrow full of bricks out of the front door. His case failed.

Here is an example of two occupations that are dangerous: driving instructors and driving test examiners.

Driving instructors have more accidents than taxi drivers. Even with dual controls they have problems and are vulnerable.

The testers of car drivers have problems too – but the motorcycle testers have more. These motorcyclists have to reach a speed in their test and then do an emergency stop. They go out of control and the examiner is in danger!

So I have seen more than my share of driving instructors and examiners as patients.

The Report

Solicitors sometimes take exception to a report although it is addressed to the court. On one such occasion I wrote that a man had consumed 17 pints of beer and then was hit crossing a road. The solicitor insisted I remove the mention of 17 pints from my report. I argued that we should write 'the truth, the whole truth and nothing but the truth'. He disagreed and declined to pay me if I did not alter the report.

I even wrote a report for my daughter, aged eight years. We were at a firework display behind the safety rope in the dark. I was carrying her younger brother in my arms. Suddenly there was a flash and a firework landed at our feet and exploded. She complained of pain. A torch was found. She had superficial burns to her thighs and her coat was ruined. I took photographs and we sued Standard Fireworks. A roman candle had burnt out through the side and was kept by the organisers for inspection. My daughter was compensated. Our solicitor and I charged no fee!

She was not scarred – but remains scared of fireworks.

* * *

Sometimes nobody is to blame for an accident and it nearly goes to court. A young girl was giving trampoline demonstrations at fetes and all sorts of meetings. She was good – coached by her father. She was practising for one such demonstration and, unbeknown to her, the trampoline had broken at one corner and been taped up.

Down she came and the trampoline tipped due to the break. The girl was thrown heavily against a wall, fracturing her skull.

265

She was admitted to hospital but remained well. Suddenly at 3am she deteriorated rapidly. She had had an extradural bleed (inside the skull). She was operated upon by a neurosurgeon. He telephoned me at home before he operated. I knew her family well. The clot was removed and she made a slow, steady recovery. She never returned to the trampoline. Nobody would admit liability. It dragged on and on. Finally, an insurance company made her an offer of compensation on the steps of the court about five years later. It was accepted.

She became a nurse and still works at our hospital to this day. She made a complete recovery.

* * *

One complainant was incensed by my report. I was of the opinion that due to his height and weight his sprained left ankle would never heal. He was six feet six inches tall and weighed a mere 45 stone. (We weighed him on the public weighbridge.)

An Interesting Case (1980)

A firm of insurers sent me a request for a legal report. Could I please see Joe and comment on whether he was burnt or not, and how this had happened. He attended a local day centre, and they had insurance. Hence his claim. He lived outside Derbyshire, in Nottinghamshire, and had learning difficulties. Could I please call and see him. In the circumstances I had to drive to him.

I arranged one evening after work to see him. So I drove to Nottingham. He had learning difficulties but recalled the pain in his leg after the injury. He had dressings by the district nurse. He had now recovered after three weeks of dressings. He had no idea how he had been burnt. The pain came on slowly after a bath.

His mother agreed that he had been burnt whilst he had been at the local day care centre. He had a bath and later went to a local hospital. Joe walked with difficulty due to cerebral palsy. He had two red areas on his calves. They were each circular, about 10 cms across. The right calf area was slightly smaller and higher than the left. These areas corresponded to two healed superficial burns. These were painful but Joe had reduced sensation in both calves and did not feel a lot of my pin pricks. Sometimes burns are not felt at once – especially chemical burns. I had no idea how Joe had been burnt. Then I received a telephone call – anonymous of course. (I thought this only happened on television.) She identified herself as a nurse and confirmed, "Joe had been burnt." She declined to give me her name!

I looked up the hospital and GP records – these recorded the burns on the calves and the various dressings for two and a half weeks. How had he been burnt and why?

I next visited the day care centre in an evening. The manager was mystified as to how Joe had been burnt and doubted it had occurred at his place. The mystery nurse was there, curious to find out what had happened. She never gave me her name! All the carers had declined to meet me. Joe had upset them by repeatedly opening his bowels into his clothes – a reason for retaliation and scalding him?

On leaving, none the wiser, I was shown the bath. "It won't help you," I was told. "The thermostat has been changed recently." Well, you would have thought that a bath is a bath, and there could be no confusion. How wrong can you be? This bath you walked into and turned round to sit on a seat (a healthcare bath). Two little doors then closed in front of you like saloon bar doors in a Wild West movie. These doors gave a watertight seal to three feet off the ground. Warm water then came in round the bather's feet.

"So the first part to be burnt would be the feet and not the calves," said the manager.

However, hanging outside the bath was a long piece of hose, an attachment for washing hair. If this was put inside the bath, it reached below my right knee. I took off my shoes and socks and rolled up my trousers. The doors were shut and the water turned on. If only the hose was used, both my calves were in direct line of fire. After ten seconds I turned it all off. I inspected my calves. I had red areas (erythema) that corresponded to the burns received by my patient. The hose was on my right side. The area of erythema was smaller and higher on my right calf compared to my left calf – just like Joe's legs.

The next day I wrote my report and sent it off. The insurance company complained I had taken nearly three weeks to generate a simple report that most doctors would have done in a few minutes. Well, you can't win them all!

As I was so 'useless' the insurance company never contacted me again. Well, I did charge a lot – £100 including petrol, postage, telephone and secretarial fees.

Court

These court cases are strange happenings. Nobody can be sure of the outcome beforehand. In 1992 I recall one case of a 40-year-old Egyptian man. He had been told by the foreman to lift a very heavy weight. He had done so, but his back gave way. He collapsed. He continued to be in pain. Investigations confirmed disc prolapses at several levels. He could not return to this type of work again. He had no particular skills.

We were told he had never been on a lifting and handling course. No lifting gear was available. He was due for compensation, or was he? At court it was recorded by the other side that he had been on a lifting and handling course! He was not just an ordinary labourer but the foreman himself! Lifting gear was available and he should have used it. Finally all this had come out in a previous internal inquiry. We knew none of all this. We lost our case.

A 38-year-old man was involved in a road traffic accident hurting his neck. I saw him two years later in 1984. He had a lot of problems with arm pains and numbness. I suspected he had damaged his spinal cord. I asked and in fact insisted on a second opinion of a neurologist. He confirmed this injury. The other side in this claim disagreed. They had video footage that showed he could travel in a car and eat in a restaurant. (The camera was poised on the next table.) This was shot secretly. The patient did not see the camera. Four years after the injury my patient was penniless. He could not work. He had lost his job in management.

In the court everything went our way. The judge and the neurologist got on very well together. The neurologist explained that the patient had spinal cord damage from this accident. The judge turned to the barrister for the insurance society representing the other party.

"Where are we getting to, Mr Jones?" (Not very far I suspected.)

Finally, after about eight doctors had given evidence, the judge concluded our client had had spinal cord damage in the accident and awarded substantial damages to him. The day before, the patient would have accepted a fraction of this.

The patient wrote me a letter of thanks – it actually made it all worthwhile.

CHAPTER THIRTY-ONE

More Law Courts

If you have a lawsuit, you get one bad lawyer, you lose your suit – you can appeal.
But if you get one bad doctor and he kills you, then there can be no appeal.

Nicholas de Belleville

There has always been some rivalry between doctors and lawyers. Which is the senior profession? I know how the other side feels from the annual Doctors v Lawyers Golf Match. Taken to the extreme, lawyers revel whenever they can call a doctor to court. Any flicker of a problem that could prevent a doctor getting there, and the poor doctor is 'served a subpoena' to appear. Failure to do so could result in a jail sentence.

So all the doctor's other commitments are cancelled at a moment's notice for him to sit around in court waiting and waiting. The judge always takes long meal breaks. I have even known one judge stop early. He had toothache and asked his attendant, to 'find a dentist'! Family cases are heard first. So, more delays. I was once called out of work at lunchtime to support a police statement of fact about a road traffic accident victim I had seen. Normally a doctor would not be called, but the policeman I had given my statement to had died. But I was still on call. I was struggling outside the court room trying to turn my hospital bleep to vibration mode. I eventually succeeded but not before three of the ushers in turn insisted: "Turn that thing off as his Lordship will be upset if it goes off."

You can imagine my delight when a doctor followed me to the witness stand. He was paid to attend by the other side's solicitors. He gave an opinion contrary to mine and then his bleep went off loudly. The judge nearly had a fit. He admonished the other doctor and later agreed with my opinion and not the other doctor's.

If a case overruns to the following day one of the barristers often stands up and says, "He is compromised." It just means he has another brief (job) and cannot come. So the case is put off till he can come. A doctor is told, if he cannot come, that he will be subpoenaed! So he has to turn up, or go to jail!

* * *

An 18-month-old girl was scalded badly whilst in a small baby bath. She had bruises to her upper arms, suggesting she had been held forcibly in such a small bath. There was also bruising to her face and under her chin consistent with an assault. At the time of the incident, 11pm, she was in the care of a man. He was a client of the child's mother. She was a prostitute who was busy at work at the time of the incident. The child's father was in Broadmoor!

I was a Burns registrar in 1975 and admitted the child that night, transferred from another hospital. There was an extensive burn to the bottom, thighs and lower abdomen. This burn was superficial. There was a line all round her trunk like a 'tide mark'. She was burnt below but not above this line.

She was admitted, given analgesia, intravenous fluids and silver sulphadiazine cream applied to the burns. As the burns were superficial she made an excellent recovery within two weeks or so. The child thrived in hospital. She loved it. She got stronger and stronger. She then systematically beat up all the other children, even four-year-olds! She came from tough stock and for fun attacked bigger children from behind!

The social worker attached to her case could not stop crying initially. Soon the child was made a ward of court. The hospital was a place of safety. The child stayed in for months and months. Doctors have to do things at all hours immediately. The law acts at a slower pace. As the admitting doctor I was called to court to give evidence of her injuries in the case against the mother's client. I was given quite a tough time.

"How hot was the water? How can you be sure?"

Answer: "House hot-water thermostats are set to about 40-50 degrees C maximum. This water, to scald, was hotter."

"How long was the child in the bath?"

"Depends on how hot the water was. 55 degrees C, probably two minutes, 65 degrees C, less than one minute."

"But surely anybody bathing such a child would be scalded too?"

Answer: "No, you can hold a child in a hot bath and not get scalded yourself, e.g., by the arms." (This is easier to do in a baby bath.)

"Children of this age fall over regularly so cannot these bruises be due to falls?"

Answer: "Not in the distribution of these bruises, round the eyes, under the chin and to upper arms. These bruises could only have been caused non-accidentally. So this child has been beaten up by somebody".

My answers were carefully noted down by all the parties. The judge then added some more questions. I was exhausted at the end and went back to work. As soon as I got to work I was called to the phone. The clerk to the court had bad news:

"During a break in proceedings, the father-in-law of the accused got chatting to one of the jurors in the men's toilets, so the court has to start again afresh tomorrow with a new jury."

I was advised to forget everything that had gone on the previous day. The next day I repeated all the answers to all the same questions. Then lots more new questions appeared. After over two hours I was told I could go. All three questioners thanked me profusely and wished me well. I relaxed my guard. This was to be my undoing!

The judge said in his thanks to me that I clearly cared a lot about children and knew a lot about them. He was of the opinion that I obviously had children of my own.

"No," I said, "I have no children as I have only been married six weeks."

"Oh," said one of the barristers. "But, doctor, just because you have only been married a short time it does not follow that you do not have any children."

I cringed and fled. (I was paid twice – once for each day!)

The mother's client went to prison. The child was adopted by her grandmother, a caring Italian lady who was very upset by what had happened. She gave the child just what she needed – lots of love in a secure home.

* * *

I was working as a paediatric casualty officer years before in the East End of London. A lady brought in her two-year-old with a painful arm. Mum was single and said she did not know how it had happened. I was suspicious. The upper arm was very tender and any movement painful.

I organised an X-ray and was present when it was taken. I watched the mother all the time. There was no bonding between the two of them. The mother tried to ignore her child. She was strange. She gave the child no cuddles at all! The X-ray showed a spiral fracture of the humerus. This is very likely to have been caused by somebody twisting the arm. Mother still said that she knew nothing of the cause of this injury. Very strange! She was not upset by the result of the X-ray being told to her.

The child was admitted. The arm healed well in a sling and the child had regular analgesics. She made a full recovery but stayed in hospital. The mother, a single parent, was interrogated by a consultant paediatrician and a consultant child psychiatrist. They had plenty to say about her. They quickly discovered that two previous children had been taken from her because of non-accidental injuries caused by her. She had been to court twice before and each time found guilty.

In court we three sat about outside for six hours and were then sent home! We went to another magistrates' court some weeks later. I went in first. We three doctors went to court to try and have this third child removed from the mother's care. I was a junior doctor at the time. This was my first attendance to court. The magistrates expressed natural sympathy for the mother who had brought her child to the hospital. Her legally aided barrister was superb. I produced the X-ray, but initially I was not allowed to use it as I had not taken the X-ray myself! I pointed out that the X-ray had the child's name and date of birth on it. After a lot of arguing the X-ray was allowed and when asked how this injury had occurred, I gave my opinion that the arm had been twisted resulting in a spiral fracture. After my two consultant colleagues had been called, the magistrates somewhat reluctantly made the child a ward of court and found the mother guilty of assault.

"Are there any previous convictions?" they asked. Only then was it revealed that two previous children had suffered similar injuries at her hands.

This child fortunately never returned to her mother.

Non-accidental Injuries (Battered Babies)

These two cases of clear non-accidental injuries to children illustrate some of the confusion and complexity of this condition. Tragic news stories in our papers and on television graphically convey the true horror of the suffering. Time and time again questions are asked: "Why did they do it?" "Why was it missed?" "How can it be prevented?" I am not clever enough to have simple answers to these questions, but I do have observations of my own.

When it is proved that a child has suffered a non-accidental injury, it is often remarked, "Well, even animals never behave like that!" This is entirely untrue. For example, in the insect world, the female is often larger than the male insect. After sexual intercourse of the praying mantis the pregnant female often looks upon the redundant male as a good source of food. She therefore eats the unfortunate male. For the only time in his short life the male experiences the ecstasy of copulation followed immediately by the harsh cruelty of cannibalism. This is an extreme example of one family member killing another, but it is for the indirect benefit of offspring. So it does serve a purpose!

In certain situations, some mammals kill offspring. The male lion is dominant in the pride that consists of females and young offspring. If another male lion takes over the pride, the first thing he does is kill the young cubs. They are the progeny of the previous male. The lionesses then quickly come on heat – for his enjoyment and to pass on his line. So he benefits by destroying the cubs.

We have bred sheep for years. One ewe always had twins. She allowed one lamb to suckle, but not the other one. Any attempt to suckle and this

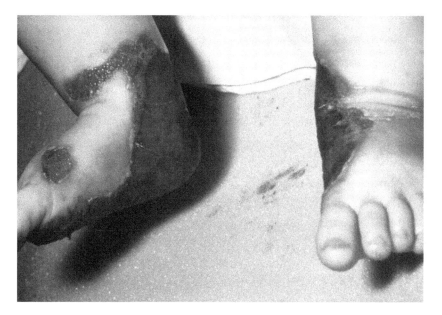

Fig 47 – Burns to the feet like this can only be non-accidental. The burns are mainly on the heels! This child was held in hot water for this burn to occur.

lamb would be kicked away violently. Farmers put such ewes in a fixed metal halter. In this the ewe can put her head down to drink and feed but can't move about. She can't turn her head to see, and smell, the lamb. So she can't recognise which one is suckling.

After a couple of weeks in this contraption we let her out, and by then she had accepted both lambs. Incidentally, her udders were always huge, indicating she had plenty of milk. Similarly, the victimised lamb is outwardly healthy. So insufficient milk for two lambs and an unhealthy lamb can both be ruled out as causes of this strange behaviour (battered lambs).

We are seeing in our society today a breakup of the family unit. Marriages for life are less common. Casual relationships are far more common. We know that where a man lives with children whom he knows (or even suspects) are not his, then like the male lion, he is more likely to abuse them (or do worse, like the lion!).

One form of torture involves sleep deprivation. Many young children subject parents to this torture. Some parents can take torture and some can't. Some mothers simply can't cope. The ewe could easily cope with one lamb, but not two she thought, hence her initial actions. Then she found she could cope with two lambs.

Abuse of children by their parents does run in families. Can some form of genetic engineering by manipulating amino acids on chromosomes remedy this? I don't know. All I do know is that child abuse is prevalent in all classes of our society today. This form of violence is taboo. Like the commoner activity of wife-beating (or even the rarer husband-beating), nobody wants to talk openly about it.

However, the perpetrators of these crimes come to health professionals with the evidence time and time again. Why so willingly and so frequently, I do not know. Are they subconsciously trying to be found out? I have studied casualty cards of young children's attendances to hospital going back years. All these particular children had suffered abuse only recently proven conclusively. Time and time again bruises and other injuries had been accepted previously with the strangest explanations. Gosh, we are gullible.

Incidentally, two of my children suffered long bone fractures when young – one sledging and one running backwards. Nobody was the slightest bit concerned. I expected a call, especially as one was less than two years old. None came! (It is thought that about 25% of children's long bone fractures under the age of two years are due to non-accidental injury.)

One last observation I make I find difficult to comprehend. It concerns some young ladies. They are particularly attracted to young men who then regularly beat them up. I have treated such injuries many times. So some ladies remain faithful to their aggressive boyfriends despite his repeated violent actions. They tell me that they will change him. By the time they find out that they can't, they often have a common bond of offspring.

"A leopard won't change its spots," I tell them. Like most young ladies they ignore the advice of an older man.

So will there always be a background of violence within families in our society? I expect so. Some of the violent traits are inherited and some acquired. To some extent we all need to be aware of this and all be on the lookout.

Domestic violence can be emotional or physical. Some poor children even suffer sexual abuse. Since I have retired there have been national studies on domestic violence and in particular non-accidental injuries to children. These reports show that domestic violence and non-accidental injuries to children are frequently undetected.

CHAPTER THIRTY-TWO

Medical Administration

My Experience of Hospital Administrators over the Years

We are the masters at the moment... and for a very long time to come.
Humpty-Dumpty, *Alice in Wonderland*, Lewis Carroll.

An obstetric consultant asked me in 1967, when I was working for him as a junior doctor, if I would like to do a caesarean section. He would assist me. I immediately agreed. It was my first (and last) Caesarean section. The patient was a West Indian lady aged 45, an elderly primip (first baby). She was hypertensive and past her expected date of delivery (term). Labour had not started. In view of the circumstances the consultant advised a caesarean section and the patient agreed. I performed the operation – all fingers and thumbs. The baby was fine. Mother and baby made a good recovery. The operation went well.

Several days later the patient was still hypertensive. She then had a stroke. She was transferred to the care of the physician on call. She made a partial recovery.

Some months later I had a telephone call from the hospital secretary. "Oh," he said, "just to let you know that that patient, Mrs X, is going to sue you for negligence. You must have done something during the operation. Anyway, she was fine before the operation and now has some paralysis. Unfortunately all of your medical colleagues cannot be found so they are just sueing you and, of course, the hospital. Just tell me that you agree negligence and I'll settle it today."

"No," I said, "but what about the other doctors?"

"Well," said the hospital secretary, "as you well know, the obstetrician in charge of her case died of a heart attack in your present hospital last week. Now, the obstetrician that assisted you has moved on and cannot recall the case. The physician who treated her took his secretary to a mobile X-ray screening. He had an X-ray too, as he was there. His routine chest X-ray showed a tumour that had spread from his thyroid gland. He has died too recently of this condition. The medical registrar has gone back to Africa."

"That leaves you, doctor. You have written all the notes and I can really read them. These things happen; perhaps a clot went into the lungs or even some air."

I repeated that I would not settle and referred the case to the Medical Defence Union. They acted on my behalf. The allegations of negligence were quickly withdrawn.

* * *

My second contact with a hospital administrator was bizarre.

It was 5pm and just getting dark. I had been on call continuously all weekend (81 hours from 8am Friday). I was a senior house officer in plastic surgery in 1973. I had treated many patients and in particular one severely burnt patient. Amongst many other things, I had to get up four-hourly to do blood tests – haemoglobin – and then act on the result, i.e., more intravenous fluids, a blood transfusion or different drugs.

I was shattered by 5pm Monday evening. I had had lots of other patients to attend to. As I opened my car door at dusk, a cardboard box prevented me from getting in. I lifted up the box and could just make out dozens and dozens of five-inch mayo scissors. They were sharp. I realised that I had parked outside the central sterile supply department. The instruments must have been left out. The department was in darkness. They had all gone home. Whilst I puzzled what to do, a man started to get into the next car.

"Excuse me," I said, "do you work here?"

"Yes," he said, "I am the hospital secretary."

"Oh good," I said. "These instruments are precious. They have been left out."

"Oh, I'll take charge of them," he said and he did and then drove off.

I later found I had left one pair of scissors out, as I had cut my nails to assess their sharpness. I presented them to my mother, a GP. She was delighted, and found many uses for them in the following months – removing stitches and dressings, etc.

Six months later I was about to leave the job. I was up most of the night with another patient, and was returning to my room at about 4am. There had been a noisy doctors' mess party. I had not been there. As I opened my room door a porter rushed up to me.

"Oh thank goodness," he said, "can you please help me?"

"Why, what is the matter?" I asked.

"Well," he said, "after the mess party there was a girl left behind. She is drunk, but not badly. She has lost her handbag, and cannot recall where she lives or who she is."

"Oh," I said. "Call the police."

"Well," he said, " she has done nothing wrong and is very well spoken. She does not want and does not deserve a police record. We have phoned the police and they are tied up with a fight near Putney Bridge."

"Well," I said, "phone an administrator; there is always one on call for the hospital."

"He cannot be found," he said. "We phoned and phoned. No reply."

"Oh," I said. (I just wanted to get to bed.) "Just put her in a room in the residency, making sure it is empty, and has no property in it."

"OK," he said.

I later learnt she had gone the next morning early. No property was missing. At lunchtime the same hospital secretary that I had met previously called me to his room urgently. He was furious with me and very, very aggressive.

"How dare you?" he kept on loudly shouting at me. "How dare you take it upon yourself to do such a thing? You should have had her locked up in the cells."

"But," I said, "she had done nothing wrong."

"Rubbish," he cried. "You were at fault. You interfered. You busybody.

You should have kept out of it. Don't ever, ever do such a stupid thing like that again… Now, get out," he said rudely.

"Oh, there is one thing," I said. "Do you recall me giving you a box of instruments outside CSSD some months ago?"

"Oh yes," he said, in a very off-hand manner, not even looking up. "They were surplus to requirements so we chucked them out."

* * *

Years later, I knew that everyday equipment, like hospital disposable gloves and some medicines, in hospitals throughout the UK often goes out of date. It is all disposed of. My daughter, as a final year vet student in 2008, wanted to go with other vets to Romania, to sterilise stray dogs and cats humanely. Devoid of finance they wanted gloves and medicines just out of date. The head of pharmacy at our hospital agreed. The hospital board disagreed because:

1. These things may get into the human treatment chain, and so the board could be sued.
2. The owners of the animals could sue the board. (The animals were all strays!)
3. The dogs could get adverse reactions from drugs just out of date. So I failed to provide them with any equipment!

* * *

Instrument packs are made up for suturing casualties in an emergency department. These cost us, the taxpayer, plenty of money. The instruments are disposed of after – thrown away! So they are only used once. What a waste! I have re-sterilised these instruments many times, so they are of good quality. I am responsible for smuggling hundreds of such instruments, which would otherwise have been destroyed, out of the hospital, and they have found their way to Africa, where they are very well received!

* * *

Some years ago in 1977, a lady doctor was driving a car. Her car was stationary at some traffic lights. From her left she saw a car back out of a house beside the traffic lights. The car backed on and on and on. She hooted her horn. The bumper of this car collided with the side of the doctor's car. The offending car was undamaged. The doctor's car was dented.

A very tearful lady driver got out of the other car. Names and addresses were exchanged. "I will tell you my insurance company if you phone," the upset lady said. She admitted full liability.

One week later, despite several telephone calls, the insurance company name had not been told to the lady doctor. Our insurance company said we might have to foot the bill if the other party withheld the information. The lady doctor found out that the insurance company details were known only to the other lady's husband. He was the 'nursing superintendent' at the hospital where this doctor worked. He was known to be a very busy and important man.

I am that lady doctor's husband and worked at that hospital too. I put on my white coat and went to see this man, the next lunchtime. His secretary refused to let me see him unless I had an appointment, and so I told her my business. I insisted on seeing him, and got to. He was disinterested, but would talk to his wife and let us have all the details that evening. He did just that. Was she too frightened about the accident to tell her busy husband?

* * *

My wife and I were living in a hospital Portakabin in 1977. My wife's job was resident, but mine was not. My wife's job contract came to an end. We expected to stay on a few days, at least, as I still worked there full-time. I was abroad on study leave when my wife worked her last day. She was then told to move the next day. She asked to stay a few more days. The administrators refused.

"You might need me for that locum," she said.

"No, we definitely will not," said the administrator in Human Resources, "and we have new doctors to move in today."

My wife found alternative accommodation and moved all our property that day. About a month later I got the final bill for electricity used the month before – up to our leaving. It was over £2,000. This was absolutely monstrous, and I thought quite impossible. *This is going to be difficult to prove as the new people have obviously moved in*, I thought. I went back to our old abode. It was deserted, and everything was just as we had left it. The meter reading had been misread. We owed a small amount. It was such a relief.

Incidentally, my wife was subsequently asked if she would do that full-time resident medical locum the night before it started! Well, that's called health service planning!

* * *

I answered a telephone call in 1976 from a neurosurgeon. "Please help," he said. "I'm stuck in theatre. I've just accepted two head injury patients, father and son, both deeply unconscious from an RTA – they drove into a stationary vehicle. Could you check them over when they arrive and transfer them to ICU? Oh, and please tell A&E and ICU about them – here are all the details. Thanks a lot. I'll see them later, on ICU. Bye."

I promptly telephoned ICU and spoke to the consultant anaesthetist in charge – a close friend.

"Look, Alistair," he said, "they both should be on ICU, but I can't, I just can't."

"Why not?" I queried.

"Oh," he replied, "we have six patients on ICU already. After my appointment five months ago the chairman of the Regional Health Authority collared me. He told me straight that if ever I exceeded six beds on our ICU, then he would personally sack me! I forbid it," he repeated. "You don't need them."

"But," I exploded, "we have the regional neurosurgical and cardiothoracic centres."

"Yes, I know," he replied. "But I need a job. My wife and kids need to be supported."

"Well," I replied, "can I help by giving you all the patients' details?"

"No, it won't help at all," he retorted.

I replied, "I think it will," and so I did.

Silence followed.

"Not, not, the Mr So-and-so," he replied.

"Yes," I answered. "The chairman of the Regional Health Board, and his son!"

More silence.

"Well, if it's for him, we have no alternative," he answered.

So two more beds were put up on ICU. These two patients slowly improved. Eventually father and son were discharged, but the father never worked again.

There was no retaliation for the two extra beds. Sometime later a bigger ICU was built.

* * *

Years later in 1980, as a consultant, I held a teaching session for the juniors. To cover the work for that time, when I was teaching, we had a general practitioner who did a clinical session in the emergency department. He then retired. We advertised and nobody applied to fill that post for weeks. Sometime later a GP telephoned me. She had applied for this job weeks and weeks ago.

"Nobody has acknowledged my application. I've heard nothing," she said.

I went to the administrator in question, who denied all knowledge of the application. Then she just opened a drawer in front of her.

"Oh, here it is," she said. "Isn't that lucky?"

The GP got the job. No apology was given.

* * *

This is nothing really. My wife worked as a doctor in a hospital for ten years before she even had a contract of employment.

* * *

There was a car parked in the senior staff car park, late on a Saturday night with no hospital pass. The car was clamped by security.

The new chief executive of the hospital was catching up on paperwork prior to the commencement of his appointment starting on the following Monday morning.

Oh dear, he was clamped.

Red-faced security men removed the clamp.

The clamping fee was waived for the chief executive!

* * *

In the UK, besuited hospital administrators have the temerity to invade the operating theatre bearing their clipboards. In Accra, the capital of Ghana, they have a remedy for this: on the operating theatre door there reads this sign:

WARNING: IF YOU MAKE A
MISTAKE AND GO BEYOND
THIS DOOR WITHOUT:
The Proper Clothes
The Proper Shoes
Or Permission
You will be forcibly subjected
to a free operation (without
anaesthetic) on the delicate
parts of your anatomy, etc.
You will certainly regret
the result.[1]

Reference:

1.   Anonymous. Mr Slop Abroad. *Ann R Coll Surg Engl* (Supp 1) 2010:92;365.

Flagrant Financial Fiddling or Confused Communication

Money is the root of all evil.

A song

Newspapers and television for a few months in 2011 have been full of the Parliamentary expenses scandal. Members of the House of Commons and the Lords have had their written expense returns scrutinised properly, for once. They are all public servants. This exercise was not cheap, or quick either! Initially no members were suspended. All members were given time to respond. Once all the evidence was viewed, many members had to repay money. Four members have been accused of false accounting. Very large sums of money are involved and they have been taken to court.

> *Let the punishment fit the crime.*
> *The Mikado.* Gilbert and Sullivan

We doctors working in the health service are also public servants. One lunchtime, a neurosurgeon, Mr Terry Hope, recalled paying for a bowl of soup and also paying for a few croutons. He was distracted at the time as his bleep went off. As he paid, he complained about his miserable quantity of croutons. He said he would return for more croutons. He put down his tray with his soup on it. After a telephone call related to his work he returned to his soup and added a few more croutons. He carried on working normally for that day, and for several days afterwards.

> *"Curiouser and curiouser," said Alice.*
> Lewis Carroll

Some weeks after this episode in the hospital canteen he received a telephone call from his secretary on 22nd March 2004: "Oh, I'm sorry to tell you this, Mr Hope, but you are suspended. You therefore can't go and do your clinic this afternoon at the Derbyshire Royal Infirmary. I will send your registrar on his own."

Confused, he went to see the chief executive of the hospital. He was his employing authority, and was in charge of the hospital. He could do nothing, and redirected the surgeon to a hotel (catering) manager.

This manager accused the surgeon of probity and of stealing croutons. The surgeon was given a video. In many hours of video there was a short snippet of video showing the surgeon paying for his soup and croutons. He did add a few more croutons later.

The catering firm were outside contractors working within the hospital to provide a service. Hence, the chief executive could not do anything! At that time, the firm's profits were soaring!

This all happened quickly. Nothing was in writing to be pored over later. The total value of the croutons – one or two helpings – was less than £1.

> *Some men are born great... and some have greatness thrust upon them.*
>
> Shakespeare, *Twelfth Night*

The surgeon was told by the hospital (catering) manager not to contact the press. He did not – but a colleague did!

This whole episode hit the front pages of newspapers. The surgeon was forced to give an impromptu interview for the BBC and ITN News reporters from his garden! Anxious patients waiting to receive major brain surgery from this surgeon were interviewed on television.

> *Confusion now hath made his masterpiece!*
>
> Shakespeare, *Macbeth*

Well, this is a classic 'storm in a teacup'. The surgeon was subsequently reinstated as a consultant, and returned to operating. What was this all about?

The surgeon was never charged with any offence. He still says that he paid for the croutons; the tape he was given confirmed it. The surgeon has not had an apology as yet, although this whole scenario was acutely embarrassing for him.

Perhaps some background information from a personal communication will help.

> *'Tis strange – but true; for truth is always strange; stranger than fiction'.*
>
> Byron, *Don Juan*

As doctors we are all taught to be observant. That is how we are trained. This surgeon was no exception. Also, as a surgeon, he naturally had an obsession with cleanliness. He had to scrub up regularly and he saw to it that all staff did so properly. This is second nature to any surgeon. He also had contact with the catering staff. He knew that as they were in contact with food, their conduct must be exemplary. He observed that they were not following ideal hygiene rules. So he had written to the catering bosses and pointed this out. He had complained to the same hotel manager who had later accused him of probity! So was he then a 'marked man'? If not, then why was he watched so carefully? Did the catering department want to get its own back? (Tit for tat.) We can only guess.

'Ay, now the plot thickens very much upon us.'
The Rehearsal, George Villiers

This story does not quite end here. As intimated above, 'the plot thickens'. I am indebted to the Freedom of Information Act. This showed that some time later, 12 people were interviewed at a meeting of staff from that hospital to discuss this episode in retrospect. Catering staff were called. The surgeon was not! To do this thing properly, two external administrative staff were drafted. Naturally, these were experienced top-class experts, and so they were paid top-class fees. Their eventual findings were that the catering bosses needed 'media training'. The cost of this exercise was modest – hardly anything at all – just under £30,000.

Well, with the catering firm's profits soaring they could easily afford this.

A fool and his money are soon parted.
Often misquoted. William Shenstone

Mr Hope has since retired from the NHS. He still teaches medical students. He himself has personally set up a neurosurgical unit in Nepal. He still pays his own expenses to go there annually to operate. In Nepal he is known as a professor. It is amazing to realise that in the 21st century this episode came about in a moment of confusion. The victim was a generous British surgeon with an international reputation.

The mere fact that he has committed a lifetime of service to our NHS counted for nothing. Today patriotic service is totally ignored, and the aura once held for a senior surgeon has been lost forever. On hospital property there was a financial dispute for less than £1. Penalty: immediate suspension and public ignominy.

Abraham Lincoln told us, quite rightly, that 'all men are created equal', but are they treated equally? In our modern society we are proud of the

British 'sense of fair play'. This should apply to public servants too. In my humble opinion the Parliamentarians were treated to a generous dose of fair play. This poor surgeon was not!

The truth is often stranger than fiction.

A fact

If they ever make a film of this, then Professor Hope may be free to star as himself. This catering firm had a guaranteed clientele – inpatients, staff and visitors. All unused, cooked food is thrown out after a meal. So there is always some considerable wastage!

I cannot mention the name of the catering firm – for legal reasons!

My Experience of an Appraisal Interview

As a casualty consultant I supervised my junior staff. They had regular teaching sessions. If there was a mistake – a missed fracture on an X-ray, or a patient sent home in error, then I would be the first to know.

One doctor started to perform badly in 1982. I was picking up her mistakes – quite a few of them. I got feedback from the nursing staff and other doctors about her – all bad. She and I were both tired at 6pm on a Friday evening. She was off for the weekend when I met up with her. I was not. We had a particularly unsatisfactory meeting where I outlined some of her mistakes and asked for explanations.

She was confused and said she had a lot of problems. One minute she talked about her husband. Then she mentioned a fiancé. I myself was confused. To have both at the same time seemed greedy. This tension gave her headaches. She had difficulty concentrating. I told her that she could see no more patients until this whole episode had been investigated.

This doctor was training to be a general practitioner. I contacted the GP course organiser who told me that he had just had a report from this doctor's previous attachment – not a good one. What was going on?

Then events took a strange turn. My trainee doctor came in as a patient that very weekend. Her headaches had got worse and her eyesight was upset. Tests of her visual fields confirmed that something was obstructing her vision. A head scan showed a tumour in the pituitary gland that had pressed on her optic nerve, causing eye problems and headaches.

This tumour was in no way malignant and responded to treatment. She made a good recovery. Her eyesight recovered, as did her headaches.

Best of all, she became a very good doctor again. No more problems. The last thing I heard was that she just had a husband (and no fiancé!).

CHAPTER THIRTY-THREE

My Experience of
Interviews for Jobs

Words are the most powerful drug used by mankind.
Rudyard Kipling

I had to shortlist candidates in 1998 for a medical post in our department – a locum middle-grade doctor. I was the only consultant around and was extremely busy. Shortlisting, however, could not wait. The only time I was free to do the shortlisting was lunchtime – usually ten minutes or so with a sandwich. Jackie brought in the bundle. I groaned. Over two hundred doctors had sent in applications. I had to look at each one and give a good reason for not shortlisting them – usually lack of necessary experience. I ploughed through them quite quickly. Most were excellent – this was not going to be easy. Then one outstanding application caught my eye. I stopped. It was outstandingly dreadful. No experience. No substantive appointments. No full registration; so if I appointed him it would have been illegal for him to work in this job.

I showed his application to my colleague who said, "You're not going to give him the job, are you?"

But what was it that was strange? Yes, that's it, this fine paper it is typed on. I puzzled for a second and then held it up to the light.

I read the watermark 'BRONCO'.

I did not keep this fine paper, but used it for the purpose for which it was originally intended.

* * *

I have read countless CVs, mostly containing truths but in amongst them were some untruths. Years ago it was the custom to bring along to an interview a copy of any medical article you had published. This should still be the case as a few doctors have boosted their chances of a job by introducing spurious articles into their CVs. Some of them even tried to fool the GMC before being struck off.[1]

Occasionally, candidates have scuppered their chances of a job by stupid remarks. For example, one locum casualty consultant had done well. He was going to get the permanent appointment,, when he was asked what percentage of patients in the department he himself personally saw. He said he saw them all – 100%, day and night. Well, even if he was always in the department, that was completely impossible. We questioned him further – he continued to repeat the impossible.

He did not get the job!

* * *

We fail to realise how interviews can change our whole lives. For example:

Anne was a qualified physiotherapist who had been going out with Chris, a medical student, for 18 months. Then in 1973 Chris qualified as a doctor and applied for a job. He was shortlisted for a job in Shrewsbury, and Anne drove him there.

Two hours later he returned to her car.

"How did you get on?" she asked.

"Oh, I got the job," he said.

"Well done," she said; "that's sorted then."

"Oh," he said, "there is a slight problem."

"What's that?" she said.

"Well, this job is compulsory for me to be resident," he said. "But they don't have any single accommodation, just married."

"Oh," she said.

"Err… yes," he said.

They sorted out this problem together. They got married!

They lived happily ever after. Although several years later Anne did go off one cold and dreary winter with 20 fit young men to the sun in the Southern Hemisphere. Chris, meanwhile, was very understanding. He stayed behind, looking after their children and working as a GP. Well, the England Cricket Team clearly needed a sport's physio of Anne's calibre.

Chris did join Anne for a holiday in New Zealand at the end of the cricket tour.

* * *

I had a phone call from John in 1985. He had been a single-handed casualty consultant for years and years. Nobody had come to work as a consultant with him. He was on call all the time as a result, day and night, week in and week out!

"Somebody has applied to join me as a consultant," he said excitedly. "She is excellent. Trained in Scotland. Please come to the appointment. You are free on 3rd July, I hope. Will you represent the college?"

"Yes," I agreed, "send me all the information."

The big day came and I set off.

"She is a really good candidate," John told me over coffee beforehand.

"She has met everybody, and we are delighted. She has done the rounds of relevant people for at least the second time. Several people told me that she is charming – a perfect candidate."

"Oh good," I said.

The interview started. I was an external, a college representative. We had a lay representative, university ones, local ones, specialty ones, the medical director, the chief nursing officer, a general surgeon and even the chief executive. We asked questions in turn, me last.

The candidate had a rather boring CV. She had done nothing interesting or different. I was puzzled – why so very bland and so uninteresting? She had spent rather a long time as a registrar in training. I was sitting at the end of the table close to her. I was by far the closest member of the committee to the candidate. It was hot. I would speak last.

Over an hour later we had had a lot of useless questions. We had had all the usual ones. There was nothing revealing about the candidate, one way or another. We really wanted to know if she was up to the job (or not). Then I smelt a funny smell, and thought it was her perfume. As she turned towards me to answer questions from my neighbour, I realised it was alcohol. The candidate must have been drinking earlier, at lunchtime! This had been her only opportunity as she had been alone for a while! What could I do?

My nose could detect alcohol. I was horrified. Poor John, I thought. If this candidate gets the job, is she an alcoholic? Better no colleague than one that drinks! I am barred from asking questions about their state of health. Similarly, and quite rightly, questions like, "Are you thinking of starting a family?" or "Are you thinking of going into private practice?" are also not allowed. What could I do? The chairman, a lay person, turned to me and invited me to ask questions.

"Err, you have spent a long time in training. Was that really necessary?" I asked.

"Oh yes," she replied. "I wanted to make sure I had sufficient experience in all the specialities relevant to our own." And then she gave me a long list I know well.

"But," I said, "other registrars complete their training in a much shorter time." She did not reply. I tried a different tack.

"Tell me," I said, "if you were appointed to this post would you offer treatment to everybody that presented to the casualty department?"

"Oh yes," she replied, "everybody."

"Well," I said, "what about alcoholics? Would you always treat them?"

"Yes," she said, not so confident now.

Out of the corner of my eye I saw one of my colleagues, the university representative, raise an eyebrow at me – just one. This close friend also gave me a 'funny look'.

"Well," I said, "what is the long-term prognosis for a chronic alcoholic today? Is it good or bad?"

"Bad," she stammered.

"No more questions," I said.

The lady withdrew whilst we deliberated. She was the only applicant. There was nobody else to interview. I felt under some pressure to appoint. The chairman commented that I had been very searching and close to the mark in my questioning.

"I can now reveal to you, as instructed by the General Medical Council, that this lady was struck off the register because of alcoholism, whilst a registrar. She received treatment as an inpatient and is now totally cured. She has been reinstated onto the medical register."

I pointed out that she smelt of alcohol and was not cured. I alone spoke against her appointment. She was not appointed. John was devastated, but profuse in his thanks. We were still good friends, thank goodness.

John subsequently got three more consultant colleagues – none alcoholics. He then retired, and rides his horses daily.

* * *

Examinations and tests are essential in all walks of life, e.g., the driving test. I read in *The Times* recently of two men who had tried to cheat in the driving test – one had impersonated the other. They went to prison!

* * *

This newspaper story reminded me of one of my junior doctors. This happened soon after I was appointed as a casualty consultant. He was very confident. He hoped to become a neurosurgeon and I asked him to give a talk to his medical colleagues on the causes of unconsciousness. At the end I asked him to clarify three of the causes.

"How does measles cause unconsciousness?" I asked. He failed to answer. "Encephalitis is rare but possible," I said. Then I said he had mentioned Marfan's syndrome – "What is it?" He had no idea. (Such people are tall, not short as he had suggested!). Finally, he had mentioned tabes dorsalis as a cause of unconsciousness.

"How does that work?" I said.

"Well," he started, "in tabes dorsalis you get…"

I interrupted. "As an examiner I don't suffer with syphilis."

They all laughed. He was deflated, but still so confident of passing the primary FRCS the following week. He had no chance at all, I thought. Of this I was certain. So this doctor had plenty of confidence – far too much. But on testing basic knowledge he failed easily.

I was a single-handed emergency consultant on call all the time in 1978. I was down to three juniors. The rest were off taking the primary

FRCS examination in Scotland, including this doctor. At 10.45pm on a Sunday evening I had just got home and was off to bed. The phone rang. The same confident doctor (in the paragraph above) was telephoning from Shannon Airport.

"I passed," he said. I was in emotional shock. "I'm off back to Canada tonight, sir."

"Oh no you are not," I said. "You are contracted to work for three more months."

"No, I don't need your reference, sir. I am off back home. Thank you, sir, and goodbye." He was gone. My blood pressure was raised.

I telephoned the surgical college of Edinburgh the next morning. It is one of my colleges, and the examination secretary was a softly spoken Scot.

"Oh, he passed all right," was his reply. "In fact his marks throughout were very, very good indeed. He was right at the top."

I was dumbfounded. What had happened?

"Oh yes, that's him," came the reply. "If only we had known, we could have caught him red-handed."

"Who?" I asked.

"Oh, the imposter," he said. "He sits the exam for others and gets them through. We know he charges £1,500 a time but we can't catch him."

So this travesty of justice had been revealed to me by the examination secretary. I knew my doctor could not have passed. He did not know even the basics. This examination had a low pass rate. For him to get good marks was impossible. I was very angry. We commiserated with each other.

Ever since then the candidates have had to produce their passports during the examination.[1]

* * *

Unfortunately, cheating in examinations is still rife in the United Kingdom. Data obtained from 61 British universities under the Freedom of Information Act shows that nurses are the most likely to cheat. Websites based abroad boast of employing retired professors to write nursing essays for a fee. Such coursework becomes difficult to detect with plagiarism software. The University of Dundee disciplined 179 students for cheating between 2010 and 2013. So, 155 student nurses were caught, but only 17 medical students and seven trainee lawyers. What happens to these cheats? Are we too soft? Well, Edinburgh Napier University caught 300 nursing students cheating. Less than five of them were referred for investigation by the 'fitness to practice' panels.[2]

Yes, I think we are far too soft. I would have thrown them all off their course.[2]

* * *

A British ophthalmologist in the United States was a pillar of society. He was an associate professor with a PhD who had risen to head a US laboratory that was pioneering stem cell research. He was found guilty of fabricating the results of a non-existent pilot experiment to obtain two federal grants. He admitted the offence and resigned.[3]

Two Argentinian doctors were fined the maximum during a GlaxoSmithKline trial for irregularities during patient selection and consent. (There were also 14 deaths!)[4]

Steven Eaton, 47, was jailed on 17th April 2013 for faking research data for a possible anti-cancer drug. He was sentenced at Edinburgh Sheriff Court to three months for falsifying test results. The clear evidence presented to the court confirmed that this crime had been going on for years![5]

It has got worse for GlaxoSmithKline! This company has admitted that its senior executives in China broke the law. They were guilty of bribery to promote the sale of drugs! Police say that the bribes totalled £323 million![6]

This follows previous identical problems! To date, GlaxoSmithKline has been fined £3 billion for illegal promotion of prescription drugs and other breaches.[7]

Is there a cure for corporate crime in the drug industry?[8]

The whole question of drugs gets more and more complicated and more sinister still. All over the globe, substandard and falsified drugs abound. This has resulted in many adverse reactions and some deaths. Urgent international action is needed to combat these criminals. There has been no agreed global treaty as yet![9]

In the 21st century we are all too aware that fabrication, fraud and falsification abounds. If we buy a car component on eBay or a drug on the net, we can find that the former is defective and the latter is a poison. Plagiarism is rife, e.g., in speeches, university applications and even theses!

Scientific research is not immune. Reputations lie in tatters after the disclosure of fraud, and the pertinent papers are ignominiously withdrawn. Eminent doctors have been struck off the medical register. Authors have been fined and even imprisoned.

* * *

Surprisingly, cheating when presenting scientific papers is not new! As long ago as 1830 a British mathematician, Charles Babbage, wrote 'Reflections on the Decline of Science in England'. He coined the phrase 'Hoaxing and Forging' when data was simply made up. He noted that if data did not fit in, it would be 'Trimmed out'.

He even found that some data was made to appear vital or important, when it was not. He called that 'Cooking'.

References:

1. *General Medical Council Newsletter*. December 2008. Medical students' professional values and fitness to practise.

2. Alex Mostrous and Billy Kenber. Thousands of Nurses Cheat in Exams. *The Times*. 19.07.16:4.

3. C Dyer. British doctor fabricated the results of a non-existent experiment, US body finds. BMJ (28.4.12):344;3.

4. A Rada. GSK and 2 doctors are fined malpractice during vaccine trial. *BMJ* 2012:344:e449.

5. Home Staff. Scientist who faked anti-cancer drugs data goes to prison. *The Times*. 18.4.13:19.

6. Emily Ford. Glaxo admits it broke law in bribery scandal. *The Times*. 23.7.13:42.

7. Andrew Jack. Another Fine Mess. *BMJ* 28.7.12;345:20.

8. C Davis and J Abraham. Is there a Cure for Corporate Crime in the Drug Industry? *BMJ* 2013;346:f755.

9. Amir Attavan et al. How to Achieve International Action on Falsified and Substandard Medicines. *BMJ* 24.11.12;345:23-26.

CHAPTER THIRTY-FOUR

The Birth of our National Health Service

Aneurin Bevan was our Health Minister in 1946. He believed that the Second World War had given Britain the opportunity to create a 'new society'. By this he meant a National Health Service in a welfare state. In the 1946 NHS Act, 2,688 voluntary and municipal hospitals in England and Wales were nationalised, and came under his supervisory control. There was some medical opposition which he overcame by 'stuffing the doctors' mouths with gold'. The crux of the NHS Act was 'free medical care for all Britons'. Mr Bevan wrote: 'A free health service is pure socialism and as such is opposed to the hedonism of a capitalist society.'[1]

The National Health Service started on 5th July 1948. Everybody who worked in these hospitals was employed directly by the state. Many hospitals were specialised – the chest hospitals, which treated mainly tuberculosis, and the mental health hospitals, with huge numbers of long-term patients. Each hospital had a hospital management board – top heavy with consultants. There was a hospital secretary who ran the hospital day to day and was answerable to the board. There were district

WESTMINSTER HOSPITAL

INCORPORATING
Queen Mary's Hospital Roehampton
Westminster Children's Hospital SW1
The Gordon Hospital SW1
All Saints' Hospital SE11

PATRON
Her Majesty The Queen

CHAIRMAN
The Rt Hon Sir John Vaughan-Morgan Bt MP

HOUSE GOVERNOR AND SECRETARY
R P MacMahon MA FHA

Telephone PUTNEY 7211

From QUEEN MARY'S HOSPITAL ROEHAMPTON LONDON SW15

LDC/MJB

13th December, 1965.

Dear Dr. Fraser-Moodie,

I am pleased to be able to confirm your appointment as House Officer in Orthopaedics at this Hospital from 1st December. This letter, which complies with the CONTRACTS OF EMPLOYMENT ACT, 1963, is to explain to you the terms and conditions of your appointment to the Hospital.

Your basic salary will be £770 per annum, (with a deduction for Residential Charge at the rate of £175 per annum) and you will be paid monthly. You are entitled to the annual leave with pay in accordance with the Medical and Dental Whitley Council Regulations, in addition to the usual statutory and National holidays. You are also entitled to certain sickness benefits which will depend on the length of your employment in the health service.

This appointment is superannuable and unless, within 13 weeks of starting your employment you are notified otherwise, you will be subject to the NATIONAL HEALTH SUPERANNUATION SCHEME. Copies of the current regulations governing this scheme, and an explanatory booklet, may be seen in the Finance Department.

All rates of pay and conditions of service will be as laid down by Whitley Councils in various memoranda: up to date copies of these are kept in the Finance Department for you to examine if you wish. New circulars affecting your salary and conditions of service will be received from the Whitley Council from time to time and will be available for you to see.

This appointment is subject to you being currently registered as a Medical Practitioner and also to your being a member of a Medical Defence Union.

The Board reserve the right to require any member of the staff to be medically examined.

I advise you to obtain smallpox vaccination from your general practitioner as a precaution against risks of infection.

Will you please sign and return to me the attached copy of this letter.

Yours sincerely,

Dr. A. Fraser-Moodie,
Dept., of Orthopaedics,
Queen Mary's Hospital.

SECRETARY TO THE BOARD.

Fig 48 – My first contract.

administrators, and above them regional administrators. The health minister was in overall charge in the Ministry of Health.

My first contract of employment in 1965 was signed by the hospital secretary (fig 48). In 1978 when I became a consultant the appointment committee could not offer me the job! Oh no, that committee could only recommend me for the post! Subsequently, at region a few days later, the regional medical officer confirmed my appointment. He could have opposed my appointment, and the appointment's process would have begun all over again – advertising the job, shortlisting of applicants and finally the convening of a committee to recommend a candidate for appointment!

In 1948, hospitals had many different departments that functioned together. The catering department fed staff and patients. The doctors, and even the sisters, had their own dining room – served by waitresses. The portering department was exclusively male. The busy telephone exchange tried to communicate to everybody. All calls were through switchboard and they all were free of charge – personal and work. But what if a doctor could not be found? In practically all hospitals initially there was a complicated system of flashing coloured lights positioned in corridors. If these flashed in one particular pattern then a doctor knew that switchboard wanted him/her urgently.

On 1st March 1978 I was appointed a casualty consultant in the accident and emergency department of the Derbyshire Royal Infirmary. The sister in charge told me to contact the sewing room, which I did. I expected that this sewing room was a 'quiet backwater' of just two or three ladies quietly sewing. I was not prepared for what I found.

On opening the door of the sewing room, the noise was deafening. In a large room, 20 'middle-aged' ladies each sat at a desk. Every desk had a sewing machine. As they chattered away they worked. There was material all over the desks, as well as under and around them.

The supervisor greeted me. She measured my height and arm length. She would make up four white coats and send them to my office. I thanked her and she briefly showed me round. Close by, a lady was turning over the end of a blanket – with blanket stitch of course. Another lady was stitching up a hole in a sheet. Her neighbour was making a pillow case.

Two ladies behind her were making up curtains. At the back, two more ladies were busy with bundles of nursing uniforms. I marvelled at this hive of activity. They all chattered to their neighbour as they worked. There were piles and piles of work to be done, and yet more work in progress. It seemed like organised chaos. I thanked the supervisor and beat a hasty retreat.

A few days later via the internal post, I received a parcel wrapped in brown paper and bound with string. It contained four white coats. They fitted perfectly and looked great. My name and department were stitched in red on the inside of the collar. So they were all mine and mine alone!

A few days later my white coat needed washing. I put it carefully in the department laundry basket and waited in anticipation. A few days later, my was coat returned to me – as clean as ever! Starched and ironed it looked as good as new. The hospital laundry had done a great job and continued to do so for many years afterwards.

Unfortunately, subsequently, three of my white coats got ruined. Two were permanently blood-stained – the laundry failed to get these marks out. A third coat was torn to shreds by a violent drunk. I returned to the sewing room. Had I been given my 'quota of white coats for life'? "Oh no, doctor," was the superintendent's reply. Her hive of activity was busier than ever. Three brand new white coats came my way. What efficiency! What kindness! What a great service!

The Central Sterile Supply Department (CSSD) sterilised instruments on site. A works department looked after the buildings. A stores department kept everybody supplied. A pharmacy was invariably small, and a doctor's prescription was rarely queried. The dispenser supplied all drugs free of charge. Out of hours, we doctors could get the keys of the pharmacy and help ourselves to any drugs at all for the benefit of our patients!

A few cleaners worked in offices and corridors under the direction of matron. The nurses themselves did the majority of the cleaning in the wards, operating theatres and outpatients. The student nurses' home was exclusively female and locked up at night. The nursing sisters' home was open all hours (personal experience), as was the doctors' residency. There were radiology, biochemistry and haematology departments – all small and understaffed.

The wards themselves were Nightingale in design in my teaching hospital (St Thomas'). Sister sat at her desk in the centre of the ward. She could see every bed from there. Screens could be pulled around the bed for the doctor's rounds. When I did my medical job in Barnet General Hospital we were relegated to Nissen huts for the wards.

The general practitioners often worked from home – as did my mother. Many practitioners had higher qualifications, e.g., MRCP or FRCS. Often they had hospital beds of their own. Some were on call for other GPs for admissions to their beds. Many general practitioners were on the obstetrics list and did home deliveries with a midwife, as did my mother. Junior doctors went straight from a hospital post to become a general practitioner. Several of my friends in general practice offered me partnerships – usually in the golf club bar after a round a golf. I refused them all.

> *"But you are selling off the family silver."*
> Sir Harold MacMillan's criticism of party policy

Soon after 1948, our National Health Service – free at the point of delivery – began to unravel, and unfortunately this continues to this very day.

The opticians had given out free NHS glasses initially and free eye tests too. This changed in 1951. Well, eye tests are all charged for now (unless there is a family history of glaucoma!). Glasses are big business, and in the high street this business is booming.

Completely free NHS dental treatment is a thing of the past today. This too changed in 1951. Even NHS dental patients today pay for their check-ups and treatments. Many dentists only take on private patients.

It is good that we have so many excellent hospitals all built since 1946. However, many are PFIs and as such technically don't belong to the NHS – well, we are still paying for them. So to my mind these hospitals belong to the big business that built them for us and that has cashed in to its advantage.

These hospitals today are run by a chief executive. These hospitals have a management board containing several non-executive (paid) directors. The medical presence on such a committee is usually only one doctor – the medical director. The district administrators have long gone. Regional administrators still exist but have little power. Foundation trust hospitals are funded directly by the government and appoint their own consultants independently. The hospitals are all computerised. Hospital administrators flourish. Hospitals are big business. The finance department is large. There is a litigation department and a hospital lawyer. Security and fire safety are major concerns – how times have changed.

Within the hospital, things have changed a lot. Yes, there is still a catering department. Everything looks just the same, but it is not. The catering is usually run by outside contractors. These firms use the same original hospital staff but put in their own managers. Profits from this enterprise go directly to the catering firm and not the NHS! Things are done differently now. According to Dr Saliha Ahmed, the NHS is buying cheap, pre –made food that they don't have to cook. This food is heated up in the microwave as there are no chefs anymore! Well, she is a registrar in hospital medicine and the BBC MasterChef winner of 2017. Times have changed. For example, sandwiches are made on site each day, are they not? Oh no, a lorry brings them each day from miles and miles away. This lorry goes from hospital to hospital. Many things are a lot different now.

Porters are of both sexes today. They are assisted by an army of volunteers. This help, I believe, will be temporary and not permanent. I can't see the next generation assisting unpaid in this manner

The sewing room closed 20 years ago, probably a casualty of some senior administrator's Cost Improvement Programme. Let me explain. Annually, hospitals are directed to make savings. This is called the Cost Improvement Programme. This is a complete misnomer and the name is laughable. Well, practically the only way to implement this CIP is to sack hospital staff. About 80% of the cost of the NHS is the wage bill. So these 20, or so, ladies in the sewing room, all not far from retirement, had been sacked en masse! The cost of the hardship to families, the redundancy payments, the increased income support and perhaps the dole money was totally ignored. All that mattered was that the health minister could stand up annually in Parliament and say that a successful Cost Improvement Programme in the NHS had saved so many million pounds annually. It mattered nothing that the permanent damage to the hospitals, people's lives and the state financially had been huge. An outside company supplied a lot more new blankets, curtains, sheets and uniforms. They continue to do so to this day. What a great cost saving, I don't think.

I soon learnt of another CIP: the hospital laundry was shut – more efficiency and cost-saving excuses (circa 1990). I suspected that this was simply another casualty of the CIP. But by now (1990) all my white coats were filthy. So I tentatively put one 'white' coat in the department laundry basket to test the new external laundry service. A week later I had not received my coat. After two weeks, still no coat. I discussed the matter with the sister in charge. "Oh, the new system is hopeless," she replied. Her prognosis for my coat was very bad indeed. I made inquiry after inquiry on the telephone. After one month I talked to the laundry supervisor from the firm that had the laundry contract. She told me straight, "If you HAD put your white coat in the laundry, then you WOULD have had it back by now!" She then inferred that I was trying to get a new white coat from them under false pretences. There was no way that she would supply me with one. End of conversation. (RIP my white coat.)

By now all my white coats were no longer white. I personally took them home and washed them in our washing machine. I then ironed them. The results were never as good as those from the old hospital laundry.

My junior doctors were required to wear white coats at work, but they could not get any. They had to beg, borrow or steal them. They then all took them home to wash. Nobody trusted the laundry.

I am not surprised that white coats for doctors were banned, because commensal bacterial organisms were grown on them. Now, if the old hospital laundry was still there, the coats would have remained sterile and safe. To my mind, CIP stands for the Cause for Increased Problems and resulted in the RIP of so many excellent departments! The fact that the two Departments of Health dress code guidelines in 2007 forced doctors to abandon their white coats is not completely backed up by scientific evidence. The first guideline, TVU1, stated that 'the hypothesis that uniforms/clothing could be a vehicle for the transmission of infections is not supported by the existing evidence'. Then the second TVU2 found 'no good evidence to suggest uniforms are a significant risk'. So why was the white coat abandoned, along with ties, watches and shirt cuffs?[2]

I am not alone in my criticism of the hospital doctor's appearance today.

Dr Campbell wrote that 'the lengths of a smart appearance (for a doctor) far outweigh the miniscule and theoretical risk that a tie would play in spreading infection'.[3]

The scruffy appearance of us doctors with no ties has not gone unnoticed![4]

Similarly, the implication of ties as a transmitter of pathogens (a fomite) lacks evidence as reported by a microbiologist![4]

Similarly, the wearing of long-sleeved white coats does not expose patients to an increased risk of cross contamination.[5] We are all told by the Ministry of Health that we must wash our hands 'bare below the elbows'. But tests show that this act does not improve the effectiveness of hand washing in reducing bacterial contamination.[6] So, we the doctors are subject to more and more ongoing draconian nonsense! The scientific evidence to back up these changes does not exist!

Quite honestly, the only reason, in my opinion, for all NHS reforms is money. The hospitals no longer have to provide white coats for doctors, or to launder them. What a colossal saving! Incidentally, the doctors themselves have also become a badly dressed group of individuals and no longer a well-dressed, cohesive force.

The telephone exchange is still there – overworked and on call still day and night. Today, the doctors, nurses and administrators are armed with a sophisticated bleep that can give audible or written messages. These allow anybody in the hospital to contact them without going through switchboard. For the record, hospital bleeps were first tried out in a small hospital (Richmond Hospital) in Richmond, Surrey in the 1950s. An antiquated system of crude heavy bleeps worked. They were the forerunner of today's system.

The central sterile supply department has left the hospital (apart from small satellite units), and it too is provided by an outside contractor. Some sterilisation is still carried out in the hospital, e.g., gastroscopes for endoscopies. However, the disease AIDS has made the sterilisation of instruments more complicated. Some instruments after some surgeries are routinely discarded.

We still have a works department, usually provided by the builder in PFI buildings – it's not cheap! Changing a light bulb is so very expensive![7]

The hospital stores department has gone completely. Well, these new PFI hospitals have next to no storage areas anywhere. There is a very large building located 20 miles or so away. This supplies stores to all the hospitals in that region twice a week. This is the RDC – no, not the Regional Disaster Centre, but the Regional Distribution Centre. I preferred the old hospital stores – a lot easier for communication (I suspect this is another result of the Cost Improvement Programme!).

We still have a hospital pharmacy. It is a lot bigger and contains a lot of pharmacists. These quite rightly question any prescription. This is appropriate, as drug interaction is rife. One of these pharmacists dared to query one of my prescriptions. Question: "Why did you prescribe an adult dose of this drug to a ten-year-old child?" Answer from me: "Well, the child is a lot heavier than me."

The student nurses' accommodation is better and not locked up. The bar has gone, along with the doctors' dining room.

A lot of hospitals have been closed down and houses built in their place. In some places, hospital farms have been sold off. Inmates from mental hospitals worked on these farms. Well, what has happened to these inpatients? Housing has been provided for these former inpatients and support at home. I once asked a social worker what exactly his job entailed. "Oh, I look after Mr X; he needs round-the-clock supervision!" I subsequently discovered that he was one of four social workers who were on a rota. Between them they looked after Mr X in the community! Oh, how efficient and cost saving is that? Mr X had been previously, for years, an inpatient in a mental hospital.

Back in 1948 each consultant has his or her own secretary. I had my own on appointment in 1978. I later lost this excellent secretary! So many of these efficient people, usually ladies, have subsequently been lost – only to be replaced by somebody from the typing pool, perhaps in the YTS? So a person who was a mine of information and the epitome of efficiency has been replaced time and time again by somebody less knowledgeable and with a poor secretarial output! The administrators are happy. They have saved money. The consultants have to try and pick up the pieces – mistakes by a secretary reflect upon the consultant, and it is the patient who suffers. Time and time again the patient telephones with a query. The consultant is on a ward round, lecturing, in theatre or inoutpatients. The old secretary knew their job inside out. This young lady from the typing pool is put 'on the spot'.

Haematology, biochemistry and radiology have all expanded –

particularly the latter. All other departments are larger, especially the number of wards and operating theatres. The Nightingale ward has long gone. The patients are nursed in bays of a few beds, or individual rooms. So now if a patient collapses it's very likely that nobody notices!

Possibly the greatest challenge to our health is obesity. The Dietetics Department was so important in 1948. Amazingly today, it is slimmed down. How strange!

The general practitioners have banded together. Many have bought their own premises. They train to become general practitioners on a vocational training scheme. After several years, if they pass exams, they become general practitioners. So they are practically all independent practitioners who work within the NHS structure and are paid by the NHS. Their wages are made up of lots of payments for work done, but not necessarily by themselves.

They receive payment for each patient on their list. However, if a patient is very old, or lives in a deprived area, then that payment is increased. Our nurses' tower block at the Derbyshire Royal Infirmary was within a deprived surrounding area. So local GPs received extra money for being the doctor for our 'fit nurses' – how ludicrous. The doctor's nurse injected patients for immunisation. Once a target was achieved, the doctor was paid a bonus. I was contracted to do minor operations for our local doctor's surgery. I did this on my days off. I was paid very well. But the doctors claimed for the service carried out in their premises, so they were paid for my work! So the government paid them a lot more! Even a general practitioner who works in his own premises is paid a rent by the government for carrying on looking after NHS patients there!

It is not surprising that a new partner in general practice is often paid twice that of a new consultant in a hospital!

References:

1. 'In Place of Fear' by Aneurin Bevan, page 106. Published by the Socialist Health Association (1952) and by the Bevan Society (2008)
2. Rhys Clements. Is it Time for an Evidence Based Uniform for Doctors? BMJ 2012:345;e8286.

3. Dr R C J Campbell Commentary. *Membership Magazine of the Royal College of Physicians.* April 2013. 9. Letter.
4. Dancer CJ. Put your ties back on: Scruffy Doctors Damage our Reputation and Indicate a Decline in Hygiene. *BMJ* 2013;346:f3211 (13 June) and *BMJ* 2013;347:f4388.
5. Burden M, Cervantes I, Weed D, Keniston A et al. Newly cleaned physician's uniform and infrequently washed white coats have similar rates of bacterial contamination after an 8 hour workday. J Hosp Med. 20. 11;6:177-82.
6. Burger A, Wijewardena C, Clayson S, Greatorex R. Bare below the elbows: does this policy affect hand-washing efficacy and reduce bacterial colonisation? Ann R, CollSurgEngl 2011:93:13-16.
7. Martin Barrow. £466 to fix a light, £184 to install a bell: The cost of getting a job done in hospital. *The Times* (23.12.11):10.

Come and See Our New National Health Service in 1948

All the world's a stage, and all the men and women merely players. They have their exits and their entrances.
William Shakespeare, *As You Like It*, Act 2

I am your guide. Come with me to 1948 and see the new National Health Service. Meet doctors from real life through the eyes of a typical patient, John Smith. He has a common problem – 'a lump in the groin'.

In 1948 John Smith comes to the evening GP surgery held in my parents' house. There is no appointment system and no receptionist. He waits his turn. He may ask to be examined by a male doctor (my father). John Smith is told that the lump is a hernia. This needs to be repaired surgically and he is referred to the hospital.

My father types a letter to the surgeon, addressing him by his first name. All the doctors know each other. They are so few. They all meet at regular clinical meetings. The surgeon is the only consultant general surgeon at the hospital. He is continuously on call.

In 1948 most people visit hospital by public transport. A few cycle to the hospital. Very few people own cars, but parking is plentiful and free at the hospital. John Smith sees the busy consultant in his outpatients and is booked in for surgical repair.

Some time later, John Smith is sent for. Mr Smith cannot get lost in the hospital as there are plenty of porters in smart uniforms to direct him. He is admitted to a large single-sex, surgical ward. It is a couple of days before the operation so that blood tests and a chest X-ray, to exclude tuberculosis, can be carried out. The bed for John Smith has been reserved for him. The ward sister told the ward clerk to do this. This is bed-blocking (it is illegal today). If there are too many emergency admissions in 1948 then the sister orders extra beds to be put up. Most wards can take six extra beds, and this too is impossible today. These 1948 beds are hard and cannot be raised or lowered.

The nursing staff clean the ward themselves, and flowers abound. Smoking is permitted for the staff and patients.

John Smith is operated upon by the consultant general surgeon, at the end of a busy list in main theatres, under a general anaesthetic. Operating lists go on until the list is finished. Patients are never cancelled. No nursing staff ever complain, as the consultant operating is on the hospital management board. The consultant may be watched, or even assisted by a visiting surgeon. These are not consultants but all of them have passed the FRCS – the surgical examination to become a consultant. This experienced pool of surgeons visits hospitals just waiting for a job. Many of these men have just been demobbed. This is 'dead man's shoes', i.e., they wait for a consultant to die, and for a surgical job to therefore become available.

John Smith recovers on the surgical ward for several days. Visiting times are strictly limited, but refreshment is available to visitors for a pittance in the hospital canteen. The new NHS has paid for everything – all Mr Smith's treatment, his drugs and his food. Complications for this general anaesthetic operation are well recognised; these include chest infections and a deep vein thrombosis that can lead to an embolus. Either can be fatal. A groin infection is uncommon, but antibiotics are only just being discovered.

John Smith has great faith in the new NHS and his surgeon. The newly qualified house surgeon is around all the time, even assisting in theatre. The ward sister works long hours. The consultant surgeon has a medical secretary who is hard-working and efficient. So between the three of them (ward sister, house surgeon and medical secretary) no notes or X-rays ever go missing, and operations are organised correctly. The house surgeon and the consultant are each insured with a medical defence organisation, as decreed in their hospital contracts. Suing a consultant or a hospital is rare. No hospitals in 1948 ever even employ a solicitor!

Come and See Our NHS Today

Once again, I am your guide. All the players are drawn from real life. John Smith presents with the same groin swelling today.

Today, John Smith telephones his general practice. He eventually speaks to a receptionist. He is asked if he needs an urgent appointment that day. He declines, and is given a routine appointment a few days later. John Smith is not aware that the eight doctors working in the surgery have been lent the money to build it by the Primary Care Trust that organises GP services. These eight doctors own the building and run the business of GP medical care. Meanwhile they are slowly paying back the money lent to them, with interest. John Smith thinks that general practitioners are employed by the NHS. No, all general practitioners are running independent businesses that are paid by the government according to targets achieved.

John Smith agrees to be examined by the new female partner. He is unaware that this lady has had to buy into the practice at great expense. She also has a massive mortgage from her new home. She is therefore 'tied' into the NHS financially. She loves all her patients but the red tape and administration is overwhelming. A friend of hers from medical school works in a practice in Australia. All that sunshine abroad, a lot more money and very little political meddling sounds very tempting.

John Smith does know that the senior partner in the practice has retired. He does not know that this doctor wanted to carry on, but appraisals and revalidation are a nightmare. His accountant telephoned him and told him to retire soon. The pensions cap that came in spring 2016 would cost him thousands of extra pounds in tax. So he has retired reluctantly. Nobody has applied to replace him. (Some suitable candidates have emigrated!) All the doctors will have to work even harder as a consequence.

John Smith may be seen by a medical student as well. This GP business gets paid more for teaching medical students. John Smith is told that he has a hernia and is being referred to the local hospital. Also, John Smith is told that as he is obese he needs to be tested to exclude hypertension and diabetes. John Smith leaves. Only eight minutes is allowed for this consultation. It overruns. When he has gone, the GP explains to the student that hypertension and diabetes need to be excluded, or John Smith could have fatal consequences. Diabetes, caused mainly by overeating, is threatening to bankrupt the NHS.

Today, referrals from a general practitioner to a consultant can be sent instantaneously electronically. Each request has a unique 12-digit identifying code – a mixture of letters and numbers. So, if lost, it can be traced online. John Smith is sent for. He parks at the hospital for a fee. He passes a sign that reads NHS hospital. He is unaware that this hospital was built five years ago by a private finance institution. So this hospital has cost us, the taxpayer, many more times than how much it was to build. Like a massive mortgage, it was signed in private. We, the taxpayer, will go on paying excessively for many years to come. It is not surprising that this hospital is in debt, as interest rates on these 'mortgages' can be 15%. All this money goes to offshore funds and so no tax is paid. As this hospital has yet to be paid for, it really belongs to the PFI building firm and not the NHS!

This is one of the 145 Foundation Trust Hospitals in England and Wales. These hospitals compete for business with all other hospitals. They enjoy some managerial and financial freedoms compared to other hospitals. Foundation Trust Hospitals have been described as a 'halfway house between the public and private sector'. They are regulated by Monitor. John Smith knows nothing of this. He is being seen in part of the NHS hospital that is called a treatment centre. He sees a consultant general surgeon – one of 20 such surgeons. John Smith is examined and placed on the waiting list for inguinal hernia repair.

Prior to surgery, the surgeon will want to check that Mr Smith is not hypertensive or a diabetic. However, any blood sugar tests carried out by the general practitioner may well have been done privately. The surgeon will not have access to them or to any GP records. John Smith's operation is subsequently carried out by a consultant general surgeon as an outpatient in the treatment centre under a spinal anaesthetic. This operation to repair a hernia benefits from the latest technology – a plastic mesh. Mr Smith is taken home that day. He is followed up at the treatment centre. He makes a good recovery.

Today, Mr Smith does not have a general anaesthetic. So chest problems do not occur. Similarly, he has not had a stay in bed in hospital. Thus a deep vein thrombosis is very unlikely. A local infection is unlikely too. Today, all surgeons publish their results from surgery. A hernia recurrence is unlikely too.

The letter from the surgeon to Mr Smith's general practitioner is typed in the Philippines. The consultant has shared secretarial support from young ladies in the typing pool. Well, it's so cheap, but an ongoing clerical disaster. All clerical mistakes reflect upon the consultant and so this boss is held accountable for them all. So notes go missing and other tests too. Patients get forgotten and follow-ups are not arranged. When things go wrong it's the consultant who is blamed. Patients nowadays are litigious. Well, so many lawyers are flourishing on a business of exposing medical mistakes. The old experienced medical secretary has been banished forever. The worried well fill GP surgeries and hospital outpatients. They complain a lot, demand tests over and over again and try to play doctors off against one another.

John Smith has been impressed. What a great service. The good old NHS again, and all free-well, apart from the car parking and his drugs to take away. Also, that Costa coffee was expensive. Boots the Chemist and Marks and Spencer's all pay the hospital to be there, and charge top rate. Well, these organisations are not charity institutions. They are in your 'NHS hospital' for a profit.

Nobody has told John Smith that the treatment centre is run by a private company. This company charges to see NHS patients on their premises (the NHS tariff). This private company, and not the NHS, pays the doctors and nurses employed there. The consultant doctors had no choice. Either they worked for this private company or they were sacked by the foundation trust. This private company says it is not profit-making. However, it is quoted on the stock exchange, and has directors that are well paid for their work.

Many functions carried out within the foundation trust hospital are pursued by private firms. The hospital kitchen is run by a private franchise. All the hospital laundry is costly from a local firm. The hospital is cleaned by another firm for a price. Even the surgical instruments are sterilised and packed elsewhere – it's not cheap.

So has Mr John Smith been treated by our National Health Service or not?

My own view is that Mr Smith has been treated by a health service that is being privatised by stealth.

The Denationalised Health Service

Definition from the Oxford English Dictionary of 'privatise':
to assign to private enterprise... to denationalise.

Yet more news – not just bad, but a lot worse – really dreadful recent news. On 27th March 2012 the Health and Social Care bill became law. The conservatives argued that they had a mandate to reform the Health Service. It was presented by politicians as the saviour of our Health Service. They talk about healthy competition being so good. The vast majority of politicians have never worked in our NHS. Yet they speak with such confidence and spin. There was opposition to the bill from doctors – and it is there today.[1]

This bill gives big business a chance to cash in on the running of our NHS; this is privatisation. The profits from this leave the NHS to line the pockets of businessmen and shareholders. Standards of healthcare will decline. Profits will soar.

We are all victims of political spin. The politicians will continue to unravel our NHS. It will soon be fully privatised – sold off to various bidders.

We will soon find ourselves victims of this web of deceit spun by confident eloquent politicians for the benefit of their chums in big business. These politicians have spun their web. We, like innocent flies, are caught in the trap. There is no going back. We will be sucked financially dry.

Well, you were warned by the doctors, nurses and royal colleges.

Why else did they speak up against this bill initially? I am not alone in my criticism. Dr Max Pemberton[2] has a new book, *The Doctor will see you now*, published by Hodder. I agree completely with his views – we both believe in the National Health Service that is being hijacked by big business for their gain and our loss.

This is profane, profligate privatisation – nothing less. The old system has been destroyed. There can be no going back. More is the pity.

Nye Bevan must be turning in his grave.

The medical press has buzzed with plenty of articles, all criticising the present government. An Editorial in the *BMJ* read 'Lansley NHS "reforms" are divisive and destructive.[3] The NHS is left at the mercy of ideological and incompetent intervention. Well known opponents of the act have been elected to the BMA Council.'[4]

There is also plenty of evidence that supports the view that big business wants to make money from the NHS. On 19th February 2012 in *The Times*, City investors were offered the chance to make huge profits from projects aimed at cutting the cost of patient care in the National Health Service. Catalyst Corporate Finance advises companies on investments. They informed private firms that the NHS is open for £20 billion pounds worth of business.[5, 6] I cannot see how standards could be maintained, if an investor took money out of the NHS on the one hand and still cut the cost of patient care with the other. These facts spell disaster to me, and a lot of other people agree!

So the doctors, nurses and all the clinical support staff remain, still the backbone of our National Health Service. The buildings and the fabric of the NHS are going (see next chapter). So are any profits. We, the taxpayers, foot the bill.

References:

1. Isabel Oakeshott. 'Spineless' Clegg under fire on NHS. *Sunday Times* 19.12.12:2.
2. Max Pemberton. Healthy Competition is a Sick Joke. *Daily Telegraph*

9.4.12:22.

3. Lansley's NHS 'Reforms' are divisive and destructive. *BMJ* 2012:344; e709.

4. Defenders of the NHS Step Up. *BMA* News 5.5.12:8.

5. *BMJ* 2012:345; e6305.

6. Jon Ungoed Thomas. Investors Urged to Cash in on Health Service. *Sunday Times* 19.2.12:2. News.

CHAPTER THIRTY-FIVE

Health Service Planning in the 21st Century

The best laid schemes o' mice an' men. Gang aft a-gley.

Robert Burns

First Let's Plan Medical Communications

All patients have a diagnosis that is coded, and kept for planning and costing. Our emergency department coded every patient and produced a computer-generated letter to the GP that the hospital doctor signed. Well, how efficient is that! Nothing can go wrong! Or can it?

I received a telephone call in 1990 from a general practitioner one day about one such letter. I was suspicious from the start, as the doctor was very intelligent. (I had trained him.) He read the letter out as he did not know how to treat this patient and had not come across this condition before!

"Mr Frederick Smith, aged 31 years, of 2 Barhouse Road, was seen today at 6pm and discharged. Diagnosis: gynaecological left elbow."

Yes, medical communication is a wonderful thing!

A New Hospital is Needed Urgently. Shall we Have a PFI?

I would never be asked to design a PFI Hospital as such architects are concerned with cost cutting. My aim would be to make such a building fit for purpose.

An International architect, Derby

So, health service planning is vital. Our last Labour Government boasted of many new hospitals, but where did the money come from? The taxpayer? Yes. However, if you look closer, the Labour Party resorted to Private Finance Initiatives (PFIs). This involved getting big business to build the hospital for you to your own specification. The hospital then pays the business a sum annually for the use of that hospital. In effect it is a big mortgage. So the hospital really belongs to the business. The hospital pays annually on and on – a permanent rent! So, after 30 or 40 years, the hospital has paid the business many many times the original cost of that building, i.e., more than it needed to. PFIs were originally introduced by John Major as Prime Minister. According to Hansard, by 2020 the annual cost of current PFIs will be many billions of pounds! My own view is that paying via the old method (cash) would have been a lot cheaper in the long run. So, the health service planning of new hospitals is, in my opinion, too expensive! Or as Michael Meacher wrote in *The Times* back in 2004, 'Picking up the tabs for the PFI – a scheme that was supposed to save money is stacking up debt for generations.'[1]

I am not alone in my criticism of PFI schemes. The British Medical Association has published some horrifying figures about the cost of these new hospitals of ours all funded by PFI. According to HM Treasury figures PFIs are funding 100 new hospital schemes valued initially at £10. 9bn. By 2048 the local hospital trusts will have paid for them. The bill will be a staggering £62.9bn.

Now look closely at each PFI. They have passed the building regulations, but does everything work and are they built to high specifications? Ask the staff working there – I have. There needs to be plenty of storage space in each department for gowns, dressings and other disposables. Oh dear, some things have to be sent for twice a day and others stored in corridors. Some bits of the hospital are busy now, and in ten years' time could we expand? No.

Are the buildings well planned? Is the main entrance too narrow? Well, that's too bad, we can't change it now. We can't expand it either to get more beds. What a shame!

One small point: if you change the use of a room with no alteration, it is called a change of use. The National Audit Office found that such changes to contracts cost the NHS £180 million in 2006, so each change of use costs us, the taxpayer, more money. It's all in the contract!

The PFI problem simply won't go away. The BMA[2] quoted 22 hospital trusts nationally. All these trusts are in trouble financially due to soaring costs of their respective PFI. In one trust alone 132 doctor posts are at risk. So, this health service money will go to big business instead of paying for doctors to look after patients!

Details of payments for work done for minor building work are excessive in PFI hospitals. Routine work could have been carried out by local tradesmen at a far reduced rate.[3]

But good news, all those PFI projects must pay plenty of money in tax! Oh no, recently a European Services Strategy Unit published a report! Over 270 PFI projects, many in the NHS, are based offshore, so avoiding millions in tax. What a disgrace![4]

References:

1. Michael Meacher. Picking up the tabs for the PFI. *The Times*. 14. 12. 04;16.
2. Jenna Pedelek. Soaring costs of PFI put scores of trust jobs at risk. *BMA News* 3. 12. 11:1.
3. Martin Barrow. £466 to fix a light, £184 to install a bell. The cost of getting a job done in hospital. *The Times* 23. 12. 11:10.
4. Kathryn Cooper and Jon Ungoed Thomas. NHS Finance Firms avoid millions in tax. *The Sunday Times* 2. 9. 12:12.

The Hospital Administrators are in Charge –
They Know Best

*I turn my thoughts to consider wisdom… and also madness
and folly.*

Ecclesiastes 2.12

They are planning a health service for a county in which a million people live. From studying previous activity they know for example that on average one-tenth of the local population will attend the emergency department (Casualty) each year. Similarly, the level of medical and surgical activity can be gauged and on average activity goes up about 10% each year. This does not take into account new activity. Indeed, when the NHS was planned by Mr Bevan it was thought that, as disease was cured, hospitals would become less busy. Many new treatments and surgical operations have been introduced since, for example, hip and knee replacements, not even dreamed of at the start.

To return to planning numbers of patients in beds, nothing is more difficult than medical admissions – chest problems, heart attacks, etc. We have an ageing population. Many factors like obesity and smoking exacerbate the picture. We are seeing a break-up of family life, and fewer and fewer family members are caring for their elderly relatives. More and more people are living longer thanks to drugs, for example, treating heart failure, hypertension, etc.

So the admission of patients to these beds is strictly controlled and regulated (Bed Co-ordinators appointed). The number of vacant beds is posted everywhere (bed meetings). The discharge of patients from hospital is streamlined (discharge lounges). With all of this in place at two hospitals, I was told by a reliable source that the system failed at each. Medical patients spilled out all over the hospital. Efforts to block beds for surgery failed. Some staff obstructed other staff to preserve their own beds. Surgical patients had to ring up on the day of surgery to see if there was a bed or not – how ludicrous is this!

So they built a big new hospital, combining both hospitals together (there have been plenty of hospitals combined in this way in the UK) – yes, you guessed it, a PFI. The cost was eventually about £400 million, before we started paying the mortgage. Now get your calculators out. If there are X medical beds in the first hospital and Y in the second hospital, and both are unable to cope with the number of acute medical patients, how many medical beds are required in the new super expensive hospital? No, no, no: X + Y = far too many, according to hospital planning. This new hospital will be super-efficient, and fewer medical beds were allotted! True.

Result: intermittent chaos. No beds? Medical patients are sitting regularly in the emergency department for hours and hours and hours. No operating at times, as the surgical beds are full of medical patients. No room for any more patients! This activity could not have been foreseen, is reported in the newspapers.

On the contrary, this activity, intermittently in my opinion, was a certainty.

* * *

I previously worked for six months in general surgery in North London. This brand new purpose-built hospital was a model of excellence. One slight teething problem – the surgical wards were a long way from the operating theatres and on a different level! How will the porters get the patients there, and then back? What is the best route?

Solution: Joan, our attractive houseman, got on a 'trolley' as a dummy patient. My registrar Peter and I pushed and pulled the laden trolley to theatre and back. What fun! Stopwatches out! Now off we go again – ready, steady, go.

We eventually found the right route.

The Four-hour Wait (or Weight)

Our previous Labour government introduced a four-hour wait policy in emergency departments. This was, and is, a great idea. To implement this, a lot more staff were appointed. So, in one hospital, for example, 16 specialist emergency consultants now perform the work that two did 15 years ago (and one did alone 30 years ago!).

Computers log patients on the system and all patients are kept on the system till they are admitted to a bed or are discharged. The system is active, i.e., in real time.

If a high proportion of casualties are discharged in four hours then the hospital is rewarded financially. So, initially, it paid a department to do badly and lots of new staff were appointed and perhaps a new department was built (and was!).

This system of the four-hour wait was just there to be abused. But how? Let us see. All of these methods have been used and DO WORK!

Ways to beat the four hour wait:

Get a big notice that looks imposing. Write on it CLINICAL DECISION UNIT and find a big empty room. Put it on the door. Now, nurse, as soon as Mrs Jones is about to breach (over four hours) just wheel her in. Yes, that's it. She has left the department so wipe her off the screen! Good, one less!

A variation of the above is just to have rows and rows of trolleys in a room somewhere and call it a ward. It is not a ward. It has no beds, no oxygen, no suction, no bed tables, no individual lights, etc. The medical doctors attend to these patients. These patients have left the emergency department and so are off the system. A few more less.

Delaying logging the patient on is common. So Mr Brown comes at 9pm and is not logged onto the system till 11pm so he has to be out by 3am (not 1am). Some ambulances have even been kept waiting outside till the department can see them! Good, eh? Yes, this still goes on in 2013. Hospital trusts guilty of leaving patients over one hour in an ambulance outside A&E have all been fined £1,000 for each patient. Newspaper headings: 100 patients a day wait an hour in an ambulance before they reach A&E.[1] Ambulance waiting rooms cost the NHS £11m. Ambulances stacked up like planes.[2]

Put the patient on the system twice. Oh, that's easy. Mrs Brown has been here three hours and 58 minutes. Wipe her off the system and two minutes later she is on again. That is two admissions, and the department gets twice the money for two patients. More importantly, the four-hour rule has not been breached. Well done.

Last night was bad. No medical beds and so the poor medical patients stacked up in the emergency department for hours and hours. There are lots and lots of breaches. Fortunately, help is at hand. I am a computer whizz. I hack into my own hospital computer. I have all the passwords – well, I work here, don't I? With my deft little mouse in my right hand I pick off all the patients from the breech list. Hey presto, last night was a good night – no breeches. Didn't we do well? (Confirmed recently at a hospital inquiry in the Midlands). In July 2013 two senior nurses from Stafford Hospital emergency department were found guilty of this. As a consequence their names were removed from the nursing register.

Let's shut the department tonight – it's just too busy. So all the new patients are redirected elsewhere, especially those ambulances with all the 'sick ones'. Two hours later – that's a lot better. I think we are in for a quiet night.

Find a bed and pop Mrs Smith into it. Empty beds are fiercely defended by staff – usually for planned admissions. In an emergency these beds can be used. It does not matter that the nurses looking after the confused sick old lady are trained in gynaecology or ophthalmology – or does it? There were nearly 136,000 more admissions in the UK in 2004-5, a probable result of the four-hour wait.[3]

Yes, all these illegal acts have been exposed and blocked. There is another way always to beat the four-hour wait, but it is a bit tricky!

DON'T TRY THIS WAY TO BEAT THE FOUR HOUR WAIT:

I was summoned occasionally by the sister in charge to 'do something'. This was such an occasion. "Do something," she said, "and get your friend out of here and quickly." There was an intense urgency in her voice that I failed to comprehend, until I turned the corner.

There was a tall, retired neurosurgeon, now a farmer, at reception. Three of his farm labourers were carrying a fourth.

"Ah, there you are," said the farmer surgeon. "This man has fallen off a ladder in the cowshed." They had all come on a tractor parked outside! They were all in overalls with big muddy boots shedding cow muck all over the place. I felt ill. The smell was dreadful. Another patient was complaining of the smell already. Thirty seconds later, after a full consultation and examination, this bevy of men had refused a wheelchair and staggered off to X-ray carrying the wounded man.

About a minute or so later they had returned from X-ray with the films. The superintendent radiographer had voiced her opinion about their smell to the receptionist already. The corridors were mucky too.

I was in the centre of our accident room surrounded by doctors, nurses and others when the landowner plonked the patient at my feet, and the X-rays into my hand. I am not used to doing a consultation in public, but we were all feeling a bit sick by now.

"Oh, he has an undisplaced fractured calcaneum," I said. Plaster, crutches, analgesics and follow-up Fracture Clinic, that I organised. Two minutes later, as he left being pushed out on a wheelchair, I talked to the surgical farmer in public.

"He's got an undisplaced fractured calcaneum," I said.

"Thank goodness it's not serious," the farmer surgeon said.

"It is serious," I said. "He will have to rest."

"But I have a farm to run," he said.

"Well, he can't work," I said.

By now several people had gathered round to see him go. The other three farmhands listened intently.

"He can't work," I repeated, "because he can't walk. He has to rest."

The doors shut; that was the end. I thought I had won. A few seconds later the doors opened again, and the surgical farmer's head appeared.

"I know what I'll do," he said. "I'll put him on the tractor."

With that he was gone – home on one tractor, all five of them!

So that's how to beat the four-hour wait, but it is not advised.

* * *

My own view of the four-hour wait is that patients have benefitted. I benefitted as my life as a consultant coming up to retirement was made easier. This is because I was given colleagues to work with. However, daft things still happened. For example, a 90-year-old man was brought in dead. He was a miracle really. He had had five previous myocardial infarcts. The ambulance and emergency staff had worked on him over and over again. He recovered each time. He was grateful on discharge. However, we are all going to die sometime. On the sixth myocardial infarct he had died, to the great surprise and sorrow of his relatives. We comforted them all at their loss, but 90 was a good age to die.

Sister telephoned the mortuary. "Oh," she said, "the mortuary is busy and the technicians are unable to take him." After four hours of waiting, this body breached the four hour wait. – yet another black mark to us!

> *I'm not afraid to die. I just don't want to be there when it happens.*
>
> Woody Allen

> *I told you I was ill.*
>
> On Spike Milligan's gravestone

As I write, the Conservatives are in power. The four-hour wait did wonders for emergency departments – lots more doctors and nurses appointed. Well, it's just like a pantomime really. In the old days, Casualty was an 'ugly sister', shunned, understaffed and criticised by everybody. After the four-hour wait it was an emergency department. So popular, busy and attractive, it became the centre of attention, just like Cinderella!

Will the four-hour wait return? Things seesaw in politics – and it just might!

No, the commissioners of A&E Services have introduced A&E Clinical Quality Indicators. This is essentially the four-hour wait made more complicated and in another form altogether!

References:

1. Nick McDermott. 100 patients a day wait an hour in an ambulance before they reach A&E. *Daily Mail* 27. 5. 13;10. Jonathan Oliver. Ambulance Waiting Rooms cost NHS £11m. *Sunday Times*. 28. 3. 10:9.
2. Chris Smyth. Ambulances 'stacked up like planes'. *The Times*. 19. 12. 13;12.
3. Beware overeager A&E staff. Anonymous. *The Times*. Public Agenda. 11. 1. 05:6. In turn reporting from the *Health Service Journal*. 6. 1. 06.

CHAPTER THIRTY-SIX

Is Working in a Hospital Dangerous Today?

Yes, it can be at times. I should know. For example: we employ security guards that work for the hospital. One large former policeman working as a security guard took a punch on his outstretched palm and suffered a fractured wrist (1).

Another security guard went to tackle a flasher. This flasher pushed him down some steps, and he suffered a triple fracture of his ankle (tri-malleolar). This needed two operations to fix (2).

Nurses are often in the front line for assaults (3). One charge nurse was punched in the face by a stroke patient. He was off work for weeks. A tall nurse working as an administrator, Janice was over six feet! She was unexpectedly attacked by a patient's relative (4). The culprit was taken to a magistrate's court. She got off by telling the magistrate she was frightened of injections. The magistrate sided with her: "Oh, poor lady," he said, and let her off. She was not even a patient so was not written up for any injections at all.

Drug addicts and alcoholics are the main instigators of violence (5). One drug addict had collapsed with an overdose of heroin. We reversed the action of this drug with nalorphine and so woke up the patient. He

Fig 49 – Now here is a lorry upside down after an accident. Those firemen have got to be careful! The lorry could roll over and kill them all.

was furious that we had cancelled out the effect of this drug. "You bastards wasted £50," he said. He went berserk, injuring several staff members (6).

A man and a lady from Derby ran out of cash and decided to hold up an off licence. He had a gun (or a replica of one). As they ran away across the road with the money, she was hit by a passing car. He brought his accomplice to the hospital Casualty. He failed to hide the gun. The receptionist informed the police. The lady was examined and sent for an X-ray. He still waved the gun about, upsetting the other patients and staff. She was then discharged. As they walked out of the front of the hospital, the armed police response team was waiting for them. They were both surprised to be caught. How naïve can you get? (7&8).

I finished a ward round one morning. We had four ladies in our ward. One of the nurses told me that they had had trouble with a middle-aged man from Burton. He had turned up late (2am). His girlfriend, a patient, had let him in through the window and the two ended up in bed together! What the other patients had thought, I had no idea! I expressed my disgust, when who should turn up but this middle-aged man in an aggressive mood. "I go where I fucking well like!" he said.

Fig 50 – If a person is trapped in a burning building then the smoke will kill that person long before they are burnt. So all rescuers need to beware of that toxic smoke. Breathing apparatus needs to be worn.

I told him to go away. I was then hit on the chin. The police were called and he was taken into custody. I gave a statement to the police. This made me late for the clinic. The nurse consoled the waiting patients in the outpatient clinic. "The doctor is very sorry, but he will be late. He is at present involved in a fight on the ward!"

This middle-aged man went back to court. There was a plethora of evidence on a galaxy of charges. He was found guilty. He went back to prison, for this and quite a few other offences. He was supposed to be under curfew and was not to go out after 8pm or before 8am (9).

He must be out by now. Thank goodness I have retired!

I had nearly finished my daily morning follow-up clinic. It was 3pm. Nobody was waiting to see me, so I rushed to the League of Friends tea bar. As I put my mug of tea down, a hand from behind me lifted it up and poured the tea over my head!!! I was amazed, and worried that this was a warning. Was I being goaded into a fight?

I turned round and there he was – a very regular attender, and a known pugilist. The previous week I had witnessed a fight in our department. He had taken on two security men. The pugilist punched hard with both hands, and would have won if a third security man had not appeared.

He got the pugilist in a neck lock from behind. So the fight was over.

The crux of the problem was that this pugilist had a 'fatal attraction' for doctors. He had been to prison twice for attacking them, and had broken one doctor's jaw.

So on that lunchtime in 1995 I simply smiled at this man. I prayed that he would not flip into all-out aggression. Well, over two stone heavier than me and over 20 years younger, he would have pulverised me in a fight. Despite my hunger, I walked away from trouble that day. I returned to the safety of the clinic.

I could feel my heart pounding in my chest.

That was a close shave!

* * *

I recall that one gang of drug pushers stabbed a member of a rival gang. This injured man was admitted to our hospital. The police were preoccupied with keeping the two gangs apart. They even wanted to take over my office. My secretary and I had a lot of work to do and so I declined consent to use the office. (Another black mark to me!) (10).

* * *

One day I was trying to find out where a man had tenderness in his left shoulder, to get a diagnosis. As I found the tender spot, he hit me with his right hand and then said sorry. He demanded treatment. With great reluctance I referred him to physiotherapy. The physio course was a very short one! (11).

We occasionally had hospital hoppers. These travel from hospital to hospital demanding drugs. I recall, in 1972, one very clearly. He mimicked pain from his left kidney where he said he had a haemangioma. This rare condition can bleed and cause pain. He had had extensive investigations and wanted no more – just pain relief, i.e., morphine or its derivative. He was very, very aggressive. He did have blood in his urine, but probably from a pricked finger! So he passed urine and added to it some blood from his finger. He then lied and said that the abdominal pain he had was from the rare 'tumour', called a haemangioma, in his kidney.

We eventually got rid of him, i.e. he was discharged. He was a white man from Zimbabwe. Another hospital, two weeks later, prosecuted him as he had hopped there. In court he admitted 53 previous convictions for trying to obtain drugs on false pretences. He was deported (12). (He did not have this rare kidney problem. It was a lie!)

Several times I have resorted to doing the one thing such patients (hospital hoppers) do not want – taking their picture. Afterwards, these patients are gone in a flash. They are frightened their picture will be all across the internet. So we achieve what we want – the patient discharged. One such hopper had a fight with security, and I took his photograph. He then went to a solicitor and demanded the photograph back. I declined as I said it was "an integral part of the hospital records" (13).

There are times when doctors contract illnesses from their patients. There are many such instances in history. Aged 23 years I contracted chicken pox from a patient. I could not sit part of my final examination as I was infectious. I lost my examination fee as a result! (14).

My late father in 1960 was operating on a very ill patient with swollen glands to the neck. My father took ill afterwards. He developed hepatitis and was deeply jaundiced. He was off work for six months. He finally recovered. His operating assistant was his registrar. He was off sick for three months with swollen glands. The patient died (15 & 16).

So, yes, working in a hospital can be dangerous. I always used to tell my junior doctors, if you are attacked just shout and run. All health workers on the front line are exposed to some danger – call security before something happens, if possible.

Some years before I came to the Derbyshire Royal Infirmary, my colleague Mr John Collins had been travelling in an ambulance. The ambulance crashed. Mr Collins suffered a fractured skull and was off work for a long time. He was left with a poor sense of smell – the commonest neurological problem after a fractured skull! (17).

The risk of a road traffic collision is up to 13 times higher for emergency ambulances, per mile travelled, than other vehicles! (In Turkey 21 people have died in such crashes!)[1]

Dermot was a medical student at Nottingham University. He is very tall and particularly well-muscled. He is the perfect build for playing rugby. He played for the university. He was outstanding. He looked fearsome as his nose is not straight, due to so many rough games. He shaved his head. He was particularly intelligent and very kind to his patients. I should know. He was one of my students. He excelled. He was a real role model. He had no trouble qualifying as a doctor. He went off on his sabbatical to Johannesburg – the world-famous trauma unit.

The area around the hospital has always been rough but inside the hospital was safe. He was there for several weeks. He loved it. He took his camera and took picture after picture. There were a lot of stabbings and shootings. He took pictures of X-rays, theatre sessions and patients generally. He had a large number of shots.

Just before he left, he slipped out one morning early to get some souvenirs of his stay. He did not concentrate. A tall, slim guy came up behind him and pulled a knife. He had to give up his wallet, and his precious camera with all the shots.

Oh, despair. *I have lost all my pictures,* he thought. All those memories gone. He cancelled the credit cards and lost a bit of cash. He was desolate that last evening. He was not paying much attention. Then a call came. There was another shooting.

He stayed for the very last time. That patient was a bloody mess but looked a bit familiar. *Oh yes, he held me up earlier today.*

The patient was rushed into the operating theatre. Blood was taken for cross-matching and he had an urgent chest X-ray. The nursing staff en route removed the patient's valuables for safe keeping.

What's that? Oh, my camera. Better news still, the memory card is still intact.

What luck.

Dermot returned home with his camera and his pictures. (18).

I was working as a locum senior house officer in 1970 in surgery at Hillingdon. I passed through the doctors' mess going to the operating theatre one evening. A junior dentist was organising a mess party. This dentist was an extrovert, but of small stature. There were tables, a bar, music and floodlights. It looked great. I could not stay. I never got there either.

This junior dentist telephoned his boss at 7am the next morning. "I have fixed up theatre for you at 9am today, sir," he said. "The case is a 24-year-old man with a fracture of the angle of the lower jaw left side with some displacement. Otherwise he is fit." "Oh fine," said the boss, "see you there. You – err, will be there to assist me?" "Well, I will be there, but…"

"Well, I'm sorry, I can't assist you," said the junior.

"Whyever not?" asked the boss.

"Well, sir," he said, "I'm sorry, but I am the patient."

Some gatecrashers had beaten him up at 2am (19).

A 12-year-old (20) was referred by her GP for removal of a 'freckle' on her chest. This was obviously benign. Her father was aggressive and irritated by having to sign a consent form. But I had to explain everything. I wanted the 12-year-old to agree herself to the very minor operation. She nodded her agreement. The father told me to, "hurry up and get on with it, I've had too much trouble with people like you. Take my dentist. He has refused to treat my daughter, just because she bit him!"

Well, the freckle was taken out in seconds, once the local had worked. I was just putting in a stitch when I noticed a sudden movement at the edge of my field of vision. I moved my left hand quickly away. Her jaws snapped shut a fraction of a second later where my hand had been. The nurses told the girl off. She said nothing.

On discharge, I mentioned to the father, "She tried to bite me."

"Oh, that's your fault," he said. "You obviously upset her!"

Human bites are no fun; I have treated many in my time. I suspect she never wanted the minor operation and this was her way of showing it. Adolescence is a strange time, and 12-year-old girls can be very odd indeed.

I can hear a criticism. I have been unfair to administrators, and anyway all these events that I have recounted may be true but our NHS can't be at all dangerous now – or can it be?

In November 2012 a lady doctor was pleaded with by an administrator. Please be on call for 24 hours – two doctors have telephoned in sick. So that lady doctor worked in a hospital in the South West, on call, for 24 hours. She was not given an on-call room. (She herself found one empty room and crashed out there!)

After 24 hours on call in the hospital, she got into her car and drove onto the motorway and back to her flat.

This contravenes European Law – the hospital did not care. The administrators got away with it? If after 23 hours she had made a prescription error, she could have been in trouble, and a patient could have died! She could have had a serious RTA on the way home. She was that tired,anything could have happened.

How do I know about this junior doctor so far away? Well, she is my daughter! (21).

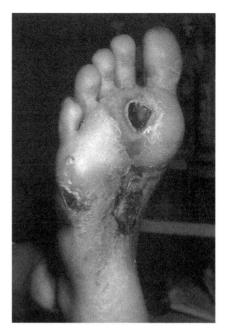

Fig 51 – An electrical burn to the foot. The electrical current must be turned off before resuscitation.

An electrical burn to the foot (fig 51) has to be treated after the power has been switched off, and the chemical causing a chemical burn can rub off on you too!

So, is working in a hospital dangerous? Yes, and the above cases confirm that statement.

_____

Reference:

1. *J Forensic Leg Med* 2012;19:474-9.

A Sore Throat

Truth, stark truth, is the word.

John Cleland

I was about to leave my job in Bristol and move to Derby in 1977. I was working out my period of notice. Meanwhile my wife's contract of employment had ended. She could not apply for another post, as she was coming with me to Derby. She did, however, accept a short locum – a general practice surgery one Friday evening.

I finished operating at 6pm and set off to help my wife out that evening. Well, if we both saw patients, we would be finished a lot quicker. Nearly 7pm on a dark, wet evening in Bristol found me looking for a doctor's surgery in Eastville, a suburb. I eventually found my destination.

I passed through a small waiting room packed to overflowing with expectant patients. Initially, when I approached the sleepy receptionist, I was told abruptly to "sit down and wait".

"No, I've come to help the doctor; I'm her husband. Didn't she tell you I was coming?" I said.

"Oh yes, follow me," was her reply. "She is our only doctor."I was led down a long passage. On both sides were deserted offices for administration of the practice. At the end of the corridor was an open area. Four consulting rooms and two examination rooms were situated around this. All was quiet.

"Your wife is in there," said the receptionist, and left.

I knocked on the consulting room door to tell my wife I had come, but I did not want to interrupt a consultation. She came to the door and was pleased to see me.

"Oh yes," she said in a whisper, "could you see the young man in that examination room. He's just a bit odd. He has a sore throat and there is a good light on the wall. I told him to loosen his collar." She gave me his notes.

I knocked on the examination room door and went in. The young man jumped as I entered. "Wwwwwhereiistthellllladyddddoctor?" he stammered.

"She asked me to see you," I truthfully answered.

This young man was sitting on the couch with his legs wide apart. He was completely naked!

"Now, let's look at your throat," I said.

"Oh, it's better now," he said.

The throat was normal. The eardrums were both normal too (throat and ear infections can get confused).

Neck – no tender glands.

Temperature – normal.

"I'm better now," he repeated over and over again. He had a perfect grasp of English. He understood me well. He was upset!

I noted there was a nicely folded gown on the little table beside the couch. The patient remained agitated and naked.

"Did the lady doctor ask you to take everything off?" I casually asked.

"Oh yes," he said. "She said that I must take everything off!"

"Oh really?" I said. "Well, I can't find anything wrong with you."

"Can I go now?" he asked.

"Yes," I said. "Your doctor can see you if you have any more problems. Just, PLEASE, put on some clothes before you go into the waiting room."

He hurriedly dressed and left.

Later that evening I told my wife about this naked man. She was shocked. "I told him just to loosen his collar," she kept on repeating, over and over again.

Now what would have happened to my young attractive wife if she had gone into that particular examination room and been confronted by that naked man?

Thank goodness we will never ever know!

So, general practice has its problems.

CHAPTER THIRTY-SEVEN

Practical Jokes and Other Funnies Over the Years

Life is a joke that's just begun.

Gilbert

I was in theatre as a senior house officer in 1970 in general surgery at St Helier. The registrar, Alan, was demonstrating an appendicectomy during my first week. It took him five minutes, skin to skin. Well, he left me to put the skin stitches in. Then I could not leave the theatre! Alan had been into the ladies, changing room. (Somehow he knew that they completely undressed before putting on their theatre clothes!) Alan removed all their knickers and bras from the changing room. There followed a stand-off for half an hour. The nurses in theatre clothes surrounded me and would not let me go! Eventually their clothes were returned and these lovely ladies released me!

A few weeks before I arrived, Alan had bleeped my predecessor Paddy at 3am in a spurious call to a patient who did not exist, to a ward at the far end of the hospital. When Paddy got back to his room after failing of course to find the non-existent patient, something was missing – his bed. It had been completely removed from his room and hidden in another room. Paddy spent the rest of the night on the floor. He knew who had tricked him and he wanted to get even.

So he set up a trap for Alan. Paddy joined three drip sets together. The initial fluid bottle was set up to a drip stand in the room directly above Alan's bedroom. Then it went outside and into Alan's room through the window that was just open. When he started the fluid flowing, it went directly into Alan's bed. He planned to start if off at about 3am when Alan was in bed. Unfortunately, Paddy was caught by Alan, and so this practical joke failed.

Paddy was popular with the female nursing staff. He was chatting on the ward with two of them when on call late one night. The ward sherry bottle was removed from the drugs cupboard. They finished it. So, to cover up the fact it was empty, a fluid was put in, called Mist Pot Cit. This is used to change the pH of urine and so prevent a lot of urinary infections. It is also foul smelling. When I started, some time later, the senior sister on this ward had an old friend recuperating from an operation in the side room. One Friday night at the end of her shift, this sister went to her friend for another chat. The sherry bottle was produced… Yes, I got the blame. Well, sometimes in life, you just can't win!

* * *

I was a surgical registrar at Ashford Hospital, Middlesex in 1972. I was also in charge of the doctors' mess. So I was their spokesman. The hospital management board decided that as their doctors' residency was such a big success, another identical residency was needed right next to the first! I thought otherwise and so did my junior colleagues. So I wrote a letter to the board as follows:

Dear Members of the Board,

I understand that plans have been drawn up for a new residency, beside the first and identical in every way. Allow me as a resident in the original building to make a few observations.

The building has very thin walls. I can hear a conversation in the next room easily. I hear my houseman getting up at night (he is in the bedroom above mine). The building is on the hospital car park, close to Casualty and the wards. Night staff come on and off duty at some very odd times. Casualties are driven in at all hours. We have a stream of cars coming and going 24 hours a day, with doors slamming and people calling out! So the construction and siting of the building is at fault.

I have problems with birds in my room – of the feathered variety. There is a ventilation grill on the inside that opens outside just below the guttering. Birds nest in this aperture, and the constant squabbling of sparrows nesting keeps me awake at night.

The plumbing is outstanding. We have copious amounts of hot water but unfortunately from the hot and cold taps. Last week, coming back at 4am from theatre, hot water was pouring down the stairs too!

My personal view is that another residency sited beside the first, and identically constructed, would be an unmitigated disaster. Please think again.

Yours faithfully,

A Fraser-Moodie
Mess President

The new residence was re-sited and redesigned.

* * *

My first job, when I had just qualified (1965), was to clerk in eight amputees on a Sunday afternoon. They had all been soldiers in the Second World War. They had returned to Queen Mary's, Roehampton for limb fitting and adjustment. They bonded together very well – far too well. Unbeknown to me, at 8pm that evening they walked out of the back door of the ward, down a short path and into the back door of a public house. They knew the way well. They had done it before. Drunk, at about 11pm, they staggered back into the ward, waking all the other patients up.

On the Monday morning I was asked to tell them all off by the ward sister. Well, I sympathised with them. They had fought for Queen and country. Between the eight of them they only had seven legs, as one was a bilateral amputee. They had carried him back!

My telling-off was mild. They grinned throughout!

* * *

I was running my daily clinic as an A&E consultant in 1991. This usually meant that a nurse assisted me. They were short-staffed. I sometimes had to start or finish a clinic on my own. Today was different and I had no idea why. Not one but three experienced nurses came to help me. *Well perhaps, just for once, they have come to realise how important I am. No, that can't be the reason.* I was yet to learn, to my cost and considerable embarrassment, that they had seen the clinic list. It meant nothing at all to me, but they knew who was on the list, and they were prepared. I was not informed, and totally ignorant.

A lady in her twenties was ushered in. She seemed just an ordinary patient. I had failed to notice that two female nurses came in too. One female nurse stayed just outside the door.

This lady had injured her left ankle. An X-ray was negative. I needed to examine the ankle. However, this lady had only taken off her sock. She still had a tight pair of jeans on. I slowly rose to leave the room. The girl started singing, and had her jeans off in a flash. No knickers on either!!!

The two nurses pulled up her jeans, to try and make her decent. She resisted this forcibly and carried on singing. The third nurse entered and quickly 'frogmarched' me out of the room.

"What is going on?" I protested.

"Tell you later," said nurse number three.

"Now stay here and don't – don't – go in." She said to me.

I felt a real wally standing about outside the clinic door. There was obviously a struggle going on inside. The third nurse rushed in with a gown.

Five minutes later: "Doctor, you can come in now." In I went and was shown the offending leg up to the knee. The lady was well gowned up. I was still very confused. I reassured the young lady that she simply had a sprained ankle. I discussed exercises, analgesia and tubigrip.

She was given a card that outlined information for patients with 'sprained ankles'. Her likely recovery time was assured.

I left her for the nurses to attend to. She later walked away from the clinic with hardly a trace of a limp.

"Well, what was all that about?" I asked my clinic nurse in a quiet moment. (I had noticed that for the rest of the clinic I was left with just one nurse.)

"Well," she said, "that girl has a bad reputation. She is a prostitute and rather brazen. If she has no clients she goes into a public house. She starts singing to draw attention to herself. Then she strips off. She gets men by the score, and takes them off with her.

"That silly bitch thought she would strip off in front of you. We knew it once we heard her sing. She never wears knickers – they slow her down!"

Now, that's why I got three nurses and not one!

* * *

A registrar was taken ill in 1988 and telephoned in sick. Ros, another registrar, had to work that night. She is very fond of animals but, poor Ros, there was nobody to look after her dog Benjie. This little terrier was quite a character. She went home and came back to the hospital with Benjie. He had a walk in the hospital grounds and was then locked up after a meal in the registrar's office with a warm rug and plenty of water in a bowl.

Whilst Ros was working, somebody came into the registrar's office, probably looking for hospital notes. Benjie saw his chance and escaped. A few minutes later Ros went to check on her charge. He was long gone. Oh dear.

Benjie went right down the corridor, then left, left again, and then smelt food. Oh good. Another left and a right. He was on the ward. Supper had just been served, and he could also smell toast.

Ros raced around looking for Benjie. Some of the offices were open, being cleaned. No, he was not there. (She checked he had not left his calling card anywhere!)

An elderly lady on the ward was going home. She was a bit confused. "I can see a dog," she exclaimed.

"Oh, don't tell fibs," said the nurse not looking up.

"I can see a dog and it's there," said the lady.

"Oh, yes it is," said the surprised nurse. She recognised Benjie.

"Whose dog is it?" said the lady.

"Oh, it belongs to some people who were involved in an accident," said the nurse, making it up hurriedly.

"Oh, in that case I will take him home with me and look after him," said the old lady.

"No," said the nurse, thinking hard. "We have a hospital policy for stray dogs. I will set the policy in motion."

"Oh, how efficient!" said the old lady.

Ros appeared and scooped up Benjie. He could easily have been the subject of an IR (that's an incident report – any untoward incident gets notified to the hospital authorities, and it would not have helped Ros's career).

Ros is now an emergency consultant in Leeds – surrounded at home by animals, including horses.

* * *

'Alcohol increases the desire for sex.'
William Shakespeare

I attended a meeting of the Derby Medical Society in 2015. An eminent neurologist called Graham gave us a lecture entitled 'Love Actually'. We were taught that, during sexual activity, one particular area of the brain is stimulated to the exclusion of other cerebral cortical (brain) activity! He illustrated this, as 20 years ago he had been the President of the Junior Doctors here in Derby. After a mess dinner, two junior doctors, one male and one female, left the party hand in hand. They walked up the main hospital corridor of the Derbyshire Royal Infirmary past several well-lit, busy wards. But at the top of the straight corridor, it was deserted and dark.

So she mounted an empty hospital trolley, and he mounted her! But this trolley had no brakes. It could not stop. Neither could they! Whoops of pure joy filled the air as this laden trolley slid back downhill, into the bright lights and past the wards. Amazed onlookers stared and stared.

The following morning it was the duty of the mess president, Graham, to go to each ward in turn and apologise to the senior sister for the disgusting behaviour of these two junior doctors.

But once this particular area of the brain is stimulated, other brain activity stops.

* * *

Robin is the kind of doctor who always has and always will be a pillar of respectability. He was happily married and working as an SHO in obstetrics at Kingston Hospital. One evening, he was on the labour ward or in theatre for hours and hours.

He knew there was a mess party. He kept well clear of the wild event. Things had got a bit out of hand, especially with Maria. She came from abroad, and was a mess cleaner. She knew most of the doctors and the layout of the mess. Maria was a bit bored.

She had seen there was a mess party advertised on the mess notice board soon after she had arrived some months before. So she went along, although uninvited. She had a few drinks. She got very uninhibited. She took all her clothes off and jumped onto a male doctor's bed. He was very, very surprised. It was with some difficulty she was thrown out, once they got her to dress. How embarrassing it was.

More parties followed. More Maria antics were repeated. She eventually was warned, and then lost her job. She left. Would she return and strip again? Everybody was apprehensive.

Robin was busy doing what he loved: obstetrics. Very, very late and very tired, he returned to his room. The mess party was over. Everywhere was quiet, at last.

As he walked along a corridor that ran beside his room, there was a window onto the corridor from his room. *That's funny*, he thought. *There is a light on in my room. Well, my wife is at home! What is going on? I am sure I turned off the light when I left.* The curtain was only partly across the window. He looked in.

Oh horror, there was a form of a body in HIS BED. What could he do?

He called night sister. She needed back up. So she called for more muscle – a porter (male). They each peeped through that window and confirmed that a body was definitely in the bed.

They cautiously knocked at the door. (Everyone was frightened of being confronted by a naked MARIA!)

No reply from the knock – so in they cautiously went.

The form of the body was in fact two pillows strategically placed. On the main pillow at the top of the bed there was a note:

"MARIA SLEPT HERE – HA HA"

* * *

An interservices exercise between two groups of British troops in the Mediterranean took place in the 1960s. Regulars and reservists were involved, but obviously no live ammunition. The senior officer on one side happened to be a surgeon. After some hours of combat, this surgeon had a problem. His side had captured many men from the opposition. He could ill afford the troops needed to guard all these prisoners. He had no handcuffs and no jail. These men could escape and rejoin their comrades. So he temporarily took these prisoners 'out of action'. Each man had his foreskin attached to his inner thigh with a large tight stitch! This immobilised them.

The next day the successful commander snipped all these stitches.

The Ministry of Defence was never informed – until now.

* * *

The heirachy of hospital doctors is ill understood by the general public. So, let me enlighten you. Medical students are at the bottom of the ladder, although final year students are encouraged to do some things under supervision. Once provisionally qualified, the house surgeon or house physician does vital work. When fully qualified, the senior house officer, the staff grade, or the clinical assistant has a lot more responsibility. The registrar grade is next and is clearly recognised as a consultant training grade. The consultant grade is the pinnacle of success for most hospital doctors. By far the most exalted grade for medical positions in hospital is the professor. These doctors are distinguished by their great wealth of medical knowledge. All professors have impeccable manners and display a mastery of medical etiquette.

I was a registrar in plastic surgery at Bristol in 1975. None of my four consultant bosses were professors. At that time I don't think we had a professor of plastic surgery in the UK. Then one visited us from abroad to see the work that we did. All the bosses – extrovert surgeons – were only too keen to demonstrate their surgical skills and show off.

I was tired and not on call on Thursday night, 9th July 1975. I had been up most of the previous night. I was glued to the television. A recording of the Open Golf Championship at Carnoustie that day was on, and one of my British golfing heroes was on the screen. He was playing well.

343

Just then my junior doctor, a lady, rushed in. "He's after me – the professor."

"Oh shut up," I said. She loved to exaggerate. How impossible. Dressed immaculately in a suit, he had been the absolute personification of good manners. I pushed this hysterical female out of the door. She was laughing as I did this.

I settled down. Oh good, he had holed that putt; I was engrossed.

The door was thrown open again. My female junior was shouting as she burst in. "Help, help, help!" she cried.

Behind her staggered the professor. I have never seen a doctor so drunk, and that night he was raving! He held both his arms out in front of himself and yelled, "Come here, come here, I want you." He was chasing after this lady doctor!

"He's drunk all the whisky in the doctors' bar," she explained quickly, and flashed out of the door to escape the professor's clutches. (He had drunk two full bottles!)

I never saw the end of the golf that night. I had to catch the professor, before he caught this female or injured himself.

It took some time and several doctors to corner him. We did not want to hurt him. At 11pm I called for reinforcements – we had six or eight junior doctors, all sober, trying to catch one professor – he thought it was a game! Then he got a second wind. He jumped over chairs and slid under tables. A rugby player crashed into a door when he was beaten by a sidestep! "Be careful," I cried, "don't hurt the professor." We finally got him into the front seat of my car. He had run out of steam at last. He was exhausted.

"I feel so ill," he said. "I think I will be sick." All that alcohol was having an effect.

I found a floor bucket and put it between his knees. I belted him up. I knew where he was staying, and carefully drove him there.

It was long after midnight before I got him there. He had lost his key. So I knocked for the landlady. I had difficulty getting him out of my car. I helped the professor up the stairs. Somehow his legs did not work properly. His sense of balance had left him. I supported him a lot, preventing him from falling. There was quite a commotion. We were very noisy. I could not stop him shouting out! We must have woken all the residents of this high-class accommodation. I finally got him into his room. With great difficulty I got this 'sack of coals' onto the bed and took off his shoes. My job done, I left at once.

The next morning found us sitting and waiting for the teaching session. Our lecturer was to be the professor. There had been quite a build up to this event. Everybody was there – all the four consultants and the juniors.

My female junior sat beside me. In a stage whisper at 8.59am she said to me, "He will never make it, will he?" This stage whisper was overheard by Paul, our senior registrar and organiser. He turned to us and said, "What's happened? Why won't he make it?"

Well, I am not one to tell on anybody. I just said, "Oh, the professor was a bit tired last night." Now, if I had said the truth: "He was raving mad and completely drunk", it would have been a bit unfair on the professor. His standing amongst his professional colleagues would have plummeted. Anyway, the look I got suggested that Paul thought that I had 'nobbled the professor' and prevented him from lecturing. The professor was telephoned, and everyone was told, "The professor is unwell." A deputy speaker spoke. Paul was suspicious of me after that.

The professor's wife then joined him. Now on the rein, he behaved well, and left. Paul still wondered what I had done to their star speaker.

Paul was my chief usher at my wedding and became a consultant in Bristol.

Contrary to Paul's suspicions, I had looked after this VIP very, very well indeed. So I was in trouble for doing a good deed!

This was not for the first, or last, time in my life.

* * *

I well recall very clearly a medical student slipping up on medical etiquette! I was an examiner in Surgery in medical finals at the time. My assistant was another male, the professor of surgery, no less! Now, as doctors we are all taught to be observant. Obversation is at the heart of being a good doctor and is, of course, an essential part of being a good examiner.

The female candidate came in wearing an ivory silk blouse and a long, navy blue, pleated skirt. She was later required to lean over the patient to listen to the heart sounds with her stethoscope. As she did this, both of us examiners had a clear view of her cleavage right down to her umbilicus!

Points for this were neither added nor subtracted. The male patient was ecstatic!

This is not the action of a proper professional lady. She was counselled later about her dress code, by a lady doctor who explained, "Medical examination is concerned with exposure of the patient's body, and definitely not that of the doctor's!"

Incidentally, she passed this examination and qualified as a doctor.

* * *

Phil was a young surgeon who loved his beer. He was affectionately known as 'Phil the Swill'! One night at a mess dinner he drank more beer than usual. He staggered out of the doctors' mess and across the corridor. He needed to rest. He got into the lift and pressed the button for the top floor. He got out and walked into the surgeons' on-call room. He stripped off and got into bed.

Unfortunately, he had pressed the wrong button. He was on the wrong floor and in a bed on a ward. The nurse in charge of the ward failed to recognise this surgeon. He was certainly not wearing his white coat or his name badge. She called security. These men walk mildly drunk people off site. Phil, in his state, was destined for the police cells. Fortunately for him, his wife turned up. Wives are good at checking on their spouses. She apologised to the nurse, helped her husband dress and drove him home.

Their marriage survived. He is now a pillar of society.

* * *

In 1995, Angus William Wallace, a professor of Orthopaedic and Accident Surgery at Queen's Medical Centre, Nottingham, was on flight 032 from India to London. Before take-off, he was called to attend to a patient with an arm injury after a fall from a bike. A sling was fashioned and the plane took off.

This patient soon had chest pain and deteriorated. Clearly, they had a punctured lung. Air was escaping inside the chest to collapse the lung (a pneumothorax). This could kill the patient quickly, especially on an emergency landing in Delhi with the alteration in cabin pressure.

Professor Wallace operated, aided by Dr Tom Wong and a rudimentary medical kit. The skin and instruments were sterilised with Courvoisier brandy. Some lidocaine was inserted to numb the skin. Dr Wong had to hold a small chest incision open with a knife and fork. A urinary catheter was inserted deep into the wound with the aid of a metal coat hanger. The catheter end was then inserted into a water bottle. Air bubbled out of the chest and into the bottle. So the treatment worked. On landing at Heathrow the patient was transferred to hospital (Professor Wallace had finished the brandy by then).

Professor Wallace published the article, 'Managing in flight emergencies, in the *British Medical Journal* in August 1995. Mrs Thatcher praised him for 'his courage, split-second decision-making and his "can do" approach'. He was awarded the Weigelt-Wallace award, and he gave the money to medical research.

I know Angus Wallace. We both sat on a committee organising medical school teaching. This extrovert retired on 2nd October 2015. He is known to this day as the 'coat hanger surgeon'. Well, as such, I believe that he was following the innovative surgical lead of Sir Harold Gillies.

* * *

I Treat By Royal Consent!
Not Another Practical Joke

For once, in 1989, I was sitting in our coffee room for five minutes between patients. Sister burst in:

"There's so-and-so (a major Royal) in the waiting room."

Everybody laughed. Yes, a practical joke – another! Ha ha!

She paused and then repeated herself.

Now nobody laughed. I went to investigate, expecting it to be a joke. But no, there was that Royal sitting in the middle of a packed waiting room. I had never seen them in the flesh before, just on television, or in newspapers. Now, I have seen second-rate sportsmen, or even third-rate entertainers, all without exception mobbed in this waiting room. No, this major Royal was left alone – unrecognised and totally ignored!

I asked them to follow me. They had been hunting in South Derbyshire and had been kicked by their horse. They had a cut to their chin and needed an X-ray. As I escorted them through X-ray, I noted several radiographers looked up, and their faces registered instant recognition and great surprise.

There was no fracture. Under local anaesthetic I cleaned and sutured the laceration. A small piece of skin was trimmed away. The bleeding was red (and not blue). The patient left, but not before they had made a careful note of my name and address. As I escorted them to the front door, I enquired if the Queen was waiting in the Rolls? No, just a redhead in an estate car was there.

My Royal's scar healed well. I followed them up on television.

Perhaps, as it was December, I would get a hamper from Fortnum and Mason's, sister suggested. She also suggested that we raffle that little piece of Royal flesh that I had trimmed. "No, bin it," I told her. (Well, a raffle was not exactly the action of a professional – good idea that it was!)

No hamper arrived.

Christmas came and went.

On twelfth night I was clearing away the Christmas cards that had arrived at our house. My eye fell on one that I had been unable to read. Well, as a doctor, I am well used to deciphering medical missives, but this cryptic communication had completely baffled me. What is the message? Who is it from? I sat down in a good light with my glasses on, and very carefully surveyed these strange hieroglyphics. Then eventually I interpreted this appalling scribble.

Alistair Fraser-Moodie and all in the Accident Department.
With best wishes for Christmas and the New Year.
With many thanks, [the Royal].

So, there is one group of individuals with worse writing than doctors – the Royals!

CHAPTER THIRTY-EIGHT

Mistakes and Mismanagement: What Has Gone Wrong? What Can We Do About It?

Any fool can defend his mistakes and most fools do.

Dale Carnegie

Medical and Surgical Errors

"Have I seen any mistakes?"

I have spent over 50 years working in our National Health Service. This included as a medical student (five years), in industry (six months), in general practice (six months,) as a junior hospital doctor (12 years,) as a consultant (nearly 30 years,) and as a clinical teacher (seven years.) I have seen mistakes, big and small, over and over again. I am not blameless. I too have made mistakes. I have seen my patients, my relatives and myself all suffer from medical mistakes!

"How do medical mistakes occur?"

In my opinion medical mistakes fall into four groups :-

- The first cause is getting the wrong diagnosis (because of the wrong history, the wrong examination or the wrong tests).
- The second cause is the wrong treatment(because of the wrong drug, wrong dose, wrong administration, wrong operation or right operation done badly).
- The third cause is a complication of this condition that is missed(often because it has not been prevented.)
- The fourth cause is an identity crisis (because one patient is confused with another).

"How big is the problem?"

A private company, Dr Foster, published a government report on our National Health Service. As reported[1], the errors make painful reading. Surgical items were left in at least 209 patients in the year 2008-9. Surgeons operated on the wrong part of the body at least 82 times as well. Many hospitals had unusually high mortality rates. Frequently, hospitals failed to investigate unexpected deaths. Dr Foster estimated that there were 5,000 avoidable deaths in our NHS in 2008.

Well, how bad are these mistakes? The BBC programme World at One[2, 3], through the Freedom of Information Act, found evidence of:

- 322 cases of foreign objects – instruments or swabs – left inside bodies!
- 214 patients had surgery on the wrong part of the body.
- 58 patients had surgery with the wrong implant or prosthesis.
- 73 patients had feeding tubes to the stomach inserted into the lungs by mistake.

But I did the latter once, after inserting a feeding tube with a radiopaque end into the lungs. Then I did an X-ray. The tube was in the chest and I quickly removed it. That was why the patient could not speak with a tube down his larynx! If this patient had been fed down this tube they would have come to harm.

Mistakes abound in our health service. For example, the victims of infected blood hepatitis C and HIV.[4] But there have been no reported cases of transmission of HIV from healthcare workers to patients in the UK.[5]

'Millions of people die each year from medical errors and infections linked to healthcare, making going into hospitals riskier than flying,' the World Health Organisation (WHO) said.

The WHO said that the chance of dying from an error in healthcare while in hospital was one in 300, compared with the risk of dying in an air crash of one in 10 million passengers.[6] (This is great news for all airline passengers, but not so good for patients on an admissions unit of a hospital).

Sir Liam Donaldson of the WHO said, "Healthcare is a high-risk business… modern healthcare is delivered in a fast-moving environment involving a lot of complex technology and people."[7]

I would put a different emphasis on this. Sir Liam Donaldson was after all an efficient medical administrator. But when did he last treat a patient? He has since retired.

"Are there any administrative errors?"

Yes, lots and lots and lots. Let me explain:

Are there inaccuracies in hospital surgical coding?[8] Such mistakes could affect the wrong payment from primary care trusts to the hospital involved.[8] The results from one surgical firm over four months showed 9% of patients were miscoded and 27% incompletely coded. This represented a loss to the hospital of nearly £20,000 over this time! So the whole hospital overall is a big-time loser! The trouble is that coders in hospitals are non-medical and so cannot read records accurately. This is another form of communication error.

Other papers found mistakes in orthopaedic day surgery, orthopaedic surgery, neurosurgery, otolaryngology, and even head and neck surgery.

Their conclusion, was that more communication was needed between the clinical and the coding staff.[9] This idea is carried on by Tucker et al in *The Bulletin* January 2016, page 34. Three orthopaedic surgeons intervened in this procedure. They educated the coders, who were non-medical, and the surgeon.

There was a definite improvement as a result.

Mr Bevan introduced us to a free National Health Service.

Now the emphasis has changed. Hospitals (and general practitioners too) have to generate income from treating patients. Do patients, or money, run the system? E.g., one heading in our local paper read: 'Cold snap leaves city NHS in Cash Black Hole'.[10]

Also, in *The Times:* 'Lives at risk as Hospitals run into Cash Crisis'.[11]

Yet More Mistakes and Mismanagement

Are hospitals safe? Are they efficient? Are we getting value for money as taxpayers? What will the changes in the running of the health service bring?

Unfortunately, the hospitals are not as safe as we would like. Our ambulances are dirty.[12] The new system of electronic patient records being introduced across England is unreliable and contains inaccuracies that could put patients at risk.[13] The NHS covers up fatal blunders.[14]

There is another danger. Privatisation. Some NHS care is provided by large multinational companies. They are taking over whole hospitals. So they are funded by taxpayers but the profit goes to shareholders.[15]

Payouts by the NHS for mistakes have trebled over the past decade to reach £1.33 billion in 2011-12, of which £230 million went to lawyers in fees.[16]

Lawyers take half of NHS damages claims.[17] The NHS wastes millions overpaying for supplies.[18] Labour has left the NHS with a £60 billion debt after building 103 hospitals on the never never (Private Finance Initiative).[19]

Human error is the main cause of most accidents. Both leaving surgical items in a patient or performing the wrong operation are due to collective human error, and the surgeon involved is ultimately responsible. Every patient must be checked before, during and after an operation. But freedom of information requests by the BBC tell us that over the past four years 214 patients had the wrong operation in England, and 322 patients had foreign objects left inside them! How can this happen? Let's go through this in detail:

A patient sees a consultant surgeon with all the investigations. The operation is decided upon, the likely complications are mentioned and the outcome outlined.

The patient is admitted, the notes obtained with investigations. The consent form is signed. The patient is marked with the area for surgery. But new doctors and nurses are often now involved.

The patient goes to theatre. But the patient is under a premedication and often confused now. The anaesthetic staff and theatre nurses are unfamiliar with the patient. Another surgeon may take over the surgery. The notes may be wrongly entered, or of another patient. The area marked may be wrong. The consent form may be wrong – it's a whole catalogue of potential pitfalls. NO, NO, NO, the surgeon should be in charge and that person does the operation.

He or she must check each patient before theatre and that everything to do with the operation is correct. They alone are ultimately responsible for the whole surgical procedure and for not leaving anything inside. The surgeon may otherwise rely on false information told to them! No, he or she must check the patient themselves.

Today's conveyor-belt surgery, where the surgeon sometimes stays scrubbed up and just does the operation, is wrong. This multiple blame culture is wrong too. Shared responsibility between health professionals for ensuring the right operation is done is not foolproof. The statistics prove this.

In 2017 there is a trial of barcodes on wrist bands in some hospitals. Will this put a stop to wrong operations and wrong drug administration? I hope so.

It all starts with medical training and there are a lot more students. These in turn have far less patient exposure than I did in the 1960s. For example, seeing a medical student on the wards or in the emergency department after 5pm is a rarity now. It used to be common.

The pass rate for the final examinations is now a lot higher. Back in the 1960s the failure rate for the finals at our hospital and the 2nd MB was 30%-40%. Nowadays the failure rate for finals is 5%. Any failure to reach this target is reflected on the medical school and clinical teachers rather than the student. The clinical teachers do the examining now, not an independent body. The examination is in-house and not external. There is an external assessor.

When I was a junior doctor – a surgical registrar – my surgical consultant was rarely called in by me in the night. I telephoned him as necessary and at his request got on with the operation time and time again. It is now imperative for surgical consultants to come in and supervise junior doctors doing emergency surgical operations. (Unless the junior is very experienced.) These juniors have to comply with the European Working Time Directive. So they have a much shorter working week (unless they opt out!)

From the 1st August 2009 the European Working Time Directive (EWTD) legislation required all doctors in training to be working no more than an average of 48 hours per week. (The EWTD originally was introduced to stop foreign lorry drivers falling asleep at the wheel!)

It is not just the 48-hour week either. If a trainee surgeon is on call for the wards, their 48-hour week is soon used up. So surgical training in particular is lacking in outpatient and theatre training.[20]

The most significant impact of EWTD is the detrimental effect on young doctors' ability to accumulate valuable life experience within the profession.[21]

This 48-hour week has compelled trusts to introduce full shifts for doctors. Research in industry has shown that shift working leads to interrupted sleep patterns, chronic tiredness and mistakes.[22] I was tired on call, but better a tired doctor who has seen it all before than a well-rested doctor who has seen nothing.[23]

More junior doctors working shorter hours have less patient contact and so learn less, becoming less experienced. There is political pressure to improve the pass rates for higher medical exams or even scrap them altogether. These same junior doctors are on fast-track training called specialist registrar training programmes. So, when they get to the end, four or five years, they are trained but less experienced than their predecessors. (I was a junior doctor for well over ten years before I became a consultant.)

So there is a knock-on effect:

Less medical student exposure to disease.

A higher proportion of medical students passing finals.

Less junior doctor medical experience.

Easier junior doctor higher exams.

Less experienced junior doctors when trained.

Less experienced consultants with an increasing workload, more technical expertise expected of them and very little medical or surgical support!

Since the EWTD was imposed, a quarter of junior doctors drop out of their NHS training after two years.[24] They were either 'quitting or taking a break'. The European Working Time directive has had a disastrous impact on training and morale.[25]

Have I any answers? Well, maybe a few ideas:

Medical students need more knowledge. They need to be attached round the clock to junior doctors F1 or F2 – more exposure to disease, more technical expertise. Medical student examinations need to be a lot harder. Back in the 1960s nurses had more anatomical knowledge than medical students of today! To put it bluntly, today we are passing students that honestly deserve to fail, and reaping the consequences. (I failed finals twice along with a lot of my friends and worked harder than ever at retakes!)

Junior doctor higher examinations need to be harder, e.g. MRCS. This has a pass rate greater than 50%, whereas the old FRCS was at times less than 10%. Any politically motivated attempts to abandon these tests can only result in more medical mistakes.

All my final year students are worried stiff about medical errors. They cannot sleep at night they tell me. They know that finals are a formality, but the responsibility of medical work is heavy. I guided them through: mistakes in history taking; mistakes in clinical examination; mistakes in X-ray interpretation; mistakes in ECG recognition; mistakes in blood test results. There needs to be greater knowledge to pass finals, with an emphasis on possible mistakes.

If I was still working as a surgeon and a patient had one good and one diseased kidney, what happens if I remove the wrong kidney?

A big row.

I might be suspended (and a locum does my work).

The hospital lawyer is consulted and eventually there is a big payout from hospital funds to the patient or his relatives or both. Millions of pounds of taxpayers' money goes out annually in this way.

At times, at least 100 consultants are suspended from duty by the hospitals involved, on full pay initially. (More taxpayers' money is gone.)

The reader may be drawn into the false conclusion that this is a short-term remedy. Not so; one of my colleagues was suspended on full pay for well over 20 years and then got a full pension!

It is about time that every consultant's contract is renewed, and reviewed annually. Then they can be sacked easily!

Once a doctor is employed by a hospital today he has full indemnity. So, if he kills anybody at work, the hospital pays out usually 50% of the claim! If the doctor kills anybody driving home he will lose his licence to drive, may well not get any more car insurance and go to jail, probably for manslaughter.

We have returned to each individual doctor insuring himself or herself for all medical work. It is expensive, but the premium can be claimed against tax. The medical defence unions already exist – several of them.

If a doctor makes mistakes his premium goes up. Eventually, he would not get insurance and so would not be able to work. I believe that if a doctor is solely responsible for a claim, then his medical insurance should pay it ALL.

The hospitals would have less bills and I suspect less mistakes. All doctors would be more accountable and I believe more careful. Premiums would rise after a mistake and some doctors would have difficulty getting indemnity insurance. Well, the results today show that too many mistakes are made in hospitals and that change is indicated. New laws were introduced in 2010 to stop the cover up of fatal blunders! I don't think that they have worked.[26] Or will we, the poor taxpayers, foot the bill as more and more doctors are turned out to make more and more and more mistakes at our expense?

The growth of the litigation culture is drowning hospitals and schools of money. £1.33 billion paid out by the NHS in 2011/12. The NHS Litigation Authority estimated potential liabilities in 2012 for outstanding clinical negligence claims at £18.6 billion.[27]

It is about time that every consultant's contract is renewed, and reviewed annually.

Well, in January 2012 the NHS Compensation Fund had a bailout fund of £185 million. When will it end? Since then, the projected bill for medical compensation has risen up and up. It is rising daily!

Finally – what is a mistake? The Dr Foster episode has dealt with the more serious cases, but this is the tip of the iceberg. Exposure to current medical records soon exposes a myriad of faults. There is an urgent need for central computerised medical records for all, including all results, X-rays and GP records. Is this beyond our capabilities and a haven for hackers? What a shame, but mistakes would be reduced by such a system, and any errors reduced.

Medical Productivity

But are market forces good in some way? Eight years after Labour introduced market forces into the NHS, the health service is still not seeing the desired returns for its investments.[28]

The European Working Time Directive – has it not helped those poor overworked junior doctors? 90% of junior doctors feel that these changes have already resulted in reduced training.[29]

Fixed shift working has been introduced. Research in other industries has shown that shift working is associated with interrupted sleep patterns, chronic tiredness and mistakes.[30]

Finally, billions of pounds have been spent on improving NHS hospitals but this has failed to improve productivity.[31] Well, I am not surprised. In my first year as a doctor I was frantic seeing patients, day and night, week in and week out. Now if I wander into the doctors' mess I see junior doctors reading newspapers at 11am. When I ask them what they are doing they often say, "My consultant is on holiday, I have no patients and nothing to do." This is lunacy. Wards empty, lists empty – what a waste!

Goodbye productivity. These doctors are paid well but have little or no work to do. More and more lunacy!

The Senior Fraud Squad had investigated a UK-based orthopaedic implant company, De Puy International.[32] This company was found guilty of making corrupt payments to Greek surgeons to induce them to buy its products for the state health service. As a consequence, nearly £5m was demanded by the UK.[33]

Reporting of safety events is improving.[34]

No: medical mistakes,, in my opinion, are often the result of communication problems, e.g., for drugs – the wrong dose, wrong method of administration, wrong drugs for that patient, or given to the wrong patient or even not given at all! The moment the drug gives the wrong response from the patient it should be noted and acted upon.

Well, why did I pick drugs as an example of medical errors? Quite simply, as an emergency consultant, I saw many patients a year with drug reactions. Failure to diagnose earlier could be fatal. Many such reactions could have been prevented.

Poorly performing doctors are unlikely to have an isolated performance issue. Only 44% of such doctors were shown to have performance issues. However, 94% were shown to have behavioural problems and 75% were shown to have communication problems![35]

What is a medical mistake?

Pitfalls in medicine abound. Let me explain by giving a classic example – the fractured scaphoid bone. This small bone is in our wrists, surrounded by other little bones. If anybody falls onto their wrists this little bone may break. Young people are more vulnerable.

There are two problems here. Firstly, such a fracture if left untreated has a 50% chance of never healing! So the young person is left with a stiff painful wrist, unless they have a complicated operation to fix it!

Secondly, this fracture is often not seen on initial X-rays! So, despite the X-rays being excellent, the fracture cannot be seen as the bone is small and wedged in by other little bones all around!

The classic solution is to put everyone where a fracture is suspected into a special plaster. The plaster is heavy and inconvenient. Then after a few days re-X-ray – often this charade is repeated over and over!

Well, for over 30 years as a consultant I was exposed to droves of these suspected fracture cases in four follow-up clinics a week. I was heavily involved in the teaching of medical students and minor operating sessions. I only got routinely onto the shop floor at work when the junior doctors were being taught!

I sought advice from a senior registrar of mine, Dr Tan, about suspected scaphoid fractures. Together we planned the treatment for these cases. We put all suspected cases in a splint held on by Velcro. It was quick and easy to put on and take off. The patients took it off to wash. I taught my juniors of this treatment and spoke at meetings in the UK and abroad. I had trips to Dublin and Sydney, funded for me on the strength of this interest! What were my results?

Over 20 years I had reviewed about 4,000 patients with wrist injuries. (Well, I alone did adult follow-up clinics.) Radiology experts were sought and they agreed that 42 patients had a fractured scaphoid bone only seen on follow-up X-rays, and invisible initially! Untreated, half these patients would have developed a stiff and painful wrist as the fracture would not have healed.

However, even in these splints initially, the 42 fracture victims were subsequently put in plaster, i.e., a fracture of this bone was seen on follow-up. Eventually all but two of them healed well. So only two patients needed an operation.

These results from this treatment were good. Not one of these 4,000 patients sued us. They all healed with no long-term problems. But I received criticism galore: "Oh, we can't do that!" they cried. So my colleagues at other hospitals continued to put droves of patients in heavy plasters – costly and time-consuming, especially as the majority just had sprained wrists with no fracture.

But guess what? In the 21st century, I have heard of several hospitals that put on this splint for a suspected fractured scaphoid. Forty years ago this was unheard of – except in Derby!

So, in my humble opinion, better training, better accountability and finally communication is needed urgently.

Another Doctor Makes Yet Another Mistake!!!

In hobbled another casualty. Oh he's a friend of mine, called Jim. He is a retired consultant histopathologist whom I have known for years.

"I've got an infection in my foot" he stated. "So could I please have some antibiotics?" he said.

Once in a cubicle, he explained: "This infection has ruined my holiday abroad in the mountains. It's been going on for weeks. I wanted to walk far, and to ski, but I just cannot. I have only been able to walk around the alpine village. Can you please heal this infection?"

Well, on examination his left ankle was red, swollen and warm. BUT ON SQUEEZING THE BONE IT HURT. (This is the classic sign of a fracture.) He denied any injury at all. "It can't possibly be a fracture." He was adamant.

"Well," I reassured him, "if the X-ray is negative, I will treat this infection."

He protested "An Xray is not necessary. It's just a total waste of NHS money."

I STRONGLY DISAGREED.

He went for an X ray, still protesting!

I should explain here of the important work that histopathologists do. They are concerned with recognising different diseases at cellular level, i.e. down a microscope. So they tell other doctors what is wrong with a patient, by studying a piece of tissue from that patient. It is highly skilled work. They are very busy people. They also perform post mortems.

But they are paid extra for going to the coroners court. They don't get called out at night, or at weekends. They can start work early, often, and just go when they are finished! But best of all, none of their patients ever complain about them (as they are dead)! Incidentally, there is a national shortage of histopathologists.

Jim was appointed a consultant in the '60s. He came with four young sons, but his wife Nancy longed for a daughter, and she became pregnant for a fifth time. Even better news, she was expecting triplets! She went into labour and delivered three more boys! Yes, Jim has seven sons, and Nancy told me she was the fastest potato peeler in the street!

Let us return to the story.

Jim came to me, now back from X-ray, clutching his X-rays.

"When did you last examine or treat a patient?" I asked.

"Oh, about 50 years ago," he admitted sheepishly. (So he was deskilled.)

"Well, it shows," I said.

The X-ray showed a nasty fracture of his tibia (shin bone) into his ankle joint!

He healed well in a plaster, combined with rest.

I often meet him today, out walking. He has no limp. He healed well, and in 2017 is over 90 years old.

References:

1. David Rose. Worst hospitals free to go on failing. *The Times*. 31.11.2009:3.
2. Tariq Tahir. The Never Events for Patients that occur all too often. *The Metro*. 10.05.2013:7.
3. Martin Barrow. Hundreds of patients suffer with serious mistakes during surgery. *The Times*. 10.05.2013:23.
4. Sam Lister. Blood scandal victims get justice at last. *The Times*. 11.01.2011. Health Scare 2 Editorial.
5. Richard Mar. Discrimination against doctors with HIV must end. *BMJ*. 2012:344;E3440.
6. Sir Liam Donaldson. Safety. *Health Service Journal*. January 2010:7.
7. Routers. Geneva. Hospital stay riskier than flying, WHO says. *The Times*. 22.07.2011:35.
8. HA Khwaja, P Kerr, C Kelley, K Patel and ED Baba. Inaccuracy in Surgical Coding. *Ann R Coll Surg (Suppl)* 2007.91:142-146.
9. A Razik, V Venkat-Raman, FS Haddad. Assessing the accuracy in Clinical Coding in Orthopaedic Day Surgery patients. *Surg Eng (Suppl)* 2013:9;14-16.
10. Kate Liptrot. Cold Snap leaves City NHS in cash black hole. *Derby Telegraph*. 20.02.2010:1.
11. Martin Barrow, C Smyth. Lives at risk as hospital run into cash crisis. *The Times*. 13.12.2011:1.
12. *Derby Evening Telegraph*. 19.02.2010:Front page.
13. David Rose. Patients' database riddled with errors. *The Times*. 19.03.2010:20.
14. Lois Rogers. Watchdog MP finds billions being wasted. *Sunday Times*. 28.03.2010:8. Robert Watts. How the NHS covers up fatal blunders. 28.03.2010:10.
15. BMA Publication. Look after our NHS.
16. Julie Henry. Blame game bleeding the NHS dry. *Sunday Telegraph*. 09.09.2012:18.
17. Sam Lister. Lawyers take half of NHS damages claims. *The Times*. 18.12.2009:3.
18. Chris Smyth. The NHS managers waste £1billion a year paying different prices for the same equipment. *The Times*. 03.01.2011:1&11.
19. *News of the World*. 27.03.2011:Front page.
20. Professor Angus Wallace. NHS shift takes surgeons away from operations.

The Times. 10.08.2009:23.

21. TWR Anderson. Limits on doctors' hours threaten patients' wellbeing. President Royal College of Surgeons, Glasgow. *The Times.* 11.08.2010:19.

22. Matthew Worrall. Surgeons in the frontline. *Royal Coll Surg Bulletin.* No7;July 2008:234-5.

23. Dr J Hardy. Tired doctors. *The Times.* 18.10.2010:23.

24. David Rose. Junior Doctors desert the NHS. *The Times.* 06.09.2010:Front page.

25. David Rose. Remedy for overworked doctors causes more harm than good. *The Times.* 06.09.2010:8.

26. Lois Rogers. How the NHS covers up fatal blunders. *Sunday Times.* 28.03.2010:10.

27. Claire Dyer. NHS compensation fund gets £185 million bail out till April as claims rise. *BMJ.* 2012:344.
    Amijas Morse. National Audit Office.17.12.2010: Management of NHS Productivity.

28. Zosia Kmietowicz. NHS has seen little benefit from reforms in market forces. *BMJ.* 06.03.2010:340;500.

29. CR Chalmers. The lost generation. Impact of 56 hour EWTD. *Ann R Coll Surg Eng.* 2010:92;102.

30. Matthew Worrall. Do reduced hours create better safety? *Ann R Coll Surg Eng.* 2090:7225&2009:9;224-5.

31. Amijas Morse. National Audit Office. 17.12.2010: Management of NHS Productivity.

32. *BMJ.* 23.04.2011:38;891.

33. C Dyer. UK Company pays £5 million order for corrupt payment to Greek surgeons. *BMJ.* 2011:342;897.

34. Adrian O'Dowd. Reporting of safety events is improving. *BMJ.* 17.10.2009:339;880.

35. *Bulletin of the Royal College of Surgeons of England.* 2012:94(Suppl)342-344. Cloi 10 1308/14. 7363512x1344851 169262.

CHAPTER THIRTY-NINE

Mistakes of Communication – More Misadventures Than Ever (Some of them mine!)

The man who makes no mistake does not usually make anything.

Edward Phelps

Doctors are good communicators. Failure to communicate properly leads to disasters (see previous chapters!) Here are a few 'misadventures' of mine and other doctors'. Lack of communication caused most of these errors.

Surgeons tend to be extroverts. They love showing off. They don't lack for confidence. It's all part of their character. They need plenty of self-belief in their own ability – built up by years of experience. Just as an actor is only as good as his/her last part, so a surgeon is only as good as his/her last operation.

* * *

Towards the end of an afternoon, a private cosmetic surgeon invited me in to see his follow-up patients. They had all been operated upon recently.

I had seen them pre-operatively. The first two patients were very happy. A third came in; she had had the bridge of her nose built up. Some ENT surgeon had operated previously and cured her ENT problem. This left the patient with a great dip in the bridge of her nose. This was very disfiguring. She had to resort to private cosmetic surgery. She sued the ENT surgeon. Would he pay her bill?

My colleague had inserted a slither of bone. The plaster was removed. The result looked good – really good. I was impressed.

The patient was given a mirror; she was ecstatic. "Oh, you wonderful man," she said. "Thank you, thank you." This lady of 40 had also acquired a new man half her age! She called him in from the waiting room. He was delighted. His new woman was more beautiful than ever. He enthused about her nose.

A second mirror was called for, so she could see her profile better. She cooed and he drooled. I had seen enough.

Then she said, "How did you do it?"

"Oh," said the surgeon, "I slipped a piece of bone in."

"Where did you take the bone from?" she said, looking around her ample body anxiously.

"Oh, it's pig bone – specially prepared," he said.

"What?" she shouted. "What did you say?"

"Pig bone," he repeated anxiously.

There was a pause and she let out a scream. Her new man rushed to her. She pushed him away and then turned to the surgeon.

"But, you stupid idiot!" she shouted. "I can't have pig bone in me; I'm a vegetarian."

"But it's only under your skin," he pleaded.

"Get it out, get it out now!" she roared.

The pig bone was subsequently removed and plastic silastic inserted.

The surgeon, the new man and the nose were all back in favour again! A communication disaster.

There are many mishaps in cosmetic surgery. The classic one is when a rather flat-chested lady goes in for breast implants. Pre-operatively she takes an A-cup. Post-operatively she has a fine 36-inch bust with a B-cup. Now, most ladies would be more than satisfied.

A few ladies – a very few however – have not been happy. They wanted bigger implants to become a D-cup. Quite out of proportion.

What a communication disaster!

But this operation has benefitted many ladies. Take, for example, Kate O'Mara, the stunning Hollywood actress. She came to a pub to push over a pile of pennies for a charity. She was wearing a low cut dress that showed off her rather ample cleavage. She caught sight of a man looking at her wares and smiled. "Darling," she said, "they cost me £180 each!"

So it's not just the patient who derived pleasure from the operation, but countless others (mainly men).[1] The Medicines and Healthcare Products Regulatory Agency reports that 30,000 ladies have breast implants annually. They reported 1,500 ruptured implants in the past two years. I suspect these implants were too big.

Is this operation expensive? Yes. It's not just the surgeon's, anaesthetist's and nursing home's fees.

The really expensive items are all those new clothes!

* * *

A little old lady was brought into Casualty. She had been conveyed by a 999 ambulance. "What happened?" I asked her.

"Oh, I fell and twisted my leg. It hurts; please help me," she said.

I turned to the ambulance crew. "Her GP was there," said one.

"Did he give her anything?" I asked them.

"I don't know," said the other crew member.

I turned to my patient. "Has your GP given you any medication?" I asked.

"Oh, I don't think so," she said.

"Is there a letter?" I asked the crew.

"No," they replied.

I inspected the leg. It was obviously fractured, as the leg was deformed.

"I'll give you an injection to kill the pain," I said.

She thanked me.

I gave her 5mg of morphine intravenously. Ten minutes later the pain was no better. We wanted to put a splint on her leg. This would really hurt. So I gave her another 5mg of morphine intravenously.

The receptionist came to me then and whispered in my ear: "The GP is on the phone. He wants you to know he gave this lady 20mg of omnopon intramuscularly a few minutes ago." She left.

I panicked. She had had a huge amount of morphine intravenously and yet more morphine in the omnopon previously.

At this point her breathing suddenly stopped – she had been given an overdose of morphine, by me. By mistake.

I intubated the lady, i.e., put a plastic tube down her throat and into her windpipe, and gave her 100% oxygen. She then had the antagonist to morphine – nalorphine. She returned to breathing normally by herself in a few minutes.

So this was a communication problem.

* * *

A plastic surgery consultant was carrying out a breast reduction on a private patient in a private clinic. It was very posh. So was the patient. Sir Harold Gillies described the condition of big breasts as similar to going through life with a heavy fish slung on each shoulder. The bra straps cut in. Weight can often be lost elsewhere in the body, but fat remains in the breast area. This is so unfair.

Such private patients are excellent for our economy. As the present top rate of tax is 50%, up to 50% of the surgeons' and anaesthetists' fees go eventually straight to the Exchequer. Nurses are employed at these private nursing homes. They gain employment and pay more tax. Finally, such patients are removed from the NHS waiting list – another gain. (Recently, such people are no longer treated under the NHS.)

There are lots of clever ways of doing this operation. On this occasion the consultant favoured removal of the nipples and reducing the size of the breasts, and then putting the nipples back on again at 48 hours. The nipples would 'take' as a full thickness graft. He was assisted by another surgeon – a senior, senior registrar! Two surgical stars!

Everything went fine. The nipples were taken off. The breasts were reduced in size. It all went very well indeed.

Two days later, the plastic surgeon did the first dressing. The nipples had been wrapped in gauze and moistened with saline. He sent for them. They should have been in the fridge. Nobody could find them! Panic, panic, panic!

Two hours later they were found. They had been thrown away and were in the rubbish bin for 'contaminated disposables'. Fortunately, this had not been collected yet. This refuse is collected and disposed of separately. In that two hours, three theatre nurses had emptied the contents of this bin and had sifted through it. They were kneeling in plastic aprons and wore plastic gloves. Now they had found those precious nipples.

Now sometimes, the nipples kept in the fridge and put on at 48 hours do not take. This is rare. But in this case the nipples had been in the warm, dirty dustbin and not the fridge for 48 hours. Dead nipples seemed likely.

The private patient sensed some delay and anxiety regarding her nipples. However, after her nipples had been cleaned a few times in saline they had been put on.

Against all the odds these two nipples, stored in garbage for two days, took absolutely beautifully – 100%.

Well, life's like that. The patient was not told anything!

So this was a communication problem between the surgeon and the scrub nurse in theatre.

* * *

A man visited a tattooist in Ripley. This tattooist is called Fred. I have never met him and don't want to either.

This client of Fred's had had a tattoo that he wanted taken off. So this is what he did.

Fred charged £50. Then he looked at the tattoo. It was the word 'Sally', but now he was going out with 'Jenny', so the client wanted 'Sally' off and a dolphin below her (fig 52).

A paste containing sulphuric acid was made. It was carefully laid over 'Sally' and the dolphin. It was bandaged on.

"Now," said Fred, "get on the next Derby bus, go to the infirmary and ask for Mr Fraser-Moodie."

Whilst on the bus the client experienced pain in his arm. Well, he was being burnt.

I was called to see my 'private patient' who had come to see me. "Hurry, he is in pain. You are not a popular doctor," said the hospital receptionist!

I had a strange meeting with this patient. He was under the illusion I was paid by Fred to see him – a shared client. Denial by me simply inflamed the situation. He did not believe me.

'Sally' had gone forever. Well, he had suffered two full-thickness burns.

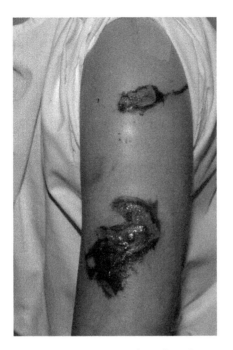

Fig 52 – The two tattoos have been burnt off with acid to leave painful raw areas.

He was so aggressive, as he was in so much pain.

I washed off the acid with copious water. The wound was dressed with flamazine.

I was prepared to do a skin graft, but he healed without one. I caught the patient telling the nurse he was a private patient of mine. I was not happy.

I had been used by Fred. I had had no communication at all! In my opinion the end did not justify the means.

Not for the first, or the last, time in my life I was in trouble for doing absolutely nothing.

Yet another communication problem. Many more almost identical cases followed.

* * *

In 1769, Captain James Cook, and his crew, were sailing the ship *Endeavour* in the South Seas. On 13th April they reached Tahiti. Here they were introduced to tattooing. They brought this custom back to England when they returned in 1771. The word tattoo is Tahitian. This 'art form' has been with us ever since.

Many celebrities have been tattooed, including David Beckham, Cheryl Cole and even Samantha Cameron. Famous people from the past have been tattooed. Sir Winston Churchill followed a family tradition and probably had an anchor on his right arm. (Some 'authorities' claim that this was a surgical scar.) Edward VIII certainly had a cross on his arm. Both George V and Tsar Nicholas II of Russia had Japanese dragons on their arms.[2]

My own personal view is that a tattoo on the face is distasteful. However, whilst working in plastic surgery we sometimes tattooed a patient's face! The patient usually had a port wine stain on the face (a noticeable birthmark). We tattooed a flesh-coloured pigment into the port wine stain that then became less noticeable!

A tattoo may record a close relationship – but this may not last. Similarly, the allegiance of somebody to a club or association may change. So the tattooed man may now support a different football team from the one adorning his chest. I have seen tattooed out-of-date telephone numbers, and even blood groups that are wrong! Surely such vital information can be stored in another form?

I have also seen the ultimate tattoo, usually on a large man's back. Down the shoulder blades gallop the huntsmen in their red coats. They chase the hounds that stream down the lower back, towards the bottom. But where is the fox? He is going to ground. Just his brush protrudes from the anus!

Tattoos can turn up in 'funny places'. Many years ago, in 1967, I was assisting my boss, a gynaecologist, in theatre with a private patient for repair of a prolapse. This old lady was outspoken and a 'snob'. Well, she was rude to everybody. This was her nature! Under a general anaesthetic her private parts were cleaned pre-operatively and the operating light turned on. Astonishingly, around the entrance to her vagina was a tattoo; it read:

'Abandon all hope, you who enter'.

(This is an inscription from Dante's 'Inferno' denoting the entrance to hell!)

Reference:

1. Norman Eshley. Kate O'Mara. *The Times*. 11. 4. 14:58.
2. Question Time: Guess who's got a tattoo at the age of 75. Patrick Kidd. *The Times*. 12. 11. 13;3.

CHAPTER FORTY

The General Medical Council

Five hundred years ago, King Henry VIII was approached by qualified physicians and qualified surgeons. The problem was that so many of the King's subjects were being treated by non-qualified personnel. The King agreed that this was wrong. The King noted that there were few qualified medical staff and the licensing of them was difficult. There are issues with the number of doctors in the UK and their licensing to this very day!

In 1858 the Medical Act laid down the minimum standards of medical education in the UK. This led to the formation of the General Medical Council (GMC).

Why did we need regulation of the medical profession?

Well, the catalyst for the regulation of the medical profession was the unprofessional behaviour of a few doctors. For example, the pioneering eye and ear surgeon Sir William Wilde was well respected professionally. He set up the first ophthalmic hospital in the British Isles, and wrote the first ENT textbook in 1853, *Practical Observations on Aural Surgery*. He was editor of the *Dublin Journal of Medical Science*. He was knighted in recognition of his contribution to medical statistics, and to his help during cholera epidemics. His public lectures were well attended.

But his private life was public knowledge. He fathered three illegitimate children prior to his marriage. He continued to stray. In a celebrated court case a young female patient, Mary Travers, accused him of seducing her under the influence of chloroform! His scandalous private life was laid bare in court! He refused to testify and was found guilty.

(Incidentally, years later Sir William's notorious playwright son, Oscar, was to die of intracranial sepsis secondary to ear disease. His father's book had shown this complication, and how to prevent it!)

Clearly, a mechanism was needed for the removal of such doctors as Sir William Wilde from the medical register. Hence the formation of the General Medical Council.[1]

Let me explain my own experiences of my contact with the GMC. In the 1980s we employed an experienced surgeon as a highly paid locum for several months. He signed the contract, worked one day and scarpered! Well, to be honest, I saw him in the distance in the canteen. He failed to answer his bleep. At 3am one morning on our ward I bumped into him. A student nurse was with him. She then rushed to me and kept close to me (this is not the usual effect I have on females). She told me later (with sister to help her) that he had propositioned her! Well, he spread his attentions liberally amongst the female staff, I was told. We men were safe.

After six months of being paid a vast amount he left. He had done nothing. I complained to the General Medical Council and went there one day to put my case. But he had killed nobody – no one had suffered. He had done little wrong. One female radiographer testified to his ardour. The chief executive from Guy's followed me. He had the same complaint as me – this doctor worked there for one morning. This doctor was not struck off then, but cautioned. He continued to stray and was struck off three years later.

My only other contact with the GMC was equally frustrating. My mother was aged 94 years in 1999, was senile and demented. After 40 years of working she had, for life, full registration of the General Medical Council. She then threatened, in an act of bravado, to do a GP locum, just to show me that she could! In panic I telephoned the GMC, giving all the details I could and identifying who I was and my relationship. My mother still had contacts and some GPs are desperate for a locum.

A receptionist at the GMC was unhelpful in the extreme. I was informed quite politely that as my mother was on the register she could do any such locum. No, age is not a bar and I definitely could not speak to any of the doctors. I informed her of the dangers of employing my mother, but to no avail. I was mortified.

Thank goodness this threat was never carried out. New regulations have now been implemented at the GMC and this loophole in the medical law has been closed! The GMC previously allowed doctors to remain on the medical register after retirement, for no fee. This changed in 2010 and all doctors now have to pay annually to remain on the register, although the fee is less if they are non-clinical.

My own contact directly with the GMC was equally frustrating. My direct debit was confirmed as set up on 11th December 2009 by the Finance Directorate of the GMC. You can imagine my surprise when I was told by the medical school where I taught, on 4th January 2010, that I was "no longer on the medical register". I had broken my contract with the medical school! I had not killed or seduced any patients, or even attacked an administrator! I had not even been informed by the GMC that I had been removed from the medical register, it was just uncovered.

The GMC's reason for this action was: "Oh, it takes a long time to arrange direct debits – we did not have enough time. Please pay another way." So, after all the money my late parents, my older sister, my wife and I have given the GMC, this is how they treat me – struck off! All because of their financial skulduggery. In a panic I telephoned the GMC and paid them over the phone using my debit card. I was reinstated onto the register. But will I remain on the medical register after this publication? Probably not!

I have since left the Medical Register.

* * *

A junior doctor in 1980 rotated to our emergency department from orthopaedics where he had previously worked. At 5.30pm on his very first day the sister in charge came to me rather upset. A student nurse had reported that this new doctor was overheard arranging a date with a lady patient. He and a male friend would have drinks with this patient, and her friend, that evening in a local pub.

I contacted him immediately and talked to him in private. He smirked initially when we confirmed the facts. He was going to meet his patient for drinks that very evening, and that was that!

I told him bluntly that he had met this patient professionally. He was barred from meeting her socially. She is a patient and as such should be treated properly. He was in a position of trust.

He only started to listen when I told him that any such meeting was likely to lead to his suspension by the hospital. He would be reported to the GMC. He suddenly took notice, and behaved after this.

The whole matter is a bit complicated. Well, I know of at least three consultant surgeons who have married their patients. The professional treatment has to finish first. Then later, they are free to make contact. My own observation is that the patient concerned is usually private, and that the doctor must do the right thing and marry her (or else be sued?).

* * *

I was retired but still teaching first and second year medical students on Introduction to Medicine sessions in 2013. I was told that doctors from the General Medical Council were coming to my respiratory session. I was nervous. I would be judged on my teaching ability and the educational content of this session!

I gave my usual lecture on the examination of the respiratory system. A routine must be followed so nothing is missed. Then we broke the 60, or so, students into groups of two or three for one-to-one bedside teaching with volunteer patients. Many of them had respiratory disorders like asthma or chronic obstructive pulmonary disease – the end result of smoking?

I was assessed on my teaching by a GMC member. But he was only just registered, and far less experienced than any of my helpers – all senior medical doctors! I taught this VIP, and my students, on a sprightly 89-year-old volunteer, whom I had not met before. I had no medical records or X-rays to help me! He told me that he had had an operation because of tuberculosis of the lung.

I noted his scars. This elderly man had had chest surgery (thoracotomy) before the Second World War! This operation resulted in a deformity from multiple right rib fractures to collapse the right lung. So his chest now failed to expand on the operated right side when he breathed in!

(One small area of his right chest went in on inspiration – called a flail segment.) What was going on?

Well, in the 1930s tuberculosis was rife, and anti-tuberculosis medication yet to be invented. This man had had tuberculosis of his right lung, treated by crushing the ribcage and often paralysing the diaphragm by cutting a nerve (phrenic).

This ancient surgical treatment is called plombage, and it had worked brilliantly. He had completely recovered from tuberculosis!

My GMC colleague had never heard of this operation. This was the first case of plombage I had ever seen.

I never had any feedback, but I presume my teaching passed!

Reference:

1. Raymond Clarke. Saints and Sinners, Sir William Wilde. *RC of S of England Bulletin*. DOI:10. 1308/147363513X135005 08920374.

Medical Confidentiality

Many people believe that what they tell their doctor – or indeed what he finds out in other ways – cannot be told to anybody else. As registered medical practitioners we have duties and responsibilities to our patients – they trust us. We also have duties to society. Here is a clear and true story:

In 1983 two elderly ladies were in a car driving along the A6 trunk road in Shardlow, South Derbyshire. At a notorious corner their vehicle was hit by an oncoming car on their side of the road. Worse was to follow. The male driver of the offending vehicle was unconscious – fitting.

The ladies called for the police and the ambulance. The man was still fitting when the ambulance arrived and had stopped by the time the police turned up. Fortunately, nobody was injured badly. They all came to our hospital. The male driver, now well recovered, was aggressive and insisted on taking his own discharge. I tried vainly to counsel him:

Question: "How are you feeling?"

Answer:	"I'm fine; let me go now."
Question:	"Do you know you had a fit?"
Answer:	"No, I did not fit."
Question:	"Are you an epileptic?"
Answer:	"No, I'm not."
Question:	"You should not drive."
Answer:	"Don't tell me what to do. I'm going to drive."
Question:	"I will tell the DVLA."
Answer:	"You do that and I will get you."

Shortly after this, he ran out, and the police were after him. I telephoned the DVLA – they had no record of him as a registered driver. I telephoned his general practitioner and talked to him. "Yes, he is an epileptic; no, he does not take his medication. He should never have been driving."

So I broke confidentiality by talking to the DVLA – it was in the public interest. I am sure the police caught up with him. The two ladies were in a dreadful state. They felt nothing but sympathy for the 'poor man'. I felt otherwise.

The new General Medical Council Guidelines are helpful. The guidance is on:

- Reporting concerns about patients to the DVLA (see above).
- Disclosing records for financial and administrative purposes, e.g., if the patient has come from abroad for treatment in the UK for free.
- Reporting gunshot and knife wounds – who will be the next victim?
- Disclosing information about serious communicable disease, e.g., HIV.
- Disclosing information for insurance or employment, e.g., an epileptic having fits should not work with machinery.
- Disclosing information for education or training.
- Responding to criticism in the press.
- Telling the coroner – he/she has a legal right to know.[1, 2]

There are plenty of pitfalls.

* * *

In 1991 I was looking for Mrs Joy Brown, a casualty with a minor injury. Several patients were in the vicinity, but the receptionist pointed her out. She was busy talking to a policeman in the corner. He took details of her road traffic accident. There was no secrecy. They talked publicly. He concluded with the words, "Thank you, Mrs Smith, I will file the report at the station."

He disappeared.

"Are you Joy Brown?" I asked (in a confused state a few seconds after he had left).

"Oh yes," she said.

Once in a cubicle I asked her why she had given a different name to the police. "Oh," she said, "I'm running away from debt and a violent husband. My real name is Joy Brown I'm from Birmingham."

I kept this information to myself. I did not break medical confidentiality.

* * *

In the 1980s I had a call from the administrator who was in charge of medical records. He explained to me about the Criminal Justice bill. If somebody is accused of a serious crime then medical confidentiality is waived if he/she is likely to be convicted on this evidence.

He subsequently introduced me to a large policeman in an impressive uniform – a chief superintendent. The police knew the identity of a man who had held up a post office with a shotgun. This man had an above elbow plaster on his right arm at the time.

I confirmed that on that date this man of that address did have such a plaster on, and that such a treatment is uncommon. I signed a legal form to this effect. The patient through his solicitor had tried to hide behind 'medical confidentiality'.

So the moral of the story is, don't hold up a post office with a distinctive plaster on one arm and a shotgun in the other.

References:

1. Confidentiality. General Medical Council. Regulating doctors ensuring good medical practice. 12. 10. 09.
2. Dr John Holden. Guidance. *MDU Journal* 25:2. November 2009:06.

CHAPTER FORTY-ONE

Local Anaesthetic Minor Operations

In life, it is better to learn from other people's mistakes than your own.

A saying

For the past 50 years I have carried out a lot of minor operations under local anaesthetic. It's all very straightforward, you think. No problem at all? After all, I was performing minor operations, under local anaesthetic, as a medical student. Nothing, nothing at all, can go wrong with such piffling minor procedures – or can it?

Local anaesthetic (lignocaine) is a wonderful drug given by injection. Well, I should know, I have had six minor operations in my whole life. (No, I am definitely not addicted to lignocaine.)

Let me explain:

Operation One:

Aged 18 years I had just started nervously as a medical student. In a physiology practical I had to stick a needle into my finger to get some blood out. I was then told to dilute the blood in a pipette and count the cells under a microscope. Well, I did too well. Blood poured out of my finger. All my so-called friends came and sucked my blood up their pipettes (Draculas!). I eventually got a sample and rushed over to my bench. As I did so, I slipped and fell, cutting my forehead on said microscope. Yet more haemorrhage. Sent to Casualty! What an ignominious start to my medical career.

I won't forget the casualty officer – so pompous. He said, "Oh, he is just a first year medical student. He needs two or three stitches. Oh, don't bother with any local anaesthetic. It's not worth it."

I recall the agony of the stitching. I felt the shame. I vowed if ever I became a doctor all my patients would have adequate analgesia.

Operations 2 and 3:

Aged 55 and 60 I had painful hammer toes. The joints stuck up and rubbed against my shoe. (My mother had the same.) It hurt when I walked. Under local anaesthetic in theatre I twice watched my friend Tony, an orthopaedic surgeon, resect some bone in my toes, so that said toes were straight again. Under local anaesthetic, it was a joy – no pain at all. It was slow to heal, but the operation was a success, always – I had it twice.

Now, local anaesthetic just blocks the pain sensation in the skin. So, I could still feel light touch, position sense, vibration and temperature. So, cold water hurt, but not the scalpel or bone nibblers! I enjoyed watching my own operation. I felt like a ghoulish bystander.

So, doctors test to see if the local anaesthetic works, with a pin and not light touch.

Operation 4:

Aged 62 I had golfer's elbow. When I used my right arm my elbow hurt on the inside. I could not play golf. I could do relatively little. I needed a cure. Steroid injections – failed. Physiotherapy – failed. I detected a little reluctance on the part of my surgeon – an orthopaedic hand surgeon. So

I suggested the ultimate operation. He hesitated. "Do you really want me to do that?" he said.

"Yes please, Peter," I said. So he did it.

Under local anaesthetic on my right elbow he cut the skin on the inside where the flexor muscles were torn and painful. He then cut right across the flexor muscles, detaching them from where they were attached to the bone at the elbow. This condition (golfer's elbow) is degenerative in cause. Under a microscope the muscle fibres are old and torn. So they won't heal or repair readily. This operation in my humble opinion gives them time to heal. The muscle slowly reattaches itself to the bone – just like a limpet sticks to a rock. Yet more ghoulish enjoyment for me.

Three months later – pain gone – scar healed – back to gardening and playing golf. I recommend this operation. No longer was I depressed or in pain. Local anaesthetic rules OK.

Operation 5:

Aged 62. Removal of sebaceous cyst from my back. These cysts are due to blocked glands in the skin. All sebaceous cysts should be removed, or sooner or later they get infected. Then they really hurt. (I have seen many such patients.)

Operation 6:

Aged 68. I have ten toes – more prominent 'knuckles' to my toes (hammer toes; another toe affected). More pain. I was a ghoulish bystander watching my own operation again. No pain, but at times the surgeon 'tickled my soul'. (Ha ha.) I am recovering now, and writing this five weeks later.

As a registrar in general surgery and then plastic surgery I did a lot of teaching about local anaesthetic operations. As a consultant I was teaching all my juniors a lot about minor operations, suturing, etc. Finally, I was in charge of teaching medical students for 20 years. This is a synopsis of what I taught them about local anaesthetics, moles, bleeding, foreign bodies and lumps and bumps of all sorts!

Local anaesthetic works in 99% of patients. So in 1% of patients it won't work at all. Doctors can easily give too much (the dose is 4mgn per kilogram) of a 1% lignocaine solution injected. The maximum dose for a 75 kilogram patient is 30mls of 1% lignocaine. Don't give more. I have seen 60ml given to a windscreen cut face. (The patient could have died from cardiac problems as a result of too much lignocaine!)

* * *

My own dentist was sent to me for removal of a lump on his side. I said, "Lie down and open your mouth. Now, what is the problem?" He was petrified. He did not laugh!

After the injection, he said, "Oh, local anaesthetic does work. I am surprised." Well, he must have given locals thousands of times. Did he not have confidence that it worked? I was very surprised!

Sometimes, local works in under ten seconds. I know of one patient where it took nearly 15 minutes to work (well, lawyers are thick skinned!).

Once in a blue moon a patient is sensitive to local anaesthetic. Usually they have had local anaesthetic before with no problems, so the surgeon (me) was lulled into a false sense of security.

I gave a local anaesthetic injection. Then…

Tingling around the mouth alerted me to trouble. I'd seen this only once. I had to resuscitate. She recovered over a few hours. So she was sensitive to the local anaesthetic. Fortunately it is very rare. She could have died!

* * *

When in doubt, I sent specimens of lumps and bumps for histology.

We all know about nasty moles. There is a lot of publicity about them. They are commoner in fair-skinned people. They are not always obvious. I ran a lot of clinics. One lady presented with what looked like an ingrowing toenail. The general practitioner said it was one. Yes, that cherry red lump by her nail looks just like granulation tissue. It's 'common as muck'. We all know how to treat this condition, ingrowing toenails.

Stop, stop, stop! This toe had normal sensation, but the patient had no pain.

She needed an excision biopsy of this, followed days later by amputation of the toe.

She did really well – she had a malignant melanoma (it was unpigmented!). See fig 56.

So the malignant melanoma looked like an ingrowing toenail.

Diagnosis precedes treatment in all patients, is a golden rule.

* * *

If the patient says, "I bled and bled and bled after a dental extraction" – watch out, he could be a haemophiliac. Get his clotting checked (and also his blood pressure).

Now, I should know, as I have had to operate on three haemophiliacs – all as emergencies, and all unknown to be haemophiliacs at presentation. Now, one was for such a minor problem. The tiddly operation in 1972 was over very quickly. He was still oozing blood over a week later, still in hospital.

All three survived – divine intervention again?

* * *

There is a funny little condition called dermoid cysts. These cysts usually are on the head and fixed to the scalp, so cannot be moved like sebaceous cysts. They are formed by problems when the scalp bones develop (fig 53). The general practitioner and junior doctor would be well advised to leave these alone. Let me explain:

One of my colleagues has a fantastic pair of hands. Fully trained in plastic surgery, he has an enormous experience of private cosmetic surgery. What a star! Just sometimes this dextrous genius cut corners. One day he regretted it.

He was doing minor operations at a private Harley Street clinic in 1978. A man from an embassy came in with a dermoid cyst. These cysts are under the skin, fixed to the skull bone. Stop. He should have been X-rayed to make sure there was bone under the cyst. He did not. He put local anaesthetic in first.

Cyst excised. No problems at all. Oh dear, oh dear. No bone underneath this cyst, just a hole. The brain and covering meninges were

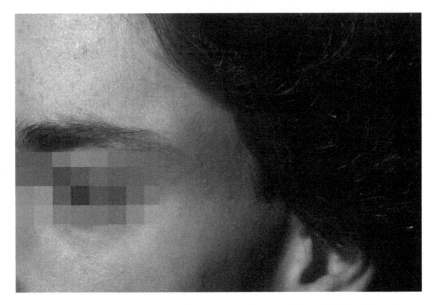

Fig 53 – External angular dermoid cyst. Just above and lateral to his left eyebrow is a swelling. This is the classic presentation of an external angular dermoid cyst. If excised there could be a skull defect underneath, i.e. no bone just brain, that could bleed.

exposed. Things got worse. There was a haemorrhage from inside the skull. Bone nibblers were needed. The artery was finally found inside the skull and dealt with. What a sweat.This was all unnecessary and under local anaesthetic. The poor patient could have died. How dangerous.

This was not right. He is a brilliant technician – but took a risk. It's not worth it.

The patient should have been sent to a neurosurgeon for a general anaesthetic. Fortunately, the patient recovered well.

* * *

I watched out when a patient came with a thick horrible scar (fig 54). After a few years these are called keloid scars, or they just might have a foreign body in them. I excluded a foreign body with an X-ray.

Now, say the thick scar is the size of a grape. You are under pressure to excise this scar. Watch out. I have seen this done. The patient is oh-so very grateful – till they return in tears.

Now the scar is the size of a grapefruit. So discuss with the plastic surgeon before an operation. (Or send this patient to be dealt with by your surgical opposition.)

Finally, don't do much under local anaesthetic if an area is infected. Infection leads to increased blood flow. The local anaesthetic is carted away by the blood. The patient bleeds and is in pain. Just drain the pus.

* * *

I was caught out three times by young ladies bitterly complaining of pain from glass in their foot. On each occasion their periods were normal and a pregnancy test negative. Each lady vehemently denied any contact recently with the opposite sex!

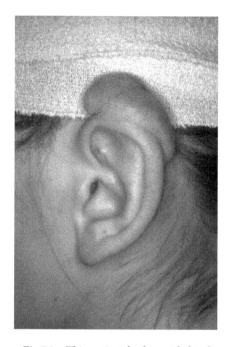

Fig 54 – This patient had a cut behind his left ear. A couple of years later and this scar had grown and grown! So this is known as a keloid scar. A simple excision can give the poor patient a far worse scar, about the size of a grapefruit.

"Oh no, doctor," one testified. "No man has been near me for a long time."

So I organised soft tissue X-rays to pinpoint the glass and how many pieces. The glass was then removed under a local anaesthetic. The patients were 'oh so grateful'. Then some weeks later they each returned. I was subjected to great abuse.

"You X-rayed me when I was pregnant." They proudly showed me the bump.

, Well, in very early pregnancy all the tests are normal. Had I failed again?

All their babies were born fit and well. They thrived and were in excellent health.

* * *

X-rays were originally discovered by accident by Wilhelm Rontgen in Germany in November 1895. He called them X as they were unknown. This man was experimenting with a cathode ray tube. After turning the tube on, he happened to put his hand in the beam. To his amazement he saw the outline of his hand bones screened on a piece of cardboard nearby.

Within a month of this, the first clinical X-ray was taken! Exposures were long and everyone was unaware of any dangers – particularly of radiation!!!

Derby County Football Club

It was a typical Saturday evening at work in the 1980s. I was pushing a child in a cot back to the emergency department from the CT scanner. A porter helping me remarked, "Derby have won again. We might not be relegated. I've got a ticket for the match next Saturday."

Derby County is the only professional football team in southern Derbyshire. They enjoy huge local support, reflected in their healthy attendance record. Whenever they lose, doom and gloom descends on the city.

I was just about to go home at 8pm when I got a phone call from a close friend, Dick, who was the doctor in charge of Derby County football team, saying, " Could you please see one of our players? He has a nasty fractured nose."

I agreed, and we met up a few minutes later. Alan, the Derby County player, had a grossly deformed nose. His nostrils were both blocked. He was in some discomfort. His nose was very tender indeed.

"Look," said Dick, "Derby County is in a mess. Alan is our third striker. Both the first two are injured. They won't be back for some time. Alan is in terrific form. If you fix his nose tonight, he will be able to train. If you agree, he might even be able to play next Saturday."

"Well, I'm not an ENT surgeon," I protested.

"No, but with your plastic surgery experience can you do something tonight, before the swelling starts? The ENT guys won't see him or operate for days, you know that," he answered.

"Let's put it another way," Dick continued. "I am the GP, and I refer this private patient to you, tonight. Can you do it?"

"Oh yes," I replied. "If the patient agrees, I can try under local anaesthetic tonight." Alan was a trained accountant, but football paid a lot better. If I fixed him that night he might play next Saturday – match fee plus possible winner's bonus? Of course he agreed.

Well, I had done this countless times before – but always under a general anaesthetic. Under local anaesthetic, with the correct instruments, I straightened the septum, then realigned the fractured nasal bones. He said he felt nothing – or was he being nice to me?

I packed the nose – to come out at 48 hours.

Then I applied a 'dinky' plaster to said nose.

Elastoplast held it in place.

Alan trained that week, and scored the following weekend. Dick kept me informed of his progress. The plaster came off at three weeks. No further injuries.

"Oh, by the way," Dick said, "make sure your bill is a big one. Derby County are so grateful."

I complied with his instructions – as always!

A Clever Local Anaesthetic Operation

It was a miracle of rare device.

Samuel Coleridge

I was waiting for a private cosmetic surgeon to perform an operation. I had seen the patient. Poor man, he was born without one branch of his facial nerve that supplied his mouth on one side. This facial weakness was not acquired through injury or infection (Bell's palsy). No, this patient was born without this branch of this nerve.

So his mouth drooped on the affected side. He could not smile symmetrically. He was very self-conscious. Now in his twenties, no-one had helped him at all. He had been teased at school. He was embarrassed whenever he met anybody. He was a very intelligent patient desperate for help.

The private cosmetic surgeon was aggressive to me, "You must know what operation I am going to do," he said.

"No, I don't," I replied truthfully.

"Oh come, come," he said. "It's in all the books."

My brain recorded no such information.

"I don't know," I said. "Anyway, you can't start, the anaesthetist is not here."

"I'm doing this under a local anaesthetic," said the surgeon, to my amazement.

The patient was very well versed. He knew exactly what was coming. I was totally ignorant.

The patient was asked to smile - deformity demonstrated.

Local anaesthetic was put in - the good side.

The muscle around the mouth is circular just under our lips, and is called the orbicularis oris.

An incision was made on the inside of the mouth on the good side. Some of the muscle on the good side was resected.

"Smile again please," said the surgeon. More muscle resected on good side.

"Now smile again please." More muscle was resected on the good side.

"Smile, thank you." After a few minutes the inner lining of the mouth was closed where the incision had been.

A mirror was brought to the patient.

For the very first time in his life his face was symmetrical - at rest. And when he talked and smiled he drooped on both sides symmetrically. I have never seen a patient so grateful. He was ecstatic and profuse in his thanks.

The private cosmetic surgeon turned to me. He is Welsh, by nationality, and they are all actors.

"Well," he said, "you don't know about this operation because I have not written it up yet." Soon after that he published this operation in the plastic surgery literature!

That local anaesthetic changed that man's life forever.

I was impressed.

CHAPTER FORTY-TWO

Surgical Rarities: Oh Gosh, this is rare, but true!

Rocking horse shit is commoner than this!

In my time I worked for four years in general surgery – one year as a senior house officer and the rest as a registrar. Then I worked for four and a half years in plastic surgery – three and a half as a registrar. Throughout all this time I saw a lot of patients with lumps for removal. As an Emergency Consultant, asked to do a minor operations list by the administrators, I saw a lot more lumps. So over 40 years I estimate I saw over 10,000 lumps of various sorts. I was confident that the overwhelming majority were benign. A few were malignant, i.e., cancerous.

The most dangerous cancers were malignant melanomas. Most of these were large black moles on ladies' legs. I referred these to the plastic surgeons, along with the keloid scars (fig 54). These three figures, 55, 56 and 57, illustrate some pitfalls in minor surgery. The mole in figure 55 was discovered on our ward on a burnt inpatient! The lady in figure 56 was referred to our chiropodist by the GP as an ingrowing toenail! Both patients had no problems after surgery.

The man in figure 57 had an even rarer condition. (I discussed all three

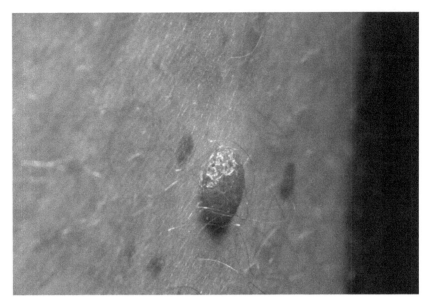

Fig 55 – Malignant melanoma with no pigment, as confirmed histologically. He was skin grafted after a wide excision and did very well indeed with no recurrence.

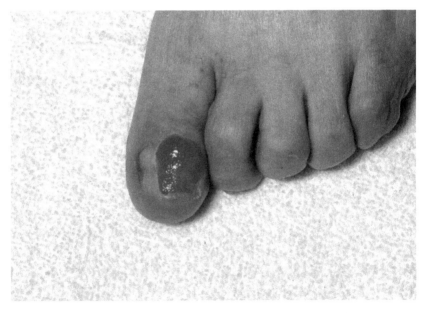

Fig 56 – A malignant melanoma of the toe, and not an ingrowing toenail. She had a biopsy that confirmed this, then her big toe was amputated. She had no recurrence of this and incidentally had no problems walking either after this operation. There is no pigment in this tumour!

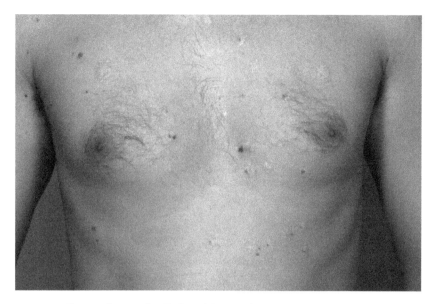

Fig 57 – Chest moles I took off a lot of this man's moles and sent them ALL off for histological examination. Each and every mole was starting to go malignant! So I took off the lot after consulting a colleague for a second opinion. There was a bad family history of very aggressive cancers in his family.

patients with the plastic surgeons.) Under a local anaesthetic in monthly sessions, I removed well over 100 in total of these premalignant (precancerous) moles. He then had to move away. He returned a year later, and I removed another dozen moles. By now one mole had progressed into a malignant melanoma on his forehead. I sent him to the plastic surgeons for more surgery. I lost him to follow-up. The prognosis was poor in this rare inherited genetic disorder.

I spent most of my time during my two hour-a week minor ops session removing sebaceous cysts (figs 61 and 62) as, if not, they became infected and very painful.

* * *

Out of this huge group of local anaesthetic patients I saw less than ten of a very rare group of soft tissue cancer called sarcomas. It is estimated by the National Institute for Clinical Excellence that a family doctor will see one case of soft tissue sarcoma every 24 years. I think this is an overestimate, as I know several general practitioners close to retirement who have never seen, or even heard of, such a case.

These malignant swellings are bizarre and difficult to spot. Whereas most cancers come from the outer layer of the body (ectoderm), these sarcomas come from the inner layer – muscle, blood vessels and fat (mesoderm and endoderm). We are trained as doctors to watch out for hard lumps anywhere that may be malignant, e.g., neck, mouth, etc. They are more frequently seen in older people. Sarcomas, however, occur in young people (twenties) and often they are soft!

For the record, I remember seeing two liposarcomas (from fat), three angiosarcomas (from blood vessels) and two fibrosarcomas (from fibrous tissue). The angiosarcomas were all seen in plastic surgery and were in patients with port wine stains. They were horrible (very rare and soft), spreading to the lungs via the blood stream very early!

> *Rarer than the unicorn.*
>
> Erica Jong

A 28-year-old man had bought a house. He was proud of his house. He worked hard to keep up the mortgage payments. He noticed a soft swelling on his left arm. Oh, perhaps it will go away. Now, this young man had no wife to nag him. So he just went to work and carried on his life normally.

In spring he decided that he would paint the outside of the house himself – a lot cheaper. He started slowly, but did not anchor his ladder in any way. One Saturday morning his ladder slipped, and he fell heavily. He slid down the wall, landing in a heap.

Dazed and confused he sat there. Nobody was about. His neighbours were out. He surveyed his injuries. He had a deep graze on his left forearm – right over that lump. It was bleeding, so he staggered indoors and put a tea towel on it to stop the bleeding. He glanced in the mirror – oh dear, a deep graze on his left temple.

He got no work done on the house over the weekend. He got some antiseptic from the chemist and some dressings. "No, I won't go to the doctor or the hospital. I am OK," he said to the chemist.

He took a few days off work. His left forearm he cleaned and put antiseptic on. Then to save time he cleaned the wound on his temple 'with the same gauze'. Both areas he thought were healing, as they stopped bleeding.

He failed to heal, and some time later he apologised to his general practitioner. "Just tell me to carry on and I will go home and do more dressings," was his opening gambit to her.

She referred him urgently to the general surgeons for a second opinion. Both wounds looked odd to her. The general surgeons biopsied both the left temple and left forearm. What was the result?

Well, the left forearm had a sarcoma of smooth muscle – a rhabdomyosarcoma – now, this is rare (I have not seen one myself). But rarer still, the left temple biopsy, also showed the identical sarcoma histologically. It is thought that this rare cancer had been transmitted unwittingly by the patient taking malignant cells from his left forearm to his left temple, when he cleaned these areas with the same gauze. So malignant cells had been transported from one area of his body to another by the patient!

This is very, very rare indeed.

(One of my juniors told me all about this case.)

Foreign Bodies from Foreign Parts

One... enriched with foreign matter.

Sir Joshua Reynolds

A 50-year-old Englishman, David (fig 58), was working in Japan for Rolls-Royce. He had qualified as an engineer. He was now no longer a shop floor worker. He was now on the board. His board meetings went on and on, and during them his right buttock became sore. He recalled that 30 years before, he had been a National Service army cadet in Wales. He had had an injection in his bottom, and the needle had broken! A plain X-ray in Japan confirmed the needle was still there, exactly where he felt the pain (fig 58).

He flew back to the UK. I removed the needle under a general anaesthetic (as a private patient) in 1984.

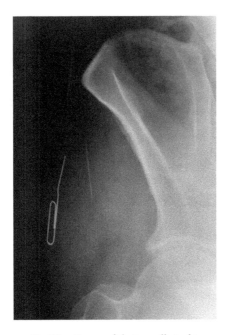

Fig 58 – X-ray of that needle in his bottom. It is seen as a fine line. Also seen is a paper clip taped onto the skin to guide me.

This needle was in him for 30 years and two months – the longest reported time I could find in the literature for broken needles. This needle had travelled 1.5 million miles. In the patient, it had visited 44 countries and been round the world three times. This needle had travelled in style. The altitude of the said needle varied between 150 feet below sea level (Death Valley, USA) to 60,000 feet, and speeds in excess of Mach 2 (Concorde).

My late father, as an oral surgeon, wrote up a series of 29 broken needles removed by him following injections by dentists. To find the needles in theatre he used 'the Fraser-Moodie Metal Detector' – of course (fig 59).[1]

Fortunately, broken needles today are a rarity. The modern hypodermic needle is disposable, sharper and of better quality (Personal Communication from M Huxley, Quality Director, Sabre International Products).

* * *

A 53-year-old African living in England was referred to my minor ops clinic in 1989. He recalled that when aged ten he was climbing a tree in Somalia. A large thorn lodged in his left thigh. He tried to remove it, but it broke off – leaving some behind.

He was fine till the area became sore some 43 years later.

I removed the remains of the thorn 2.5 cm long – under a local anaesthetic.

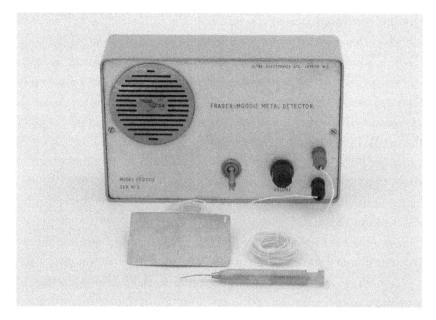

Fig 59 – My father's metal detector. He used it many times in theatre. Yes, he always found that broken needle, to the relief of the patient and the dentist!

* * *

A 30-year-old housewife was referred to me by her general practitioner in 1991. She had only recently developed a small painful lump below her right eye.

I explored the area under a local anaesthetic. I removed a small piece of wood. She then recalled that another girl had hit her there with a stick 27 years previously. At that time she was aged three and living in Melbourne, Australia.

* * *

These three cases of foreign bodies from foreign parts were presented to the Fifth International Conference of Accident and Emergency Medicine (London) 1994. All the patients recovered well.

The African's thorn that was in him for 43 years was the longest time that a foreign body had remained in situ prior to removal. Previously the longest had been a swab.[2]

This African also waited 43 years after an accident before he consulted a doctor. This must be one of the longest delays before consultation!

The 50-year-old Englishman, David, had a reputation as an after dinner speaker. About six months after his operation, I met somebody who had been at such a gathering (he did not know I knew the speaker). He recounted how the after dinner speaker had told everyone the story of the needle in his bottom for over 30 years. Then the after dinner speaker produced the said needle from out of his pocket in a little glass container (well, I had given him the evidence in a glass specimen bottle). As soon as the needle was produced, some of the assembled audience were a bit shocked. And felt ill!

The raconteur was surprised that I laughed so much. "You don't know the after dinner speaker," he enquired, "or do you?"

"I'm sorry," I said, "but I simply can't comment. Medical etiquette; I'm sure you understand."

References:

1. W Fraser-Moodie. A Series of Broken Needles. *Br Dent J.* (1958):105:79-85 and W Fraser. Location and localisation of metal in the tissues. *Br J Oral Surgery* November 1966:4:2;99.
2. A C Macey et al. Unusual soft tissue tumour. *BMJ* (1989):299;1567.

More Foreign Bodies and More and More

Children love to insert foreign bodies into various orifices. The commonest trick is to swallow coins. They just pass out the other end, but not before mum has had a few sleepless nights. Some toddlers stick small objects up their nose. My medical colleague, Dr Joe Zammitt, showed me a clever trick. If such a toddler is taught to inhale pepper they often sneeze, then the impacted plaything is delivered 'hey presto'. One red-haired boy had a noise in his left ear. On inspection out crawled an earwig! One blonde girl had a vaginal discharge. She recovered on removal of the goldfish!

Adults are attracted to foreign bodies too. Objects like razor blades, open safety pins, biros and batteries play havoc with our bowels, and have to be removed. One prisoner from Wormwood Scrubs swallowed a toilet brush. He could not speak. The bristles protruded from his mouth. Another surgical emergency!

One story I have heard over and over again goes like this: "I was up steps in my pantry – naked, of course. I fell off, and somehow this jam jar got into my back passage!" I always had difficulty keeping a straight face. The poor surgeon is often needed again, and an anaesthetist. Sometimes, if the open end of the jar is visible, then a stick and plaster of Paris can be inserted. Once the plaster is set, the solid object can be removed. The glass jar is then less likely to break.

Body piercing is so popular. I can't understand why. Bits of metal are inserted into sensitive,

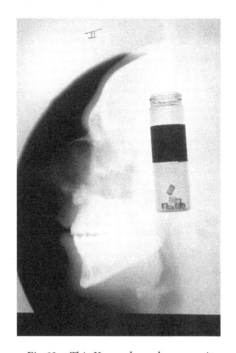

Fig 60 – This X-ray shows how easy it is to leave glass in a wound. This man was in an RTA. He went through a windscreen. All he suffered was a tiny cut on his upper lip. He was not stitched. A long time later I saw him with a lump on his upper lip. It was a lump of glass pieces from his RTA. I removed this lump and put them all in this little bottle.

and sometimes private, areas with no anaesthetic! This, to my mind, is tantamount to torture! The real pain starts if the piece of metal moves, or part is lost into the tissues.

The victims' cries are loud. Strong analgesia and frequently a general anaesthetic are demanded. Once cured, the patient is not deterred from putting it back again!

Earrings for ladies are acceptable. We had one male doctor who wore a large gold earring in one ear (he obviously could not afford two earrings). He took the said earring off before an examination. Well, he had to face the examiners. It has not been put back. Now, as a consultant

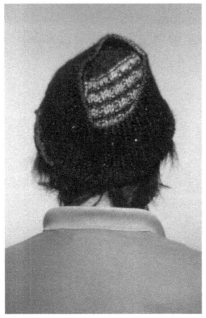 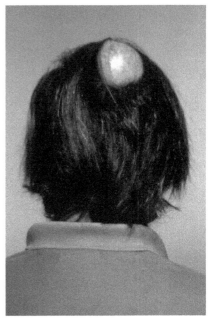

Left: Fig 61 – This man wore a hat to my clinic. He kept it on, and was reluctant to remove it. Why, oh why?

Right: Fig 62 – Oh, that is why! Once I removed this little cyst, he took off his hat.

anaesthetic, I have seen him speak on television – minus the earring. This seems to have been a phase that he went through in his life.

Tattooists sometimes cause infections. The poor patient is then treated under the NHS. A few patients are allergic to the dyes used – especially the red one. Are any needles reused? I hope not, because the HIV virus is difficult to kill off. There have been many instances of transmission of the virus through repeated injections!

Hair transplant centres are also a source of patients. One technician tried to sew new hair into a scalp (ouch)! The large needle got stuck. I removed it.

Fishermen commonly get fishhooks in their fingers. The barb makes it difficult to remove, and often has to be cut off.

Well, it makes good small talk:

Question to fisherman: "What did you catch today?"

Answer: "Myself."

Do It Yourself Accidental Operations

The greatest pleasure I know is to do a good action... by accident.

Charles Lamb

Some patients inflict purposeless injuries upon themselves, e.g., slash wrists. Occasionally, these self-inflicted injuries have a purpose, e.g., to burn off a tattoo. Ganglia, especially around the wrist, have disappeared following accidental trauma. However, I report three cases of patients on waiting lists for minor operations, each of whom successfully did the operation themselves, by accident! Such events are rare!

A 58-year-old ambulance control officer was referred to me by his GP for removal of a sebaceous cyst on his scalp. I examined this man's cyst and placed his name on my minor operations waiting list for this operation.

A few days later he was driving home wearing a seat belt. Whilst crossing the Derby ring road, his car was driven into from the right side by another car. He suffered a jagged laceration to his right parietal area (temple), presumably due to the impact against the driver's door and window. He was brought to our accident and emergency department, where he greeted me with the remark, "Sorry, doc, I've done your op!"

Lying freely on the wound was the intact sebaceous cyst, which he picked out. The scalp wound was sutured and he made an uneventful recovery.

* * *

A 71-year-old lady was referred to me with a sebaceous cyst on her forehead. The very day of her appointment she forgot about the cyst, whilst combing her hair. The teeth of the comb dug into the cyst and lifted it out! I saw her a few hours later with the cyst. Histology confirmed it to be a sebaceous cyst. She too made an uneventful recovery (fig. 63).

* * *

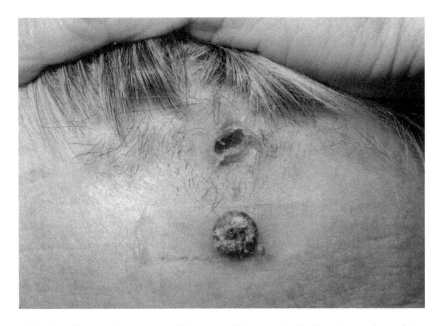

Fig 63 – Here is that tiny cyst. I have taped it onto her forehead. Just above this cyst is the little hole out of which it had popped.

A 42-year-old man had a blocked right nostril from a polyp and was awaiting surgical removal. His nose was then hit whilst playing rugby football, causing an epistaxis. At the end of the game he blew his nose and out came the polyp. He then presented to our accident and emergency department. His nose was tender and swollen but not deformed. The obstruction had been relieved! An X-ray showed fractures of the nasal bones and lateral cartilages.

His nose healed, and nasal surgery was thus avoided.

* * *

These three cases illustrate the fact that some patients can successfully 'operate' upon themselves by accident. I can find no record of such an event in the medical literature, up to now. Today's surgically active doctor would suffer if the incidence of this type of operation increased.

This is another reason for reducing waiting times for minor operations (before the patient does the operation themselves).

DO IT YOURSELF ACCIDENTAL INJURIES

COME ON, DO THAT JOB YOURSELF.
IT'S SO CHEAP.
IT'S SO EASY.
ANYBODY CAN DO IT.
JOIN THE FUN.

IF THINGS GO WRONG,
DIAL 999 (IF YOU CAN).
A FREE AMBULANCE IS WAITING.
IT GOES TO A & E OFTEN.
IT WILL TAKE YOU THERE, TODAY.
LOTS OF DIY PATIENTS ARE THERE ALREADY.
IT'S FREE TREATMENT FOR DIY PATIENTS.
JOIN THE FUN.

I'VE GOT IT NAILED

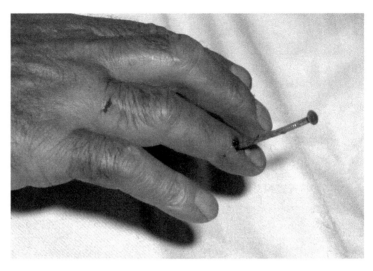

Fig 64 – Now, here is a sorry tale of two friends. This man helped his friend to hammer in nails. He held the nail each time for his friend to hit it with the hammer. Yes, they were a team. But this time his friend was too quick for him. So he hit the nail too quickly. This was the result! This team did not last after this episode.

NAILED IT AGAIN

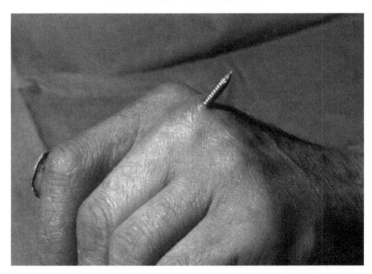

Fig 65 – Nail guns are such fun; so powerful they shoot nails into wood, walls and even each other!

JUST JOINED THE CHAIN GANG

Fig 66 – This man was joining up a chain with a power press. Somehow he managed to get joined up too. This is another patient who was unable to drive to the hospital!

YOU'VE BEEN FRAMED!

Fig 67 – The guard of a machine only works when it is switched on. Wake up – you've been framed!

A STITCH IN TIME – SAVES?

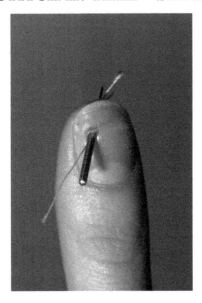

Fig 68 – Turn the sewing machine off before you adjust it. This put an end to all those repairs that you were going to do!

CHUCK IT TO ME

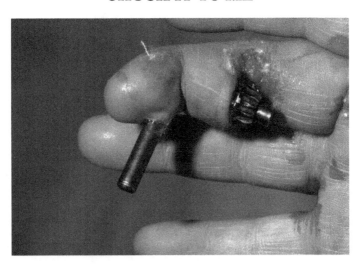

Fig 69 – This keen man got his drill out and tightened up the drill piece with the chuck. He was in such a hurry that he failed to remove the chuck before starting to drill. Oh no, that chuck went round and round in the drill. It embedded itself in him. He could not carry on with his work. He could not drive to our department.

I'M INTO METALWORK

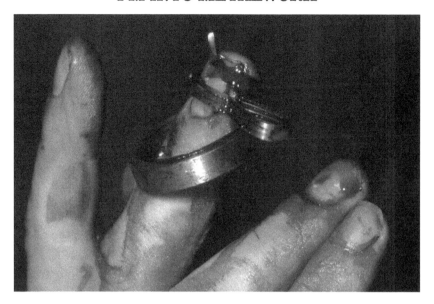

Fig 70 – Keep your fingers away from swarf. It really really hurts. This patient regrets his hobby of DIY very much indeed.

Mad as a Hatter

Everything's got a moral, if you can only find it.
Lewis Carroll, *Alice in Wonderland*

Late one evening a very junior doctor was working in an emergency department in 1992. A black elderly man came, and he complained of a swollen painful forearm. On examination he was acutely tender just below his elbow. This area on the front of his arm fluctuated on pressure. There were no puncture wounds.

The doctor injected a little local anaesthetic. Once this area was numb, he incised the tender area, expecting pus from an abscess. No – out came mercury! The registrar, Ros, was called. A lot more mercury was drained.

An X-ray of his forearm revealed the presence of still more mercury. So this area was excised and closed, primarily under a general anaesthetic.

The patient was investigated. Mercuric emboli were seen in both lungs on X-raying his chest. Over two months serial measurements of his blood and urine showed raised levels of mercury, but not to toxic levels. Lung and kidney function was unaffected.

One month later, he complained of a headache. A skull X-ray showed flecks of mercury, so the mercury had passed through his lungs and he had intracranial deposits. He was treated with penicillamine.

Now, throughout this whole escapade the patient continued to deny any knowledge as to how the mercury got there. He remained very well. As he said his occupation demanded a certain strength of stature.

Now, what was going on here? There is no doubt at all that he, or a friend, was injecting mercury into his body. Deliberate intravenous injection of mercury into the body, to gain strength, is a strange phenomenon thought to emanate from South America. There are other such cases reported in the literature. We thought our man was such a case. We tried to explain that mercury is in fact a poison, and could kill him. We thought he understood this.

Perhaps the injection of mercury into his arm was a suicide attempt. (It has been reported as such in the past medical literature.) This black man was seen again in our emergency department and was referred to a psychiatrist.

The hatter in *Alice in Wonderland* was depicted as mad. This is a play on occupations. Many hatters in Victorian times were suffering from mercury poisoning from handling hats. This occupational hazard made many of them a 'trifle' mad.

A Hand Case

"Now, just a little prick is coming."
A common saying by nurses giving an injection!

A 19-year-old girl was brought by her mother to a clinic of mine in 1991. She had been crying and looked a mess.

"What is wrong?" I said.

"Oh, I got drunk in the pub last night, with my friends," the girl said.

"She wants them all out today please," said her mother. "She needs to go to work."

It transpired that, encouraged by her so-called friends, she had inserted several needles into the back of her hand. She was the cabaret at the local pub. This cabaret star was rewarded with more drinks. The more needles she put in, the more they cheered, and the more drink she was given. Morning had brought reality. The hand would not function.

An X-ray confirmed five long needles embedded in the back of her left hand. She was referred to the hand surgeons for a general anaesthetic.

But she protested: "I put them in with no anaesthetic – that's not fair!"

The hand surgeon struggled to remove these needles embedded so deeply. A general anaesthetic was mandatory.

Her hand function then recovered.

A Chip Pan Fire

Chips themselves are not bad for you, but the hot fat they are cooked in is!

A fact

A 43-year-old housewife in 1991 suffered a chip pan burn to her right forearm – about 10cm x 12cm in size. She had pain and it was blistering, so the burn was superficial. This type of burn should heal in two weeks. The treatment of choice, at that time, was flamazine, made by Smith and

Nephew Pharmaceuticals. This cream contained a sulphonamide. She was not sensitive to sulphonamides.

This housewife had daily dressings of flamazine. It's a wonderful cream. It takes the pain away, and heals burns well. Unfortunately, for the only time I have ever seen, this cream did not work. The poor lady was in severe pain. Instead of healing quickly, this burn was unhealed at three weeks. She was in agony throughout. The cream was changed to a Vaseline gauze. This burn then healed.

I was mystified. The cream that always works – did not. In fact it made her worse. We discussed this amongst ourselves. The patient, mystified too, asked the question, "What's in the cream?"

"Oh," I said, "it's 1% silver sulphadiazine."

"That explains it," she said. "I'm allergic to all metals."

She could not wear any metal close to her skin. She taped over the metal on her brassiere. She wore gloves for housework, as even her broom had a metal handle. The most surprising thing of all was that she could not have a metal wedding ring.

She showed me her chunky plastic wedding ring!

Skin patch tests later confirmed that this lady was indeed sensitive to silver.

According to Smith and Nephew, this is so rare – it is only seen in one in 5,000 people![1]

> *"With this plastic ring, I thee wed."*
> With apologies to the wedding ceremony

I sympathised with this lady. I have twice been given the antibiotic tetracycline. Each time I developed an urticarial, itchy rash. I was confused. This lasted several hours. So I am allergic to tetracycline (I was given it twice, as nobody believed I could be sensitive to this drug!) This is uncommon.

Well, we are all different.

Reference:

1. W Fraser-Moodie. Sensitivity to Silver in a patient treated with silver sulphadiazine (Flamazine). *Burns* (1992) 18:74-75

A Bizarre Self-Inflicted Injury?
The Square Wound

This is rare.

Countless professionals – doctors and nurses – have been baffled by this phenomenon.

I cannot recall reading of this in the world medical literature ever.

Is this another first?

Square Wounds

I have only seen this condition half a dozen times. Each time is similar. Sometimes the patient has been referred to my clinic. At other times I have discovered the patient in the dressings clinic, or the patient may be seen by the tissue viability nurse.

The patient always has a strange square-looking wound. This is usually situated on the shin, but I have seen it on the back of the hand. Despite numerous dressings of various sorts, this wound fails to heal. The staff, the patient and all the relatives are amazed.

Quite simply, a square wound is not natural. These wounds are caused by the patient rubbing or scratching their own skin – consciously or subconsciously.

I cured each and every patient by telling them, quite rightly, that the wound needed to rest and then heal.

So I put the injured area in a plaster. This should cover the joint above and the joint below. So, for the shin, this plaster went from above the knee to below the ankle – all round.

This plaster was kept on for three weeks and then removed.

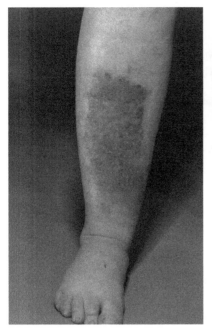 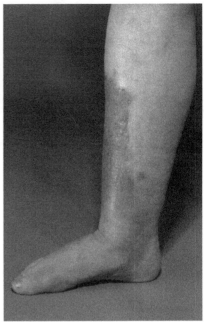

Fig 71 – How square can you get? It looks so very odd to me! All the relatives were so worried too.

Fig 72 – Another view of this strange square wound. A square wound like this is not natural!

The wound was always healed and the patient discharged.

So once the cause of the wound is stopped, the patient heals quickly.

The patient realises that they have been rumbled and usually does not do the interfering again!

CHAPTER FORTY-THREE

Appendicitis

That abdominal pain is here again,
Is it perforation, or constipation?
Acute nephritis, or just cystitis?
Is that renal colic, in the alcoholic?
An appendix mass, in this pregnant lass?
We'll do a scan, if we can,
Repeat that test, while they rest,
Stop running about, THEY'VE JUST WALKED OUT.

I dedicate this 'terse verse' to the memory of Mr James Angell FRCS. He was the author of 'The acute abdomen in rhyme', and a boss of mine.

Appendicitis was frequently fatal before the advent of surgery and antibiotics. Frederick Treves, the surgeon, performed one of the first appendicectomies in England on 29th June 1888. He advocated waiting a few days before operating, to drain the pus. His younger daughter Hetty even died of a perforated appendix in 1900, as a direct consequence of this delayed treatment.

Appendicitis postponed Edward VII's coronation in 1902 for two months. The king was not happy at this postponement, and insisted to Frederick Treves that it was not necessary. Treves famously replied,

"Then, sir, you will go as a corpse". Eventually Treves operated and was rewarded for his successful surgery on the King, with a baronetcy and trips to Balmoral![1]

Oh, what a straightforward condition today is appendicitis, I am told. So easy to diagnose and treat. Well, no; in my opinion it is full of pitfalls for the unwary.

As a senior house officer in surgery at Northwich Park Hospital, a 14-year-old boy had appendicitis. His symptom – diarrhoea. He got antibiotics galore.

Weeks later, still in hospital, the boss explored his so-called pelvic appendicitis. He was horrified – pus and pus and pus came out. His appendix had pointed down to his pelvis and burst. The boy recovered slowly but completely.

(We had to treat the boy even though he was an Arsenal supporter!)

* * *

At the end of a ward round my pleasant good-looking registrar said he had a lump in his tummy. He had a huge lump low down on the right side. We thought it was an appendix abscess. After weeks of antibiotics the remnant was explored. More and more pus drained from around his appendix. He made a slow recovery, but needed intravenous fluids for two weeks and lost nearly two stone in weight.

Note, he had no pain, just a lump.

* * *

A Spanish kitchen porter at Northwich Park Hospital spoke no English. Jesus was his Christian name! He had tummy pain. He was fed analgesics by his mates (all Spanish), till he could take no more.

Dehydrated and in extremis, we saw him 72 hours later in the same hospital. Appendicitis is a real killer. This fit 17-year-old very nearly died. We operated that night and drained the pus again. What a close shave!

* * *

Finally, I was sent a definite case of appendicitis by the local gynae hospital when I was a surgical registrar. In she came in a 999 ambulance. I was not at all happy. She was sick and perhaps an ectopic. At operation she had an ectopic pregnancy in her right tube that she lost at surgery. She recovered well.

She could easily have bled to death (not a good idea to pop such a patient into an ambulance for this journey).

* * *

Then, another appendicitis certainty. A really tall well-built lady presented with lower abdominal pain in 1986. Diagnosis: appendicitis. She was shocked and in pain.

I tipped her head down because of her shock. She got shoulder tip pain. This is a sign that the undersurface of her diaphragm had been stimulated, and the pain is referred to her shoulder: both areas have the same nerve route (bizarre, but true). The only thing that I could think of that would do this would be blood in her abdomen in her case. So this really massive lady had bled into her abdomen, and so had an ectopic pregnancy too. I was correct! (She was six feet four inches tall and weighed over 20 stone!)

* * *

An experienced medical practitioner, Ian, developed indigestion one night in 1991. So he treated himself with aludrux (aluminium hydroxide). The first dose had little effect on his indigestion, so he gave himself a proper therapeutic dose the second time (and not a homeopathic dose like the first one). He tried to sleep, but the indigestion would not go away! Another dose of that white medicine was needed.

The next morning he washed off that rim of white around his mouth and manfully struggled through the morning surgery. At the end of the morning that indigestion still had not settled, so he sought a second opinion from his senior partner in the room next door.

Diagnosis: Appendicitis.
Treatment: Appendicectomy, that day.

He returned to work two weeks later.

What a tough Yorkshireman!

* * *

After a year of paediatrics I was a senior house officer in surgery. One night a colleague remarked that a child with suspected appendicitis had had a normal appendix removed. I listened to the child's chest. The tell-tale signs were there. Pneumonia can mimic appendicitis, especially in children!

* * *

Finally, one man had pain high up over his right kidney: Diagnosis appendicitis due to appendix in the wrong place. (Oh, that's not fair!)

* * *

Around 50 people die from appendicitis in the UK annually! The differential diagnosis can be vast. I have seen two people with their appendix on their left side – complete situs inversus. The mortality from appendicitis is higher in the extremes of age. The very young and the very old are vulnerable.

Babies under one year often get gastroenteritis. I followed up such babies when I did paediatrics. One small baby, however, had appendicitis. Initially she looked like all the others with gastroenteritis. She nearly died. Post operatively she was small enough to be treated in an incubator.

* * *

Appendicitis is a product of our Western diet. Denis Birkett, a surgeon, worked in Africa for many years. He reported that Africans on a high roughage diet in Africa did not get appendicitis (or even diverticulitis!). Once such an African went to New York, his chances of appendicitis went right up on the Western diet!

'Prevention is better than a cure.'

A saying

'Should conservative treatment of appendicitis be the first line?' asked a recent article in the *BMJ*. Conservative treatment meant antibiotics and rest, as well as computed tomography to exclude perforated appendicitis.

It concludes, "However… appendicectomy will probably continue to be used for uncomplicated appendicitis." My response is to say, "Thank goodness."[2]

References:

1.   Louise King. Saints and Sinners. Sir Frederick Treves. *Royal College of Surgeons Bulletin*. September 2012:94;284.
2.   Olaf Bakker. Should conservative treatment of appendicitis be first line? *BMJ* 2012:344;e2546.

Wounds to the Neck

The most unkindest cut of all.

Shakespeare, *Julius Caesar*

Wounds to the neck are deceptive. Just a simple laceration can't be dangerous. Or can it be? There are a lot of important structures in the neck. Any surgeon doing any neck surgery must have intimate knowledge of all of them. There is a golden rule with neck lacerations – if the wound penetrates the muscle under the skin – called platysma – then operate and explore under a general anaesthetic. This rule is very old, and still applies as much today as when I was told it as a medical student. Here are four cases in chronological order:

Case One:

I had only been working as a surgical registrar for two weeks in 1971. A man presented. He had acute depression and had tried to commit suicide by cutting his own throat. This was a serious genuine suicide attempt, in no way a sham.

The man, in his fifties, had several deep horizontal cuts across the front of his neck. He was bleeding and in pain. He was depressed and apologetic. I telephoned my consultant. "Oh, you can do that" he said. (Well, my boss was still in plaster!)

Under a general anaesthetic I controlled the bleeding first. The cuts were very deep indeed. I looked for some important nerves (recurrent laryngeal). The anatomy was so distorted I could not find them. The windpipe (trachea) was cut across. But what was this strange fluid welling up deep in the wound. It was not blood.

"I'll put a tube down his oesophagus," said the anaesthetist. "Perhaps that stuff comes from there." A brick-red plastic tube was inserted down the oesophagus (gullet).

I saw a flash of red deep in the wound. So he had cut his oesophagus. I sewed up his oesophagus. I repaired the rest as best I could and sutured the skin (draining the wound).

I expected all sorts of problems. I suspected nerve damage to his larynx. He confounded me. He recovered quickly. He deeply regretted his actions. He returned to his family, picked up the pieces of his life and told the psychiatrist he was better!

His swallowing and speech were fine. He was discharged. I was truly amazed.

Case Two:

I was a surgical registrar in 1973. I was far more experienced by then. A man presented with another suicide attempt. In his sixties he had inflicted deep horizontal cuts to his neck. He had bled and stopped bleeding. I urgently cross-matched blood and arranged for an anaesthetist. He came quickly. We needed an operating theatre. None were free.

I then had a frantic time for over one hour. I had already explained the urgency to the repentant patient and anxious relatives. In that time I had telephoned every theatre in the hospital. None were free. All were busy. Nobody would make way for this emergency!

My own consultant was the only one doing major surgery that would last for two hours. I strongly suspected that I could have broken into another surgeon's lists, but to do so would have created havoc. The list would have overrun and cases been cancelled. Hence their refusal.

Then tragedy struck. This poor patient suddenly bled profusely – an arterial bleed. Despite a blood transfusion already going on, the poor chap bled to death. I was upset.

Case Three:

I was working as an emergency consultant in 1979. A young lad of 16 was seen as a minor injury. He had just a small cut on the left side of his neck, 1.5 inches long. He had sat waiting to be seen. He felt fine, and looked fine.

On questioning he was asked, "Now, your mate stabbed you when you were larking about, is that right?"

"Oh yes," he said, "my mate is upset. He is waiting for me now. Can I go?"

"Well, just a few questions," I said. "How long was the knife?" I asked.

He held his two index fingers about ten inches apart. I gulped.

"How far did it go in?" I said.

"Oh, all the way," he casually remarked. The patient was transferred to a trolley, and blood taken for cross-matching. He was not shocked. He seemed fine throughout.

X-rays of his neck and chest showed a punctured lung (pneumothorax) on the other side of the chest.

Oh dear, I thought. I just knew that this knife had passed very close to all sorts of vital structures across his neck.

The consultant general surgeon on call, David Thomas, was contacted urgently by me.

The surgeon exposed the chest, splitting his breast bone under a general anaesthetic in theatre, and the aorta was repaired. After 12 pints of blood the patient was stable.

This lad, who wanted to go home, had only had his aorta (main artery out of the heart) nicked by the knife!

He recovered very well.

The surgeon was upset like me. Gosh, that was close.

Case Four:

The seat belt law had yet to be passed. *Oh, those politicians are so slow*, I thought (1979). A 20-year-old lady had gone flying through the windscreen of her car. She had not bothered to do up her seat belt. There were several cuts that zigzagged up her neck to her face. A loose dressing had been applied.

She had come in at 5am. I came to work as an emergency consultant, and saw her on my ward round at 8.30am. She was still bleeding but had had a blood transfusion.

"I need to operate urgently," I said, and I promptly arranged this.

This lady had bled for three hours in the hospital, previously in the ambulance and at the scene. I put in a lot of stitches and repaired the wounds. We suspected she had cut a major artery. In fact she had just cut a small vein (facial vein). Blood had oozed and oozed from this little vein!

She recovered well, but will always be scarred.

And they are the ups and downs of neck wounds. They are always to be respected and, if deep enough, always to be explored under a general anaesthetic.

CHAPTER FORTY-FOUR

Tropical Medicine

It Ain't Half Hot Mum

TV programme

Well, the furthest south I have worked was in Surrey! How have I seen any patients from the tropics? Well, the answer is that air travel has shrunk the globe. Tropical diseases present to doctors working in the UK. These patients are 'different', but don't always have a label on them that says 'Beware Tropical Disease'!

Malaria is by far the commonest and most well known tropical disease to occur in the UK. This is despite the eradication of malaria in large parts of the world. Travellers to, in particular, Africa, India and South America need to take prophylaxis for an adequate period and use mosquito nets to sleep under at night. Failure to do so may well result in malaria. This condition is characterised by persistent fever and malaise, occasionally even rigors. A blood film confirms the presence of the parasite. Sometimes the parasite is resistant to initial chemotherapy. (The AIDS patient is particularly susceptible to malaria.)

So we see a trickle of patients with malaria in each district general hospital. Once diagnosed, treatment is usually straightforward. We need a vaccine to prevent this condition.

One hundred million dollars hopes to be raised by the Malaria Capital

417

Campaign. This would provide everyone at risk with net beds and anti-malaria drugs.

At present nearly a million children in Africa die annually from malaria.[1]

(As I write this in September 2016, it is reported in *The Times* that avian malaria spread by mosquitoes has infected the penguins in Exeter Zoo!)

Bill and Melinda Gates have also done a fantastic job using their billions, and know how to fight malaria.[2, 3]

GlaxoSmithKline have introduced a vaccine to fight malaria, as reported by the World Health Organisation in April 2017. It is being trialled in three African countries, and has been shown to reduce the incidence of malaria, rather than eradicate it altogether.

* * *

As a very junior doctor in my first registration year I had been 'volunteered' by my orthopaedic surgeon to help the rheumatology and rehabilitation consultant (his junior had developed tuberculosis!).

Quite simply, I did what I was told. I expected to see a lot of patients with various forms of arthritis. Not so. I was working in Queen Mary's Hospital, Roehampton in 1965-66. This rehabilitation consultant was following up men who had been prisoners of war under the Japanese.

These poor men had outwardly recovered from their starvation and beatings. They initially had returned to the UK, I was told, full of diseases and parasites. They were treated for these. They had all subsequently put on weight and seemed healthy 20 years later. These men each had physical examinations by me. Then they had a chest X-ray. They were still vulnerable to tuberculosis and other infections. Apart from routine blood tests they had stool examinations and cultures. I was told that they all had been 'riddled with amoebae and intestinal worms'. There was a real danger that intestinal amoebiasis could recur even after repeated courses of treatment. We treated such recurrences, but they were uncommon.

* * *

The Brits were returning from their holidays in the Med, the Caribbean and the Indian Oceans. After all, it was September and for most people their summer holidays were over. My minor ops list in 1987 was supplemented by four such patients. They were all keen swimmers and had explored the shores and deeper waters, to their cost. Each had managed to tread on a sea urchin, or two. They had extensive spines still embedded in their feet. I took some time under local anaesthetic to remove all the offending spines, to the grateful relief of all the respective patients.

Some spines are neurotoxic and deaths have been reported as a consequence!

I have seen the marks on the skin inflicted by Portuguese man-o-war and the even more toxic Indian jellyfish. By the time such patients get back to the UK they are usually better. Fatalities have occurred from both.

* * *

A 40-year-old hairdresser in 1989 returned to her country of birth, Mauritius, for a holiday. She was paddling in the sea on a busy holiday beach when she unfortunately stepped on a stonefish. These fish are so called because they sit on the bottom of shallows and to a bather look like a stone. Unfortunately, these fish have longitudinal spines on the dorsum of their whole body that are poisonous. When stepped on, these spines inject a powerful exotoxin into the recipient. This is the strongest exotoxin known and has a definite mortality rate (snakes in comparison inject endotoxins through their fangs). This lady screamed in pain and was helped out of the sea. She received antivenom. She needed antibiotics for an infection up her right leg to her groin. The pain continued despite analgesia. She had amputation of her right big toe for necrosis. On return I gave her a skin graft to the dorsum of her right foot for an area measuring 4 x 3 inch of skin loss. She healed slowly but eventually was able to walk in normal shoes.

So this is not a true bite, but a poison injected by the sharp fish spines. As in her case, immediate antivenom does not prevent necrosis. A tourniquet applied immediately helps to stop the spread of venom throughout the body. Immediate immersion of the affected part in water up to 50 degrees C denatures the venom. This injury can be prevented if bathers in the Pacific and Indian Oceans wear sandshoes.

Local fishermen are particularly at risk. If the stonefish spines inject this exotoxin, the recorded mortality is nearly 10%![4]

I recall in 2012 seeing three young men who had just returned from Thailand. They had coryza, headache, conjunctivitis and backache. Their eyes were sore and one had had a rigor. They all had dengue fever. This is caused by a virus carried to man by a mosquito. Treatment is symptomatic, and mortality is nil. The patients all got better.

Another tropical disease, the West Nile fever, is also spread by mosquitoes. The prognosis is good. There were only 10,000 cases in the UK of this in 2012!

* * *

I was on holiday in Kenya with my wife in 2009. We stayed in a modern hotel just north of Mombasa. The scenery was beautiful, but all around us was extreme poverty. Even those few employed, like our waiter, had frequently not been paid for months. A guard with a dog patrolled our campus at night to keep out the locals.

One morning after breakfast we decided to walk inland half a mile or so to the local village. The bored locals stood about in the shade. They had nothing else to do. The local shops had a few local wares, some overripe fruit and cheap alcohol. As we walked past some stalls, my wife hurried on. Alone, I was suddenly accosted by a young African lady. She wore bright clothes in contrast to all the other Africans. As she jumped up and down to attract my attention she called out to me, "I give you special massage!" I hesitated. Well, this was an invitation to taste the delights of Africa. After massage, what else indeed…? So what price would I pay for this treatment at about 10am on a very hot morning? Well, prostitutes in Africa have a very high incidence of human immuno deficiency virus. Ladies in this, the oldest profession, working in the United Kingdom have conversely a low incidence of HIV. Apart from HIV what else could I get for my money?

Well, gonorrhoea could play havoc with my 'nether reaches'. Non-specific urethritis and chlamydia, yes, I could definitely develop those too. There were also a few spin-offs from such an encounter – fleas, lice, viral warts – this list is a long one.

Was I missing out on anything else – any more 'presents from Africa'. Well, anybody with AIDS has a higher risk of tuberculosis and hepatitis.

They can't form resistance to infection and are so vulnerable. I could be introduced to these two diseases after a close encounter with such a lady.

I hesitated, not because she was attractive, but simply because she stood right in front of me, barring my way. Politely I declined her generous invitation and moved on.

I rejoined my wife who was engrossed looking at trinkets on a nearby stall. She had not missed me. "There's nothing here for us," she said. We walked slowly back to the hotel.

Half an hour later I was travelling on a dilapidated dhow sailing across the lagoon to the reef. Once there, Jacob the boatman anchored. The Pacific breakers crashed on the rocks 20 yards away; in contrast, the lagoon inside the reef was calm. I was the only passenger. I slipped into the cool, clear, water, 20 metres or so deep. I snorkelled for over half an hour. Jacob and his son kept a look out. Nobody else was around, not even the sharks.

Later, at Jacob's request, I held onto a rope as the dhow flew through the water back to the shore. The underwater world that opened up to me was idyllic. This was a taste of the delights of Africa that I would definitely not turn down.

The cost that I paid was £5 for the boat and the two of them for one and a half hours. I tipped Jacob generously, because I gave him my top.

* * *

AIDS started in Africa and is an important export to other countries all round the world. So it originated as a 'tropical disease'.

A BBC travel programme in February 2011 quoted that one in 20 British holidaymakers returned home from abroad still experiencing something very special – a sexually transmitted disease!

In the Second World War the German soldier was fully armed. He was issued with condoms! The US and Britain were the only countries not to arm their soldiers in this way. Sexually transmitted disease was, as a consequence, seven times higher in British soldiers than in the Germans!

Today the British government boasts of its foreign aid programme. Look at the small print – we spend nearly £20 million on condoms for Kenya alone. Africa needs a lot more condoms to prevent the spread of HIV. Well, annually they are 6.5 billion condoms short.[5]

* * *

Back in the 1970s an American philanthropist funded contraceptives for the Third World by creating a lucrative pornography business in the United States.[5]

Safe sex campaigns warn against unprotected sex and so reduce the danger of sexually transmitted disease and unwanted pregnancies. I applaud such initiatives that have done so much good worldwide. But just occasionally such actions have backfired, for example, when to the propaganda leaflet, a free condom was stapled!!!

* * *

Successive governments all over the world have wrestled with the problem of prostitution. It is an integral part of the black economy. The sex trade in France is said to be worth £3 billion annually. Should prostitution be banned and their clients fined? The trade would go underground. Or should prostitution be regulated, then at least they could pay tax on their earnings and have regular health checks?

* * *

Tropical diseases can turn up in the most unexpected places and in strange ways. They are now not solely confined to the tropics. My interest was aroused over 30 years ago by such a case. I was a surgical registrar on call at the Hammersmith Hospital in 1973. My bleep had called me all over the place. I had missed breakfast. Everybody else was enjoying their lunch, but I had one more call to follow up. This was to endocrinology outpatients. (I never got my lunch either.)

When I got there, everybody had left, apart from one junior nurse. She gave me some cursory notes and pointed me towards a patient. The patient was a Jamaican lady with acute abdominal pain. She had been unwell for months with vague central abdominal pain. She now had vomiting, with abdominal distention and constipation. She had lost eight kilograms in weight. She had twice coughed up blood and once noted blood in her stool. She had come to England 13 years before and had had three young children in the UK.

On examination she was in pain. She was ill. She was thin and dehydrated – dry tongue and skin. Her pulse was fast (90 beats a minute) and her blood pressure was low (90/70 mmhg). By contrast, her abdomen was relatively soft. No masses palpable. She had normal bowel sounds. Now, most people with acute abdominal pain have some tenderness, a lump and/or poor bowel sounds. Not this lady – she was so different. What was wrong?

Now, this hospital is the Royal Postgraduate Medical School. There are a lot of clever doctors there – physicians, surgeons and professors. This lady had the benefit of seeing a lot of them. We all knew she was ill but what with?

She had many tests. These were abnormal, but initially we did not know why! She was not anaemic. She had slightly more white cells than normal, suggesting an infection, but of what? Blood tests showed the salts in her blood (electrolytes) were mildly deranged. A chest X-ray was normal and her plain abdominal X-ray showed a few fluid levels – probably from her small bowel. So had had an infection of her small bowel, giving her dehydration and salt (electrolyte) imbalance. But what?

She had a tube inserted into her stomach and this was aspirated to empty her stomach. Fluids – salt and potassium – went into her blood to correct the salt imbalance and dehydration. Her abdominal pain continued, but her tummy was still soft. Oh, so soft!

Some small amount of barium was introduced into the stomach. This is opaque on X-ray and showed a grossly dilated first part of her duodenum. An endoscopy showed an abnormal duodenum with large villi. Aspiration of the duodenal contents showed large numbers of larvae. There were identified and confirmed later to be of a notorious tropical worm that rejoices in the name of Strongyloides stercoralis. (So it's not just botanists who love to tie you up in long words – it's doctors too.) She recovered well with the appropriate oral treatment.

But what on earth had happened here? What was the connection between this Londoner and the tropics so far away? She had lived here for 13 years! What had happened?

Well, this worm lives in the soil in the tropics, including the West Indies in one form. As she had walked about barefoot as a girl it had penetrated her foot. Once inside her body it had entered her gut and matured. Here the worm had lived for 13 years at least. A review of her obstetric records show she had it then – ten years before.

423

After living for many years in harmony with this host, this worm multiplied and multiplied to finally obstruct her bowel. A review of the medical literature showed this hyper infestation was not only rare but usually fatal. Her survival was unique. Two professors from the London School of Tropical Medicine and Hygiene visited her as she recovered in the hospital. Although they had written the authoritative textbook on the subject of tropical medicine, they had never seen a case of hyper infestation with this worm (or anything like it!).

This lady made a complete recovery and went home to her family. My boss followed her up for many years to ensure there was no reinfestation. There was not, but her immune system became deficient. So her ability to fight infection was reduced, perhaps accounting for this problem.[6]

* * *

A general practitioner contacted me in 1996. A 70-year-old man was referred to me privately as an emergency. He was a retired Rolls-Royce engineer. He had recently returned from a holiday in Costa Rica. Whilst in the jungle he had been bitten on his left wrist. This wrist was painful and swollen.

On examination of the wrist there was a lump about 1.5 inches x 1 inch with a small discharging hole. The patient exclaimed that the 'lump moved'. I replied to this: "Oh, how interesting". Well, you have to humour these private patients, or you may never get another one, ever.

Clinically, the lump looked like a sebaceous cyst; however, on removal, the wall was a lot thinner. I could see an insect inside just bunched up. I sent the specimen to a friend of mine, a professor of entomology. He identified the insect as Dermatobia hominis "with enormous hooks on the second instar larva". He told me that "one of my students had two of these following an expedition to Peru. They were agonisingly painful when they moved inside the sinus".

* * *

My insect could have escaped and flown all around Derbyshire biting people. (TRUE!)

These references total six cases of Dermatobia hominis – all seen in the UK. [7, 8, 9, 10]

This is not the only insectivorous holiday souvenir. The larva of the botfly loves to burrow into patients' backs. This is normally a parasite of sheep and horses, but sometimes uses us as a host. I know of one case from Peru. The larva was cut out under a local anaesthetic.

* * *

After finishing my obstetrics and gynaecology job in 1967 I still had large painful tonsils. I saw an eminent ear, nose and throat surgeon; he advocated tonsillectomy. I agreed.

Post-operatively, I wandered round the Central Middlesex Hospital. I knew a lot of staff as I had worked there recently. I chatted to a few people. A third person told me that they were in theatre when I had had my operation. Each said the same story: "You coughed, and the anaesthetist could not be found!" I know he was reading the newspaper and doing the crossword round the corner. I knew the anaesthetist too well!

My so-called recovery was very slow indeed. I was off sick for weeks until antibiotics cured my post-operative throat infection. I then recuperated by doing my mother's general practice locum, and visited food factories as a doctor. (My mother paid me very well!)

Workers in food factories must have medical examinations. Workers with persistent productive coughs or carriers of disease are not suitable for work in a food factory. It was my job to see that the workforce was healthy in this respect.

A worker from India, about to start in the creamery of the factory, was found to have typhoid bacilli in his stools. He was asymptomatic. So he was a carrier of typhoid and could pass this disease on to fellow workers, or even into the cream – an ideal culture medium. I refused to allow him to work there. His union objected, but he needed eradication of his carrier status. This would involve further treatment and often removal of a diseased gallbladder. He left and never returned to the factory.

The commonest form of typhoid seen in emergency departments today is Salmonella typhimurium. This can be acquired in the UK, but is more likely to develop on holiday in the tropics. I recently saw a West Country seamstress with this infection, who had just returned from a holiday in Cuba. Even after treatment her bowels had not returned completely to normal six weeks later!

* * *

I was doing a follow-up clinic in 2005. A tall black man came in. I discovered he was from the Horn of Africa and had been in the UK for less than one year.

He complained of some numbness to his left hand. However, on careful examination he had some sensory loss to the fingers that was mostly partial and some complete. Both his median and ulnar nerve distribution was involved. This confused me immensely. He had no injuries or scars. There was no evidence of something wrong with his neck or arm. Something pressing on or damaging the nerves to his left arm seemed unlikely, e.g., cervical spondylosis, carpal tunnel syndrome or an accident.

I had no idea what caused his numbness as I had seen nothing like this before. I paused and then had a guess.

"Have you had any treatment for leprosy?" I asked. (This was a complete stab in the dark). "Oh yes," he replied. "I had some treatment in Africa, but I did not return for follow-up as I was cured. I stopped the treatment."

I told him that, in my opinion, he still had leprosy. I referred him to a hand surgeon. In a friendly letter back, the hand surgeon agreed with me over the diagnosis. He added: 'We see quite a few cases of leprosy in our clinics.' I showed this to my consultant colleague and we both had a laugh about this remark!

In all types of leprosy the textbook informed me that peripheral nerve involvement (that he had) is a constant feature. Treatment is effective with chemotherapy, but needs to continue 'for one to two years'. There are probably 10 to 20 million cases of leprosy scattered throughout the globe. To develop leprosy there is usually a history of prolonged exposure to this infection. The incubation period can be years!

So, our present treatment for leprosy usually works but can take up to two years – a rather long time.

Now compare this treatment:

426

Jesus was going into a village when he was met by ten men suffering from a dreaded skin disease (leprosy). They stood at a distance and shouted, "Jesus Master! Take pity on us." Jesus saw them and said to them, "Go and let the priests examine you."
On the way, they were made clean.

Luke 17, verse 11

NOW THAT'S WHAT I CALL A MIRACLE!!

∗ ∗ ∗

Influenza comes to our shores, usually in the winter and often originating in the Far East. We tend to treat it with contempt – 'just flu'. But the elderly (my age group) and infirm may well succumb. We tend to forget that in 1919 in the pre-antibiotic era a virulent influenza virus caused the death of 1% of the world's population!

References:

1. Grace Mukasa. AMREF Better Health for Africa. 17. 11. 10.
2. *BMJ* 7. 2. 2009:338;b454.
3. Bill Gates. Reduce child deaths and end overpopulation. *The Times* 23. 10. 10:24.
4. A Fraser-Moodie. Minerva *BMJ* 13. 1. 90:300;134.
5. Helen Rumbelow. Lie back and think of England. *The Times* 19. 3. 10:65-66.
6. G Royle. A Fraser-Moodie. J Spencer. Hyperinfection with Strongyloidesstercoralis in Great Britain. *Br J Surg* (1974) 61:498-500.
7. Bowry R. *J AccidEmerg Med* 1997:14;177.
8. Kitching J. J AccidEmerg Med 1997:14;178.
9. MacNamara J. *J AccidEmerg* Med 1997:14;179.
10. A Fraser-Moodie. *J AccidEmerg* Med 1997:14;411.

Rabies

I have never seen a case of rabies. However, cases of rabies have been reported throughout the continent. It has not crossed the English Channel yet! Well, other invaders like the Romans and the Normans had several tries before they succeeded. There are several ways rabies could get across. A rabid rat could board a cargo vessel abroad and disembark at a British port. A seal could be swimming in Roscoff Harbour one day and bite a swimmer in Folkestone Harbour the next. Finally, an infected fox could streak through the Channel Tunnel to cause havoc in Kent. Let us hope this never happens.

As an emergency consultant I have seen countless British holidaymakers who have been bitten abroad. Typically, the bite is from a stray dog in India. Over the years the animals implicated have been varied. This disease is deadly. The virus of rabies has killed thousands of people worldwide. The incubation period is from three weeks to several months. Once bitten there is time therefore for the holidaymaker to return home and have treatment. The vaccine combined with immunoglobulin assures immunity.

Let's hope this virus never reaches the UK.

CHAPTER FORTY-FIVE

Yet More Diseases From Abroad(?)

Three Cases – One Diagnosis

"Curiouser and curiouser," cried Alice.

Lewis Carroll

I was asked by a sister to look at a patient's leg in 1980. The leg was not healing with dressings. I was introduced to a 40-year-old Irishman.

"My leg's not healing right, doctor," he said. "You need to do more."

On his right calf were two ulcers (an ulcer is simply a raw area). There are lots of causes of ulcers. I looked at two snake-like ulcers, each 5cm x 5cm. The bases were wet and the walls thickened. The leg was otherwise healthy. He had no pain. I stared and stared.

"Don't you know the cause?" he asked.

"No, I don't," I said.

"Well, I need to see a better doctor," he said.

Ignoring this remark I arranged for several swabs to be taken and sent to the laboratory at once. "If we find nothing I will do a biopsy," I said to the sister.

As I left I heard him complaining to the nurse, "That doctor does not know what he is doing."

Events then became a bit chaotic about two hours later. Long after the patient had left, the microbiology consultant telephoned. We then had a diagnosis.

* * *

The second patient with the same problem presented differently. An intelligent black lady in her thirties had really acute abdominal pain. Bizarrely, her abdomen was very soft and non-tender. She had no pyrexia and the bowel sounds were normal.

I was not the admitting doctor, but I worked in the Emergency Room. I was not quiet in my opinion to the junior surgical team that she had a medical acute abdomen. As I wrote in the records and said, "She needs to see a physician and have an endoscopy." (I was on the point of leaving this hospital for good at that time).

I later learnt from a third party that the lady had died after an operation.

* * *

Finally, a young Indian lady presented with acute shortness of breath in 2009. She had recently married and attributed this to her loss of weight.

On examination very little air was going into the right side of her chest. A chest X-ray showed she had punctured her right lung (pneumothorax), but how?

All these three patients were suffering from the same condition – tuberculosis.

The Irishman had tuberculosis ulcers on his leg. In all three patients the infection probably started in the lungs and then spread.

The Irishman was likely to spread this infection to whoever looked at his ulcers. On interrogation, later, he had walked out of treatment in Ireland, even though he was told he had tuberculosis. He had kept this quiet initially, to see if we reached the same conclusion! So, he wanted a second opinion and got one. Luckily none of our staff were infected, but I don't know who else he had been in contact with. He recovered.

The lady with abdominal pain had extensive tuberculosis of her bowel. This, I understand, is usually fatal. She died.

The Indian lady had tuberculosis of her lung. The infection caused the lung to puncture. She had a chest drain inserted and this allowed the collapsed lung to expand. She healed well on treatment, just like the Irishman.

These patients are all so very different, but there is one common denominator. None of these three patients were born in the UK. None of them had been immunised against TB! They all had contracted tuberculosis abroad. A lot of the tuberculosis patients come from abroad. Our previous health secretary Andrew Lansley has publicly said this, and blamed the recent rise in cases on immigration.

Strangely, airport checks with chest X-rays for all immigrants have been recently scrapped.[1] So, immigrants with respiratory tuberculosis are free to enter this country undetected and are likely to infect others!

Conversely, our same government has a very active programme detecting tuberculosis in another susceptible group. The Department of the Environment and Rural Affairs ensures that veterinary surgeons check all cows annually. If tuberculosis is found in any cow – or even suspected – then that animal is put down immediately! (I can't see any of my patients agreeing to that treatment.) Surely immigrants should be more carefully looked at. Tuberculosis is becoming a commoner condition again!

So tuberculosis is one of the prices we have to pay in the United Kingdom for attracting immigrants to our shores.

Stories about tuberculosis come back to haunt us again and again. This disease refuses to go away. 28,000 cattle annually test positive for bovine tuberculosis and so are slaughtered in the UK. These carcasses are now being introduced into our food chains! They are sold to schools, hospitals or the military. Some meat is put in pies.[2, 3]

So this is what meat inspectors, veterinary surgeons, health and safety workers and executives from the Department of the Environment, Farming and Rural Affairs have agreed. Well, they are all paid by the government!

The first vaccine against tuberculosis was given as recently as 1927. This vaccine was not given out widely and tuberculosis flourished.

In 1953, France and Scandinavia started immunising children again tuberculosis. They reported that after 50,000 children had been injected there was an 80% reduction in infection rates. Supported by this evidence, our new National Health Service commenced vaccination routinely in all secondary schools.

When I started as a medical student in 1960 I was asked if I had been immunised against tuberculosis. I had to have a test to see if I had developed immunity (mantoux). Finally, as medical students, we had to have yearly chest X-rays to check we had not caught tuberculosis.

Now, the modern schoolchild is not routinely immunised against tuberculosis, unless they have been in contact with a case. Similarly, medical students don't have chest X-rays routinely or tests to see if they have any immunity to the disease.

This may all change.

I wrote the above in March 2011. In June 2011 the government announced the reintroduction of vaccination against tuberculosis for the newborn in some areas, e.g., London.[4]

Too little, too late? We will wait and see.

Immunisation has proved to be a big success. As a result, smallpox has now been totally and completely eradicated worldwide. Less than a century ago it was rife in the United Kingdom. The campaign against smallpox was at its height. For example, in 1922 there was a fresh outbreak of smallpox in Gloucester.

The Health Committee released the figures locally:

Total admissions for smallpox	350
Unvaccinated cases	319
Cases vaccinated a long time ago	18
Cases vaccinated during incubation period	13

These figures speak for themselves.

In December 1965, when I started my first medical job, the secretary to the board sent me a letter that complied with the Contracts of Employment Act 1963. At the bottom of the letter was this sentence:

'I advise you to obtain a smallpox vaccination from your general practitioner as a precaution against risks of infection.' So this was at the commencement of my very first contract of employment.

Diphtheria is another immunisation success. I have never seen a case, of even heard of one case. All babies are immunised against diphtheria, yet as recently as 1940 there were 60,000 cases in the UK, with 3,283 deaths.

So immunisation works.

There are three important diseases in the United Kingdom that have come from abroad. All three are serious and difficult to treat. I have mentioned tuberculosis and human immunodeficiency virus (HIV). But in the last four years, 95% of all cases of hepatitis B have come from abroad to this country.[5] This condition can be fatal, sometimes by producing liver cancers. Mass immunisation is effective, as has been shown in the United States.[6]

I recently read an abstract entitled, 'Should universal hepatitis B immunisation be introduced in the UK?' It read, in its entirety, 'Yes, but how?'[7]

References:

1. Airport TB Docs axed by Health Protection Authority. *News of the World* 23.1.11:2.
2. Jonathan Leake. Thousands of TB Cows sold as Food. *The Sunday Times*. 30.6.13:1.
3. Hannah Devlin. DEFRA sells diseased cattle for human consumption. *The Times*. 1. 7. 13:5.
4. Chris Smyth. Mass jabs for babies to check TB surge. *The Times* 3. 6. 11:1&10. A Dickensian disease that came back from the dead.
5. Daily Mail. Migrants blamed for diseases. Www.dailymail.co.uk/health article. 191209/migrants-blamed-diseaseshtml#ixzz2lbKSzkRg (31.1.13).
6. Science-based Medicine. Why Universal hepatitis B Vaccination isn't quite universal, 2009, www.sciencebasedmedicine.org/index. php/why-universal-hepatitis-b-isn't-quite-universal.
7. English P. Should universal hepatitis B immunisation be introduced in the UK? *Arch Dis Child* 2006;91:286-89.

CHAPTER FORTY-SIX

Some Problems with Alcohol and Drugs

Every form of addiction is bad, no matter whether the narcotic be alcohol or morphine.

Carl Jung

Alcohol

Alcohol is one of the oldest and most widely used drugs. Well, beer was being produced in Mesopotamia from barley and hot water in 8000-6000 BC.

Today, alcohol is the nation's favourite. Taken in moderation at all meetings. Taken to excess regularly. The NHS had more than a million admissions due to alcohol last year.[1] Twenty thousand people die annually in the UK due to drink related causes. Alcohol misuse costs the NHS and the justice system about £25 billion each year.[2] More needs to be done. Perhaps a different approach to alcohol and drugs, especially heroin, is called for?

Between February 2008 and December 2009 the last Labour government hired nearly 80 celebrities. These role models were used to endorse campaigns outlining the dangers of alcohol, amongst other things. These people were paid well – over £300,000. Is this the very best use of taxpayers' money?[3]

British householders in 2010 spent about £70 billion on alcohol. As a consequence, hospital admissions due to alcohol soared to over 250,000. These include the toxic effects, alcohol liver disease, as well as mental health and behavioural problems.[4]

As a gynaecological senior house officer in 1967, I once organised a party for the doctors' mess with the help of a friendly Pakistani doctor. We were returning some hospitality we had enjoyed from other doctors. On our evening off we organised a variety of drinks, a few nibbles and some music. At 11pm, after an enjoyable evening, we were both clearing up. My Pakistani friend had told me fondly of his upbringing in the foothills of the Himalayas, now covered in snow.

I picked up our very large gin bottle. It had been full, but now it was empty! But my co-organiser had been the only one drinking gin! He can't have finished it alone! He then confessed "I am a Muslim and an alcoholic. I can't go home. My life is a mess," he said. He was the first of several medical alcoholics I met. Several general practitioners, and even one medical school dean, were affected. Their work suffered and they all tried to hide their habit.

Drink Driving

We think that the laws imposed on us concerning drink driving are new. Not so. In 1872, the Licensing Act made it an offence to be drunk while in charge of carriages, horses, cattle or steam engines! The penalty for which was a fine of up to 40 shillings or imprisonment with, or without, hard labour of up to one month.

1925- Criminal Justice Act. It became an offence to be drunk in charge of any mechanically propelled vehicle in a public place. All guilty parties could face a fine up to £50, and/or imprisonment up to four months, and disqualification from driving for at least one year.

1967- the Road Safety Act introduced the first legal maximum blood alcohol: 80mg alcohol/100 ml blood. This is also known as the breathalyser act.

1983- more accurate breath testing machines were introduced. High risk offenders were targeted. The DVLA won't give them their licence back until they are satisfied that they have overcome any drink problem.

2010- a UK government report suggested:

1. The current legal limit could be reduced to 50mg of alcohol per 100ml blood.
2. Permanent disqualification for repeat drink driving offenders.

Yes, as an emergency consultant I have seen many drunk drivers who have been involved in road traffic accidents. The damage, once again, had already been done. Sometimes an innocent victim's life has been lost due to their loss of control. The driver will then have to live with the consequences.

I recall Stirling Moss, the motor racing driver, interviewed on television in 1967. It was at the time of the introduction of the breathalyser act. His response times were tested before and after a drink of alcohol. The results were startling. He was slower to respond after a very small amount of alcohol.

When will we learn?

* * *

On 17th of April 1963, I was 21 years old. I was given a large golf bag. This was by far my best present. Then a disaster occurred. In August 1963 this new bag, and all my golf clubs, were stolen from my locker at Royal Mid Surrey Golf Club. The lock had been forced. This act was reported to the police so two uniformed policemen drove to my parent's house in Richmond, in a patrol car, to take a statement from me.

My late mother was there too and desperately wanted to be hospitable. She overdid this hospitality, but that was typical of her generation! First she offered them tea or coffee – they refused. Then she offered them whisky! They hesitated, as they were obviously on duty. But then they accepted !!!

I was very concerned. My late mother did not drink whisky. She never touched a drop, unlike my father. She poured it out like lemonade, and filled two large glasses full of neat whisky. By now I was really worried. Could my mother be charged with aiding and abetting an offence (drink driving)? Alternatively, my mother could be charged with bribing, not one but two, policemen whilst on duty, with alcohol, i.e., attempting to pervert the course of justice.But my mother was a registered medical practitioner. Such a charge could cause her to lose her licence to practise medicine.

I signed my statement concerning the theft. Then the huge whiskies went 'down the hatch' very quickly indeed. The patrol car drove off.

The bag and clubs were never recovered. But this golf equipment was insured. So I got a new bag and better clubs from the insurance payment. I presume that the generous whiskies caused no repercussions???

* * *

In 1967, when the breathalyser act was introduced, the captain of the rugby at St Thomas' just happened to be invited to the grand opening of a new public house. Not surprisingly, he attended, and found all his medical student mates were there too. What a surprise! Well, the beer was free!!!

Unfortunately, I did not hear about this.

But I do know that some hours later a car approaching St Thomas' just happened to strangely veer left off the road, across the pavement, and collided with the wall of the mortuary!

The driver and passenger were the only people involved. They were quickly conveyed to Casualty barely 100 metres away. The police were hot on their heels bearing the new breathalyser. The casualty officer told the police that unfortunately the breathalyser could not be used on these two casualties for technical reasons. Both these people were so bad that he had to resuscitate them with a stimulant – alcohol. So the police were thwarted. (Our rugby captain and the publican had 'got away with it'.)

* * *

I was one of four golfers who had just played a round of golf. We would now eat a meal together.

"Would you care for a glass of wine?" asked my medical golfing partner .

"Yes thank you," I replied.

I expected two glasses of wine, one each. Instead, he produced a bottle. Our opponents each had a beer, and so refused wine. I was driving home later, so I was only going to drink one small glass of wine. I had just finished the starter of our meal, when my golfing partner announced: "I'd better get another bottle." He left to get one. Well, where had all that wine gone? I was still on my first little glass of red! I started to take notice.

I refused a top-up to my glass. Over the next few minutes I watched this second bottle of wine disappear down my golfing partner's throat! We finished the meal. Then a friend tapped my partner's shoulder and said, "She's here." He shook hands all round, and left. He was driven home by his wife, who had just arrived.

I paid for one bottle of wine. (That was my most expensive glass of wine ever!) Then a friend remarked to me, "What a pity your golfing partner has lost his driving licence. Such rotten luck. His poor wife has to drive him everywhere. Even to visits."

I thought, *Thank goodness he's not driving home tonight,* and also, *How long will he last on the medical register?*

* * *

Should the legal limit for alcohol for drivers in England be lowered from 80mgm to 50mg/100mi, in line with Scotland? Well, the number of accidents in Scotland fell by 20% when the new limit was imposed. This limit is in line with other European countries and could save 200 lives each year.

Other Drugs

When I was a medical student in 1963, a motorcyclist was seen in Casualty. He had been in a road traffic accident. He seemed well – very alert indeed. He had been riding his motorcycle down Whitehall and had collided with the Cenotaph. You would have thought that a structure as large as that, and fixed, could have been avoided! No, he argued, it should not be there – why so aggressive? So, in his opinion, he was definitely not to blame. Whoever built the Cenotaph should be held to account!

He remained talkative and agitated. We could not shut him up. Then he admitted it. He had taken purple hearts. None of the doctors knew what they were. However, I knew that the Americans took them in the Second World War. They are amphetamines.

So this driver had crashed whilst under the influence of drugs, not alcohol. He was the first driver I ever saw under the influence of any such drugs. Many more similar drivers were to follow.

Prior to this I had seen a few barbiturate addicts and morphine addicts. This patient was the first of a new type of drug addict that was to plague me for the rest of my career.

This man was suffering more from amphetamines than from the road traffic accident.

He recovered well.

* * *

A 39-year-old lady had already been assessed by the triage nurse in 1993. The diagnosis was a groin infection. A man, I presumed to be her husband, preceded her. He was wearing a smart brown leather coat with a sheepskin collar. The lady slunk in slowly. He sat down and she stood behind him. She looked a lot older than her age.

"She has a groin infection that needs to be treated," he confidently pronounced, and she remained silent.

"Excuse me," I asked, "but are you the patient's husband?" He laughed and slapped his thigh.

"Me, married to her, never," he said, and glanced at her.

"May I see the problem?" I asked, pointing to the couch.

"Are you leaving?" I asked him.

"Oh no," he said smiling. "I know the problem well."

"Is that all right with you?" I asked her. The slim, tired, badly dressed lady just nodded again. She was so depressed.

She had evidence of puncture wounds over the femoral veins on both sides of the groins. So, needles had been inserted to put, probably, heroin directly into her blood stream. Frankly, both groins were a complete mess, with infection and profuse discharge bilaterally.

"She needs to be admitted for treatment," I said. "She will be given dressings several times a day and intravenous antibiotics."

"No, she can't be admitted," he said.

"Well, what about you?" I said, turning to the patient.

She looked so dejected and just said, "I do whatever he says."

I took swabs for culture and sensitivity. As she was not allergic to penicillin, I gave her a high dose of a broad spectrum. She was given dressings, and both groins were dressed.

He refused a follow-up appointment for her. "I'm not coming here again," he said confidently. "Come on, hurry up," he said to her and left.

So the poor lady was a prostitute, and trapped. She was addicted to heroin, and self-injected heroin. He was her pimp – what a bully! He wanted her working, so he got more money. She needed to work to fund her habit.

Poor wretch, she looked years older than her chronological age. I was absolutely amazed that any man would be attracted to her in that state. But some men must be, for her to continue working. She was likely to pass on hepatitis C to them, amongst other things, and her life expectancy was poor.

* * *

A young couple in a car had been involved in a high speed collision, in 1991, with a lamp post. Their car was badly damaged. He had a fractured right femur, and abdominal injuries probably caused by the steering wheel. She had a fractured right arm, and chest injuries caused by the seat belt. This had been a high speed impact according to the ambulance man – "the lamp post was flattened".

Now both these people in their late twenties needed resuscitation. He needed a blood transfusion. They both needed intravenous fluids.

Oh, there is a technical problem – nobody can find any veins in either of their arms. We searched around for one, to take a blood sample and give them intravenous fluids. Everybody is born with veins under their skin – where were they? The real worry here was that both patients were candidates for internal bleeding, and they could take a turn for the worse.

Finally the penny dropped. "Do you inject anything into your bodies?"

"Oh yes," she confidently remarked, "we both take heroin. We love it."

Multiple injections cause the veins to clot and shrivel up.

Some clever doctor eventually found a small vein in each of them. They were both given fluids via this tiny vein. They were both admitted and recovered well.

We usually see the end result of drug addiction in hospital. Well, this is the start. Both these patients had good jobs and a good income. The pushers target such people, offering them heroin. "Oh go on, just try it; this stuff will give you a high." Soon after, they are hooked. The pusher has an income. When they lose their jobs, he will turn to crime to fund his habit, and she might turn to prostitution.

* * *

A man in shabby clothes was ushered in to see me in 1996. He had two companions, both uniformed – customs men from the East Midlands Airport. The patient was handcuffed to one of them. "Please can we have an X-ray?" said a customs man. "We have reason to believe he is carrying drugs inside him."

I turn to the captive. "Well, er, how are you?"

"OK," he said, looking dejected at being caught.

"We need to do an X-ray," I said.

"I don't want an X-ray. I refuse. I want a lawyer now. Do you hear? Now!" he replied.

"I'm sorry," I replied. "An X-ray is in the public interest. Anyway, if you are carrying drugs a packet may burst, and you will be very ill."

I made out the X-ray form in the name on the man's passport. It may well have been a false name on a false passport. I did not know.

Five minutes later they were back with the X-ray. I glanced at the

X-ray. His abdomen was full of packages. It was very obvious indeed (fig 73).

"Is that them packages?" asked the customs man looking at the x-ray.

"Yes," I said, "he's full of them."

"Thanks doc," and the three of them were gone. I did not see this man, or his minders again.

This patient was a body packer or mule. In a recent article from the United States, the experience of customs apprehending such people at JFK Airport over 20 years was reported.[5] 1,250 people were caught and a lot more probably made it through. Seventy per cent of those caught were male with an average age of 33 years. Most of them were South American.

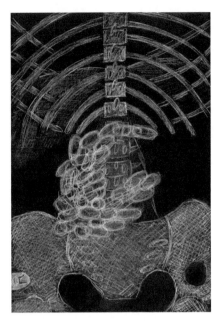

Fig 73 – An artist's impression of the X-ray of this man. Each oval represents a condom. If any of these had burst he could have died.

They each carried between 40 and 150 packets of drugs taped up in condoms! The usual drug was heroin, but sometimes cocaine. The value of these drugs in each patient could be up to $1 million.

The packets rarely burst and were usually subsequently passed down below with the aid of an aperient.

In a few cases surgery was necessary to remove these packages.

* * *

I was thinking about going home. It was past 6pm on a Sunday evening. I had been there all day in 2004. Then in hobbled another 'football injury'. He had twisted his knee that day. He had obviously sprained his knee. His symptoms exceeded those expected with the clinical findings. He was sullen and silent. He was accompanied by a tired-looking older man, who denied a connection. "Are you a relative?"

–"No" – "Are you a neighbour?" – "No." *What is going on?* I thought. *What am I missing?*

They both had Glaswegian accents. So I blindly said, "Do you support Rangers?"

Suddenly these two sprang to life. The knee forgotten they started to sing a partisan song as they danced around the cubicle together. "Rangers, Rangers, Rangers," they called out.

"So what is it between you two?" I asked.

Now the ice was broken and the story was told.

"I'm a heroin addict," he said, "or I was last week. This is Brian; he is my minder at Jericho House. In there they will help me get clean and stay that way."

Brian was an ex-junkie – a lot younger than he looked, but heroin makes you age prematurely.

There are Jericho Houses all over the UK. It is a charity started by a Scottish minister. He dried out some alcoholics in his vast manse before he told his bishop! This treatment worked.

Current Treatments for Drug and Alcohol Addiction.

Let the punishment fit the crime.
                    Gilbert and Sullivan, *The Mikado*

So now there are plenty of outlets giving treatment to many people for drug and alcohol addiction – similar to the NHS, but outside the NHS – each is called Jericho House.

I have visited the Jericho House in Derby twice, and I subscribe to their charity. The road to recovery is a slow one. They are watched all the way. That is why Brian was there. That explains his presence,, stopping the patient from getting a fix behind his back.

Once clean, heroin addicts are watched locally in a flat. Weeks later they are let out – back into society.

The set-up is not big time. It is small and expensive in Derby. It is not NHS-funded but from donations like mine. Over a year or two, 19 heroin addicts were treated. One year later, 17 are still clean. This sounds poor to you, but actually it is very good.

The rules are tough. No methadone (a heroin substitute), no mess and no fights. The police are called to the house very occasionally. All those in charge are ex-addicts, so they know the score. Is this a model for future NHS establishments? I suspect the NHS could learn from Jericho House to cure alcohol and drug addicts.

Could there be help for heroin addicts with a vaccine? The Scripps Research Unit in the US is clinically testing vaccines for cocaine and nicotine users. Designing such a vaccine has been difficult but clinical testing has started.[6]

But how effective are other treatment centres for drug and alcohol addiction? Amy Winehouse died in 2011 after a vodka binge. She had received treatment at the Causeway Retreat on Osea Island in the Blackwater Estuary, Essex. Mitch Winehouse, Amy's father, called this residential centre 'useless' despite its fees of £10,000 a week. It has since been closed down.

The Winehouse family has set up a charity to promote education about drug and alcohol problems in schools throughout the UK, in collaboration with the organisation Addaction.[7] Children are more exposed than adults and need stronger protection.

Could the possibility in the UK, of a minimum price for units of ethanol, actually work and reduce deaths from alcohol? Well, in British Columbia since 2002, the minimum price of alcohol has been set per litre without reference to the strength. Between 2004 and 2009 there was a significant reduction in deaths due to alcohol. These included deaths due to acute situations, e. g. poisoning, fatal injuries whilst drunk, and chronic problems like cirrhosis.[8]

Many celebrities have taken drugs, including even Rudyard Kipling[9] and Mick Jagger.[10] Jail sentences do not cure drug addicts – well, it's sending them to a land of plenty. We all need to engage in reality.

Drug use amongst teenagers is in decline. But what about cannabis? It is usually grown in the UK and is very strong and affordable to teenagers. An increasing number of teenagers are being treated for cannabis abuse.

An 'at risk' child develops a personality change – they may be dishevelled, consistently late and unable to get up in the morning. Over 13,000 teenagers needed help for a problem with cannabis in 2011-12.[11]

There are many beneficial uses of alcohol – in medicine, solvents, dyes, industrial resins and even rocket fuel. It could be argued that without the rocket fuel to propel him, and the tax revenues from alcohol, man could not have explored space!

Now, alcohol is not all bad. The farmers of South West France have proved this. I have seen them each tip one glass of cheap red wine into their soup. They stir in the wine. The majority of them as a direct consequence live to an old age. This was confirmed in a leader in the *BMJ* on their longevity in 2009.

There is scientific proof of this too. For those who consume light to moderate amounts of alcohol (about one drink a day), the news is good.We are told in the *BMJ* that such consumption is associated with a reduced risk of cardiovascular disease – reduced mortality, and reduced incidence of coronary artery disease and strokes.[12]

Also in the same *BMJ* (above), on page 490, we are reminded that 4% of our adult population are alcohol dependent. Over 26% of all adults today consume alcohol in a way that is potentially, or actually, harmful to their health.[13]

Yet currently, of all those alcohol dependent, only 6% receive treatment; this is too little, too late. Would the creation of a minimum price for alcohol benefit big business rather than the 'blighted boozer'? Let's hope that eventually this legislation is adopted universally and does bring about real benefits.[14]

But it's not all bad news. Currently there are nearly 200,000 heavy alcohol drinkers in Scotland. A new drug, nalmefene, has been licensed in Scotland, and this reduces the craving for alcohol.[15]

Also, a US study from Yale University and published in the Journal, 'Alcoholism: Clinical and Experimental Research', in August 2013 by Sherry McKee, showed that taxing cigarette smokers more made them drink less alcohol. They looked at 21,000 alcohol drinkers and this was more marked amongst men, the poor and the young!

The reader may easily be lulled into a false sense of security about drugs. "Well, surely this drug problem affects a tiny section of our community. Our government has it under control and it has no relevance to the reader."

However, some anonymous urine samples from the general public were analysed. These samples were collected in Central London from four-person, portable urinals with no flushing mechanism, and so were not diluted. Twelve urinals were collected. These represented the urine from 48 persons, and any metabolites detected indicated drug use, and not drug disposal. So this is a 'snapshot' of drug activity in one area of London.

All 12 urinals had evidence of hordenine (a 'legal high'), cocaine and cannabis. Eleven urinals were positive for ecstasy.[16]

In susceptible individuals the long-term effects of illicit drugs could lead to personality and psychiatric disorders. But referrals to the psychiatric service are already high! In November 2014 the Office of National Statistics reported drug deaths up from 1,636 in 2012 to 1,937 in 2013.

Money paid for these drugs funds the black economy. This is untaxed and booming. We unknowingly reward the drug pushers and cannabis growers with unemployment benefit and income support. Drugs have to be paid for! This black economy in drugs is funded by thefts, burglaries, muggings, shoplifting and scams of all sorts. A lot of these crimes go unreported and ignored.

Well, for 40 years I treated the victims of violent crimes. A brick to the head ensured that the mugger got that mobile phone. Those brave passers-by tried to apprehend a shoplifter, one was stabbed in the guts and another was run over.

I have met and been lectured to by the local police drugs squad. They do a brilliant job. Unfortunately, police funding and police numbers are on the decline!

Incidentally, our prison numbers are at an all-time high. Despite Chris Huhne being given an eight-month sentence, he was out in two months. How strange is that? These people are all detained at great expense to the taxpayer. It can cost over £200,000 to keep some teenagers behind bars.[17] Unfortunately, three-quarters of teenage criminals reoffend within one year.[17] If these teenagers are drug addicts then they have easy access to drugs whilst in prison! Also, while the criminals are in prison their families are well supported by the state as well!

I have been in six prisons – in a professional capacity, of course! The gardens in the open prisons are fantastic. Well, the inmates act as gardeners. I have visited two high security prisons. Obese, middle-aged, male guards in drab uniforms with huge bunches of keys passed me from one to another as a succession of doors was unlocked. Yes, these places, quite rightly, seem secure and very inhospitable. The last time I visited such an institution I was greeted in reception by a young slim lady in a very tight-fitting dress! She introduced herself as Carol and shook my hand. She was stunning and very friendly. She waved as I left. I asked the man on the gate who she was, thinking that she was a secretary.

He smiled and lowered his voice. "That, doctor, is the governor," he replied.

Well, prisons are so expensive and don't seem to work, especially with teenagers, perhaps criminals could be fined instead? Well, there is a trend that criminals today get off scot free by ignoring fines.[18] Let us hope that things never get as out of hand as in the United States. There, female prison officers in Baltimore were accused of long-term sexual relationships with prisoners. They also helped a gang run a drug trafficking and money laundering scheme from inside jail, it was alleged by prosecutors![19]

So, fines and imprisonment fail! There is no deterrent – flogging, deportation and hanging are all obsolete. Are we too soft on the criminal? Fortunately, in 2015 the British government launched a screening programme of all visitors, to stop drugs and weapons getting into prisons. I hope this works.

* * *

Many doctors think that we have tried, and failed, to eradicate drugs! A new approach is needed NOW. The police, armed with the full force of the law have failed badly. No, today drugs abound. The pushers are happy. Crime funds the drug habit. Our courts are busy with drug addicts, and our prisons are full. We the taxpayer are paying a heavy price for drugs in our society over and over again. We need a fresh approach NOW.

There is a start already. There are free injection centres springing up, where no questions are asked. Where addicts are helped to inject into veins, and resuscitated if they collapse. But drugs need to be decriminalised NOW. The police and the courts should no longer be involved. The work of Jericho House should be expanded and replicated all over our land.

VILLAINS, VIOLINS, AND VIRTUOSOS.

Who plucked their heartstrings? Who is on the fiddle?

Villains are not known generally for their super intelligence. One burglar from Derby stole a violin from a retired paediatrician's house. He tried to sell it for £50 at a local music shop. But why did the salesman know it was stolen and so called the police? The startled burglar was dumbfounded. After protesting his innocence, he finally owned up to the theft. The answer was that the salesman just happened to recognise the violin – as a Stradivarius!

Not bad value for £50.

Min-Jin Kym, the South Korean concert violinist, also lost a Stradivarius, valued at £1.2 million, and a bow worth £62,000. She was in a cafe (Pret a Manger at Euston Station) on her iPhone. Oh dear.[20] She failed to notice that her precious violin was gone, for a few minutes! She later joked that she had purchased the world's most expensive sandwich!

The thieves were soon caught. They had been unable to sell the 1686 instrument for £100. It took three years for the British Transport Police to finally track the violin down and return it. However, by then Min-Jin Kym had cashed in the insurance policy. She could no longer afford to buy her beloved instrument back. So she had lost it.

In July 2016 another violinist, Krysia Osostowicz, had her £200,000 violin snatched while she was locking her bicycle outside Brixham Station. True to form, it was recovered when a lady tried to pawn it for £50. So the IQ of villains has not improved, and the value of preowned, priceless, purloined violins on the black market is still £50![21, 22]

In August 2016 the violinist Jane Gordon left her violin on the train on the luggage rack. This instrument was valued in excess of £100,000, as the 17th-century piece was from an Italian master craftsman. Fortunately, after a lot of publicity it was returned.[21, 22]

These episodes suggest to me that the female of our species may not be as good at multitasking as they have led us to believe. Amazingly, the three virtuosos got their timing all wrong, and all failed to note where their violins were.

Who says that history does not repeat itself?

References:

1. Tim Spanton. Million Bingers Injured. *The Sun* 20.1.11:27.
2. K Chand. Is it too late to crack down on the country's favourite drug? *The Times*. 2.11.10:25.
3. Alcohol and Celebrities. *The Daily Telegraph*. 22. 2. 10:9.
4. John Appleby. Drinking Nation – Have we had enough? *BMJ* 2012:344;e2634.
5. N Mandava et al. Establishment of a definitive protocol for the diagnosis and management of body packers (drug mules). *EMJ* 2011:28:98-101
6. Tariq Tahir. Jab for Heroin Addiction could offer hope to 10 m. *The Metro*. 7.5.13;21.
7. Isabel Oakeshott. Drug lessons in class – yes, yes, yes. *The Sunday Times*. 10. 3. 13:7.
8. Gerard Hastings and Nick Sheron. Alcohol Marketing: Grooming the next generation. *BMJ* 2013;346:f1227.
9. Theodore Dalrymple. Intoxication for Happiness. *BMJ* 2012:344;e3188.
10. Lucy Bannerman. From Showboat to Satisfaction via a Landmark Leader. *The Times* 31.12.12:9.
11. Rachel Carlyle. Teenagers and Cannabis; what every parent needs to know. *The Times* 10.11.12;6-7.
12. Jacqui Wise. Deaths from alcohol fall with rise in minimum price, study finds. *BMJ* 2013:346;f825.
13. H Jacques et al. Is it all bad news? *BMJ* 2011;342:478.
14. P Ronksley et al. Association of alcohol consumption with selected cardiovascular disease outcomes. A systematic review and meta analysis. *BMJ* 26. 2. 11:342;478.
15. S Tilling et al. Diagnosis assessment and management of harmful drinking and alcohol dependence. *BMJ* 26.2.11:342;490.

16. Ausian Cramb. Drug to cut craving for alcohol approved for use. *Daily Telegraph.* 8.10.13:2.
17. *Quarterly Journal of Medicine.* 2013:106;147-152. *BMJ* 2013:346;1535.
18. Graeme Wilson. £200K to lock teen yobs up. *The Sun* 14.2.13:2.
19. Mark Macaskill. Criminals get off scot free by ignoring fines. *Sunday Times.* 10.2.13:5.
20. Rhys Blakeley. Prisoner 'had sex with five of his guards'. The Times 26. 4. 13;39. 20. Adam Fresco. Stradivarius worth £1. 2m stolen as violinist sits in station cafe. *The Times* 7.12.10:12.
21. Valentine Low. Proms Musician's Treasured Violin Snatched on Train. *The Times.* 26.8.16:5.
22. Jonathan Paige. Case Closed. £120K Violin Found in Road. *The Times.* 27.8.16:19.

CHAPTER FORTY-SEVEN

Smoking

In 1492 Columbus sailed the ocean blue.

A fact

European planters exported dried tobacco leaves from America to Europe in the 16th century. Celebrities like Sir Walter Raleigh promoted smoking. Smoking remained the pursuit of the rich until the Crimean War in 1854-6. British soldiers acquired the habit from the Turkish troops. Anti-smoking campaigns were ignored. For example, in 1604 James I of England condemned tobacco and published 'A Counterblast to tobacco.' In the Second World War, Hitler vehemently opposed smoking. It was not until Austin Bradford Hill and Richard Doll published their findings in 1950 that the true dangers of smoking became realised.[1] Richard Doll was originally a smoker himself. He continued to publish papers about smoking causing diseases for 55 years. Many authors followed his lead.

I was a medical student aged 20 years and had just started to learn about medicine on the wards. I met a 28-year-old garage mechanic. This unfortunate West Indian sat in a wheelchair. He smoked and had bilateral amputations above his knees. "How can I go back to being a mechanic?" he argued. "Why me, why me?" he said over and over again. I sympathised with him.

I raced to my textbook and read about his diagnosis. He had Buergers disease. This is a condition of young people – his age exactly. It is caused by smoking. My textbook read 'total abstinence from smoking is imperative, i.e., you can have your cigarettes or your legs, but you can't have both'. So he had chosen cigarettes, to his cost. Poor guy what a cost. What a life.

I feel immensely sorry for cigarette smokers. In the early part of the 20th century smoking cigarettes had been advised by doctors to 'calm the nerves'. The damage it can cause to your body, sometimes years later, was yet to be realised.

Cigarettes are poisonous. There is enough nicotine in two cigarettes that if put directly into your blood stream would kill you.[2]

Our hospitals are full of smokers, ex-smokers and passive smokers. Then they suffer from mouth and lung cancers, asthma, coronaries, circulatory problems, chronic pulmonary obstructive disease, back disc problems, strokes, hypertension – the list is never-ending, and growing still. If people did not smoke we probably would not have a bed problem in hospitals and the NHS would cost a fraction of what it does. A large survey of 30 years' survival for smokers and non-smokers was published in 2009. This showed that after 30 years, if you did not smoke, your chances of surviving was 20%–30% higher than if you did smoke. This were true for men and women.[3]

Smokers are addicted to smoking. Withdrawal leads to a craving. Smokers don't face up to the dangers. If a patient is going to get better then we need their co-operation and support. Perhaps we need no- smoking holidays. Here smokers are taken on holiday where they are given a galaxy of treatments to stop smoking, ranging from nicotine gum to hypnosis, acupuncture, etc. Up to now, free nicotine replacement therapy and telephone support has had a disappointing result. Smokers finally quit more often without professional or pharmaceutical assistance.[4] Vaping is popular today. It is less damaging than smoking. Vaping could cause lung damage, if used for a long time.

Unless a patient is fully committed it simply won't work. They could also be lectured on the dangers of smoking with evidence. Are children ever taught the true dangers of smoking?

Our NHS could fund these holidays.

The crux of the problems of addiction – smoking, alcohol or drugs – is that treatment will always fail unless the patient wants to get better. We lack willpower. The participants enjoy smoking, taking alcohol to excess or the effects of drugs!

The exclusion of smokers in the UK nowadays from public buildings is only the start. In parts of the United States, smoking has been banned in public parks and on beaches. Exposure to secondhand smoke is an established cause of coronary heart disease, lung cancer and premature death.[5]

The non-smoking areas are likely to expand all over the world.

But why are governments all over the world reluctant to take action against smokers, and so naturally *for* non-smokers? Well, it's not a vote winner for them. They stand to lose the smoker's vote. Secondly, smoking provides valuable revenue, although the cost to health, and overall production by smokers, is ignored. Thirdly, important funds are invested in the tobacco industry, e.g. government workers' pension funds.[6]

So, ethics is a minor issue.

But good news for shareholders of two of the biggest tobacco companies – British American Tobacco and Japan Tobacco International. Revenues for both colossal companies are up 5%.[78] Not such good news for Bangladesh, Pakistan and Vietnam. Here sales are booming. Can these countries afford the long-term health costs of smoking?[7]

But what about cocaine? Is it safeor is it not? This recreational drug is becoming more popular. How the young love to experiment. Well, they have 'money to burn'. No, there is a definite incidence of myocardial infarction in the use of cocaine, a lot younger than the usual coronary age group![87]

Well, cannabis is not dangerous, or is it?

The National Treatment Agency for Substance Abuse treated over 10,000 teenagers with problems from cannabis in 2011-2012. "Cannabis is an integral part of mainstream teenage culture," says Mandy Saligan, co-founder of the Charter Day Treatment Centre in Harley Street. "The modern-day cannabis is much stronger than it used to be. Its use is linked to the development of schizophrenia, psychosis and bipolar disorder. Most children have some exposure to the use of cannabis and risk these problems!"[9]

Outside every public place in the United Kingdom, including hospitals, are smokers furtively lighting up. Has the smoking ban had any effect on our health?

Research from the University of Bath has shown that emergency admissions for asthma fell by 4.9% for adults for the first three years following the introduction of the smoking ban in July 2007. This study looked at over half a million admissions in England over this time, and other variables were taken into account (it referred to asthma and no other respiratory disorder).

Nearly 6% of our population have asthma. Other countries have shown that no-smoking laws can lead to up to a 40% reduction in emergency asthma admissions.[10]

In the United States recently tobacco taxes were put up. A review then of 21,000 alcohol drinkers, who also smoked, showed that cigarette taxes were effective in reducing smoking and also alcohol consumption! These effects were most obvious in vulnerable groups to alcohol-related disorders – male heavy drinkers, young adults and low income drinkers.[11]

To my mind, smoking very occasionally has been beneficial to me. Once playing golf and once fishing – the smoke got rid of the midges! Otherwise I am a non-smoker.

So, to summarise these last two chapters we need:

- Greater education in our schools of the dangers of smoking, drugs and alcohol. Could any of this be incorporated into Biology GCSE?
- More places like Jericho House to help drug addicts, smokers and alcoholics.
- No smoking, drugs or alcohol in our prisons – what a deterrent!
- To increase cigarette taxes and alcohol prices, as well as reduce tobacco investment.
- To increase no-smoking areas in our country, and to stop all publicity about smoking by introducing plain packaging of cigarettes. (This is successful in Australia.) In 2015 our government at last introduced plain packaging of cigarettes in the UK. About time too. Now we have it in 2017.
- To decriminalise drugs – it could help a lot.

The really bad news about smoking is the increased sales of cigarettes to the Third World. There will be increased medical problems for these smokers. The good news is the American courts awarding billions of dollars in compensation to widows of those who have died from smoking. Could the tobacco industry go bankrupt?[12]

Will such court actions spread to the UK?

References:

1. Richard Doll, Mike Daube and Simon Chapman. The legacy of the tobacco colossus. *BMJ* 2012:345;e7311.

2. *Harrison Principles of Internal Medicine* 6th Edition. Published by McGraw-Hill, page 658.

3. *BMJ* 2009:338;B480.

4. BMJ 2012:344;e1732.

5. Exposure to secondhand smoke is an established cause of heart disease, lung cancer and premature death. US Department of Health and Human Services. 'The health consequences of involuntary exposure to tobacco smoke. *BMJ* 2009:338;a3070.

6. Jonathan Gornall. How the New Guardians of public health are investing heavily in tobacco companies. *BMJ* 1.12.12:345;22-23.

7. Tanya Maric et al. Prevalence of cocaine use among patients attending the Emergency Department with chest pain. *Emerg Med* J 2010;27:548-550. doi10 11 36/emj 2008 070581.

8. Alex Ralph. Asian sales keep fire burning under BAT. *The Times* 26.4.13;21.

9. Rachel Carlyle. Teenagers and Cannabis. What every parents needs to know. *The Times*. 10. 11. 12:Body and Soul:6.

10. Ella Pickover. Health Smoking Ban linked to drop in asthma cases. *The Independent*. 16.4.13:21.

11. Chris Smyth. Cigarette taxes 'cut alcohol consumption'. *The Times*. 10.8.13:5.

12. Rhys Blakeley. $23. 6 bn damages for widow of smoker who could not quit. *The Times*. 12.7.14:32.

CHAPTER FORTY-EIGHT

Size Matters – Too Thin

Yond Cassius has a lean and hungry look.
Shakespeare. *Julius Caesar Act 1*

Hunger is the world's number one health risk. Every year, it kills more people than AIDS, malaria and tuberculosis combined.[1]

I received a telephone call from Oxfam on 25th January 2011. A young lady asked me, politely, if I would consider increasing my monthly subscription to that excellent charity. Her argument was strong and persuasive. She explained that today one billion people, one-seventh of this planet's population, are undernourished. Worse still, over 25,000 people die weekly from starvation alone. You would have thought that such people live away from the land – the source of our food. Not so: three-quarters of the people who starve to death live in rural areas!

Oxfam has run an agricultural project in Honduras for the past few years. Some experts in farming went in and trained ten local farmers. This would take at least a year as different things needed to be done at certain times – preparing the ground, sowing, looking after the crop, harvesting, storing and transporting, etc. There would be no guarantee it would work the first or even subsequent years. The weather can wreak havoc as any gardener knows to their cost! Several years on, this project has been a success, and the local farmers in Honduras are now training other local farmers.

Oxfam wanted more money to finance similar projects in other parts of the world – Ethiopia, Kenya and target areas in Asia. What works in one area is not guaranteed to work in another. There are huge variations in the weather, local facilities and soil. In 2013 I met an American Christian missionary; we were both passengers on the same aeroplane. He was neither preaching nor medical. He was going back to the States, where his business was growing trees on a large estate. He had spent three months in Africa teaching the locals how to grow trees of all sorts.

If we are going to help the starving millions of this world we need more projects like these. We produce enough food for everyone at present.[2] Some food rots in the ground. More food is stored incorrectly or is not eaten soon enough and goes bad. Nine million hospital meals in England annually are wasted.[2]

So nearly 900 million people – one in eight of the world's population – go to bed hungry every night, and more than two million children die from malnutrition annually.[3]

Size Matters – Too Fat

I'm fat, but I'm thin inside... there's a thin man inside every fat man.

George Orwell

It is a well-known fact that about 90% of the food produced goes to about 10% of the world's population.[1] Food is even transported from the starving Third World to feed fat Westerners. For example, green beans in the UK supermarkets now have a carbon footprint as they have been flown from Kenya. Pundits tell us that many fish stocks are running low. However, when we buy cod or tuna we are reassured by the fishmonger that they are always from 'sustainable sources'. There is an unacceptable waste of food in so called developed countries. In 1967 I was convalescing from illness. I worked as a short medical locum in two factories producing bread, biscuits and cakes (McVities, Park Royal, London).

If a product was too heavy or too light then, for no other reason at all apart from weight, the Health and Safety Inspector decreed it cannot be sold. So such food – excellent as it was – had to be destroyed or alternatively given away to staff. (My weight increased!) Similar experiences are shared by anybody in the catering industry. Large quantities of unwanted or unused food are thrown away daily. This food should at least be going to our pig farmers, or for compost, but often it is not. Each and every household in Britain in 2010 threw away an average four kilograms of food and drink each week.[4] Our supermarkets are full of 'two for the price of one' offers. So we all buy too much food and a lot is wasted. In the media in October 2013, Tesco admitted that half their food is thrown away. This supermarket cannot be alone!

One huge supermarket in Cannock in July 2014 had the answer. Food that cannot be sold is sent to charities or to feed pigs. The rest is converted to methane that heats the store!

Now, what effect has all this food had on our UK population? Working as a doctor in an emergency department over the past 30 years has made this painfully obvious. The incidence of diabetes and myocardial infarcts has soared. Obesity is a major factor in both conditions. Obesity leads to hypertension, that in turn leads to strokes and heart failure. Our emergency departments are full of ageing patients. They are frequent attenders on multiple medications. The common factor in many of their complaints is simply obesity. Chest complaints, backache and joint pain fill our GP surgeries and hospital outpatients. Unfortunately, obesity is frequently a major factor in the development of all these conditions too. Obesity was responsible for 11,173 hospital admissions in the UK and over 25,000 days in hospital in 2009-10.[5]

Tam Fry from the National Obesity Forum in 2013 informs us that 26% of adults in the UK are obese according to their body mass index. By 2050 over half of our population will be obese.

Total and complete denial of the problem, and frequently downright aggression, greets the honest physician when the patient is confronted by the truth. "My surgeon refuses to operate on me till I lose two stone in weight at least." I have often heard this complaint about the poor surgeon who loves to operate and is frequently a workaholic. He does, however, know well that the complication rates and the recovery times for the grossly obese are high. In October 2016 the clinical commissioning groups, both for Harrogate and the Vale of York, are withholding some surgery for at least six months. Patients with a body mass index above 30, or smokers, will not be given routine surgery – for example, hip or knee replacements.

This active discrimination may seem harsh. But such patients have a high complication rate, a slow recovery and, particularly the obese, have a low level of satisfaction following this surgery. When patients are over 30 stone the hospital needs hoists, help from the fire service to lift patients and sometimes special beds. (I hear more complaints from the patients and relatives.) Patients over 25 stone don't normally fit into a scanner. In February 2011 the ambulance service nationwide is spending more money on bigger wider stretchers and more hoists for the increasing number of patients who are over 30 stone in weight! Please, please don't tell the politicians. (I can see a bill making it illegal to discriminate against anybody on account of their size.) Bigger scanners and bigger beds would only compound the problem. Stop stop stop. In Lincolnshire they are planning supersized graves at great expense to ease the burden on undertakers! (Oh help!)

In a moment of quiet reflection recently I turned on the television. There have been plenty of clips on television – flashbacks to our past. These usually record special events like the start of the Second World War or the birth of our present health service. There are numerous crowd scenes. Now I looked carefully at each scene and looked again. There may be fat people in shot, but very few. Conversely, when I pop into the local supermarket today I see hordes and hordes of them. They fill their baskets with cake and beer. Obesity is a disease. This serious life-threatening epidemic is spreading, and as a consequence our society today is suffering badly.

So what is the cost of obesity? Mike Kelly, director of NICE's Public Health Excellence Centre, wrote: 'Obesity rates in this country are rocketing. Physical inactivity in England alone results in costs of more than £8 billion.' This is the direct cost of treating diseases linked to lack of activity, and indirect costs such as absence from work because of sickness. He estimated that a sedentary lifestyle results in 54,000 premature deaths a year in England alone. NICE calls for young people to exercise for 60 minutes a day.[6]

Mike Kelly also wrote that the number of children not taking part in physical activity is increasing. He recommended a long-term (minimum five years) national campaign to promote physical activity among children and teenagers. I strongly suspect that many of these young people have been lulled into a false sense of security regarding their own physical activity. This is because they turn on the television and see athletes breaking world records – running, jumping and swimming. The implication here is plain to see. They see a professional athlete who probably does little else but train all day long. They don't know that. The television conveys the impression that the human race is getting fitter, when for the vast majority of us the reverse is true.

Studies show that childhood obesity has reached epidemic proportions. Childhood obesity, defined as a high body mass index, is directly linked to cardiovascular disease in adulthood – our nation's biggest killer![7]

There are a few instances where the fitness of this generation can be directly compared with previous generations. For example, all infantry recruits to the British Army are trained and tested for physical fitness at Catterick Camp in Yorkshire. For many generations recruits have had to go round the same assault course in the same time limit. If they fail to get round in that time, they are told that they are not physically fit and have to train some more.

The records held there show that years ago the majority of recruits achieved this time easily after a short period of training. Recently, however, fewer and fewer recruits achieve this time initially. So these recruits have to spend more and more time training. This rarely happened 20 or 30 years ago. So this generation is less fit than previous generations. They have been compared by the same 'yardstick'.[8]

Do gluttony and laziness that cause obesity have to cost so much to so many? These two sins are not going away. They are with us to stay. We all need to engage in reality. For far too long we have been blasé and disinterested. The fat person is unable to see their own body image. Obesity blinds them to reality. Educational interventions are unlikely to work because obese people aren't unhappy enough to lose weight.[9]

The simple fact is that we each have only one life. All lives are valuable. In our so-called sophisticated society, that boasts of so many technical achievements, we are failing the obese. Something needs to be done urgently to prevent the situation getting worse still.

What thoughts or answers do I have to this dilemma?

One simple way of losing weight that often works is to drink a glass of water before each meal. The stomach then tends to get fuller quicker and less food is consumed. There is another way that is more proven but a bit tricky! Read on:

* * *

Farid Saad from the Gulf Medical University in the United Arab Emirates presented a paper to the European Congress on Obesity in Lyon, France in April 2012.

He treated men with erectile dysfunction by giving them testosterone injections. This treatment had some unexpected results! Of 251 men treated, 95% were overweight! Over five years of treatment these men lost an average of 16 kilograms each! So their body mass index was reduced, as was their waistline, cholesterol and blood sugar levels. All good news.

Were these men adequately counselled before this prolonged treatment? (There must have been an increased risk of testicular tumours fuelled by higher testosterone levels.)

Also the wives of these men – were they counselled too? Did they consent to this treatment? Many of these ladies perhaps would have preferred a rotund husband with little, or no, sexual activity. Instead they found themselves married to a slimmer husband, with suddenly a significant sexual appetite! These ladies may have been totally unprepared for such activity. What a surprise!

* * *

There are many contributing factors in obesity. Lack of exercise is one, hereditary factors are another, and diet is one more. Is the diet of today's teenagers healthy? My answer is NO. Let me explain.

Over 50 years ago, when I was a teenager at school, you had a choice. Either you ate a school dinner or a packed lunch. We were at school and stayed there all day.

Recently, I have been frequently in supermarkets. Well, at midday the local comprehensive school empties. Large numbers of schoolchildren flood the local shops mostly for food. I have been in the 'lunch queue' behind them. They eat chocolate bars, sweets, crisps, etc. So their diet is high carbohydrate, high fat, low protein, low vitamins and low minerals.

They supplement this diet with top-ups of the same before and after school. They are made of money and spend it on junk food. Obesity is not a surprise but a certainty. This junk food addiction is widespread throughout the UK. Incidentally, if both parents work then the eating habits of their teenagers are even less supervised. Result: both parents working make the chances of their child being obese six times more likely.[9] Tam Fry from the National Obesity Forum informs us that today in the UK 20% of children are obese.

Doctors were warned about sugar over 40 years ago by John Yudkin of Cambridge University: 'Added sugar increases heart disease risk.' [10]

In October 2011 Denmark introduced a tax on foods high in saturated fat, e.g., butter. France and Hungary have a tax on sugared drinks and junk food. There has yet to be a cost benefit analysis of any such 'health tax'.[11]

In the UK we have just started to plan a tax on sugary drinks, sweets and other foods, announced in 2013 to start soon. But I do not know how the drinks industry will cooperate? What effects will this have on our population? Nobody knows. But an American study over 24 years proved that a high sugar intake was a significant risk factor in the development of type 2 diabetes.[12] Well, type 2 diabetes is becoming very common in the UK.

Fizzy drinks are making our children fat.[13]

In 2005 McKesson started running Medicaid – a medical treatment programme for the poor in Illinois. They trawled through lots of information. They identified the people most at risk of getting ill. They then gave them intensive treatment at home and monitored them. Diet and exercise prescribed for all! This reduced unplanned admissions to hospital and saved millions of dollars.[14]

In a recent study of 500,000 Swedish men, it was noted that the obese aged 18 years were significantly less likely to be married at 40, compared to men who fell within the normal weight range. Stigma, discrimination and emotional problems were blamed. (I think that nobody talked to the ladies. I guess I know what they preferred.[15])

So there is an epidemic of obesity, and a major factor is a lack of physical exercise, which results in long-term health problems with frequent premature deaths. Doctors are losing the battle against the effects of obesity, and also losing against another common condition – premature mental decline. This frequently leads to dementia. In our NHS, early onset dementia is investigated with blood tests and a brain scan. If the results are normal the patient is given advice on strategies to improve the memory and brain-stimulating drugs.[16] Could there be a connection between obesity and dementia?

In Toronto, Canada, researchers have reviewed and evaluated 32 different treatments to combat dementia. Brain exercises like Sudoku and crosswords were found to reverse dementia and improve memory. So, lack of physical exercise leads to obesity. Lack of mental exercise leads to dementia![17] We probably need regular physical and mental exercise. Professor Erickson at the annual meeting of the American Association for the Advancement of Science in Chicago in February 2014 showed that regular physical exercise improved the functions of our brain.

Some stupid hospital trusts have spent £1,000 on buying a 'fat suit'. Once donned, health service workers know what it feels like to be fat and so show sympathy for those so affected. This is a 'waist' of time and money – hospital administrators are good at that.

You are more likely to die on your sofa than on your bicycle.
A Danish saying

Measures to Combat Obesity

Our lifestyles and our society need to change. We all need to walk more and exercise generally. I have thoughts on this.

The chancellor could quadruple the duty on petrol, leading to less car use and quieter roads – less accidents.

This would also lead to more use of public transport – more walking , more cycling. The money raised from the duty could make public transport cheaper and more efficient.

We should be weighed with our luggage when flying abroad. There should be a maximum weight – exceed it and you pay!

I applaud British Airways and Eurostar. Both companies refused a 35-stone passenger. BA stated it was not possible to safely accommodate the customer.

A Eurostar spokesman said, "We have worked tirelessly to find a solution." So basically it was not safe for him to travel. He was going to sue them in the courts. What problems he caused these companies.[18]

- Governments should subsidise sports clubs. But I can't see the chancellor paying my golf club subscription.
- More traffic-free zones in all cities.
- Should we all return to some form of rationing? It might be the only way.

Thoughts on Cycling

At work I had free parking for my bicycle – car users have to pay. I sometimes got a free breakfast for cycling to work.

A bicycle is cheaper to buy and run than a car. (An average household in the UK spends a sixth of their income on travel.)

Cycling is less polluting than car travel. It can be quicker in a city! (Two kg of carbon are saved for every short bicycle journey compared to a car.)

Regular cyclists are as fit as an average person ten years younger. An article in the *British Medical Journal* in April 2017 by Doctor Jason Gill looked at the health of cyclists. He followed up 250,000 people over five years. The cyclists had a dramatic drop in the incidence of cardiovascular disease and cancer, when compared to non-cyclists!

On average, cyclists live two years longer than non-cyclists.[19]

Cycling is safer on the Continent as their roads are better designed especially the roundabouts.[20] The first cycle-friendly roundabout is coming to the UK soon – to be in London. We need more cycle lanes on our roads and fines if they are obstructed. Helmets need to be compulsory.

On a personal note, as an emergency consultant for 30 years I saw a trickle of cyclists who had been injured whilst cycling. I never saw a fatal injury, if the cyclist had been wearing a helmet!

In my 30 years as an emergency consultant I saw at least 12 cyclists from RTAs – *all dead and none wore a helmet.*

The British roads are overcrowded. Overtaking parked vehicles, turning right, large lorries and above all roundabouts are all dangerous on a bicycle on our roads. Canada found the beneficial effects of cyclists wearing helmets to be minimal and attributed a reduction in cycling head injuries to improved road safety measures and safety campaigns! I have cycled and driven extensively on their roads recently. Their traffic is far less dense, cycling lanes abound and after many thousands of miles of driving I have yet to see a Canadian roundabout! So their data is valuable but has little relevance to our roads![21]

In the Netherlands, traffic congestion on their roads has been lessened by more cyclists. 27% of all journeys in the Netherlands are made by cyclists, compared to just 2% of journeys in Britain! In the Netherlands they spend over £400 million annually on cycle lanes, etc., whereas in the UK we have spent as a maximum £139 million.[22]

Well, the Dutch do have thousands of miles of dedicated cycle lanes. We have so-called cycle lanes. These are not solely for cyclists; often cars are parked on them and as soon as the road narrows there is a sign that reads 'End of cycle lane'. Our cycle lanes are a farce. Our cyclists are not protected. Will more government money help and protect cyclists more? We will wait and see! Incidentally, currently in France if a motorist overtakes a cyclist he has by law to leave a full car width between his car and the bicycle!

We do however spend £5 billion annually solely on obesity related conditions! Going Dutch on cycling could cut £1.6 billion from our health budget.[23]

As a car driver, and as a cyclist, I have noted a fair amount of animosity towards cyclists generated by frustrated car drivers. Car drivers feel that they have paid to be on the road whereas cyclists are freeloaders who have not paid a penny. Car drivers pay Vehicle Excise Duty which is linked to emissions and so this is not applicable to cyclists. After a lifetime of contact with patients and road traffic accidents I know of many drivers who have avoided Vehicle Excise Duty and car insurance. Hence the purge by police on such people. Road maintenance is funded from income tax and council tax. So, most adults, including cyclists, pay this.[24]

Car drivers who kill cyclists on our roads need to have sentences that fit the crime. Such an action demands more than hours of community service and a paltry fine.[24] Only 10% of such offenders get a jail sentence.[25]

Any car driver in our country can't have failed to notice teenagers on a bicycle endangering their own life by venturing dangerously onto our roads. Usually unhelmeted and in dark clothes they enter traffic at some speed, often at night with no lights on. Is there no answer?

Surprisingly, there is one. In 2012 less than half the children in England and Wales will receive the free cycle training to which all children are entitled by law, despite evidence that the courses help to save lives.[26]

Another way of treating obesity is to appoint bariatric physicians – to evaluate obesity and co-ordinate treatment.[27]

_____

References:

1. Christian Aid leaflet 'Count Your Blessings'. 2013. UK registered charity no 1105851.
2. Daily Telegraph reporter. £22m NHS meals waste. *Daily Telegraph*. 11.10.11:11.
3. Loretta Minghella. *Christian Aid News* Winter 2013. Enough for Everyone. Pg. 12.
4. Christian Aid leaflet 'Count Your Blessings'. 2011.
5. HES on… Obesity. HES onlineTM. http//www.hesonline.nhs. uk/Ease/servelet/contentserver? siteID=1937&catego vy/D+857
6. S Mayor. NICE calls for young people to exercise for 60 minutes a day. *BMJ* 2009:338;314.
7. *BMJ* 2012:345;e5457 and BMJ 2012:345;e6516.
8. Personal communication from Major S Vinall – a relative.
9. Monica Galetti. Food and Drink. BBC2 17.2.13.
10. Geoff Watts. Sugar and the Heart – Old ideas revisited. *BMJ* editorial 2013;346:e7800.
11. *BMJ* 2012:345;e8487.
12. *BMJ* 2012:345;e6885.
13. *American Journal of Clinical Nutrition* 2013:97:155-56, cloi:10. 3945/ajcn. 112. 048603

14. Anna Moore. The fructose timebomb: it's drinks that are making our children fat? *The Times* 13.3.13;2.

15. Nick Sneddon. Learn from the US: Put patients before doctors. *The Times* 29.8.12:18.

16. *BMC Public Health* 2012:12:833, cloi 10. 1186/1471. 2458. 12:833.

17. David Rose. Watchdog Sanctions drugs for early treatment of Alzheimer's. *The Times* 7.10.10;3.

18. Sudoku. Wits help. The Sun 27.4.13;12.

19. Rachel Dale. P & Obese Ferry. Home at last… 35 stone man too big for BA and Eurostar. *The Sun*. 21.11.13;27.

20. Why cycle? Sustrans leaflet:www. sustrans.org.uk

21. Jessica Dennis et al. Helmet legislation and admissions to hospital for cycling related head injuries in Canadian provinces and territories: interrupted time series analysis. BMJ 15. 6. 13;346:15.

22. Kaya Burgess. Give Cyclists a headstart with Dutch-style safety on British roads, campaigners urge. *The Times* 13.5.13;19.

23. Kaya Burgess. Going Dutch on cycling 'could cut £1. 6 billion a year from health budget'. *The Times* 13.6.13;19.

24. Letter. *The Times* 21.4.12:15.

25. Phillip Pank. Tougher sentences demanded against drivers who kill cyclists. *The Times* 25. 5. 12:15. Kaya Burgess. Drivers avoid prison over cyclists' death. *The Times* 20.1.14:News. 23.

26. Rhoda Buchanan, Ruth Maclean. Children are denied free cycle training by council's apathy. *The Times* 13.4.12:11.

27. Paul Grant et al. The Bariatric Physician. Clinic Medicine. *Royal College of Physicians*. 14. 1:30.

Dangers of Exercise

The wise, for cure, on exercise depend.

Dryden

We are all told we need to exercise more. So, we get into our cars and drive to a gymnasium. Thus we burn precious fuel, increase our carbon footprint and pollute the atmosphere. Then we attach ourselves to various machines with various weights and do various exercises. Many try to move static rowing machines or static bicycles. Before we drive home again we must pile into the restaurant to put the calories back on again. Well, our blood sugar is low and we need to justify spending so much money a month keeping up our membership of the gym. Somehow I feel this habit we have fallen into is a good way to lose pounds, but in money not weight!

Case One:

A 63-year-old housewife presented with severe abdominal pain worse on coughing. There had been an acute onset and she had vomited twice. There was a tender mass on the right side of her abdomen. She was observed in hospital. Bruising appeared around her umbilicus. Several blood tests showed that her level of haemoglobin fell. She never became anaemic. She settled with several days in hospital.

Case Two:

A 61-year-old laundress had had severe acute abdominal pain for two days. She was in acute pain on examination, with a tender mass in her lower right abdomen. She had a general anaesthetic and at laparotomy; it was found that she had ruptured an artery (inferior epigastric). There was a blood clot. This clot was cleared away and the artery ligated. She stayed a few days in hospital.

Case Three:

A 49-year-old man had a lump and soreness in his abdomen for several weeks. On examination he had a lump in the muscle wall of his abdomen (rectus muscle). This lump was still there at a second outpatient attendance. The lump was explored under a general anaesthetic. It was found to be a fibrous nodule and histology showed it to be traumatic in origin.

All three patients recovered well.
So what did all these three have in common?

They were all using an exercise wheel when the pain started. Case One had been using the exercise wheel for the first time. Cases Two and Three had been using the wheel for several months.

The exercise wheel was a small wheel about eight inches in diameter. On each side of the wheel is a handle. Using one hand on each handle, one can exercise. One exercises horizontally with the body weight shared between the wheel and the toes. I tried this: my abdominal musculature was sore in a few minutes!

So, exercising in this way can cause problems.

All these patients stopped using the exercise wheel.[1]

When these cases were written up, this exercise wheel was all the rage. My houseman was tall and very fit. "What nonsense," he said. "This thing can't hurt anybody!" He gave a demonstration in sister's office. Then he had acute back pain. He was off sick for two weeks with a prolapsed disc.

* * *

Even Hippocrates recommended walking for longevity!

* * *

Last Christmas I drove to the local railway station to drop off a relative. On turning round at my destination I spied an old man staggering under the weight of a very heavy suitcase. I offered him a lift. He took it with reluctance. He told me he was not used to having lifts! I was going his way anyway. As I drove him the half mile uphill I was amazed that he was intending to lug that heavy suitcase all the way. (I had difficulty putting it in my car boot. It was full of Christmas presents.)

"What's your secret of fitness?" I said.

"Oh, I'm 89," he said. "All my life I have made it a point always to walk at least three miles a day."

Yes, it showed.

* * *

469

Will today's children really live this long? The answer is yes, provided that they exercise regularly. The National Institute for Health and Clinical Excellence (NICE) tells children and teenagers to do 60 minutes minimum of moderately intense physical activity each day.[2]

Extreme physical activity can be dangerous unless the participant is very fit and under 40. For example, the television presenter Andrew Marr suffered a stroke that he attributed to an over energetic workout! Well, how far do some athletes go? Well, my son James is an elite mountain biker. He is an amateur, racing against professional mountain bikers! In his thirties and a doctor, James monitors his heart rate during a race! His heart rate goes way over 180 beats a minute. He keeps it up for as long as he can. He has been doing this for years.[3] A word of advice to the reader: don't do this yourself!

An independent survey in 2013 found that cyclists travelling to work were a lot happier on arrival compared to non-cyclists. Cyclists were less tired and more motivated.[4]

References:

1. A Fraser-Moodie and S Cox. Haematoma of rectus abdominis from the use of an exercise wheel: A report of three cases. *B J Surgery* (1974) 61:577.
2. *BMJ* 2009:338;b373.
3. A personal communication from James Fraser-Moodie FRCS (Orth.).
4. Cyclists get a head start in the workplace happiness stakes. *The Times*. 21.10.12:2.

CHAPTER FORTY-NINE

What is wrong with me, Doctor?

We have all heard this remark over and over again. The most likely diagnosis is at times greeted with incredulity by the patient. I recall twice being in queues at shops and being the captive listener to confidential medical matters. Once, in a queue for the butcher's, one lady in front complained to her friend. "Well, my doctor has told me that my weight loss is due to diabetes. He must be wrong. Nobody in my family has ever had diabetes before. These tests will prove him wrong. I think it is my glands!" she said.

On another occasion in a supermarket queue a husband had just met his wife. "What did the doctor tell you is the cause of your headaches?" she asked.

He replied, "I have hypertension. She has given me some pills."

"Oh nonsense," said his wife. "What you need is new glasses."

Well, diabetes can present commonly with weight loss, and hypertension often gives rise to headaches. Sometimes out of the blue a patient attends with one condition and goes home suspected of having another one – completely unrelated! We are taught as students to look at the whole patient. So let me explain what happened on two such occasions.

A young man aged 30 had an ankle injury from football. He had an X-ray that showed no fracture. He would recover quickly.

This was a cold, dreary December. The patient looked so brown.

"Have you always looked this brown?"

"Yes," he replied.

"Have you been abroad recently?" I asked.

"Not for years," he said.

"Well," I said, "what does your wife say?"

"Oh, she is so pale. She is so jealous."

Yes, he looked tanned and fit – a picture of health. But all my other patients were as pale as can be (unless they had been abroad recently).

I glanced at his palms. There were deep pigmented creases. So the distribution of the pigment melanin was abnormal. I sent him to endocrinology outpatients. His adrenal glands were under-functioning (Addison's disease). Another gland tried to stimulate his adrenals. As a result he produced too much melanin.

I saw him several times after this. Each time he was an emergency admission and each time he was worse. He greeted me warmly, "You saved my life," he said over and over again. I had diagnosed failure of a pair of glands. He had failed to respond to treatment. I was upset. His quality of life was poor. He had been so well initially. So very well!

But he may well have died suddenly if not diagnosed quickly.

* * *

Another man had a hip injury. He too was healing well – no fracture or other problem.

As he talked to me his eyes were protuberant. They stuck out, making him look strange.

"How are you?" I said.

"Oh, I'm fine," he said, "no problems."

"Well, what about your appetite?" I said.

His wife, who had an ample figure, butted in, "Oh, he eats like a horse and won't put any weight on."

This man had a fast pulse at 90 beats/minute. He was nervous and sweating with a palpable thyroid gland. He had an overactive thyroid gland (thyrotoxicosis). He responded well to antithyroid drugs prescribed by a consultant physician. I never saw him again. He got better.

Do I always get the correct diagnosis? Answer: No.

I treated one elderly diabetic lady with a leg wound that was slow to heal. After dressings and antibiotics the skin eventually healed. But I missed the fact her shape was changing. Her face was round and she had put on weight in her trunk. Her consultant specialising in the treatment of diabetes eventually diagnosed an overactive adrenal gland producing too much steroid. She received treatment eventually. I kicked myself for missing the obvious (Cushing's syndrome).

Recently one of our horses developed Cushings syndrome. (I missed that too!)

* * *

In March 2015 I was unwell with a cough and chest pain. I was in Scotland and was seen at the emergency department of the Glasgow Royal Infirmary. My X-ray showed pneumonia. I received a powerful, broad spectrum penicillin. I recovered quickly. Thank you, Glasgow, and thank you ,Alexander Fleming.

I needed a follow-up X-ray to confirm I had recovered. Today we are high tech. All X-rays are digital and stored on a computer disc so they can be easily retrieved and never lost. My X-ray was lost, along with my summary of attendance that never reached my GP.

I needed a scan to confirm my chest had recovered.

As a digital dinosaur I am sceptical of all modern ideas until I am won over. Well, 20 years ago I often sent for X-rays from all over the UK, so that I could write a medico-legal report. These X-rays were often slow in coming, but never lost.

The really worrying feature here is that all the doctors and nurses treating me were not at all surprised that the X-rays had been lost, so it must be happening a lot in our NHS. Such is the cost of progress.

My scan was clear.

* * *

In December 2016 I had a further bout of coughing up sputum and difficulty breathing. We were instructed in the press not to contact our GP unless absolutely necessary. Three weeks later, still bad, I was given a telephone consultation with my GP. I suggested and they agreed to my sputum being examined. One week later, a purulent infection was confirmed and antibiotics were suggested. But I was prescribed tetracycline – the one antibiotic that I am sensitive to (I get an itchy rash and feel dreadful). I expected I would recover quickly on a different antibiotic. And I did.

* * *

One local GP brought one of his own patients to the hospital for an urgent admission. Then this doctor asked me directly if we had seen many chest pains that day. "My chest is sore," he said, rubbing his own chest!

"Lie down and we'll do your ECG.," I suggested.

"Oh no, I can't be ill, I'm on call," he protested vehemently.

"Lie down now on this couch," I insisted…

Subsequently he recovered well from the coronary thrombosis and promptly retired.

* * *

Most doctors are better than this at self-diagnosis.

* * *

One doctor palpated his own paunch expecting to feel fat. He felt a hard lump and correctly diagnosed his own cancer. (Unfortunately both the above doctors were heavy smokers and should have known better.)

* * *

Another doctor brought a new stethoscope. He was so eager to try it out that he had to listen to his own heart sounds. Then he heard the typical murmur of a leaking mitral valve. The surgeons fitted a new valve, and he was a 'new man.'

CHAPTER FIFTY

How and Why did Mike Hawthorn Die?

His motor car was poetry, and tragedy.

Sinclair Lewis in *Babbitt*

Mike Hawthorn was my childhood hero (fig 74). Now I am retired and find myself with some free time I decided to look into the matter. I have studied all the witness statements from the coroner's inquest, with the coroner's findings and the pathologist's report. I have studied newspaper reports, and Daniel Gee of the *Farnham Herald* has helped too. Melanie Sambells of *The Mirror* has assisted me, as well as the Surrey History Centre. Finally, Anthony Pickering helped me with the missing piece. Thank you, one and all.

Please allow me to take you, the reader, back over 50 years on a 'detour of medical misadventure' to reflect on what did happen. In the 1960s I lived near the A3 and was often driven on this road.

Am I qualified to discuss this accident? Well, I have been an advanced motorist for over 50 years. My driving licence has been clean throughout. I have driven motorcycles, cars and lorries, and even towed caravans. Apart from the UK, I have driven in many countries abroad. As the leader of the Derby Accident Flying Squad I attended countless road crashes with the police, fire and ambulance services. Personally, I have taken thousands of histories of accidents from patients, and then examined the crash victims before investigating and treating their injuries.

In turn I have given medical opinions on injured patients in coroners', magistrates', county and higher courts. They call me an 'expert medical witness' and seem quite impressed with my medical qualifications!

Yes, I know something about accidents, and a lot more about people and injuries. Nobody can know everything, but I know sufficient relevant facts to have published a lot in the medical press about accidents. In 1973 I

Fig 74 – Mike Hawthorn, the World Champion driver. Yes, he had many admirers and a big female fan club.

was awarded a prize from the Royal College of Surgeons of Edinburgh. This was for an illustrated essay of 5,000 words on the subject, 'Accident Prevention, How and When to Educate'.

I have read a number of statements from people about the cause of Mike's accident. Various theories have been put forward. These include an epileptic fit, a car race, the wet road, the high wind, and mechanical failure. Each possibility has been greeted with enthusiasm and eventually discarded as it does not fit the facts! Let us explore the relevant facts together. I have taken advice from Mr Peter Ashworth a retired solicitor. Peter was the deputy coroner for South Derbyshire from 1986 to 1990, and then the coroner until he retired in 2007. I have drawn from my experience of coroners' courts, and my own observations.

It is universally accepted that, for road accident collisions, there are just three main causes – the vehicle, the environment and the driver.

John Michael Hawthorn's Fatal Accident:
22nd January 1959

THE VEHICLE:

This was a dark green Jaguar 3.4 litre saloon index VDU 881. So this was a powerful motorcar. Mike ran a nearby garage – the Tourist Trophy Garage at Farnham. His manager at the inquest said the vehicle was in 'good mechanical condition'. None of the witnesses suggested that there was any mechanical failure associated with this accident. An automotive engineer confirmed that the brakes, and tyres, were perfect. So on the balance of probabilities was this vehicle to blame for this accident?

Not according to the coroner's inquest.

Now, looking back over 60 years:

Did this car have disc brakes? No, although in 1953 the Jaguar C type racing car had 'primitive' disc brakes. It was many years before the four disc brakes were fitted on the inside of the wheel in any production model.

Did this car have power-assisted steering? No, this did not come out in a production car until 1970.

Did this car have a modern gearbox? No, a very outdated one.

I don't suppose this car had any electronic anti-skid system? No, not a chance. It did have overdrive – to make it go faster!

The tyres were 'perfect'. But 60 years ago the quality of the rubber compound was relatively poor. Modern tyres have a better grip.

Did the Jaguar have side impact bars or a crumple free zone? Answer: no.

Did this car have seat belts or airbags fitted? No, but seat belts were available to be fitted in any car 'as an extra'. Air bags came in years later.

THE ENVIRONMENT:

The weather was clear, although it had rained earlier. At the inquest, witnesses commented on the spray from the road, and the fact that there was a 'very strong wind'. So when Mike's Jaguar car started to skid, the rear end moved sideways, perhaps influenced by that 'very strong wind'?

This particular stretch of the A3 Guildford bypass was notoriously dangerous. A police inspector at the inquest testified that there had been two other fatal accidents nearby in the previous two years!

PC Keefe at the inquest said that this stretch of the A3 was approximately 45 feet wide. There were bollards and islands down the centre of the road, with two lanes on each side. He stated that there was nothing on the road, like mud, that could have caused this accident .There was no mention of any skid marks or marks from braking. How strange! Perhaps there were none? Nowadays in any fatal collision all the tyre marks are recorded with lasers and interpreted electronically!

Now, looking back over 60 years:

So, in 1959 just bollards and traffic islands separated the two streams of traffic. Nowadays, for a busy trunk road like the A3, there is a crash barrier down the centre of the road. Also, each lane in 1959 was just over ten feet across – rather narrow.

A coroner is a judge, and an important part of our legal system. I have heard of coroners who have asked police inspectors at inquests if a particular road could be made safer, and how. Coroners are not to be ignored, and can ask the Highways Authority, the councils and the police to work together to make a road safer. At Mike Hawthorn's inquest the coroner said, and did, nothing of this nature unfortunately.

In retrospect, if Mike's car had hit a safety barrier in the middle of the road, then it is unlikely that it would have crashed into the truck coming in the opposite direction, and then gone behind it into the opposite ditch! So a safety barrier could well have saved his life.

Now looking back, there were quite a few cars on the road that day. None of these other vehicles crashed, or even skidded! There was a wind and the road surface was wet, but driving that day was not particularly dangerous.

THE DRIVER:

Everybody infers that as Mike was the World Motor Racing Champion, he was immune to error. So there must be another cause of this accident. I disagree strongly.

Mike Hawthorn overtook Robert Walker, who gave evidence at the inquest. As Mike overtook his friend Robert, he waved at him. Mr Walker

Fig 75 – Mike Hawthorn's car. What a mess!

slowed down. Mr Walker said, "his speed (Mike's) increased all the time". Nobody will ever know how fast Mike was driving downhill on the wet road. One witness, Arthur Hill, estimated Mike's speed at 80 miles per hour.

Mike's car went out of control – it hit a bollard before crossing the road. Then it hit a glancing blow to a lorry coming in the opposite direction and then impacted into a tree at speed (fig 75). All the witness statements tally. Rob Walker braked. There is no mention of Mike's car decelerating, or the brakes screeching! The final fatal impact of the car was catastrophic.

The onlookers found Mike's body on the back seat of the saloon. The pathologist recorded that bone had 'penetrated his skull'. He died of a severe head injury. There was 'no evidence of any other physical trouble'.

A verdict of accidental death was recorded by the jury at the coroner's inquest.

Now, looking back over 60 years:

Mike Hawthorn would have passed his driving test, as this was first introduced in 1934. This consisted of some questions on the Highway

Code, and a practical demonstration of driving skill. The written test on driving was not introduced until fairly recently. So to pass his driving test Mike would almost certainly have read the Highway Code that was first published in 1931. This explains about stopping distances that get longer with increasing speed. Several witnesses at the inquest commented on the spray from passing vehicles. The Highway Code clearly states that stopping distances are longer in the wet. Mike obviously ignored this.

But travelling so fast and exceeding the speed limit would have meant that, if caught, Mike would have lost his driving licence. Well, I was driving my Lambretta 125cc at the time. I had been driven all over the UK by my parents in their cars for years. There were speed traps employing a policeman at each end of a stretch of road, and another later on to stop the vehicle. These speed traps were few and far between (my late father was caught speeding in one of these traps near Folkestone around 1960). Radar guns did not come in until the '80s, and speed cameras were introduced in the 1990s. So a speeding motorist was unlikely to be prosecuted in the 1950s, but would soon be caught today!

Finally, something is missing from the pathologist's report. In 1959 they did not do blood alcohol levels on fatal road traffic accident victims. They do now. We will never know if Mike did have 'one for the road' on leaving work and before his meeting. One alcoholic drink can affect one's judgements. Nowadays all 'fatals' are screened routinely by the police for drugs.

A brief reflection solves the mystery.
William Stubbs (letter to JR Green, 1871)

There is no doubt at all in my mind that driver error was the main cause of this road traffic collision/accident. He drove too quickly down that wet road and paid the ultimate penalty – a fatal head injury.

Today, looking back, we can easily exclude a lot of causes by going through the facts. The road was wet, but that is all. So the road surface was fine. There was a wind. but no other cars were affected by it .Mechanical failure has been excluded by an expert. Mike was well that day and had never had an epileptic fit in his whole life. When Mike overtook his friend Robert, this driver slowed down. This does not seem like a race. So a lot of theories about the cause of this accident do not fit the facts!

Today's drivers are no better. They still drive too fast in the wet, overtake too readily and follow other cars too closely. When will we learn?

But the roads and the cars today are a lot safer. We forget too readily how seat belts and airbags have saved countless lives. Poor Mike had neither. He was found in the back seat so he must have been thrown around like a ragdoll.

We forget too easily that back in the 1950s only about 20% of households had a car. People walked to work, went by public transport or cycled. Looking back, ours was the only household in our road with two cars, as both my parents were working doctors. So the roads of the UK were less busy. Very few cars on the roads were as powerful as Mike's 3.4 litre Jaguar.

So naturally, with fewer cars on our roads, you would expect fewer accidents. But this is not true. Back in the 1950s we had 5,000 fatalities a year on our roads.

Now, in 2017, we have less than 2,000 deaths, with a high proportion on A roads, and fewer on motorways as they are safer. To my mind, today's drivers are no better than in the 1950s, but the roads and the cars are a lot better. Unfortunately, personal error remains as the main cause of road traffic fatalities!

But all of this does not explain this simple fact: Mike Hawthorn raced all around the world in dangerous car races. Then he is killed on a road in the UK not racing, i.e., in a far less dangerous situation!

To explore one possibility we need to digress. I apologise, but experience from one accident may throw some light on another.

Twenty years ago, working as a consultant in the emergency department, we were often called out to trapped drivers in vehicle accidents. One such Sunday afternoon stands out in my memory because I did not understand what had happened! A man aged 31 years was alone driving his car on the Derby ring road. The weather was clear and bright. No other vehicle was involved. His car, in a 40mph zone, careered off the road to his nearside over some grass, and into the stone support of an overhead road bridge. There were no skid marks on the five yards or so of grass. The impact with the bridge support was colossal. His small saloon was concertinaed! He was wearing a seat belt (no airbags fitted). His upper body was unharmed, but both his femurs were shattered. He could have died from blood loss.

I was the only doctor in attendance. I gave him plenty of morphine intravenously. He had fluid expanders in a drip intravenously. Blood was ready for him when he had been extricated from the vehicle, and he was taken to the hospital in traction splints. He was admitted to our hospital and operated upon.

Then I had a chance meeting with him in our department three months later. Well, he recognised me, and hobbled over to say his thanks – particularly for the analgesia. As he left he paused and blurted out, "You know it was a suicide attempt, don't you?" I had had no idea and was dumbfounded. "Oh yes," he said, "I was fine when I woke up, but then had a big row with my live-in girlfriend. It's silly looking back but I just 'flipped' and decided to end it all."

So this was a suicide attempt. I never would have thought it! How strange!

I have since read a lot about such accidents, and discussed suicides with a former senior police officer concerned with fatal collisions. Some commentators have guessed that about a third of all people killed in road traffic collisions have committed suicide. Suicide in this way is a lot commoner in men than in women. The men are often in their twenties and thirties, travelling alone, and usually no other vehicle is involved. When a driver normally is about to crash, he will practically always brake hard. This is the 'self-preservation reflex'. Suicides, however, turn this reflex off and DON'T BRAKE.

They don't want to kill anybody else. So nobody else is in their vehicle and no other vehicle is involved usually!

(The word suicide was introduced originally in the 17th century by a doctor, Sir Thomas Browne.)

SO LET'S RETURN TO THE MAIN PLOT:

Mike Hawthorn was driving alone.

No other vehicle was involved. He had overtaken another car. He had waved at his friend, as he passed him. Was he waving goodbye? Out of control, his car had a glancing blow to a lorry. That is all. No other person was in any danger.

He was aged 30 years. Yes, he too was a male aged 30, travelling alone. But why, oh why, would he want to commit suicide? Any reasons?

He was an extrovert. Extroverts tend to have mood swings – highs and lows.

He was no longer doing what he loved – motorcar racing. He had retired. (It's only when you retire that you realise how you miss your work – especially if you love it.)

He had a lovely fiancée and a job running a successful garage. He was due to be taking on a partner. So work was fine, and his personal life. He had a beautiful fiancée but she was not with him that morning to lift his mood. So, you would have thought that as one avenue, racing, had stopped he would continue happily running his garage and getting married.

Well, no. Death was all around him. His father had been killed in an RTA and died a tragic death a few years before. People don't forget how their parents died, particularly as this should have been avoided. Mike was going to meet Mrs Collins later that day. Her husband had died on the Nurburg ring the previous year. Then there is himself. Well, you think that a 30-year-old is fit and healthy. He looked it.

But he had a congenital deformity of both kidneys. One had already been removed as it was non-functioning and may well have given him pain. He had been given a few months to live by his surgeon. This was discovered by chance a few months earlier when he was burnt in a motor race accident. One blood test, a blood urea, was raised, indicating renal failure. He was then given a dye intravenously. This dye is radio-opaque and excreted by his kidneys. They were shown to be small kidneys, and not functioning well. All he could do was keep his fluid intake up and he would have been advised on a diet. He may well have had pain, perhaps that very day, from the remaining kidney. Renal transplantation was in its infancy. Tissue typing had not been properly worked out, and rejection of a kidney was a real possibility. It all depends on what is defined by a successful renal transplant. The technical bit of the arterial and venous anastamosis of the vein and artery was not difficult for surgeons to perform, then the ureter was implanted into the bladder. A success was hailed whenever urine was produced. But after days, or a few weeks,the kidney was rejected. It was not until 1960 that the UK had a really successful renal transplant.It was performed by Mr Michael Woodruff between living identical twins.

His blood test, called a blood urea, would have to be repeated over and over again to monitor his condition of renal failure. His general practitioner would be in charge of this. Mike would have advised to have a special diet to help the kidneys function. This diet is bland and boring. It is low protein. So, little meat, and that means no steaks, burgers, bacon or sausage! His urine would have to be tested regularly to exclude infections, that are common in this condition. His blood pressure could go up, and needed to be checked regularly. He did see a surgeon, who removed one kidney. That kidney was either very sore or non functioning at all. He may have been offered peritoneal dialysis. This is a slow treatment that can last hours. It involves putting a tube into the abdomen and running in some fluid. The blood urea is lowered as a result. The artificial kidney, the forerunner of the modern dialysis machine was still being developed.He may have been attached to an early artificial kidney. This too would have been boring! So Mike would have been fed up seeing his GP, having blood tests and check ups. In his condition he would have to be followed up carefully. This was mandatory! Also, patients with a raised blood urea feel unwell. I should know as I chatted to many of them when I was a registrar on the transplant unit at the Hammersmith Hospital in the 1970s. Once they had been treated on the dialysis machine, their blood urea was back to normal. They then felt fine. So Mike's blood urea may have been up that day. We will never know.

It is possible that he had a mood swing. He would try and keep outward appearances up. He had been into work that day.

Mike knew he had only a short time to live because he only had one poorly functioning kidney. So he knew and felt he was in the early stages of renal failure. Such patients find themselves drinking copious amounts of fluid. When Mike Hawthorn retired from motor racing the press asked why he had retired so young. If the governing body of motor racing had known he was in renal failure, then they would not have let him race. So he would have had to retire months earlier, and everybody would have known of his kidney problem, that he tried to hide.

His mother knew him well. She did not give evidence at the inquest. This inquest, held only days after the accident, seems very quick – especially with a jury. Well, the accident happened at midday on Thursday 22nd January, and the inquest, with a jury, was held on the evening of 26th January! This is four days later. Mr Ashworth commented to me, "That is far too quick."

There was considerable publicity about this inquest.

At a coroner's inquest the coroner, practically always, chats to the pathologist and reads his post mortem report before the inquest. This is not illegal. The coroner is in charge of proceedings, and it is helpful for him to know what is going to be said. I have little doubt that the two solicitors – the coroner and the family solicitor – had such a meeting prior to the inquest, and agreed that the state of Mike's remaining kidney should not be made common knowledge. Mr Ashworth told me that family solicitors usually attend inquests if there is a medical problem. THERE WAS A MEDICAL PROBLEM HERE. YES, THAT ONE REMAINING KIDNEY! The coroner's post mortem is always thorough, and the whole body is inspected. There is always a statement about the kidneys. This fact (ONLY ONE FAILING KIDNEY) would be irrelevant to the cause of death, and upsetting to Mike's mother. So, I guees that is why this problem was kept quiet. (Both men were local solicitors, and would know each other well.)

So the coroner just asked the pathologist for the cause of death. That is all. The family solicitor just asked a question about the possibility of an adverse camber. There was no adverse camber. The jury brought in a verdict of accidental, death as instructed. But how strange for a champion racing driver to crash his car while not even racing!

So despite the fact that he had a beautiful fiancée and an excellent job, I believe Mike knew he would not live long to enjoy life. His life already had been close to death a few times. His father had died needlessly in an accident. He was due to meet the wife of a fellow racing driver who had died the previous year in an accident.

I think Mike, an extrovert, had a low mood that day. It possibly was triggered as he felt the onset of renal failure with thirst and maybe kidney discomfort. Then behind the wheel of his beloved Jaguar he had a thrill. This is what he loved – motor racing. Why had he retired? He overtook a friend. The friend braked. He waved goodbye to him. This is what Mike lived for – SPEED. He did not have long to live for anyway!!

"Oh, hang it," he said to himself, and put his foot down hard on the accelerator and flicked on the overdrive. He mentally turned off his self-preservation reflex. Joy of joys – what a way to go! He lived… and died… for this. Faster – faster, faster, BANG!

POSTSCRIPT:

So, did Mike Hawthorn really commit suicide by crashing his beloved car on purpose?

We will never ever know for certain but, considering all the facts, on the balance of probabilities, in my humble expert opinion he did! Male suicides are more common than female suicides. Suicide is the commonest cause of death in men below the age of 50.

I finished writing about Mike Hawthorn in 2016, and spent ages trying to finish this book. In January 2017 I read of the research of Colin Pritchard. He is a professor of psychiatric social work at Bournemouth University. He has analysed the coroner's cases where cause of death was undetermined. He commented correctly that, "Coroners are obliged to use the criminal level of proof, beyond reasonable doubt, rather than the civil 'balance of probabilities' to deliver a suicide verdict." He went on to say that, "Coroners are also keenly aware that families can be comforted by the thought that their relative did not mean to end their life." He also said that, "It is the stuff of nightmares when a young person dies by their own hand. A family will never get over that. They feel guilty and ashamed. Parents who have lost their children to suicide are devastated and broken". He concluded that the true number of suicides reported by coroners in England and Wales is underestimated by "as much as 50% in young people".

I believe that the work of Professor Pritchard supports my opinion that *Mike Hawthorn committed suicide by crashing his car.*

I suspect that Mike's mother knew him best of all. Well, parents know, and love, their children. She attended the inquest but did not give evidence. I think she knew, or at least suspected, that this crash was suicide. That is why she wanted the cause of the crash, the kidney problem, definitely NOT to be mentioned.

The only other person who knew Mike well was his GP. He knew the score very well indeed. His general practitioner was not called to give evidence.

So the conspiracy to keep his suicide quiet, in my opinion, has worked, until now!

CHAPTER FIFTY-ONE

My Hereditary, and Other, Problems

Problem One – Dyslexia – Hereditary?

Anyone who can only think of one way to spell a word obviously lacks imagination.

Mark Twain

One of my children was having some problems at school. The school asked our consent for a test. My wife and I agreed. The test showed the child had dyslexia. Schoolwork improved with specialist teaching.

Our child showed me their test paper. It rang bells in my ears. I realised I had it too and had passed it onto my child. My own modification of learning techniques had helped me get through some examinations with a low pass rate. So, by myself, I had learnt to partly overcome my dyslexia.

Perusal of a book, *Study Skills for Dyslexic Students* by Sandra Hargreaves, published by Sage Publications, confirmed my diagnosis.

I quote, with permission, from this book:

'Note taking… can be difficult for dyslexic students as a number of different tasks have to be performed simultaneously – listening, reading, comprehension, processing and writing.'

Oh yes, I took copious notes in a lecture and nothing was remembered after!

'Reading is hard.' Gosh I had difficulty reading aged five, six and seven!

'Problems with spelling.' Oh, gosh, yes. I could not spell inoculation and changed it to vaccination in my finals! (I have spelling problems to this day!)

'Dyslexic students often have trouble with the maths content of a course – procedures involved, not concepts.' Oh, yes again. I had two or three private lessons of maths tuition before Common Entrance – I was expected to fail by the master. I score 92% overall for three maths papers. 'Truly an amazing result', he wrote in my school report! I had had help with the procedures.

Dyslexia caused me to fail so many examinations – an A level, 2nd MB, 2nd MB (Conjoint) and finals twice. I got through in the end. There must be a lot of undiagnosed dyslexics out there.

I only got through by using my own auditory revision technique, i.e., I closed the book I had been reading and tried hard to remember fact after fact. With practice and after a lot of study, I could get up to three or four hundred facts! Then these facts were cemented in my memory bank. (My so-called friends said that I was asleep!)

But I am in good company. Leonardo da Vinci and Albert Einstein are both believed to have been dyslexic![1]

Hereditary Problem Two – The Fickle Finger of Fate (Dupuytrens)

I was in my sixties. For some years I had noticed fine thickening bands under the skin of both my palms. I knew that they were called Dupuytren's contracture. I do not know of any of my relatives with this condition, but it is inherited. I was not bothered by this. My use of my hands was unaffected until…

I was about 12 feet up in a barn full of small bales of hay. I needed to get two bales for horses down. One bale was sticking out of the haystack below and to my right. I kicked it free, and it fell. Unfortunately the bale I was standing on was supported by the bale I had just kicked away! I found myself free falling all of a sudden!

I landed on my palms on the ladder I had climbed up. My right palm was sore for weeks and weeks. As I suspected, an X-ray showed no fracture. The fine bands of firm tissue in my right palm thickened. The skin was drawn in, and a nodule formed. What had my stupidity accelerated? What had happened?

Dupuytren's disease is an inherited disorder almost exclusively found in northern Europeans. Scandinavians have a high incidence. The chances of developing Dupuytren's are increased if you are an alcoholic or epileptic. I am neither. Heavy manual workers have a higher chance compared to clerical workers.

Three of my grandparents were Scottish – one came from the Western Isles of Scotland. Here the disease is prevalent, possibly introduced by the Vikings, who settled and intermarried. Exacerbations of this condition can occur by micro trauma (tear-like interruption of longitudinal fibres), with proven deposits of haemosiderin due to bleeding. So it is likely that micro trauma caused bleeding and an exacerbation of this condition.[2] So, my fall accelerated an inherited condition! Dupuytren described such an outcome.

My stupidity again!

Reference:

1. A A Gill. Is this how to face up to Dyslexia. Cover story. *Sunday Times Magazine*. 2012.
2. Palmar fibromatosis (Dupuytren's contracture). Ultrastructural and enzyme histochemical studies of 43 cases.
    Iwasaki H et al. Virchows Arch A Pathol. AnatHistopathol1984. 405. 41-53.

A Synopsis of My Medical History

To see ourselves as others see us.

Robert Burns

In this medical journey what have I learnt about myself? Well, quite a lot.

As a schoolboy I thought that I would like to be a doctor. I went through medical school. Once qualified, I loved it – the best job in the world.

On the London to Brighton walk I learnt about the value of adequate analgesia. Well, as a student I had not been given local anaesthetic when my face was stitched. It was agony. As a doctor I never stitched anybody up without analgesia. Later in life I had several local anaesthetic procedures. Hammer toes, golfers elbow and a sebaceous cyst – they all were cured, and subsequently gave me no problems. This London to Brighton walk taught me that fatigue predisposes to accidents – I was nearly run over in Brighton. I also learnt the value of analgesic tablets.

I was unusual. I had a sensitivity to tetracycline. It is just one of those things in life. But lots of my patients had drug sensitivity.

I kissed a lot of attractive nurses as a casualty officer, and so contracted glandular fever. The first part of the previous sentence was fun, the latter part was not! I was very concerned until I knew I had glandular fever. (The differential diagnosis included agranulocytosis and leukaemia.)

I contracted chicken pox from a patient and could not sit my finals. My father nearly died from hepatitis contracted from a patient.

Tonsillectomy as an adult was an experience I wish I could have missed. Nobody ever told me that the recovery would be as slow!

I could not see a fast ball at cricket as I had a curved lens (astigmatism). An optician found this out for me.

I could easily have become an alcoholic when I had fractured ribs. I treated myself with alcohol to kill the pain. When the ribs had healed I needed the alcohol. I stopped just in time. My body recovered. The craving for alcohol left me.

It took me a long time to find out why I could not spell, or remember much from lectures – I had dyslexia. I was never tested for this!

Just before retirement I injured my right palm. Painless lumps appeared under the skin in my palm. The condition called Dupuytrens followed. For this I have to thank my Scottish ancestors. This condition is always hereditary. My hand function remains unaffected.

Aged 65 I returned from a walking holiday in Scotland to find my left tendo-Achilles was painful and swollen. A diagnosis of Achilles tendonitis was confirmed when an ultrasound showed new blood vessels!

How do you treat this? Nobody knew. An orthopaedic friend told me, "surgery gives poor results!" Finally ultrasound physiotherapy cured me!

In conclusion I have suffered from dyslexia, astigmatism, tetracycline sensitivity, glandular fever, chicken pox, tonsillectomy, local anaesthetic operations and Dupuytrens. I recently had a hernia repair. The spinal local anaesthetic was brilliant (painless). The hernia was the price I paid for generating the logs to keep two wood burning stoves going 24/7, for six months a year, for the last 30 years. Achilles tendonitis threatened to ruin my retirement!

My GP one day checked my blood pressure and told me it was borderline for treatment. I STRONGLY disagreed. So I arranged for a blood pressure recording device to be attached to me for 24 hours. It went off regularly throughout that time! Bleep, bleep, bleep. In choir practice the organist stopped playing and said, "What`s that?" My wife refused to sleep with it in our bed! A shop assistant told me that my phone had a strange ring. Luckily it proved that I was NOT hypertensive, thank goodness.

Am I really such a hypochondriac? As I age I seem to have more and more and more conditions. I try and play golf. This strange game does involve looking down and focussing on a small ball. But both my eyes are filled on cold days with pools of water. The trouble is, I know too much. These little holes on the inner aspect of my lower eyelids, out of which the water drains from my eyes, are not applied to the eyeball – hence water accumulates. This is not serious – just a big nuisance. If I could only operate on myself, I could tighten up the muscle and water would drain away. This senile condition I have cured when I did plastic surgery. Yet another minor operation beckons. Am I addicted to them??

I have had pneumonia and been cured with penicillin.

So a study of medicine has lead me to understand a little of the workings of my own body – as well as everybody else's body!

The best doctor is he that has been well hacked himself.
Chinese Proverb

I still read the *British Medical Journal,* and recently discovered that a review of multicentre trials concerning coronary heart disease, considers a cholesterol level over four to be a definite coronary risk factor. They have 'moved the goalposts'. My cholesterol level of five was not considered to be a risk factor, until now! Last year, I had to stop taking a statin as it gave me severe muscle pains. Could I take a different statin that would not cause this side effect, and also lower my cholesterol?

I made an appointment, and attended the surgery. The doctor was young enough to be my granddaughter! She knew me too! Well, ten years ago, I had taught her as a medical student! What a role reversal. I left clutching the prescription. I knew I had to take the statin regularly. So for one month I took the tablets daily. What joy – no muscle pains at all!

One month later, my tablets ran out, so I handed in my repeat prescription at the local pharmacy. The bald pharmacy assistant said, "Look, we are very busy. Could you please come back later?" The place was deserted as I left that Friday afternoon! I returned on the Monday morning.

I was greeted by bedlam. There was a geriatric queue out of the door, and people everywhere! I patiently waited. My bald friend was harassed beyond words. This invasion was causing work overload. Finally I reached the front of the queue. After scurrying around and checking up, my friend handed me some medicine. "There you are," he said.

"But," I protested, "this medicine has someone else's name on it."

"Are you sure?" he said. "Well, what is your name?" he asked yet again.

I told him my name for the third time that day.

"Well," he said, "the computer says you have received the medicine already."

He then called for reinforcements.

An utterly charming Indian lady then greeted me and politely informed me that she was the pharmacist.

"Don't worry," she said, "you are confused."

"No, I am not," was my reply.

"Yes, you certainly are," she replied. "I know you are. Now, go home and check in the drawer where you put the medicines. It will be there. Our computer says that you already have the tablets. Goodbye."

I left confused, with my tail between my legs. The queue was relieved to see the back of me – a troublemaker, no doubt about it.

I waited several days and then cautiously returned to the pharmacy. It was deserted apart from the same assistant. "I still haven't any statin," I announced.

"Oh, have you lost them?" he replied.

"The computer says that you definitely have received them," he confidently announced. He checked again. "No, they are not here," he said. "You must have them somewhere."

I left in disarray again. Was I confused? My wife and I went away for a few days.

I then returned to the pharmacy. My friend, the assistant, was again adamant. "The computer says that you have the tablets."

Finally, he observed, "Well, if you have lost them, you might get another prescription?"

So, I queued up and asked the doctors' receptionist for help.

"Well," she said, "this is very unusual. The computer says that you can't have any more tablets till next month!"

I pleaded with her.

Finally she made out a request for the doctor to sign a repeat prescription. Two days later I returned.

"Oh," said the receptionist. "He is far too busy. He has not had time to sign it, but if you like I'll make it urgent."

Two days later – no prescription. My wife and I went to visit grandchildren in Scotland.

On my return, after more than four weeks without the statin, I cautiously re-entered the pharmacy. This time I knew the assistant, Beverley. She is an attractive blonde, married to a golfing friend of mine.

"Oh hello, Alistair," she said. "How can I help you?"

"Well," I said, "I just wondered if my tablets, a statin, have come in yet?"

She did not even touch the computer, but marched straight to the shelf.

"Oh yes," she said, "here they are. But there is another lot of tablets here for you. Oh, you naughty boy," she said, "you should have picked these up a month ago."

I left with a double supply of statin.

Clearly there is a major flaw in their organisation. It can't possibly be that having a double-barrelled surname they looked under F for some medicine that was filed under M! No, whoever is in charge should be held to account, exposed or replaced. I have no doubt at all who that is – it's that chatterbox computer!

* * *

But what about my mind? It's crammed full of medical facts, coupled with life's rich experiences. But is that all? As an ignorant 18-year-old I embarked on medicine. Now, over 50 years later, clouded by dyslexia and old age, how differently am I emotionally, and why? Has my attitude to different people changed?

I have worked closely with many other professionals – just thrown together. As long as the doctor cares about the patient and puts them first, then I get on with everyone, whatever colour, nationality or creed. I got on very well indeed with Aspi, an Indian surgeon.

However, I have seen in fellow doctors other activities get in the way of clinical judgement, then I get 'mega' upset. These other activities include various sports, a mistress or two, alcoholism, laziness and the ambition to succeed. Fortunately, I have avoided all these traps.

Patients are different too. Most patients are sane, sensible and I empathised with them. I got on very well with James Partridge, whose face is disfigured.[1] Similarly, I have great sympathy for the transgender patient with the mind of one sex and the body of another. I hated the pimps, the pugilists, the prostitutes, the pyromaniacs and the paedophiles. Yes, I saw far too much of such people! Some patients lied to get drugs, a bed for the night or to cover an offence! But they ALL had a right to access medical treatment. I could not refuse!

So my long medical career has bred some tolerance in me, and some insight and understanding of other people. But we are all different, and that's something I find fascinating. I struggled to keep my medical knowledge up to date. But I took, and passed, the Advanced Trauma Life Support examination on my own initiative in my sixties!

I continued to play that strange game golf for fun and exercise until now, aged 75 years. I got down to a five handicap in my twenties and lasted for ten years in single figures. My happiest moments were playing in two club competitions at Royal Mid Surrey golf Club when we won knockout foursomes competitions. I played once with my father and once with my sister. In 1988 I won a knockout singles competition at my favourite golf course, Saunton, in Devon. This is called the plate, and I won seven games in one week! (It nearly cost me my marriage, but my wife forgave me.)

But of all the golf games that I played over many, many years one still remains in my memory to haunt me! Let me explain this bizarre happening. I had qualified to play in an inter club singles competition organized by the *Evening News* newspaper. One sunny day a third round match was arranged at Royal Mid Surrey Golf Club. My opponent turned up with three supporters. I was not expecting this.

As I went to drive on the second hole, I had to stop. Smoke filled the air. I coughed and coughed. I looked up and one of his supporters, who was smoking, was missing. Was he behind me? I took a step back and a fast practice swing. I heard him fall right off the tee behind me. (He might have been decapitated!) The smoke cleared. He had been behind me, blowing smoke at me to put me off!

Our game continued, but each time I went to play a shot one of his supporters coughed, laughed, dropped a club or moved quickly. So they did anything to upset my game. All three of them gave my opponent advice. This is contrary to the rules. A golfer is only allowed one caddy. This is not in the spirit of the game. If I had complained, I had no proof. I did not want to upset my game. I was in front, and a rematch would have to start again all square. So I looked for a way to get my own back. This barracking continued over and over. Even on the putting green they tried to distract me by walking behind, and suddenly I was in their shadow. How unsettling it was, for me! Twice my opponent hit the ball into deep rough. At once his three caddies bounded off to find the ball. Under normal circumstances I would have expected a lost ball. But no, his ball was found, always at once, in a very good lie. How strange is that!

I was seething inside. Then I was given an opportunity to get my own back on the twelfth hole. I was two holes in the lead. We each had played 4 shots, and our respective golf balls were close to the hole. My opponent was given eight shots by me in the handicap system. One of these shots was at this hole. So he had won this hole if he used this stroke

Cheekily, and casually, I offered him a halved hole. The fool accepted this. I raced to the next hole and we agreed that I was two up, as we stood on the tee. After we had hit our second shots on that hole I casually asked him why he had not claimed his free shot on the last hole? He went ape. He shouted abuse at his 3 caddies. They abused him back. My opponent got tense, and he then played worse and worse. I won easily. They walked away, and went home.

Over all my years of playing golf I have enjoyed every single round with this one exception. I shall never know the correct way of dealing with such an opponent.

Two rounds later I was knocked out of the competition by a county golfer on top form. He deserved to win. We had played before, and we became good friends. I congratulated him on winning our match, and wished him well in the next round.

Now, it is in this spirit, that golf should be played.

I was, always, interested in lectures on human embryology. We learnt that we all developed from one cell, that in turn divided, and divided, into specialised cells. The developing embryo traces our development through primitive forms of life to eventually emerge as homo sapiens. So at one stage in the embryo we all develop gills like fish, our ancestors. This was important, as rarely these gills do not disappear, but remain in the neck of a newborn baby. This hole is called a branchial fistula.

Each time an embryo develops, the same events occur over and over again. Take the thyroid gland for example: this organ produces a chemical (thyroxine) that regulates our activity. The thyroid gland is programmed to develop in our mouth – clearly the wrong place. So it moves, in our development, to the front of our neck. Rarely, this move fails and a baby is born with a thyroid gland in the mouth. We each have a brain. This is our own complex computer with megabytes of memory.

So each human baby is a miracle. Our development is not haphazard, but logical, complex and controlled.

Defects are uncommon. The lecturer taught us all the facts, with one exception. Who planned our development, and who co-ordinates it today over and over again?

So I worked as a doctor, and knew very well that I was no different physically to anybody else. I marvelled at embryology. Each one of us is formed from one single cell. What a miracle our development in utero is, and also our birth. Lectures in anatomy told me of our intricate detail. Physiology showed me how each organ functioned, and how they each is fit for purpose. Biochemistry is an amazing eye-opener. Chemical formulae interact over and over again to keep us alive. It's all so fascinating, and most people think that it all has happened by chance. How? Absolutely impossible!!!!

As a doctor I know very well what our society is like. Time and time again I saw my patients at death's door from major trauma or illness. Then frequently I saw them recover. Doctors arrange treatments. It is up to our bodies to respond to these treatments, and recover. All patients expected to recover, unless they were suffering from a terminal illness. Patients expected the doctors and nurses to heal them, and not the workings of their bodies to do it.

What did I learn about my patients?

Am I proud of the society that I have tried to serve? Are people happy today?

So many people are obsessed with acquiring money and material things. They idolise billionaires, successful sports stars and well-known entertainers. The media encourages us to be healthy and happy. The average diet is high sugar and high fat, so the incidence of diabetes is soaring! We read in the press of some of our role models having multiple sexual partners of both sexes! Today illegal drug use and alcoholism is widespread, our prisons are overflowing, convictions for rape and domestic violence are soaring, and one in five pregnancies end in abortion.

No, our society is sick but refuses to accept it.

Then in my thirties I read the Bible, and things fell into place. Jesus taught us that a love of money is the root of evil. Jesus was a miraculous healer, far better than any doctor today. I became a Christian and have not looked back. I don't believe that I am better than anybody else – just different. Jesus has helped me write this book. I know that I am not perfect, but Jesus accepts me as I am. I strongly believe that if fewer people turned their back on Jesus, then this world would be a much better place. So I will follow Jesus for the rest of my days. As a Christian I am considered odd by the rest of society. A pariah? So be it.

I am sure that what I have just written has upset a few readers. So I leave you with some facts that Jesus said 2,000 years ago, that are still relevant today. You may disagree with me for the above, but not this!

In his gospels Jesus is quoted as saying, 'there will always be wars, natural disasters and famine'.[2] How did a poorly educated Jew from the Middle East know this 2,000 years ago? He went on to say, 'there will be strange and terrifying things coming from the sky' (i.e., bombs).

Well, he knew this 2,000 year ago because he is God. Jesus died on the cross. There were witnesses to this, and many to his resurrection. He paid for all our sins on that cross. Those who commit their lives to Jesus have the promise of eternal life in Heaven with him.

References:

1. James Partridge. Disfigured are being given new rights to face up to prejudice. Equality 2010. *The Times*. 24. 3. 10.
2. Luke. *The Bible*. Chapter 21 verses 10 & 11.

My Contemporaries:
Well, What Has Happened to the Rest of my Medical Year?

The reader may recall that 51 of us started as students at St Thomas' in 1960. As I write, most of us are still alive. However, three former students have all died prematurely from the same condition – cancer of the pancreas.

Well, for six days a week for the first 18 months we were 'tied' to the anatomy room. We wore no gloves. We washed our hands after each dissection, but the smell of formalin (formaldehyde) lingered for hours afterwards on our hands.

Martindale, the authoritative textbook on drugs and poisons, informed me on reading recently that formaldehyde is now an established carcinogenic substance. Inhalation of formaldehyde predisposes to cancer of the nasal passages.[1] Is it perhaps possible that as the formaldehyde was on our hands, we subsequently ingested small amounts when eating?

The formaldehyde from our hands could easily have then been absorbed into our body. Absorption of substances from our food mainly occurs in the small bowel. The pancreas is closely applied to the small bowel and secretes enzymes that aid digestion. The minute quantity of formaldehyde so absorbed could have acted as a cumulative poison predisposing in these three to cancer of the pancreas.[2]

Nobody knows today if that did occur.

We might know in the future. In a recent article in the *BMJ* on pancreatic cancer, formalin or any similar substance is not mentioned.[3]

* * *

Henry, a consultant physician from my medical year, had retired. Now well into his seventies, he was very active, but could no longer prescribe drugs as he was off the medical register. His interest was horticulture, and he was very knowledgeable. He had an attack of shingles. He diagnosed it himself. As the spots settled he was left with pain. This has a medical name (post herpetic neuralgia), and it hurts! So he consulted his general ptactitioner, who was young enough to be his granddaughter .He was told to take paracetamol, and nothing stronger. He was very unhappy. The treatment did not work, and the pain stopped him sleeping.

Then his eye alighted on one of his favourite flowers, the poppy. He knew that the sap contained a powerful mixture of strong analgesics. He did not want to suffer an overdose. So he made a small vertical cut on the fine stem just below a seed. He squeezed out a small blob of sap onto his thumbnail. He ate this on bread with marmalade to disguise the bitter flavour. Half an hour later he was pain free. He slept well, at last, that night. He repeated this a few times till he was better.[2]

* * *

A professor of gastroenterology of my vintage was about to retire, having spent a lifetime not only treating patients, but also doing research and lecturing often abroad. Before a long-haul flight to a meeting he followed the accepted advice to prevent a deep vein thrombosis. This involved wearing support stockings during the flight and taking one low dose aspirin before.This tablet reduces platelet stickiness, making a clot less likely.

This doctor had enjoyed good health up to then. But after the flight he had blood in his motions. This bleeding continued and failed to settle. He eventually was hospitalised and investigated. No serious cause could be found for his bleed!

The only possible cause for his bleed was that one low dose aspirin irritated his stomach and so caused his haemorrhage. This can occur, but is very rare at such a low dose.

He has now retired and is in excellent health. This therapeutic hiccup shows that things can go wrong even if the correct treatment is followed. This eminent physician was the victim of his own iatrogenic complication! It's cases like this that will always make medicine so fascinating.

References:

1. *Martindale* 36th Edition, page 1644.
2. A personal communication from Dr Henry Oakley FRCP, Garden Fellow, Royal College of Physicians, Regents Park, London.
3. Giles Bond-Smith et al. Pancreatic Adenocarcinoma. *BMJ* 2012:344;e2476.

My Last First-aid Lecture

"Should auld acquaintance be forgot"

Robert Burns

My golfing friend Ron asked in 1990 if I would possibly give a talk on resuscitation to the Rotary Club of Belper. He was the president (fig 76). There were about 20 members. There had recently been two sudden deaths locally and his members wanted advice on resuscitation. I agreed, and we fixed a date for Wednesday lunchtime at 12.30pm at the Talbot Hotel, Belper. "We will give you a bite to eat first," said Ron.

My clinic was due to finish early, at my request, at midday, but several people came late – congratulating themselves on getting there at all. At 12.30pm I was leaving. Ros, my registrar, told me, "You must take the new dummy; the old one is falling apart." I rushed into the registrar's office. There was a shiny new resuscitation dummy's case. I lifted it up – yes, the dummy was inside, it was so heavy. I would impress my friends with a brand new dummy. She is called Annie.

Two minutes later, I was off to Belper. I have lectured on resuscitation many times before. I had not lectured on first aid for several years. As an emergency consultant I am frequently involved in resuscitation, so I get plenty of practice in it. My greatest achievements occurred when my first

Fig 76 – Mr Giffin the President.

aid students came back to me and said that they had resuscitated somebody successfully away from my hospital. That gave me a buzz. I was looking forward to showing off in a subject I knew well!

I drove quickly to Belper. When I got to the Talbot Hotel there were cars everywhere – parking was difficult. There must be a function on, I thought. Lugging the case carrying Annie, I was directed to the annex. On opening the door it was bedlam. The room on two levels was full of men supping soup. Many of them greeted me warmly. Most had pints of beer. This was a party in full swing. What a crowd!

I had a reserved place on the top table. Ron explained, "Your talk is so popular that two other Rotary clubs have come along. I hope you don't mind."

I left Annie in the corner of the room, and had a fine bowl of soup and a roll. I was replete. I thanked my neighbour. "Oh, that's just the start," he said. "The main course is coming up." Well, I was used to a round of sandwiches and a cup of tea at lunchtime. This larger meal might be a struggle. I refused a pint of beer, too! Many were on their second pint already! Banter with my neighbours soon told me that the majority of men in the room had retired. Well, if this is what retirement is all about I need to get into training!

Soon, an ample plateful of pork and stuffing was put in front of me. My attention was caught by a friend at a nearby table. When I came to my plate again, it was piled high with vegetables, including about eight potatoes, cauliflower, peas and apple sauce!

Well, I did not want to offend my hosts. I finished the lot. Well, if this is what retirement is all about I will HAVE to go into training. I'm simply not prepared for such colossal, calorific cuisine!

Then I had a nasty experience – acute abdominal pain. The remedy –

I loosened my belt by two notches. Relief was immediate. There followed pudding – blackberry and apple crumble with custard (my favourite). I tried to refuse twice, but some well-meaning soul put one in front of me, when I was distracted by another friend.

I tried refusing coffee – but still got one.

I stood up to get Annie from the corner. I felt faint. I took my tie and jacket off. I glanced down. I looked and felt pregnant!

I had a nasty shock getting Annie out – one of her legs fell off. Oh no, I have the wrong dummy. This could be grim.

After my preamble about "looking for absent breathing and no pulse", I explained and demonstrated mouth to mouth resuscitation. Then I did cardiac massage. Things were dire. On mouth to mouth, the dummy's chest should expand. It did not. Why was there air blowing onto my left cheek? Oh yes, she has a hole in her chest. Similarly, on chest compression the ribcage collapsed.

I would press on. I tried bigger breaths, but just more air escaped. Some feathers from inside of Annie's chest flew into the air. I caught the first few and then gave up.

Annie's left arm fell off. "Is that supposed to happen?" asked the comedian on my left. (I ignored him.)

I was feeling ill. Commentating and resuscitating is hard work anyway. I was running out of puff. I cleaned the dummy's face and somebody else took over. Despite plugging the big wound in the chest wall with my hand, more feathers than ever flew into the air. I sneezed, and so did the man on the other side.

Several other Rotary members tried resuscitation with Annie. Then eventually we stopped. I was thanked, and beat a hasty retreat.

I felt guilty going back to the hospital. I was going to have to work till at least 7pm to make up for my absence. I did not see a dustbin big enough on the way back, or I would have willingly abandoned Annie.

As I staggered into the hospital, dragging Annie, I met Ros. "Good meal?" she asked.

"Oh yes," I said, "too good," trying to hide my pseudo cyesis.

I had been guilty of gluttony.

Don't be greedy for fine food… Or you will vomit up what you have eaten.

Proverbs 23

I Perform my Penultimate Minor Operation

I had formally retired but found myself teaching medical students in my old emergency department. I had a contract with Nottingham University to teach and a medical registration certificate for this alone.

A golfing friend of mine called Paddy presented to our emergency department in 2009. He is a large genial fellow. He had lost an argument with some electric hedge clippers, and had suffered cut fingers. He just needed simple suturing.

There was an annoying delay in treatment, and I detected some baffling reluctance of the staff to do this suturing! Why? Paddy and I were frustrated. I explained to Paddy that despite my experience I was unlicenced, and uninsured.

Finally in desperation – heavily coerced by the patient – I quickly performed the simple suturing under a local anaesthetic, and dressed at last those bloody fingers.

"Now," I said, "you're not playing golf in the medal on Saturday, are you?"

"Oh, I've booked 7.40am to start my round," said Paddy.

Somewhat unprofessionally, I threatened Paddy with violence if I found out he was playing at the weekend. He, somewhat reluctantly, decided not to play.

Once the possibility of golfing sabotage was removed, Paddy's fingers healed well.

I thought that Paddy would be my last case.

CHAPTER FIFTY-TWO

Medicine Today

The Modern Interview for
Medical School Graduates

I have had experience of sitting on the other side of the table with two other people, selecting candidates for medical school. There had to be at least one doctor, one lay person, and often the third person is a lecturer at the university. We were first vetted and, if we passed this test, we were then given a lecture on how to conduct the interview.

"It has to be a structured interview," I was told. We were shown videos of actual interviews. All the applicants were graduates who had to have at least a 2:2. Then they had to sit and pass a long multiple choice paper. Some basic scientific knowledge, good general knowledge, and an ability to solve problems was needed. At interviews candidates are all anonymous, to be absolutely fair, so we did not know their names and addresses or see their CVs! But we did know their test score.

We were told the subjects on which we should ask questions and what we should be asking, but not on the precise wording of each question (I understand that all these questions are now on the internet and so all applicants have access to them, as previous applicants have divulged this information). So, they know what is coming. Well, some have applied before, but only once as a maximum.

Basically, we could not ask what we liked, but had to score applicants on their answers to the set questions. In particular, these applicants had been screened medically beforehand. So hopefully we would not be interviewing a schizophrenic. (Some schizophrenics are very bright, but from bitter experience I know that they are unlikely to make good doctors.)

So even if we get the feeling that somebody is not an ideal candidate, we cannot ask the questions we want to, but just score them on the standard set ones. This can be tricky, but we are told that this is in the interest of fairness. The interviewers cannot take any notice of age or sex. (Elderly people, i.e., over 60 years of age, tend not to apply.) Disabled people tend not to apply. One doctor I know well has a thalidomide-type-deformity of one arm. He is an excellent general practitioner and never considered surgery.

An ability to communicate in English is desirable but not mandatory. I have worked with two doctors who are excellent, but both had a severe stammer. Medical relatives are completely ignored – don't even mention them! Ladies who want to impress with low-cut tops and short skirts, or men in casual jeans, are not banned from entry but don't do themselves any favours.

The students are also screened for any police record. It would not be a good idea to admit anybody to medical school who was, for example, a convicted paedophile, drug pusher or violent offender. So this modern medical school interview is anonymous, repetitive, not ageist or sexist and completely ignore any medical connections. So it is narrows minded and at times boring as the panel cannot ask the questions that they want to. Although the modern interview is a lot fairer, I still think that at times we don't screen out the wrong people. Once students, these wrong people create problems and are allowed to carry on. What sort of doctors will they become?

This modern interview seems very politically correct and sterile. This is a far cry from my medical school interview 50 years and more ago. Nowadays the council of heads of medical schools and the General Medical Council acknowledge that students with a blood-borne virus (HIV, hepatitis B or C) should be allowed to study medicine, and qualify with a suitable career plan that does not pose a risk to patients! It is now easier for medical students with depressive disease and ill health to study medicine. Gays, lesbians and bisexual applicants are protected from any form of discrimination.

Incidentally, my original appointment to the hospital predated any police checks. So there I was working with unlimited access to children for 30 years at the hospital and no, repeat NO, CRB check! (CRB is an abbreviation for Criminal Records Bureau and has recently been superseded by the DBS (Disclosure & Barring Service check.) I was asked recently to help out in the crèche at my church. No CRB check – then you can't do it!

The modern interview can't be ageist. It is an offence to discriminate against anybody on the grounds of age. Recently, in 2013, the number of people aged 65 and over in work in the UK hit one million for the first time (the Office for National Statistics). Well, government ministers have advised people to retrain. Anti-age discrimination laws make it unlawful to impose age limits on students to study medicine. This prompted a 69-year-old lawyer from Market Harborough, Anthony Davis, to re-apply to retrain as a doctor. He was invited by Nottingham University to sit his entrance examination in August 2013. But even if accepted he could not qualify until he's 74 years old. His career aim was oncology. It would take at least ten years from qualifying to achieve this. Our brains all age as we get older, and the normal retirement age for doctors is 65 years. Insurance cover for doctors aged over 70 is very, very difficult. I think there was a case here for refusing this admission on the grounds of age. Common sense prevailed. A younger person benefitted. Legislation here was stretched far too far, and Mr Davis was given false hope of a second career, that was impossible to achieve.[1]

Reference:

1. Sian Griffiths. Solicitor aims to qualify as a doctor aged 74. *Sunday Times* 16.6.13;9.

Changes to the Medical School Intake

Good doctors have at least three things in common: They know how to observe, they know how to listen, and they're very tired.

Gregory D Robert, *Shantaram*, Page 206

There has been an explosion of new medical schools. There has also been an explosion in the number of medical students. If you have a medical relative, that is a disadvantage at interview. Well, at least those with medical relatives had some idea what they were letting themselves in for. (Incidentally, I would not have got into medical school by today's standards. As I had failed A-level Physics, I would have been 'passed over' at least for that year. Somebody else would have taken my place!)

We now have a lot more female medical students than male. This ratio has gradually changed over the years. Now it seems there are two or three female students to every male. Will the male doctor become extinct like the dodo? Who knows?

When I started medical school, overall in the UK there were 500 female medical students on that intake to 1,500 male medical students. The female intake subsequently leapfrogged the male intake. By 2008 there were nearly 5,000 in the female intake compared with 3,500 in the male intake.[1]

* * *

The history of female doctors in the UK officially started in the 1860s. A group of medical students (all male of course) were being quizzed by a visiting physician at a London hospital. None could answer one question and then, from behind them, a lady gave the correct answer. The male medical students petitioned for removal of this lady. This was one of her many obstacles to qualifying in medicine. But in 1865, she became the first lady doctor to officially qualify in the United Kingdom. She qualified at the Society of Apothecaries. She was told afterwards by two of the examiners that she had scored higher than all the men in the examination. She was Doctor Elizabeth Garrett Anderson.[2]

Dr Anderson was allowed to sit the examination only because the constitution allowed all medical students to do so after six years of study. (They could have been sued if they had not let her take the exam.) These men then subsequently changed the constitution, excluding any further ladies from sitting the exam. But she had passed already. Well done! She went on to marry, and have children too. So she was fulfilled in her personal and professional life. First a physician, then a wife and finally a mother of three children.

So Doctor Elizabeth Garrett Anderson is officially recorded as the first female doctor to qualify in the United Kingdom. She succeeded because of her perseverance in the face of active male discrimination against women, in a male-dominated society. The truth here, however, is stranger than fiction. Another lady did qualify in medicine before her. She used another strategy – deception!

This is recorded accurately, in detail, and illustrated by HM du Preez in the *Edinburgh College of Physicians Journal* 2012.[3]

Michael du Preez and Jeremy Dronfield have recently done research into 'James' Barry. They have published a book on her entitled, '*Dr James Barry. A Woman Ahead of her Time*'. I quote facts from their writing, with their permission.

Miss Margaret Ann Bulkley was born in Cork in 1789. The family became bankrupt, and so her father was sent to prison. Even before Margaret Bulkley became a male medical student, she was raped by her uncle and bore a child! Her mother, Mary Anne (nee Barry), sought assistance from her brother, James Barry, a London-based artist. He died in 1806, leaving money to his sister, Mary Anne, and niece, Margaret Ann. So these two ladies travelled to London 'to give Margaret an education'. Here she was tutored by Dr Edward Fryer, physician to the Duke of Sussex. She was found to have an intellect more suited to a profession than to a governess, her likely future. Several close friends of her late uncle took a keen interest in Margaret, including Lord Buchan who was well known, and well connected, in Edinburgh.

At the end of November 1809 Margaret was 'transformed into a male', taking the name of her late uncle, James Barry. 'He' travelled to Edinburgh and enrolled as a late student at the university. James was one of 900 medical students in Edinburgh – safety in numbers? James avoided 'his' fellow students and wore a surtout – an overcoat with long skirts. James also had a youthful appearance, and feared the dark. James worked hard and qualified in medicine in July 1812. (So the length of study to become a doctor was less than three years!)

She was the first ever lady to qualify in medicine in the UK, and the first to pass a difficult examination and become a member of the Royal College of Surgeons (98 years before they allowed women to sit the test!). In 1826 'he' performed the British Empire's first successful caesarean section – mother and baby survived. Dr James Barry was godfather to this child, named James Barry Munnik! So 'he' was an eminent surgeon, with a healthy temper, who rose to become Inspector General of Hospitals, a rank equivalent to Brigadier General. 'He' served with distinction in 11 different parts of the Empire. 'He' was a personal physician to the governor of the Cape colony – Lord Charles Somerset. 'He' cured him of cholera, and they 'fell in love'. Lord Charles' wife, Lady Somerset, was naturally upset by this 'homosexual affair'. Lord Charles was recalled to London urgently.

'He' was outraged by the atrocious conditions in Scutari, and then taught Florence Nightingale the fundamental need for hygiene. Dr Barry clashed with Florence Nightingale at Scutari. James Barry implemented many hygiene and sanitation measures.

'His' true sex was once uncovered when 'he' was ill with malaria in Trinidad in 1842. The two discoverers were fellow surgeons, who were then sworn to secrecy, which as gentlemen they honoured!

'He' was retired on medical grounds in 1859. James died in July 1865.

After death 'his' body was laid out by a female servant, Sophia Bishop. She discovered 'he' was female and this was confirmed by others. The truth was revealed to an astonished world, and an embarrassed Army! Had James Barry gone into the Army on purpose? Here 'he' would then avoid female patients. Well, ladies are more observant and intuitive. James had trained in medicine surrounded by men. 'He' probably felt safer in the Army still surrounded by more men. Well, it finally took a female to discover 'his' true sex![3]

So Margaret Bulkley, alias James Barry, was unofficially the first female doctor to practise in the United Kingdom. She was also the first female member of the Royal College of Surgeons and the first female general in the British Army!

* * *

Elizabeth Blackwell was another female doctor. She was born in Bristol in 1821. Her family emigrated to America. She feigned studying medicine as a ruse to put off an ardent suitor. She became interested in medicine but was turned away by many medical schools. Finally, she was accepted to train as a doctor by Geneva University in upstate New York. This school was in disarray at the time. Well, medical students were put in charge of the admissions process, and accepted Elizabeth Blackwell as a joke! She graduated top of her year in 1849 and was ostracised by society. She returned to the UK to found the London School of Medicine for Women in 1869 (now called The Royal Free Hospital). So she was the first lady doctor to officially work in the UK.

Incidentally, I am possibly the only male doctor to have the complete set of female relatives who became doctors: my mother Christina (qualified at the London School of Medicine for Women); my older sister, Janet, a GP (qualified at the Middlesex Hospital); my wife, Christine, a consultant physician and gastroenterologist (qualified at Cambridge and The London Hospital); and my daughter, Lindsay, a qualified doctor (Leeds graduate) now working in Australia. As time has passed, discrimination against female doctors by male doctors, and patients alike, has lessened.

By 2017 the majority of medical doctors in the United Kingdom will be female, as reported by the Royal College of Physicians.[1] So, do women make better doctors? This is a really contentious issue, and I am definitely not going to take sides. But the National Clinical Assessment Service (NCAS) receives and reviews complaints about all doctors, both male and female. Interestingly, over the last eight years 490 male doctors were banned from seeing patients, compared with just 79 female doctors.

Finally, medicine is one calling where women are making giant leaps. Elsewhere this is not universally recorded. It is reported that it will take women 55 years to reach equal numbers with men in the senior judiciary, and 73 years for women directors in the FTSE 100 companies.[4]

References:

1.   Elston M A, Women in Medicine. Royal College of Physicians. June 2009 and BMJ Careers 29.9.12:2.

2.   Jo Martin. *Elizabeth Garrett Anderson*. Published by C & A Black.

3.   du Preez H M. Dr James Barry (1789-1865): The Edinburgh Years. *J R Coll. Physicians Edinb.* 2012:42;258-65. http:/dx. doi. org/10 4997/JRCPE 2012. 315. c) 2012 Royal College of Physicians of Edinburgh.

4.   Sex and Power. The Equality and Human Rights Commission (2008)

Our National Health Service – Today and Yesterday

Things ain't what they used to be.

Ted Parsons song (1941)

As far as our National Health Service goes we have good news and bad news. The good news is that after over 60 years we still have an NHS. But is it free at the point of delivery? No. We pay for prescriptions and for dental treatment. Also, the bad news is that we no longer treat some conditions like varicose veins surgically, or even do breast reductions. But, good news – we can now treat obesity surgically!

The good news on training is that we are turning out a lot more doctors from more medical schools. Once the successful candidate gets to medical school there is no formal physical examination. There are no formal chest X-rays – I had both! Good news abounds in training. There are more formal lectures. There are feedback forms after teaching. All lecturers put lectures on the web and are given feedback by the students after their lecture. (Good news!) The students have books into which they record their clinical experiences and patient contacts. (Good news!) About 10% of a consultant's salary comes from the medical school in recognition of teaching. So, in theory, if a consultant refuses to teach, his salary could be cut. Audits and reviews have shown that some of the surgery that I was taught does not work, and so is not practised or taught, e.g., surgery for lymphoedema. Medical students nowadays are not normally seen out of hours. (Bad news!)

Yet more good news – the pass rate for medical students is sky high, especially for finals. As an examiner recently, I was told at the briefing prior to the exam that of the 340 students sitting medical finals only about

5% of students were expected to fail. Out of these 5% of students only 25% would fail the resit a few weeks later, because they had received help and further training. If more than that failed it reflected very badly on the medical school and all the staff. In my day it was really tough. We were failed in our droves. Nobody counselled us. We did not know why we had failed. We just got back into the library and onto the wards. We worked and worked till we passed. I got through my university finals after working an extra year. In that year I practised as a doctor, having qualified another way. Is this high pass rate good or bad news for the patient? Nowadays, are there any medical students qualifying in medicine who are unfit to practice? Only time will tell.

Medical examinations today have changed in one small respect compared with years ago. When I was a student it was forbidden for any examiner, in medical finals or higher examinations, to have any connections to a candidate when assessing their knowledge in a viva. Above all, it was very important that no examiner was related to any such candidate. Consultants went to great lengths to ensure that this was the case. Several times I saw examiners greet candidates for a viva and realise that they were connected in some way. As a frequent attender to examination halls, I then witnessed one examiner change places with another examiner from a different table. This charade guaranteed impartiality and fairness.

In 2001 I was teaching medical students prior to their final examinations. One student was called Miss Darvell. Now, I had three Scottish grandparents but only one 'English' grandparent. My grandmother's maiden name was Darvell (French originally). My student explained that her grandfather came from my grandmother's birthplace – Chorleywood, Hertfordshire. Oh dear, we were related. I therefore informed the university office that I was related to this student, and so was barred from testing her in finals. I thought that they had understood this, until I was the examiner on my own in the 'head and neck section' of the final examinations. In walked Miss Darvell. I gave her distinction – the only candidate I rewarded in this way all morning. Prior to the examiners' meeting I sought out the external assessor. I confessed to my crime and unburdened my soul! I told him of my dilemma, of how generously I had rewarded my relative! "That does not matter at all," he explained. "Besides, everybody else has given her distinction too." I was reassured. How times have changed.

NEPOTISM RULES OK

The junior doctors are in training for general practice or to become hospital specialists. Has the European Working Time Directive (EWTD) helped or hindered their progress? Well, 90% of junior doctors feel that the EWTD has resulted in reduced training.[1, 2] Fixed-shift working has been introduced. Research into this in industry showed that shift working is associated with interrupted sleep patterns, chronic tiredness and mistakes[3], so episodes of sick leave amongst juniors increased.[4] Another study showed that implementation of the EWTD resulted in few trainee surgeons being involved in operations.[5, 6]

Let's look at the practical application of this. As a direct consequence of this EWTD, it is possible to do a junior surgical job just after qualifying, and never get into theatre. What bad news this is! But today there is 24-hour haematology, biochemistry and microbiology support. So the juniors of today don't have to do their own blood tests, as I did. (I had to do the blood tests for the haemoglobin of my gynaecological emergencies on admission, and stain the cerebra-spinal fluid of my lumbar puncture patients in paediatrics, and interpret the results!)

There are record clerks employed round the clock. I spent a lot of time in 1966 trying to find the medical records of the poor patient I was about to see. I had to unlock the medical records building, and lock it up afterwards, returning said key to a central point. What a hassle! (All good news today.)

The modern junior doctor in training has annual reviews and a trainer – all good news. I had nothing like this.

Let's look at the modern training of the middle grade doctor, called a registrar. They are in post for five or more years. These posts rotate – good news. The medical or surgical registrar 40 years ago was on call for emergencies every other night. It was onerous, but the experience was valuable. Nowadays, there are more doctors in training. So we have a lot more registrars. This doctor today may be on call once a fortnight.

The whole emphasis on medical training has altered in the past 40 years. When I first qualified I had no introductory course, no tutor and no lectures for over a year. The important emphasis then was the medical work that needed to be done. That is why I was stuck in Casualty on my own as an orthopaedic pre-registration house surgeon one morning. I was dealing with desperately ill patients. I could not call anybody. I was told that the hospital cardiac arrest team did not come to Casualty. Just get on with the work! I had a lot of informal teaching. I went to lectures in the evening. These were primarily for general practitioners, but as a hospital doctor I could attend too. I had no formal feedback on my registration year. Nowadays, the emphasis is on the further training of the junior doctor, particularly during their provisional registration. How times have changed.

Oh, I was told one important fact. Never telephone a consultant unless he asks to be called. So I never, ever telephoned my boss at all for the first six months.

Similarly, the surgical registrar on call today has a better rota. However, this doctor has far less operating experience. The operating is largely left to the consultant. The registrar assists, but does not get the experience surgically of his predecessor. Out of hours operating today can't be done by a junior on his own. No, a consultant comes in and has to be there. To save time he, or she, often operates. In training, I recall often telephoning my boss to tell him what I was going to do. He just said: "Good, I am sure you can do that." I replied, "Yes, sir," and got on with it. There is little wonder that the new surgical consultant today is less experienced.

One surgeon in training recently was recommended to go to India.[7] The surgical experience was excellent. He did a lot of operating. He learnt more in the last two months in India than he did in the ten years before, working in our NHS. Another trainee had a similar experience in Colombo, Sri Lanka.[8] So today, going abroad gives greater experience in surgery than staying in the UK.

When I first qualified, and for 20 years after, Indian doctors came to the UK for experience and examinations. Will there now be a reverse trend? Well, the formation of the European Union hampered the employment of Indian doctors here. Now the European Working Time Directive might send our local trainees on a reverse 'passage to India' or Sri Lanka! After Brexit maybe EWTD will no longer apply.

The juniors today are given several jobs in a rotation, and not one stand-alone job after another as I had. Fewer doctors come from the British Commonwealth, but some arrive from the European Union. The hospital accommodation is a lot better but they are in the hospital for shorter hours. So one on-call room is used, when each of a group of doctors is in the hospital, for one night on call. Years ago as a junior doctor I was on call a lot. I had my own room as a consequence.

The junior doctors working as registrars now have annual assessments. This is largely a paper exercise. Well, if there are the correct 32 pieces of paper in the folder when it is presented, then the doctor is likely to pass. After five years or so, the doctor sits an exit examination in his specialty, and if he passes he gets his accreditation certificate. I was a junior doctor for 12 years. I never had an annual assessment! I never had a mentor, as a junior doctor or a medical student. Times have changed. (Good news.)

The net has helped today's doctors – particularly the new juniors in the emergency department. On their iPhones they can access their hospital guidelines. These are likely to mirror the national guidelines and NICE guidelines, which are also on the net. The doctor has to be careful that they follow the right guidelines, e.g., they could confuse those of Newcastle (UK) with those of Newcastle (Australia).

Most current medical textbooks are on the net. The *British National Formulary* (BNF) is there too. This is a concise pharmacopoeia with indications for medications, modes of action, dosages, alternatives, contraindications, complications and even drug interactions. Finally, the doctor can find help on the net to recognise some conditions by photographs, such as skin rashes or eye conditions.

So, the successful applicant for a consultant post today is congratulated at interview. Then later this surgical doctor is taken into a little room by one of his new colleagues. The new consultant then lists all the operations he can't do but should be able to do for that post. Yes, this is bad news indeed. So inevitably, the range of surgery performed by a specialist becomes less. But the surgeon may become a 'specialist specialist' and only do a few operations, e.g., mainly knee surgery. If he does little else but knee surgery, his results will be very good indeed. (Good news.)

The good news on specialties is that we have a lot more. For example, when I qualified as a doctor, Casualty had no proper consultant cover. This has now gone. We have modern emergency departments with emergency consultants. We also have stroke consultants, and the treatment for strokes has dramatically improved outcomes. So we have more specialist surgeons and more specialist physicians – all very good news. The bad news is that a specialist knows a lot about their specialty, but if one of their patients has something else wrong with them outside their expertise, will it be recognised and treated? (Bad news?) After all, *the definition of specialist is somebody who knows more and more about less and less.*

There has been an expansion in consultant numbers, plus an expansion in their specialties. For example, we now have ophthalmic physicians. We also have psychiatrists with an interest in deliberate self-harm, and dermatologists with an interest in minor surgery. Out of all the specialties, anaesthesia and radiology have changed the most. There are anaesthetists who give only paediatric anaesthetics, or their main duties are on the intensive care unit. Radiologists are appointed with a particular interest in ultrasound. A few specialist positions have been lost forever – thank goodness. For example, Dr Cyriax's post – no consultant in orthopaedic medicine any longer exists.

The good news is that we have many more clever investigations. This is the digital age, and it is here to stay. Radiology departments are busy. CT and MRI scans are carried out frequently at all hours of the day and night (all good news). But these scanners are not cheap; they have significant running costs, they break down occasionally, need to be upgraded and after a few years are obsolete (all bad news). There are plenty of clever blood tests. But the bad news is that the junior is tempted to reach for the form before performing an examination and taking a history properly. So, could the art of history taking, or examination, be lost forever – it is possible (bad news).

Today's modern doctor – consultant or GP – is less likely to be a maverick. After all, they are now working in groups and not alone as before (good news). There are plenty of refresher courses and lectures that we all have to go on – more good news. Some courses are interactive with, for example, simulators for resuscitation or an anastomosis workshop. Many of these courses are very expensive (bad news). The journals are more scientific, with excellent trial data. Each hospital has plenty of protocols, usually based on national guidelines, to follow, e.g., chest pain protocol – all very good news. But the bad news is that, despite all this, we are making more medical mistakes than ever (bad news). For example, the unlawful killing of David Grey in February 2008.[9] We must question therefore whether our doctors are given the necessary experience. And are they accountable for their actions?

One classic error is wrong route drug errors. The UK leads the world in preventing them.[10] The GMC has shown us how errors in prescribing can be avoided.[11] In November 2014, a report by the British Pharmaceutical Society said that at any one time 8,000 NHS hospital beds are taken up by patients suffering adverse drug reactions! (Bad news.)

Surgeons have to publish their results of surgery (good news). I know what they are worried about: will like be compared to like? For example, some orthopaedic surgeons specialise in redoing hip replacements. Their results will be poor, compared to surgeons performing the first hip replacement operation. There are cancer centres. Cancer surgeons have to work at these centres. The treatment of cancer is multidisciplinary and co-ordinated. All good news.

The patient has changed a lot over the past 50 years. The doctor is not held in such high esteem anymore – bad news. The doctor was universally adored by the Victorians – good news. But the rot started in 1910. Dr Crippen drugged and murdered his wife. He buried her in the basement. He fled to the States with his more attractive mistress. He was caught using the new wireless telegraph. A certain Dr Bodkin Adams was struck off in the 1950s as he had managed to benefit from many of his patients' wills. Finally, Dr Harold Shipman has not helped us at all. He hastened the demise of many patients with drugs. Interestingly, he had been struck off previously by the GMC for drug offences and later reinstated. (I think our present GMC is a big step forward.) So it is hardly surprising that many patients do not treat their doctor with any respect at all – what bad news.

Many patients are not registered with a GP. Working in an emergency department many patients lie about their identity. How do I know? Well, I followed up a lot of patients, largely for medical research. So often an address did not exist, or nobody of that name had lived there! Are they an illegal immigrant or did I see their face on TV – on *Crimewatch*? We each need a national identity card to be presented at the start of all GP or hospital treatment. The cost would be high, but the benefits to our society even greater. But could we do it? Well, we failed to implement an NHS computer. So we have already failed on electronic patient records, and this IT project has cost billions.[12] The patients' database is riddled with errors, we were told.[12] Another similar project on national identity cards could fail too.

Patients – How They Have Changed

The Worried Well

A classic patient does present
Apprehensive and troubled
So many tests are sent
Their fears are quickly doubled.

All tests normal, this I cry
Please do so lift your gloom
They are dissatisfied and pry
They want to meet their doom.

So frequently my phone they ring
More fractious than ever
Their relatives they bring
Abnormal tests, no never.

On normal tests they thrive
Second opinions sought
Amazed they are still alive
Ill health cannot be bought.

Two years later, more aggressive
Hysterical and odd
But their weight gain is excessive
They still can't do a job.

The NHS, what a cost
Keeping the sick alive
Some of the very ill are lost
The worried, well, they thrive.

Four out of ten patients (39%) check medical symptoms online before seeking professional help. This gives many patients (24%) more confidence when visiting a doctor. Women are more likely to go online than men, particularly when the complaint is embarrassing, or their children are involved.[13]

Once patients have a particular condition, they now can choose to go online and communicate with other patients suffering that condition. Dave de Bronkart did just that, to his immense benefit. He got facts and practical advice that to this day don't exist in any journal article or establishment website.[14]

But finally, it depends on which website they visit! Is that website giving an overview of a condition and its treatment? Or is that website biased in any way so it can be misleading?

There is far too much paperwork for the poor general practitioner. They are submerged in it. But one government initiative is very, very worrying. It has not been noticed, as yet, by the media. It goes on under the radar. It is this: some general practitioners are rewarded financially by cutting down on referrals for prescribing.[15]

This is immoral and intrusive, in my opinion, and litigation may wipe out any cost saving. This bribery of doctors could spread and spread. So, less and less work gets done, and possibly the whole NHS grinds to a halt.

The family unit of the 1950s and 1960s has gone – bad news. There is pressure on hospital beds. The general practitioner is no longer a telephone call away at midnight. So elderly patients, many with longstanding conditions, present to the emergency department. *The Times* newspaper showed that hundreds of thousands of patients are discharged from hospital between 11pm and 6am.[16] This is a sign of the times we live in. There are not enough hospital beds (bad news). There are far too many patients, particularly elderly ones (bad news again). Nursing home care for the elderly is both expensive and in high demand (bad news over and over again). But the new NHS Clinical Commissioning Group rewards 'speedy discharge' from hospitals. Life in hospitals is complicated, especially for the staff dealing with patients who need complex care. The morale of hospital staff, the patients and their families is poor.

The patient has changed and become more litigious. They are aided by wealthy medical negligence lawyers. Yes, the patient of today has high expectations. Failure to fulfil these high expectations leads to the courts. More doctors and hospitals are being sued successfully. I have discovered that, in March 2012, the NHS Litigation Authority estimated its potential liabilities for outstanding clinical negligence claims at £18.6 billion (that is one-sixth of the annual health budget!).[17] Many patients and their relatives cannot come to terms with the fact that we will all die for certain – sooner or later. It gets worse still. Many GPs and specialists are plagued by neurotic patients who have been over-investigated and display no evidence of organic disease. The worried well abound. Expectations are high. Normal investigation is followed by normal investigation. The patient gets more and more upset. Complaints abound. Well, everybody is going to die someday. That is a certainty. But patients don't want to face up to this.

In January 2013 there was a surge in complaints by patients, as recorded by the General Medical Council. This is particularly true for general practitioners and surgeons. But few doctors have been suspended, perhaps due to the emerging complaints culture.[18] Money is wasted on the NHS in many ways. The Private Finance Initiatives are a prime example. Clinical negligence is another.

It gets worse and worse because any change in the running of our NHS is mega expensive. I have seen change after change in the past 50 years – all under the banner of efficiency. As I write, the Conservatives are 'tinkering' with our sacred NHS. Will more privatisation follow in one form or another? Poor Nye Bevan must be turning in his grave.

One NHS hospital has already gone private – for a while – Hinchinbrooke. I am not alone in thinking that the proposed changes to our NHS are not reforms. They are hailed as efficient, competitive and directly benefitting the patient. I call them expensive, introducing privatisation. So, big business will gain financially. They will keep any profits. We will no longer have a National Health Service as such. It will soon become a Privatised Health Service. Bad news over and over again. One small point – confidentiality. This is governed by English Common Law of Confidentiality, Article 8 of the Human Rights Act (1998), Data Protection Act (1998), NHS Confidentiality Code of Conduct and the Caldicott principles. But one private company that is heavily involved in running hospitals has the notes and letters typed in the Philippines!

Changes to the NHS in England are providing private companies with business opportunities worth £20 billion. Well, that would pay for a lot more staff.[19] Bad news maybe, but Circles Health has improved

Hinchinbrooke Hospital in less than six months. It is cleaner, and now meeting targets for waiting times and cancer. How did they do it? Well, a tier of management was sacked. More complaints were listened to. More clinicians run the hospital. Operating theatres are now efficient and Unison is happy. Things have gone full circle, as this is how hospitals were run 40 years ago.[20]

Unfortunately, this was short-lived. Circles Health still runs services at three hospitals in the UK, but is about to be taken over (April 2017).

But the modern doctor has better treatments than ever before. Good news abounds over and over again. The doctor has better equipment,e.g., disposable plastic syringes and needles that won't break. Our doctor has better drugs that have been evaluated properly. All significant adverse drug reactions are recorded as originally outlined in the Dunlop report. The thalidomide disaster was a catalyst for this. Drug and treatment advice abounds from many sources – the Royal Colleges, the Audit Commission and the National Institution for Clinical Excellence. This is all very good news indeed. But why do we still make mistakes? Hence the litigation. We, the taxpayer, foot the bill for these mistakes. Most doctors are now medically insured so his/her medical insurance could pay for each mistake.

A consultant post in the NHS today is time and time again a job for life. But in the Cleveland Clinic in Ohio, impressive outcomes are published annually for all 'major disease areas'. All the doctors are on a one-year contract. Any failing doctor is sacked pronto. Our NHS could learn from this.

One of the most fascinating things about medicine is that it is always changing. Even in my own lifetime I have seen changes galore. Here are a few of the many milestones:

1948   5th July. The birth of the British National Health Service. Everybody is eligible, and services were provided free at the point of use.

1953   Seldinger described his technique – still the basis for modern vascular intervention. So the arterial tree can be explored safely, usually through the groin. This can be life saving; for example, to unblock coronary arteries. Similarly, bleeding cerebral aneurysms are cured by this approach.

1954 Harold Hopkins described the fibre optic bundle that makes up our flexible endoscopes. So our entire gastrointestinal tract can be viewed. So diagnosis, and often treatment, can be carried out without surgical intervention.

1958 Vaccination for diphtheria and polio was introduced for all children. A dramatic reduction in both diseases followed.

1959 Sir John Charnley gave a lecture on hip replacements. Two years later, he published the first results. Now this operation is commonplace. The elderly population of our nation is more mobile – many on new hips or knees.

1960 First very successful kidney transplant in the UK in Edinburgh (from an identical twin).

1960s Godfrey Housfield, and independently Allan McLeod Cormack, described the theoretical basis for computerised tomography. CT was in place by 1971 and whole body scanning by 1975. A non-invasive investigation, but it involves some radiation to the patient. The management of many conditions has been revolutionised as a result – for example, head injuries.

1968 Britain's first heart transplant in London.

1973 First Magnetic Resonance Imaging, invented by Sir Peter Mansfield and published by Paul Lauterbur. This test shows soft tissue well and involves no radiation. This test allows the doctor to see many more conditions without intervention, e.g., a ruptured vertebral, or meniscal (knee), disc.

1975 Kohler and Milstein published work on monoclonal antibodies. Many new clever diagnostic blood tests are based on this work.

1978   World's first test tube baby born, Louise Brown.

1979   First bone marrow transplant at Great Ormond Street Hospital.

1986   World's first liver, lung and heart transplant at Papworth Hospital.

1988   Robotic surgery begins – prostate surgery (Guy's and St Thomas').
21, 22, 23

Many of these inventors are non-medical. They have a scientific background usually. Some have made multiple inventions. Some inventions have been superseded by others more recently. A few inventors benefitted from their own inventions, like Mr Ridley in Chapter Four.

Sir Hiram Maxim, for example, invented the machine gun that fired 666 rounds per minute. He also suffered from bronchitis in the poor London air of late Victorian times. He then invented (and benefitted from) an inhaler, that was efficient. Many other sufferers were treated with his inhaler, which he made freely available. But he wrote in his autobiography: 'It is a very credible thing to invent a killing machine, and nothing less than a disgrace to invent an apparatus to prevent human suffering.' Modern inhalers have superseded this one.

This strange bizarre coincidence, that several doctors have personally benefitted from their own inventions, continues to this present day. Professor Alan Mackay-Sim was director of the Australian National Centre for Adult Stem Cell Research for a decade. He was named Australian of the Year by their premier Malcolm Turnbull in 2017. But this professor was recently diagnosed with multiple myeloma, a form of leukaemia. He himself has benefitted greatly from a stem cell transplant!

Not everybody benefitted from their own inventive genius, as occasionally it was ignored. Mr Hamilton Bailey was such an individual. When I was studying surgery his textbooks were compulsory reading. If you could quote Mr Hamilton Bailey accurately in a viva then you would pass. Unfortunately, in retirement, the great man developed an abdominal condition. And yet his treating doctors had not read Mr Hamilton Bailey's own textbook! If they had then their eminent patient's fatal complications would have been avoided.[24]

A few medics made inventions outside medicine. Sir Harold Gillies was a keen golfer. He invented a new driver with a huge head. This super club enabled him to outdrive all his fellow competitors. Then the Rules Committee of the Royal and Ancient Golf Club of St Andrews outlawed this club. This stipulated the dimensions of a golf club head, and can be found in the preface to the rules to this day. So Sir Harold was thwarted.[25]

Endoscopy is a prime example of how medicine has progressed over my lifetime. Modern endoscopies are flexible and have better and better fibre optics, thanks to Harold Hopkins. Perforation of the patient at either end is a rarity. Endoscopy is used for diagnosis and in some cases for treatment. For example, if a patient has a haematemesis from oesophageal varices, then this can be treated through the endoscope with a rubber band. Thank goodness that maverick treatment of stypven and adrenaline has been stopped. (Well, it did work.) At the lower end, some polyps can be snipped off through an endoscope. There is a chance that otherwise they could become malignant.

My golfing partner from medical school, Peter, went to Japan in the 1960s to learn endoscopy. After a spell as a consultant at the Middlesex Hospital he was lured to the States. Professor P B Cotton, MD, FRCP, FRCS is Director, Digestive Disease Center, Medical University of South Carolina, Charleston, South Carolina, USA. He has lectured worldwide and written so many textbooks – quite a colossus in gastroenterology. My old teacher, Mr 'Pasty' Barratt, has not been forgotten even today. No: the eponymous terms of Barratt's oesophagus, and Barratt's ulcers, are still quoted in medical practice today.

Nowadays new drugs abound. Of the myriad of new drugs today my favourite is the statin. Well, it reduces cholesterol and has dramatically reduced the incidence of coronary thrombosis. (It has helped my cholesterol too!) Some drugs have been banned, with a few exceptions! One of my favourites was – butazolidin. It was banned for prescribing to humans as rarely it caused a blood abnormality. Well, one group can prescribe it still – veterinary surgeons happily do so. Every day new drugs are coming in and are repeatedly carefully evaluated. So, such drugs for multiple sclerosis, the alcoholic and malaria are on the way.

There are many more milestones; these are but a few.

So, there are new treatments not even dreamt of at the conception of our NHS. Indeed, in his maiden speech in 1948, Mr Bevan told us all that as disease is cured by the new NHS, then hospitals would all become less and less busy. Well, as we all know, politicians can get it wrong! Today new treatments abound – joint replacement, microsurgery and thrombolysis. So more and more conditions are treated successfully. I was so fortunate back in 1970 to work with Bob Acland. He was interested in microsurgery in the UK. He has operations, techniques and instruments named after himself. A real pioneer. Similarly, Sir Harold Gillies, whom I met as a student, is called the father of plastic surgery. Even today, operations are performed and instruments are used that he invented. Sir Harold even suggested something unheard of: "Why don't anaesthetists give the anaesthetic gas into the windpipe via a tube?" Initially greeted with incredulity, but now, like microsurgery it is practised widely throughout the world. This is all very good news. The bad news is that we still can't cure some conditions, e.g., Crohn's disease. Also, our hospital and GP surgeries are busier than ever – bad news! All the children I treated with leukaemia died. Now the prognosis is so much better. Good news again.

Will cloning and new vaccines open up the floodgates for more conditions to be treated which have been hitherto untreatable?

The different conditions that patients present with have changed. The news is partly good and partly bad. Well, some conditions that I saw as a junior doctor are far less common; for example, the infection erysipelas and acute osteomyelitis. Other conditions, like leukaemia or rheumatoid arthritis, have not changed in frequency. However, thanks to modern treatment, the prognosis in both these conditions is a lot better – good news indeed. Some conditions have become a lot more common in the last 20 years or so. These include malignant melanoma (from sunbathing) and chronic obstructive pulmonary disease (from possibly smoking, but many patients have never smoked!). A few conditions that were previously almost unheard of present more often today in the UK. The classic example is malaria – yes, air travel has shrunk the globe. (Even celebrities are not immune.)

Taken overall, psychiatric disorders are far more common today, especially depression. Modern treatments tend to help but not cure depression. I recall diagnosing anorexia nervosa on a patient of my mother's when I sat in as a student at one of her surgeries. My mother had been a GP for over 30 years. This was her first patient with this condition.

She had never heard of it! Anorexia is commoner today. Mental health problems abound today – all bad news.

Not only have the doctors, patients and treatments changed – so have all the nurses. When I trained as a student we feared the ward sisters. They ruled the ward. The consultant dared not venture onto her ward without her permission (bad news). But once on her ward an experienced nurse HAD to go and help the consultant (good news). The Salmon Report (1966) changed all this – bad news. Nowadays, nurses have become specialised, and treat patients – advanced nurse practitioners, stroke nurses, for example – good news. Today, cleaners clean the wards, and not nurses. Infection rates are unacceptable – bad news.

Nurses used to be involved in the cleaning of the wards. Sister inspected their cleaning – she was so strict! Would we have today's infection rate if the old-time sister was in charge? But the nurses today are doing treatments and diagnosing, especially in the emergency department. The nursing is left to the health care assistants.[26] Oh, bring back the old sisters and the battleaxe matrons and scrap Salmon. Nurses in the 1960s just did nursing, and kept the ward, and theatres, clean. These nurses were disciplined by sister. They had no time off at Christmas, wore no make-up, their long hair was pinned up and the only jewellery allowed was a wedding ring. The student nurse had to ask matron's permission to get married! How times have changed!

Today the ambulance personnel are better trained. Their training and equipment have improved. They have lifts, hoists and pat slides. So they don't suffer with bad backs as previously (good news). They can resuscitate, give drugs and even defibrillate – all good news. So, the Derby Accident Flying Squad is obsolete, as ambulance personnel have taken over – good news. However, they occasionally spend too long trying to resuscitate at the scene – Princess Diana was a classic example (bad news). So sometimes the old fashioned 'scoop and run' to the hospital is called for. This is confirmed, as analysis of data from 19,000 patients presenting to a level one trauma centre revealed increased mortality if the scene time was greater than 20 minutes in cases of penetrating trauma.[27]

Finally, let's carefully look at the doctors themselves. More and more are female. The white coat has gone – bad news. So has the waistcoat for men. Men now have open-necked shirts and no tie, apart from bow ties.

Sleeves are bare to the elbow. I have even seen a paediatrician wearing jeans and running a clinic – bad news. The watch can't be worn on the wrist. Does the doctor smile? Does the doctor greet his patient? Or are they conceited? Do they go around with their nose in the air thinking, *Oh, aren't I important?* I think this matters – many doctors don't smile or greet their patients.

What about the morale of all the hospital staff. Oh dear, it's low – bad news. We have targets that are difficult to achieve, and at times downright impossible. They may be good news for the patient, but can be bad for the morale of the doctors. Productivity is everything. Billions have been spent on our NHS (good news). Well, a percentage of the income tax that we all pay goes back in turn to pay for the NHS itself. The National Audit Office showed that productivity has fallen (17.12.10), and this was confirmed in the *BMJ*[28] – what bad news! Productivity in the NHS fell nearly 14% in ten years. How unexpected! The national press, politicians and administrators are all at a loss to explain this. But I have answers.[28] These are, on balance, all bad news.

Bad news – The Reasons

Reason 1

Multiplicity of consultants. For example, 17 consultants struggle to run one emergency department in 2017. But I ran it alone in 1979. Do these 17 actually do 17 times the work I did?

Reason 2

Shorter working week. As a direct consequence of the French lorry drivers, we are all stuck in a 48-hour week (EWTD). How logical is that? So much less work gets done. The patient does not get continuity of care (mistakes?).

Reason 3

The consultant is too often not there. The consultant goes on holiday, has meetings or mandatory study leave – all lists and clinics are cancelled. We used to do tons of operating whilst the boss was away. It was our list. Now the juniors watch TV whilst the consultant takes his holiday. (I recall that in the good old days in the early 1970s we got all those difficult cases off a certain consultant's list!) Oh, surely not, I hear the reader cry. The consultant is primarily a doctor and his main function, whatever specialty he works in, is to see patients and treat patients properly. Nothing at all should interfere with the work of this highly trained and expensive individual, but a lot does:

"You can't work normally today."

"Why?"

"Oh, mandatory training."

"What does this mean?" – Read on:

- Appraisal sessions – I appraised junior doctors and was appraised myself by another consultant.
- Multidisciplinary meetings with radiology, biochemistry, orthopaedic, haematology, etc., etc., etc.
- Clinical governance meetings. I was lead for the emergency department in clinical governance for years and attended meetings, including infection control, regularly.
- I was expected to do audits for my appraisal meetings.
- We had to attend the fire awareness meeting.
- Courses on conflict resolution.
- Courses on equality and diversity.
- How to conduct an interview meeting – all these meetings were absolutely mandatory, often irrelevant and universally boring (core corporate training!).

For well over ten years I was lead for:

- Training medical students in the department. So, plenty of formal and informal training of students. Then I attended a trainers' course for teaching.

Oh yes, there was local and…

- Regional medical student training meetings.
- Trainers' meetings for those training registrars, i.e., me.
- I was the only consultant for over ten years at the local medical committee liaising with general practitioners.
- Initially, in the 1980s' I was chairman or vice chairman of my division (Casualty, ENT, Ophthalmology and Maxillo-facial surgery).
- I was later chairman of the Medical Advisory Group, giving advice to Southern Derbyshire Health Authority. This took a lot organising with agenda meetings.
- I went to plenty of meetings in my own time – lunchtime or evening. These included trainers' meetings for the Vocational Training Programme (General Practice) or…
- Medical Executive or…
- Medical Advisory Committee.
- Failure to attend was a serious sin. Oh yes, there were shortlisting meetings and appointment committees for…
- Junior and…
- Senior doctors.
- It went on and on and on. Theatre users' meeting.
- Examinations for training nurse practitioners to work in A&E.
- Department meetings.
- Trauma meetings.
- Mortality meetings.
- Major disaster planning meetings.
- Accident Flying Squad meetings.
- Department annual review meetings.
- Lectures for introducing courses for new doctors and lectures for medical students.
- Meetings about complaints – locally and nationally.
- Consultant training meetings, etc., etc., etc.

Reason 4

A new consultant is appointed. That should be good news, but… Now the

money is tight, what can we do? Oh, let's save money. We will give that doctor no middle grade cover and a secretary on the YTS from the pool. This penny pinching is an unmitigated disaster. It leads to overwork for the consultant, who has to check everything. There are mistakes made. The intelligent, thoughtful secretary who co-ordinated the work of her consultant for a pittance has been lost forever. More is the pity.

Reason 5

The use of hospital surgical beds is abused. For example:

- The patient arrived starved four hours ago – good news.
- The patient is fit for the general anaesthetic – good news.
- The surgeon and his staff and all the nurses are here – good news.
- The theatre is empty and booked – good news.
- The anaesthetist is ready and keen to go – good news.
- All the hospital notes are here – good news. Consent signed, tick.
- No more tests need to be done. They are here – good news.

Well, that's everything is it not?

No, one small point:

A drunk with a head injury was admitted to our patient's bed at 5am today.

So, no bed – send the patient home! Goodbye. We will send for you again.

This bad news scenario is not rare. It is very, very common!

Well, tens of thousands of patients had operations cancelled in 2013. This is the highest total for a decade.[29] This is a direct result of fewer beds for our population compared to other 'developed' countries.

So, there are not enough beds for so-called emergencies and they block everybody else! What a farce! This also explains why 400 patients are kicked out of hospital beds every night.[30]

Reason 6

The morale of doctors needs to be improved.

Morale is low for many reasons. When I was first a consultant, the doctors ran the hospital. We had evening meetings (Medical Advisory Committee Meetings). Practically all the consultants went. We argued and thrashed out problems. These could be disagreements about consultant expansion, or which new equipment to buy, or arguments over beds, etc. These were serious discussions and money was tight. The chairman always held a vote at the end. So we ran the hospital. Today, hospital administrators run any hospital.

The planning of acute medical services has also been taken out of medical control by the experts – professional planners, politicians and hospital administrators. Take an example of the chaos that follows: In April 2012 University Hospital Lewisham (UHL) opened a newly refurbished emergency department (with suitable hospital acute services on site). Within six months there was a draft proposal for the closure of all this from our 'government administrators'.[31]

It continues to this day. NHS watchdogs covered up their failure to investigate baby deaths.[32]

The medical influence is slight and often completely ignored. One of the last large medical meetings I attended was a discussion about a new hospital. A PFI, of course. The vote in favour was astounding – practically unanimous. Only one fool had the temerity to vote against. He was soundly ridiculed as he left, by a senior colleague who was so much better informed. This fool now pens this paper. The current hospital administrators are trying to re-negotiate the PFI – as it's too expensive.

But this PFI – it's just a finance problem, is it not? Clinical care won't be affected. Oh no: 'Lives at risk as hospitals run into cash crisis.'[33] This was in part because these hospitals have a greater exposure to the private finance initiative. It gets worse. 'Soaring costs of PFI put scores of trust jobs at risk.'[34]

I believe that the financial mess the health service is in can be blamed on the politicians and hospital administrators. The very expensive PFIs are partly to blame. The NHS computer fiasco is another financial disaster. The database was axed, but we, the poor taxpayers, face a further bill of £2 billion. What for? A white elephant.[35] Yes, working in the casualty/emergency department for over 30 years, we treated droves of patients in transit from all over the United Kingdom. Access to health service records would have been of direct benefit to us and the patient alike. Bad news

Fig 77 –Me as Father Christmas with sister on my ward in 1965.

and yet more bad news. The hospital administrators are paid bonuses and golden handshakes. Good news for them, but very bad news for us taxpayers.

But good news, surely, that all those PFI projects must pay plenty of money in tax. Not likely! Recently, a European Services Strategy Unit published a report stating that more than 270 PFI projects, many in the NHS, were based offshore, so avoiding millions in tax. What a disgrace![36]

When I first qualified, I looked after the doctors' bar. Now, our local hospital is alcohol free (Well, apart from my locker). Where have all those mess parties gone? The Christmas Revue. All those cocktail parties, and dinners for doctors, nurses and staff – bad news. Well, many of the junior doctors lived full-time in the hospital. We were so frequently on call. Weekends did not begin till Saturday lunchtime. Saturday morning was part of the working week – everybody in the hospital was at work. Not so today – bad news. Today the weekend starts at 5pm Friday.

Hospital work was the life for many doctors. They hardly left the place. But there was plenty going on socially. Take Christmas, for example. During my first Christmas in hospital I had to be Father Christmas – sister told me so! I wore my red kilt under my red coat (fig. 77). I gave each patient a present and each nurse a kiss (well, not the male nurses). I carved the turkey. All doctors' immediate relatives came in for an extended party and lunch with patients.

A prominent urologist has only just left the council of the Royal College of Surgeons of England. This present-day pillar of society and sobriety was once a junior doctor, of course. One Christmas, just before a large gathering of hospital staff at the London Hospital, he had a chat with

Fig 78 – A Burns Night at the hospital. Such events are now rare, more is the pity.

Fig 79 – Me dancing with my wife at a Burns Night.

matron. He persuaded this senior figure to swap clothes with him (well just the outer garments). So he appeared in a uniform as matron. She was a junior doctor. What fun. What high jinks. Yes, the hospital social life today is sterile. Oh, how boring.

The doctors met and discussed patients (and gossip) in the doctors' dining room. This networking was good news. We felt we were a united team all pulling together. The dining room was labelled elitist and has gone. So has unity. Medicine used to be fun for the patients and the doctor – never at the patient's expense (figs 78 and 79). In the 19th century, the Harveian Society of Edinburgh regularly awarded the degree of Doctor Hilaritatis (doctor of mirth).[37]

We have lost all this fun. Jokes are out. Such a shame, as they relaxed the patient and doctor alike. Occasionally, jokes escape even today... Professor Greenhalgh is a fair-haired lady. Whilst lecturing at an international conference abroad she was told, "All lecturers are required to be made up." So she was. On getting home her children explained it all to her. Why did the blonde have foundation on her forehead? To make up her mind![38]

The consultant of today is stereotyped in manner and dress. The eccentrics of yesteryear are gone, but not forgotten.

The endless tedium of mandatory committees discussing irrelevant topics of no benefit to you or your patients was once livened up. A loquacious Scottish surgeon who loved arguments had, for the first time in living memory, lost one. The winner was matron of the Children's Hospital and he was outvoted. In retaliation for his defeat he shouted, "Well, put up your fists, madam, we will sort this out for good in the car park!" Chaos ensued. The poor lady chairperson eventually restored order. Well what on earth was this about? Quite simply, the Scotsman had started this pantomime as a ruse – a simple ploy in the hope that the original discussion would be eventually forgotten. Amazingly, it was not, and he had to admit that we all thought he was wrong. The issue was very minor.

Eccentricity in manner and dress abounded, and no more so than in psychiatry or close specialties. One neurosurgeon always wore a striped blazer when he was in a rather manic mood. One physician with an interest in mental problems of the elderly was well dressed in a white shirt. He was much loved by all his patients. But we all could see the black bra he wore underneath his shirt.

Finally, a psychiatrist called me in one night to certify a patient. This is largely a matter of common sense. Such patients are not under the influence of drink or drugs, but are not responsible for their own actions and can be a danger to themselves. I was met by a very tall man, with black hair down to his shoulders. He wore a large black coat, unbuttoned at the front. His black boots protruded from under the coat, and he strode around with huge steps. He had a loud Irish voice, and was paranoid on questioning. Had this patient just escaped from playing Captain Hook in Peter Pan? No, this was the psychiatrist! (The patient was a lot more disturbed – poor chap!)

Dr Asher was a consultant physician with an interest in mental health at the Central Middlesex Hospital, Park Royal. He was well known for his eccentricity, and high intelligence. One day he was about to lecture to some medical students. He appeared clutching some papers. He then asked one student for some help. He explained that he did not understand a form. Could the student please fill it in for him? He then handed the startled medical student his tax return form and all the relevant information. The lecture followed.[39]

We now have a lot more medical staff. We don't know each other and all rush to get home. There has been an explosion in consultant numbers. This expansion cannot be sustained. But more and more students are qualifying as doctors. Medical unemployment beckons for many of them, unless they go abroad.

The government changes to the NHS in England came into force on 1st April 2013. 'They will result in creeping privatisation and destroy the public service "ethos".'[40] What a clever move. Put the general practitioners in charge of the funding locally of the NHS – then underfund them, and blame them when it does not work!

Have I any thoughts on the current crisis in the emergency department all over the UK? Headlines abound: 'A&E staff can't cope'; 'The A&E wait is too long'; 'Bank holiday chaos in Emergency Department'; 'The emergency wait is too long'; 'Minor A&E department to close'; 'Doctors dismiss blame for A&E crisis'.

Quite simply, at nights and weekends these hospital staff are exhausted. The patients and the relatives wait hours. It's the same, daily, all over the

UK. There are no hospital beds either. Thirty years ago, this was not a problem of this size. What has happened?

The answer is that there are a large number of patients that are a core of the chronically ill, or very old, and often both. They have had a lot of investigations, and often previous admissions. Most can't cope normally at home. Many are on multiple medications and are within a short time of dying.

So the junior, relatively inexperienced, emergency doctor is presented out of hours with a variety of these clinical problems that are rarely new, but often difficult to treat. The mere fact that each of these patients is still alive today to my mind is a triumph of medical treatment. We doctors are the victims of our own success. Are we to blame? Yes, say the politicians and the media. Well, it's easy to shift the blame onto someone else.

As stated, many of these patients can't cope at home. The GP who knows the patient well is not around, and community beds are scarce. The new GP contract stopped the GP being on call for his or her patients at night. Many times I have seen these patients admitted to a medical ward for urgent investigation and treatment. A week or two later they are discharged on treatment. The relatives are still unhappy, so they take their relative straight round to the emergency department. The whole episode starts all over again.

I recall another complaint from a relative that a patient was 86 years old, so must be the oldest patient in the department and must be seen first. This relative was surprised to hear that 17, yes 17, patients were older who were waiting that day! Two men were well over 90 years.

Targeting this core group of chronic patients for intensive treatment has been successful in the States. Also, denying more very old, demented patients urgent hospital referrals could be the kindest thing for them. This is in place for a few patients already. More urgent slots in specialist medical outpatients is a possibility. Without a concerted effort, and more long-term beds for the elderly, this 'problem' that had to be dumped on emergency departments everywhere will only get worse and worse. It won't go away. Actions speak louder than words. True emergencies, like heart attacks, broken legs and pneumonias, have to wait, whilst chronic problems with alcoholism, old age and mental health – all of some considerable duration – hijack the doctor's time. "Yes," say the relatives, "this emergency is acute." "What rubbish," I say to myself.

But what can we do about the walking wounded patient presenting to the emergency department all round the clock buoyed by a huge sense of entitlement? Many patients attending A&E are not true emergencies. When the Kegworth plane crash happened, the entire waiting room was told of the imminent influx of real emergency cases from the crash site. The patients there all got up and left. So how urgent were they?

But many of these people are (as my transatlantic cousins would say) freeloaders, i.e., never worked and never will work. Absorbed by their mental state, drug addiction and self-helplessness their condition seems acute after waiting two hours. Some sane responsible person should give them on arrival an appointment within 48 hours with their GP. Some patients are frequent attenders at least once a week and others refuse to register with a GP. Perhaps we should have general practitioners doing triage in the emergency department round the clock? But many general practitioners are in short supply and busy. The abuse of the emergency department by the non-urgent and those with chronic conditions must end. The floodgates are open wide for all and sundry. This modern culture of ours, which demands 24-hour petrol, 24-hour shopping and 24-hour television, is also seemingly demanding 24-hour medicine. This government wants to open the floodgates even wider. So, to appease the electorate, and to lighten the burden on emergency departments, the Conservatives recently introduced Saturday morning hospital clinics and told the receptionists, nurses and doctors to run them. Unfortunately, droves of patients failed to attend. As a direct consequence, the cost of the NHS for non-attenders has swelled to nearly £1 billion annually. Yes, we the taxpayer, pay again and again. And the Conservative manifesto prior to the party's victorious 2015 General Election campaign pledged 24/7 healthcare by 2020. Well, politicians are pandering to the electorate – they always do. It's their job! If 1) the elderly were targeted and 2) the abusers thrown out, then the emergency doctors and nurses could get on with their real emergency patients. About time too, as the stress in the job is sky high. Watch out for a meltdown of all staff involved. Current government initiatives can only make it worse.

I would be happy to help, but I refuse to work for nothing. This government is obsessed with spending millions of our taxpayers' money expanding this service – a recipe for disaster, to be sure. This emergency service in the 21st century needs to be tailored and streamlined for the true acute emergency patient. Them, and them alone. Jeremy Hunt, our Health Secretary, appears to have the right aims (good news). Good luck to him.

I have worked night shifts as a consultant, following straight on from my day shift. Some recent research from Sheffield showed that an emergency consultant on the shop floor at night was beneficial. Patient outcomes of a consultant night shift were compared to those of a middle grade night shift. Although the consultant night shifts on average were a little busier the median, waiting time was less, and fewer patients were admitted. There was no difference in the reattending patients within the following week.[41]

So a senior presence on the shop floor of an emergency department through the night is beneficial. But with respect, we need to keep inappropriate attenders away from an emergency department. Triage nurses nowadays do not have enough clout to send inappropriate attenders away. As a senior doctor I would send away such patients by the score. For example, "I've been limping for over a month now." (Go to GP.) "I've lost my tampon – is it inside?" (Go to GP.) "My piles ache." (Go to GP.) "I've come now as my outpatient appointment was last week." (Reappointment made.) "Am I allergic to my cat?" (Go to GP.)" I've nowhere to sleep." (Go to local hostel)." I can't go home, my husband threatens to hit me." (Go to police.) Etc., etc. I have seen all these complaints and lots of others that I would discharge with advice, e.g., "I can't sleep, my willy won't work and I can't get on with my GP – although I see him/her at least once a week with different complaints!"

The facts written in this chapter reflect the current state of our health service. I believe that we could do better. So please read on!

References:

1. C R Chalmers et al. The Lost Generation: The impact of the 56 hour EWTD on current surgical training. *Ann CollSurgEngl* 2010:92;102.
2. P J Wraighte et al. The impact of European Working Time Regulations on Orthopaedic trainee Operative Experience and *Ann R CollSurgEngl (Suppl).* 2012;94:156-158. A Consensus statement. London ASGBI:2008.
3. *Coll SurgEngl* 2009:7;225.

4. McIntyre H F, Winfield S, Te H S, Crook D. Implementation of the European Working Time Directive in an NHS Trust. Impact on patient care and junior doctor welfare. *Clin Med* 2010:10;134-7.

5. The impact of the European Working Time Regulations on orthopaedic trainee operative experience. *Ann R CollSurgEngl (Suppl)* 2012:94;156-58.

6. P J Wraighte et al. More trainees and less operative exposure: A quantitive analysis of training opportunities for junior surgical trainees. E C Toll and C R Davis. *Ann R CollSurgEngl (Suppl)* 2010:92;170-73.

7. Peter Davis. Could a passage to India be the way to get more surgical experience? *BMJ* 13.10.12:345:18&345;e6637.

8. D J Pournaras et al. Colombo-Taunton Surgical Trainee Exchange Programme. *Ann R CollSurgEngl (Suppl)* 2009:91;140-141.

9. *BMJ* 2010:341;c6814.

10. *BMJ* 2012:344;e3826.

11. Mistakes Happen. *GMC Today*. Nov, Dec 2009:8-9.

12. Dominic Kennedy, Chris Smyth, Laura Pitel. Exclusive NHS Computer Fiasco still costing billions. *The Times* 8.12.11:1.

13. David Rose. Patients database 'riddled with errors'. *The Times*. 19.3.10:20.

14. Boots Webb MD.com. Patients go online to spare embarrassment. A collaboration between Boots and the online health site Web MD. *The Times* 10.4.13:15.

15. Dave de Bronkart. How the ePatient community helped save my life. *BMJ* 13.4.13:346;24-25.

16. Caroline White. Giving GPs cash to cut referrals is unjustifiable, says BMA. *BMJ* 2012:345;e6445.

17. Chris Smyth. The Times 13. 4. 12:3. Lansley pledges action on NHS scandal. We didn't know about patients thrown out at night.

18. Julie Henry. Blame Game. Bleeding NHS dry. *Sunday Telegraph* 9.9.12:18.

19. Casebook www.medicalprotection. org. uk. casebook-january2013/ complaints-culture.

20. Private firms are told that NHS in England is open for £20bn worth of business. *BMJ* 2012:345;e6305

21. Private treatment is curing a sick hospital. *The Times* 16.8.12:23.

22. Camilla Cavendish. *Royal CollSurgEngl (Suppl)* Derek Anderson. 2011:93;158-160.

23. Matthew Whitaker. *R CollSurgEngl (bulletin)* Sport and Surgery 1948-12122012:No6. 94;204-205.

24. Derek Anderson. *Royal CollSurg (Suppl)* 2011:93;158-60.

25. Adrian Marston. Mr Hamilton Bailey: *Bulletin R C of S.* July 2012:94;238-239.

26. Personal communication from Sir Harold (1956).

27. Chris Smyth. Army of NHS carers a 'disaster in waiting'. Nursing leader demands tighter regulations. *The Times* 27.9.11:1.

28. Ref:Ann. Emerg Med 2013;61:167-74.

29. Zosia Kmietowicz. *BMJ* 6.3.10. NHS has seen little benefit from reforms in market forces.

30. Stephen Adams. Billions spent on extra NHS wages but productivity falls. *Daily Telegraph.* 17.12.10:1.

31. C Ejimofo. We love Lewisham Hospital. *Emergency Medical Journal.* June 2013; 1-2.

32. Frances Gibb and Chris Smyth. NHS Scandal Watchdogs 'should face prosecution'. *The Times* 20.6.13;1.

33. Martin Barrow and Chris Smyth. Lives at risk as hospitals run into cash crisis. The Times 13.10.11:1.

34. *BMA News.* December 2011.

35. Kathryn Cooper and Jon Ungoed-Thomas. NHS finance firms avoid millions in tax. Sunday Times 2.9.12:12.

36. Doctor Hilaritus BMJ 31.7.10:341;256.

37. Trisha Greenhalgh. All made up. *BMJ* 2010:340;158.

38. Personal communication from my late father Dr W Fraser-Moodie FDS RCS, also a consultant at the Central Middlesex Hospital.

39. David Hunter. Will 1st April mark the end of the NHS? BMJ Editorial 30.3.13:346;14-15.

40. E Christmas et al. The Impact of 24 hour consultant shop floor presence on Emergency Department performance: A Natural Experiment. *EMJ.* May 2013;30:360.

CHAPTER FIFTY-THREE

Today – Our National Health Service – The Cost

Lord Hunt

Money is the most important thing in the world.
George Bernard Shaw, *The Irrational Know*

W e hear many grumbles about our National Health Service. "It's too expensive" is a common complaint. Lord Hunt of King's Heath is Shadow Deputy Leader of Lords and an expert on our NHS. He wrote to *The Times* on 30th December 2017 and I quote 'The NHS has been remarkably resilient in the face of the population increase of more than 7 per cent since 2003 and an ageing population. The average annual real terms funding increase over the last parliament was less than 1 per cent compared to a historic average of 4 per cent since the birth of the NHS in 1948.

A recent analysis shows that 24 countries spend more on health care as a share of GPD than we do. Not surprisingly, we have per capita fewer doctors, nurses, hospital beds and access to sophisticated medical equipment than any comparable country.'

This is a robust, informed response to any criticism of our NHS on financial grounds. But there is plenty of room for improvement in our

NHS. In a report in *the Lancet* in May 2017 health service data from 192 countries was compared. The UK came 30, mainly because of poor outcomes in cancer care. Please read on.

TODAY – OUR NATIONAL HEALTH SERVICE – THE PRODUCTIVITY
Lord Carter

I have recently read Lord Carter's ideas on how to make the NHS more efficient. It is called 'Operational Productivity and Performance in English NHS acute hospitals.'

This is an excellent top-down, trouble-shooting review that is wide-ranging and interesting. Each topic that is covered is looked at under four headings – greater central grip, greater transparency, greater standardisation, and greater leadership. It will promise to provide substantial cost saving once implemented. The cost of such an implementation won't be cheap.

My ideas, conversely, are definitely bottom-up, and many so cheap to implement. I believe that we need to value our staff and patients more, or we may lose our NHS.

I will send Lord Carter a copy of this book. I wonder if he will ever read it?

HOW CAN WE ALL HELP OUR NHS?

1. WHAT THE BRITISH GOVERNMENT CAN DO FOR THE NHS

In April 2016 the NHS was hit by the introduction of a single state pension. The abolition of the second state pension removed the 3%-4% National Insurance rebate that employers offered final salary schemes.

This means that in the next financial year the Treasury will claw back over £1 billion as a result. The NHS will have to pay. This money can only come from us – the taxpayers.

The government has another ruse to make money. In April 2016 they introduced the £1 million pension rule. Savers will be penalised. The Treasury won't have to pay out such big pensions. I think that this is so shortsighted. Experienced professionals will be, and are, retiring as fast as possible to beat the drop in pension. We can ill afford to lose all these people at once. We as a country will pay the price for this. The experienced professional will be replaced by somebody less able and less experienced, perhaps from abroad.

Now, if the pensions cap was removed we would get these people working for ten or more years. They would pay tax on their pay. I am now nearly 76 and paying 40 per cent tax on my pension. My generous pension predated this cap. The pension cap will reduce the amount of tax these early retirers will pay in the future. Before the pensions cap, many GPs worked until they were 75 years old, or even older. But not now.

* * *

There are ways in which our government has tried to 'improve' our NHS. Recently, general practitioners were told to provide weekend appointments. Then not enough patients turned up. Patients had better things to do at a weekend than to see their GP. So as a result most weekend clinics have now closed.

This is a clear example of government failure.

* * *

One way the NHS can save money is by penalising patients who do not turn up to an outpatient appointment or, even worse, for a planned admission. A freedom of information request showed that, in 2014-15, 16,803 patients failed to attend an outpatient appointment five or more times! Each 'Did Not Attend' costs the NHS £120.

What have the government and the hospital administrators done to ensure the notice of the appointment is sent prior to the appointment date? I know that it is sometimes sent late. All such requests are sent second class. Finally, is there enough parking at the hospital? Or did some of these non-attending patients arrive early, but could not park anywhere at the hospital? So some patients were forced to drive home! Is more car parking at hospitals possible?

As a hospital doctor I recall that often we arranged a theatre list with one big case. Then this patient failed to attend. What a shambles. The cost for non-attendance for an operation is enormous. We had no plan B. Several times the patient would turn up days later and demand treatment. No, such a patient should be penalised financially.

* * *

Is our government blind to health tourism? There is plenty of evidence that health tourism is costing us, the taxpayer, a lot of money. People are coming to our country to get treatment for different conditions in our NHS, and we are oblivious to this fact. Mr Merion Thomas is a retired surgeon who has investigated this problem. He describes the Immigration Health Surcharge as the cheapest travel insurance on the planet! He has looked into this, and the cost of health tourism is set out in the May edition of the *Bulletin*, a journal of the Royal College of Surgeons of England.

* * *

This government and future governments can't stop tinkering with the running of the NHS. Each major upheaval of the NHS must cost many billions of pounds. So many top executives are paid off only to be re-employed elsewhere the next week. It's a farce. Every time a new government is formed there is a complete revision of the NHS. What it costs each time – nobody knows!

Well, we pay the politicians; they are answerable to us, the electorate. We have a right to know the full cost of any government reorganisation!

Professor Sir Bruce Keogh is medical director of NHS England. He is keen to rationalise our current NHS. Perhaps this means closures of A&E departments? Interestingly, in July 2014, in California, researchers looked at the effects of such a closure. They looked at ten million emergency admissions. Such an A&E closure had an adverse effect. Heart attack deaths increased by 15% and stroke deaths by 10%.[1]

* * *

The government gets in private firms to run parts of hospitals, or in some cases whole hospitals. This, to my opinion, is an admission of failure. All the profits go out of the NHS – forever. If the administrators appointed to run a hospital can't do it properly, they need to be replaced. In November 2016, Virgin was awarded a £700 million contract to provide NHS Care Services. This is a blatant privatisation. It is not cheap and will only get more costly.

* * *

Now, have we got enough hospital beds in 2017? We know that our population is increasing annually. In the past 6 years official figures show that the number of beds free in our hospitals nightly has fallen from 144,455 in 2010 to 129,458 in 2017. It gets worse and worse. In the past year £17 million has been spent by the health bosses in efforts to reduce jobs in the NHS. It gets worse still. In 2015 in figures just released, there is a rise in annual deaths and a fall in life expectancy for the over 65s. In the journal of the Royal Society of Medicine failures in the health and social care system were to blame inciuding missed targets in A & E, and staff shortages. It went on to say that the missed targets are due almost entirely to hospitals being swamped with very old patients, all of whom have been suffering from chronic illness for some time.

So our beloved NHS struggles on. Compared to other countries, we are underfunded, understaffed and have fewer beds. As a direct result of serial changes in government policy we could face a meltdown of our precious NHS. I hope that this never happens.

* * *

The government has an obsession about the weekend working of doctors, and the higher mortality of patients at any weekend by 16%. It's crazy to think that if you generate more doctor hours then this mortality rate will fall. GPs and hospital doctors practically all work weekends anyway. There has not been a trial run of an alternative staffing structure to reduce weekend deaths. We need one NOW. Are these mortality statistics correct?

545

Let's look at this rationally. There is not the back-up of numbers at the weekend. So technicians, secretaries and administrators are absent. The hospital consultant and the GP each can't get the back-up that they require. It would cost the hospital, or the GP, a lot of money to get all these people to work weekends. Then these people would need time off in the week in lieu. In some respects, therefore, it would be self defeating.

Also, let's look at this yet another way. I have worked a lot of weekends and nights in my time. Over my lifetime, I have worked over 1,000 Saturdays or Sundays for the NHS. I saw a lot of patients. I feel that the type of patient presenting after midnight, or at weekends, is iller overall compared to those patients presenting in the day every weekday. We know from studying trauma statistics that trauma victims presenting at 2am have a higher mortality than in the daytime. So, at weekends, there will always be a higher mortality, as we are not comparing like with like. Yes, there will always be peaks and troughs of mortality statistics. We can't escape from them. We accept these results as fact. But as more and more doctors are made to work weekends and nights, I do not believe that the statistics will improve overall.

* * *

Our government has yet to produce an air quality plan and implement it. We need one that works. Air quality in our cities is dreadful. Diesel cars produce vast quantities of nitrogen oxides, up to 20 times the legal limit. So we know the cause of this pollution. Tens of thousands of premature deaths annually in our country have been linked to this pollution. Yet our government has been woefully slow to act. It has taken a high court action to produce a draft plan for discussion. This draft plan passes the buck to local authorities, and is useless. ACTION IS NEEDED NOW, TO STOP MORE PREMATURE DEATHS.

* * *

We have had a new General Medical Council for several years, with greater powers over doctors, paid for with increased annual subscriptions.

Each doctor in the United Kingdom is subject to annual appraisals and regular revalidations. This is to weed out the poorly performing doctor.

I am not aware of any such doctors that have been picked up from this charade. On the contrary, it is possible to attend medical educational talks and learn very little. Similarly, it is possible to find patients and colleagues who will vouch for your capabilities. What is the overall cost of the annual appraisal in medical time? Firstly, each doctor in the UK has to do some paperwork. Then he, or she, meets with another doctor who is the appraiser. If the participant passes the test, the clinical director, or the equivalent from general practice, signs off this document. Finally, the annual appraisal is lodged at the General Medical Council. So there is plenty of paperwork, hours of work, and to what end? Our government has extended annual appraisals to include nursing and midwifery staff. This is a paper exercise that is supposed to take about 35 hours. This is an underestimation of the time involved, in my opinion. This test is billed as 'designed to ensure that the 700,000 nurses and midwives maintain their skills'. I would question this statement too.

What is involved in these annual appraisals?

The nurse or midwife or doctor obtains feedback from fellow staff members and patients. It's so easy to 'cherry pick' staff members, to pass the scrutiny of this test with flying colours. The incompetent nurse can easily go unrecognised. Surely it would be better to look at any complaints against a certain nurse or doctor, or include more feedback from patients. Those written and verbal complaints together would provide a better picture of competence, in my opinion. In 2010, only 16,000 nurses and midwives had been tested, but many have not been able to complete this paperwork. We are already short of staff, and when a nurse fails this test, for whatever reason, they won't be able to work.

I fear that this whole ambitious system is likely to drown in a sea of paperwork, and to what end? Appraisals have continued for nurses, but I have been unable to find out nationwide if they are up to date with them.

* * *

The poorly performing doctor or nurse has flourished in our NHS. He or she has only been picked up following complaints from patients, or as a result of the actions of a whistleblower. Complaints from patients are not taken seriously enough. Too often the well meaning whistleblower has suffered over and over again.

Jeremy Hunt announced in March 2016 that, in an attempt to make the NHS the safest healthcare system in the world, a new investigative branch of the NHS is to be created, modelled on airline accident inquiries. The department has legal powers to keep revelations secret. So we have disciplinary panels regulating doctors that have to discover the facts independently of this new investigative branch. Frankly, I am puzzled; the doctors who made the mistakes might go unpunished. Mr Hunt reminded us that there are potentially 150 avoidable deaths in UK hospitals every week. Gary Kaplan is the Chief Executive of the Virginia Mason Hospital in Seattle. He set up the aviation-style system of reporting and learning in 2004. This has transformed this hospital into one of the safest in the world. So Mr Jeremy Hunt may be right after all. We have to wait and see.

* * *

Let's hope that this government and all its successive ones never again go down the private finance initiative route. It has been, and continues to be, crippling to our economy. Can't the Inland Revenue look at these contracts and see where our money goes? If it goes offshore and pays no tax then surely something can be done. We are talking about billions of pounds, and no tax paid on any of it. Is the Inland Revenue completely powerless?

My own hospital, the Royal Derby Hospital, cost £334 million to build. But the final cost to the taxpayer was over £2 billion. What a disgrace!

* * *

Our government has taken some action on obesity. More action is needed now. One way would be for every general practitioner to record all their patients who are grossly obese. This patient could then go on a diet and exercise regime. If that patient then returns as a result to a normal weight, the GP and the patient could be rewarded financially. This policy would save us money in health costs.

Originally, our government had plans to restrict advertising and promotion of junk foods. These have been scrapped. However, there are plans to reduce the sizes of some portions of food. For example, some pizzas are huge – high calorie and high fat. As we argue, manufacturers are making more and more money. Our children are suffering now. Obesity leads to diabetes and often an early death.

* * *

We have suspected for many years that veterinary antibiotics given to farm animals are dangerous. A study published in 2016 in *Environmental International,* by Dr Ying of the Chinese Academy of Science, showed that 80% of Chinese schoolchildren had traces of veterinary antibiotics in their urine. Those children with high levels of veterinary antibiotics were two or three times more likely to be obese than children with lower concentrations. This research confirms what has been suspected for years. Mixing antibiotics into the feed of animals to make them bigger has an adverse effect on the bacterial flora in our bowels. This change in the flora makes it more likely that the eater of meat becomes obese. The widespread use of antibiotics has also encouraged the emergence of antibiotic-resistant strains of bacteria. Antibiotics bought online has made this worse.

I strongly believe that our government needs to discuss this internationally. If the United Nations as a whole banned this practice then we would benefit two ways. Firstly, there would be less childhood obesity and also fewer antibiotic resistant infections. These infections currently are very expensive – time off work, hospital stays – and have a definite mortality rate. As this is a worldwide problem, the pharmaceutical industry in Davus in 2016 called for more to be done. The World Health Organisation has called for antibiotics given to animals in this way to be banned. It is easy to test animals for antibiotics in their meat after slaughter. So the banning of this practice can be easily monitored.

In 2017, Antibiotics UK tells us that 44,000 Britons die of sepsis each year.

* * *

When is our government going to publish a meaningful strategy against obesity? At present we don't have one. There are plenty of ideas. We need to target the young.

There needs to be more regular exercise in schools. This is especially true for primary schools. In Stirling, Scotland, all primary school children were asked to run one mile a day round the playground. They felt better for it, and said so. This experimental scheme needs to be rolled out in every primary school in the UK, now. Nicola Sturgeon is a strong supporter of this.

A tax on fizzy sugary drinks was introduced in the Budget in March 2016. This is long overdue. This sugar tax does not go far enough and won't start till 2018. A similar tax in Mexico showed the sales of such soft drinks fall 12% as a result, as reported in the *BMJ*. France and Finland have a sugar tax on fizzy drinks already. Hungary taxes sweets and snacks as well. I believe a sugar tax is a step in the right direction and it is just the start. We need, now, a sugar tax on all food and drink. This would embrace smoothies and fruit juices, sweets and chocolates, cereals and coffee. The health of our nation could be improved at the expense of the profit margin of some retailers.

Clearer labelling of all food and drink is needed now to show how much sugar has been added. This is advocated by Jamie Oliver and James Cracknell.

I believe that all schoolchildren should either have lunch at school or go home for lunch. So, more schoolchildren should stay in school at lunchtime. Daily I see droves of children released from school at lunchtime spending money liberally on crisps, sweets and chips. This is a recipe for one thing – obesity. Some children today order takeaway meals to be delivered to them at school!! Junk food by phone!! Their parents are not aware that their child is obese! However, Dr Angela Jones of Nercastle University has produced projected computerised images of obese children as they develop into adulthood. Parents have been shocked, and started giving their children more healthy food.

In March 2016 our government announced that 100,000 overweight patients will be offered cookery classes and exercise annually on the NHS to help prevent diabetes. This is excellent news, but will such weight losses be sustained? We will have to 'weight' and see.

* * *

In August 2016 we learnt that the British government's strategy to fight childhood obesity had floundered. The lobbyists from the food industry had persuaded the government not to make food healthier or even curb the marketing of unhealthy food. So, although currently about a third of children are too fat on leaving primary school, there are no plans for curbing junk food. An amazed chief executive of Sainsbury's, Mike Coupe, said "We need compulsory and measured targets for the reduction of sugar (and other nutrients such as saturated fat). Nothing less will work".

So our children are getting fatter. Then they suffer in adult life and have a reduced life expectancy. Everyone involved – the parents, the children, the teachers, the doctors, the food retailers and the government itself – all blame each other!

What else can we do? The scouts have introduced an 'anti-fat badge' for their youngest recruits. This won't be nearly enough. Does the answer lie in 'high-tech'?'

Gail Ganney from Kent is a mother of four, a former school governor and civil engineer, as well as an entrepreneur. She has set up a web-based computer program currently used by nearly 500 schools. The teachers can track the progress of a child through primary school in four areas:

Sport and physical activity.

Health and nutrition.

Collaboration.

Creativity.

Parents are involved too, and the child learns about their health.

Is this the way forward? Well, with obesity costing the NHS £15 billion a year, I think this system is well worth a try and could be rolled out nationally.

Parents need to know what the 'pocket money' they give to their offspring is spent on.

Greater parental control is needed now.

* * *

Every hospital has a different system of working with completely different IT systems. So not only are foundation hospitals competing against one another, they are also spending a fortune on training and retraining staff on IT, moving from one hospital to another. Many junior doctors are on rotation jobs. The GP has no access to the hospital computer. Likewise, the hospital doctor has no access to the GP computer. It is obvious, to the reader, that one hospital won't have access to another hospital's computer!

The different IT systems and their different ways of working account for mistakes that can be very costly. Surely this can be remedied, or is it an ongoing disaster? Mr Hunt tells us to embrace technology. Independent IT consultants tell us that the IT systems in hospitals are very poor. I think I know who is correct!

* * *

Clear segregation on our roads is needed now to keep other traffic away from cyclists. A white line on the road is all that separates the cyclist from cars and lorries! Safer roundabouts for cyclists and stiffer penalties for drivers injuring a cyclist are needed now. If you attack somebody in the street and kill them, you are likely to go to prison for many years. If you turn your car left without looking and kill a cyclist, you get a telling off in court and community service. It's not fair. On the continent of Europe, cycling is a lot safer. When a cyclist is overtaken by a car on the Continent, a full width of the car is supposed to be between them.

Compulsory cycle helmets would save lives; I should know. All the dead cyclists I saw from accidents had significant head injuries, and none wore cycle helmets. Compulsory cycle lessons for all children are long overdue. Compulsory hi-viz jackets and compulsory lights at night are needed for all cyclists too.

* * *

There is no doubt that there are far too many hospital admissions due to alcohol. Could a minimum price for alcohol reduce the alcohol problem? The answer is yes. However, the European Court of Justice has ruled recently that imposing a minimum price for alcohol could breach European law! Long live Brexit. Goodbye Europe.

An alternative ploy might be to disqualify anybody from driving if any alcohol is found in their blood. Similarly, the police could adopt a more aggressive policy, by screening more drivers for drugs. They now test drivers if they suspect that they have taken drugs. Over 50% of those suspected of taking drugs have proved positive. So, of 5,857 drivers tested for drugs in 2015, 3,718 tested positive. So, drug driving arrests have soared 800% in the past year since the law was introduced.

In all big cities, we need alcohol and drug treatment centres. These are separate from A&E. There is one in Cardiff. Sydney, Australia had one of the first centres.

* * *

Our government needs to come to terms with 'bed-blocking'. The think tank, Res Publica, has called for greater investment in social care to reduce the number of hospital beds taken up by patients who are medically fit to leave. A study published in February 2016 showed that, daily, 8,500 patients are trapped in NHS wards. This has a knock-on effect. Medical patients spill out all over the hospital and block surgical beds. The medical ward is full, and emergency department patients can't leave for the ward as there are no beds to put them in! The four hour limit is now breached! Bed occupancy in many hospitals is approaching 100%. Relatives refuse to take some patients home, or just take them from the ward on discharge directly to the emergency department to be reassessed! Some NHS hospitals are opening their own care homes. Well, a bed in a care home costs a lot less than a bed in a hospital. Who will pay for the care home bed? I think that the patient or his relatives should pay. People will try and get out of paying – at any cost.

If these care homes were all run by the NHS, then the income from them should go to the NHS.

Bed-blocking currently costs the NHS nearly £1 billion annually. Every district general hospital should have a Crisis Intervention Scheme. This should be made compulsory. This is a short remedy for elderly patients, to try and prevent hospital admission. In such a team, a large number of nurses, physiotherapists and home helps are referred a patient. This team then works together to keep the patient at home. These have proved to be successful. Some general practitioners don't use this service. It may not be a service that is widely known in the community. I think that this should change.

* * *

The government should introduce at each hospital a clinic that doctors themselves can self refer to. Many doctors won't contact their own general practitioners. Many doctors suffer with stress. This includes recently qualified doctors, right up to senior physicians and surgeons. The pressures are immense. Mistakes occur as a result.

We used to have doctor's dining rooms and coffee rooms for us to meet and discuss problems. The GPs had a lot of meetings to go to. I should know, as I went with my mother. Well all this has stopped as it was labelled elitist. The net result is work, work, work. We are dealing with people's lives every day. Between doctors there may be issues, and competition for beds and theatre time. We are competitive between ourselves. There is stress, stress, stress. Burnout is rife. Are you, the reader, surprised?

* * *

As I write this in April 2017, the British Government is obsessed by the election, Brexit, the possible breakup of the UK, and fighting in the Middle East! But there are other problems. One concern of mine is the pollution of our seas with plastic. In Britain we use, daily, 35 million plastic bottles, but only recycle 20 million. How many bottles end up in the sea? There is a group called Plastic Oceans that is lobbying to cut usage of plastic. They estimate that annually worldwide we produce 300 million tons of plastic. Half of this is used once for less than a year. So, they estimate that eight million tons annually ends up in our seas. Plastic fragments of all shapes and sizes are generated daily, and a lot end up in our sea. These include nurdles (pellets the size of lentils) that are spewed out by our factories, and look like fish eggs. Millions of microfibres of plastic are in the water after washing polyester, nylon or acrylic clothes. Microheads are in toothpaste and facial scrubs. So our oceans have vast floating islands of big plastics, and in the depths there is pollution of tiny microplastics. Many mammals and sea birds have died as a consequence. The fish that we eat are contaminated. So, we are eating microplastic. Some bits are too small to filter out.

- All plastic bottles used in the UK to be made of biodegradeable plastic.
- Penalties for not recycling. Nurdles to be filtered out of the water from factories.

- Clothes to be treated to stop microfibres escaping.
- Microheads to be banned from toothpaste and facial scrubs. But this is not a vote winner. I am interested for the sake of my grandchildren. This problem is sortable and won't go away!
- I wrote this and then read of the work at Imperial College London. A Mr Lee is developing an edible, biodegradeable capsule to convey fluids of all sorts. There are problems, as the capsules feel wet, and could be tastier, but this is a start. Good luck to him.
- Then I read in *Current Biology* recently that researchers in Spain and Cambridge have discovered that wax worms used in fish bait can digest plastic.
- A Dutch inventor, Mr Slat, hopes to employ long, high-tech, sea surface booms quite soon, to scoop up the plastic floating in our seas.
- Our Environment Minister Michael Gove is to introduce a bill in Parliament to outlaw the use of microbeads in cosmetics. But will the European Commission ratify this? Finally, such a legislature won't stop plastic being in the fish that we eat, or getting into our bodies.

So, one way or another, I hope that man can solve this problem of plastic.

* * *

There are 'grey areas' of costs to any hospital. If these 'grey areas' were cleared up then the NHS would cost a little less.

One grey area is the cost of interpreters. Currently, it's an open house. Many patients who have lived in the UK for over 20 years can't speak one word of English. They then demand interpreters regularly. I strongly believe that interpreters for patients who can't speak English should only be available for those people who have lived in this country for up to one year.

The second grey area is for those who have travelled abroad for surgery, especially cosmetic surgery. Then there is a 'botch-up'. The upset patient falls back on the good old NHS. So they return to receive urgent medical and surgical treatment! I believe that any such patient should be treated privately on their return, and not by the NHS.

* * *

There are also grey areas in general practice. I know that many patients have no general practitioners; they tell us this when they attend A&E. There are currently 54.3 million people living in England (2011 census). But currently, official figures from NHS Digital in September 2016 show over 57 million people are registered with a GP in England. Each GP is paid £141 a year, at least, for every patient, and more for some patients, e.g., elderly. Even allowing for the population going up in the past five years, this difference is rather a lot. If every patient in England is registered with a GP, then we are overpaying GPs by about £400 million annually. Basically, if a patient dies or moves, the GP may not be informed. Many patients are not registered with a GP.

As a 'guestimate' I think that GPs are probably being overpaid for this 'list inflation' by about £1 billion a year!

* * *

There is another grey area – dental problems. Quite simply, medical treatment is free. Dental treatment is not. Dental charges were introduced in 1951. So, if you suffer from toothache, don't bother the dentist, but go straight to your GP or emergency department. At first hand, as a general practitioner years ago and recently as an emergency consultant, I was plagued with dental patients, often after midnight.

The conversion went like this:

Question from me: "Have you got a dentist?"

Patient's reply: "No."

Question: 'When did you last see any dentist?'

Patient's reply: "'I don't know.'"

On examination of the mouth, there were usually widespread cavities.

As doctors, we can advise on mouthwashes, analgesia and even prescribe antibiotics. We can't do fillings, drain apical abscesses or do extractions. My own view is that these patients are inappropriate attenders, and should be referred to a dentist.

This whole question of dental emergencies is not as cut and dried as you would think. Patients with dental problems can present as facial swellings, earache or even pain in the joint between the top of the jaw and the skull (tempero-mandibular joint). The attendance of such patients to a doctor is worthwhile initially.

* * *

My late father decided in 1930 to explore different medical specialties. In 1930 for a few months, he was a ship's doctor. His ship had just passed through the Suez Canal when the captain received an urgent message from a town nearby: 'Stop immediately, we need your doctor to attend to an emergency'.

The ship anchored. My father went ashore. A local sheik had toothache. Luckily my dad was a dentist too. He cured the toothache with an extraction. The tooth could not be saved. After thanks, the ship was allowed to proceed.

* * *

Our government has failed to attract enough doctors into general practice. What has happened? There are swathes of unfilled GP posts all around the country.

Firstly, a lot of GPs have recently retired, many to beat the pension cap. The NHS Business Services Authority, which administers NHS pensions, said that 1,400 GPs retired in 2014. I know that a few years ago many GPs worked into their seventies, like my mother. This no longer occurs.

Secondly, the British Medical Association knows only too well of the pressure that GPs are under to achieve government targets. So, recently, 3,500 GPs have applied for certificates to do this job abroad. There are no targets there.

Thirdly, there is a fundamental flaw in selling general practice to medical students today. The hospital specialists look down on GPs and many criticise their referrals. I have worked in general practice, and as an emergency medicine consultant. I, too, was a generalist. A GP has a demanding job.

General practice is a business as well. Doctors are not business men and women. We are not trained that way, and probably should be.

Our government is totally out of touch with this problem. Their £10 million recruitment scheme for GPs has floundered. This included 'golden hellos' of £20,000 for each new GP and a high-profile publicity campaign. Our government needs to go back to the drawing board before emergency departments all drown in a sea of GP patients.

Why are we so short of GPs in our country? What has gone wrong and why? Well, as an emergency consultant, I trained a lot of GPs. Initially I trained two at a time. Then, after political pressure, I was training more and more. I was training six at one time eventually. Where have they gone? GP numbers should have soared. Why not?

Fourthly, let's remind ourselves of the rhetoric of politicians. Their speeches are recorded (and then forgotten). But one of the first things that Mr Cameron said on being appointed prime minister was a pledge to reduce paperwork. Last week I asked my GP what was wrong with her job, and she replied at once "Far too much paperwork!" So start by scrapping appraisals and revalidation for all doctors and nurses. All complaints could be looked at independently, looking for trends (i.e., bad doctors).

Fifthly, let that GP get on with his job. Politicians are ignorant of the stresses involved, and are hell bent on making things worse. So, the politicians say, lets not take on the food manufacturers that are killing off our children. LET'S NOT REDUCE SUGAR IN OUR DIET. Oh no let's just pass the buck and overburden the GPs. Let them be the scapegoats. Tell the overworked GP to cure obesity. Then when it does not work we know who to blame. Not the politician, oh no, we can blame the GP!

There could be a meltdown of our NHS SOON! WHY? Well the signs are there already and our government is largely to blame. The work of the doctors and nurses has altered beyond measure and the pressure on them is on. Watch out, Mrs May, it could go pear-shaped! Well, Salmon in 1966 destroyed the authority of our ward sisters, and we have suffered with dirty hospitals and less authority on our wards ever since. So we plunder trained nursing staff from countries that can ill afford to lose them. The consultant staff ran the hospital initially. We now have the other extreme with very little medical input and targets everywhere. New contracts are imposed. What about that GP contract of 2004. The GP WAS NO LONGER RESPONSIBLE FOR 24-HOUR CARE. So, expensive locums run the show. They don't know the patients. As a consequence we get a lot of stupid referrals to A and E, or problems sent back to the GP to sort out the next day! Gone is the doctor's white coat, falsely blamed for causing infections. Gone is the doctor's and sister's dining room. We were a well informed, cohesive body. Now morale in the NHS is AT AN ALL TIME LOW. We are haemorrhaging junior doctors abroad. That imposed contract was a victory for our government, and a death knell for our NHS.

But the pressure is being racked up more and more. Is our government oblivious to the stress and strain of the system? Simon Stevens is head of NHS England. He wants GPs to do a lot more. He means more clinics for mental health, etc. It won't work. The House of Lords wants ALL GPs to be employed directly by the government. The NHS property services have put up the rents for no reason. This affected 1,400 practices. As I write this, our government is short of revenue by quite a few billion and is trying to save money. So what services will they cut? A few more beds? But occupancy is nearly 100%. But the Freedom of Information Act showed that in 2016 there were 57 GP practices that shut completely, and 34 surgeries closed because of mergers. Ministers have promised another 5,000 GPs by 2020, but I think that is not going to happen. Well already in the last three months official figures released by the government show that GP numbers are down by nearly 1%, to only 41,475. So, pharmacists and nurses are plugging the gap. I know that non-doctors, like nurses or pharmacists, doing the GP role is not good enough. The GP training has been shortened from three to two years. A new GP was enticed by a substantial bribe. Pressure was put on hospitals to train more GPs. But all to no avail.From January to March 2017, 830 GPs left, but only 789 joined!

Finally, a study in the *BMJ* of doctors in South West England showed that about two in every five GPs were thinking of retiring in the next five years. Now this could spell DISASTER FOR OUR NHS. This is a time for our government to be proactive, and NOT too late and reactive. The latest idea is to recruit GPs from Europe, Australia or New Zealand. Well, all I can say to that is that such a recruitment drive will fail for certain. Mr Simon Stevens, head of NHS England, recently said, "If general practice fails, then the NHS fails." You have been warned. Our government is to blame for the mess that I believe is inevitable!!!!! A MELTDOWN OF OUR PRECIOUS NHS IS LIKELY SOON. WATCH OUT IT'S COMING. I KNOW WHAT IS HAPPENING. ARE OUR POLITICIANS GOING TO BE PROACTIVE NOW? IT WILL BE TOO LATE IN FIVE YEARS' TIME. MY FRIENDS ARE RETIRING TODAY, NOW, IN THEIR DROVES, IN THEIR FIFTIES. HELP OUR NHS, NOW! NOW! NOW! (2019 will be crunch time for the NHS!)

THERE COMES A TIME WHEN EVERYBODY IS TIRED OF BEING BULLIED, PUSHED AROUND, OVERWORKED AND

DROWNED IN A SEA OF USELESS PAPERWORK. ALL THIS FUELS STRESS, AND THE DOCTORS WANT OUT NOW.

The reader may think that this is impossible and I am just sensationising all this to sell my book. Oh no, this is what will happen sooner, or later. All the GPs are busy and short-staffed now. Many patients can't find a GP today, as they are in such demand and some practices have shut.An extra lot of GPs retire, and then more and more. The GP service is at breaking point now.It can collapse at any time, and the emergency departments will be flooded out. All those GP patients turn up to the nearest emergency department en masse demanding to be seen now. There will be a possibility of medical gridlock. I should know as I was an Emergency consultant for many years. We had intermittent gridlock at all hours. Once the emergency department is stuffed full of patients, there will be problems inside, and outside, the hospital. The illest patients will be seen first. So other less ill patients will have to wait, and wait, and this will cause friction. So patients referred to other specialties by the emergency doctors may well be sent to medical or surgical admissions units to give us more room. This would cause friction between doctors. (In April 2017 the NHS had over half a million emergency hospital admissions. This is a record. Incidentally the target for routine surgery of 18 weeks is being achieved by fewer and fewer patients. The four hour wait is lost over and over again. Less than 90%of patients are treated in that time in April 2017). Most hospitals currently are running at nearly 100% bed occupancy today. Yet our government is trying today, and succeeding to cut bed numbers overall. All those PFI hospitals cannot be expanded! Well, they were designed NOT to!

Outside the hospital I can foresee, in the near future, ambulances stacking up right down the road. This can cause a hospital to grind to a halt. No patients, or relatives, can get in or out of the hospital grounds. All the beds are full, and more patients are waiting to be admitted, but there are no beds! The administrators will run around like headless chickens giving orders, but to no avail. The hospital ceases to function.

I hope that I am so very wrong. But I feel passionately that I will be very, very correct. This chaos will cause a lot of acrimony. Productivity in the NHS will fall dramatically, and the politicians and administrators will blame it on the doctors!!!

I rest my case, and hope that I am wrong.

Reference:

1.   John van Radowitz. Closing A&E Units increases Deaths. *The Times Supplement*: Pg19;15.08.2014.

2. WHAT THE ADMINISTRATORS OF THE NHS CAN DO FOR THE NHS

There are some costs the government tries to hide. The first is an NHS reshuffle or reorganisation. Always billed as cost effective, but so often they have been 'money down the drain'. We are never told the cost of such an exercise, but we the taxpayer foot the bill. Successive governments tell us that they have a mandate to carry this out as it is 'in their manifesto'. I have lost count of such exercises. They are accompanied by phrases like 'payment by results'. I think it is time to call a halt to these charades and go with the status quo. We can't afford any more hiccups in the running of our NHS.

In 2010 it cost £15 billion to administer and run our NHS. I expect by now that it is a lot more.

We need administrators who care about people – staff and patients alike. So many administrators are just obsessed with targets. Many are not interested in the wellbeing of patients or staff. The creeping privatisation of our sacred NHS is, in my opinion, a direct consequence of administrative failure over and over again!

* * *

It would help hospital administrators if all consultants were employed on annual contracts. This would make it a lot easier to sack a consultant, i.e., at the end of the year. It's very difficult today to sack a consultant. Many such consultants are suspended on full pay for years and years. Up to 100 consultants are suspended at any one time. They may be struck off the register. Then they can appeal to the House of Lords, and appeal to the European Court. Perhaps everybody employed by the National Health Service could be on an annual contract, including the chief executives.

* * *

561

The mandatory attendance of doctors at various compulsory lectures annually is expensive in time and money. What a farce. The vast majority of these lectures are a complete waste of time. We have to attend. The administrators tell us to. There is a roll call! This all should stop now.

* * *

Some people say that Jeremy Hunt the minister, or the prime minister, is in charge of the NHS. Other people say it is Simon Stevens, the NHS England chief executive. In each individual department the administrators think that they are in charge. Some are intelligent and sensible, other administrators are not. Quite simply, I believe the doctors are in charge of the NHS, as they and they alone are responsible for the patient's treatment. The administrators and the government need to accept this and stop pushing doctors around, or they will all emigrate, or retire.

I wonder what use annual appraisals and regular validations serve. Surely these time-consuming exercises are a farce? At each hospital there is an annual review of every department. The workload of each consultant can be viewed from computers. Outcomes and problems are there. Also, complaints can be seen and collected. The general practitioner can also be scrutinised in this way. They have complaints too. So there are better ways of looking at a doctor's work. Complaints from staff and patients should show up a poorly performing doctor.

There are so many vital meetings that drag a consultant away from his work. I have listed them in detail elsewhere. Surely, when a consultant is absent from his, work there is some way of keeping an operating list open. Major surgery can be replaced by routine operations from a competent surgeon, i.e., registrar, standing in for the consultant and performing basic surgery.

So the theatre is not left idle. The junior doctors at present are idle too, and the hospital beds empty when a consultant is absent. This is one of many reasons why productivity in the NHS is not better.

* * *

One of the problems in our health service is that there is no slack in the system. So, if a doctor or a nurse is sick there is a hole in the rota. A locum is found through an agency – at great expense sometimes. In retrospect, after a locum has been employed, it often would have been better to close ranks and for everybody to do a bit more, than spend all that money on that locum.

The locum often does not want to learn. They tend to do things their way and may not fit into a team. They leave the moment their shift is finished and not when their last patient has been discharged.

The government has capped locum pay. This has not worked.

What if locum pay was double the ordinary rate and only open to doctors working in the department that is shortstaffed? (This works in Australia.)

When a doctor leaves, for whatever reason, there is often a delay of months before the post is advertised. This process needs to be speeded up.

3. WHAT THE CONSULTANTS DO FOR THE NHS

Now the consultants are all on annual contracts, they each can be sacked easily, i.e., their contract is not renewed the following year.

Mr Hunt is to introduce a 'no blame culture,' that has proved to be successful in the aviation industry and in some hospitals in the United States. But I believe that each and every doctor working in the NHS still needs to be covered for their work through insuring with a medical defence organisation. Currently, the hospital, as the employing authority, pays at least 50% of any damages awarded by a court to a patient. I think that this should change. If a surgeon amputates the wrong leg, or removes the one healthy kidney, then I believe that the surgeon's own medical insurance scheme should pay 100% of all the costs and damages. If a medical insurance scheme has paid for a consultant's mistake then his or her next premium will be loaded. Eventually the consultant will be unable to afford insurance cover and so won't be able to work.

* * *

Mistakes abound in our health service. One conservative estimate is that 7,500 people die annually as a result of NHS mistakes. I, too, made mistakes. Many of the patients that I treated had x-rays taken. Initially I reviewed these X-rays, then, later, a consultant radiologist reviewed them. This X-ray specialist recorded that I made a significant error in my reporting once every 700 X-rays. I admitted my mistakes and always apologised if I met the patient. The consultant radiologist had plenty of time and no distractions. I did not. We as doctors don't get feedback on our mistakes. This should change.

* * *

Well, is there enough clerical support for the consultant or the general practitioner? In October 2015 a study by the NHS Alliance and the Primary Care Federation pointed out that large chunks of the family doctor's time could be freed of duties, such as changing appointments or chasing up test results, which could be handled by other staff. Hospital consultants too are under pressure to see patients as quickly as possible.

They too are chasing results, finding hospital records and covering up for mistakes by inexperienced secretaries. There is no doubt that there is an urgent need for better secretarial support for both consultants and family doctors. That faithful medical secretary, who checked everything, was pensioned off years ago. Mistakes abound as a consequence, and the doctor has less time with the patient as a direct result of government targets.

* * *

We need to bring back the white coat for all hospital doctors. There was never a good reason for scrapping them in the first place. This would give back doctors their uniform and clear identity. The hospital would have to provide the white coats and launder them.

* * *

Consultants, junior doctors, administrators and general practitioners spend far too long each day with their eyes glued to a computer screen. On return from a holiday they each have hundreds of emails. Many of these communications are frivolous, or simply advertising. There should be a way of monitoring how long such a valuable person spends on his computer or phone each day, and a way of cutting out junk emails.

4. WHAT THE JUNIOR DOCTORS CAN DO FOR THE NHS

All junior doctors, and consultants too, are now insured with a medical defence organisation. So if a junior makes a mistake then this medical insurance pays for that. If the mistake can be attributed to that one doctor, then I believe that the doctor's insurance should pay all the costs and damages.

These junior doctors are the principal general practitioners and the senior consultants of tomorrow. These doctors have given the best years of their lives to study and train for medicine. I took my last examination (Advanced Trauma Life Support) in my fifties and passed.

Today most junior doctors qualify in medicine with a debt of at least £50,000.

They will have to work hard to pay that back. So one reason why the negotiations with the government over their new contract were so vital was that the juniors are in debt.

I have a particular interest in the wellbeing of junior doctors as my daughter is one. She is currently gaining valuable training by seeing another health service in Australia. We all expected, and hoped, that this would be for a few months. She had plenty of experience in the UK prior to leaving. She has liked Australia a lot. She is a paediatric registrar on the middle grade training ladder. It's not just the sunshine and the beaches. Her rota is excellent. So different from the UK. She is better paid and better appreciated too. A medical qualification is a passport to many countries.

My daughter is surrounded by British graduates in medicine. Many have emigrated. The Organisation for Economic Co-operation and Development says that there are four million British people living abroad; 1.5m of them are graduates or similarly trained. This figure does not include millions of British graduates who have emigrated abroad and relinquished their British citizenship. So we need to keep our doctors in the UK. The battle with Jeremy Hunt has sent some abroad! This is the fall-out. Politicians to blame yet again!

* * *

Our present government was involved in long talks with junior doctors over terms and conditions. What was it all about? There were a few sticking points. For example, our government was calling a shift that finished at 2am a DAYTIME SHIFT. What rubbish. The new junior contract will be imposed on the junior doctors by the government. That has made the junior doctors rather deflated and upset. Do they still want to go on working for the government? They could apply for jobs in Wales or Scotland where the new terms and conditions don't apply. Applications to work in these countries are soaring!

* * *

No, I think that these junior doctors deserved better. They have committed their working lives to the NHS. They should not have been the butt end of political rhetoric.

It is of note that when 50,000 junior doctors were balloted on the question of industrial action, 98% voted in favour. Also of note is that official statistics show that within ten days of Jeremy Hunt announcing the new contract for them, no fewer than 3,468 of them applied to the General Medical Council for registration to practise abroad! Yes, our government and our administrators need to copy the Australian government. The on-call rotas in the UK could be so much better. We could find UK graduates flocking back. In 2011 official statistics from Australia showed that 22% of specialists appointed and 13% of GPs were from the UK.

* * *

Our government does not understand junior doctors. Each and every one of these doctors is a success story. They have passed GCSEs with sometimes as many as 10 or 11 A*s. They then have passed A levels with the top grade. They have survived a gruelling time in medical school and competed over and over again against each other. So these junior doctors are resilient and committed to working for our NHS.

* * *

But once qualified, high rates of psychological distress, depression and suicide have been reported amongst doctors.[1] This stems from the workload of doctors. For example, the president of the Royal College of Physicians says that 60% of medical registrar trainees found their workload heavy and 37% found it to be unmanageable.[2]

A census of trainees in medicine for the Royal College of Medicine in December 2014 showed that 8.5% were dissatisfied or very dissatisfied with their career choice. But why? The answer I believe is found in the Medical Protection Society's survey of the mental health of UK doctors in 2015. They received 631 responses to a questionnaire: 75% of doctors had experienced stress. 49% had had anxiety and 57% had had sleep disturbance all during their medical careers. Also, if they had a significant mental health issue, only 56% were confident enough to inform the GMC!

Peter Williams is chairman of the Medical Defence Union. In their annual report published in 2016 he says 'what with the growing demands of the services provided by doctors and the rising tide of complaints against healthcare professionals generally, more doctors than ever before were leaving the profession and a growing number were becoming unwell or suffering burn out'.

The junior doctors are under pressure to make decisions about patients. They don't want to make any mistakes. A lot of these doctors still have a debt to pay off from being a student. They are also expected to pass yet more examinations to gain promotion in general practice or hospital medicine. Now I ask you, has the decision of our government to impose a new contract on them lessened or worsened the stress that they are under?

* * *

It is a well known joke that doctors themselves have a significant incidence of alcohol and/or drug addiction. I believe that the cause of this is stress. We doctors work in teams. When one member of a team makes a mistake then all members are accountable. International studies estimate that

10% of hospital patients suffer an adverse event. The workload of doctors is driven today by government targets all invented by politicians, none of whom are working doctors. These targets are adored by the media as they provide plenty of information. This information is widely reported by the media. The bar has been set high on purpose – cancer waits and A&E four-hour waits, etc. The workload is going up, patient expectations are high, litigation abounds and consultation times are getting shorter and shorter. What is the result for the doctors themselves?

Dr Michael Blackmore has the answer. He was a practising general practitioner for 20 years. He suffered stress, anxiety and depression. He still carried on working as a doctor, but his mental state triggered drug and alcohol addiction. Finally he had to stop work, and is now fully recovered. Today he lectures widely to health care professionals about his drug and alcohol addiction.

* * *

When I was training in the 1960s at St Thomas' Hospital there was a discreet hospital clinic for doctors to self refer to. Many doctors with a problem don't want to go to their GP or the General Medical Council. Should the hospital clinic for doctors to self refer to be reinstated?

References

1. S Feeney et al. Practise what you preach: health behaviour and stress amongst non consultant hospital doctors. *Clinical Medicine* 206: Vol 16 No 1:12-18.
2. Professor Jane Dacre. President's message commentary. *Royal College of Physicians*. Feb 2016.

I Digress about Stress

Yes, here I digress about stress. What is stress? It's all just in the mind. An insight into my own personal stress and also into the stress suffered by medical colleagues.

As I write this in 2016 I recall the 50 or so years that I spent in the NHS, from being a medical student in 1960 to fully retiring in 2015. I was always concerned for my patient. This was paramount. In my short time in general practice I found that the treatment my patients received, if I referred them to hospital, at times fell short of my expectations. That is why I then pursued a career in hospital medicine.

What is the workload of a doctor? Well, in 2017 many European countries recommend that the maximum number of patients that a doctor sees in a day is 25. But a BMA spokesman, and friend of mine, Dr Peter Holden, rightly points out that currently in 2017 an NHS GP can see up to 60 patients in a day! Well, it gets worse in emergency departments where over 500 new patients can be seen in a day! I did a ward round, then a daily clinic and then onto the shop floor seeing new patients! I could easily see 100 patients or more in a day. I have counted them at times to prove it!

In my training as a junior doctor I worked for two consultants who each had breakdowns due to stress of work. One was a paediatrician who returned to work but needed support. He only worked one outpatient session with me. To gain support he brought along to out-patients his own four-year-old son. The presence of his own son at work gave him support. It probably would not be allowed today, but in the 1960s it was allowed.

Two years earlier a lady obstetrician had stopped work for nearly a year due to stress. She then returned to work. I did not work directly for her, as my consultant was on call on alternate nights to her. I knew that although she was on call and an obstetrician, nobody called her out at night. So she had not been called in at night for two or three years. She worked in the daytime but was rather shy and withdrawn.

One night while I was on call, a private patient of this lady consultant came in. She was in labour. I found myself looking after this lady, as the midwives said that she was not their patient. At 1am I telephoned the obstetrician. I reminded this sleepy lady who I was, and that this private patient she had was about to deliver. The consultant replied that she was 'coming in'.

At 2am I delivered a healthy baby girl with the assistance of a student midwife. At 4am there was nothing left to do. The placenta was intact. The baby had been examined by me and then bathed and dressed by the student. The baby was a good size so I had to make a small cut to the mother to aid delivery (called an episiotomy). This I had repaired surgically. The parents were overjoyed and the baby was fine.

Then round the door came the head of the lady obstetrician. She did not come into the room! Her hair was a mess. She kept her coat on.

She asked, "Is everything all right?"

I replied, 'Yes'.

She nodded at the parents and they muttered, 'Yes, thank you'.

Then she left.

I expect she put a bill in, but I received nothing. But that is life.

Looking back with the value of hindsight, I do not think that the paediatrician or the obstetrician were fit to practise. But they had to work. There is no halfway house. These doctors either worked or were prematurely pensioned off.

You may think that years later as a hospital doctor I had a cushy time. Well, I did have two days off a fortnight – Saturday and Sunday, alternate weeks. I worked normally the 12 days and was on call alternate nights.

Over the years, A&E departments got busier. So I was called in to see patients if the waiting time to see a doctor was greater than one hour. The patients were not ill but usually had a very minor problem. Yes I was called into the hospital by the sister in charge of the department, as directed by the administrarors, at 2am, 4am etc., on and on. It was a nightmare. Guess what? I felt tired the next day. Well, I had had little or no sleep. I fell asleep at the end of the clinic the next day. Then I was told 'you are sick' by a bossy administrator. Well, she had had a good night's sleep.

No, this calling me in at all hours for minor non-urgent cases was a farce. This is typical of the administrator's mentality. Plenty of concern for the waiting time to see a doctor, and no concern for the staff. This has to stop.

At the time, I was being called in frequently. I knew that there was one doctor, from outside the hospital, who had a responsibility for the wellbeing of the hospital staff (a staff doctor). I contacted this doctor and he referred me to a psychiatrist. The psychiatrist and I had a pleasant chat. He was horrified that I was being treated so badly. I don't know what he told the administrators, but thereafter I was only called into the hospital to see properly ill patients. I was less tired in the daytime.

The psychiatrist recognised the stress that I was under and put a stop to it.

* * *

As an Emergency Medicine consultant I was heartened, as time and time again the patients leaving my care to be admitted to our hospital were obviously going to be treated properly. My responsibility to them finished once they had left our department. But occasionally I too was very stressed when the junior doctor's plan of action for that patient did not correspond with mine. Each time I was not content to keep quiet, but openly voiced my concerns to the junior doctor. Usually common sense prevailed, or I contacted a more senior doctor to take control.

> *I confess my sins. They fill me with anxiety.*
> *The Bible.* Psalm 38 verse 18.

However, in my old age, now fully retired, I am still haunted at night by the clear recollection of two cases, both surgical. I openly criticised both junior doctors as they left our department with the patient. The junior doctors adopted the wrong treatment plan, but I was no longer responsible for the patient now that they had been admitted to our hospital. So my work was finished.

In each case I tried but failed to contact the relevant consultant on call. One consultant was operating on a private patient elsewhere, and I never got through on the telephone. The other consultant was in a very important meeting with general practitioners. I telephoned his personal assistant. She told me confidently in perfect diction that my patient was not ill and that she had no intention of calling her consultant nearby to the telephone. I implored her, but she refused over and over again. I myself was stuck in a clinic at that time with nobody to relieve me. After ages on the telephone, failing also to contact the surgical registrar, who was operating, or that surgical consultant in the meeting, I gave up. Pressurised by the nursing staff and patients, I reluctantly started my daily follow-up clinic (this was why I was criticised by my colleagues for not seeing patients on the shop floor. This clinic was often five hours long). On this particular occasion, when I wanted to tell my consultant colleague about this patient with a rare and dangerous condition, this was a clinic from Hell. When I had finally finished it was time for my evening ward round. I was exhausted and very fed up. I had failed.

On each of these two occasions, I was to learn days later, down the hospital grapevine, that the patients had died. On each occasion the coroner's post mortem showed that the cause of death could have been prevented with the right treatment, exactly as I had suspected. Well, I am trained in surgery. One patient bled to death. The other surgical patient was suffering from a medical condition that killed him.

I never knew what evidence the junior doctors had given to the coroner at the inquest. Each doctor had ignored my advice and as a consequence the patient had died. I was ignorant of this until days later. Well, my testimony, and my emergency department records, would have shown up both sets of junior doctors and that mouthy personal assistant to be the idiots that they were. I know that the relatives witnessed my outbursts to the junior doctors to 'call the consultant on call'. I wish now, when it is all far too late, that I had risked being sacked and walked out of the emergency department on each occasion to communicate with those two consultant surgeons, wherever they were. Such an act would have caused uproar, but so what? Stress is the downside of being a doctor. We care a lot. My late father felt some stress in his old age. Many years earlier he had been the victim of grossly unfair criticism in the press. Professional etiquette forbids any response to such events. My father could not come to terms with these memories.

A close medical friend was a doctor. He was presented with a patient with vague nondescript symptoms and no clinical signs of any significance. Unbeknown to him, the patient had a rare condition – a tumour of the heart. The clinical signs are often intermittent, as in this case. He was sued for missing the diagnosis. The lawyers had a field day. There was publicity. The legal case dragged on well into my friend's retirement. The stress of it all fuelled my friend's hypertension. He could not enjoy his retirement as he had this case hanging over him. He was never the same man as a direct consequence of this experience. It was so sad, as I knew him to be an excellent doctor.

* * *

Patrick was one of my former junior doctors. He was also a golfing partner and a brilliant general practitioner. He recently committed suicide. In his obituary his wife, a former physiotherapist, wrote that he could not come to terms 'with his demons'. I knew what she meant. Another friend of mine is a nurse. He is currently off sick with depression, brought on by stress. He may never work again!

* * *

We don't look after health workers well enough. Clinics they can self refer to are needed now. Many of these doctors do not want to contact their GP, their college or the General Medical Council. Surgeons are a lot better than other health workers at coping with stress. Even if the surgeon does nothing wrong, there can be unforeseen complications beyond their control.

There is another way to alleviate stress. Dr Danielle Ofri founded the *Bellevue Literacy Review* at the Manhattan Hospital, New York. Medical students, nurses and doctors express themselves in poems and stories to alleviate stress. The response to this publication has been overwhelming.

We have not come to terms with stress in the medical or allied professions. More needs to be done. Now.

5. WHAT CAN THE PATIENT DO FOR THE NHS?

But the patient is perfect. He or she can't be blamed for anything. You forget that I have been a patient too. Politicians are all scared stiff to say anything against the poor patient. If they do, then the patient may not vote for them in the next election.

* * *

The poor smoker is vilified. He or she wants to smoke everywhere, but can't. Smoking costs the NHS £2.7 billion annually. Cancer of the lung, coronaries and arterial disease due to smoking is so common. Yet the young smoker is openly heaping up medical problems for tomorrow. More needs to be done in schools to communicate the dangers of smoking, drugs and alcohol.

* * *

Is the patient registered currently with a general practitioner? There is very little pressure on anybody to register. So, often, hospitals are treating conditions that should be treated by a GP. All patients should be compulsorily registered with a GP. All GP receptionists should give patients an appointment within a week!

* * *

I understand that there are plenty of illegal immigrants in our country. There are quite a few people running away from the police, usually for good reason. When they need medical treatment it's easy. They just go along to the nearest emergency department. They give a false name and address and receive treatment.

When we open a bank account, or see a Solicitor, we show our passport and/or driving licence. Are we gullible in our NHS? I know from trying to track a few people down for research purposes that their names and addresses are spurious. Why? What have they to hide?

* * *

Time and time again my heart goes out to a patient. This scenario is too frequent. An elderly lady is seen who can't cope at home. She has been struggling on for years and finally things become too much for her. A ridiculous diagnosis is made like 'off legs'. She can't walk. Her home is a mess. The relatives have given up and may well be belligerent.

These patients are admitted as acute patients. No, this has been something that has been coming on for years.

Elsewhere, in the United States, there have been initiatives for such folks. Early timely intervention and mobilisation have reduced admission rates. You may tell me that this is already practised in the UK. Well, why are we still getting these patients in our emergency department in 2017?

Their problems are chronic (and not acute). There needs to be better publicity for crisis intervention schemes.

* * *

The elderly infirm patient who does not fully recover is a huge problem for our NHS. That poor elderly person ends up spending their life savings on private care in a nursing home.

The emergency departments and the medical wards are full of elderly patients who can't go home, but the doctors say they are fit for discharge. These patients fill the hospital beds and have nowhere to go. There are insufficient beds for them, acute beds blocked and operating lists cancelled. The government needs to provide more beds for the elderly.

The think tank Res Publica published a report about 'bed-blocking' in February 2016. They found that 8,500 patients were medically fit for discharge from hospital at any one time, but there was no care home bed to accommodate them. Currently this costs up to £900 million annually. There is a knock-on effect of this. This elderly patient may be on a general surgical, gynaecological or even ophthalmology ward. No other patient can use this blocked bed. So as a consequence a slot on an operating list may be cancelled and a surgical patient turned away! Res Publica called for greater investment in social care, as bed-blocking will get a lot worse!

Finally, what can the patient do for the NHS?

The answer is simple:

GET FITTER.

AND NOT FATTER.

Gross obesity is a form of slow suicide.

Please read on…

My advice for anybody wishing to go on a diet is contained in Appendix A.

6. WHAT I WOULD DO FOR THE NHS –
(THIS WAS A REAL DREAM)

We all dream. In my dream recently the Minister of State for Health, Jeremy Hunt, retires suddenly for personal reasons! There is a hiatus. The media is clamouring. Who is going to take the post over? Nobody is keen to. Is it a poisoned chalice?

Simultaneously, I find myself elevated to the Lords!!! This is in response to some mutterings from ex-patients about 'a life dedicated to serving humanity'.

Well, I have met a lot of important, influential people and tried to treat them all equally. However, as a consultant in Casualty/emergency consultant, not all my patients were top drawer. I saw plenty of prostitutes, perverts and pugilists. It is difficult to treat everybody the same in the circumstances.

As a surprise in my dream, I find myself suddenly in charge of our National Health Service. Unbeknown to me, a lot of other people refused the job. I was the last choice!!!

So here I am in charge at last. The first thing I do is to put a large photograph on the wall of my hero, Nye Bevan. This upsets the Conservatives, but so what. I renationalise the NHS. All those contracts to privatize bits of the NHS are cancelled by me. (No compensation to be paid.) This would include all those PFI contracts, but so what, they have been so lucrative up to now. If they object I can get the Inland Revenue to investigate all their tax affairs.

Then I would stop treating some conditions in our NHS. They would all have to go private.

Hospital-run care homes, that I organised, have stopped the bed crisis in hospitals. If nobody can pay for this care then this cost, plus interest, is taken from the patient's estate when they die. (The average length of time spent in a care home before a person dies is 18 months.) Many elderly patients have been labelled as terminally chronically ill (i.e. they are NOT CANCER SUFFERERS) but they are now barred from A&E attendance, because everything treatment-wise that could be done for that patient has already been done. The decision not to admit such patients to hospital is made by a medical consultant. They are still looked after by their GP. Emergency departments are less busy immediately.

All patients with obesity will no longer be treated for obesity related problems. If the obese want treatment for cancers or arterial disease they will have to pay. These obesity units to be set up and paid for by the food industry. For the first time this century, the size of the obesity problem is slimmed down.

All smokers and smoking related illnesses to be treated elsewhere. Special private treatment for smokers and their illnesses to be funded by the tobacco industry.

Those alcoholics that flood into emergency departments time and time again would be banned. Alcoholics, and those with alcohol related illnesses, would have to go elsewhere. Such treatment to be funded by the drinks industry. Amazingly, emergency departments are now quiet.

These alcoholic people would be treated in specialist alcohol units with strong links to an expanded Jericho House, so their alcohol addiction can be cured. The drinks industry to fund these places.

The drug addicts that pay dealers a fortune for their fix would also go. Well, the drug addicts themselves often fund the habit by stealing, or the ladies resort to prostitution. Emergency departments, and police stations, are even quieter! Drug addicts are now registered at last. These drug addicts then receive their drugs at a drug treatment centre. The police are no longer involved unless people are selling drugs or manufacturing them. The injection centres have been expanded to become drug treatment centres. Currently in the Bristol area the police run a successful programme re-educating drug addicts and curing them. This programme to be expanded. (This free supervised access to drugs by drug addicts is not new. For example Calgary, Alberta in Canada has set up 4 supervized consumption sites for drug users. These have support, on site, from primary care, counselling and mental health. All drug treatment and the centres to be funded by the pharmaceutical industry.)

Before my colleagues could stop me I would flood the market with free condoms for all under the NHS. Better sex education to be introduced in schools nationwide. So hopefully fewer teenage pregnancies. Simultaneously I would introduce licensed brothels in our country. All prostitutes to be medically checked regularly. Profits to go to our NHS. The revenue would flood in! Gosh, those brothels really swell the coffers. The chancellor is delighted, and wants to lower taxes for everybody, including you and me! The incidence of venereal diseases would plummet from the present high level.

But licensed brothels are not desired in the UK in the 21st century, you may say. Well, let's look at this another way. It is exactly 100 years since our government passed the Venereal Diseases act of 1917. In this act it says that only doctors can treat venereal disease (and not quacks.) Now, 100 years later, gonorrhoea and syphilis, that was rife in Victorian times, is still with us! (Public Health England recorded over 5,000 new cases of syphilis in 2015 in the UK!) This is despite penicillin being invented. We also now have AIDS to contend with and other venereal diseases. We are losing the battle against venereal disease today, so drastic measures like licensed brothels are called for. We need them. Prostitutes are in the oldest profession. We will never get rid of them. They have been driven under cover today. This is one reason why venereal disease is rife! I dream on.

Licensed brothels exist today in several developed countries, for example Australia and America. I have visited Sydney and New Orleans. Both cities have licensed brothels. By chance, looking back, my wife and I have walked there in the red light districts. There were no girls on the streets. There were good restaurants there, and in New Orleans the best jazz!

Diesel cars to be banned from all cities. Air quality is improved. There would follow an increased use of public transport and cycling. Hospitals will report fewer respiratory admissions. We are told that thousands of premature deaths can be attributed to air pollution. Somebody needs to do something about it NOW. I dream on.

The stock market has gone down! Well, shares in all food retailers have crashed and so have all the brewery and whisky shares. Cigarette shares are down too. Clothing retailers are not happy as they can no longer sell extra, and extra extra, large clothes. Their shares are down as well. I am entirely responsible, and pension funds in these shares have been hit hard. The stock market finally crashes triggering worldwide panic. The mere fact that the nation has for once decided to become fitter, and not fatter, matters not at all. Sports clubs are booming. Sales of vaporizers and Nicorette chewing gum have soared.

Finally, before I am certified insane by a medical lynch mob, I would help the training and workload of doctors. There has been about £15 billion of savings annually by my refusal to treat smokers, alcoholics and drug addicts. The coffers are full. A lot more medical students are to be trained. So we won't be so short of doctors ever again. I would decree better rotas for doctors, no rude administrators, Jeremy Hunt's contract for junior doctors to be burnt, and excellent return to medicine courses for all those doctors who have had to stop work, many to have babies. All appraisals and revalidations to be stopped for doctors and nurses, but more attention paid to complaints. So that badly performing doctor is spotted earlier. A lot more junior doctors working abroad clamour to return. This includes those who have emigrated to Scotland.

I have saved the NHS. Before I am certified insane and locked up in the Tower of London, to be tried later by my fellow peers, I WAKE UP. Oh

no, I am not in charge. ALL THOSE 'MEDICAL PARASITES' ARE
COSTING OUR NHS A FORTUNE.

MY THOUGHTS ON RETIREMENT

Looking Back and Looking Forward

Writing this book has helped my brain to continue working, reduce my
degree of dementia, but I am gradually slowing down. I still have many
interests, but today the golf ball does not travel far (fig 80) and my skiing
is unsteady. My vegetable marrows and squashes are unbeaten in local
produce shows (fig 81), but that is not enough. This year I have fished in
the South Pacific (figs 82 and 83) and the north of Canada. My brain still
works – hence this book. I need to do more and more. So I have returned
recently to singing. Over 60 years ago I was the only member of a large
class to pass the audition to get into the school choir. For the next nine
years I sang in that choir. Just before I left school the choirmaster decided
we basses needed auditions to thin our numbers. He slung me out of the
basses into the tenors. Then I sang in the choir at St Thomas' as a tenor.

My favourite composer is Handel, and in particular the Messiah. I
also have a personal reason for liking this music. I have sung the Messiah
in its entirety in the chorus four times. Once as a treble, once as an alto,
once as a bass and once as a tenor, (Is this another record?) Handel's
music is demanding, but I just love it.

I have been blessed with five children and recently five healthy
grandchildren. Oh, what joy they bring.

But will the publication of this biography get me into trouble? The
new General Medical Council won't be too pleased with me for giving
morphine to patients while still a medical student! Similarly, I operated
on my friend Paddy whilst only registered to teach. What will they say?
The police will discover that I smuggled morphine through customs, and
also operated on a sheep whilst I was not a veterinary surgeon. I even was
driven to bend the rules of golf. What will they say at my golf clubs? More
and more crimes revealed. It could cost me dear, but perhaps through the
publicity generated more books could be sold. Who knows?

Fig 80 – My prize-winning squash that weighed over 22 kilograms.

Fig 81 – I won the Lindsey Cup for golf in 2014, for the fourth time!
A competition amongst Derbyshire doctors.

I have been at the cutting edge of medicine in our country for years. I have seen Mr Bevan's original idea of a free health service for all dissolve. Pure socialism replaced by capitalism in the form of privatisation. We have paid and continue to pay a high price for this – materially and practically. Money now runs the service, and not patient needs. More is the pity. Will our NHS survive the next few years? There is a real possibility that it might crash! I hope that I am wrong, but the signs are ominous !!!!!

But what about disease itself? What have I learnt? I am confused. Let me explain some of my dilemmas.

As a Christian I appreciate that I am in a strange minority in the United Kingdom – a pariah – and also recognise that science and religion often appear strange bedfellows. However, freedom of religion and freedom of speech are cornerstones of our society. So I expose my thoughts to the reader – 'warts and all'.

The Bible teaches us that we are created in God's image. So why did He create congenital abnormalities, inborn errors of metabolism or horrible hereditary neurological disorders? Some of these are more common if the parents are related! Most are not related to consanguinity.

Secondly the Bible teaches us also that God created all things and that nothing was created without Him! So God created all those nasty bacterial infections and even viruses like HIV. Why? Bacteria are not all bad. Those bacteria in our bowels are beneficial to us!

Finally, has God created cancer? Well, many cancers are the result of human stupidity – for example, smoking leads to an increased risk of cancer of the lung. But what about leukaemia in small children? They have done nothing wrong.

Well God has secrets, still. We know life has problems, and we don't have answers to many questions in and out of medicine. But God has given us all brains and bodies. We need to exercise both frequently. We don't. We should eat properly too – not rubbish, high fat and high carbohydrate. We do adopt strange ways that poison our valuable bodies – drugs and smoking, for example. It is well recorded in the Bible that Jesus was tempted by the Devil. He said, "Get thee behind me, Satan." So the Devil's temptation did not work on him. I believe the devil tempts us all still today." Go on, smoke that cigarette, or eat that cream cake, they won't hurt you!" Similarly, our body image can be distorted, leading to anorexia, or our mood affected by minor things leading to depression! Can the power

Fig 82 – Fishing off Lord Howe Island in the South Pacific. This is a trevally.

Fig 83 – More fishing at Lord Howe. This is a king fish that took ten minutes to haul in. BBQ tonight.

of Christian prayer combat any of these afflictions? I believe so. Jesus' miracles are well recorded in the Bible but largely ignored by modern society! Why? The greatest healer ever? We call ours a Christian society, yet only about 1% of our population attends church regularly. Our idols are pop, sport and film stars, instead of the God that created us!

He also gave us brains to exercise. Very good and valuable assets to be turned on. He gave us senses to input information into our brains. He gave us all an ability to communicate with one another and to share ideas. So, I believe, He has given us the wherewithal to sort out all these medical problems, including cancer. So slowly and surely we are combating disease, or at the very least mitigating its effects. As a result, in my lifetime, childhood leukaemia has a much better prognosis!

The dream of immunisation for all may become a reality. Could the viruses of AIDS and influenza be finally beaten? Cancer needs to be detected earlier. Gene therapy promises a lot. Will it deliver? Eventually, even diseases that have baffled us as yet will be overcome. One example of this is Crohn's disease. It is an inflammatory condition of the small bowel mainly. Could it be due to a deficiency of a mineral within our bodies? Maybe – who knows? In time, some brain will fathom it all out, to great acclaim.

So, I have spent a lifetime working for the NHS as a junior doctor, a senior doctor, and been exposed to administration as well. The future of this huge organisation is uncertain. The bills are mounting daily, fuelled by increased spending in healthcare and clinical negligence. The ethos that the nursing and medical professions are caring has been eroded by a whole series of scandals. Scientific improvements have grabbed the limelight quite rightly. But the structure and organisation of the NHS have changed out of all recognition from 1948. This has happened by a whole series of reorganisations labelled as improvements. Is it fit for purpose? Waiting lists and complaints are up.

But I remain a strong supporter of the NHS, which has had some necessary changes forced upon it. The alternative to the NHS is a medical insurance scheme. This is bureaucratic, costly and not all-encompassing. It would create more problems for the future, and solve very little. Long may our NHS survive!

In this book, I have made sweeping statements about staff and patients alike. The very fabric of the NHS has been criticised. What will the GMC or BMA say? Will it matter if I am struck off? Well, I can't be. I'm not on the register at all anymore! Will I still get my pension? I am likely to be a patient in the NHS soon – surgery beckons on more than one front. I have a booking reference number and a password – how impressive is that? But how many people have I upset with my ramblings? Quite a few very possibly. Will the staff still greet and treat me? I will have to wait and see.

In my opinion, everything written in this account is true. I apologise for any errors that are unintentional. I have simply expressed my opinion that may upset a few people. Apologies for this.

> *To write one's memoirs is to speak ill of everybody except oneself.*
>
> Henri Petain (1946)

Postscript

O h dear, I have forgotten to mention the most important people in the NHS and some of the best paid. The hospital administrator. Gone are the days when the hospital secretary ran the hospital with the help of somebody in Personnel. More is the pity – bad news.

There are droves of administrators. Health is a business and the finances are complicated – bad news.

I have found many of them caring, considerate and conscientious. But far too many administrators had their own agenda and delusions of grandeur. Most have nine-to-five jobs with weekends off, plus a generous salary. Many change jobs like cabinet ministers. Their redundancy payments are often kept secret as they are beyond any normal worker's wildest dream, e.g., a million pound pay-off for a couple who are soon re-employed![1]

The true cost of NHS administration is taboo – until now! Administration has always been the biggest expenditure in the NHS. In 2010 the cost was over £15 billion.

So, for 2017, this cost has probably risen to £20 billion, which is the approximate cost of the HS2 rail link from London to Birmingham, or roughly half the UK education budget. Are we getting VFM – Value for Money? I think not.[2]

So I leave you with something I heard myself. This sums up the priceless contribution to our NHS by some administrators.

Mr John Collins MBE was president of the Casualty Surgeons Association. He was in the chair at our national conference. A question from the floor came: "Mr President, how do you like hospital administrators?"

Response by the president: "Fried."

I disapprove of what you say, but I will defend to the death your right to say it.

Voltaire

References

1. Chris Smyth. Lucy Bannerman. £1m pay off then NHS brings back managers. *The Times*. 1.11.13:1.
2. Bohumil S Drasar. NHS admin costs. *The Times* 9.7.14:27.

THE FUTURE

Thank you, the reader, for looking at my recollections, mutterings and thoughts.

If this scribble of mine ever makes any money it will all go to my grandchildren. This would be in the form of an educational trust for their future.

Their names are Angus, Louisa, Thomas, Rory and Mirren. Currently, their ages range in 2017 from three years to eight years (fig 84).

Fig 84 – My grandchildren, from the left: Mirren, Louisa, Thomas, Angus and Rory.

Appendix A

OUR 'SWEET' LIFESTYLE

What has gone wrong?

Can we save money on the NHS by us all adapting a better lifestyle?
Genghis Khan advocated the death penalty for obesity. Fortunately, for a large portion of our population, he died in 1227.

Obesity is our biggest health risk today. Currently in the UK, one in four adults is obese with a body mass index over 30. A body mass index is reached by referral to a chart. There is a simpler method of measuring obesity. Try the tape measure test. Is your waist measurement less than half your height? If it is not, then you are obese! Obesity is a global problem, killing more people worldwide than malnutrition. How and why has this come about?

To answer these questions I believe it is helpful to look back to our ancestors. We have all descended from prehistoric man who had a completely different lifestyle. Prehistoric man was short of food. He ate root crops, leaves, fruit and berries. So he had a high roughage diet of mainly carbohydrate, natural sugars, starch and fibre. There are some fats in vegetable oil. Occasionally, if he was fit and could run fast enough, he might be able to catch an animal. Then he and his family would get some protein from the meat.

Over time the amount of food available to man has improved dramatically. We kept animals and grew our own crops. Historians tell us that the biggest change in our diet happened in the 19th century. The amount of sugar in our diet increased dramatically. It has continued to rise ever since. Our food and drink today is a lot safer than it used to be! For example, Coca-Cola was sold as a safe healthy drink from 1885. But it still contained cocaine until 1929.

Today we still need carbohydrates from plants and vegetables, as sugar, starch and fibre. We get fat from meat and some vegetables. Protein is essential too. It is found in red meat and fish as well as eggs and hard cheese. So we need all three, carbohydrate, protein and fat, in the right properties. A balanced diet will give us all essential minerals and vitamins too. Each adult should have a daily intake of three litres of water. A lot of this water is in our food. Well, we are nearly 60% water. We absorb all these good things from our gut. An average adult doing an average amount of exercise needs 2,000 – 3,000 calories a day.

There is a new word banded about – it is new to me anyway – AUTOPHAGY. After 12 hours of no food, our starving body starts to burn up damaged cells, tumours and viruses. So, unexpectedly, a lot of sick paients have felt better. A Japanese scientist called Ohsumi has received a Nobel Prize for this work. This study clearly shows that we can miss meals, and even benefit from this! Most people, in comparison, eat too much too often.

What has happened is that our normal daily diet is no longer balanced. It is unbalanced. Most of us are taking in far too much carbohydrate. The food industry has 'tricked us all'. Extra sugar has been poured into many of our foods. We are gullible. This extra sugar is to our liking. So we eat even more sugar. We have developed a 'sweet tooth'. Once we have a liking for sugar we want more and more and more. If you don't believe me just look and read the labels on jars, packets and containers. The writing is small, but the amount of carbohydrate, fat and protein has to be displayed. This writing is there to help you!

Once you get used to reading the small print on the food packet then everything becomes clear. Comparing cereals is an example. We soon find out how many grams of sugar has been added to each packet. It's that sugar that our taste buds want. The yoghurt that advertises on the front of the tub that it is low fat is another catch. It tastes so good too because it has been loaded with sugar. So, eating low fat yoghurt, like this, makes you fatter, as you have consumed extra calories in that sugar. The reverse is also true. A cereal packet may display on the front in big letters that it is low sugar. You think that this is what you want. Just read the small print of the actual nutrition. Yes, it is low sugar, but often the product has extra fat, instead of sugar. So read the small print.

Biscuits and jam tend to be loaded with sugar. Some jams have far less sugar, and those are the ones to buy. Try eating jam made for diabetics – I like it. To explore our eating habits in the 21st century all you have to do is to stand at the supermarket checkout. You recall that our ancestor prehistoric man lived off berries, fruit and vegetables. Today, processed foods abound, so cake and beer with high sugar contents are being purchased to consume. Fresh fruit and vegetables are not so popular.

So we love sugar in our diet. We absorb this sugar into our bloodstream. We need sugar in our blood in small amounts to keep us alive. This sugar is carried all round our body in the blood stream. We produce insulin that lowers our blood sugar. So sugar passes into the cells of our body, or is stored by our body. But today we overload our blood stream with sugar. Our resting blood sugar level as a result rises and rises. In time, insulin has less and less effect in lowering our blood sugar. We take less exercise so we need less sugar for our metabolic requirements. We don't burn up any fat. We get fatter.

Eventually the patient's blood sugar rises so high that they become a diabetic. A diabetic is somebody who has lost their ability to control their blood sugar. If they don't go on a diet, often combined with medication, then their blood sugar level will continue to rise. Diabetics die if their blood sugar level is not controlled.

The walls of the arteries of diabetics are full of fat. This leads to hypertension. A diabetic has a higher chance of heart attacks, strokes and amputations as a direct consequence. Blindness and dementia are common. The life expectancy of a diabetic is reduced.

What is the Cost of a High Sugar Diet to the NHS?

The cost of a high sugar diet for the majority of people in the UK is high. The obese cost the NHS £9 billion annually. The number of people with diabetes in response to a high sugar diet (type 2 diabetes) has risen by 60% over the past decade to 3.3 million. Diabetes has many complications and consequently costs the NHS currently almost £10 billion a year, about a tenth of its budget. Soon, one in six beds in our NHS will be filled with a diabetic!

Obesity itself is a major health risk. As a former Emergency consultant I know only too well that the overweight person, not yet a diabetic, who falls heavily is very likely to suffer broken bones. The obese person is also likely to have skin infections, frequently needing admission.

So obesity alone brought on by a high sugar diet has its medical problems.

My late father was a dentist. He knew only too well that the high sugar diet causes dental disease. In the Middle Ages the inhabitants of the United Kingdom had a low sugar diet. Their skeletons today show no evidence of dental disease. Current government statistics show that dental disease is the most common reason for a child aged five-nine to be admitted to hospital in England. In 2012-13 the NHS in England spent £30 million on dental extractions.

In 2014-15 the NHS in England provided multiple dental extractions under general anaesthesia for nearly 46,000 children.

OBESITY – MY THOUGHTS

Are there any alternatives to a diet?

STARVATION

Back in the 1960s a very few patients I witnessed with gross obesity were admitted to hospital. They were allowed to drink as much water as they liked each day. Each patient ate one orange each day! That is all. Not surprisingly their, weight reduced!

WIRING OF JAWS TOGETHER

It was noticed that if a patient fractured their jaw and needed their jaws wired together, then they healed but also lost weight. If your jaws are wired together, you always lose weight. Dentists now refuse to do this for weight loss. It is also not a safe practice.

GO ON AN EXPEDITION

Several of my friends have gone on extended expeditions. Two went to Antartica for a year. They had essential supplies, but not unlimited access to goodies like chocolate bars or beefburgers and chips. Expeditions involve a lot of exercise. They both lost weight.

DRUGS

There have been patients who were desperate to lose weight. Instead of discussing this with their general practitioner, the patients purchased drugs through the internet. Fatalities have occurred. The pros and cons of appetite suppressants are best discussed with your general practitioner. My own view is that appetite suppressants are best avoided, as side effects can be severe. To my mind, such drugs purchased through the internet are taboo.

WEIGHT WATCHERS

Commercial programmes like Weight Watchers are more successful than dieting by yourself as they provide plenty of support.

PSYCHOLOGICAL SUPPORT

There may be an underlying problem like depression. Once that depression is treated then the overeating may be curbed. Hypnotherapy has been advocated for obesity, but I know nothing about this.

BARIATRIC SURGERY

This is the 'in' treatment for weight loss. People talk of it as being perfect. It is billed as being the ideal way to lose weight. Before you rush to have this done you should be aware of some facts:

It is major surgery and as such it has a major complication rate of nearly 5%. Post operative deaths have occurred!

You have to have a BMI of greater than 30, be over 18 years and have tried to diet unsuccessfully.

There are a huge variety of surgical procedures. About 30% of these will need a second surgical procedure.

After surgery, weight is lost slowly. It can take up to a year for a patient to lose up to 60% of their excess weight.

After surgery, patients may suffer from discomfort after eating. They have to learn to live with this.

Patients after bariatric surgery are expected to continue with their diet.

I have experience of patients after bariatric surgery coming to the emergency department late at night. Each time they had had the procedure performed privately and had problems. They could not contact their general practitioner, or their specialist surgeon. Each time I had no idea what surgery had been performed. Each time the patient was at the end of their tether. They usually demanded injections to inflate their gastric bands and/or intra-gastric balloons. I was unwilling to do this as they had no information with them, and I had no access to their notes. So follow-up after bariatric surgery has some hiccups.

Bariatric surgery cannot be reversed. So there is no going back to a 'normal stomach'. It is a 'one-way treatment'.

Bariatric surgery can be expensive. Apart from the cost of the operation there are all those new clothes!

After bariatric surgery most patients have abdominal scars and some patients have emotional scars. There is a small risk of suicide.

Not all patients lose weight after bariatric surgery! Some patients after gastric bands or intra-gastric balloons do not lose weight. You are more likely to lose weight after partial gastric resection.

Are you Obese?

If you are, let me help you to lose weight.

You have to recognise that you have a problem. You must commit yourself to action. A half-hearted attempt at a diet is useless. The number of obese people today is huge. One in ten people are currently at risk of developing diabetes (type 2). Diabetes type 2 has a long list of complications. About 22,000 deaths a year in the UK are attributed to diabetes. Even if you have diabetes type 2 already, it has been shown that you could be cured of diabetes with the right lifestyle.

You need to adopt a balanced diet. So a diet is a way of life. You have put on weight over a long time – perhaps years. It is unrealistic to think that we can lose a lot of weight in a short time. You need to be focussed, realistic and determined from the start. Don't stop weighing yourself and don't stop discussing things with your buddy partner. It won't be quick or easy to return to a normal weight.

A balanced diet contains protein, carbohydrate including sugar and fat, all in the right amounts. We need to drink plenty of water. Cups of tea and coffee don't count, as the plant substance in them makes you pee more and so dehydrates you. We are supposed to drink three litres of water a day. Some we take in our food, but most should be as drinks. Try diluting water with no added sugar squash. Soft drinks are laden with sugar. Just look at the nutrition labels in small print. Some soft drinks are not laden with fat or sugar. Those are the ones to go for, if you hate squash. I like ginger beer. Some ginger beer bottles are full of sugar. There are some with little sugar and little fat and they still taste great!

So we know why we have to lose weight. The grossly obese are either the pre-diabetics with a high fasting blood sugar or the diabetics type 2 with loss of control of their blood sugar. The challenge of getting back to a normal weight is a daunting one. Researchers at King's College London in 2015 found that an obese man on a diet had a one in 210 chance of getting back to a normal weight. Obese women however had a one in 124 chance of achieving this with a diet. So the odds are stacked against you from the start.

Let me help you shorten these odds.

First, adopt a routine. Weigh yourself on the bathroom scales, or elsewhere, at the same time each day. Don't forget. Remember that weight, or record it some other way. It only takes a few seconds. Don't slip up. Do it daily. Record your weight in a little book.

Secondly, have you somebody to be a buddy? This might be your partner or your wife. Perhaps they have a weight problem too? It could be your neighbour, or a friend at work. This is why and how Weight Watchers is successful. A close friend or relative might be easier to confide in. You two might have a competition? Emotional support from someone regularly, or even a group of you, will improve your chances of success.

Then thirdly, you need to adopt the correct diet. The word diet came from the Latin and Greek words that when translated means a 'way of life'. So a diet is not a quick fix. We hear stories of people who lose weight in a few days. I am doubtful about this. A diet is a long-term commitment. To be perfectly honest, unless you are prepared for this, for the rest of your life, please don't start a diet. If you are hell bent on returning to cakes, beer and fry-ups regularly after the diet, then definitely don't even start. Yes, if we get back to a normal weight these can be occasional treats, but definitely not your staple food.

There are so many types of diet. Some are starvation diets and so are relatively quick. Some are slow. Many are weird. For example, there are diets dictated by your religious beliefs and others by your blood group! One of the modern fads is the gluten free diet. The only reason at all to go on such a diet is if you are in the 1% of people sensitive to gluten. So don't go on a gluten free diet unless you have been diagnosed by a specialist with this condition, known as Coeliac disease. It's little wonder that patients are confused with diets and don't know where to start.

May I suggest that you eat three meals a day – breakfast, lunch and supper. Preferably these meals should be at the same time each day, so your body gets used to these times. There must be no snacking between meals. Don't give in to these temptations. If you have to eat between meals then you can have a piece of fruit. Never eat quickly. Chew your food a lot before swallowing.

Before each meal, drink at least one glass of water. This is what your body needs to help to fill your stomach. Once again, you could flavour the water with 'no added sugar' squash. In 2015, scientists in Birmingham showed that drinking a pint of water before meals increases weight loss. So this has proven scientific value and reduces your appetite.

For breakfast, after a drink of water have some fruit – grapefruit, an orange or strawberries. Then a bowl of cereal (low fat and low sugar) plus low fat milk. There are dairy free alternatives. An alternative food is porridge made with water, perhaps flavoured with low fat, low sugar yoghurt. Or some fruit on your porridge.

Lunch should start with a drink of water. Then two poached or boiled eggs with salad. So, in this, could be lettuce, tomatoes, avocado, radishes or peppers. Don't reach for the salad cream or mayonnaise. They are loaded with fat and sugar.

An alternative for lunch is beans or tomatoes on toast.

What about a mushroom or tomato omelette? Another alternative.

The evening meal should start with that drink of water. Then a mugful of low calorie soup (watch out, some soups have cream in them, especially in restaurants).

An alternative is a slice of melon or a corn on the cob. Then eat a piece of chicken or fish with vegetables. Choose two vegetables from swede, peas, carrots, marrow, squash, broad beans, runner beans or green beans.

Some evenings, try a grilled steak instead, with vegetables.

These menus form the basis for your diet. You have done your homework. You have read all these small print labels. Those foods you love have been left out. Well, eating too much of them has got you into this state. So